Money, Credit, and Economic Activity

The Irwin Series in Economics
Consulting Editor   Lloyd G. Reynolds   *Yale University*

Money, Credit, and Economic Activity

CHARLES D. CATHCART, Ph.D.

Vice President
Citibank, N.A.

RICHARD D. IRWIN, INC.

Homewood, Illinois 60430

Irwin-Dorsey Limited
Georgetown, Ontario
L7G 4B3

1982

ISBN 0-256-02491-X
Library of Congress Catalog Card No. 81–82215

Printed in the United States of America

1 2 3 4 5 6 7 8 9 0 **H** 9 8 7 6 5 4 3 2

To my father, James A. Cathcart, Jr.
with love, gratitude, and admiration.

This book was written primarily for the beginning college course on money and banking. It is expected that students will have completed one or two semesters in the principles of economics. But, recognizing that the backgrounds of students will be varied and that some time may have elapsed since their introductory course work, I have provided review materials in key places and a glossary at the end of the book. Mathematical equations in the text are restricted to elementary algebra and are always accompanied by verbal descriptions. Other student aids include cross references between chapters, problems and suggested readings at the ends of chapters, and extensive applications of concepts to historical and current events. Many applications and supplementary readings in the book are drawn from *The Wall Street Journal*. I have found the *Journal* to be extremely valuable for student parallel readings during a course, so I have provided a student's guide to *The Wall Street Journal* in an appendix at the end of the text.

Preface

The content of this text is distinguished from the standard text in several ways. First, it devotes several chapters to more detailed analysis and description of the credit markets, including specific yield calculations and major credit market instruments. Instructors teaching business majors may find this particularly valuable material, and it may make the text a suitable addition to a capital markets course. At the same time, instructors who wish to concentrate on topics in monetary theory and policy can skip this material (Chapters 4 through 7) without interrupting the flow of the book.

A second area receiving more exhaustive treatment is the analysis of alternative monetary systems and the supply of money—important material for courses emphasizing money, particularly in view of the recent revival of interest in the gold standard. For courses where these topics are less important, Chapters 9 through 12 can be omitted. It should be noted that the text is up-to-date on important changes in 1979 and 1980, including the Federal Reserve's shift to a reserve aggregates strategy in October 1979 and the Depository Institutions Deregulation and Monetary Control Act of 1980.

Other distinguishing features are an early chapter presenting a simplified supply-and-demand-for-money analysis (Chapter 3); an earlier-than-usual placement of a chapter on international finance (Chapter 8); and the incorporation of a chapter on aggregate supply (Chapter 18) within the standard material on the Keynesian model.

This book was written over a span of seven years which bridged academic and business occupations for the author. During the first three years, I was a member of the faculty at Pennsylvania State University, and during the past four years I have worked principally as a business economist and financial forecaster in New York City. In the course of drafting and redrafting chapters, I have benefited from the suggestions of many students, colleagues, reviewers, and friends. Two students, Jeffrey Sanderson and Toby Kimura, read the complete text and provided detailed comments of great value. Among colleagues and friends who read the text or parts of it, I am particularly indebted to Frederick Meltzer, Bluford Putnam, Sykes Wilford, James Rodgers, Lucy Edwards, and Paul Brody. Reviewers included Edward Day, Stephen Miller, David Schutte, Anthony Santomero, William Wilbur, and Robert McLeod. My beloved wife, Evelyn, was an important contributor as an editor, glossary and index compiler, and, above all, chief source of encouragement despite the severe encroachment of the project on family time. The two principal typists of the final draft, Carla Kanatake and Manny Lopez, also deserve thanks.

My intellectual debts are many, but Leland Yeager was a most important mentor, both as an exemplary teacher and as a monetary theorist. None of the foregoing credits, of course, in any way absolves me from responsibility for any errors or deficiencies which remain.

Charles D. Cathcart

Contents

PART THREE • ANALYSIS OF MONEY AND MONETARY SYSTEMS

Two views of the money-supply process and lagged-reserve account-
ing.
APPENDIX: RECORD OF POLICY ACTIONS OF THE FEDERAL
OPEN MARKET COMMITTEE: MEETING HELD ON OCTOBER 6, 1979

PART FOUR • AGGREGATE SUPPLY AND DEMAND ANALYSIS

PART FIVE • ISSUES AND PROSPECTS

Empirical studies of the relative strength of monetary and fiscal policies: *The St. Louis studies. The FRB--MIT model.* Inside lags, outside lags, and policy instability: *The inside lag. The outside lag. Policy instability. Unemployment versus inflation. The costs of inflation. The costs of unemployment.* Internal versus external stability: *Mundell's strategy. The global expansion approach.*

Introduction to money

Introduction

The study of money and credit may appear in your college catalog as just another field in economics or finance, but it is an especially important field which involves some unique and interesting problems and which encompasses some heated controversies. Controversies in this field are due to the special importance of money and credit to the economy, to the institutional characteristics of the monetary system, and to the various interests that have evolved in the financial sector.[1]

Many issues in money and credit will be dealt with in relative isolation in various chapters of this book. However, there are two broad, related problems which will be of concern throughout this book. These are: (1) what government regulations and policies are

---

[1]Serious misunderstandings of material covered in this book often arise because of confusion regarding definitions of terms being used. This is especially true of the term *money*.

Webster includes the following among other definitions of *money:* "wealth reckoned in terms of money" and "the first, second, and third place winners in a horse or dog race" (*Webster's New Collegiate Dictionary*, 8th ed., © 1973 by G & C Merriam Company, s.v. "money"). Other, more colloquial definitions abound. The problem is not helped by the fact that economists and financial analysts often use the term in different senses (though not as the winners of a horse race) and, as explained in the next chapter, there are even different definitions of money within the limited sense of the term as used in this book. *(continued on next page)*

required to keep the financial sector from excessive fluctuations and possible collapse? and (2) what are the government policies in the area of money and credit which will produce the least inflation (or deflation) and lost output in the overall economy? Unhappily, there have been periods when government regulations have been inadequate and periods when government policies have tended to destablilize the economy. The section below describes one particularly severe example of government regulation and policy failure. It is presented in this chapter to illustrate the importance of the material covered in the text.

THE GREAT DEPRESSION AND THE BANK HOLIDAY OF 1933

Beginning in the summer of 1929, the U.S. economy suffered probably the worst decline in its history. The banking system played a role in this decline as banks were affected by the weakening economy and, in turn, contributed to the fall in income. Banks passed through a series of serious crises as the economy deteriorated. The final and most severe crisis occurred in early 1933.

During the Great Depression and earlier crises, fears of bank failures led to runs on banks. In a run, depositors convert deposits into currency, causing banks to call loans and contract credit.

As you probably already know, banks keep reserves equal to only a small fraction of their deposits; hence no bank has enough reserves to meet a run by all of its depositors. Once a bank showed signs of weakness during the Great Depression, this was a signal to depositors to get their money out before it was too late. Depositors' fear of a bank failing was capable of causing even an ordinarily sound bank to fail unless it was permitted to restrict withdrawals temporarily. In late 1932, runs spread to such a degree that governments of many states instituted special bank holidays which permitted banks to suspend or restrict withdrawals of deposits temporarily. It was hoped that this would give time for panic to subside.

Runs on banks and bank holidays

During the three years prior to 1932, over 5,000 banks had gone out of business, many with insufficient assets to cover their liabilities. (See Figure 1–1.) As a result, depositors lost almost $800 million in savings.[2] Those banks which had not failed became increas-

---

To avoid confusion in the discussion ahead, the term *money* will always refer to whatever is used in making payment in transactions in the economy, unless otherwise indicated. In particular, money is not credit, and it also is not income or spending.

Other important terms with which the reader is assumed to be familiar include *GNP*, the *price level, real income, capacity output,* and the *business cycle.* An appendix to this chapter provides a review of conceptual and empirical definitions of these and some related terms. For a general, quick reference for definitions of terms encountered frequently in the text, see the glossary at the end of the book.

[2]One problem, as we will explain more in a later chapter, was that there was no deposit insurance in those years.

FIGURE 1–1
Number of commercial banks in the United States

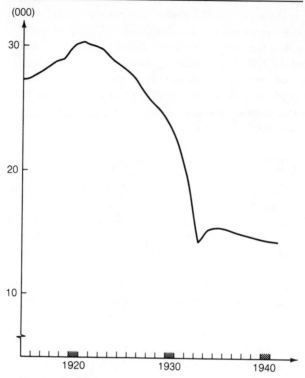

Note: Much of the decline in the number of banks in business which began in 1920 and accelerated in 1929 represented mergers with no loss to depositors.

SOURCE: *Historical Chart Book* (Board of Governors of the Federal Reserve System, 1973).

ingly unable to convince depositors that deposits were safe. Savings and loans and other thrift institutions were also experiencing heavy withdrawals and failures with losses to their depositors. By late February 1933, fear among institutions and depositors was so pervasive and strong that there seemed to be nothing that could prevent a collapse of the whole financial system.

The lack of meaningful policy response

The Federal Reserve, the nation's central bank which had been created in 1913 mainly to prevent such bank panics, could not decide what to do, and its officials took no ameliorative action. The Hoover administration was also stymied. Because he was about to end his tenure, Hoover felt constrained unless a concerted plan could be worked out with President-elect Roosevelt; but the incoming president did not want to be associated with the previous administration or its policies.

International aspects of the crisis

Further complicating and compounding the problem of the public's fear of bank failures was a second fear—a fear that the United States under Roosevelt was going to abandon the gold standard.

Under the gold standard, the government was committed to exchange a fixed quantity of gold (coin or bullion) for its paper and deposit money liabilities on demand. If this commitment were abandoned by the new administration and Congress, the value of paper and deposit dollars might fall in terms of gold. Fearing this, foreigners and many Americans rushed to convert these dollars into gold, reducing gold reserves in the Federal Reserve Bank of New York to a level below the then legal minimum. (More will be said about the gold standard in later chapters.)

On Saturday, March 4, 1933, in an atmosphere of extreme crisis, Franklin D. Roosevelt was inaugurated. Acting swiftly and dramatically, at 1:00 A.M., Monday, March 6 he issued a proclamation which ordered every bank in the country closed for all but essential transactions for a period of four days. All banks were to be examined, and those determined to be sound would be licensed by the federal government to reopen. Withdrawals and exports of gold, silver, or currency were prohibited under maximum penalty of $10,000 or 10 years in prison.[3] Subsequently, the bank holiday was extended to a week to allow more time for banks to be certified to reopen.

Moves to restore confidence

During the business week of March 6–11, the country had to make do without transfers or withdrawals of bank deposits except for limited, essential needs. Personal credit and scrip (emergency currency—not permanently legal tender) partly cushioned the shock, but most normal transactions were disrupted. Over the next few weeks most banks were permitted to reopen, and in place of runs, many depositors returned their hoards of gold and currency to the banking system.

However, at the end of the year more than 1,500 banks still remained closed by government order and another 1,000 had gone out of business causing severe losses to depositors. Partly because of bank closures and partly because of panic reactions of the public and banks, there had been a sharp reduction in the nation's supply of money and credit. The fall in the money supply between mid-1929 and the spring of 1933 was about 28 percent. This decline in the money supply unquestionably contributed to the severity of the depression.

The effect on the supply of money

By the spring of 1933, the economy was reeling with an unemployment rate of 25 percent, production at only two thirds the 1929 level, and prices 25 percent lower than they were in 1929. If more money and credit had been provided to stimulate demand, production and prices probably would have declined less severely and recovered more rapidly. Instead, financial and monetary collapse ex-

The effect of the money supply on the economy

---

[3]Roosevelt claimed authority to issue these orders based on the Trading with the Enemy Act of 1917. Congress, in a special session, validated that claim four days later.

acerbated the economic collapse.

Recovery from the Great Depression was agonizingly slow. By 1940, the unemployment rate was still 15 percent, and full employment was not reached until the nation mobilized for World War II.

INTRODUCTION TO ARTICLE

Since the Great Depression, failures of banks and other depository institutions have never reached anywhere near the proportions experienced during those grim years; however, depository institutions still fail. When they do, most depositors of "insured" institutions are covered by Federal deposit insurance which was introduced in the mid-1930s and which now guarantees deposits up to $100,000.

Despite this protection for most depositors, the safety of the depository institution system cannot be taken for granted. As the following article in *The Wall Street Journal* describes, losses among thrift institutions as a result of high interest rates and doubts about the capacity of the federal insurance agencies to rescue the system were a source of considerable concern and a spur for new legislative initiatives in the spring of 1981. There is probably little chance that a crisis of confidence and a full-fledged financial panic on the order of the Great Depression will again grip our economy, but such an event cannot be ruled out altogether.

Saving Plan: Bill to Aid Sick S&Ls Could Eventually Lead To Interstate Banking

To handle growing insolvencies among savings institutions, uneasy federal regulators are seeking potentially radical changes in the way that they and the whole financial system operate.

From its founding during the Depression until last year, the Federal Savings & Loan Insurance Corp., the main insurer of deposits at savings and loan associations, had to deal with an average of about one thrift-institution failure a year. It did so either by liquidating the S&L and reimbursing depositors or by paying another S&L to take over part or all of the insolvent concern. Sometimes, the FSLIC itself would buy the loan assets of a failed thrift if their yields were so far below market rates that disposal of them would cost the agency a bundle.

But no longer is sole reliance on these tactics possible, because of the sheer number of S&Ls being endangered by high interest rates.

In March alone, the FSLIC added 114 S&Ls to its problem list—increasing the total of troubled thrifts 86% to 246. The agency concedes that 120 may be left with little or no net worth by year-end and that another 100 could be in the same fix in 1982.

"The FSLIC is swamped," says a former official of the Federal Home Loan Bank Board, the agency's parent body.

Problem of confidence

Testifying before the Senate Banking Committee last month, Richard Pratt, new chairman of the Bank Board, acknowledged that the amount of the FSLIC's spending this year "could have an unsettling effect upon public confidence in the insurance fund." He added, "We are at the point . . . where truly significant increments of assistance must come from Congress."

The thrift regulators, including the Federal

Deposit Insurance Corp., which insures commercial- and savings-bank deposits, formally asked for the help last week. To relieve the strain on their funds, they proposed a bill that would let them use new tactics, including a highly controversial plan to begin to permit some interstate mergers between and among banks and S&Ls.

The FSLIC would be able to auction off failing S&Ls to commercial banks or other thrifts eager to enter new markets, at prices that could cut its losses. The FDIC would be able to sell off failing banks with assets exceeding $2 billion. Conceivably, the plan could eventually pave the way for large-scale interstate banking.

"What they have in mind is the auctioning of market-entry rights," says an S&L economist privy to federal officials' thinking. "It will be the only way institutions that want new out-of-state markets can get them. They'll say to Citibank that you can enter this market for this price"—that is, at the price of acquiring a sick S&L.

Keeping them going

The FSLIC also plans to let some S&Ls continue to operate with "essentially zero capital," it says. Mr. Pratt says the agency will infuse technically insolvent thrifts with enough capital to keep them going until interest rates fall and merger partners can be found. Federal regulators have never had a program for pumping money into failed financial institutions on a large scale, but internal studies indicated the FSLIC couldn't afford another approach.

In the bill submitted to Congress, the FSLIC and FDIC sought other changes. The FSLIC asked for an increase in its line of credit from the U.S. Treasury to $3 billion from $750 million; its insurance fund totals about $6.5 billion, compared with the FDIC's $11.5 billion. Both the FSLIC and FDIC sought broader authority to lend money to troubled thrifts well before any collapse—thus perhaps avoiding or postponing an expensive liquidation. Down the road, the Reagan administration and the Bank Board are likely to push to give savings institutions the right to enter the most profitable kind of banking business—corporate loans and deposits, which now are reserved for commercial banks.

If these new strategies fail and the FSLIC runs out of cash, it still plans to pay off insured depositors with advances from the U.S. Treasury. Uninsured depositors may get hurt, however. In a liquidation of a Chicago S&L that began Monday, the FSLIC indicated that the uninsured depositors could lose one-fourth to one-third of their unprotected funds.

Fight on Capitol Hill

The FSLIC will soon begin its plan to nurse a group of "essentially zero capital" S&Ls. But its plan for a distress auction through interstate banking faces a fight on Capitol Hill. Trade groups for thrifts and small banks oppose interstate banking, at least of the kind that would let money-center banks gobble up everybody in sight. Moreover, Congress is reluctant to face this contentious issue.

Faced with determined opposition by the trade groups, the regulators may see their bill significantly modified by Congress or even defeated. "I'm told it's a close call, 50-50," says one investment banker who has conferred with the FSLIC.

But the regulators have a powerful trump card: They can confidently say that if current interest rates persist a few more months, the FSLIC insurance fund will be hit with sizable losses or be tied up with below-market assets purchased from failed lenders to an extent that may jar public confidence in the financial system. "The current plight of the thrift industry is sufficiently severe, and the stakes sufficiently high, that interim action is imperative," Mr. Pratt told the Senate panel.

Reprinted by permission *The Wall Street Journal.*

Last year alone, the FSLIC spent $1 billion of its $6.5 billion fund buying the assets of just three S&Ls. (The fund nevertheless grew because of premium payments, earned interest and maturing securities.) Now, the thrifts' problems are far worse. The recent surge in short-term interest rates has put the S&Ls' cost of funds even further out of line with the low returns from their many old mortgages and seems sure to devastate many of them.

The thrift industry already is locked into a first half loss of $1.5 billion to $1.75 billion, according to Dale Riordan, chief economist for the National Savings and Loan League. And Jonathan Gray, an S&L analyst for Sanford Bernstein & Co., a New York securities firm, believes that the red ink may run to $2.5 billion in the first half and, without a break in interest rates, to $6 billion to $8 billion for the year.

"Interest rates are literally crushing this $800 billion industry," Mr. Gray says. "The situation is without precedent in a half-century."

SOURCE: G. Christian Hill, "Saving Plan: Bill to Aid Sick S&Ls Could Eventually Lead to Interstate Banking," *The Wall Street Journal,* May 21, 1981.

CONFLICTING VIEWS OF THE ROLE OF MONEY AND CREDIT

What have we learned from the performance of the financial system and the economy during the Great Depression? It was clearly understood at the time that the U.S. financial system required some major reforms of its institutions and of government policies to prevent future economic collapse; but there was considerable uncertainty as to precisely what the central problems were and what reforms were essential. (The money and credit reforms that were enacted in the 1930s and further discussion of the events that led to them will be covered in Chapter 12.)

Some students of the period emphasize that the sharp decline in the supply of money and credit during the early 1930s was the major factor accounting for the extreme severity and duration of the Great Depression. Among those who subscribe to this view are the *monetarists*. Monetarist economists hold that changes in the supply of money in the economy have powerful effects on interest rates, real income, and prices. A sharp fall in the money supply will cause a fall in real income followed by a fall in prices; a sharp rise will cause an expansion in real income followed by inflation. Monetarists further believe that the officials of the Federal Reserve have the technical power to make the money supply whatever level they want it to be and should have done more to arrest and reverse the fall in money during the 1930s. Other government policies are of far less consequence for real income and employment (in the short run) and prices (in the long run) according to this school.

The monetarist view

Other economists do not place as much weight on the supply of money and credit and have less confidence in the Federal Reserve's ability to control money, especially in periods of depression. In the *General Theory of Employment Interest and Money,* a now classic book written during the Great Depression, John Maynard Keynes argued that efforts by the monetary authorities (such as the Federal Reserve) cannot by themselves prevent or correct a severe depression. Keynes, who was a brilliant and influential British economist, felt that higher deficit spending by governments combined with monetary expansion is the most effective way to combat a depression.

Keynes won over the majority of economists in the United States during the decade following publication of his book. As these economists, the *early Keynesians*, applied his ideas following World War II, however, they were inclined: (1) to ignore the importance of money, and (2) to extend his notion of the overriding power of fiscal policy (government spending and taxes) to hold for an economy close to full employment as well as for an economy in deep recession. During the 1950s and early 1960s the view also developed among Keynesians that moderate inflation was a price that had to be paid to achieve low unemployment.

The early Keynesian views

Beginning in the late 1960s, the United States and other countries began experiencing a sharp increase in inflation combined at times with high unemployment. For a variety of reasons that would be premature to detail now, aspects of this experience were not consistent with Keynesian theory. At the same time, new studies by Milton Friedman and other monetarists at the University of Chicago and by economists at the Federal Reserve Bank of St. Louis began to spark a revival of interest in money. Subsequently, monetarists' ideas have had a substantial impact on many economists and on government policy.

Recent experience and current views

If forced to choose sides, probably most economists would still consider themselves Keynesians, and certainly most continue to assign considerable importance to fiscal policy. However, Keynesian views have been modified somewhat. There is at least as much emphasis placed now on monetary policy as on fiscal policy, together with other factors, in Keynesian explanations of inflation and unemployment.

Neo-Keynesian views

As we shall see later, the controversy between Keynesians and monetarists has shifted from a focus on whether monetary policy is important at all to debates on the degree of importance of fiscal policy and on the appropriate response of monetary and fiscal policies to business fluctuations. But it is time to conclude our discussion of these debates at this point with the observation that there is wide agreement today at least that the money supply is a very important factor affecting interest rates, real income, and prices.

BENEFITS OF THE FINANCIAL SYSTEM

The foregoing sections have focused on money and credit in disorder because of this book's concern with policy, and because it is in disorder that we perceive most the importance of policies which preserve order. A less dramatic, but equally important concern of this text is the ways in which a properly operating financial system provides vital benefits to the economy. Contributions of the financial system to our standard of living are vast; at the same time, by their nature, these contributions are subtle and difficult to measure. Consequently, we can include only a few rough suggestions of their characteristics and magnitudes in this introductory chapter.

Benefits of the financial system derive from: (1) our advanced payments system, (2) our efficient credit allocation mechanism, and (3) our extensive financial-information system. These benefits are largely provided or enhanced by private financial intermediaries and a number of government agencies.

One way to convey an impression of the benefits of our payments system is to consider how the economy would operate without it or with a less efficient system. The alternative to a money payments system is barter, which is a time-consuming and costly mechanism. This is a topic which will be expanded in Chapter 2.

The payments mechanism

Another way to approach the same topic is to examine some data pertaining to the volume of money transactions in the economy. No one knows the value of all the transactions in currency each year. Based on available bank data, however, there was approximately $50 trillion in debits to bank demand deposit accounts in 1979. These debits required the processing of roughly 40 billion checks and many millions of wire transfers. The efficiency of alternative payments media are described in Chapter 9.

In terms of benefits related to borrowing and lending, the financial system channels great quantities of credit from entities seeking to place funds to those wanting or requiring them for a period of time. In this manner, households, firms, and governments are able to gain greater rewards from saving and to engage in activities that either would not be possible or would have to be postponed otherwise. Real gross national product and the enjoyment of income are vastly higher as a result. (Quantifying this increase would be guesswork, however.)

The improvement of spending choices and income through credit

Some idea of the use of credit can be obtained from flow-of-funds data published by the Federal Reserve. Raw data on the flow of funds among entities reflect inflation as well as the real value of the funds transferred; but these data are impressive nonetheless. In 1979, almost $400 billion in new funds was raised in the credit markets by nonfinancial entities. The size and distribution of these flows of funds were largely determined by market responses to economic variables such as interest rates, expected inflation, and the level of economic activity. The ratio of this total flow of $400 billion to nominal GNP or final money spending was roughly one to six. Approximately 75 percent of these funds was channeled through private financial intermediaries.

In the area of information, the last area mentioned above, there are several contributions. First, the financial system provides us with a unit for general pricing (a unit of account)—the dollar. We will elaborate on the use of a unit of account in Chapter 2 to show how it saves tremendously on information required to make transactions.

Second, the financial system provides us with information about the economy. As already implied by earlier discussion in this chapter, the money supply is considered by most economists and business analysts to be a valuable indicator and source of information about the current and prospective state of the overall economy. Many other financial variables are followed as well for insight into this, variables such as interest rates, credit volumes, the stock market, and the exchange rate for the dollar. Individual interest rates, of course, are crucial to the decisions of borrowers and financial investors.

Lastly, because of certain economies of size and specialization and by their very functions, financial intermediaries and government agencies involved in the financial sector are natural sources of information and interpretation of economic conditions for local areas and for the economy as a whole. In fact, for many financial institutions, directly or indirectly, information is a principal product.

Information provided by the financial system

ORGANIZATION OF THIS BOOK

The book is presented in five parts. Part I concentrates on money. It explains several important concepts and facts about money and provides a preliminary analysis of the effects of money on interest rates, real income, and prices in the economy. Financial, institutional, and macroeconomic detail are omitted from Part 1. (This is not because these details are unimportant, but because there are certain fundamentals of money which can be presented before such detail is introduced and which create a useful perspective for the rest of the book.)

Part 2 covers credit and finance, including key concepts in credit, the functions of finance, analysis of the credit market, and, importantly, international finance. (At one time international finance could be postponed to the end of a text on money and credit; but financial markets now are so globally integrated that this is no longer practical.)

In Part 3 money again occupies center stage. Additional concepts in the topic of money are presented, and the money-supply process is developed for several monetary systems, ranging from simplified but historically meaningful systems to our current complex system. The institutional features of modern financial intermediaries and their regulation, and the monetary policy tools and operational behavior of the Federal Reserve are explained in this part. In the final chapter of Part 3, the major theories and empirical findings concerning the demand for money are presented.

In Part 4 the analysis shifts from one centered on money and credit (with implications for the macro behavior of the economy) to a more direct and general analysis of inflation, real income, and employment. This part presents the Keynesian aggregate-demand, aggregate-supply model which incorporates fiscal policy as well as monetary policy and shows adjustments in consumption and investment, the major components of private spending, to changes in policy. The analysis in this part is also used to trace the effects of special shocks to the economy such as the oil-price increases in 1974 and 1979 by the Organization of Petroleum Exporting Countries (OPEC).

The final part of the text, Part 5, is comprised of two chapters which pull together and expand upon policy issues appearing repeatedly and treated partially in the analytical sections of the book. These issues include: the relative importance of monetary and fiscal policy, the appropriate response of policy to economic fluctuations, and regulation and reform of the financial system.

CONCLUSION

This first chapter has introduced two broad problems in policy that have especially concerned analysts in the area of money and credit—the maintenance of stability in the financial sector and the management of monetary policy for the best possible inflation and employment conditions in the economy. In connection with these problems we described some key aspects of the controversy between Keynesians and monetarists over money and credit. This chapter has also described our concern in this book with the benefits of the financial sector to the economy. These will be recurring topics in the chapters to follow.

The emphasis of this chapter on just two topics in policy should not be construed as an indication that they are the only important ones in the discussion ahead. Government policies in the areas of the allocation of credit among competing interests, international exchange-rate adjustment, and the efficiency of the U.S. payments system are three more that will receive considerable attention.

ADVANCED READING

Friedman, Milton, and Anna J. Schwartz. *A Monetary History of the United States*. Princeton, N.J.: Princeton University Press, 1963, pp. 299–419.

Temin, P. *Did Monetary Forces Cause the Great Depression?* New York: W. W. Norton, 1976.

APPENDIX

GNP, THE PRICE LEVEL, REAL INCOME, POTENTIAL GNP, AND THE BUSINESS CYCLE

This appendix is a review of some important definitions and concepts which are usually treated in an introductory macroeconomics principles course. It is intended as a quick refresher.

GNP

Gross national product is the market value at current prices of all final goods and services produced in the economy over a specific period. Intermediate goods and services are not counted because this would introduce double (or more) counting of their value as they pass through the process of becoming final output. Current-dollar GNP is the broadest measure of the economy's nominal output (output at current prices). Quarterly estimates are constructed and published by the Department of Commerce. (See Figure 1–1A.)

FIGURE 1–1A
Gross national product (annually 1929–1946; seasonally adjusted annual rates, quarterly, 1947–)

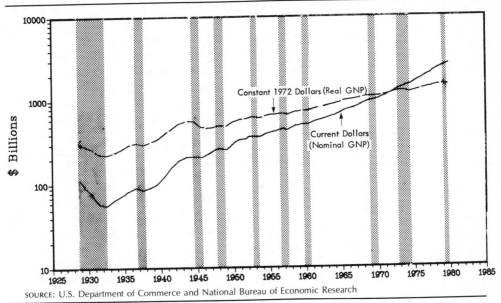

SOURCE: U.S. Department of Commerce and National Bureau of Economic Research

If we subtract sales taxes and an allowance for depreciation on capital goods from GNP, we arrive at a figure very close to national income—the sum of wages, salaries, profits, rent, and other forms of individual and corporate income. This follows from the fact that the production of goods and services yields income to individuals and firms, and this income is roughly equal to what their output is or would be sold for except for sales taxes and expense on plant and equipment maintenance. We may, therefore, refer interchangeably to changes in nominal output and changes in nominal national income, for the two move together and, except for minor concerns such as those just identified, are even essentially the same thing. As a nation, our income is essentially what we produce.

We must be careful, however, not to interpret a change in nominal output as necessarily an equivalent change in the real physical quantity of goods and services produced or a rise in real income. The GNP may change partly as a result of price changes, and this part of a change in GNP adds nothing to our material well-being. We will return to the topic of real income after a discussion of the price level.

The price level

In any year, quarter, or month some prices are higher and some are lower than in a previous period. The price level refers to a weighted average of individual prices in one period and is used to make comparisons among overall prices in different periods. The two most commonly cited measures of the price level are fixed-weight indexes—index numbers which express weighted prices in the current period as a percent of prices with the same weights in a base period. These popular indexes are the consumer price index (CPI) and the producer price index for finished goods (PPI).

Fixed-weight indexes are constructed with weights reflecting a certain quantity mix (basket) of goods in either the current period or the base period.[4] (Not all relevant prices and quantities are recorded; samples are used.) Since in actual fact, products and services change in the proportion in which they are used and new ones are always being introduced in the economy, it would be better to adjust the weights for composition changes and quality changes more often and more accurately than is done for fixed-weight indexes. For these reasons and others, there is a margin of error and, to some extent, an upward bias to the inflation recorded by fixed-weight indexes.

As to coverage, the CPI is designed to measure changes in the prices of goods and services purchased by all urban workers. It is constructed monthly by the Bureau of Labor Statistics, and different CPIs are available for different large urban areas. The PPI, which is

---

[4]If the quantities of the current period are used, the index is a Paasche index. If the base period's quantities are used, it is a Laspeyres index. Most price indexes are of the Laspeyres type.

also constructed monthly by the Bureau of Labor Statistics, is intended to measure changes in the prices of intermediate commodities.

In contrast to the CPI and PPI, which have rather limited and specialized coverage, the gross national product implicit price deflator is a gauge of price changes for all goods and services which comprise the gross national product. It is derived indirectly from nominal GNP and a real GNP series (explained below) such that it does not have the type of bias of a fixed-weight index. The GNP deflator is not completely free of bias, however. For reasons beyond the scope of this review, increases in the GNP deflator tend to understate inflation. Its usefulness also is reduced somewhat by the fact that it is available only quarterly from the Department of Commerce. The charts in Figure 1–2A on page 16 show the rates of increase (rates of inflation) for these indexes since World War II.

Real income and output

As mentioned earlier, GNP and national income are nominal aggregates, and changes in them usually reflect price as well as "real" (physical volume) changes. Comparisons of real output in different periods are obtained by an adjustment of the components of nominal GNP for price changes. This is done by the Department of Commerce to derive the components of real GNP. These components are then added up to obtain total real GNP, the value of GNP in terms of a benchmark year's prices or dollars (1972 prices or dollars, for example). Finally the estimate for total real GNP is used to calculate an overall GNP implicit price deflator as follows:[5]

$$\text{GNP deflator} = \frac{\text{GNP}}{\text{Real GNP}} \times 100$$

Note that we can rearrange the expression above to the following:

$$\text{GNP} = (\text{Real GNP}) \times \frac{(\text{the GNP implicit price deflator})}{100}$$

In general, nominal output (or income) is equal to real output (or income) times the price level, properly expressed.

Ordinarily, of course, we are far more interested in real-income and price-level changes than changes in their multiple, nominal income. There is no benefit to an individual from a rising nominal income if that rise is fully matched by a rise in the price level. A rise in real income means more employment and a generally higher standard of living; a rise in the price level, however, probably yields no net benefits to the populace as a whole and can cause hardship for some individuals and disrupt the economy.

[5]The ratio of nominal to real GNP is multiplied by 100 in the expression above because the GNP deflator is constructed as an index number on a base of 100.

FIGURE 1–2A
Comprehensive price measures (change at annual rates; seasonally adjusted, quarterly)

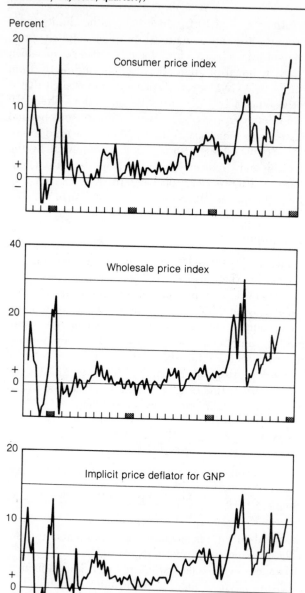

SOURCE: Historical Chart Book (Board of Governors of the Federal Reserve System, 1980).

**"True, eight years ago I promised to marry you when you made
ten thousand a year... sounds ridiculous now, doesn't it?"**

Reprinted by permission *The Wall Street Journal.*

Potential GNP

Potential GNP (also called capacity output) is the level of real
output of the economy at the full employment of its labor and capital
resources. This means that it is the maximum sustainable rate of
output under normal conditions. Actual real output can exceed potential GNP for brief periods but not indefinitely.

Growth in potential output can be attributed to growth in the
labor force, growth in hours per week per employee, and/or improvements in productivity. The United States experienced a period of lower growth in potential output in the 1970s due to lower
gains in productivity relative to earlier years. In 1977 and again in
1979 the President's Council of Economic Advisers revised downward its estimates of recent and future rates of growth in potential
GNP for the United States, as shown in Figure 1–3A. In the 1979

Economic Report of the President, recent (since 1973) and future growth in potential GNP were estimated at 3.0 percent, down from 3.5 percent estimated in the 1977 report, and 3.9 percent estimated in the 1976 report.

FIGURE 1–3A
Actual and potential gross national product

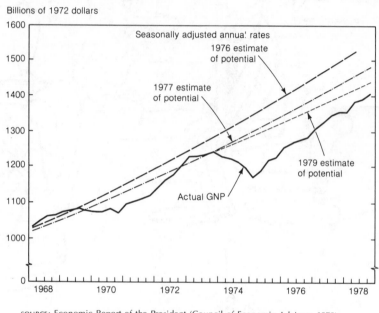

SOURCE: Economic Report of the President (Council of Economic Advisers, 1979).

The business cycle

Economists and business analysts who have compiled data measuring the pulse of economic activity, have found discernable patterns of expansion and contraction in historical data. For a while in the early 1960s it was felt that new macroeconomic policies had made periodic swings or business cycles obsolete, but experience has revealed that this was not to be the case. Today it seems that the cycle will be with us for the foreseeable future. Better government policies may be able to reduce its amplitude, but few today believe that it can be eliminated.

Real GNP is the broadest indicator of general economic activity, but more information is needed to identify business cycles. Based on a number of indicators, the National Bureau of Economic Research has broken down the historical experience of the economy into periods of expansion and recession (contraction) dating back to 1854. The average full cycle in this century has been a little over four years, and expansions have tended to last roughly twice as long as contractions. On the chart in Figure 1–1A—which shows real GNP in 1958 dollars (prices) and nominal GNP in current dollars since 1929—are shaded areas representing contractions as designated by the National Bureau; the unshaded areas are expansions. Note the severity of the contraction from 1929–33.[6]

---

[6]A rough guide to the occurrence of a recession or contraction in recent times is two consecutive quarters of declining real GNP. There is no official distinction between a recession and a depression, and the description of certain severe recessions as depressions is simply a matter of popular agreement.

Some economists have offered the criterion of double-digit unemployment for a depression. There is also, of course, the old quip, "a recession is when my neighbor is out of work; a depression is when I am out of work!"

Some key concepts and facts about money

The concepts and facts about money in this chapter are necessary to the analysis in the chapter that follows on the supply and demand for money. In the first section we describe the functions of money in the economy. These will be helpful in explaining the demand for money in Chapter 3; they also provide the conceptual basis for various empirical definitions of money, which are described in the second section of this chapter. The last section summarizes the role of the Federal Reserve in our money-supply process.

THE FUNCTIONS OF MONEY IN THE ECONOMY

There are three functions traditionally attributed to money or to parts of what is considered the money supply. These are a medium-of-exchange (or transactions) function, a unit-of-account (or standard-of-value) function, and a liquid-store-of-value function.

The medium-of-exchange function is crucial in a sophisticated market economy. We use paper currency, coins, checkable deposit balances and travelers checks to complete almost all transactions in the United States. Hence these are our media of exchange or means of payment. The alternative to using a medium of exchange is

2

20

barter—trading the goods or services you have to offer in direct
exchange for what you want, trading your stereo for a guitar from a
fellow student, for example. Barter works reasonably well for some
isolated transactions such as this, in very primitive economies
where the variety of goods and services is small, and between governments of planned economies where package deals involving
swaps of a wide range of goods can be arranged.

The medium-of-
exchange function

It would be exceedingly awkward and inefficient in a complex,
free-market economy to arrange most transactions as barter, however. Finding suppliers of what we want *and who want just what we
have to offer* would be a highly time-consuming, costly process.
Having a medium of exchange frees us from having to find such
matches. When we find a source of what we want, we offer money—
a medium of exchange—which is *generalized* purchasing power.
Ordinarily, the supplier plans to spend the money he obtains on
something we could not have offered in return, but this does not
interfere with our transaction. Likewise, in transactions where we
are the supplier and offer our labor or goods, it is necessary only to
find a demander who wants what we have to offer and who will pay
the required amount of generalized purchasing power. It is no matter to us if the demander cannot satisfy our ultimate wants.

It is doubtful that a market economy could reach a very high
stage of development without a medium of exchange. Even most
primitive economies adopt some form of transactions medium. But
is the medium-of-exchange function of money the essential property
of money from the standpoint of spending decisions, inflation, and
fluctuations in the economy? Some scholars believe that it is;
however there is no agreement on the answer to this question. The
other functions that money serves may be as or more essential in
this regard.

The unit-of-account or standard-of-value function of money is
identical to the function provided by our system of physical measures and weights. A dollar of currency is our accounting measure of
value. Goods are priced in terms of a standard unit, dollars, for the
same reason they are measured physically in terms of a standard
unit such as inches. Loans, as well, usually specify payments in the
standard unit of dollars, and hence dollars provide a unit of account
for deferred payments and interest.

The unit-of-
account function

The alternative to using a unit of account for transactions requires
pricing each good in terms of every other good. (This does not necessarily mean barter since a medium of exchange could still be used
for actual trades.) Each good would then have as many prices as
there are goods. Assuming uniform prices for each good, the number of prices in the economy would almost equal the square of the
number of goods! [1] With one good selected as a unit of account, all
goods are priced only in terms of the unit-of-account good and there
are only as many prices as there are goods (counting the unit-of-

account good). We find the prices of goods in terms of each other by comparing their unit-of-account prices (one Heineken's at $1.92 is worth two Budweisers at 96 cents each).

The unit of account for prices does not have to be a unit of medium of exchange—it could be bushels of wheat—but it almost always is because this eliminates the comparison we would otherwise have to make in each case between the price of the good we want to buy and the price of our basic medium of exchange. By making the currency or deposit dollar the unit of account, the price of a good or service tells you both the price and the amount of the medium of exchange with which you must part. However, using the money unit as a unit of account is beneficial only so long as the value of a unit of money does not change too drastically or in unexpected directions. Such changes are analogous to having an inch which fluctuates in actual length from time to time. (Chapter 3 provides an analysis of changes in the value of money in terms of the supply and demand for money.)

The liquid-store-of-value function

The third function of money is not difficult to appreciate. Money provides a liquid store of value because it is so easy to store and so easy to spend. This is certainly true for a medium of exchange. Whether it is travelers checks in your billfold, currency stuffed in mattresses, or a checkable balance ensconced safely in a venerable financial institution, it is convenient for many to hold some savings in this form. There are other assets in the economy beyond the media of exchange, however, which serve as liquid stores of value and have one advantage over travelers checks, currency, or checkable deposits in that they pay higher interest. (Currency and travelers checks, of course, pay no interest, and checkable deposits pay either no, or relatively low interest.) Alternative liquid assets include savings and time deposits at commercial banks, and shares or time deposits at savings and loans, mutual savings banks, credit unions, and money-market mutual funds. It is only a little less easy to spend by drawing on these assets than on a medium-of-exchange balance.

Liquid assets play an important role in the economy because they provide individuals and firms with security. With a suitable cushion of liquid assets there is security that financial difficulties can be weathered, and also there is assurance that attractive future buying opportunities can be exploited easily. By providing this service, liquid assets free individuals and firms to engage in activities that they otherwise would avoid because of risk. Problems can arise for the

---

[1]For one good there would be no need for any price. For two goods, say beer and cheese, we would have P_{BC}, the price of beer in terms of cheese (e.g., one beer is worth a half pound of cheese) and P_{CB}, the price of cheese in terms of beer (e.g., one pound of cheese is worth two beers). For three goods, beer, cheese, and Alka-Seltzer, there would be P_{BC}, P_{CB}, P_{AB}, P_{BA}, P_{CA}, P_{AC}. In general, for n goods, there would be $n^2 - n$ prices. (Only half of these prices are independent since $P_{BC} = 1/P_{CB}$, and so on.)

whole economy, however, if there is a sharp change in the overall supply or demand for liquid assets; as we shall see, such changes can affect spending in an undesirable way. (The characteristics of assets which make them more or less liquid are described in Chapter 7, and analysis of the supply and demand for liquidity is covered in that and several later chapters.)

INTRODUCTION TO ARTICLE

Money is such a "magnificent improvisation" that it is usually adopted in even the simplest of economies. In what has become a classic article for economics students, R.A. Radford described the development of markets and a commodity money—cigarettes—among British soldiers in a World War II prisoner-of-war camp. The excerpt below describes the use of cigarettes as a unit of account (standard of value), medium of exchange, and store of value. (Another excerpt from this article appears in Chapter 10. The full article is extremely enlightening but is not reproduced here because not all of it is directly relevent to the topics of this book.)

The Economic Organisation of a P.O.W. Camp

Very soon after capture people realised that it was both undesirable and unnecessary, in view of the limited size and the equality of supplies, to give away or to accept gifts of cigarettes or food. "Goodwill" developed into trading as a more equitable means of maximising individual satisfaction.

We reached a transit camp in Italy about a fortnight after capture and received one quarter of a Red Cross food parcel each a week later. At once exchanges, already established, multiplied in volume. Starting with simple direct barter, such as a non-smoker giving a smoker friend his cigarette issue in exchange for a chocolate ration, more complex exchanges soon became an accepted custom. Stories circulated of a padre who started off round the camp with a tin of cheese and five cigarettes and returned to his bed with a complete parcel in addition to his original cheese and cigarettes; the market was not yet perfect. Within a week or two, as the volume of trade grew, rough scales of exchange values came into existence. Sikhs, who had at first exchanged tinned beef for practically any other foodstuff, began to insist on jam and margarine. It was

realised that a tin of jam was worth one-half pound of margarine plus something else; that a cigarette issue was worth several chocolates issues, and a tin of diced carrots was worth practically nothing.

In this camp we did not visit other bungalows very much and prices varied from place to place; hence the germ of truth in the story of the itinerant priest. By the end of a month, when we reached our permanent camp, there was a lively trade in all commodities and their relative values were well known, and expressed not in terms of one another—one didn't quote bully in terms of sugar—but in terms of cigarettes. The cigarette became the standard of value. In the permanent camp people started by wandering through the bungalows calling their offers—"cheese for seven" (cigarettes)—and the hours after parcel issue were Bedlam.

The inconveniences of this system soon led to its replacement by an Exchange and Mart notice board in every bungalow, where under the headings "name," "room number," "wanted" and "offered" sales and wants were advertised. When a deal went through, it was crossed off the board. The public and semipermanent records of transactions led to cigarette prices being well known and thus tending to equality throughout the camp, although there were always opportunities for an astute trader to make a profit from arbitrage. With this development everyone, including non-smokers, was willing to sell for cigarettes, using them to buy at another time and place. Cigarettes became the normal currency, though, of course, barter was never extinguished.

The permanent camps in Germany saw the highest level of commercial organisation. In addition to the Exchange and Mart notice boards, a shop was organised as a public utility, controlled by representatives of the Senior British Officer, on a no-profit basis. People left their surplus clothing, toilet requisites and food there until they were sold at a fixed price in cigarettes. Only sales in cigarettes were accepted—there was no barter—and there was no higgling. For food at least there were standard prices: clothing is less homogeneous and the price was decided around a norm by the seller and the shop manager in agreement: shirts would average say 80, ranging from 60 to 120 according to quality and age. Of food, the shop carried small stocks for convenience; the capital was provided by a loan from the bulk store of Red Cross cigarettes and repaid by a small commission taken of the first transactions. Thus the cigarette attained its fullest currency status, and the market was almost completely unified.

SOURCE: from R. A. Radford, "The Economic Organisation of a P.O.W. Camp," *Economica,* 12 (1945).

CONCEPTUAL DEFINITIONS AND EMPIRICAL MEASURES OF THE MONEY SUPPLY

The different functions of money may seem to suggest alternative definitions of the money supply, depending upon which function is stressed. In fact, they do. The most closely followed definition equates money at a conceptual level with whatever serves as a medium of exchange. At a practical or empirical level, this implies that money is comprised of different assets in different historical periods

Money narrowly defined

and in different economies. Assets that have served as media of exchange range from cattle in pastoral societies to promissory notes written on playing cards in 17th-century French Canada. Through time and across societies metals such as gold, silver, and copper, have been widely used, almost universal media. As world economies have developed, however, paper media have tended to displace metals, and checkable deposits in turn have largely displaced paper.

Most transactions in the United States today involve payment in U.S. metal currency (coins), paper currency, checkable deposit balances, or travelers checks. This suggests that an appropriate empirical measure of the money supply in the United States—based on the medium-of-exchange criterion—would be an aggregate of all these assets. Because alternative measures of money include a wider range of assets, measures based on the medium-of-exchange criterion are referred to as *money narrowly defined*.

The M-1 measures

In actuality, because of ongoing institutional changes in the monetary system, there are presently two medium-of-exchange measures calculated and published by the Federal Reserve. For a long period ending in early 1980, there was only one medium-of-

exchange measure, labeled M-1 and defined as currency plus commercial-bank demand deposits owned by the "nonbank public"
where the nonbank public referred to anyone except domestic commercial banks, the Federal Reserve, and the U.S. Treasury.

This definition became increasingly obsolete in the late 1970s as
new forms of checkable deposits developed and spread at banks and
other intermediaries. In February 1980, the Fed introduced M-1A,
which is virtually the same as the old M-1 measure except that it
excludes deposit holdings of foreign commercial banks and foreign
official (government) institutions, and M-1B, which adds new forms
of checkable deposits and (as of June 1981) travelers checks to M-
1A.[2] The new checkable deposits are negotiable-order-of-withdrawal
(NOW) accounts and automatic-transfer-savings (ATS) accounts at
banks and savings and loans and share drafts at credit unions.[3] Starting in January 1981, NOW accounts were authorized nationwide;
previously they were authorized only in New England, New York,
and New Jersey. The two M-1 money-supply measures, M-1A and
M-1B, will be retained by the Federal Reserve during a transition
period following this institutional change. Subsequently, there
probably will be a single narrow measure of money very close to the
present M-1B and labeled, once more, simply M-1. Both narrow
money supply measures are shown for 1979-80 in Figure 2–1.

The second conceptual basis for money-supply measures is the
liquid-store-of-value function. Clearly, any measure of money based
on this function should include all medium-of-exchange assets and
more. The difficulty is in knowing where "more" stops. One measure includes M-1B and, among other assets, savings deposits and
small-denomination time deposits at all depository institutions. Naturally, this measure is designated M-2.[4] Another, M-3, adds mainly
large time deposits at all depository institutions to M-2.[5] Finally,
there is L, which is the broadest measure of liquid assets published
by the Federal Reserve.

*Money broadly
defined and
related measures*

---

[2]Often subscripted Ms are used for the different measures of money: M_1, M_{1a}.
M_{1b}, etc. However, subscripted Ms are also frequently used to refer to different
levels of the money stock in graphical supply-and-demand analysis, as we do in Chapter 3. Hence, as above, hyphenated Ms are used to distinguish the M measures of
money in this text.

[3]NOW accounts are essentially demand deposits which bear interest and carry a
different label to get around federal regulations which have prohibited interest payments on demand deposits. ATS accounts are savings accounts which permit funds to
be switched to and from checking accounts automatically, for a fee. Except for the
fee, they are essentially the same as NOW accounts.

[4]Other assets in M-2 are, in order of size, money-market mutual fund shares,
overnight repurchase agreements issued by commercial banks, and overnight Eurodollar deposits held by U.S. nonbank residents at Caribbean branches of U.S. banks.

It would take more space than warranted to explain these assets here, since together they constitute only 5 percent or so of M-2, and there is conceptual material
we must cover before it will be apparent why they are included in M-2. Descriptions
and analysis of these assets and certain other assets included in the other broad
measures of money are presented in Chapters 6 and 7, and all of the specific assets in
the various definitions of money are set out in tables in Chapters 7 and 14.

[5]Large time deposits are those issued in denominations of $100,000 and above.

FIGURE 2—1

Money stock (M-1A) (averages of daily figures seasonally adjusted)

$ Billions

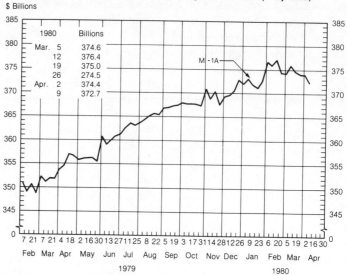

1980	Billions
Mar. 5	374.6
12	376.4
19	375.0
26	274.5
Apr. 2	374.4
9	372.7

M-1A

Money stock (M-1B) (averages of daily figures seasonally adjusted)

$ Billions

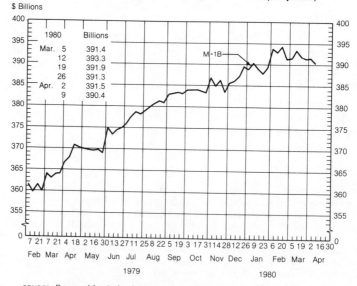

1980	Billions
Mar. 5	391.4
12	393.3
19	391.9
26	391.3
Apr. 2	391.5
9	390.4

M-1B

SOURCE: Prepared by Federal Reserve Bank of St. Louis.

How do we choose among so many broad measures of money? Partly because of the difficulty in establishing the appropriate empirical counterpart to liquidity, most economists and analysts who stress the liquidity services of money still seem to prefer to define money as one of the M-1 measures or M-2.

For reasons of convenience, of the author's own judgement, and of the judgment of the majority of monetary economists, the medium-of-exchange function of money will be the criterion for measures of money in this text. *For the present system, we will identify the appropriate measure of money as M-1B or, once the Fed changes notation, the new M-1, which consists of currency, travelers checks, and checkable deposits held by the nonbank public.*

INTRODUCTION TO ARTICLE

The controversy between Keynesians and monetarists as to the importance of the money supply is complicated by several related minor controversies, one of which involves the appropriate definition and measure of money. Monetarists and Keynesians do not divide along clear lines in this controversy: most Keynesians prefer a narrow definition of money, but some prefer a broader definition; the dominance of opinion among monetarists is not clear, though Milton Friedman has been a strong advocate of an earlier version of M-2 which focused on deposits at commercial banks.

An unfortunate consequence of this minor disagreement and of uncertainty as to the appropriate definition and measure of money is that on occasion there can be conflicting opinion and uncertainty as to what money is doing—hence all the more disagreement and uncertainty as to what money is doing *to the economy*. The *New York Times* article below describes the controversy as it existed in 1975, during the Ford administration when there were even more monetary measures in use. Though the monetary measures published by the Fed have been revised, the same basic issues persist today.

The Many Faces of Money

WASHINGTON—Quiz. The following was said last week by a public figure:

"The facts are contrary to the facts that you've stated. M-1, 2, 3, 4, 5, 6 and 7—all of them—show an increase." Who said it?

1. Milton Friedman.
2. Henry Reuss.
3. Edward Teller.
4. Gen. George S. Brown
5. Gerald Ford.
6. Hubert Humphrey.

The answer is No. 5, the former center from Grand Rapids, Mich., became last week the first President of the United States to show himself, if not a monetarist, a user of the jargon of the monetarists. It was an event in the history of economics of probably greater moment than the much quoted statement of Richard Nixon that "I am a Keynesian."

President Ford made the remark in answer to a question at one of his increasingly frequent regional, nontelevised news conferences. It did not make news as such, but it put a Presidential imprimatur on the mysterious "M." "M" stands for money.

It is fairly familiar ground by now that monetarists think that the economy's course—inflation, recession and the like—is largely determined by the rate of change of the money supply, usually in terms of M-1 or M-2, and that the Federal Reserve, which controls the money supply, is skeptical of this view.

Is there some "truth" anywhere in all of the argument about "M"? The main truth, most economists would probably agree, is that uncertainty is a hallmark of discussions of the subject. But beyond this there are serious and respectable, if sometimes conflicting, facts and viewpoints.

In probably the most detailed effort to date to discredit the supposedly crucial importance of M-1, George W. Mitchell, a member of the Reserve Board, illustrated in a speech early this year all the ways in which both businesses and consumers have learned to economize on their demand deposit balances by holding their checking accounts to a minimum because they may not earn interest. He concluded:

"To seek improved control by reliance on a variable, M-1, whose characteristics and significance are undergoing rapid change, involves unknown exposures. In my opinion, the concept of the narrowly defined money supply is becoming less appropriate even as a proxy for monetary action."

Definitions of eight monetary aggregates

Includes	M-1	M-2	M-2'	M-3	M-4	M-5	M-6	M-7
Currency	X	X	X	X	X	X	X	X
Demand deposits	X	X	X	X	X	X	X	X
Time deposits except large certificates of deposit		X	X	X	X	X	X	X
Large certificates of deposit				X		X	X	X
Deposits in saving and loan associations and savings banks				X	X	X	X	X
Savings bonds and credit union shares					X	X	X	X
Short-term governments							X	X
Commercial paper								X

Milton Friedman, the father of monetarism, and Alan Greenspan, the chairman of the President's Council of Economic Advisers, implicitly accept some of the problems of M-1 but believe that many of these are solved by using M-2. Mr. Greenspan has pointed out in Congressional testimony that there is a remarkable parallel between the growth of M-2 and the growth of the current-dollar gross national product. By this test, if M-2 grows faster than "real" G.N.P. can grow, the result is bound to be inflation.

The Federal Reserve can directly control only the total of bank reserves (some would use a roughly equivalent magnitude called the monetary base). What happens after a given amount of new reserves is pumped into the banking system is beyond the Federal Reserve's control. If the public wants to hold more currency—as has been the case in the last year—this "uses up" more reserves than if money is held as demand deposits, and M-1 growth will be less.

But if there is a shift toward commercial bank savings deposits, or large corporate certificates of deposit, then less reserves are "used up" and more M-1 can be created.

Regardless of all these various subtleties and caveats, serious economists continue to look at M-1. Witnesses before Congressional committees such as Otto Eckstein, head of Data Resources, Inc., and Wall Street analysts such as Sam I. Nakagama, economist at Kidder, Peabody & Co., do not hesitate to specify numbers—such as 8 to 10 per cent—as the needed growth in M-1 this year to assure economic recovery.

The same is true of the economists in the "Shadow" Open Market Committee, a group of monetarists who respectfully try to tell the Federal Reserve what to do. And the same goes for the growing monetarist group in Congress. Representative Henry S. Reuss, the Wisconsin Democrat who is the new chairman of the Banking Committee, hailed as "excellent progress" earlier this month the fact that M-1 had grown fairly rapidly in the most recently reported four weeks, thus putting himself squarely in the corner of President Ford.

Dr. Burns himself has let it be known that he rather likes M-5 or, for some purposes, M-2 prime. While these preferences are no doubt genuine, there is an implied gamemanship involved. Designed or not, this is obviously a promising ploy for confusing the attacker. If one can show that M-5 is doing very well, one can scoff at a weak performance of M-1.

Whether all of this amounts to an advance in knowledge or wisdom is difficult to say. A decent humility about many of these matters characterizes not only private economists but also people in the thick of the battle, including Dr. Burns. But in any case, a President has blurted out M's with a proper sense of their importance.

SOURCE: Edwin L. Dale, Jr., "The Many Faces of Money," *New York Times*, March 23, 1975. © 1975 by the New York Times Co. Reprinted by permission.

THE ROLE OF THE FEDERAL RESERVE IN THE MONEY-SUPPLY PROCESS

This final section of Chapter 2 gives only a brief description of the most important role of the Federal Reserve in the financial sector. A full treatment of the Federal Reserve's procedures and the money-supply process is not presented until Part III. At this point the following summary must suffice until more background material has been covered.

The Federal Reserve was established by Congress in 1913 to serve a number of regulatory and central banking functions. These functions and the tools and strategies used by the Federal Reserve to achieve them have undergone significant changes over the years.

The Federal Reserve's chief responsibility today is the establishment and implementation of monetary policy. In conducting monetary policy, the Federal Reserve sets targets for the growth rates of several of the monetary aggregates. These targets are designed to be consistent with the Fed's general objectives and perceptions regarding inflation and real output in the economy. And under legislation passed in 1978, the Federal Reserve has been explicitly charged with reporting these targets to Congress and adhering to inflation and employment objectives consonant with those of the administration and Congress.[6]

As the nation's central bank, the Fed has actions that it can take to expand or contract reserves available to depository institutions with strong effects on interest rates and the supply of money in the economy. Its actions are taken principally through *open-market operations* (purchases and sales of government securities), but it can also change *the discount rate* (the interest rate it charges on loans) and alter *reserve requirements* for depository institutions.

The Federal Reserve's tools

Additions to the supply of reserves through open-market securities purchases or loans tend to reduce interest rates and encourage growth in credit and the money supply; Fed actions to drain reserves through open-market security sales tend to raise interest rates and reduce the rates of growth of the monetary and credit

[6]This legislation was the Full Employment and Balanced Growth Act of 1978, also called the Humphrey-Hawkins Act.

aggregates. A reduction in the discount rate encourages depository institutions to borrow reserves from the Fed to expand credit and deposits; a rise in the discount rate discourages reserve borrowings and credit and deposit expansion. A decrease in reserve requirements frees up reserves, stimulating bank loans and monetary expansion, and an increase in requirements freezes funds in reserves, curbing growth in loans and money.

As direct as these linkages sound, they, in fact, involve a number of complex interactions and adjustments which take time and introduce uncertainty to the process, complicating the Fed's job. Complications are created by the following facts: (1) the Fed does not have precise, current information as to how rapidly system reserves and the monetary aggregates are growing; (2) there are factors not under the Fed's control which influence system reserves and the monetary aggregates; and (3) there is a lag before Federal Reserve actions take effect on money growth.

Guides to appropriate Federal Reserve actions

Yet, despite these problems, the Fed must decide on a current basis what actions to take. During the 1970s, the Federal Reserve used a narrow target range for the *federal funds rate* as a guide to appropriate open-market operations in the very short run.[7] Periodically, the narrow target range for this rate was adjusted to influence the growth of money and credit.

It was found that there were drawbacks to the 1970s approach to monetary control, however, as explained in later chapters. In response, in October 1979, the Federal Reserve began permitting a wider range to the federal funds rate and vowed to key its actions more directly to the behavior of bank reserves and the money supply. Additionally, in March 1980, new legislation provided for a phased-in extension of Federal Reserve reserve requirements to virtually all depository institutions.[8] The October 1979 operating approach has not achieved the stability in money growth many analysts had hoped for, though the Fed has expressed satisfaction with it. For reasons explained later, some critics of the Fed feel that still further changes in the Federal Reserve's operating procedures are necessary. Changes brought by the March 1980 legislation, the Depository Institutions Deregulation and Monetary Control Act, are still in the process of being implemented, and it is too soon to tell whether these changes will prove beneficial.

As we shall discover, difficulties presented by monetary control are not the only problems the Fed faces. Others include uncertainty

---

[7]A detailed analysis of the federal funds rate must be postponed. Here we will simply identify it as the rate of interest charged on unsecured, short-term loans of funds, principally among banks, and point out that the Federal Reserve is able to influence this rate by adding or draining reserves from the monetary system via open-market operations.

[8]In the 1970s and earlier, Federal Reserve reserve requirements applied only to "member" banks, roughly two thirds of the nation's banks which elected to be members of the Federal Reserve system.

about the state of the economy, the fact that Federal Reserve officials generally have different backgrounds, points of view, and even objectives, and that the Federal Reserve may be subject to conflicting pressures from the administration, from Congress, and from various economic interests—and such pressures may be in conflict with the Fed's own view of appropriate policy.

CONCLUSION

This chapter has described the key functions of money in the economy, the closely followed empirical definitions of money, and the role of the Federal Reserve in the money-supply process. In Chapter 3, we will develop a supply-and-demand analysis for money which draws on the concepts and definitions of this chapter. Much of the present chapter and all of Chapter 3 are essentially previews to more detailed material in later parts of the text.

PROBLEMS

1. Describe the major definitions of money employed by economists and policy advisers. What difficulties might possibly arise as a result of there being more than one definition in use by policymakers?
2. Construct a hypothetical example of an economy with a unit of account separate from the unit of the medium of exchange. What would be the advantages and disadvantages of such a separation?

ADVANCED READINGS

Brunner, K., and Meltzer, A. H. "The Uses of Money: Money in the Theory of an Exchange Economy." *American Economic Review* 61 (December 1971) 784–805.

Yeager, L. B. "Essential Properties of the Medium of Exchange." *Kyklos* XXI (Fasc. 1, 1968); 45–68.

Supply and demand analysis of money: A preview and some applications

Why does money affect interest rates, real income, and prices as indicated in Chapter 1? A preliminary, simple analysis of the effects of money on the economy can be developed using the model of supply and demand which is so useful for analyzing the determination of prices and quantities of individual goods and services.

In this chapter we will first cover some basics of the supply and demand model. Much of this will be a review of introductory material; the presentation here will be the same as, or slightly more advanced than in your introductory course. However, some of the material is especially geared to providing background for the analyses of money and other topics in the remainder of the book.

Next the supply and demand model is applied to money, and the effects of an increase in the supply of money are explained. This is a very preliminary and summary analysis which will be expanded upon in later chapters.

The third section describes the timing of the effects of money on the economy. Finally, in the last section, a comparison is drawn between money and the outstanding quantity of a corporation's common stock to illustrate some unique characteristics of money.

3

32

THE SUPPLY AND DEMAND MODEL: BAREST ESSENTIALS AND X-RATED MOVIES

The fundamental components of the model are a demand function, a supply function, and an equilibrium condition. The demand function states all the important variables which we think influence the quantity of a good or service consumers (or others) desire to purchase. The supply function states all the relevant variables which are likely to affect the quantity producers (or others) desire to sell. Finally the equilibrium condition defines the state of rest for the market, that is, the situation where there is no tendency for change.

The demand function

Components of the model

To illustrate the bare essentials, we can take a peep at the market for X-rated movies. Imagine that the quantity of admissions to X-rated movies that people desire is determined by the price of admission, X-rated moviegoers' incomes, the price of parking in the movie house area, the price of *Playboy,* and so on. (We implicitly assume that X-rated moviegoers want to get the most satisfaction they can from their incomes across a variety of goods.) For brevity it is convenient to express our demand function symbolically as,

$$X^D = f(P^X, Y, P^R, \ldots)$$

where X^D is the quantity of admissions demanded, $= f(\ )$ indicates "is a function of" or "is influenced by" the variables within the parentheses, P^X is the price of admission to X-rated movies, Y is income, and P^R stands for the prices of related items such as parking and *Playboy.* The dots stand for all the variables we have left out of the analysis.

This expression as it stands tells us nothing about the *direction* or the *relative strength* of influence for each variable within the parentheses, though we may have definite notions about these. The variable on the left-hand side of our demand function is the *dependent* variable; the variables within the parentheses, on the right-hand side, are *independent* variables.

We may want to focus on one particular independent variable, say P^X, and examine the direction and strength of its influence. To do this we assume the other variables are constant and consider the values of X^D that would tend to occur at different hypothetical values of P^X. The relationship between the two variables, our dependent variable and our one independent variable, can be labeled D^X and represented graphically as in Figure 3–1.

The demand curve

The values along the axes were picked just for illustration. (Instead of identifying numerical values such as a price of $2 and a quantity of 5,000, we could have used P^X_1 and X^D_1 to indicate a certain combination of price and quantity demanded; P^X_2 and X^D_2 could replace a price of $4 and quantity of 4,000, and so on.) The relationship D^X in Figure 3–1 is usually, but not always what economists are referring to when they use the term *demand curve.* It describes the

FIGURE 3–1   Demand for admissions

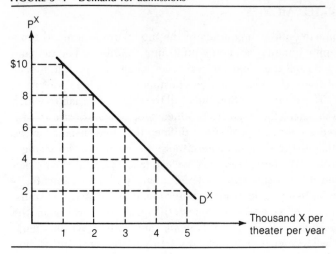

quantity ¦demanded at each price over a range of hypothetical prices.

The demand curve is downward sloping (as most are), which indicates that the direction of influence of price on quantity demanded is inverse; that is, a rise in price causes a decrease in the number of admissions demanded. The strength of influence of P^X on X^D is also apparent from Figure 3–1. This influence is gauged best by the percentage change in quantity demanded divided by the percentage change in price, which is called the *price elasticity* of demand. For a rise in price from $4 to $6 the arc measure of the price elasticity of demand is −5/7, and for a rise from $6 to $8 the arc measure is −7/5.[1] In the first case demand is *inelastic* (elasticity less negative than −1), and in the second, demand is *elastic* (more negative than −1). If the demand elasticity were equal to −1, demand would be *unitary elastic*.

Price elasticity

Note that the elasticity of demand changes along a straight-line demand curve. A demand curve of constant elasticity would be nonlinear unless that elasticity is zero or infinity. A special demand curve that will be of interest later has a constant point elasticity

---

[1] Arc elasticity calculations are made across discrete changes in price and quantity, using the averages of the prices and quantities for the base in each percentage:

$$\frac{\dfrac{X_1^D - X_2^D}{(X_1^D + X_2^D)/2}}{\dfrac{P_1^X - P_2^X}{(P_1^X + P_2^X)/2}} \quad \text{or} \quad \frac{\dfrac{X_1^D - X_2^D}{X_1^D + X_2^D}}{\dfrac{P_1^X - P_2^X}{P_1^X + P_2^X}}$$

where X_1^D and P_1^X are initial quantity and price and X_2^D and P_2^X are the "changed to" quantity and price.

Point elasticity calculations are made at a single point on a demand or supply curve, using the slope of the curve and a single price and quantity:

$$\frac{\Delta P}{P} \bigg/ \frac{\Delta Q}{Q} \quad \text{or} \quad \frac{\Delta P}{\Delta Q} \bigg/ \frac{Q}{P}.$$

FIGURE 3–2   Unitary elastic demand curve

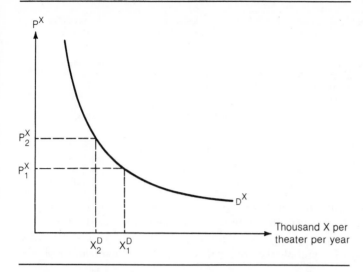

equal to -1 and is shown in Figure 3–2. Its geometric form is that of a rectangular hyperbola.[2]

It is important to remember that the relationships in Figure 3–1 and 3–2 are drawn *assuming the other variables which affect the quantity demanded are constant.* This assumption is known as the *ceteris-paribus* (other things the same) assumption. It means that the relationship shown may not accurately describe the quantity demanded for each possible price if one or more other independent variables change. A change in one of the other variables will shift the demand curve to the right or left depending upon whether the other variable exerts a positive or negative influence on quantity demanded. For example, a rise in moviegoers' income will probably result in an increase in the quantity of admissions demanded *at each price*, and hence a shift to the right in the demand curve in Figure 3–1.

The ceteris-paribus assumption

The box at the top of the next page provides a summary of the demand function as we have described it. The demand function is repeated in symbols above the box for convenience.

Now we move on to consider the supply function. Using our example of X-rated movies, we can reason that the quantity of admissions supplied by movie houses in a competitive market is determined by, among other things, the price of admission they charge, the rental fee for films, the cost of projection equipment, employees' wage rates, and the risk that the local authorities will fine the movie houses or shut them down. (We implicitly assume that movie

---

[2] A constant elasticity demand curve can be represented by the equation $X^D = a(P^X)^b$ where a is a constant and b is the constant elasticity of demand (usually negative). When $b = -1$, this is the equation for a rectangular hyperbola.

$$X^D = f(P^X, Y, P^R \ldots)$$

Influenced (dependent) variable	Influencing (independent) variables	Direction of influence
X^D: the quantity of admissions to X-rated movies demanded	P^X: the price of admission to X-rated movies	Negative or inverse
	Y: moviegoers' income	Positive
	P^R: the price of related goods	Positive for substitutes; negative for complements

houses are out to maximize profits at some tolerable level of risk.) Movie houses vary the number of admissions per year they are willing to supply by varying the number and length of runs of X-rated movies. In symbols the appropriate supply function could look like this:

The supply function

$$X^S = f(P^X, C, K, \ldots)$$

The following box explains the symbols and the influences.

Influenced variable	Influencing variables	Direction of influence
X^S: the quantity of admissions supplied to X-rated movies by movie houses in a competitive market	P^X: the price of admission to X-rated movies	Positive
	C: the expected unit costs such as the rental fees for films (marginal costs are the relevant variable)	Negative
	K: the risk of un-expected costs such as fines for violating local moral ordinances	Negative

The supply curve in Figure 3–3 represents the relationship between quantity supplied and price for a range of hypothetical prices, assuming the other independent variables are constant. The direction of influence of P^X on X^S is positive. We could calculate elasticities of supply to show the strength of influence. (Any supply curve which is a straight line out of the origin has a constant elasticity equal to 1.)

FIGURE 3-3   Supply of admissions

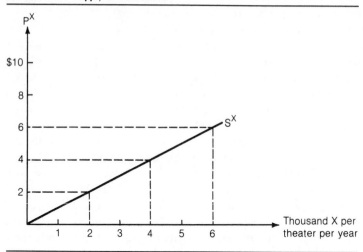

The supply curve is a ceteris-paribus relationship. If the rental fee for X-rated movies were to rise, the curve would shift upward or to the left to reflect the fact that movie houses would require a higher admissions price (to offset the higher rental fee) at each quantity of admissions supplied. Alternatively, we could say that they are willing to supply a lower number of admissions at each price.

FIGURE 3-4   Supply and demand for admissions

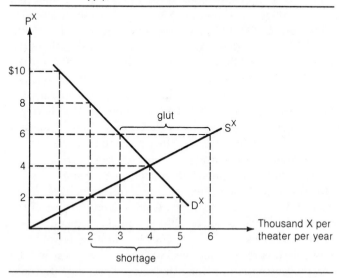

The demand and supply curves can be drawn on the same graph as in Figure 3-4. We are not quite ready yet to use the model for analysis, however, because an equation which defines an equilibrium for the market is missing. If the market is free of legal restric-

The equilibrium
condition

tions on the price that can be charged or the quantity that can be sold, the appropriate equilibrium condition is $X^D = X^S$ because, when this condition occurs, there will be no tendency for P^X, X^D, and X^S to change. This is often referred to as a *market-clearing equilibrium.* Such a condition occurs at $P^X = \$4$ and $X^D = X^S = 4,000$ in Figure 3–4. If the price were to rise higher than \$4, say to \$6, $X^D = 3,000$ and $X^S = 6,000$, and a condition of excess supply would exist (excess supply $= X^S - X^D$). Movie houses would book more nights of X-rated films at \$6, and moviegoers would purchase fewer admissions. The result would be a persistence of vacant seats for the movie houses. In a perfectly competitive market, movie houses would tend to cut the price of admission (so that X^D would rise) and the number and length of runs (X^S would fall) until $X^D = X^S$ again.[3]

A fall in price below \$4, say to \$2, would cause X^D to rise to 5,000, X^S to fall to 2,000, and a condition of excess demand (excess demand $= X^D - X^S$) to emerge. This would mean that admissions sold would fall below the profit-maximizing level and movie houses would tend to raise price and expand scheduled showings to eliminate the excess demand.

Effects of market
restrictions

Other equilibrium conditions are possible if there are price or quantity restrictions imposed on the market. If, for example, there is a maximum legal price (price ceiling) for admission to movies of \$2, the equilibrium condition for price would be $P^X = \$2$. In this case, the market may not eliminate excess demand; a permanent condition may exist where some are unable to find seats. In such a condition of shortage, as shown in Figure 3–4 by the difference between 5,000 and 2,000 at \$2, the price moviegoers would be willing to pay is higher even than the price that would exist without the legal ceiling. We can find this price from the demand curve; it is the price at which moviegoers would desire only 2,000 admissions per year, \$8. Since this represents the value of an additional admission to an X-rated movie to someone denied admission by the shortage, someone else lucky enough to obtain tickets at \$2 could make a handsome profit by reselling them to the frustrated customers at \$8. This type of extralegal exchange constitutes a black market.

Conversely a minimum price (price floor) of \$6 would create a more or less permanent state of excess supply or "glut of smut," you might say. In this case, the frustration would be on the part of the movie houses which would not be able to find the demand for admissions they would like to have at \$6. No doubt they would attempt to remedy this with "come-ons" such as free popcorn and the like. That would essentially reduce the price of the show to those who enjoy popcorn with porn.

---

[3]Many movie houses operate in markets with a limited type of competition known as monopolistic competition. Theaters in such markets may operate with persistent excess capacity.

We will not go into quantity restrictions, and we will assume for further analysis that there are no price restrictions on our market so that the appropriate equilibrium condition is $X^D = X^S$, and our complete model in symbols is,

$$X^D = f(P^X, Y, P^R \ldots) \tag{1}$$
$$X^S = f(P^X, C, K, \ldots) \tag{2}$$
$$X^D = X^S \tag{3}$$

The complete model

This is a system of three simultaneous equations. Our analysis assumes there are three unknowns, X^D, X^S, and P^X, and the other variables, Y, P^R, C, and K are known from outside the model. (We ignore the other independent variables represented by the dots in the parentheses.) X^D, X^S, and P^X are *endogenous* variables (determined within the model), and Y, P^R, C, and K are our *exogenous* variables (determined outside the model).

The graph in Figure 3–4 which shows a solution for $X^D = X^S = 4,000$, holds for certain values of Y, P^R, C, and K. If one of the exogenous variables changes, this solution will change. For example, suppose income rises. This might shift the demand curve to the right from D_1^X to D_2^X as shown in Figure 3–5. This creates a new solution to the model, $P^X = \$6$ and $X^D = X^S = 6,000$.

Shifts in the curves

FIGURE 3–5
Increase in demand

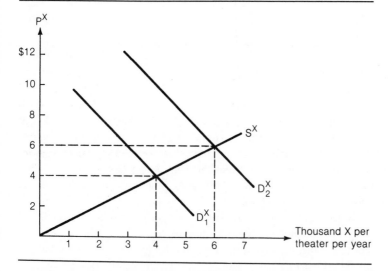

Our analysis assumes that any difference between X^D and X^S will be removed by a change in P^X, and that certainly seems reasonable. It is possible to proceed differently, however, and assume that another independent variable, say moviegoers' income, always adjusts to equate X^D and X^S. That may strike you as unlikely, but let us consider it for a moment to make a point. In Figure 3–6, we show

Plausible and implausible results

two curves relating X^D to income and a vertical curve representing X^S at various income levels. (This S^X curve is vertical since income does not enter into our supply function.) We will still call these demand and supply curves even though they no longer relate price and quantity. Using the demand curve D_1^X, equilibrium occurs at an average annual income level of $10,000 per moviegoer and at $X^D = X^S = 4,000$. Our analysis assumes X^D, X^S, and Y are endogenous and P^X, P^R, C, and K are exogenous.

FIGURE 3–6   An implausible result

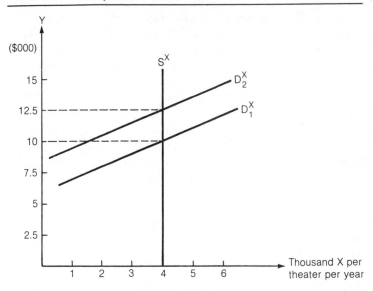

Now let the price of *Playboy* fall. This might shift our demand curve in Figure 3–6 to the left, assuming consumers tend to switch from X-rated movies to *Playboy*. X^D no longer equals X^S at Y = $10,000. If other things remain the same (including P^X), our model says that income would have to rise to $12,500 to restore equilibrium in our X-rated market; that is the new solution. What would tend to cause X-rated moviegoers' incomes to rise to $12,500 to achieve such an equilibrium? There is no plausible reason for such an adjustment in Y. Hence the approach of this analysis is not useful—at least not for X-rated movies.

There is nothing wrong with our model in that it shows what the required adjustment in income would be under the ceteris-paribus conditions imposed. The problem is simply that there is nothing about consumer or movie-house behavior under a condition of $X^D < X^S$ that suggests that income will tend to rise. On the other hand, profit-maximizing behavior on the part of movie houses does suggest an adjustment in P^X when $X^D < X^S$. And P^X is likely to be the only independent variable in the demand and supply functions to adjust. In the supply and demand analysis of the next section several variables adjust, temporarily if not permanently, to establish equilibrium; and these adjustments are reasonable responses to a state of disequilibrium.

INTRODUCTION TO ARTICLE

The Wall Street Journal article below seems to suggest that the usual inverse relationship between price and quantity demanded (known as the law of demand) does not apply to X-rated movies. However, it might instead provide an illustration of the importance of remembering that the demand curve is a ceteris-paribus relationship. Could a change in some other variable account for the increased business despite higher ticket prices?

Last Tango in Myrtle Beach: Or How A State Tried to Tax its Way to Virtue

South Carolina is learning these days that achieving social goals through tax incentives isn't so easy as it may sound. In June 1971, the state imposed a 20 percent tax on admission tickets to X-rated movies. It was hoped that making the films more costly to see would discourage people from patronizing them, according to State Tax Commission Chairman Robert Wasson. But if the law has had any impact at all, it apparently has succeeded only in making sexy movies more tantalizing.

The number of theaters showing X-rated fare has dropped to about 20 from over 80, but those remaining are doing considerably more business than the originals were two years ago. At the current attendance rate, the tax could generate $360,000 in revenues for the state treasury in the fiscal year ending next June 30, up from $300,000 the previous year and $250,000 the first year of the tax. "Our biggest month," Wasson says, "was August (1973) when 'Last Tango in Paris' was showing at two theaters in the state," including one in the Myrtle Beach resort area. The August tax take was $30,000.

A suit has been filed challenging the constitutionality of the X-rated film tax. Asked if he feels the tax is constitutional, Wasson says: "That's difficult for me to say I wouldn't want to comment directly"

SOURCE: "Last Tango in Myrtle Beach: Or How a State Tried to Tax Its Way to Virtue," *The Wall Street Journal*, October 10, 1973.

SUPPLY AND DEMAND ANALYSIS OF MONEY

Supply and demand analysis can be applied to money as well as X-rated movies, although it requires a little more imagination since we do not consciously buy or sell money. Remember the definition of money adopted in this book: the total nominal value of private checkable deposits and currency and travelers checks held by the nonbank public. We will want to set out a demand-for-money function, a supply-of-money function, and an equilibrium condition for this money aggregate.

"What other qualifications do you have besides a genuine love of money?"

Reprinted by permission *The Wall Street Journal*

What would tend to affect the desire for checkable-deposit, travelers-check, and currency balances? These balances are held mainly by households and firms; and, of course, for individual accounts they fluctuate from day to day as income is routinely received and payments are made. However, for most accounts, the *average* amount held over a month does not change so radically over time. This average *will* change, but for different reasons than the normal mismatching of receipts and payments that accounts for daily fluctuations in cash balances during the month. The top part of Figure 3–7 shows a hypothetical pattern for an individual's actual balances of checkable deposits where income is received once a month and payments are made during the month. The monthly average of the deposit balance is shown in the bottom part of the figure. It is *desired changes in the normal monthly average for checkable deposits and in the monthly average for currency and travelers-check holdings* that concern us.

The desired average cash balance

The higher the average holdings of money, the more convenience money affords in terms of transactions and liquidity services. (These services are related to the medium-of-exchange and liquid-store-of-value functions of money.[4]) There is a less chance, for example, of temporarily running short of cash, having to make additional trips to the bank, or having to pay special fees to switch funds from a time-deposit account. We will go into the motives for holding money in more detail in Chapter 15. For now, it is enough to recognize that the average size of your cash balances yields transactions and liquidity services, and more of these services are preferred to less, other things being the same.

The demand variables

Consider some variables now that are commonly encountered in the case of the demand function for a good or service. We will want

---

[4]The unit-of-account service of money does not depend on how much money is held by an individual or in the entire economy.

FIGURE 3–7
Checkable deposit balances

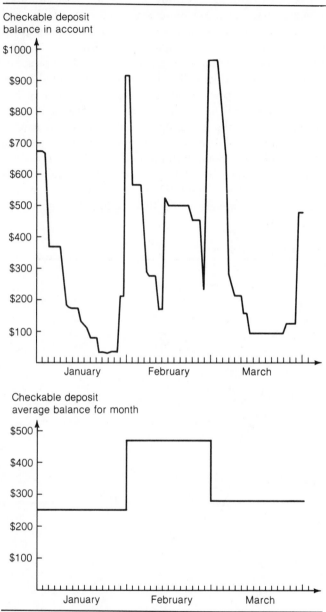

Checkable deposit
balance in account

Checkable deposit
average balance for month

to identify their possible analogues in a demand-for-money function. These variables are: the price of the good or service under
analysis, the income of those who desire it, and the prices of related
goods.

The first variable requires some careful thought for money. The
price of a good is usually the amount of money required to obtain it

since money is the unit of account and medium of exchange. The money price of money, though, is always one, which makes it rather useless for our analysis. It makes more sense to turn the tables and value money in terms of goods. In other words the analogue of price when it comes to money is best thought of as the quantity of goods that must be foregone to obtain one unit of money. This price, or *value of a unit of money* as we will call it, may be calculated as the reciprocal of the average price of all other goods and services. For example, suppose all goods for sale had a uniform price of 10 cents per unit. Then it would take giving up 10 units of goods to acquire one dollar. The value of a dollar's worth of money would be 10. On a more practical level and for comparing values between periods, we can obtain an index of the value of a dollar as the reciprocal of some broad index of prices such as the GNP implicit price deflator. The history of the value of money since 1929, using the deflator, is shown in Figure 3–8.

FIGURE 3–8   The value of money

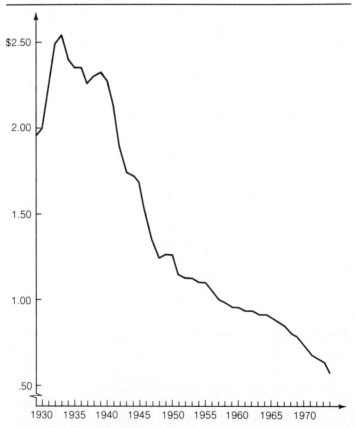

*An index of the quantity of real goods and services one dollar would buy in each year as compared to what it would buy in 1958. Index was calculated as the reciprocal of the GNP implicit price deflator times $100.

DATA SOURCE: U.S. Department of Commerce.

The influence of this calculated value on the quantity of money demanded is the same in direction as the influence of price in most demand functions, though for a different reason. When the price of a good falls, more of the good is desired to enjoy a higher level of satisfaction from that good. It is also the case that, if the value of a dollar falls, average monthly cash balances desired will rise. However, this rise in money demanded will not result from a desire to enjoy more of what money provides in terms of services, but from a desire just to keep level of money services *the same*. A fall in the value of a dollar means there has been a rise in the level of the prices of goods. With higher prices for goods, more money is required to engage in the same real transactions at the same level of convenience.

This is easily grasped when you consider what would happen to your own average needs for cash over a month if the prices of the things you buy suddenly doubled. Chances are your desired average cash balance would also increase. In fact, it would tend to double if your nominal income adjusted along with the prices of goods so that you could afford the same quantities of goods as you could before (in other words so that your real income remained constant). *As a general proposition, the relationship between the desired quantity of money and the price level is proportional;* that is, a given percentage increase in prices leads to an equal percentage increase in desired cash balances, other appropriate things (such as real income) being the same.

Translating this into a value-of-money, money-demand relationship and adding up for all demanders, we say that the relationship between the value of money (per dollar) and the total quantity demanded is inversely proportional or unitary elastic. This means that a 10 percent fall in the value of money leads to a 10 percent rise in the quantity of money demanded in the economy. This relationship is depicted by the rectangular hyperbola in Figure 3–9, where P stands for the price level and D^M is the demand-for-money curve which relates the total quantity of money demanded, M^D, to the value of money, $1/P$.

This relationship is so accepted by economists that they often automatically adjust money balances for price-level changes to obtain what are called desired *real (money) balances* and proceed to analyze the demand for money with this as the dependent variable. Desired real balances are calculated simply by dividing desired money balances by the price level, that is, M^D/P. Presumably, desired real balances are not influenced by the level of prices but only by the other variables in a demand-for-money function.[5] For most of our analysis in this book we will work with desired money or nomi-

Real balances

---

[5]Desired real balances are constant along the demand curve in Figure 3–9. A rectangular hyperbola subtends a set of rectangles of constant area, and the area of all rectangles subtended by the demand curve in Figure 3–9 gives M^D/P.

nal balances, but reference to real balances also will be made from time to time.

FIGURE 3–9
Demand for money and value of money

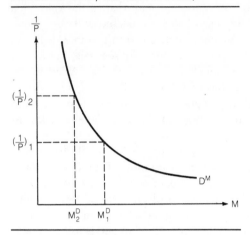

The real income variable

The second important variable in our demand-for-money function is more straightforward. As hinted by our care to keep it constant above, the demand for money is influenced by real income, just as income affects the demand for a good or service. The more real income we have, the more we can afford to enjoy the services that cash balances provide, and the more we find these services useful. Hence individually and in the aggregate, the higher the level of real income, the greater our desired average money balances.[6] This is shown graphically for the whole economy in Figure 3–10 where y stands for real national income. Note that $1/P$ and any other variables that affect the demand for money are assumed constant along this demand curve. Since it is a straight line out of the origin, the curve shows a positive unitary elastic relationship between income and the demand for money. In contrast to our previous relationship, which related M^D to $1/P$ with a negative unitary elasticity without qualification, there is less reason to be confident as to the size of the elasticity in this case; we have chosen unitary elasticity just for illustration.[7]

The interest rate variable

Desired money balances are also influenced by the level of market interest rates. This variable might be viewed as the analogue of the price-of-related-things variable in an ordinary demand function. It is a special type of price which is relevant to any financial asset such as money. As mentioned in Chapter 2, currency and travelers

---

[6]Some economists prefer to use real wealth instead of real income as the variable that accounts for these types of changes in desired cash balances.

[7]As described later, in Chapter 15, empirical studies have indicated different elasticities over different periods for the United States.

checks do not bear interest, and checkable deposits bear no interest or lower and less flexible interest than other available assets.[8] Therefore, when currency, travelers checks, or checkable deposits are held instead of an asset such as a savings certificate, the higher interest that could have been earned is foregone. The greater the interest foregone the more inclined people will be to reduce their average cash balances and hold more of the higher-interest-bearing assets. Imagine your own reaction to an extremely high interest rate on savings certificates of, say, 100 percent per week. It would be worthwhile to cut way down on your average cash holdings to take advantage of the opportunity to double your money every week. The same influence exists for less extreme interest rates and for interest rates on assets other than savings certificates.

FIGURE 3–10
Demand for money and real income

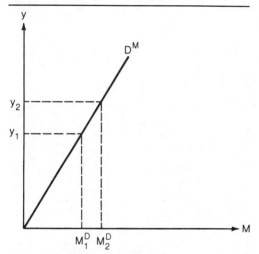

We show the relationship between the aggregate demand for money and market interest rates in Figure 3–11, where i stands for the level of interest rates on competing assets. This graphical relationship is not intended to convey either an especially strong or an especially weak influence of interest rates on the demand for money. As we shall see later, the actual strength of this relationship was at one time a matter of considerable disagreement between monetarists and Keynesians; and, according to many economists, it remains an important issue for monetary policy in a deep depression. The reason will become apparent in later chapters.

Certainly there are other variables which affect the demand for money, and some will be discussed in a subsequent chapter. For now we will not go beyond consideration of just these three. Our demand-for-money function, then, can be expressed as:

---

[8] If cash did bear significant and variable interest, we could simply put the interest rate on cash in our demand function as a separate variable.

FIGURE 3–11
Demand for money and the interest rate

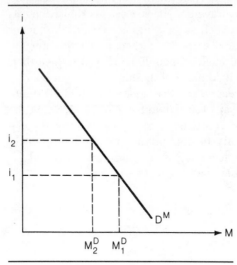

$$M^D = f\left(\frac{1}{P}, \; y, \; i, \; \ldots\right)$$

Influenced variable	Influencing variables	Direction of influence
M^D: the quantity of money demanded	$\frac{1}{P}$: the price or value of money, which is calculated as the inverse of the price level	Negative and proportional or unitary elastic
	y: the level of real income in the economy	Positive
	i: the level of market interest rates on assets which compete with money for a share of asset-holders' portfolios	Negative

The rest of the model

The next step is to determine what our supply-of-money function should include. To keep things as simple as we possibly can and still achieve our objective of providing an explanation of why money affects prices, real income, and interest rates, we are going to make a strong assumption here that the quantity of money supplied is fully controlled by the Federal Reserve and is exogenous. In other words, we assume that the quantity of money is not a function of any variables that we have or might want to have in the model. This is an assumption that we will be dropping for a great many chapters later in this book. In Parts III, IV, and V we will be quite concerned with

specific variables in money-supply functions, with slippage in the
Fed's control, and with endogeneity in Federal Reserve behavior;
but for the time being we will ignore these problems. It is convenient at this point to assume that, despite the problems described
briefly in Chapter 2, the Federal Reserve has all the technical
power and political independence it needs to determine the trend of
the quantity of money in the U.S. economy such that the money
supply is independent of other economic variables.[9] Our supply-
of-money function can be expressed in symbols as

The supply of money

$$M^S = M_1,$$

where M_1 is our exogenous quantity of money.[10]

We are a short way now from being able to apply our model. We
need only an equilibrium condition. If the economy is relatively free
of controls on relevant variables, the appropriate equilibrium condition is $M^D = M^S$. In other words, the model assumes that we have
an equilibrium for money when the quantity of money demanded
equals the quantity supplied. The whole model now is represented
by the three expressions

$$M^D = f\left(\frac{1}{P}, \; y, \; i, \; \ldots\right) \tag{1}$$

$$M^S = M_1 \tag{2}$$

$$M^D = M^S \tag{3}$$

The complete model for money

To proceed now with our analysis, let us focus first on the variable
$1/P$ and hold y and i constant. In Figure 3–12, the same demand
curve we showed in Figure 3–9 is reproduced; and, in addition, we
have a vertical supply curve for money at $M^S = M_1$. A vertical supply curve reflects the fact that the quantity of money supplied is not
influenced at all by the value of money. Equilibrium occurs at
$1/P = (1/P)_1$, which implies a specific price level, P_1, for goods and
services in the economy; and $M^D = M^S = M_1$.

Why are $(1/P)_1$ and M_1 equilibrium values? At a higher value for
money, $(1/P)_2$, the quantity demanded, M_2^D, is less than the quantity
supplied, M_1. This means that people have more cash balances than
they desire at prevailing levels of prices, real income, and interest
rates. It seems reasonable that, consequently, they will spend more
on goods and services, and that this will tend to drive the value of
money down (drive the prices of goods up). The lower the value of
money (the higher the prices of goods) the greater the quantity of
money demanded so that the economy tends to move down along

The process of adjustment to an equilibrium

---

[9]Making assumptions which are admittedly not wholly correct, such as our assumption here that the money supply is fully exogenous, and then subsequently
relaxing them to see whether they affect our conclusions is the essence of analysis—
breaking things up into manageable parts.

[10]Recall that in this book the notations M_1, M_2, M_3, etc. refer to specific quantities
of money.

D^M until we reach a point where $M^D = M_1$ and $1/P = (1/P)_1$. At that point people are just willing to hold the quantity of money in existence.

FIGURE 3–12 Supply and demand for money

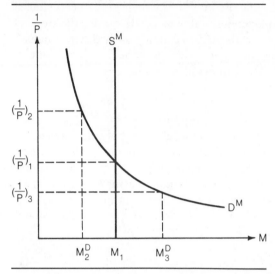

To restate the process, starting from $(1/P)_2$ and M_2^D, individuals attempted to reduce their excess cash balances by spending them. This they were unable to do in the aggregate because, as one balance was reduced, another was increased for someone receiving the cash spent. In the process of attempting to reduce their balances though, people bid the prices of goods up, and this increased the desired quantity of money so that the excess supply was eliminated.

If the value of money were lower, say $(1/P)_3$, the quantity of money desired, M_3^D would be greater than the quantity supplied, and the same process just described for an excess supply situation would work in reverse. In an attempt to add to their cash balances, individuals would cut back their spending. This would tend to raise the value of money (lower the prices of goods), and so on.

Suppose we begin from a state of equilibrium now and consider the effect of an increase in the quantity of money supplied from, say, $M^S = M_1$ to $M^S = M_2$, as shown in Figure 3–13. At the old value of money, $(1/P)_1$, there now exists an excess of cash equal to $M_2 - M_1$. This, we assume here, will be spent and tend to lower the value of money to $(1/P)_2$, where people are content to hold the new larger quantity of money. Here the percentage fall in the value of money (rise in the level of prices of goods) will just equal the percentage increase in the quantity of money. Hence we have our first proposition about money in the economy: *an increase in the quantity of money tends to raise prices in the same proportion, ceteris paribus.* This is the essential relationship between money and inflation in the economy.

Proposition I:
Money and
inflation

FIGURE 3–13
Increase in money supply: effect on value of money

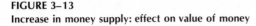

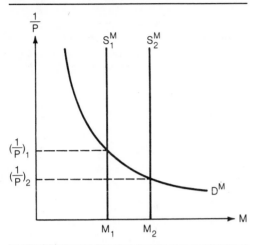

INTRODUCTION TO ARTICLE

By convention, when the price level in some economy has risen at a rate of 50 percent per month (12,875 percent per year—with compounding) or more for some time, the episode earns the dubious distinction of being classified as a hyperinflation by monetary economists. Among the dozen or so of these bizarre episodes identified by economists, the best known is Germany's experience following World War I. In November 1923, prices were more than 10 billion times higher than they were 16 months earlier, August 1922. The average rate of inflation for those 16 months was over 3 billion percent as an annual rate.

The explosion in prices in Germany was preceded and produced by an explosion in the money supply of similar proportions. The supply of currency grew at a rate of 2.5 billion percent per year. Prices rose more than in proportion to the rise in money because, when inflation is persistent and severe, it is recognized as a cost of holding cash balances. When prices rise and *are expected to continue rising,* the demand for nominal balances of money will tend to rise but not fully in proportion to the rise in prices. People make do with less of the convenience money provides because it is costly to hold money which is losing its purchasing power.* So, if the money supply grows by 100 percent, prices have to grow by more than 100 percent to make people content to hold the new money. In other words, desired real cash balances decline. Real balances of domestic currency in Germany ultimately declined to 3 percent of their value at the beginning of the period.

As fantastic as the German episode is, it is far from the most ex-

---

*In more normal circumstances, the effect on the demand for money of expected inflation is mostly accounted for through the interest-rate variable.

treme experienced. In Hungary following World War II, between August 1945 and July 1946, prices rose at an annual rate of 381 octrillion percent.†

These figures boggle the mind. Why do such episodes occur and what is it like to live through one? The following excerpts from an article in *The Listener* give some idea of why money exploded in Germany and report some of the experiences of three who lived there during the period.

---

†Calculations for Germany and Hungary are based on Phillip Cagan, "The Monetary Dynamics of Hyperinflation" in *Studies in the Quantity Theory of Money*, ed. Milton Friedman, (Chicago: University of Chicago Press, 1956).

The Great German Inflation: Remembering a Nightmare

The Treaty of Versailles in 1919 deprived a beaten Germany of one seventh of her population and one tenth of her industrial territory, and also imposed an astronomical bill for war reparations. The German economy was already in deep trouble. The Germans had expected a short war, for which the defeated Allies would foot the bill. They had not reckoned with the fearful costs of four years of war production or a new kind of war. They met those costs not, as the British did, by increased taxation, but simply by printing more money. What was it like in Germany during the great crash that followed? The story is told by some of those who lived through it. First, William Guttmann, writer and journalist.

William Guttmann: Until 1922, the meaning of the word 'inflation' was not really understood. Then it became clear, even to the most unworldly, that something mysterious and frightening was happening in Germany. Money was dying. It became increasingly difficult to buy food. Merchants and farmers were reluctant to part with their produce and sell it to customers who could only pay in depreciating money.

In June 1922, Walter Rathenau, The Foreign Minister, was assassinated by extremists while driving in his car. He was the one man who might have been able to pull Germany out of the morass. He had just returned from a round of international conferences, and his death — and the manner of it — destroyed confidence abroad in the stability of the new Germany. The dollar was the yardstick against which the

value of the mark abroad was assessed. In 1914, this was 4 marks 20 pfennigs to the dollar. By the beginning of 1922 the value of the mark had already sunk to 191. Now, after the murder of Rathenau, it plunged to 490, and in the following month, to 1134 to the dollar.

As the value of the country's notes decreased, so the quantity of notes needed grew. The Reichsbank became more and more hard pressed to meet the ever increasing demand for paper money. For their customers, suitcases replaced wallets. The government, as usual, resorted to the printing presses to ease the situation. There was an even more dangerous device. Towns, villages, big businesses — all kinds of organizations — were allowed to print their own currency.

Guttmann: It was really the original license to print money. Some of these notes were made of various materials — silk, linen, cotton, even leather. But the insidious thing about them was that they were circulating side by side with the ordinary Reichsbank notes, and helped to swell the flood of money. Foreigners flocked into Germany, where they could live very cheaply. There was an enormous influx of tourists who stayed at the best hotels. In Freiburg, which is very near the Swiss frontier, ordinary people would come for a day's outing with their Swiss francs. They would fill all best restaurants and have all the best girls. They would buy anything they could lay their hands on. We poor natives — students — couldn't compete with them. For instance, some foreign students in Germany were able to buy houses — whole rows of houses — out of their allowance.

I remember that some years later, when I was a lawyer in Berlin, I had a client, a Spanish doctor living in Madrid, who owned a very valuable block of flats in Berlin which he had bought during the inflation when he was a student there.

Our own attitude to money changed. In the past, it had had a sort of value, with which you hoped to buy something in the future. Now, it was something you wanted to get rid of at any cost and as quickly as possible. One day, I went to a café where I found out that the cost of a cup of coffee was 5,000 marks. I sat down and read my paper, had my cup of coffee, spent an hour or so there, and then asked for my bill. The waiter came and presented me with a bill for 8,000 marks. The mark had gone down in the meantime.

At the banks, it was no longer a question of suitcases. The great volume of paper money handled by industry and commerce had to be collected almost daily in handcarts, taxis, lorries. Every day was payday and wages were rushed to factories by the truckload. Willy Derkow remembers.

Willy Derkow: At about 11 o'clock, the siren sounded and from all over the departments literally thousands of people streamed into the factory forecourt, where a five-ton lorry was drawn up, brimful with paper money. On to it climbed the chief cashier and his assistants. They read out names and just threw out great bundles of notes. As soon as you had caught one, you made a dash for the nearest shop and bought anything you could lay your hands on. This was essential, because at noon every day the new exchange rate came out, and if, by then, you had not converted your paper money into goods, you stood to lose a third or more of your salary.

Guttmann: The whole German people were in the grip of a collective insanity produced by this whirl of fantastic figures. To illustrate this, let me tell you the experience of my brother, who was a doctor at a psychiatric clinic in Munich. They used to do a simple test there to find out whether a new patient was an obvious mental case or whether he was normal. They asked the person a few simple questions, such as how old he was, how many children he'd

got, and so on. And in those days they would get answers like '25 million years old' or '115 thousand children.' So there was really no saying whether a man was just befuddled by those enormous figures which were always around, or whether he was raving mad.

This insanity was apparent also in the actions of official bodies. For instance, in the annual report of the Reichsbank for the year 1923, you read that the gross income for the year amounted to 63 trillion, 730,223 billions, 49,075 millions, 939,638 marks, and 97 pfennigs. If these figures, which, after all, are only bits of history today, strike you as crazy, you can imagine how mad we Germans were when confronted with such figures—which to us meant something very real, namely whether we would have enough to eat or not.

The impoverishment of the middle classes was the most dangerous and far-reaching effect of the inflation. They mostly lived on state salaries or pensions or interest from investments. Their incomes were tied to the value of the old mark and depreciated as fast as the currency. Their capital was eaten up and their prudent provision for the future annihilated.

Guttmann: Take, for instance, the case of my father. When he retired and sold his business, he invested a large portion of the proceeds by lending it to a local landowner—this loan, of course, was secured by a mortgage of some 300 thousand marks. The interest was 5 percent, so the income would have produced a very comfortable income for a family in those days. But as inflation proceeded, of course, the income dropped until, in the end, it dwindled to almost nothing. Finally, the landowner was able to repay the capital with completely valueless money. An army of malcontents was created. And, of course, they turned against the state, which they thought—rightly or wrongly— was responsible for their misfortunes. The state was the young Weimar Republic. Therefore they became enemies of the republic. They became nationalists. They—and even more their sons, who felt themselves deprived of their birthright, a good life—turned to the radical parties and especially to the Nazi party. In the end, they formed the cadres of the future Nazi party.

Derkow: Germany at that time was dancing on a volcano. Nobody knew whether he would have anything to eat or live on the next day, and that, of course, led to complete demoralization. The consequence of this state of affairs was a fantastic increase in petty crime. Not a copper pipe, not one brass armature, not a sheet of lead on the roofs was safe—they just vanished overnight.

The pit into which the mark was falling seemed bottomless. By September, the rate was 98,860,000 marks to the dollar.

Dorothy Henkel: Two women were going to the bank with a washing basket filled with notes. They passed a shop and saw a crowd standing round the window, put down the basket for a moment and hurried forward to see if there was anything going that could be bought. Then they turned round and found that all the notes were there, untouched. But the basket had gone.

Now things completely replaced money as the medium of exchange. Services were rendered in return for food. The cobbler mended shoes for sausages. Cinema seats were paid for with lumps of coal.

Derkow: You very often bought things you did not need. But with that in hand you could start to barter. You went round and exchanged a pair of shoes for a shirt or a pair of socks for a sack of potatoes, some cutlery or crockery against coffee, tea, butter. And this process was repeated until you had in hand what you actually wanted.

Guttmann: Economic life came almost to a complete standstill. There was stagnation, despair, chaos. It was no longer a matter of living with inflation but of dying from inflation. So

currency reform became a matter of life and death. But a currency is only as strong as the faith people have in it. How was it possible, then, to create a new currency in which the people would trust, which they would hold and accept? What really did the trick was the psychological phenomenon which has become famous as the 'miracle of the Rentenmark'.

The psychology of the new mark was that its backing was declared to be all the farmland and industrial land of Germany—a 'stable' value. This was, however, a fiction. Unlike the traditional backing of gold, the backing of the Rentenmark could not be used abroad to regulate foreign exchange, nor could it be turned into cash. But all that mattered was that the people should believe in the Rentenmark. They wanted to believe in it, and they did. The mark was finally stabilized at one million million times its prewar value.

The relics of inflation were turned into pulp. As the financial position stabilized, so did the political one, almost at the same moment. Within a few days of the issue of the Rentenmark, Hitler and his followers made their abortive bid for power in a beer cellar in Munich. It was crushed–for the time being. At last Germany seemed set on the road to recovery. The French had withdrawn from the Ruhr, Agreement had been reached with Britian, France, and America for a solution to the reparations problem. Postwar Germany began to settle down.

Guttmann: Yet I cannot help thinking that some of the seeds of Hitler's war were sown during the dark days of the inflation.

From 'The Year Money Went Mad', broadcast on the BBC on 1 May 1973 and published in The Listener (September 19, 1974).

We can take another approach with this model now. We can hold the value of money and interest rates constant (only hypothetically of course) and permit real income to change following a change in the quantity of money. Holding these other two independent variables constant allows us to work with a single demand curve, as in Figure 3–14. The supply-of-money curves in Figure 3–14 are vertical as before because we assume that the quantity of money does not

FIGURE 3–14
Increase in money supply: effect on real income

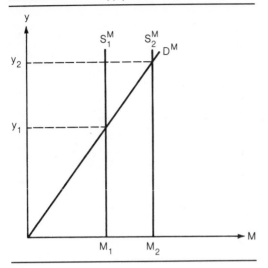

vary with real income. At $M^S = M_1$, we have an equilibrium, provided $y = y_1$.

Now let S^M increase from S_1^M to S_2^M. This creates an excess supply
of money at the real income level of y_1 and the prevailing levels of
prices and interest rates. As before, we assume that individuals will
spend more on goods and services in an attempt to reduce these
excess balances; in contrast to before, however, assume that instead
of raising prices in response to this higher spending, firms now raise
their output. Higher output of goods and services means, of course,
that employment and income tend to be higher. And this raises the
quantity of money demanded. Income will continue to rise as long
as $M^D < M_2$; therefore, equilibrium is reestablished only once income has reached y_2. This leads to a second proposition about
money in the economy: *an increase in the quantity of money tends
to raise real income (we cannot say necessarily proportionately),
ceteris paribus.*

Proposition II:
Money and real
income

It should be apparent that we can carry our analysis still another
step further. We can experimentally hold the value of money and
real income constant and permit interest rates to change. In Figure
3–15 we have the same demand curve we had in Figure 3–11 and,
additionally, our supply-of-money curves. Starting initially with S_1^M
and then increasing the supply-of-money function to S_2^M, we have
again an excess supply equal to $M_2 - M_1$, at the initial level of i and
the prevailing levels of 1/P and y. In this case, we now assume that
holders intend to invest these surplus cash balances in interest-
bearing assets such as savings certificates, instead of spending them
on goods and services. As increased funds flow into assets which

FIGURE 3–15
Increase in money supply: effect on interest rates

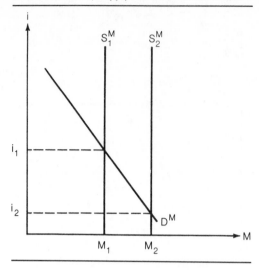

Proposition III:
Money and
interest rates

compete with money, the rate of interest they offer will tend to fall (simply as a consequence of the increased demand for these assets). As the level of interest rates falls, the quantity of cash desired increases (to enjoy more convenience since less interest is foregone). Interest rates will continue to fall and desired cash balances will continue to rise until $M^D = M^S = M_2$. The amount by which interest rates would have to fall to equate M^D and M^S depends upon how elastic the demand curve in Figure 3–15 is. The more elastic (the more sensitive the quantity of money demanded to the level of interest rates) the less interest rates would have to fall. Our third proposition about money in the economy makes no judgment on this question of how great a change would have to occur: *an increase in the quantity of money tends to reduce interest rates, ceteris paribus.*

The three conceptual experiments we have just completed are all logical possibilities. Following an increase in the supply of money, prices only could change (proportionately), or income only could rise, or interest rates only could fall. The tendencies and behavior each experiment described seem reasonable. But, as described, each case excludes the others. It seems possible that all three tendencies could hold, with an attentuated, equal impact on each variable in the demand function: the price level, real income, and the level of interest rates. Or, more likely, the relative impact on each variable will be different and change over time. That is, the brunt of the equilibrating adjustment will be performed first by one variable, say interest rates, then the second, and finally the third. In fact, this sort of shift in the equilibrating role of these variables is evident in the typical paths these variables seem to follow after an increase in the money supply, as explained in the next section.

Before moving on to consider the actual timing of the responsive changes in these variables, however, we must make one important observation. So far, we have ignored other things which cause changes in prices, income, and interest rates, and we will continue to do so in the rest of this chapter to keep things as simple as possible. But it is hard to ignore the fact that normally real income tends to increase over the long run due to factors quite unrelated to money: natural growth in the labor force, growth in the stock of capital goods, and technological change. In our model, this underlying growth in real income is exogenous. It creates an increase in the quantity of money demanded, which is represented as a movement upward *along* the demand curve in Figure 3–14 and as *shifts* to the right in the demand curves in Figures 3–13 and 3–15. Hence it tends to create an excess demand for money unless the supply of money grows by an appropriate amount. If the supply of money did not grow, prices would have to fall, real income would stagnate, or interest rates would have to rise to keep the quantity of money demanded equal to the fixed quantity supplied.

A glossed-over complication

Unfortunately, it would take a great deal of trouble to account for this complication at every step of subsequent analysis in this book. Hence in the next section which describes actual changes in these variables, and for the most part thereafter, something which is not always stated should be understood. By an increase in real income we mean an increase beyond the increase attributable to the factors described in the previous paragraph, and by an increase in the quantity of money we mean an increase relative to the growth of money that would be necessary to evenly match the growth in the quantity desired induced by the long-run growth rate of real income.

THE TIMING OF PRICE LEVEL, INCOME, AND INTEREST-RATE RESPONSES

Assume that for some reason the Federal Reserve generously arranges it so that each of us receives by special delivery tomorrow morning a surprise package of some newly printed currency which is exactly equal to the quantity of money we hold as of 12 P.M. tonight. The currency, let us imagine, is simply printed up with ink and paper, with no backing, and given away.[11] In other words, suppose the quantity of money in the economy were to double tomorrow with no change in our real resources. What would happen to prices, real income, and interest rates tomorrow? Would people spend the extra money or save it? Our earlier analysis suggested

---

[11]None of the Federal Reserve's currency we carry today is backed in any meaningful way by gold or other form of reserves. It is printed up and issued through private depository institutions in exchange, effectively, for government securities. It could not legally be given away by the Fed as we assume here; but there is nothing to prevent the government from doing the same thing via the Treasury and proceeds from its securities sold to the Fed.

that, if it were spent, prices might rise. By how much? Would prices double tomorrow? "Probably not," you say. How about income? Would production levels (incomes) change in response to higher spending the first day? You may think "probably not." Would some money be used to purchase interest-earning assets, and, if so, would interest rates change? "Probably?" Would results be different by the day after tomorrow? A week later?

Well it is really hard to say for sure how all these things would sort out, especially in the short run. We have never had such an extreme experience. Surely it would take time for things to respond. And surely interest rates, income, and prices all would be affected at one time or another before it was over. The specific reaction pattern would no doubt depend upon the current state of the economy in terms of inflation, recession, past monetary changes, etc.

Though we never have had the experience of a sudden doubling

FIGURE 3–16   Effects of a higher money supply level

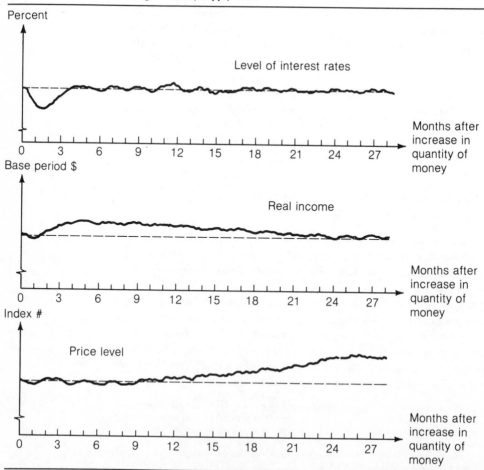

of the money stock, economists have studied the pattern of the economy's response to less extreme changes in the quantity of money. In Figure 3–16 we describe how, according to many studies, things would tend to evolve for a moderate, once and for all increase in the supply of money, assuming we start from a state of close to full employment and zero inflation. It should be noted that the time paths shown are suggestive and not simulations from any particular study. One reason for this is that studies showing these types of results do not agree on the exact months in which key changes tend to occur or, especially with respect to interest rates and real income, the size of the effects.

A higher level of the money supply

The first variable to change substantially is the level of interest rates. Most studies agree that interest rates tend to fall within the same month that the quantity of money increases. Afterward, real income begins to rise; there is disagreement as to how soon: somewhere between one and eight months following the increase in the money. As income rises, the negative effect of the increase in money on interest rates abates, and, shortly thereafter, interest rates return to their original level or close to it. With a substantial lag—between 9 and 18 months after the increase in money—prices show some substantial effect. As prices begin to rise, the positive effect on real income tapers off. The positive effect on real income ends or becomes very slight between 12 and 24 months after the money-supply increase. At that point, all or almost all of the adjustment to the increase in money is in terms of an increase in the price level. To summarize: the major impact of an increase in the quantity of money is first on interest rates, then on real income, and finally on prices. The impact on interest rates tends to be temporary, which may or may not also be true for real income.

Keynesians generally argue that there is a lasting impact of money on real income, especially if we modify our assumption that we are starting from a position of close to full employment and assume instead considerable unemployment. Also, Keynesian studies tend to show a long lag of six months or more before real income rises. A Keynesian view of the final outcome, starting from close to full employment, would be: interest rates slightly lower, real income up slightly, and prices up almost in proportion to the increase in money. Monetarists, on the other hand, are more inclined to view the effects on real income and interest rates as fully temporary. If this is the case, then the final result would be: interest rates the same, real income the same, and prices higher in proportion to the increase in money.

Disagreements between Keynesians and monetarists

Now the foregoing description is for a one-time increase in the quantity of money. How about a higher *growth rate* of money? That is, suppose there is a continuous increase in the quantity of money so that, for example, there is 10 percent more money each year. What would happen to interest rates, real income, and prices? Well,

FIGURE 3–17   Effects of higher money growth

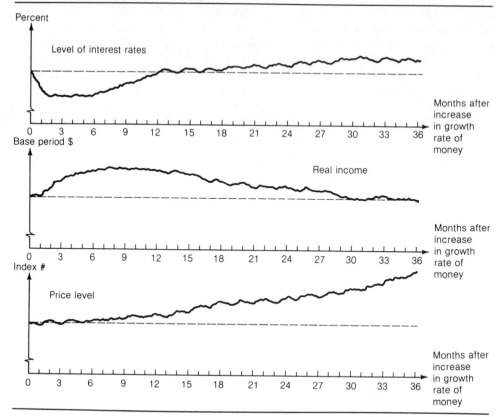

Percent

Level of interest rates

0   3   6   9   12   15   18   21   24   27   30   33   36
Base period $

Months after increase in growth rate of money

Real income

0   3   6   9   12   15   18   21   24   27   30   33   36
Index #

Months after increase in growth rate of money

Price level

0   3   6   9   12   15   18   21   24   27   30   33   36

Months after increase in growth rate of money

A higher growth rate in money

The Fisher effect

studies suggest that, though most of the tendencies described for the case of a one-time increase in money still hold, there are some important differences. As shown in Figure 3–17, interest rates tend to fall and then rise back as before, but it takes longer for them to rise back in this case of ever more money. More important, later on, interest rates tend to rise above their initial level. (We will describe why in just a moment.) Real income tends to rise sooner, and it takes longer to fall back. Prices rise sooner *and they continue to rise* as long as—in fact longer than—the increases in money persist.

When prices continue to rise over time, an important phenomenon called the Fisher effect eventually causes interest rates to rise higher than they otherwise would be.[12] Inflation erodes the purchasing power of funds loaned, and to offset this, financial investors demand an inflation premium in the interest they receive. Borrowers are willing to grant this premium because they anticipate being able to pay off loans in cheaper dollars. The longer inflation has

[12]The Fisher effect takes its name from Irving Fisher, a brilliant economist who near the turn of the century studied the effect of inflation on interest rates. The Fisher effect will be discussed again in Chapter 5, and Fisher's name will come up once more in another context in Chapter 15.

persisted, the more both borrowers and lenders will tend to anticipate inflation and hence the greater the tendency for interest rates
to include an inflation premium.[13] This makes for an interesting
reversal in the impact of a higher growth rate of money on interest
rates: in the near term interest rates are lower, and in the long term
they are higher. The same process, we might point out, works in
reverse; that is why it is often said in policy discussions that, in
order to get interest rates down, we first must get them up.

Figure 3–17 shows prices rising out of sight, which may suggest
to you at least visually that things eventually get out of hand. However, if money increases at a higher but constant rate, most economists think the economy will tend to reach a sort of equilibrium with
inflation varying around a rate approximately equal to the excessive
growth rate of money. Prices tend to rise continuously but within
reasonable range of a constant rate. There is no reason based on
experience to think that this cannot go on indefinitely. To sum up
the final results of a higher growth rate of money: real income is
almost the same, inflation is higher roughly by the increase in the
growth rate of money, and interest rates are higher approximately
by the increase in the rate of inflation.

INTRODUCTION TO ARTICLE

In comparison to hyperinflation and many historical U.S. and current foreign inflationary experiences, inflation in the United States in
the 1970s was tame. Nevertheless, the lagged impact of higher growth
in money was evident. The chart and description in the following
Business Week article of March 3, 1975 make this point for the double-
digit inflation experienced in 1973–74. The article also makes the important point that other factors contributed to the inflation burst of
1973–74. The forecasts in the article of lower inflation in 1975–76
turned out to be correct.

Subsequently, in 1976–79, the rate of growth of the money supply
reaccelerated (based on the new M-1B definition); and with the customary lags, inflation returned to the double-digit range in 1979–80.
Once again, oil-price increases were a contributing factor but only
after general inflation had passed 10 percent. Money growth slowed
beginning in the fourth quarter of 1979. What does the record show
about subsequent inflation? After how long?

Forecasting the End of Double-Digit Inflation

Among economists, it is a truism that price
forecasting is difficult. No economist, for example, succeeded in predicting accurately the
onset of double-digit inflation in the U.S. in

---

[13]Investors also tend to react to the causes of inflation such as higher growth in the
money supply. Such a reaction is called "rational expectations." Chapter 16 includes
a discussion of different ways expectations might be formed in the economy.

How money supply changes forecast the inflation rate

▲ Percent (seasonally adjusted annual rate)

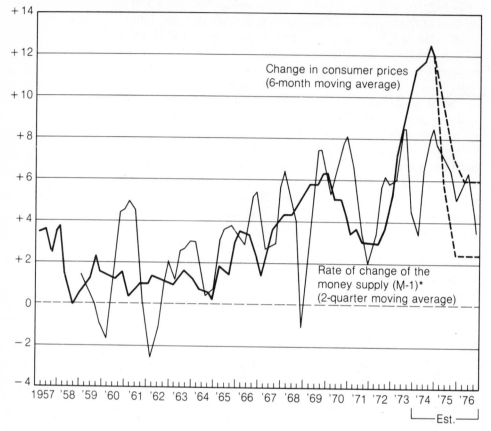

Change in consumer prices
(6-month moving average)

Rate of change of the
money supply (M-1)*
(2-quarter moving average)

1957 '58 '59 '60 '61 '62 '63 '64 '65 '66 '67 '68 '69 '70 '71 '72 '73 '74 '75 '76

└──Est.──┘

*M-1: sum of currency and demand deposits
*Lagged two years

DATA: Federal Reserve Board, Bureau of Labor Statistics.

late 1973 or its continuance through 1974. Yet to say that price forecasting is difficult is not to say that it is impossible. One method has been used with some success in the past and thus may provide insight into what prices may do over the next couple of years. That method indicates that the U.S. inflation rate is headed down, and may be headed steeply down (chart).

The chart reflects the idea that changes in economic policy affect the workings of the economy only after they have had a chance to filter through the system. Statistical analysis indicates, for example, that a change in the

monetary growth rate does not have maximum impact on prices for two years. Thus, the sharp monetary acceleration in the election year 1972 did not give its maximum boost to the inflation rate until 1974.

Similarly, the swing in 1973 toward monetary restraint cannot have its maximum impact on prices until this year, and the extreme restraint of 1974 will not show its full depressing effect on prices until next year.

Interpetation

The chart has been constructed to show the implication of this two-year lag between a change in monetary growth rate and its impact on prices. The green line shows the rate of change in the consumer price index since 1956, plotted on a real-time basis. The black line shows the rate of change in the money supply, plotted not on a real-time basis, but rather for the quarter in which statistical analysis indicates that it had its maximum impact on prices, taking into account the two-year lag of maximum effect. Thus, the money-supply growth rate plotted for the first quarter of 1973 is actually the growth rate that occurred in the first quarter of 1971, and so on.

The projection of the two-year lag is the basis for the forecast of declining inflation that is contained in the chart. Rates of change in the money supply that took place during the past two years of monetary restraint are projected to the period when this restraint should have its maximum impact. For example, the extreme restraint of the final quarter of 1974 shows up in the final quarter of 1976.

If the past represents any guide to the future, the U.S is headed for a lower inflation rate. For, as the chart shows, the Federal Reserve has been steadily squeezing down the rate of monetary growth since the end of 1972, pointing the inflation rate to a slide starting this year.

Negative factors

How much of a slide? This would be difficult to answer under the best of circumstances, but it is especially difficult in the light of the double-digit inflation of late 1973 and all of 1974. This inflation was not predictable on the basis of money-supply change, or on the basis of any other forecasting method, for that matter. No economist yet professes to be able to explain fully why prices zoomed out of control in the past two years. The answer probably lies in "a negative cluster of random events" that boosted prices: crop failures in Eastern Europe, the disappearance of anchovies (a major source of high-protein animal feeds) off the coast of Peru, the devaluation of the U.S. dollar, and—most important—the quadrupling of the price of oil.

The implications of the great 1973–74 inflation outbreak are hotly debated among economists, and each economist's position on the implications shapes his price forecasts. One group believes that the sharp rise in the inflation rate in 1973 to a pace that cannot be explained by fundamental movements, say of monetary policy, implies an equally sharp crash in prices. No one quite has the nerve to predict this crash in so many words. The group at New York's First National City Bank comes closest, predicting that the inflation rate will be down in the 2 percent to 6 percent zone in the second half of 1975. The midpoint of its forecast forms the lower boundary of the 1975–76 price channel in the chart.

At the other end of the scale is the official forecast of the Council of Economic Advisers, which sees a 7 percent inflation rate by the end of this year. Offical forecasts of inflation have been cautiously pessimistic this year, partly to justify a cautious policy that many economists feel is inadequate to get the unemployment rate down.

Even if the least optimistic forecast on a price slump proves to be right, double-digit inflation clearly is dead, and inflationary pressure in the U.S. this year and next will be a mere shadow of what it was in 1973 and 1974.

What happens beyond 1976 depends on how rapidly monetary policy swings toward ease. So far, both the Federal Reserve and the other world central banks have moved with extreme caution. There could, of course, be a drastic, sharp reversal of policy later this year as unemployment rates soar. However, even if monetary growth reaccelerates to, say, the 6.8 percent trend that was characteristic of 1970–73, it is highly unlikely that double-digit inflation will recur in this decade.

SOURCE: "Forecasting the End of Double-Digit Inflation," *Business Week,* March 3, 1975. Reprinted from the March 3, 1975 issue of *Business Week* by special permission, © 1975 by McGraw-Hill, Inc. All rights reserved.

What accounts for the tendency of prices to feel the major impact of an increase in money? And what accounts for the delay in this impact and the tendency for real income and interest rates to be affected the way they are before prices rise? In the next section, we draw a comparison between money and corporate common stock to provide a logical explanation of the tendency for prices to be proportionately and permanently related to money and for the protracted delay in this relationship.

A COMPARISON BETWEEN MONEY AND AT&T COMMON STOCK

Consider, for a moment, the supply and demand for AT&T shares. We can express the demand function for these shares as follows:

$$AT\&T^D = f(P^{AT\&T}, E^{AT\&T}, W, e^R, \ldots), \quad (1)$$

where $AT\&T^D$ is the quantity of AT&T shares desired, $P^{AT\&T}$ is the price of an AT&T share, $E^{AT\&T}$ is AT&T earnings, W is real wealth, and e^R is the ratio of the earnings per share to the price per share of related stocks.

You should recognize a strong similarity between this demand function and our demand-for-money function. It includes the value of an AT&T share, real wealth, and the earnings rate on related assets, all of which are counterparts to variables in our demand-for-money function. It includes one extra variable, the financial earnings of AT&T; this is not a counterpart of a variable in our demand-for-money function only because we have not allowed for interest earnings on cash balances.

Our supply of AT&T shares function is very simple:

$$AT\&T^S = AT\&T_1 \quad\quad\quad (2)$$

This states that the quantity of shares outstanding is exogenous, reflecting the fact that AT&T controls this quantity and does not change it for reasons we want or need to take into account. We have a direct comparison with our simplified analysis of the money supply function. Our equilibrium condition is also essentially the same as for money, $AT\&T^D = AT\&T^S$.

Now let us conduct an experiment directly analogous to the experiment with which we began the previous section (a doubling of the supply of money). Suppose AT&T declares a two-for-one stock split. What would happen to the price of an AT&T share and how soon? As most know who have followed the stock market even casually, the price of an AT&T share would tend to fall *by one half immediately* when the actual split occurs.

A two-for-one
stock split

Figure 3–18 shows what this reveals about the demand function for AT&T shares. If the share price falls by one half when the stock of AT&T shares is doubled, the desired quantity of AT&T shares is inversely proportional to the per-share price, ceteris paribus. Just as for money, *the demand curve must be a rectangular hyperbola.*

FIGURE 3-18   A two-for-one stock split

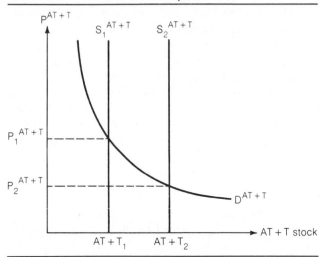

Now this event of a two-for-one stock split is commonplace and not especially noteworthy because nothing real has changed, and stockholders and others know it. Nothing has happened to the total value of AT&T shares (there are now twice the shares at half the price) because nothing has happened to change the value of the company. Nothing happens to the earnings-price ratio on related stocks, and nothing happens to real wealth.

To return to our analysis of money now, there is a similar logic which suggests that a doubling of the quantity of money should cause its per-unit value to fall by one half since nothing real has changed in the economy by the doubling of the money stock. But for this to happen with speed comparable to the adjustment in the price of AT&T shares, prices in the economy would have to double at the opening of business on the very morning the supply of money doubled. This just could not and would not happen. It is costly to adjust the prices of most goods, and the information that prices should be doubled would not be communicated or understood widely by merchants and others. Consequently, much of the new cash would be invested in interest-bearing assets to await future expenditure, and most goods would continue to be sold at old prices for a while. Later, expenditures would rise, production would rise temporarily, and ultimately prices would tend to rise proportionately.

The costs of adjustment and information

Some economists believe this protracted process of adjustment results from the simultaneous functions of money as the medium of exchange and unit of account. Because money is the medium of exchange, there is a demand and supply for it, and hence a need for adjustments in its value. Because it is the unit of account, its value can change only by changes in the prices of goods and services throughout the economy. When such changes are unanticipated, real economic relationships tend to be affected. Hence, money stands in marked contrast to AT&T stock which has its own price and is exchanged in a very efficient market.

Much remains to be understood about money, and, as suggested in Chapter 1, there is disagreement as to whether the medium-of-exchange and unit-of-account functions of money are responsible for the effects that money has on the economy. This comparison with AT&T stock merely gives an example of some of the ideas that are undergoing active debate and development by those who feel that these are the key functions of money. The role of liquidity will be examined later.

CONCLUSION

Our analysis of money in this chapter has been designed to give a preview and provide a perspective for later chapters related to the supply and demand for money to come in Part III. In these later chapters, we will modify the simplified supply and demand analysis of this chapter to take into account factors which have been ignored here. The analytical sections of this chapter provide an organizing framework for some later material. For example, such-and-such a factor may be described in Chapter 10 as important in determining the quantity of money supplied. You should then register in your mind that this is important because it has implications for prices, real income, and interest rates; and you might want to stop for a minute and run through the simplified analysis of this chapter to be sure you understand why. It will be particularly important to keep separate in your mind the factors which affect the quantity of money supplied and the factors which affect the quantity of money demanded and why.

It is necessary to stress in concluding this chapter that supply and demand analysis of money does not provide a complete analysis of the determination of interest rates, real income, or prices. It only examines the impact of money on these important economic variables. It makes clear that interest rates, real income, and prices must exist in some combination so that $M^D = M^S$. As indicated by our earlier discussion of factors unrelated to money which induce long-term growth in real income and by the *Business Week* article in this chapter, a complete analysis of the determination of these variables requires a much more complex analysis than an examination of the supply and demand for money, even at a more sophisticated level, can provide alone. In Part IV the basics of one approach to a more inclusive analysis are developed.

PROBLEMS

1. Consult recent issues of *The Wall Street Journal, Business Week*, or similar publications to build your knowledge of the current state of the economy and recent and past monetary policy. Then use the supply and demand analysis of money presented in this chapter to explain as best you can the current rate of inflation and level of unemployment in the United States. (Hint: keep in mind the timing of repercussions following money-supply changes.) Be sure your answer reveals an understanding of the supply and demand for money.

2. The *Listener* article on the great German inflation in this chapter describes how rapid inflation causes the demand for money to fall—the economy reverted to barter wherever possible. Yet the demand for money must have been rising too, because ever larger amounts were held. How can you reconcile these seemingly contradictory statements?

3. Suppose new legislation were passed which permitted banks to pay interest on all demand deposits beginning next January 1. Would this tend to have any effects on the overall economy? Use the supply and demand for money model to analyze this question.

ADVANCED READINGS

Cagan, Phillip, and Gandolfi, Arthur. "The Lag in Monetary Policy as Implied by the Time Pattern of Monetary Effects on Interest Rates." *American Economic Review* 59 (May 1969):277–84.

deLeeuw, Frank, and Gramlich, Edward M. "The Channels of Monetary Policy." *Federal Reserve Bulletin* 55 (June 1969):472–91.

Gibson, W. E. "Interest Rates and Monetary Policy." *Journal of Political Economy* 78 (May/June 1970):431–55.

Keynes, John M. *Tract on Monetary Reform.* New York: Harcourt Brace, 1924. Chapters 1 and 2.

Analysis of credit

Credit and finance: Some definitions, concepts, and uses

4

This chapter introduces certain key definitions, concepts, and background information necessary to an understanding of the credit markets. The following topics are covered: credit and equity finance, different methods of credit finance, surplus and deficit entities, financial intermediaries, and the functions of finance for different entities. An appendix to this chapter reviews several basic accounting tools, the concept of national wealth, and definitions of saving and investment which are used in this chapter and in later chapters. The material in this chapter lays the foundation for a supply and demand analysis of the credit market in Chapter 5.

EXTERNAL FINANCE AND CREDIT

External finance is the drawing by one entity on the current resources of another to meet current expenses, and credit is the major form of external finance used by households, firms, and governments in the economy. Credit finance encompasses any financing which requires unconditional payment or payments in the future. A familiar type of credit finance involves a loan of money from a financial institution to an individual or a firm. In return, the borrower

70

agrees to make regular payments until the principal and interest are paid. This is the usual arrangement for an automobile loan or a home mortgage loan, for example. There are many other types of arrangements, however.

The terms of a credit arrangement may specify payment on demand or by a certain date. Although you may not have thought of it as such, your checkable deposit with your bank, savings and loan, or credit union is effectively an extension of credit by you to the depository institution. The institution "repays" its debt to you *on demand*. An auto loan from a bank usually calls for fixed, periodic payments until the loan and interest are fully paid. A business or personal loan, on the other hand, often specifies a single payment at the end of the period of the loan.

Credit need not involve money or goods now for money later: some arrangements call for money now for goods later, and goods now for goods later. It is not hard to think of examples. In this text, however, we will be concerned primarily with financing through loans or issues of securities which oblige specified future payments in money.

Two types of contracts

A credit transaction may take place under a *general agreement* which provides for some flexibility in the amount and/or timing of the credit—credit-card charges, for example. In this case, the amount of the obligation is recorded only as an entry on a ledger or in a computer file. Your checkable-deposit balance, representing a depository institution's obligation to you, is a useful example once again.

Alternatively, the terms of a credit transaction may be spelled out in a *debt agreement specific to that transaction*. Usually in such cases the agreement takes the form of a document, security, certificate, or "paper" which states the amount and the due date of the debtor's obligation. In credit-market terminology any such evidence of specific obligation is a *debt instrument*. A personal note is an example.

Debt instruments

Debt instrument financing is effected either by the *private placement* or *public "sale"* of the debt instrument. A private placement usually involves a privately negotiated credit at a prespecified interest rate, with the lender initiating terms and drawing up or receiving the debt instrument as evidence of the borrower's obligation. In a public sale, normally all of the terms of the obligation except for the effective interest rate are prespecified by the borrower. The debt instrument is then sold, often through an investment bank as an agent, at a market-determined price and thereby market-determined interest rate.[1]

Some debt instruments are *bearer* instruments which means that mere possession of these instruments confers to the holder the right to payment. Other debt instruments are *negotiable* which means they can and must be signed by the creditor to transfer payment rights to another party. And some instruments are *nonnegotiable* or *nonmarketable*—by prior agreement or by law they cannot be transferred to a third party.

Bearer, negotiable, and nonnegotiable instruments

A few examples will help clarify the terminology introduced in the paragraph above. A certificate of deposit (CD) is a type of debt instrument issued by banks and savings and loans (also a type of time deposit "accepted" by these institutions) which, by government regulation, may be negotiable if in denominations of $100,000 or more. Nonnegotiable CDs can be issued in any denomination. Certificates of deposit ordinarily are not bearer instruments.

A standard home-mortgage agreement is a type of debt instrument often held by the original lender until the obligation of the home buyer is fulfilled. However, under a normal mortgage contract, the original lender, say a savings and loan association, may sell the mortgage to another lender, which simply may be another financial institution. The mortgage is signed over, and the homeowner, either directly or indirectly, makes payments to the new lender. Hence mortgages normally are negotiable instruments.

You may recognize the fact that a signed check is a negotiable debt instrument until it clears the bank on which it is drawn. The creditor's claim to payment from the depositor's account, which the check certifies, may be signed over to another party without the depositor's agreement or knowledge.

A U.S. Treasury bill is a particular type of government security which used to be exclusively in the form of a bearer paper instrument. Today Treasury bills often are in the form of a deposit balance with the Treasury. Treasury bills confer to the owner the right to payment of a certain sum from the Treasury (the minimum denomination of Treasury bills is now $10,000) on a certain date in the future (three months to one year from the date of issue).

To conclude this section, a debt instrument is a legal statement of a debtor's obligation which may be issued and sold like a commodity to provide a vehicle of credit. Many debt instruments are bearer or negotiable instruments with organized primary or secondary (secondhand) markets. A number of instruments and their markets will be described in Chapter 6.

Equity finance

For corporate firms, credit finance is only one of two methods of external finance. The second, much smaller in volume but still very

[1]The relationship between market price and market yield on a debt instrument will be explained in Chapter 6.

important in the United States, is equity finance. *Equity finance* | Equity finance
involves financing through the issuance (sale) of new shares of own- | defined
ership in a corporate enterprise: common or preferred stock.

Shareholders have more limited rights to payments from the corporate firm than creditors have since dividend payments depend, in the final analysis, on the profits of the firm; and, if the firm is liquidated, the claims of creditors must be met before funds from remaining assets, if any, are distributed to shareholders. Consequently, equity shares tend to be more risky than debt obligations from the standpoint of the financial investor.

SURPLUS AND DEFICIT ENTITIES AND FINANCIAL INTERMEDIARIES

Who draws on external finance in the economy and who extends it? Most households, firms, and governments do both. Yet on balance some entities are normally net providers of funds and some are normally net absorbers; others are quite active in facilitating the flow of funds without being important net providers or absorbers. More specifically we can distinguish *surplus entities, deficit entities,* and *financial intermediaries.* Each of these types can be identified quickly by reference to a statement of changes in financial position such as that shown in Figure 4–1.[2]

FIGURE 4–1

Campus Slop Cafeterias
Statement of Changes in Financial Position
(January 1, 1979, to December 31, 1980)

Sources of funds:		Uses of funds:	
Sales of meals	$1,000,000	Wages and salaries	$ 250,000
Sales of used equipment	31,500	Purchases of food and materials	500,000
Dividends and interest on securities held	5,000	Purchases of new equipment	45,000
		Interest on loans	200,000
Total sources of funds	1,036,500	Dividends to stockholders	20,000
		Total uses of funds	1,015,000
		Changes in gross and net financial assets:	
		Cash	−500
		Securities	17,000
		Less change in liabilities	−5,000
		Change in net financial position	$21,500

---

[2] It is assumed that the reader is familiar with standard accounting statements such as the statement of changes in financial position. See the appendix to this chapter, from which Figure 4–1 was taken, for a review.

A surplus entity is simply one for which the entry under "change in net financial position" is positive; a deficit entity is one for which this entry is negative; and a financial intermediary is a firm for which this entry is normally small despite substantial activity in both the raising and placing of funds. Hence a household which is setting aside income and investing in financial assets is a surplus entity; a firm which is borrowing to finance capital expenditures is a deficit entity; and commercial banks and "thrifts" (savings institutions) which are conduits in the flow of funds, are financial intermediaries. Specific examples with accounting statements for each of these cases are provided in the appendix to this chapter.

Types of financial intermediaries and their role in the flow of funds to deficit units

Financial intermediaries normally funnel roughly 75 percent of the new funds extended to deficit entities in the economy each year, as suggested in Figure 4–2. Most financial intermediaries engage in *credit intermediation;* others, such as investment companies, specialize in *equity intermediation.* Credit flows to deficit units represented by the shaded channels in Figure 4–2 are reported by source for 1979 in Figure 4–3.

FIGURE 4–2
Flow of funds

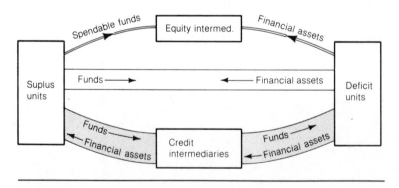

Among the individual types of financial intermediaries shown in Figure 4–3, commercial banks accounted for the largest share of credit supplied to deficit units in 1979, about one fourth of total credit from all sources and roughly one third of the credit funds advanced by financial intermediaries. Most loans and investments of commercial banks are short-term in maturity (i.e., one year or less). The dominance of commercial banks among intermediaries is attributable to their demand-deposit base and to regulatory provisions which restrict the lending activities of competing institutions to narrower lending areas.

Commercial
banks

FIGURE 4–3
Credit flows to deficit units

Sources of credit to deficit units	1979	
	Billions of dollars	Percent of Contributions to total
Commercial banks	$121.1	25.2%
Insurance companies and pension funds	92.9	19.2
Savings institutions and money-market		
mutual funds..................................	82.3	17.1
Savings and loan associations	54.6	11.3
Money-market mutual funds	19.8	4.1
Mutual savings banks	5.2	1.1
Credit unions	2.7	0.6
Sponsored credit agencies and		
mortgage pools.................................	57.7	12.0
Finance companies	23.1	4.8
Federal Reserve banks	7.7	1.6
Other financial, net.	−1.9	−0.4
Total Financial Intermediaries	$382.9	79.5%
Households	63.5	13.2
U.S. Government	22.6	4.7
State and local governments	16.6	3.4
Nonfinancial business	9.9	2.1
Total nonfinancial entities	$112.6	25.2%
Rest of the world	−14.1	−2.9
Total credit all sources	$481.4	100.0%

SOURCE: Based on *Flow of Funds,* Federal Reserve Board of Governors. (February 1980).

Demand deposits provide a low-cost source of funds to commercial banks because, by federal law, they bear no interest. This competitive advantage has waned in recent years with the authorization of interest-bearing ATS accounts at commercial banks and of NOW accounts at all depository institutions, and with a slower rate of growth in the public's demand for transactions balances in general relative to high-yield time deposits; but by virtue of their existing size and their lock on business transactions accounts, commercial banks are likely to continue to dominate the payments process and retain some benefit from associated lower cost funds in the future.[3]

In most years, insurance companies and pension funds generate substantial flows of surplus funds from premiums and contributions. Surplus funds are needed by these entities to build reserves against future claims and to obtain investment income to pay annuities. As a source of funds, these entities accounted for almost one fifth of the

Insurance companies and pension funds

---

[3]Commercial banks' other competitive advantage, the broader scope of their lending activities, may also wane in the years ahead, because other depository institutions gained authorization in 1981 for some expansion in their activities in the loan and trust services areas. This authorization was provided in the Depository Institutions Deregulation and Monetary Control Act of 1980. Early indications suggest that nonbank depository institutions are not moving aggressively into new lending and service areas, however.

credit funds provided to deficit units in 1979. The maturities of their investments are usually long-term, that is, five years or longer. Casualty and fire insurance companies invest heavily in obligations of state and local governments (municipal bonds) because of tax advantages. Life insurance companies, which are not taxed on investment income used to pay annuities, invest their funds mostly in federal and corporate debt obligations, in equities, and in real estate. Pension funds, most of which are managed by employers, unions, or life insurance companies, have investment patterns similar to those of life insurance companies.

Savings institutions (thrifts) constitute a category which includes savings and loans, mutual savings banks, and credit unions. These institutions accept savings deposits or "shares" from households and invest these funds in mortgages and consumer loans. The savings and loan institution was originally organized in early U.S. history as a cooperative to finance local home building. Now most savings and loans are profit-making institutions, but tax and other legislation has continued to focus their lending activity in the home building area. Mutual savings banks are depository institutions located principally in the northeast states. They were originally organized as nonprofit institutions designed to encourage thrift among the working class. Traditionally and in response to incentives, mutual savings banks have concentrated their investments in mortgages; hence they are very similar to savings and loans. Credit unions are cooperatives which are usually sponsored and implicitly subsidized by employers for their employees. Credit unions issue shares which earn interest and grant consumer loans and mortgages to members.

Money-market mutual funds represent a relatively new and fast growing credit-market intermediary which competes directly with savings institutions for households' funds. In contrast to most savings institutions which are restricted in the interest rates they can offer by federal and state regulations, money-market mutual funds are able to pay market interest rates net of a small management fee. They are organized mostly by brokerage houses along the lines of investment funds, but they provide more liquidity than most investment funds. Shares are offered to the public in denominations as low as $1,000. Share balances can be drawn upon on short notice, even, in some cases, with checks. Funds are invested in high-yield, short-term debt instruments such as Treasury bills and large negotiable CDs.

Several credit intermediaries have been created or sponsored by the federal government to benefit certain sectors of the economy, particularly housing. Sponsored credit agencies include the Federal Home Loan Banks and the Farm Banks for Cooperatives. These agencies borrow in the credit markets by issuing their own debt instruments, and they invest the proceeds in mortgages, farm loans, or other obligations which meet the special objectives of each

Savings institutions and money-market mutual funds

Sponsored credit agencies and mortgage pools

agency. Government-sponsored mortgage pools perform a similar function by packaging mortgages and selling participation certificates to the public.

Finance companies offer home, auto, and other loans to households and businesses. Funds are obtained from debt issues in the credit markets and from commercial banks.

Finance companies

Federal Reserve banks purchase government securities and so provide credit to the federal government at the same time that they create reserves for depository institutions, in a manner detailed fully in Chapter 14. Federal Reserve banks also supply credit to depository institutions in the form of reserves loaned through the Fed's discount "window." The funds provided are financed mostly by issues of currency to the public and reserve deposits of depository institutions held at the Federal Reserve banks.

Federal Reserve banks

Other financial intermediaries include brokerage firms and investment banks. Brokerage firms lend to customers who buy stocks and bonds on margin. These loans and their own inventories of stocks and bonds are financed mainly with bank borrowing. Investment banks arrange debt and equity issues for customers for fees and carry inventories of these issues for brief periods in order to facilitate their distribution. Investment-bank inventories are financed internally and by borrowing.

Other financial intermediaries

Sector relationships

In Figure 4–4 estimated domestic credit-market assets (financial assets less equities) and liabilities in the economy at the end of 1979 are broken down in matrix form by sector. Under each sector there is a figure for net assets. This entry corresponds to accumulated net financial assets except for equities and foreign assets and liabilities. The net credit-market asset positions in Figure 4–4 show that households are, as a sector, generally surplus entities, whereas nonfinancial businesses and governments historically have been deficit entities. It also indicates the essentially neutral posture, already stressed, of financial intermediaries. Hence though intermediation obscures the relationship, households, as a group, are the principal ultimate source of funds for deficit spending by business and government. Of course, this does not deny that individual households tend to be deficit units at certain stages or that governments and businesses may be surplus units from time to time. The foreign sector may be a net supplier or absorber of funds; during the late 1970s it was a heavy net supplier, and this is reflected in the net positive position for this sector as of 1979.

THE FUNCTIONS OF EXTERNAL FINANCE

Why do certain sectors tend to be net absorbers of funds and

FIGURE 4–4

Estimated Credit Positions of Major Sectors
December 1979
($ Billions)

		Households	Business	Governments	Financial intermediaries	International and foreign entities
Households:						
Assets 2,920	Owed by:	204	112	317	2,287	—
Liabilities . . .1,681	Owed to:	204	31	139	1,307	—
Net 1,239						
Businesses:						
Assets 736	Owed by:	31	485	14	119	87
Liabilities . . .1,785	Owed to:	112	485	135	989	64
Net . . . .−1,049						
Governments:						
Assets 830	Owed by:	139	135	266	241	49
Liabilities . . .1,306	Owed to:	317	14	266	585	124
Net . . . .−476						
Financial intermediaries:						
Assets 2,991	Owed by:	1,307	989	585	61	49
Liabilities . . .2,821	Owed to:	2,287	119	241	61	113
Net 170						
International and foreign entities:						
Assets 301	Owed by:	—	64	124	113	*
Liabilities 185	Owed to:	—	87	49	49	*
Net 116						

NOTE: Nonprofit institutions and personal trust funds are included with households; Federal Reserve and sponsored credit agencies are included with governments; foreign bank and agencies' offices in the United States are included in financial intermediaries. Some cells are overestimates due to insufficient detail in source data; therefore, totals for assets and liabilities for each sector include some double counting; and all estimates could be considered only rough approximations constructed for illustration of basic relationships of the sectors.

*Data not available and not included in totals.

SOURCE: Based on *Flow of Funds* Federal Reserve Board of Governors, (February 1980).

others net providers? Why do various entities both lend and borrow? These are questions which are addressed in this section.

Functions for households

For the household, the functions of borrowing, lending, investing in securities, or drawing on financial assets include at least the following: (1) providing for medium-of-exchange service, (2) providing for shocks and absorbing shocks and windfalls, (3) supplementing labor earnings with interest, dividends, and capital gains on financial assets, (4) redistributing consumption spending over the household's life cycle, and (5) estate building. The first function is provided by holding checkable deposits, currency, and travelers checks. Recall that it was described in Chapter 2 as one of three traditional functions of money; its relevance to this chapter is that holdings of checkable deposits, travelers checks, and currency pro-

Medium-of-
exchange service

vide external finance to private financial intermediaries and to the
U.S. government.

The second function is a rather obvious one. A household's expectations of its income and expenditures can be wrong and produce
an unexpected shortfall or surplus of funds. In the case of a budget   Providing for
shortfall, if borrowing is not possible or desirable, financial assets   shocks
may be drawn upon. If this is done, it will be important to the
household that such assets be liquid; therefore, money balances are
often held to be available as a shock absorber. (Recall that a second
function provided by money, among other assets, was the liquid-
store-of-value function.) Again, the relevance here of holdings of
money and other assets for this purpose is the external finance
thereby provided to other entities.

FIGURE 4–5
Household lifecycle earnings and spending

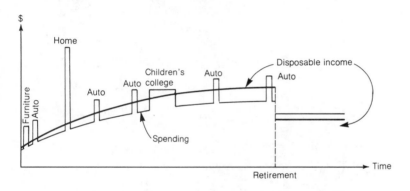

Except for currency and travelers checks and most checkable   Supplemental
deposits, financial assets usually provide earnings and hence supple-   income
ment the household's labor income. (These earnings are called "un-
earned" income in the National Income Accounts.)

A household uses borrowing and financial investment to allocate
its expected available funds over its lifetime so as to achieve a preferred pattern of spending. Figure 4–5 shows a representative   Life-cycle
household's lifetime expectations for earnings and for spending from   consumption
family formation to the period of retirement of the head of the   redistribution
household. Expected disposable income rises smoothly through the
working years of the household parents and then drops sharply at
their retirement. On average, spending, including purchases of
autos, a home, and other items normally financed by borrowing
(shown as spikes in the graph), exceeds earned income in the early
years in anticipation of higher earnings later; then it drops below
earnings in the peak income years, and finally exceeds earnings in
retirement.

During its early years, the household is a deficit entity, absorbing and spending funds supplied by other entities in the economy to purchase furniture, a car, etc. These debts of the household, of course, create financial assets for surplus units. Subsequently the household becomes a surplus entity, paying off debts and building a stock of financial assets and pension credits in anticipation of later, higher expenses such as college expenses for children and for retirement. In retirement, pension benefits and a nest egg of financial assets can support a level of spending in excess of income, and the household usually reverts to deficit status.[4]

Estate

Finally, financial assets normally constitute a substantial portion of the household's planned estate. This is convenient for distributions to heirs and for payment of estate taxes.

"We never would have been able to afford this vacation if our son hadn't
busted out of college in the first semester of his freshman year."

Reprinted by permission *The Wall Street Journal.*

Functions for nonfinancial firms

External financing has the following major uses for nonfinancial firms: (1) providing for medium-of-exchange service, (2) providing for shocks and absorbing shocks and windfalls, (3) supplementing operating income, (4) production and inventory financing, and (5) capital-expenditure financing. The first three of these are essentially identical to the first three listed for households and require no additional comment, except to note in connection with the third function that income from financial assets normally constitutes a small part of the nonfinancial firm's revenue.

A nonfinancial firm which has a production cycle will have many

---

[4]Accumulations and sales of real assets are an alternative way to achieve this objective, of course.

current outlays during the production run—for payroll and materials, for example—which it will not recover until some time after the product is delivered. Retail firms with seasonal sales have similar periods of negative cash flow due to expenditures for inventories. Drawing on financial assets can bridge the gap if the firm has sufficient cash reserves to begin with; otherwise, borrowing is necessary. Either way there is a finance cycle which conforms to the production or retail cycle: the firm is a deficit entity during a certain period and then, on sale of the goods, a surplus entity.

Production-and-inventory financing

Firms, of course, have requirements also for longer-term finance. Most begin as deficit entities and rely on long-term borrowing or stock issues to cover a substantial portion of start-up costs. Subsequent expansion may see further resort to external finance. A firm may also finance expansions out of financial assets which have been accumulated from current and past earnings. As a firm grows, its permanent borrowing ability increases, and it may choose to roll over continually a certain amount of long-term debt. Investors in the firm's debt and equity issues will be interested in the firm's ratio of interest payments to income, or alternatively, its debt-to-equity ratio. These indicate, to some degree, the firm's ability to weather setbacks without failing to meet its contractual obligations to lenders and normal dividend payments to stockholders.

Capital-expenditure finance

Functions for financial intermediaries

External finance operations of financing intermediaries are for: (1) providing for media of exchange, (2) income, (3) providing for shocks and absorbing shocks and windfalls, (4) portfolio financing, and (5) capital-expenditure financing. The first three are, by now, familiar, but require some additional comment in this case. For the first, as described earlier, commercial banks, of course, provide part of the checkable-deposit component of the money supply used by the non-bank public and some banks issue travelers checks. For their own transactions, commercial banks use demand deposits with each other (called interbank deposits), reserve deposits with the Federal Reserve, and currency. Other financial institutions use demand deposit balances at commercial banks, reserve balances with the Fed, and currency.

Medium of exchange

The income function is listed second for financial intermediaries to highlight the fact that these firms derive most of their income from investments in financial assets. They seek to achieve, within legal constraints, the best possible combination of high return and low risk on these investments. The credit intermediary must be especially concerned about the likelihood of repayment of principal on its financial investments because it has a very high ratio of debt to equity. Significant losses on its portfolio could easily cause it to become bankrupt.

Primary income

Providing for
shocks

Another important risk most financial intermediaries face is an unexpected exercise of financial claims—a withdrawal of deposits, for example. Hence, the liquidity of depository institutions' portfolios is particularly important. To cover unexpected claims and, in most cases, to meet legal requirements, depository institutions invest part of their portfolios in highly liquid financial assets which constitute their reserves. An alternative solution to an unexpected drain is to borrow, either from a government authority created for that purpose or from another source, if one can be found.

Portfolio
financing

The portfolio financing function refers simply to the dependency of financial intermediaries on borrowing, attracting new deposits, selling insurance, or issuing stock to finance their portfolios of loans and investments. Management of the "liability side" of their intermediation activities has received increased attention from commercial banks and thrifts in recent years. Their objectives in liability management may be to achieve *the lowest expected interest expense over a period of time, low risk of an unexpected rise in interest expense, or low risk of an unexpected outflow of funds.*

Capital-
expenditure
financing

Our final use for financial intermediaries, capital-expenditure financing, is not significantly different from that function described for nonfinancial firms. Financial intermediaries also have capital outlays for structures and equipment which may require external finance.

Governments

The uses of finance are not so easily cataloged for governments. They are quite different, for example, for the federal government and state and local governments. And for the federal government, distinctions must be drawn between those functions as they pertain to the U.S. government's budget (as set by Congress and the President, with external financing implemented through the Treasury), those of the Federal Reserve system, and those of the so-called off-budget federal and federally sponsored financing agencies. Our discussion of the U.S. government's uses of external finance through the Treasury and the Federal Reserve will anticipate much more detailed discussion and analysis in later chapters.

Among other duties, the U.S. Treasury is responsible for (1) collecting taxes and (2) finding ways to finance the federal government's deficit, or, as the case may be, to utilize the federal surplus. Also, (3) since there is a substantial amount of U.S. debt outstanding, the Treasury must be concerned with the management of this stock of obligations. (Some obligations are always falling due and must be "rolled over" or otherwise refinanced unless the government happens to be running a sufficient current surplus to pay them.)

The functions for the Treasury

The principal uses of external finance from the perspective of the U.S. government's budget and the Treasury are: (1) providing for media of exchange, (2) war financing, (3) discretionary stabilization, (4) cyclical finance, (5) seasonal finance, and (6) financing budgeted loan programs.

The government's transactions are handled mainly through two types of deposit accounts. The first type consists of government demand deposits in accounts with commercial banks which are called *tax and loan accounts*. These accounts are used as initial depositories for most government receipts. The second type is demand deposits with Federal Reserve banks from which most government expeditures are made; these are known collectively as the U.S. *Treasury general account*. Normally the Treasury tries to keep the general account balance reasonably low and stable, for reasons that will be explained in Chapter 14. As expenditures are made, the general account at the Fed is replenished from tax and loan account balances and other financial assets. Tax and loan account balances provide external finance to commercial banks, and the general account provides external finance to the Federal Reserve (and, hence, effectively back to the government itself).

Medium of exchange

Until recent years, truly substantial government deficits occurred only during war years. And it was once thought that debt accumulated to help pay for a war should be eliminated through postwar government surpluses. (We will note later in Chapter 12 the effects of surpluses run by the government during the latter half of the 19th century to reduce the Civil War debt of the Union.) Roughly half of the government's current outstanding debt was accumulated during World War II; and Korea and Viet Nam added substantial amounts. There is little sentiment today for reducing this accumulated debt, however.

War finance

In fact, since World War II concern has focused more and more on the rate at which government debt is growing (the level of the government deficit) without much concern for the level it has attained because of historical deficits. Our focus on the deficit, or surplus, as the case may be, is because the deficit has important implications for inflation and unemployment. As we indicated in Chapter 1 (and as we will be elaborating later) Keynesians place emphasis on an increase in government spending or a cut in tax rates to stimulate the economy in a recession and vice versa to cool an excessive expansion. In 1964 and in 1975, the government cut taxes substantially to combat unemployment, and in 1968 taxes were raised to combat inflation. These measures had significant effects on the deficit and hence on government borrowing.

Discretionary stabilization

Even without discretionary changes in the government's budget, there is a strong tendency for the federal budget to go into deficit in

Cyclical and
seasonal finance

a slack economy and to move into surplus in a boom period. This happens because federal tax receipts vary with the levels of personal income and corporate profits. Also, federal payments for unemployment compensation fall as the economy expands and go up in a recession. (Because these changes in government tax receipts and spending are built-in and have a beneficial, counter-cyclical effect on total spending in Keynesian analysis, they are termed *automatic stabilizers.*)

Similarly, there are seasonal fluctuations in government borrowing. These are partly due to the fact that tax payments are due quarterly from businesses and some individuals; and, most importantly, there is the annual tax settlement for individuals on April 15th.

Budgeted loans

The federal government extends credit directly to households, businesses, and other governments under a wide variety of programs. These loans are usually at low interest and benefit disaster victims, small businesses, and other entities. Such loans are financed out of general tax revenues and via Treasury borrowings. In the latter case, the government is operating, if effect, as an intermediary.

The Federal Reserve

To elaborate on earlier discussions, the Federal Reserve System consists of several entities. There is a central policy and regulatory unit, the Federal Reserve Board of Governors, and there are 12 regional Federal Reserve banks which also have policy and regulatory responsibilities. The regional Federal Reserve banks operate in cooperation with each other and in response to directives from the Board of Governors and the Federal Open Market Committee—a committee comprised of the governors and several reserve bank presidents. (These units will be described in still more detail in Chapter 13.)

The Federal Reserve regional units have many of the characteristics of private credit intermediaries. Their assets are predominantly financial and highly balanced by financial liabilities, and their portfolios provide earnings. The Federal Reserve banks even issue stock to their private member banks. Hence from a mechanical perspective our list of the uses of finance for the Federal Reserve banks is identical to the list for private financial intermediaries, except, perhaps, for the second item in that list which refers to providing for shocks.[5]

Despite mechanical similarities to private credit intermediaries, the basic objectives of the financing and other operations of the Federal Reserve banks are quite different from those of private intermediaries, and we now turn to a brief summary of these.

The basic functions of the Federal Reserve's financial operations

Federal Reserve financial operations are mainly geared to the following: (1) targeted growth for the money supply, (2) technical-factor correction, (3) financial-market stabilization, (4) exchange-rate stabilization, (5) "even keeling," and (6) last-resort lending. As described briefly in Chapter 2, Federal Reserve actions, especially transactions in government securities, are the major determinants of the rate of growth of the money supply. The Fed's desired growth rates for money and credit are determined by the anticipated course of the economy, the Federal Reserve's priorities in terms of inflation and unemployment, and the perceived timing of Federal Reserve actions and the economy's response.

Targeted growth of the money supply

If the Federal Reserve controlled the money supply completely, its operations could be devoted mainly to smoothly expanding the Fed's holdings of government securities and, thereby, reserves and the money supply. However, there are a number of short-run "technical" factors which tend to affect bank reserves or otherwise affect the money supply independently of Federal Reserve control. (A detailed development of this topic is provided in Chapter 14.) Consequently, on a day-to-day basis, Federal Reserve operations often are directed toward correcting for these technical factors.

Technical factors

Conditions in the financial markets usually are determined by the basic economic factors motivating the supplies and demands for funds. However, because the future is uncertain, at times market psychology can be a destabilizing factor. If the markets become disturbed, say by the bankruptcy of a major corporation, the Federal Reserve may act aggressively with loans or other actions to stabilize market conditions.

Financial stabilization

As we will explain in more detail in Chapter 8, foreign money is traded against the dollar in the foreign-exchange market; and the exchange rate between the dollar and other currencies is determined in this market by the supply and demand for the dollar in relation to other currencies. The Federal Reserve and the central banks of other countries can affect exchange rates through direct operations in this market, and occasionally this is done to stabilize exchange rates. (The Federal Reserve can also affect exchange rates

Exchange-rate stabilization

---

[5]The Federal Reserve banks currently have no concern regarding the effects of a sudden withdrawal of deposits on their ability to lend, as private intermediaries do, because the Fed has virtually unlimited power to issue Federal Reserve notes—our dominant paper currency and "legal tender for all debts, public and private"—to meet withdrawals. Holders of these notes have no recourse to payment from the Federal Reserve in anything but other Federal Reserve notes. The legal reserves of the Federal Reserve banks are mainly government securities. Functionally, no domestic reserves are necessary, however. (This was not always the case. As mentioned in Chapter 1, prior to March 1933 the Fed had to supply gold on demand in exchange for Federal Reserve currency, so a domestic reserve of gold was necessary.) The only reserves of any purpose at the Fed are those of foreign exchange which are used sometimes to influence the international value of the dollar.

indirectly by increasing the money supply at a faster or slower pace, as we shall explain in Chapter 8.)

Even keeling

Among its many duties, the Federal Reserve serves as the U.S. government's agent for sales of government securities. New issues of government securities are sold through the Federal Reserve at competitively determined prices or yields. If there is an unusually large issue being marketed, the Federal Reserve may purchase some government securities to avoid market "indigestion," that is, to preclude too much reaching the market at one time, needlessly driving up interest costs to the Treasury and destabilizing the debt markets. The idea is that the issues bought by the Fed can be sold later under more favorable circumstances, creating a leveling effect on interest costs to the Treasury and on the general level of interest rates in the credit markets.

Lender of last resort

Last, but by no means least, the Federal Reserve can extend substantial credit through its discount window to depository institutions as a lender of last resort. This has the beneficial effect of aiding a particular institution in difficulty. It can also add to the total supply of reserves at an undesirable time, however. Discount-window loans are supposed to be temporary. They carry an interest cost—the discount rate.

Free government finance through Fed operations

To return now to our earlier discussion of the Federal Reserve banks as financial intermediaries, we can identify them as mainly intermediaries in a flow of credit from the private sector to the U.S. government. Their portfolios are dominated by U.S. government securities. These are financed chiefly by issues of Federal Reserve notes and by taking in reserve deposits of depository institutions. Normally, these liabilities do not bear interest.[6] Consequently, the Federal Reserve has substantial net earnings. These net earnings, equal to more than 90 percent of the interest earnings on the Federal Reserve's holdings of government securities and amounting to approximately $10 billion in fiscal 1980, are returned to the Treasury. In the final analysis, creation of currency and reserve deposits through Federal Reserve open-market purchases represents essentially a costless way for the government to borrow, and a particularly tempting source of finance for the government in time of war. However, except in unusual situations such as war, the Federal Reserve resists making purchases of government debt for the purpose of providing free funding to the Treasury because this leads to excessive money expansion and, ultimately, higher inflation.

---

[6]In 1980, as a part of the Depository Institutions Deregulation and Monetary Control Act, Congress authorized the Federal Reserve to pay interest on a limited amount of required reserves.

Government off-budget and sponsored financing agencies

As described earlier in this chapter, the federal government, and a few state governments also, have set up a variety of off-budget, government-owned or government-sponsored financing agencies to benefit specific borrowers. These agencies directly or indirectly borrow in the private credit markets and relend to segments of the private sector. In some cases, the government explicitly guarantees the debt of the off-budget agency; in other cases, the market has interpreted government ownership or sponsorship as an implicit moral guarantee of the agency's debt. As a consequence of their government ties, these agencies are able to borrow at lower interest rates than are available to completely private intermediaries. The funds are then placed at lower interest rates and, often, at greater risk than other intermediaries would be willing to accept.

The most important of those agencies owned by the federal government and having a government guarantee for their obligations is the Government National Mortgage Association (GNMA or "Ginnie Mae" in market jargon), which buys mortages. Another government-owned agency is the Student Assistance Loan Association ("Sallie Mae"), which buys college student loan paper from commercial banks. In addition to the two federally sponsored agencies mentioned earlier, the Federal Home Loan Banks, which lend to savings and loan associations and mutual savings banks, and the Farm Banks for Cooperatives, which finances qualified private farm activities, there are the Federal National Mortgage Assistance (FNMA or "Fannie Mae") and the Federal Home Loan Mortgage Assistance ("Freddie Mac") Corporations, which buy residential mortgages; and there are two more organizations which lend to farmers—the Federal Land Banks and the Federal Farm Credit Banks.

The functions for state and local governments

State and local governments engage in external finance principally for (1) media-of-exchange services, (2) seasonal finance, and (3) capital-expenditure finance. The first two uses require no special comment for state and local governments. State debt and local government debt (both called municipal debt) ordinarily are issued to finance capital expenditures.

There are two principal types of municipal debt: (1) government-guaranteed bonds (general obligation bonds), and (2) nonguaranteed, self-financing bonds (revenue bonds). The first type might seem a fairly safe investment, but it is not as safe as federally guaranteed debt because, when in a bind, state and local governments do not have the vast taxing power of the federal government and cannot fall back on the power to create money and borrow at zero cost via

Capital-
expenditure
financing

the Federal Reserve as the federal government can. In the 1930s many state and local governments defaulted on their general obligation bonds, and a number of local governments have approached default in recent years. The second type also is less than risk-free; in the past 25 years several toll roads financed by municipal revenue bonds have failed.

INTRODUCTION TO ARTICLE

In the fall of 1975, New York City came perilously close to defaulting on its debt obligations. Federal government loans and a moratorium on some debt payments have since bought time for the city, enabling it to improve its budget and regain its ability to borrow. The origins of New York City's difficulties are complex, but it is clear that the city was relying too heavily on credit to finance its current expenditures on a continuing basis. This *Business Week* article discusses the situation at the height of the crisis in 1975. What would the effects of a New York City default have been on financial markets? Should the Federal Reserve have stepped in to lend directly to New York City if the Treasury had not? The issues are still open to debate.

New York City: The Pros and Cons of Default

This week, New York City was once again speeding down what has become a too-familiar road to financial disaster. With the last of August's billion-dollar financing delivered on Aug. 21 to pay $792 million of notes due the next day, the Comptroller's office reports that the city will be $70 million short on Sept. 2—much too soon for a third public offering to be arranged. On Sept. 15, the city will need an additional $433.6 million to repay notes that mature. And even if the city failed to pay all of the $595 million debt service due in September, it would still be $310.7 million short of meeting its other obligations, such as payroll, welfare, and suppliers. In October, much the same financial picture will exist.

That kind of gloomy outlook has rekindled a bitter debate in the financial community as to whether or not the city should default on its debt service. At least four different points of view are being aired.

Treasury Secretary William E. Simon believes the impact of any default could be temporary and negligible. In fact, government officials keep pointing out the "positive" aspects

of default. The head of one regional Federal Reserve bank reasons that default would force the city to balance its budget and accomplish more to clear away the uncertainties in the municipal bond market than any assistance from the Fed. This group believes that it makes more sense to let the city topple than to continue to teeter on the brink of financial disaster.

The exact opposite view, expressed by people such as Felix Rohatyn, chairman of the Finance Committee of the Municipal Assistance Corp., and a partner of Lazard Frères, is that a default by the city would be catastrophic. It would force the state to default as well shortly thereafter and ruin the credit of other cities, such as Detroit and Newark, which are having their own financial problems. At the least, default would raise the cost of borrowing for every municipality and state agency in the country. Default, this line of thinking runs, would remove New York City from the financial markets for years. In addition, the banks that hold so much New York paper, particularly the ones in the city, would experience a serious liquidity pinch because a large part of their assets would be frozen.

Since the threat of default is so openly discussed, some out-of-town bankers fear that, in fact, default by New York City on its outstanding notes or bonds is likely and would trigger litigation that would tie up the tax revenue stream backing MAC bonds. As a result, these bankers consider MAC securities too risky to buy, despite the allocation of New York City's share of its sales and stock-transfer taxes to pay them off.

Still other banks insist that the Federal Reserve Board in Washington will not allow the city to default. The Fed, through Vice-Chairman George W. Mitchell, has said that the New York financial community is rich enough to handle the city's current cash shortage. But these bankers are convinced that if local interests are unwilling, other banks will be persuaded quietly to help, just as the Fed has moved quietly to ease other serious credit problems that have faced the banking industry in the past, particularly those associated with the real estate investment trusts.

At best, New York City is caught in a no-win situation because it must raise so much money so quickly. In establishing MAC last June, New York's Governor Hugh L. Carey hoped to restructure New York City's debt, extending $3 billion of it from short-term to long-term, thus buying time for the city to straighten out the fiscal mess that led to the current crisis.

A tough sale

However, MAC was unable to sell all the bonds it planned to and what was sold was done with great difficulty. Says one of the 14 managing underwriters of MAC's last offering: "We did it. But we did it with mirrors again. Where will the money come from in September?" Some of the $37 million in bonds that were offered publicly out of the $960 million financing in August—even though they yielded as much as 11 percent—might have gathered dust on dealers' shelves except for the report that Arthur F. Burns, chairman of the Federal Reserve Board, had told city officials the Fed would stand ready to help rather than see the city default. The entire $37 million was sold by dealers before the Fed issued a quasidenial.

All this "will-the-city-make-it-or-not" atmosphere has pushed municipal bond yields to record highs and has helped produce unsettled conditions in all the U.S. financial markets.

A major factor contributing to the uncertainty is that no one knows what happens legally when a city the size of New York goes under. Federal bankruptcy statutes are inadequate for a city so large, and no one knows just how the courts would rule in adjudicating conflicting claims among lenders, employees pensioners, welfare recipients, and others.

The city's continuing shortage of cash ($ millions)

Projected receipts	September	October
Real estate tax	$ 313.1	$ 276.2
General fund		
City taxes	177.8	169.7
State taxes	74.9	195.8
Welfare aid	135.8	117.8
Other state aid	37.0	67.4
Other federal aid	21.1	32.3
Miscellaneous	9.1	15.0
Total receipts	$ 708.8	$ 874.2
Projected expenditures		
Payroll	501.7	389.0
Debt service	595.3	553.6
Welfare, including		
medicaid	259.6	260.6
Transit Authority,		
Housing Authority,		
Health &		
Hospitals Corp.	43.9	47.0
Pensions, insurance,		
Social Security	97.9	147.5
Construction	102.9	99.0
Vendors and		
miscellaneous	73.5	88.7
Total expenditures ...	$1,674.8	$1,585.4
Projected		
deficits	$ 903.0	$ 711.2

DATA: New York City Office of the Comptroller.

The procedures for an orderly disposition of city assets to all its creditors are just not in place. The current federal bankruptcy statute would permit the city to go into court prior to default to announce that it is seeking the consent of 51 percent of its creditors to a bankruptcy plan. But it is unlikely that the city could contact 51 percent—which the law would most likely construe to mean not only debt holders, most of which hold bearer certificates, but employees, pensioners, and welfare recipients.

It is also difficult to predict with any accuracy how a New York default would affect other municipalities. New York Senator Jacob K. Javits fears that a city default "would completely destroy the municipal market" and lead to "crushing borrowing costs." Some cities have already postponed or reduced the size of new offerings.

Financial officers in such cities as Detroit and Philadelphia—which have been paying much more for their borrowings because of fears that New York might fail—wonder where they would get the money they need if a New York default closed the municipal market to them. "If it came on suddenly, it could be tough for us," says Edward G. Rago, administrative budget analyst for the city of Detroit. "There could even be some payless paydays."

National impact

Beyond the social and economic implications for New York and other cities, there is the danger to New York City bank liquidity from a New York default—not to mention the strain on the entire banking system should a whole string of cities go under. These problems are intensified by the loans to REITs and other corporations that already stuff some bank portfolios.

The 12 largest New York City banks have about $1.4 billion of New York City debt in their $6.5 billion in municipal holdings. In addition, they hold some $1 billion in MAC paper not included in that $6.5 billion. In fact, their holdings of MAC and city paper account for about 25 percent of their $9.4 billion in total capital.

With a default, says one analyst, no one knows how far the banks would have to mark down these securities. Judging the financial strength of these banks would therefore be difficult, making it even tougher for them and their holding companies to sell certificates of deposit and commercial paper at a reasonable price to finance their operations. Federal bank regulators, in fact, have instructions ready to send to the banks should the city default, including accounting rules to permit the banks to write off their losses over six months.

Banker's view

As the day of reckoning draws nearer, some previously implacable outside New York bankers now concede that if necessary they would do their bit to avoid a city default. "The banks around the country would not let New York City go down the tube," says Richard L. Kattel, president of Citizens & Southern National Bank. "It's just too damn important. It's the financial center of the country." C&S owns no MAC bonds, and Kattel is still unimpressed with the credit of those bonds. But his point is that if the New York banks ran out of the capacity to save the city—something which he does not expect—then his bank "would do its part to help them." He says: "But we'd look at it as if we were making a loan. We'd send people up there to check the books and look over the numbers."

And Moncure G. Crowder, senior vice president at First National Bank of Atlanta predicts that his bank—which did not buy any bonds in the first two offerings—will probably own some by the end of the year.

Still, Kattel sounds a little more friendly toward New York than some of his counterparts across the country. Indeed, the confusion surrounding the whole question of New York City's finances leads some bankers to make some tough statements. Preston Luney, executive vice president of Harris Bank in Chicago, insists he has no interest in buying MAC paper even if the Federal Reserve were to step in.

In an almost hopelessly confused situation, nothing is more confusing than the attitude of the Federal Reserve Board. Robert Mayo, president of the Chicago Federal Reserve Bank, is one well-informed observer who insists that Chairman Burns has decided that even indirect assistance from the Fed is "inappropriate." Still other bankers, like John Bunting, head of First Pennsylvania, who spent 14 years at the Fed, says the New York banks have received an "intuitive understanding" from the Fed that "they should be a little more courageous than a pure economic analysis of the figures would allow them to be" in their purchase of MAC bonds. "It's the same thing they did with the REITs," he says. "And there weren't phone calls telling you what to do."

Given the secretive manner in which the Fed usually operates, it is likely that no one will ever find out whether Burns has passed or intends to pass his wishes to the New York banks, however indirectly. Many observers would find such secretive behavior on the part of the Fed highly objectionable because, for one thing, it would permit the banks to lock up some very high-yielding investments with full knowledge that the Fed stands ready to bail them out if real problems develop with their own liquidity.

But New York City does not have time to ponder these broad considerations. Without some sort of federal or state assistance, it almost surely will default on its obligations. And for the city, default is a no-win proposition. Even if it foregoes payment of interest and principal on debt coming due in September, it will still be $310.7 million short of meeting its cash needs for payroll, welfare, pension costs, and other operating expenses. In October, that shortfall will be $157.6 million. Once the city defaults, it is unlikely to find anyone willing to lend it the money to fill the gap between revenues and expenses. Then the city would be forced to miss its payroll, pension, or welfare commitments.

Bankruptcy plan

Meanwhile, almost every day new city trou-

bles come to light. The comptroller's office estimates that the city has accumulated a deficit of $2.5 billion to $2.8 billion in the past 10 years. This year, under current accounting practices, that deficit could grow another $700 million—without considering the effects of any of the city's crisis cutbacks or the incredible borrowing costs that the city has incurred through the MAC offerings.

And that does not include the bills from suppliers on which the city is sadly in arrears —not because the city chooses not to pay its bills but because the bureaucratic process is so cumbersome. Normally, bill-paying takes at least six weeks to two months. The effects on suppliers can be drastic. Airport Motors, a Chrysler dealer in Jackson Heights, N.Y., does about half of its business with the city. And according to Howard Koeppel, vice president, the city currently owes the company close to $2 million. The thought of a default obviously troubles him. "It could put us out of business," he says.

SOURCE: Reprinted from the *Business Week*, September 1, 1975, by special permission. ©1975 by McGraw-Hill, Inc. All rights reserved.

CONCLUSION

In this chapter we have explained the functions of credit in the economy from the perspective of the economy as a whole and also from the perspective of individual sectors. Credit enables households to achieve more preferred spending patterns, facilitates production and investment, and so contributes to national productivity and welfare. Without credit, choices in the economy would be severely constrained, and the savings of surplus units could not flow as effectively to their most productive uses. These are the positive aspects of credit. In later chapters we will consider the problems raised by the possibilities of financial collapse, inefficiency, and inequity in credit markets.

Although the nation is wealthier as a result of credit finance, the stock of domestic credit assets in the economy does not constitute a part of national wealth; neither, necessarily, does it reflect the accumulated value of economic investment expenditures in the economy. For a refresher on the distinctions between investments in credit assets and economic investment, and between individual and aggregate wealth relationships, see the appendix to this chapter.

ADVANCED READINGS

Gurley, John G., and Shaw, Edward S. "Financial Intermediaries and the Saving-Investment Process." Journal of Finance 11 (May 1956); 257–66.

Kendrick, John W., "Measuring America's Wealth." Morgan Guaranty Survey, (May 1976); 5–13.

PROBLEMS

1. Distinguish credit finance from equity finance.
2. Compare the functions of external finance for nonfinancial firms and for private financial intermediaries.
3. Suppose New York City were able to print and issue money to pay its debt. What would happen to income and prices in New York City? In the rest of the country?
4. Discuss the consolidated balance sheet for the U.S. economy given in the appendix to this chapter, identifying the entries which constitute net contributions to national wealth.
5. After reading the appendix, identify each of the following as adding to, subtracting from, or not changing net national wealth and explain your choice:
    a. A student loan to finance a year at college.
    b. The production of a nuclear submarine.
    c. The issuance of a new $10,000 currency note by the Federal Reserve.
    d. Declaration of bankruptcy by New York City.

APPENDIX

ACCOUNTING TOOLS AND WEALTH CONCEPTS

The balance sheet and other accounting tools

Balance sheets for two types of firms

To keep track of financial transactions and their economic meaning, three standard accounting frameworks or slightly modified versions of them are used in this text. The balance sheet is the familiar accounting statement which presents, *according to certain rules*, the economic position or worth of a firm at a specific moment in time. There are two types of firms which can be distinguished by balance-sheet characteristics: *financial intermediaries* and *nonfinancial firms*. In Figure 4–1A we show a simplified balance sheet for a financial intermediary, the Leaky Till National Bank, and another balance sheet for a nonfinancial enterprise, Campus Slop Cafeterias, Inc. We will refer to some characteristic differences between these balance sheets in a moment.

As shown in Figure 4–1A, the balance sheet is organized into three major categories: assets, liabilities, and owners' equity or net

FIGURE 4–1A
Balance sheets for a financial intermediary and a nonfinancial firm

LEAKY TILL NATIONAL BANK
Balance Sheet
(December 31, 1980)

Assets		Liabilities	
Financial:		Demand deposits	$21,000,000
Loans and		Time deposits	8,000,000
financial		Total	
investments	$25,500,000	liabilities	29,000,000
Reserves	4,000,000	Net worth	
Real:		(capital)	1,100,000
Buildings and			
property	500,000		
Equipment	100,000	Total	
Total assets	$30,100,000	liabilities	
		and capital	$30,100,000

CAMPUS SLOP CAFETERIAS
Balance Sheet
(December 31, 1980)

Assets		Liabilities	
Financial:		Loans	$ 2,000,000
Cash . . . . $	50,000	Total	
Securities	100,000	liabilities	2,000,000
Real:		Net worth	
Buildings	3,000,000	(capital)	2,150,000
Equipment	1,000,000	Total	
		liabilities	
Total assets . . . . $	4,150,000	and capital	4,150,000

worth. *Assets are rights to current or future resources.* Subcategories of assets can be designated according to the purpose at hand. In these statements we have created subcategories of financial and real assets. *Financial assets consist of money or rights to future money payments.* Hence loans and investments in debt instruments made by a firm, such as Leaky Till's mortgages on real estate in Underwater, Florida, are part of that entity's financial assets. Corporate stocks are also considered financial assets in the balance sheet of the investing firm. *Real assets represent rights to physical services.* For a firm, they include physical structures, inventories, and equipment owned by that firm—Campus Slop's taste extractor equipment, for example. Note that the assets of the Leaky Till National Bank are primarily financial whereas those of Campus Slop are primarily real.

Liabilities are specific claims on the resources of the firm which can be exercised either currently or at some time in the future. Debt owed by the firm is one form of such obligations. Tax obligations accrued and not yet paid is another (not shown in Figure 4–1A).[7]

Assets: financial
and real

Liabilities

[7]There is some question among economists and accountants as to how corporate equity shares should be treated in the balance sheet of an issuing enterprise. Some argue that, because they are financial assets of individuals, they should be treated as liabilities of the firm; but the prevailing custom is not to do so. As described later and

Net worth

The last major category in the balance sheet is usually referred to as *net worth* by economists; it is often labeled owners' capital or just capital by accountants. The entry here is obtained by subtracting liabilities from assets; to the extent that our accounting of assets and liabilities is an accurate reflection of true economic values, it represents the net economic value of the firm.[8]

Although the balance sheet is most familiar as a statement of a firm's net worth, it can also be applied to a household, to a govern-

FIGURE 4–2A
Balance sheets for a household and a municipal government

HOUSEHOLD OF B.S. MANNER, M.D.
Balance Sheet
(December 31, 1980)

Assets		Liabilities	
Financial:		Loans	$ 50,000
Cash	$ 1,000	Total liabilities	50,000
Time deposits	5,000		
Life insurance (cash value) and Securities	250,000	Net Worth	$1,616,000
Real:			
Home	100,000		
Autos	20,000		
Other durables	40,000	Total liabilities	
Human wealth	1,250,000		
Total assets	$1,666,000	and capital	$1,666,000

SPEED TRAP, GEORGIA MUNICIPAL GOVERNMENT
Balance Sheet
(December 31, 1980)

Assets		Liabilities	
Financial:		Sewage system bonds	$3,000,000
Cash	$ 10,000	Total liabilities	$3,000,000
Time deposits	90,000		
Real:		Net Worth	$1,350,000
Buildings and property	4,000,000		
Equipment and vehicles	250,000	Total liabilities	
Total assets	$4,350,000	and capital	$4,350,000

shown in Figure 4–6A, this customary treatment necessitates an adjustment for equities in a consolidated balance sheet for the nation so as not to overstate net national wealth.

[8]Accountants must contend with severe information problems—not the least of which is what the future portends—in gauging the net worth of a firm. To achieve comparability, they have devised a set of rules for valuing assets and liabilities. Because the future is uncertain, these rules conform to the accounting principle of *conservatism*, which means that they are intended to err on the low side in valuing assets and on the high side in valuing liabilities. Also, many intangibles are left out of the balance sheet.

For these and other reasons, the value of a firm as reported in its balance sheet may depart significantly from its value as assessed by the market—the current price of the firm's shares times the quantity of shares outstanding. Nevertheless, for most purposes, standard accounting measures are the best information available to economists and business analysts.

ment, and to an entire economy. In Figure 4–2A, we show simplified balance sheets for a physician's household and a city government. Note the types of real assets owned by the household of our physician, Bedside Manner. For a household, real assets should include, as you might expect, the home, if the household owns one, the automobile, and other durables (goods with a life of more than one year); but also included is the present value of the household's future labor income—*human wealth.* An accounting of the real assets of a government, such as the municipal government of Speed Trap, Georgia, should include government land, buildings, and equipment.

Often we are more interested in changes in the economic position of an entity over some period of time than in its position at a point in time. Balance sheets for the beginning and ending dates of the period could be compared explicitly, but a more convenient approach is to simply subtract balance-sheet data for the beginning date from data for the terminal date and present a "changes in" statement for balance-sheet entries. This is known as a *flow balance sheet* and is shown for our cafeteria company in Figure 4–3A. Note that this account refers to a period of time, whereas the balance sheets in Figure 4–1A refer to a point in time.

The flow balance sheet

FIGURE 4–3A

CAMPUS SLOP CAFETERIAS
Flow Balance Sheet
(December 31, 1979 to December 31, 1980)

Changes in Assets		Changes in Liabilities	
Financial:		Loans........................	$–5,000
Cash ....$ –500		Total	
Securities 17,000		change in	
		liabilities..............	–5,000
Real:			
Equipment $35,000		Changes in	
		net worth	$56,500
		Total	
		change in	
Total change		liabilities	
in assets $51,500		and net worth	$51,500

For many purposes, it is useful to focus directly on levels and changes in financial entries in the balance sheet, and it is useful to have more information about the operations of an entity which have had a bearing on its financial position. For these purposes accountants have developed the *statement of changes in financial position.*

The statement of changes in financial position

The organization of the entries in this statement depends upon what type of financial position one wishes to highlight. In this appendix we will use it to analyze changes in an entity's (or a sector's) *net financial asset position—financial assets minus financial liabilities.*[9] Our headings in this statement are labeled as follows:

---

[9]The common practice among accountants is to organize the categories to show changes in either cash or working-capital positions.

Reprinted by permission *The Wall Street Journal.*

sources of funds, uses of funds, and changes in gross and net financial assets. See the account for Campus Slop Cafeterias in Figure
4–4A for an example. Sources of funds include mainly revenue from

FIGURE 4–4A

CAMPUS SLOP CAFETERIAS
Statement of Changes in Financial Position
(January 1, 1979 to December 31, 1980)

Sources of funds:

Sales of meals	$1,000,000
Sales of used equipment	31,500
Dividends and interest on securities held	5,000
Total sources of funds	$1,036,500

Uses of funds:

Wages and salaries	$ 250,000
Purchases of food & materials	500,000
Purchases of new equipment	45,000
Interest on loans	200,000
Dividends to stockholders	20,000
Total uses of funds	$1,015,000

Changes in gross and net financial assets:

Cash . . . . $	−500
Securities	17,000
Less change in liabilities:	−5,000
Change in net financial position	$ 21,500

current sales for a firm, labor earnings for a household, and tax revenue for a government. Also, funds may be obtained by selling real assets, of course. Examples of uses of funds would be payroll expense or an equipment purchase for a firm, a car purchase for a household, and expenditures on highway construction for a government.

Obviously, the net result of the actions detailed under our sources and uses headings has to be an increase in net financial assets if sources exceed uses and vice versa because, by construction, change in net financial position is simply the difference between our totals under sources and uses. This increase can also be calculated from the relevant flow-balance-sheet data in Figure 4–3A which are repeated as detail under changes in gross and net financial assets in Figure 4–4A.

Financial assets and national wealth

Now that we have established the necessary terminology and accounting frameworks, we can demonstrate their use with an analysis of some important ultimate economic relationships that emerge from individual credit transactions.

We begin, as usual, with an example. Suppose Campus Slop, which owns four cafeterias adjacent to colleges, decides to expand to five cafeterias. It figures it can commit no more than $200,000 out of current earnings toward the new cafeteria, but a new building and necessary equipment will cost $1,000,000, so considerable external financing is required. A commercial mortgage for $750,000 is available from Leaky Till National Bank. A physician and head of the household in our earlier example, Bedside Manner, happens to be a friend of one of the owners of the cafeteria company and agrees to provide Campus Slop with $50,000 in exchange for a promissory note (a debt instrument which simply states the amount owed plus interest and the date by which it must be paid). This $50,000 represents accumulated savings from B.S. Manner's medical practice over the past year and together with the $750,000 mortgage on the cafeteria placed with Leaky Till makes the necessary external financing possible. Leaky Till National is able to accept (purchase) the mortgage and extend funds to Campus Slop because it has recently received a substantial inflow of new deposits. Figures 4–5A and 4–6A show the relevant changes in the economic and financial positions of Campus Slop, the Bedside Manner household, Leaky Till National Bank, and the depositors of Leaky Till, as well as consolidated changes for these four entities. (For convenience, only the changes described above affect the economic and financial positions depicted.)

As revealed in Figure 4–6A, there is a consolidated change in the net worth of the community of $1,090,000. This can be accounted

Figure 4–5A

FLOW BALANCE SHEETS
(DECEMBER 31, 1980–DECEMBER 31, 1981)

Campus Slop Cafeterias
($000)

Changes in Assets		Changes in Liabilities	
Financial	0	Unsecured loan	50
Real	1,000	Mortgage loan	750
Total changes in assets	1,000	Total changes in liabilities	800
		Change in Net Worth	200

Memo: Economic investment equals 1,000; saving equals 200.

Household of B.S. Manner, M.D.
($000)

Changes in Assets		Changes in Liabilities	
Financial:			
Unsecured loan	50	Total changes in liabilities	0
Real	0		
Total changes in assets	50	**Change in Net Worth**	50

Memo: Economic investment equals 0; saving equals 50.

Leaky Till National Bank
($000)

Changes in Assets		Changes in Liabilities	
Financial:		Deposits	840
Reserves	90	Total changes in liabilities	840
Mortgages	750		
Real	0	**Change in Net Worth**	0
Total changes in assets	840		

Memo: Economic investment equals 0; saving equals 0.

Depositors of Leaky Till National Bank
($000)

Changes in Assets		Changes in Liabilities	
Financial:			
Deposits	840	Total changes in liabilities	0
Real	0		
Total changes in assets	840	**Change in Net Worth**	840

Memo: Economic investment equals 0; saving equals 840.

Consolidated Account
($000)

Changes in Assets		Changes in Liabilities	
Total financial	1,730	Total	1,640
Total real	1,000		
Total changes in assets	2,730	**Change in Net Worth**	1,090

Memo: Economic investment equals 1,000; saving equals 1,090.

Figure 4-6A

STATEMENTS OF CHANGES IN FINANCIAL POSITION

Campus Slop Cafeterias ($000)

Sources of Net Financial Assets		Uses of Net Financial Assets	
Operating revenue	1,500	Operating expenses and taxes	1,300
Total sources	1,500	Expenditures on new cafeteria	1,000
		Total uses	2,300

Changes in gross and net financial assets

Financial assets	0
Less liabilities	800
Change in net financial position	−800

Household of B. S. Manner, M.D. ($000)

Sources of Net Financial Assets		Uses of Net Financial Assets	
Disposable income	125	Consumption spending	75
Total sources	125	Total uses	75

Changes in gross and net financial assets

Financial assets	50
Less liabilities	0
Change in net financial position	50

Leaky Till National Bank ($000)

Sources of Net Financial Assets		Uses of Net Financial Assets	
Dividends and interest	3,000	Interest	700
Total sources	3,000	Operating expenses, losses, and taxes	2,000
		Dividends	300
		Total uses	3,000

Changes in gross and net financial assets

Financial assets	840
Liabilities	840
Change in net financial position	0

Depositors of Leaky Till National Bank ($000)

Sources of Net Financial Assets		Uses of Net Financial Assets	
Operating revenue and disposable income	100,000	Operating expenses and consumption spending	96,160
Total sources	100,000	Total uses	96,160

Changes in gross and net financial assets

Financial assets	840
Less liabilities	0
Change in net financial position	840

Consolidated Statement of Changes in Financial Position ($000)

Sources of Net Financial Assets		Uses of Net Financial Assets	
Total of All Sources	104,625	Total of all uses	104,535

Changes in gross and net financial assets

Financial assets	90
Less liabilities	0
Change in net financial position	$90

for by the $1,000,000 investment in a new cafeteria by Campus Slop plus an increase in cash reserves of $90,000 held by Leaky Till National Bank. The remaining changes in assets are increases in financial assets which are balanced out by increases in liabilities as the consolidation is made. (Note the increase in net financial assets of only $90,000 in the consolidated statement of changes in financial position in Figure 4–6A.)

As this example demonstrates, with minor exceptions, increases in financial assets in the national economy will be matched somewhere by increases in liabilities or other entries which should be subtracted from total assets in calculating net worth or wealth in a consolidated balance sheet for the entire economy.[10] *In the final analysis, economic wealth is the ability to provide consumption services directly or indirectly, and the nation's capacity in this is represented principally by the value of its owned stock of real assets: inventories, plant, equipment, land, and human capital.* There is no equivalence or necessary connection between a nation's stock of financial assets, which represents mainly claims of some citizens on the wealth of other citizens, and its net stock of wealth or real assets. One can rise or fall independently of the other.

Estimates of total U.S. wealth are not easily constructed. One major difficulty is that of measuring human wealth—the productive power of American labor. Perhaps more reliable are estimates solely of nonhuman national wealth. In Figure 4–7A we present a balance sheet of nonhuman assets, liabilities, and net wealth for the U.S. economy at the end of 1973 adapted from a similar compilation by Professor John W. Kendrick. (Notice that national nonhuman wealth may be found to be equal to total domestic nonhuman real assets plus the small items identified in the note to the figure.)

Definitions of investment and saving

Economic investment can be defined as the quantity of current income devoted to the maintenance and growth of the stock of real wealth or capital.[11] There are two important facts to note about economic investment. First, as measured in the National Income Accounts (NIA) of the Department of Commerce, investment in the

The nation's wealth

Economic investment

[10]One minor exception is the stock of non-interest-bearing monetary assets supplied by the government (including Leaky Till's reserves). Most monetary economists feel that non-interest-bearing reserve balances of depository institutions and currency held by the nonbank public should be counted as part of net national wealth, even though they are treated as liabilities in the balance sheets of the issuers, the Federal Reserve and the Treasury.

Net financial claims on foreigners represent another financial contribution to net national (but not world) wealth and are included in the calculation of net national wealth which follows in the text of the appendix.

[11]Economists distinguish between *gross investment*, which includes all final spending on real assets and *net investment*, which adjusts this spending for estimated depreciation on the existing capital stock. Net investment represents the amount by which the nation's capital stock is estimated to have increased.

FIGURE 4–7A

NONHUMAN WEALTH IN THE UNITED STATES
Consolidated Balance Sheet
December 31, 1973
($ billions)

Assets of U.S. Residents		*Liabilities of U.S. Residents and Corporate Equities*	
Domestic financial assets		Liabilities................$4,192.0	
Demand deposits ....$	216.4	To U.S. residents‡	4,028.5
Currency*..................	65.3	To foreigners...........	163.5
Member bank reserves.......	35.1	Corporate equities§	896.7
Time and savings		Total	
accounts................	703.1	liabilities	
Insurance and pension		and	
reserves.................	458.1	corporate	
Corporate equities...........	896.7	equities $5,088.7	
Government obligations......	612.1		
Corporate bonds............	247.4	*National Nonhuman*	
Mortgages..................	429.8	*Wealth* $4,819.5	
Other credit			
instruments..............	788.8		
Security and			
trade credit	261.6		
Other†....................	310.9		
Total domestic			
financial			
assets............. $5,025.6			
Domestic nonhuman real assets			
Gold assets of			
monetary agencies	11.7		
Inventories.................	564.6		
Structures.................	1,042.1		
Equipment	2,202.1		
Land	848.4		
Total domestic			
nonhuman			
real assets......... $4,668.9			
Foreign assets	213.7		
Total			
nonhuman			
assets........... $9,908.2			

NOTE: The non-interest-bearing monetary liabilities of the federal government (currency plus member bank reserves) equal $100.4 billion and are not included in U.S. liabilities for reasons described in footnote 10 in the text; hence, they are part of U.S. wealth. Net foreign assets equal $50.2 billion (foreign assets less liabilities to foreigners) and are a part of U.S. (but not world) nonhuman wealth.

*Includes Treasury assets with the International Monetary Fund.

†Includes interbank claims, taxes payable, and miscellaneous.

‡The breakdown of this aggregate is the same as the one shown for domestic financial assets, except for corporate equity shares, which are shown separately, and currency plus member bank reserves, which are not included for reasons described in footnote 10 in the text.

§Although not treated as such in corporate balance sheets, corporate equities are a charge against net worth from the perspective of the nation.

SOURCES: John W. Kendrick, "Measuring America's Wealth," *Morgan Guaranty Survey,* May 1976, and various issues of the *Federal Reserve Bulletin,* and the *Treasury Bulletin.*

United States is accounted for by business spending on real assets such as inventories, plant, equipment, and housing.[12] Second, as we shall see in Part 4, such spending plays a key role in the determination of real income and employment in the economy. Therefore, when economists use the term investment, especially in connection with such concerns as the level of real income, it is usually spending on real assets by business which is being identified.

Financial investment

In business parlance and from an individual's perspective, on the other hand, investment often refers to acquisitions of certain financial as well as real assets, the purchase of a government security, for example. Where it is not clear by context, we refer to acquisitions of financial assets as *financial investment,* and if the term investment is used without this modifier and not in an obvious financial context, it means business spending on real assets.

Saving

Saving is another term which has a particular definition in economics. In general, *saving is available income which is not spent.* It is comprised of three parts. The first is *personal saving:* personal income less taxes, transfers, interest expense, and consumption spending. In the NIA this corresponds to the net increase in financial assets for households. The second part is *business saving:* depreciation, wage accruals less dispursements, the corporate inventory valuation adjustment, and retained profits (gross profits less taxes and dividends).[13] Here saving may take the form of acquisitions of financial or real assets. Finally, there is the *government surplus or deficit (−).*

Despite the different definitions of economic investment and saving, at the aggregate level they are virtually equivalent conceptually and almost equivalent as measured in the NIA. This can be seen if we refer back to the notes at the bottom of the balance sheets of Figure 4–5A where economic investment and saving are identified for each entity. Note that the saving for each entity is equivalent to changes in net worth. Compare this to economic investment by each entity, and it is apparent that investment exceeds saving for Campus Slop, but saving exceeds investment for Bedside Manner and the depositors of the Leaky Till National Bank. In the consolidated statement for these four entities, however, saving less the increase in reserves at Leaky Till National equals investment.

The equality of aggregate saving and investment

The close equivalence between investment and saving in our consolidated account is suggestive of the equality between saving and investment that tends to emerge in the accounts for the national economy *despite imbalances in individual accounts.* This equality

---

[12]Increases in real assets held by governments should be but are not included in national investment as recorded in the NIA. The only spending on real assets by households which is recorded as investment is household spending on housing; however, in the organization of the NIA, when making such expenditures, households are considered businesses, not households.

[13]This is gross business saving. Net business saving excludes depreciation.

would be exact if there were no government or foreign sectors to complicate the accounts. It is an important relationship to remember. It applies to actual values of saving and investment and holds regardless of the state of the economy. (In Part 4 we will show, however, that, since in an economy with financial markets, individual savers and investors are to a great extent separate decision-making entities, there can be a difference between *desired* levels of aggregate saving and investment—with disturbing effects on equilibrium real income and employment.)

The credit market: An aggregate analysis

The last chapter set the stage for a supply and demand analysis of the credit market by explaining credit and the great variety of uses of external finance by specific entities in the economy. This chapter provides, first, an analysis of the total supply and demand for credit in relation to major economic variables. (The equity or stock market will not be discussed, except as it affects our analysis of credit, because it is not central to the topics of this text.) Our supply and demand model is then applied to an examination of the major factors determining the general level of interest rates.

THE SUPPLY AND DEMAND FOR CREDIT

You should be able to recall from Chapter 3 the bare essentials required for a market model: a demand function, a supply function, and a state of rest, or equilibrium, condition. Our market analysis in this case will focus on the total flow of new credit, or loanable funds.

First, a warning: the economy's total demand for new credit is affected, in part, by the same economic variables that affect the demand for the money stock (checkable deposits, travelers checks, and currency), but for quite different reasons; hence it is easy but

5

important not to confuse the demand for new credit (the demand for a *flow* of funds, usually *spent quickly* and representing new *liabilities* for demanders) with the demand for money (the demand for a *stock* of *spendable assets* held to facilitate transactions and for indefinite periods) and vice versa. Confusion also arises because these terms—money and credit—are used interchangeably in business parlance. The same warning applies to the supply of new credit and the supply of money.

The demand for new credit

The total demand for new credit reflects the current external financing requirements of deficit entities—households, firms, and governments. What major economic variables affect these requirements—or better, these demands—and in what way? The variables analyzed here are: the price level, real income, the interest rate, the cost of equity finance, expected inflation, and fiscal policy.

Prices exert a positive effect on the demand for credit. This is because the higher prices are, the greater the external financing needed to fund the same real expenditures for inventories, housing, automobiles, etc. *So the demand for credit is positively related to the price level; and, if other variables we are going to specify are constant, this relationship should be roughly proportional*—a 10 percent increase in prices causing a 10 percent increase in the demand for new credit.[1]

The price level

The second important variable affecting the demand for new credit is real income. *The aggregate relationship between real income and credit demand is also a positive one.* It might surprise you, but the higher household real income is, the more households tend to incur debt. This occurs because, as long as there are no recession clouds on the horizon, households recognize that, with higher income, they are better situated to pay off debt in the future. Likewise, firms experiencing high demand for their products tend to add to plant and equipment, and at higher production and sales

Real income

[1]This discussion ignores some complications. The relationship, in fact, may be less than strictly proportional for two reasons. The first is that an unexpected increase in the price level may cause an increase in the wealth and the propensity to borrow of deficit entities if these entities already, on balance, owe debt. This occurs because an unexpected increase in the price level reduces the real amount (the real burden) of debt they already owe. (This wealth gain by borrowers is about equal to a corresponding wealth loss by lenders.) Such an increase in wealth may induce deficit units temporarily to increase their demand for credit less than proportionately to the change in the price level.

The other reason is that a rise in prices increases government tax receipts more than proportionately because of progressive income-tax rates. Recall that nominal income equals the price level times real income, so a rise in the price level means that nominal incomes rise with the price level, pushing individuals into higher tax brackets. This means that the government's deficit will tend to fall in real terms, thereby making the increase in the government's demand for nominal credit less than proportional to prices.

levels more production and inventory financing will be demanded. State and local governments may also increase borrowing in prosperous times. The federal government, in contrast, tends to borrow less as real income rises because, with the rise in real income, there is a rise in tax receipts, and there are reduced expenditures for unemployment compensation. Despite this automatic decline in government borrowing, the total demand for credit usually rises significantly as real income increases in a period of prosperity.

The rate of interest

The rate of interest, of course, represents the cost of credit to the borrower and undoubtedly affects the quantity of credit demanded. *The higher the interest cost of credit, the lower will be the quantity demanded.*[2]

The cost of equity finance

A less important variable is the cost of equity financing. When a firm issues stock, it is issuing claims against future profits of the firm. (Of course, these profits should go up as the funds obtained by the stock issue are invested by the firm.) The expected future earnings per share of stock divided by the current price per share of stock (the expected-earnings/current-price ratio) represents the cost of equity finance to the firm and is the equity counterpart to the interest-rate cost of credit finance.[3] *The higher the firm's cost of equity financing, the greater will be its demand for credit, ceteris paribus.* This occurs because credit finance is a substitute for equity finance.

Expected inflation

Another factor affecting the demand for credit is expected inflation. As mentioned in Chapter 3 in connection with the effect of expected inflation on interest rates, when borrowers expect that prices are going to be higher in the future, they will anticipate being able to pay back loans in "cheaper" dollars; hence the real cost represented by the same market, or nominal, interest rate will be lower the higher the expected rate of inflation. This means that *the demand for credit will be higher the higher expected inflation, other relevant things being the same, including, of course, the market interest rate.*

Fiscal policy

A final influence is fiscal policy. We have already accounted for the automatic tendency for the government deficit to decrease as income increases. As described in Chapter 4, fiscal policy involves discretionary changes in tax rates or government spending; these

---

[2]As stated in Chapter 3, although there are many different market interest rates—and we will investigate in some detail the factors that account for differences among interest rates later, in Chapter 7—most interest rates tend to move up or down together over time. When we refer to *the* interest rate in relation to the aggregate demand or supply of credit or other variables, it is the general level of interest rates over time to which we are referring.

[3]In comparing equity and credit costs to the firm, an adjustment has to be made for taxes. Under current federal tax law, interest costs are tax deductible, but dividends are not and must be paid from after-tax earnings of the firm. Hence after-tax comparisons usually make credit financing less costly to the firm. The advantage of equity financing, of course, is that the firm does not have to pay earnings if it does not realize any, whereas interest payments are obligatory.

affect the deficit over and above the automatic changes in tax receipts and spending referred to earlier. Because they are not automatic and have identified policy objectives, we account for such changes separately. *Expansionary fiscal policy (a cut in tax rates or an increase in spending) increases the federal deficit and, hence, the demand for credit.*

We can summarize all of these influences now with the following demand-for-credit function and the box below it.

$$L^D = f\left(P, \ y, \ i, \ \frac{e^*}{p}, \ z^*, \ D, \ \ldots\right)$$

Influenced variable	Influencing variables	Direction of influence
L^D: the quantity of new credit demanded	P: the price level	Positive and roughly proportional
	y: real income	Positive
	i: the interest rate	Negative
	$\frac{e^*}{p}$: the expected earnings/price ratio on equities	Positive
	z^*: the expected rate of inflation	Positive
	D: government deficit due to discretionary changes in tax rates and spending	Positive

There are quite a few variables to account for here; but, as we shall see, only four will be emphasized in the market analysis section in this chapter (the price level and the expected earnings/price ratio on equities will not be of central concern to us there).

The supply of new credit

We turn now to the supply of new credit. Most of the variables to be considered here are the same as those just described for demand; but one is different, and the repeated variables affect the supply of credit in a different direction or in different degrees.

First, *the price level affects the supply of credit positively and roughly proportionately,* as it did demand. This occurs for the household's supply because, with a rise in the price level, wages and other earnings will tend to rise; hence household nominal income will be higher, and this will induce the household to add to its financial assets for all of the reasons suggested by the functions of finance for households. Firms will also experience higher nominal earnings and tend to add to financial-asset holdings.[4]

The price level

---

[4]Again, we have ignored a complication in the text. If the price-level increase was unexpected, and suppliers of new credit were already net holders of debt, suppliers suffer a wealth loss because they will be receiving in the future dollars of lower value than those they loaned in the past. Such a wealth loss may cause the supply of new credit to increase *more* than in proportion to the increase in the price level as surplus entities strive to rebuild their real wealth to its previous, desired level.

Real income repeats as our second influencing variable. *As real income rises, the supply of credit increases* because households and firms will save more and add to their stock of financial assets at a higher rate. This positive effect on the supply of new credit is not as strong as it is on demand, however, and, as a result, changes in real income have a net effect on interest rates, as we will bring out later in this chapter.

The rate of interest is still another variable shared by supply and demand. However, the direction of influence in the case of supply should be exactly the opposite of that for demand. *The quantity of credit supplied should increase as the market rate of interest increases,* of course, because this means, ceteris paribus, that the rewards are higher to household and business savings.

It is possible for households to react differently to an interest rate rise and save less. This can occur because higher interest rates mean that households can save less and still achieve the same stock level of savings in the future. One hundred dollars at 6 percent interest will yield virtually the same stock of savings one year from now as $101 at 5 percent; so if the interest rate increases from 5 to 6 percent, households can "afford" to save 1 percent less per year. Although such an inverse relationship between the interest rate and personal saving can happen, it is not likely to be strong, and the total supply of credit should still respond positively to the market interest rate because a higher interest rate will induce an increase in business saving. Consequently, the supply of credit can be characterized generally as positively related to the market rate of interest.

To continue our discussion of supply variables, *the expected earnings/price ratio on equities should affect the supply of credit inversely,* that is, in a direction opposite to the influence on demand, because financial investors will be inclined to invest more in stocks and less in credit-market assets the higher the expected yield on stocks, ceteris paribus.

Expected inflation will affect the supply of new credit inversely, another influence opposite to that on demand. This occurs because, at the same market rate of interest, higher expected inflation reduces the expected real earnings on financial investments.

Our final variable affecting supply represents the effect on the supply of credit of monetary policy, or Federal Reserve monetary actions. As indicated briefly in Chapter 2, by expanding bank reserves or reducing reserve requirements, *the Federal Reserve can cause the total supply of money and credit to increase.* The effect of these actions on the supply of new credit, a flow, is temporary unless expansionary actions are repeated.

Note that Federal Reserve monetary policy is not a variable which was present in our demand-for-credit function. (And note that fiscal policy does not appear in our analysis of the supply of credit.)

Our supply-of-credit or loanable-funds function is summarized as follows:

$$L^S = f\left(P, \; y, \; i, \; \frac{e^*}{p}, \; z^*, \; A, \; . \; . \; .\right)$$

Influenced variable	Influencing variables	Direction of influence
L^S: the quantity of new credit supplied	P: the price level	Positive and roughly proportional
	y: real income	Positive
	i: the interest rate	Positive
	$\frac{e^*}{p}$: the expected earnings/ price ratio on equities	Negative
	z^*: the expected rate of inflation	Negative
	A: Federal Reserve expansionary actions	Positive

The equilibrium condition

Our remaining step now is to specify the equilibrium condition for the credit market. Interest rates in the United States are relatively unconstrained except for (1) federal controls on deposit interest rates at banks and savings and loans, and (2) state usury ceilings on certain lending rates. Even these restrictions have been muted by recent legislation, described in later chapters. For now we will assume that "the" interest rate (i.e., all market rates) is free to change. "The" interest rate represents the variable most directly affected by and affecting the demand and supply of credit. (Note that it is directness and not strength of influence stressed here.) Although other variables also affect and may be affected by an imbalance between the quantity of credit supplied and the quantity demanded, if the interest rate is free to adjust, it is reasonable to assume that this variable will move so as to ensure that the quantity of credit demanded equals the quantity supplied. If this is the case, we have as our equilibrium condition which completes the market model:

$$L^D = L^S$$

Of course, at the same time that the interest rate adjusts to determine the quantity of credit demanded and the quantity supplied in accordance with the equilibrium condition, this variable is itself being determined. This is shown in Figure 5–1 which depicts the supply and demand for credit in relation to the level of market interest rates, the equilibrium quantity, and the equilibrium interest rate.

If the interest rate is the price of credit and is determined by supply and demand conditions in the credit market, how does our

FIGURE 5–1
Credit-market equilibrium

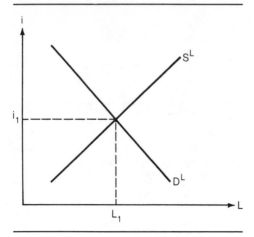

analysis of the interest rate in Chapter 3 square with the analysis in this chapter? More specifically, what are the major factors affecting the level of interest rates through interactions of the supply and demand for credit, and have we seen them before? These questions are addressed in the section which follows.

MAJOR FACTORS AFFECTING THE LEVEL OF INTEREST RATES

Recall from our review of supply and demand in Chapter 3 that the supply and demand curves in Figure 5–1 assume all variables except the interest rate are constant. These curves, therefore, will shift in response to changes in the other variables in our supply and demand functions. By examining shifts in the independent variables which appear to exert the most influence on the supply and demand for credit over time, economists can explain a great deal of the past movement in the level of interest rates. Forecasting interest rates, which is a primary occupation of many business economists, requires anticipation of the future paths of these determinants.

The liquidity effect

Our market analysis of credit identified Federal Reserve monetary actions, A, as a determinant of the supply of credit. In actual experience, these actions are one of the most important determinants of the supply of credit and can exert a considerable influence on interest rates. Federal Reserve actions to increase the quantity of reserves held by depository institutions permit these institutions to increase their deposits and loans and hence the supply of credit in the economy. This is shown by the shift in the supply curve in Figure 5–2 to the right. Given no change in any of the other determinants of the demand for loanable funds, the interest rate must fall to attract an increase in borrowing which depository institutions seek when new reserves become available. (You may recall mention

FIGURE 5–2
The liquidity effect

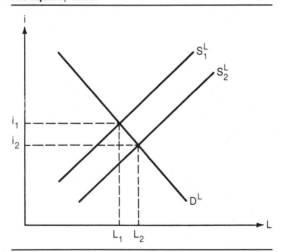

of the federal funds rate in Chapter 2. It will be the first to fall.) In the process of expanding reserves, loans, and the supply of deposits, liquidity is increased. Hence, *this effect of Federal Reserve actions on interest rates has become known as the liquidity effect.*

You should be able to recall the section of Chapter 3 which described an initial tendency for interest rates to fall following an increase in the supply of money. In that chapter, interest rates fell to equate the demand for money with the new higher supply. Here, we are analyzing the same relationship—only from a different perspective, i.e., the supply and demand for credit. The liquidity effect, not explicitly labeled as such in Chapter 3, can be analyzed in either context.

A tendency of the liquidity effect to be later offset was explained in Chapter 3 by subsequent movements of other variables in the demand for money function. These same variables will affect the demand for credit, increasing it, to offset the liquidity effect at later dates. So, viewed either way, the liquidity effect is principally, but perhaps not completely, a short-term effect.

Real income was identified in the previous section as a variable affecting both the supply and demand for credit positively. It was also pointed out, however, that an increase in real income tends to increase the demand for credit more than it does the supply. This causes interest rates to rise with a rise in real income. Figure 5–3 shows the supply and demand shifts and the effect on the interest rate. Note that the quantity of credit also rises.

The *income effect* on the level of interest rates can be very important and accounts in part for the fact that interest rates tend to rise and fall over the business cycle in phase with real income.[5] In fact, interest rates are considered roughly coincident indicators of

The income effect

FIGURE 5–3
The income effect

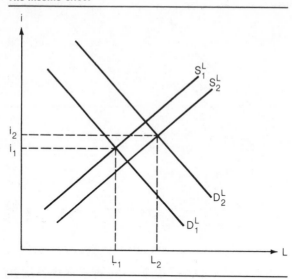

The Fisher effect

the business cycle. (See Figure 5–4. The dates of business-cycle peaks and troughs are indicated at the top of the figure by Ps and Ts. The shaded periods are recessions.)

Expected inflation, which appears in both the supply and demand functions for loanable funds, can have a very strong impact on interest rates, known as the *Fisher effect*. Investors and borrowers appear to respond to current and past inflation in forming expectations about future inflation, though other developments in the economy, such as economic policy, also are important.[6] Whatever the determinants of expected inflation, however, its effect on interest rates is clear and can be shown in terms of shifts in the supply and demand curves for credit, as in Figure 5–5.

Irving Fisher, who developed a careful analysis of the effect of expected inflation on interest rates around the turn of the century (before the advent of income taxes) and for whom the Fisher effect is named, expressed the market interest rate in terms of two principal

---

[5]The income effect can explain why the negative effect on interest rates of an increase in the supply of money tends to be reversed shortly after the increase in money, as described in Chapter 3. Recall that, after a short lag, an increase in the money supply tends to raise real income. It should be stressed here, however, that the income effect on interest rates holds for a change in real income from a variety of causes—not just from an increase in the money supply.

[6]If market participants are rational and wise, they will key their expectations of inflation to the fundamental determinants of inflation, including growth of the money supply. As a result, a higher growth rate for the money supply might cause the Fisher effect, which we are about to discuss, to operate and market interest rates to rise more quickly than suggested in Chapter 3. Such behavior is termed *rational expectations*. Rational expectations are discussed in Chapter 16.

FIGURE 5–4
Cyclical indicators: Economic process and cyclical timing

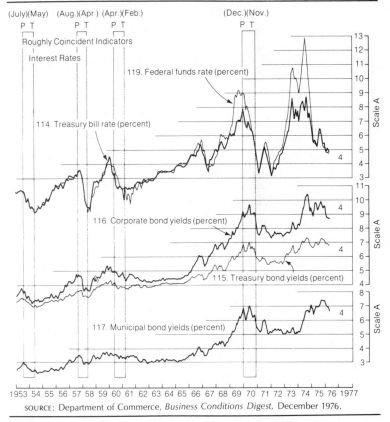

SOURCE: Department of Commerce, *Business Conditions Digest*, December 1976.

parts: the expected rate of inflation and the expected real rate of interest

$$i = z^* + r^*$$

where z^* is the expected rate of inflation and r^* is the expected real rate of interest.[7]

What happens to market interest rates and the expected real rate of interest if expected inflation rises? In line with Fisher and our market analysis, we can reason that if no other influencing variables have changed, if borrowers and financial investors have the same expectations about higher inflation, and if income taxes are ignored, the market rate of interest should rise by the same amount as an increase in expected inflation, Δz^*, and the expected real rate of interest should remain constant. This is because the real rate of

---

[7]Actually, this equation is an approximation of the relationship Fisher derived, which was $i = z^* + r^* + r^*z^*$ with each variable expressed as a decimal; the last term in this expression is small enough to ignore in most cases. See Irving Fisher, *Appreciation and Interest* (Cambridge, Mass.: American Economic Association, 1896).

return on financial investments is what should count to investors in their decisions about investing. Likewise, the real rate of interest cost is what really counts to rational borrowers. Therefore, if the expected rate of inflation rises and nothing else changes, the supply and demand curves each should shift up by the increase in expected inflation, keeping the quantities of loanable funds supplied and demanded the same at each level of the expected real rate of interest, as shown in Figure 5–5.

FIGURE 5–5
The Fisher effect

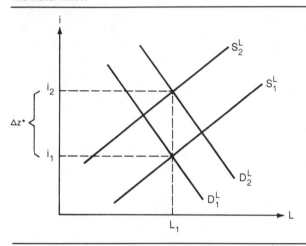

Fisher found that the market rate of interest does adjust, but only after a long lag and not completely. Studies of the Fisher effect during more recent periods suggest that today interest rates adjust more rapidly to higher expected inflation than in Fisher's time, but still not completely. And some of these studies have stressed that this is particularly evident when taxes are taken into account, as they should be.[8]

Figures 5–6 and 5–7 show recent history for actual inflation, the market rate of interest on three-month Treasury bills, the actual real rate of return on three-month Treasury bills (that is, after adjusting for actual inflation), and the actual after-tax, real rate of interest on

---

[8]If there is a simple percentage tax rate of t on interest income, the after-tax return version of Fisher's equation becomes

$$i(1 - t) = z^* + r^*$$

or

$$i = \frac{z^*}{1 - t} + \frac{r^*}{1 - t}$$

where r^* is now the expected after-tax real rate of return.

It can be seen from this formula that market interest rates have to rise by $\dfrac{\Delta z^*}{1 - t}$, which is more than the rise in the expected rate of inflation, to keep the expected after-tax real rate of interest rate constant.

FIGURE 5–6
Three-month Treasury bill rate and inflation, 1960–1981

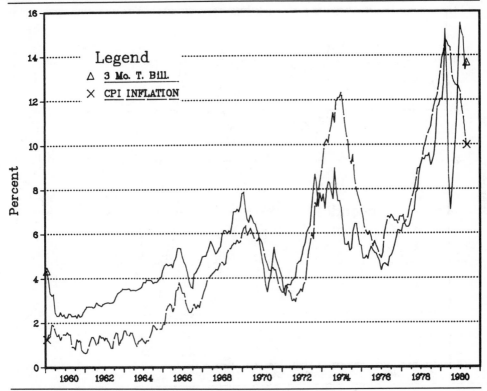

three-month Treasury bills.[9] (Technical characteristics of the yield on Treasury bills and similar instruments are described in the next chapter.)

It is not surprising that a rise in actual inflation in the late 1960s reduced the real rate of return for a while, but the persistence of negative after-tax real rates of return on Treasury bills and other securities in the late 1960s and for most of the 1970s is surprising and may be evidence of under adjustment to expected inflation in market interest rates. In any case, the reasons for such a decline in real interest rates remain a matter of some debate among economists.[10]

---

[9]We assumed a tax rate on interest income of 0.5 (50 percent). The corporate tax rate has been just under 50 percent since 1964.

[10]The after-tax, real rate of return on savings deposits has been even more negative, of course, because interest-rate ceilings have kept the nominal interest rate on these deposits artificially low.

For one explanation of the tendency for real rates of return to fall on financial investments not constrained by ceilings, see Robert Mundell, "Inflation and Real Interest," *Journal of Political Economy,* June, 1963, pp. 280–83. See also Charles D. Cathcart, "Why Inflation Reduces the Real Rate of Interest," *The Money Manager,* October 13, 1980.

FIGURE 5–7
Real rates of interest on three-month Treasury bills, 1960–1981

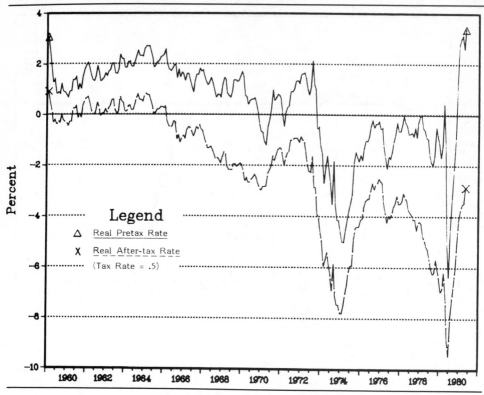

FIGURE 5–8
The crowding-out effect

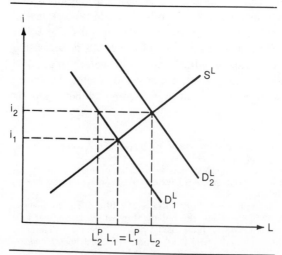

The last effect we will discuss involves the influence of fiscal policy on market interest rates. Expansionary fiscal policy increases the total amount of borrowing in the credit market, as shown by the shift in demand in Figure 5–8. If monetary policy is not also expansionary so that Federal Reserve actions shift the supply curve to the right, interest rates will rise, a result called the *crowding-out effect*.

The crowding-out effect

Although our primary concern in this chapter is not the objectives of fiscal or monetary policy, the crowding-out effect on market interest rates has been of considerable concern to policymakers because it implies that expansionary fiscal policy may tend to crowd out private borrowing, particularly borrowing to finance spending on housing and on plant and equipment. This can be seen in Figure 5–8 if we assume that all borrowing before the expansionary fiscal policy was private borrowing, L_1^P, and is associated with points on the original demand curve, D_1^L. Now, at the higher interest rate, after government borrowing, i_2, we can find that private borrowing has declined from L_1^P $(=L_1)$ to L_2^P. When this happens, it implies that private borrowers are cutting back on their spending, and that the expansionary effects of fiscal policy on income and employment will be offset somewhat. This and other forms of possible crowding out are a matter of active debate between Keynesians and monetarists and will be more fully discussed in Parts 4 and 5.

INTRODUCTION TO ARTICLE

Expected inflation has been the principal cause of a rising trend in interest rates since the early 1960s. *The Wall Street Journal* article below focuses on this factor. It was written in March 1974, a time when there was considerable concern among policymakers that expected inflation might escalate credit demands and push up interest rates. As it turned out, these concerns were well founded; interest rates jumped sharply over several subsequent months in response both to expected inflation and to Federal Reserve actions to curb growth in the money supply. The same experience was repeated numerous times in 1978–80.

Speaking of business

Interest and inflation

In past years Federal Reserve Chairman William McChesney Martin used to shake everyone up by warning, now and then, that all was not right with our economic world. On one occasion he pointed to some similarities between the present and 1929; stock prices plummeted and the headlines proclaimed the "Martin market."

Last week Mr. Martin's successor, Arthur Burns, shook up a market, too, but this was the market for short-term money. Short-term interest rates had been declining this year, and most people figured they still had a distance to go. But Mr. Burns told the Joint Congressional Economic Committee that rates just might head upward.

If inflation continues surging, the chairman said, the country is in for record interest rates. "If we go the Latin American way—and that is the way we seem to be going—we will have interest rates on Latin American standards" or "a good deal higher than at present" and higher than ever experienced in the U.S.

Rep. Wright Patman, chairman of the committee and a man who favors low interest rates all the time, apparently didn't think he had heard right and asked Mr. Burns to repeat his statement. Mr. Burns did.

The Fed chairman in his testimony emphasized that he thought government could prevent any such development by gradually bringing inflation under control. But both short and long-term markets acted as though they expected the worst—rates moved higher.

If we head off into accelerating inflation, there is no doubt that interest rates will go right along upward with prices. But as A. A. Groppelli, economist for Cowen & Co., says, interest rates and inflation do not move in lockstep from week to week.

If they did, there obviously would have been no decline in short-term rates this year at all. Consumer prices in January were climbing at a seasonally adjusted annual rate of 12 percent, well above current levels of most key short-term (or long-term) interest rates.

When anyone makes a loan, he would of course like to be sure that the dollars he gets back will buy as much as the dollars he lends. Why, then, have a lot of people been lending money for less than the going inflation rate?

Part of the answer is that the inflation factor in interest rates is based not on the current inflation rate but on the inflation rate the lender expects to prevail in the period until the loan is repaid. What counts, in other words, is inflation expectations.

And the fact is that few people right now expect that 12 percent January inflation rate to prevail indefinitely. The oil increases were bad but now—the reasoning goes—they are largely behind us. With good crops this year, the future food price increases are not likely to be as sharp as those in the recent past. Such assumptions may be wrong, but the prevailing forecast is that the inflation rate will slowly

decline over the next year or two.

As the foregoing suggests, accuracy of information is uneven. Some lenders may think they are offsetting inflation when they actually aren't even coming close.

Even if a lender knows exactly what is going to happen to inflation, he may not be able to get the inflation premium he wants. Financial institutions, for instance, have a large and steady cash inflow that must be invested somewhere at once, whatever the market. And the market is under the influence of the demand for and the supply of credit.

In an economic slowdown such as the present one, the demand for credit softens. If the Federal Reserve System continues to keep the banks well supplied with funds, there will be some downward pressure on rates.

You can get into lots of argument on whether the Fed is keeping the banks well supplied with funds, but it seems hard to argue that the Federal Reserve is drying up credit. The narrowly defined money supply, consisting of currency and bank checking accounts, did decline in January, but it has been moving up smartly since then.

There seems little question that Mr. Burns and his colleagues at the Federal Reserve will try hard to chart a course that will neither stop the economy nor permit a new acceleration of inflation. The chairman has at least made it clear that such is his intent.

In his testimony before the Economic Committee he said that the Fed "could stop this inflation in a few months dead in its tracks" by severely tightening its grip on money and credit. But "we have no intention of doing it" because of the economic hardship that such a policy would cause.

One of the unhappy facts about inflation is that the longer it persists the harder it is to curb. Once again the problem is those expectations. Mr. Burns thinks that expectations and the inflation itself can be ended "over the next two or three years without going through a protracted period of heavy unemployment," but even a gradual cure will not be painless.

Will the Fed press ahead with even a gradual cure? While the System makes quite a point of its semi-independence, it is after all a creature of Congress and tries to avoid making too many political enemies. And Wright Patman is not the only Congressman who, in election campaigns this fall, would not enjoy hearing constituents complain of tight money and high interest rates.

One thing that is certain is that the money market in coming weeks will be highly sensitive to what the Federal Reserve says and even more so to what it does. As Chicago's Continental Illinois Bank & Trust Co. said recently:

"In the current economic context it seems likely that market reactions to even minor Federal Reserve shifts to ease credit conditions will be large, and probably even greater than the Fed would like to see. The broad consensus of private forecasts suggests that with the economy slowing interest rates—particularly in the

short-term markets—will drop much further. The only problem for market participants is that the Fed will try to control the degree of ease because of their justifiable concern over inflation."

So if anyone wants to know what is going to happen to interest rates, the answer is that it all depends. It depends on the future level of economic activity and the resulting loan demand. It depends on the way the Federal Reserve handles perhaps its most difficult monetary management job. And it also depends on what the public thinks all of this will do to prices at the supermarket.

SOURCE: Lindley H. Clark, Jr., "Speaking of Business," *The Wall Street Journal,* March 4, 1974.

CONCLUSION

This chapter has outlined the supply and demand for new credit in the economy and analyzed the major factors affecting the general level of interest rates. In Chapter 6, we will turn to some details of the key markets for large borrowings, including the calculation of interest rates (or yields) on two common forms of credit arrangements and debt instruments.

PROBLEM

1. Explain the current general level of market interest rates in terms of the major factors outlined in this chapter. Information on current interest rates, Federal Reserve actions, the state of real economic activity, recent inflation trends, and the level of government borrowing can be gleaned from current publications such as *The Wall Street Journal,* the *New York Times,* or *Business Week.* (See the appendix at the end of the book for a student's guide to *The Wall Street Journal.*)

ADVANCED READINGS

Gibson, W. E. "Interest Rates and Monetary Policy." *Journal of Political Economy* 78 (May/June 1970). 431–55.

Carlson, Keith M., and Spencer, Roger W. "Crowding Out and Its Critics." Federal Reserve Bank of St. Louis *Monthly Review* 57 (December 1975). 2–17.

Conceptual and institutional features of the markets for large borrowings

6

Before proceeding with further analysis of the credit market, and particularly the relationships among individual market interest rates, it is necessary to cover certain features of standard arrangements for large borrowings. The markets for large borrowings are important because they are the key area of the credit market in which we can readily observe certain effects of monetary policy, and because these markets are highly sensitive to the state of the economy.

The first section of this chapter explains *two major types of credit arrangements and yield calculations.* In each we will demonstrate *an important inverse relationship between the price and yield to maturity for conventional debt instruments,* and we will identify the difference between *yield to maturity* and *realized yield* for these instruments. The second section shows how *the strength of the price/ yield-to-maturity relationship is greater, the longer the maturity of the debt instrument.* In the last section, descriptions are provided of *specific debt instruments and markets for large borrowings.*

This material largely concerns institutional information and is fundamental to an understanding of actual developments in the credit markets. It is key material particularly for our analysis of liquidity and interest-rate spreads in Chapter 7.

120

TWO CONVENTIONAL TYPES OF CREDIT ARRANGEMENTS AND THEIR RETURN CALCULATIONS

We have already pointed out that credit contracts can be arranged in different ways. Two particular ways are used widely for large borrowings: the discount-rate arrangement and the interest-to-follow arrangement.

The discount-rate arrangement

When funds are advanced under the discount-rate arrangement, interest is calculated on the face value of the obligation and deducted (discounted) from that value to arrive at the amount of funds initially extended. The standard interpretation of this arrangement is that interest is prepaid by the debtor. *The discount rate, or yield, is the rate of discount applied to the face value of a discount credit.* (We will explain later that the discount yield is less than the equivalent yield on an interest-to-follow basis because it ignores the time value of the payment of interest at the beginning of the borrowing period.)

The discount yield

In the case of a marketable debt instrument conforming to a discount arrangement, the debt instrument conveys no explicit interest but is sold at a discount from its par or face value. In calculating the yield on the instrument, the difference between the market price and the par value of the instrument is treated as interest on the par value. Discounted instruments generally mature in one year or less.

The formula for the annualized discount yield, d, is:

$$ d = \frac{1}{v} \left(\frac{\$100 - P_D}{\$100} \right) $$

where v is the maturity of the instrument as a fraction of a year, $100 represents the par value, and P_D is the market price of the instrument. Multiplying by $\frac{1}{v}$ is necessary for annualization.[1]

A U.S. Treasury bill will serve as an example. A Treasury bill is a government obligation, payable at dates ranging from 90 days to one year from the date of issue. It has a minimum denomination, or par value, of $10,000 and is sold at a discount from $10,000.[2] There is no return to an investor other than the return implicit in the discount—

---

[1]For the purpose of calculating v for most discount instruments, and for some other instruments maturing in less than a year, the common practice is to assume a year has 360 days. "Months," similarly, have 30 days each. This makes for easier computations. It means, however, that annualization is not quite complete. For example, for an instrument which matures in 90 days (three "months") v = .25; yet 90 days, of course, actually represents .2466 of a year.

[2]The minimum denomination of $10,000 was adopted by the Treasury in 1970 to discourage small savers from shifting funds out of deposits at banks and savings and loans into Treasury bills which carried a higher yield at that time.

the excess of the face value over the purchase price.

Suppose you are an investor/student with roughly $10,000 and you are considering the purchase of a Treasury bill in mid-January. Your broker tells you that you can buy a six-month bill (one which matures in mid-July) at a price of $96.25 per $100 of face value ($9,625 for a $10,000 Treasury bill).[3] Armed with a pocket calculator you quickly solve the formula for d:

$$d = \frac{1}{.5} \left(\frac{\$100 - \$96.25}{\$100} \right) = 7.5\%$$

It is clear from the formula and this example that the yield on a discount instrument of a given maturity is determined entirely by its market price. If the price of the six-month Treasury bill in our example were $95.50 instead of $96.21, the yield would be 9 percent, 1.5 percentage points or 150 *basis points* higher than in the earlier illustration.[4] As these calculations show, *the relationship between the market price and yield on a discount debt instrument is inverse*, that is, the lower the price, the higher the yield and vice versa.

A second point to be emphasized is that the yield calculated from the formula is the discount yield you will earn only if the instrument is held until maturity. Consequently, it is frequently termed the *yield to maturity*. In our discussions, yield will always mean yield to maturity unless identified otherwise. The following example illustrates what can happen if an instrument is sold before maturity.

Suppose at the same time that you learn that a six-month bill is selling for $96.25 (yield = 7.5 percent), your broker tells you that a three-month bill would cost $98.19. Using the formula for d, you find the yield on the three-month bill to be 7.24 percent. Because you do not anticipate needing your $10,000 nest egg before summer school in mid-July and because of the higher yield, you decide to purchase the six-month bill.

Three months later, however, while on a spring vacation trip, you stumble upon a great opportunity to invest in a ski shop in Haiti. You decide to call back to the states to have your broker sell your Treasury bill, which has three months remaining until maturity.

A sale is quite easily completed with Treasury bills since they have an enormous secondary market. Based on the price of a three-month bill quoted to you in January, you anticipate selling your bill for $98.19. Your broker tells you, however, that market conditions have changed; since you bought your bill, interest rates in general

The price/yield relationship

The yield to maturity

---

[3] Actually, for small investors, purchases of new issues of government securities from a Federal Reserve bank are usually more attractive than purchases of "seasoned" issues from brokers because the broker's commission is thereby saved.

[4] Interest-rate changes and spreads are usually quoted in terms of basis points, each of which is 1/100 of a percentage point.

have risen. Consequently, the price for a three-month bill in April is lower than the price for a three-month bill was in January. Your bill is sold for $98.00 (and you get $9,800), more than you paid but less than expected.[5] At $98.00, the yield to maturity is 8 percent for the investor who buys your bill from you. Your *realized yield* on your investment is considerably less than this and less than the yield to maturity on your six-month bill when originally purchased.

The realized yield on a debt instrument is the yield for the actual holding period for the investor. The important distinction is that the realized yield may turn out to be less or more than the yield to maturity at the time the instrument was purchased, depending upon the selling price of the instrument.   The realized yield

The discount yield formula can be used to find the *realized discount yield* by substituting the sale price for the par value and substituting the holding period for the term to maturity in our original formula. In other words the realized discount yield, d', is given by

$$d' = \frac{1}{h} \left(\frac{P_S - P_D}{P_S} \right)$$

where h is the holding period as a fraction of a year and P_S is the sale price of the instrument. For your six-month bill sold after three months

$$d' = \frac{1}{.25} \frac{(\$98.00 - \$96.25)}{\$98.00} = 7.14\%$$

Had you known that you were going to need the cash after three months and that market interest rates were going to rise so much, you would have been better off to buy the three-month bill with a discount yield of 7.24 percent in January.

To repeat the point of this illustration, standard yield formulas for an instrument apply only if that instrument is held to maturity. If a marketable instrument is sold before maturity, the realized yield may be less or more than the yield to maturity at the time the instrument was bought, depending upon the price the instrument fetches in the market. The example also illustrates how market conditions can change over time, affecting the prices of marketable instruments. Of course, there is no way of knowing for sure ahead of time what market conditions will be and, hence, how realized yields will turn out if assets are sold before their maturity date; but market participants usually have expectations about such conditions and make decisions accordingly.

The interest-to-follow arrangement

The second type of credit arrangement is more familiar in form, if

---

[5]Our examples ignore brokerage fees and differences in bid and offer prices.

not in name. It is called an *interest-to-follow (ITF) arrangement* and conveys interest at the end and, in most cases, periodically over the life of the credit. The yields calculated for these arrangements are called *interest-to-follow yields* or, often, *bond yields* because bonds are a common interest-to-follow type of credit.

The interest-to-
follow yield

Unfortunately, the technical definition of the ITF yield is a mouthful. *It is that annual rate of interest which, when applied directly to the original investment and compounded annually, would produce the terminal value of the instrument, assuming all interim income is reinvested at that same rate of interest.*[6] It might help to describe the ITF yield less technically, and only slightly less accurately, as the interest rate you would have to have on an ordinary time deposit—an ITF credit—with annual compounding to be equally as well off as you would be with the investment in question.

An ITF instrument carries periodic explicit interest payments—frequently in the form of detachable coupons which are redeemed for face value as they mature.[7] The explicit payments over a year frequently are expressed as a percent of the par value of the instrument; this refers to the contractual "interest," or coupon rate, stipulated for a bond, for example. On ITF instruments with variable market prices, however, one must allow for more than explicit payments in calculating the effective yield to maturity of the instrument. This is due to the fact that, if the market price of the ITF instrument departs from its par value, there will be a capital gain or loss on the instrument over its life. If the market price of the instrument is below par, there is a capital gain over the life of the instrument. If it is above par, there is a capital loss. This additional element of return is taken into account in the ITF yield formula.

The formula for the yield to maturity on an ITF instrument of n years to maturity is complex. We will present it two ways below to help explain its form. The first version has the terminal value of the instrument on the left-hand side to make its conformity to the ITF yield definition apparent:

$$\$100 + C + C(1 + b) + C(1 + b)^2 + \ldots + C(1 + b)^{n-1}$$
$$= P_M (1 + b)^n$$

where $\$100$ is the assumed par value of the instrument, C is the yearly explicit fixed-dollar interest (coupon) payment, b is the ITF yield, and P_M is the market price for the instrument. The sum of the terms on the first line is the terminal value of the investment n years from now, that is: the par value of the instrument, $\$100$, plus the

---

[6]Students who have encountered the *internal rate of return* in economics and finance literature will recognize the ITF yield, used in the credit markets, as virtually identical to the internal rate of return.

[7]On most bonds, coupons are payable twice a year. Our ITF yield formula given below and some standard bond yield formulas ignore the advantage of having one half the year's coupon payment at midyear.

nth year coupon, C, plus the previous year's coupon including one year of interest, $C(1 + b)$, plus the coupon payment for the year before that including compound interest over two years, $C(1 + b)^2$, and so on, up to and including the first year's coupon and compound interest over n − 1 years.[8] The original investment is P_M. And b is the unknown yield which, with annual compounding, will make this original investment rise in value over n years to equal the terminal value of the investment.

The formula above can be rearranged in a second, more standard, and perhaps familiar, presentation by solving for the original investment, P_M on the left-hand side:[9]

$$P_M = \frac{C}{1 + b} + \frac{C}{(1 + b)^2} + \ldots + \frac{C}{(1 + b)^n} + \frac{100}{(1 + b)^n}$$

"For short-term gains, I recommend Blueboy in the fifth at Hialeah!"

Reprinted by permission *The Wall Street Journal*

---

[8]We assume in the text that the reader is familiar with the usual expressions for values with annual compound interest such as $(1 + b)^2$. Here is a quick explanation in case you are not: One dollar invested at an interest rate b, payable annually, will be worth $1 + b$ dollars one year from now. If those $1 + b$ dollars are reinvested at the same interest rate for a second year, you will have your investment of $1 + b$ plus interest of $b(1 + b)$ at the end of two years. We can rearrange $(1 + b) + b(1 + b)$ to $(1 + b)^2$. If you invest $(1 + b)^2$ dollars for a third year you have $(1 + b)^2 + b(1 + b)^2 = (1 + b)^3$ at the end of that year, and so on.

[9]Students familiar with present-value formulas will recognize this equation. The ITF yield formula differs from the present-value formula, however, in that it is used to solve for b, the unknown interest rate which enters every term on the right-hand side, using a known value on the left-hand side. A present-value formula is used to solve for an unknown value on the left-hand side (the present value of an investment) using a *known*, or assumed, interest rate for b in each term on the right-hand side.

Calculating the
ITF yield

Except for two special cases, the ITF yield formula cannot be rearranged so that the ITF yield, b, appears by itself on the left-hand side of the equation. Consequently, the ITF yield usually cannot be found by direct calculation; instead, it must be found by trial and error. Approximate solutions for a wide range of years, coupon rates, and market prices are available in books of bond tables. Also, many modern business calculators have a present-value calculating capability which helps immensely with the iterative search for an ITF yield, and some have the ability to search for an ITF solution automatically.

To keep the problem of solving for b simple in this text, our examples will be developed using two special cases for which direct calculations can be made. A one-year instrument, one of the two special cases, is discussed below. We will discuss the other, an infinite-maturity instrument, and we will illustrate the use of a bond table for a 20-year instrument in the next section.

To return to the beginning of our earlier example, recall your hypothetical position as a student in mid-January with roughly $10,000 to invest. Suppose your friendly broker gives you, in addition to the bill information described earlier, a quote on a one-year U.S. Treasury note. Treasury notes are ITF-type instruments with coupons. They range between 1 and 10 years in maturity when issued, and they are available in denominations as low as $1,000, which puts them within reach of small savers.

The dealer's quote on the one-year Treasury note is $99 and 2/32 for a 7 percent coupon note.[10] Noting that the formula for b in the case of a one-year instrument reduces to

$$P_M = \frac{C}{1 + b} + \frac{\$100}{1 + b}$$

you dexterously rearrange terms

$$b = \frac{(C + \$100) - P_M}{P_M}$$

and solve with the values in the example for the Treasury note

$$b = \frac{(\$7 + \$100) - (\$99 \ 2/32)}{\$99 \ 2/32} = 8.01\%$$

As this calculation reveals, the yield to maturity on the Treasury

---

[10]Care is needed in interpreting price quotations for ITF instruments of one-year and longer maturities. The conventional dollar fraction for these ITF instruments is 1/32nd; and, making things more confusing, prices are frequently quoted using the point, as in decimal expressions, but indicating instead, with left-justified place, 32nds of a dollar. For example, the price for the Treasury note quoted above would appear in *The Wall Street Journal* as $99.2, and a price of $99 and 30/32 would appear as $99.30. (See the sample provided in Problem 1 at the end of this chapter.) In 1/10th (decimal) notation, $99 and 2/32 would be $99.0625.

note is higher than its coupon rate of 7 percent and, in fact, is roughly equal to the coupon rate plus the rate of capital gain over the year.[11]

What about the inverse relationship between price and yield we observed for discount instruments? The same relationship holds for ITF instruments. Observe that, at a market price equal to par, the ITF yield on the Treasury note would equal the coupon rate of 7 percent. A price above par would be associated with a yield below 7 percent.

The inverse price/yield relationship

It should be noted also that, as in the case of the discount yield, the yield calculated from the ITF yield formula is a yield to maturity. It will not necessarily be the realized yield if the note is sold before maturity. An investor, for example, who purchased the 7 percent coupon Treasury note at $99 2/32 and sold it at par or higher because market interest rates had fallen, would reap a capital gain over the holding period, a period which could be quite short. The formula for the realized yield on an ITF instrument, b', is derived from the formula for the yield to maturity with the holding period, h, substituted for years to maturity, n, and the sale price, P_S, substituted for par value, $100, that is

The realized yield on an ITF instrument

$$P_M = \frac{C}{1 + b'} + \frac{C}{(1 + b')^2} + \ldots + \frac{C}{(1 + b')^h} + \frac{P_S}{(1 + b')^h}$$

Now, before concluding this section, we want to point out the principal difference between the standard discount and ITF yields. For a one-year discount instrument, the formula for d reduces to

$$d = \frac{\$100 - P_D}{\$100}$$

This may be interpreted for the investor as the terminal value of the investment less the original amount invested *divided by the terminal value.*

Compare this to the ITF yield for a one-year ITF instrument

$$b = \frac{(C + \$100) - P_M}{P_M}$$

which may be read as the terminal value of the investment less the original value *divided by the original value.* Hence, from a mechanical point of view, the difference in calculation of discount and ITF yields for assets of the same maturity is due to the fact that different denominators or bases are used. From an economic point of view, the difference is due to the fact that, as mentioned earlier, the discount yield ignores the time value of prepaid interest.

The discount and ITF yields compared

A discount yield can be adjusted almost fully to an ITF, or bond-

---

[11]The rate of capital gain over the year is $\dfrac{\$100 - \$99\ 2/32}{\$99\ 2/32} = 0.95\%.$

yield, equivalent by multiplying by $\dfrac{\$100}{P_D}$, an adjustment which raises the yield more the longer the term to maturity of the instrument. As an example, consider a one-year Treasury bill selling for $92.00. The discount yield on this bill is 8 percent. However, on an approximate ITF basis, the yield becomes 8.7 percent. This adjusted yield tells you within a fairly narrow margin of error what a one-year Treasury-note yield would have to be to compete with a one-year Treasury-bill discount yield of 8 percent.[12]

THE PRICE/YIELD RELATIONSHIP AND THE MATURITY OF THE INSTRUMENT

If we return to our basic yield formulas again, we can show that *the market price of an instrument must change more to effect a given change in yield the longer the maturity of the instrument.* As explained later, this phenomenon is important to participants in the credit markets when there are expectations of interest-rate changes. The topic receives further attention in Chapter 7 which is concerned with liquidity and interest-rate spreads.

The relevance of instrument maturity to price/yield sensitivity can be seen directly from the formula in the case of the discount yield:

$$d = \frac{1}{v} \frac{(\$100 - P_D)}{\$100}$$

Maturity and the discount relationship

Recall that v is the maturity of the instrument as a fraction of a year. Clearly, the larger the value of v, the larger the change required in P_D to effect a given change in d. We found earlier that if v = .25, for example, the price of a Treasury bill must decrease by only $.19, from $98.19 to $98.00, to raise the discount yield from 7.24 percent to 8 percent. If v = 1, on the other hand, the price on a Treasury bill must fall by $.76, from $92.76 to $92.00, to effect the same change in yield. Such a difference may sound slight, but on a $10,000 Treasury bill it amounts to a $76.00 versus a $19.00 change in market values. And the difference is far more dramatic for greater differences in maturity, as we will show for ITF yields.

The reason for the strong impact of an instrument's maturity on its price/yield sensitivity is very simple. For longer-maturity assets, the yield that is changed applies to longer periods of time. This means that price changes are amortized over longer periods and

---

[12]There are two further minor adjustments which we have ignored in the text. One adjusts for the 360-day year assumption in the discount yield. The other adjusts for the time value of the midyear receipt of the half-coupon on a Treasury note. After adjustment for these, the ITF-yield equivalent for our one-year Treasury bill with an 8 percent discount yield is 8.63 percent. See *Handbook of Securities of the United States Government and Federal Agencies,* 28th ed. (New York: First Boston Corporation, 1978), p. 190.

hence must assume larger values in the current period (the period of adjustment) to accomplish a given change in yield.

Now for ITF yields, compare a one-year instrument with one which never matures. Our example of such an investment is the British government consol. The consol provides an explicit payment each year indefinitely with no provision for redemption at a par value. The usual ITF formula applied to consols with annual coupons is an infinite series:

$$P_M = \frac{C}{1 + b} + \frac{C}{(1 + b)^2} + \frac{C}{(1 + b)^3} + \ldots$$

Through a few mathematical manipulations, this series can be replaced by the following simple equation:[13]

Maturity and the ITF relationship

$$P_M = \frac{C}{b}$$

or, solving for the yield,

$$b = \frac{C}{P_M}$$

The extreme maturity of the consol together with its simple yield formula make it particularly convenient for our comparison with a one-year ITF instrument.

Consider the one-year instrument first. Suppose the coupon rate is 8 percent and the one-year instrument is selling at par. The yield then also would be 8 percent. How much of a price increase would be necessary to reduce the yield to 7 percent? We can find from the first formula that a $.93 increase would do it.

How about the consol? Well, imagine for a moment that consols have coupons of a certain amount of *dollars* per year, say $8.00; and the current market price of a consol is $100. (Of course, in fact the coupons and market price of consols are denominated in British pounds.) Then the current yield on a consol would be 8 percent. What price increase would lower the yield to 7 percent? The answer is quickly found from the consol yield formula: $14.29. In other words, the one-percentage-point change in the yield of a consol in this example is associated with a more than 14 percent change in the market price. A similar change in the yield on a one-year note requires less than 1 percent change in its market price. We chose to examine declines in yields and rises in prices in these examples, the

---

[13]If the infinite series equation above is multiplied on both sides by $1 + b$, we have

$$P_M (1 + b) = C + \frac{C}{1 + b} + \frac{C}{(1 + b)^2} + \ldots$$

Then, if the original equation is subtracted from this one, we get

$$P_M(b) = C$$

and solving this for P_M gives the simplified equation which follows above.

same orders of magnitude hold for increases in yields and declines in prices.

There is no counterpart to the British consol in U.S. credit markets, but the change in market price required to effect a given yield change is almost as great for a U.S. government long-term bond of 20 years to maturity as it is for a consol. A 20-year bond with an 8 percent coupon rate and yielding 8 percent would have to rise by $10.68 in current market value to fall to a 7 percent yield, as identified by the arrows in the table in Figure 6–1.

FIGURE 6–1
Bond yields
(Coupon rate 8 percent)

Yield to maturity	Prices by Years and months							
	18–6	*19–0*	*19–6*	*20–0*	*20–6*	*21–0*	*21–6*	*22–0*
7.00	110.29	110.42	110.55	→110.68	110.80	110.92	111.03	111.14
7.10	109.19	109.31	109.42	109.54	109.64	109.75	109.85	109.94
7.20	108.11	108.21	108.31	108.41	108.50	108.60	108.68	108.77
7.30	107.04	107.13	107.22	107.30	107.38	107.46	107.54	107.61
7.40	105.99	106.07	106.14	106.21	106.28	106.35	106.41	106.47
7.50	104.96	105.02	105.08	105.14	105.19	105.25	105.30	105.35
7.60	103.94	103.99	104.03	104.08	104.12	104.16	104.20	104.24
7.70	102.93	102.97	103.00	103.04	103.07	103.10	103.13	103.16
7.80	101.94	101.96	101.99	102.01	102.03	102.05	102.07	102.09
7.90	100.96	100.98	100.99	101.00	101.01	101.02	101.03	101.04
8.00	100.00	100.00	100.00	→100.00	100.00	100.00	100.00	100.00
8.10	99.05	99.04	99.03	99.02	99.01	99.00	98.99	98.98
8.20	98.11	98.09	98.07	98.05	98.03	98.01	97.99	97.98
8.30	97.19	97.16	97.13	97.10	97.07	97.04	97.01	96.99
8.40	96.28	96.24	96.20	96.16	96.12	96.08	96.05	96.02
8.50	95.38	95.33	95.28	95.23	95.19	95.14	95.10	95.06
8.60	94.49	94.43	94.37	94.32	94.26	94.21	94.16	94.12
8.70	93.62	93.55	93.48	93.42	93.36	93.30	93.24	93.19
8.80	92.76	92.68	92.60	92.53	92.46	92.40	92.34	92.28
8.90	91.91	91.82	91.74	91.66	91.58	91.51	91.44	91.38
9.00	91.07	90.98	90.89	90.80	90.72	90.64	90.56	90.49

SOURCE: *Expanded Bond Values Tables* (Boston: Financial Publishing Co., 1970).

Price/yield sensitivity and the realized yield

The reason the price/yield relationship is important, you should recall, is that, should market conditions change and should the instrument be sold before maturity, the realized yield on the instrument can vary from the yield to maturity. Our example earlier in the chapter was for a six-month bill held for three months. The original yield to maturity (discount basis) was 7.5 percent. Market interest rates rose over the three-month holding period such that the three-month bill yield rose from 7.24 to 8 percent, and the realized yield on your original investment turned out to be 7.14 percent. Suppose, instead, that you had invested your funds in a consol paying 8 percent, and the yield on consols declined over the course of a year to 7 percent, at which point you sold yours. The realized yield, b', would be handsome indeed:

$$b' = \frac{\$8.00}{\$100} + \frac{\$14.29}{\$100} = 22.29\%$$

THE INSTRUMENTS AND MARKETS FOR LARGE BORROWINGS

Large borrowings, associated debt instruments, and their markets are usually described by two classes of maturity: *short-term*, i.e., overnight to one year; and *long-term*, i.e., more than one year. Sometimes, however, there are three classes distinguished: *short-term*, overnight to 1 year; *intermediate-term*, from 1 year to 10 years; and *long-term*, more than 10 years. In this section we will refer only to two classes: short- and long-term.

Short-term credit instruments and markets[14]

Federal funds have become a key area of the short-term credit market in the postwar period. As mentioned briefly in Chapter 2, federal funds are short-term unsecured loans of immediately available funds among private financial institutions. At the end of 1979, there was $91 billion in federal-funds and repurchase-agreement borrowings outstanding at large banks.[15] Banks are the major participants in this market, using it as a means to manage short-term borrowings, investments, and reserve positions, but there are other participants including nonbank bond dealers. The term *federal* funds is used because this market originated as a market in reserve deposits at the Fed.

Federal funds

The federal funds market is a market which deserves special attention because the rate of interest on federal funds, the federal funds rate, is monitored closely by the Federal Reserve, and changes in this rate have been used in the past as a policy variable intended to influence the rate of growth of bank credit and the money supply. Changes in the federal funds rate can motivate changes in the growth of bank credit and in other market interest rates because the federal funds rate represents the cost of one important source of funds to banks, and changes in banks' costs affect the interest rates they charge on loans. Changes in bank loan rates spread to other interest rates through cost and substitution effects.

---

[14]The organized short-term credit market, where large quantities of funds are readily loaned or borrowed, is often referred to as the "money market" in business parlance. In general, we will avoid using the term money market in connection with this market because it invites confusion with supply and demand analysis of checkable deposits and currency. We cannot avoid using it altogether since it is incorporated in the very name of a class of intermediaries, money-market mutual funds.

[15]Repurchase agreements are explained later below. Separate data for federal-funds and repurchase-agreement borrowings are not available.

(The mechanism by which federal funds rate changes are thought to influence money-supply growth is explained in Chapter 14.)

Federal funds are loaned mainly on an overnight basis and in volumes of one million dollars or more. Overnight funds are remitted to the lender on the next day with interest, so a federal funds loan is an interest-to-follow arrangement, and the federal funds rate is an ITF yield.

Treasury bills are an exceptionally important instrument in the short-term credit market because of their volume, their liquid secondary (resale) market, and the credit worthiness of their issuer, the U.S. government. At the end of 1979, there was $173 billion in marketable Treasury bills outstanding. The key characteristics of Treasury bills as a credit arrangement have already been described and need no further elaboration.

Treasury bills are auctioned almost every week through the Federal Reserve banks. Principal investors include commercial banks, the Federal Reserve, and foreign central banks.

Repurchase agreements (RPs) are very short-term (often overnight), secured loans effected through simultaneous purchase and later-dated sale arrangements for debt instruments. Funds loaned through a repurchase agreement between two financial institutions can be made immediately available via Federal Reserve wire facilities.

The Federal Reserve frequently engages in repurchase agreements for Treasury bills when it wants to add reserve funds to the banking system, particularly if the additions are intended to be temporary. It buys the Treasury bills at a specified price from a securities dealer (often a bank) with an agreement that the dealer will repurchase the bills at a prespecified higher price a day or so later. Through this transaction, the Fed effectively lends deposit balances at the Fed to the other transacting party for the term of the RP. The interest rate is implicit in the price difference for the Treasury bills.

The advantages to the Fed of using a repurchase agreement for a temporary reserve injection are: (1) it is a transaction which is reversed automatically; and (2) the market is made aware that the Fed's intentions are to augment reserves only temporarily. The Fed also will engage in temporary sales under a repurchase agreement; in this case the Fed arranges simultaneously a later-dated purchase of the securities sold, and reserve funds are decreased temporarily. Effectively, the Fed is borrowing from the banking system. When, in a case such as this, the borrowing party initiates a repurchase arrangement, the transaction is called a *matched sale-purchase* or, in market parlance, a *reverse repurchase agreement*.

Other participants in the short-term credit market have found RP transactions a convenient way to borrow against securities and to lend available funds for short periods. From the point of view of the lender the advantages are: (1) surplus funds can be invested on an

Treasury bills

Repurchase
agreements

immediate, overnight basis with low transactions costs; and (2) the loan is secured by the debt instrument. Two advantages to the borrower are: (1) funds obtained via repurchase agreements are, usually, immediately available funds; and (2) such funds are normally less expensive than alternative sources of funds if the borrower has the necessary collateral on hand.

Large certificates of deposit (CDs) are a major source of funds for commercial banks and a less important source for mutual savings banks and savings and loans. Banks had $218 billion outstanding at the end of 1979. Described briefly earlier, they run in denominations of $100,000 and higher and may be negotiable or non-negotiable. Negotiable CDs are the major type, generally having denominations of $1,000,000 or higher, and are traded in an organized secondary (resale) market. CDs are ITF instruments with maturities from one month (30 days) to more than a year.

Large certificates of deposit

Depository institutions must set aside non-interest-bearing reserves for most CDs, and insured institutions must pay insurance fees on CDs to the FDIC or another agency. Both of these requirements raise the effective cost of CD funds.[16]

CD interest rates are ITF-type yields.[17] Under federal regulations, including Regulation Q at the Federal Reserve, ceilings can be placed on CD interest rates. However, rate ceilings for large CDs have been suspended since mid-1973, and other Regulation Q ceilings are being phased out under the Depository Institutions Deregulation and Monetary Control Act of 1980.

CD costs are a major part of banks' total costs of funds, and CDs are viewed by most banks as their major source of funds over which they have some control, in other words, their marginal source of funds (also termed "purchased funds" or "managed liabilities"). Federal funds and repurchase agreements are other types of managed liabilities. If more funds are needed to satisfy loan demand, banks tend to respond by issuing additional CDs to raise the funds. Consequently, changes in CD interest rates represent changes in the marginal cost of funds to banks. Such changes usually lead, within a matter of a few weeks, to changes in the bank prime lending rate. (The prime rate is described in the paragraph on bank commercial and industrial loans below.)

The *Eurodollar deposit* market is related to the CD market; it will be described briefly here as a source of funds to depository institutions lending in the United States and discussed again in connection with foreign financing in Chapter 8. Eurodollar deposits are dollar-denominated time deposits available at foreign branches and

Eurodollar deposits

---

[16]The effective cost of reservable CD funds to an insured depository institutions is equal to $(i_c + f)/(1 - r_c)$ where i_c is the interest cost of the CD, f is the cost of FDIC insurance, and r_c is the required reserve ratio for large CDs.

[17]CD rates are similar to most discount yields in that they assume a 360 day year, however.

international banking facilities of U.S. banks and at some foreign banks abroad. Domestic banks often tap this market through their foreign offices; at the end of 1979 there were $930 million in net borrowings by domestic banks. From time to time in the past, the Federal Reserve has imposed reserve requirements on such borrowing by member banks, and permanent reserve requirements are now being phased in for all depository institutions.

The interest rate on Eurodollar deposits is an ITF-type rate. London is the major center for Eurodollar deposits, and the three-month rate offered among banks in the London Eurodollar market has become the base rate for a great many international loans. This Eurodollar interest rate is known as the London interbank offered rate, or Libor, and its use as a base rate for bank loans has begun to spread to the United States.

The Caribbean Islands are another center for Eurodollar deposits, one with an important advantage over London for U.S.-based banks and nonfinancial entities—it is in the same time zone as New York. This advantage is considered sufficiently important by the Fed to count overnight Eurodollar deposits held by U.S. residents at branches of U.S. banks in the Caribbean as part of the M-2 money supply measure, whereas similar Eurodollar deposits in London and other centers are included in only the broadest measure, L.[18]

Commercial paper

Commercial paper refers to unsecured promissory notes issued by large nonfinancial firms and financial companies with high credit ratings. It has been the most rapidly growing area of the short-term credit market in recent years, with $111 billion outstanding as of December 1979. Commercial paper is sold at a discount from par, either through dealers or directly to investors. Yields on commercial paper therefore are discount yields. Maturities usually range from three days to nine months. Three important facts about commercial paper issues are that: (1) there is no organized secondary market for them; (2) for prime borrowers they represent an alternative (usually cheaper) to conventional bank loans; and (3) banks which are members of the Federal Reserve can rediscount their holdings of "eligible" commercial paper with the Federal Reserve at the discount window.

Bankers' acceptances

Bankers' acceptances are still another significant type of short-term instrument. In December, 1979 there was $45 billion of these outstanding. The largest proportion arises in connection with international trade, representing credit extended to importers. The importer's bank accepts responsibility for payment of the obligation in the event the importer cannot pay, hence the name banker's acceptance. The obligation is discounted; consequently, the banker's acceptance yield is a discount yield. Although it represents credit extended to importers and other firms, the acceptance has the credit

---

[18]See Figure 7–2.

FIGURE 6–2
Short-term interest rates for business borrowing (prime rate, effective date of change; prime paper, quarterly averages)

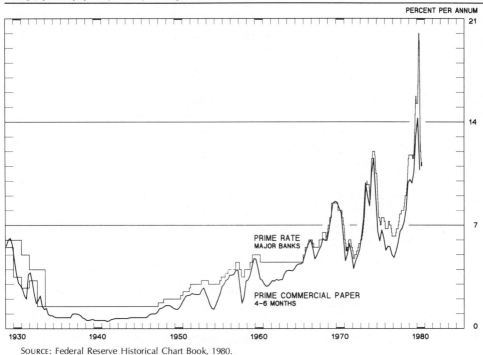

PERCENT PER ANNUM

PRIME RATE
MAJOR BANKS

PRIME COMMERCIAL PAPER
4–6 MONTHS

SOURCE: Federal Reserve Historical Chart Book, 1980.

rating of the bank which has "accepted" it. This feature and the fact that acceptances have an active secondary market make them a low-risk investment. The Federal Reserve occasionally purchases bankers' acceptances when adding reserves to the monetary system. Individual banker's acceptances may be small in value, but sales in the secondary markets usually involve large blocks of acceptances aggregating to substantial sums.

Bank commercial and industrial loans (C&I loans) are not uniformly large in terms of individual transactions, yet C&I loans often involve credits sufficiently large to be syndicated among several banks. With $158 billion at large banks as of December 1979, they represent an important segment of the short-term credit market, and they compete directly with commercial paper and bankers' acceptances as a source of funding for nonfinancial firms.

C&I loans

Bank loans to commercial and industrial firms are used to finance inventories of goods, and they are also used for plant and equipment expenditures, and for the financing of acquisitions and mergers. *The prime bank rate is the "base" rate for most C&I loans.* To be more specific, most loans are made on a floating, multiple-of-prime basis. For example, a six-month loan to Stench Quench Deodorant Company for $1,000,000 might be priced at 1.07 times the lending bank's announced prime rate, at whatever level develops for that rate over the period of the loan. Borrowing firms frequently are required also to leave a portion of the loan as unused non-interest-bearing deposits (called compensating balances) with the bank, effectively reducing the amount of the loan and raising its cost to the borrowing firm.

When not actively changing, the prime bank rate tends to be at the same level throughout the banking industry. Because the prime rate is a publicly announced base rate, not the actual lending rate (not even necessarily to the best corporate customers of a bank), and because banks' profits are protected to a degree from rising interest rates on borrowed funds by compensating balances and normal demand-deposit balances (on which banks pay no interest), banks can leave the prime rate unchanged when small changes in their marginal cost of funds occur. Consequently, the prime rate is changed infrequently (and then usually by steps of one-quarter of a percentage point or more) except in an environment in which other market interest rates are changing persistently and rapidly in one direction.

Prime-rate changes often receive considerable public attention because of the impact of such changes on the cost of funds to a broad segment of the nonbank sector of the economy, and because of the infrequency of such changes. These changes also are often viewed as an indication of the outlook among bankers as to the trend of short-term interest rates in the immediate future.

The long-term market

U.S. government securities comprise a significant portion of the long-term market. U.S. Treasury notes were described earlier in this chapter. U.S. Treasury bonds are usually issued with maturities in excess of 10 years, and denominations run from as low as $1,000 to as high as $1,000,000.[19] Treasury bonds carry coupons just as Treasury notes do. The volume outstanding of marketable bonds at the end of 1979 was $75 billion.

Standard Treasury bonds

Quotations on Treasury bonds should be interpreted carefully because there is a special feature of some of these bonds which can influence their yields significantly. Until fairly recently, the offering rate on new Treasury bonds was restricted by law to a maximum of 4.25 percent. As a result, few of these bonds were issued in the late 1960s and early 1970s when prevailing interest rates were higher, but many were issued in the early 1960s when interest rates were lower. Treasury bonds in those years carry low coupon values and so tend to trade at substantial discounts to make their yields competitive with the high yields available on other investments. However,

Flower bonds

---

[19]Students should not confuse these bonds with U.S. savings bonds which are low-interest, nonmarketable government securities sold to small savers.

these older bonds do not have to be fully competitive in yield to maturity because they have a special advantage in that they may be redeemed at face value in advance of normal maturation when presented in the payment of estate taxes. This means they can bring a substantial death-related capital gain to an estate. As a result, these bonds are associated with death cheerfully like flowers on a grave. More to the point, because of this feature, "flower bonds," as they are known in the market, convey lower yields than other, otherwise comparable Treasury bonds; stay away from them unless you are terminally ill or live dangerously.

Another special factor is "callability." Some Treasury bonds are callable, i.e. subject to early retirement at face value, five years before maturity, and this may influence their market yields, depending upon expectations as to whether they will be called and whether yields are quoted to maturity or to the earliest date of possible call.

Mortgages are a more familiar long-term instrument. They differ from most other securities in that they are secured by specific property, and payment of the principal as well as interest usually is distributed over the life of a mortgage. Mortgages also are more subject to prepayment. The outstanding level at the end of 1979 was $1.3 trillion. Contractual mortgage interest rates are ITF-type yields.

Mortgages

As described in Chapter 4, a number of government and government-sponsored agencies support investment in mortgages to encourage home building. In addition, there are federal regulations and tax breaks for thrift institutions and investment trusts which cause them to channel a high proportion of their funds into real estate-related loans or instruments. In recent years there has been phenomenal growth in one particular federal program, resulting in the emergence of a truly national market in home mortgages. (In the past, because of the heterogeneity of local real estate markets and laws, private investors in home mortgages have been mainly thrift institutions and commercial banks in the same locality as the real estate mortgaged.) This is the Government National Mortgage Association (GNMA) pass-through securities program. "*Ginnie Mae pass-throughs*" are certificates representing shares in pools of government-guaranteed (FHA and VA) mortgages. Timely payment of principal and interest are guaranteed and passed through by the GNMA to holders of the certificates. The minimum denomination of the certificates is $25,000. Yields are determined by the market price of the certificates, which may be above or below par. Thrift institutions have been able to invest in these certificates and treat them as mortgages for tax purposes. This advantage, the government's guarantee, and an active secondary market have greatly encouraged the flow of funds into mortgages. Ginnie Mae's at the end of 1979 came to $76 billion.

Ginnie Mae's

Corporate bonds

Corporate bonds are basically the same type of instrument as Treasury bonds, with the exception that some are convertible to stock. They may be issued in the public markets or placed privately. Credit ratings are assigned to most issues in the public market by two rating firms, Moody's Investors Services and Standard & Poor's. Average bond yields by each credit class, by newly issued versus seasoned bonds, and by industrial versus utility firms are available from Moody's. Insurance companies are major holders of corporate bonds. Corporations had $40 billion in bonds oustanding at end 1979.

Municipal bonds

Municipal bonds were described briefly in Chapter 4 in connection with state and local government finance. Credit ratings are provided for these bonds, just as for corporate bonds, by Moody's and Standard & Poor's. Data for average yields are available from Moody's and in *The Bond Buyer*, a trade newspaper.

Major holders of these bonds include commercial banks, fire and casualty insurers, and high-income households, with total holdings of general obligation bonds coming to $281 billion at the end of 1979.

INTRODUCTION TO ARTICLE

It is difficult for an outsider to imagine how the markets for government securities and other large-volume debt instruments actually operate. For government securities there are dealers who carry inventories of securities and quote buy and sell prices to any interested parties—mainly the Federal Reserve, commercial banks, other financial intermediaries, and nonfinancial firms. The dealers' market is very fluid, and prices in this market set the standards for other transactions in government securities. The following article from *The Wall Street Journal* describes this dealers' market from the personal perspective of an employee in the trading department of a bank with a dealer operation as of mid-August 1975.

The Trader: Treasury-bond dealer finds job more hectic as the market gyrates

CHICAGO—Even to the financially sophisticated, Federal Reserve monetary policy often remains an abstraction, half remembered from some introductory economics course.

But to Mike Rigg, the Fed constitutes an important daily reality. He spends much of his time checking money market rates and pouring over Federal Reserve statistics and other economic reports, just to get an inkling of current Fed thinking. Among the 30 buttons on his desk phone console, he watches most closely the direct line from the Federal Reserve's trading desk in New York. When it lights up, he drops whatever he is doing to answer it.

Mr. Rigg's preoccupation is explained by the fact that he is the head trader in government securities for Continental Illinois National Bank & Trust Co., one of some 25 primary dealers in federal debt securities in the U.S. As such, his correct assessment of the current drift of Fed monetary policy spells the difference between a large profit or nasty loss in the bank's multimillion-dollar government securities trading account.

"The government market is incredibly sensitive to even the slightest action taken by the Fed; within 60 seconds any news is already reflected in market prices," says the 32-year-old Mr. Rigg. "All I want to be is 30 seconds faster than everybody else, because then I know I'll make money."

Bigger than big board

The government securities market is massive. Each day some $4 billion to $6 billion of U.S. Treasury bills, notes, and bonds, and government agency securities change hands—a daily dollar volume several times that of the New York Stock Exchange.

Continental Bank and other dealers such as Morgan Guaranty Trust Co. and the New York securities firms of Merrill Lynch, Pierce, Fenner & Smith and Salomon Brothers perform a crucial role in the market.

They buy a large portion of the debt issues offered at periodic auctions to finance government operations. The dealers then distribute the debt by selling it to longer-term holders such as bank investment portfolios, insurance companies, savings and loan associations, and corporations. Dealers also maintain a secondary market in government issues by standing ready to buy back government securities from holders.

Even more important, the dealers are the focus of the Fed's open-market operations—its primary weapon of monetary policy. When the Fed decides that economic activity is lagging, it purchases government securities, mainly from the supplies that dealers have on hand. This soon has the effect of increasing bank funds, as the non-bank dealers deposit the proceeds of their securities sales in their commercial bank accounts and the bank-affiliated dealers get credit from the Fed against their reserve accounts. Thus, the money supply tends to expand, making credit cheaper and more available.

Conversely, to cool an overheated econ-

omy, the Fed sells government securities, draining funds from the banking system, and usually driving up interest rates. In the bond markets, prices rise when interest rates fall and decline when rates rise.

Treasury's huge demands

The pressures on the government securities market in recent months have been intense. By most estimates, the Treasury alone is borrowing about $80 billion in new money this calendar year to finance the federal budget deficit, compared to new borrowings of $12 billion last year. Moreover, the average maturity of the outstanding government debt has shrunk markedly in the past decade to two years, nine months from about six years.

Consequently, more than $100 billion of publicly held, marketable debt is coming due in 1975 and must be refinanced. "The financings are coming at an incredible pace." says Edward Roob, senior vice president in charge of the bond department of First National Bank of Chicago and formerly a Treasury official. "Every time we get through digesting one offering and look up, there's another one coming. It's enough to give you ulcers."

So far, this year's massive government financings haven't caused any drastic "crowding out" of less credit-worthy private and public borrowers in U.S. capital markets, as some financial experts feared. Banks and savings and loan associations have sharply stepped up their purchases of government securities, primarily because the recession has pared loan demand by businesses and the construction industry.

But some observers see a possible credit crunch next year, especially if the expected recovery in the economy is at all robust. "What we have to hope for is a nice, gentle recovery. Otherwise, the Fed will have to pump more money into the economy than its noninflationary target of 5 percent to 7.5 percent in monetary growth to accommodate increased credit demands," says Tilford Gaines, economist and senior vice president of Manufacturers Hanover Trust Co. in New York.

In any case, the task of trading government securities, which Mr. Rigg and his fellow traders face daily, has become more difficult in recent years. The market has become more volatile because of the general economy's more violent swings between hyperinflation and recession and the Fed's growing emphasis on controlling money supply growth at the expense of interest-rate stability.

"In the early 1960s a one-point move in the prices of intermediate and long-term government issues was a major move that would take weeks to develop," Mr. Rigg observes. "Today, bonds can move that much in an afternoon, so you really have to be nimble to keep from getting hurt." He also notes that between August of 1974 and early this year, yields on the three-month Treasury bills dropped from a record 9.9 percent to under 5 percent (currently yields are back to more than 6¼ percent).

Also, the price swings in government securities have become less predictable, according to some observers.

A Fed economist suggests that in the last few years the Fed has had a less sure influence over the course of the economy because of its greater difficulty in controlling growth in money supply. And recent research at the University of Chicago's Graduate School of Business indicates that inflationary expectations may be the primary determinant of short-term Treasury security interest rates as well as long-term rates and not the factors traditionally watched by Treasury securities traders, such as Fed policy and credit supply and demand.

Not surprisingly, the new, more volatile environment has exacted a toll among dealers. In early 1974, Lehman Brothers closed its government dealer department, reportedly because of trading account losses. Chase Manhattan Bank posted a loss of $29.2 million on government bonds in 1974.

The market forces are evident at the Continental's government desk on the bank's wood-paneled fifth floor. Here, Mr. Rigg and the four traders under him sit hunched over their telephone consoles from 8:30 a.m. to 3 p.m. CDT during the hurly-burly of daily trading.

Traders' specialties

As in most other dealer operations, the traders specialize in certain maturity ranges. One, for example, deals only in Treasury bills, or short-term government debt maturing in a year

or less. Two others trade in securities issued by agencies such as the Federal Home Loan Banks and the Federal National Mortgage Association. Another trades in intermediate-term Treasury securities, and Mr. Rigg personally handles the longer-term bonds and notes. The longer-term securities are generally riskiest because the more distant the maturity, the greater the impact a change in interest rates has on price.

Surrounding the trading desk are some 15 salesmen, who deal directly with the Continental's "retail" customers, such as the investment portfolios of other banks, insurance companies, corporations, and savings and loan associations. The salesmen and traders have a symbiotic relationship: the traders are constantly shouting the latest price quotations to the salesmen to relay to their customers; in turn, the salesmen furnish the traders with a minute-by-minute estimate of retail demand for specific issues.

Acting through the salesmen, Mr. Rigg and his fellow trades frequently sell government securities to customers directly from the bank's trading account (or they buy from another dealer to fill a customer's order). If Mr. Rigg is bullish on the market, he will quickly replace any securities sold from the bank's supply by buying from another dealer. Or, if he is bearish, he may let his securities inventory dwindle. Correspondingly, when Mr. Rigg buys securities from a customer, his view of the market dictates whether he will keep the issues or quickly dump them.

Much of Mr. Rigg's day is spent phoning other dealers and government securities brokers, special intermediaries between dealers, to check their price quotations on the two dozen maturities he watches closely. These "runs," plus Mr. Rigg's intuitive feel for the direction of the market, determine his own price quotations.

No $5 million gambles

Mr. Rigg's quotes are necessarily never frivolous, for under the rules of the game, a trader is compelled to buy or sell up to $5 million of an issue at his quoted price if a customer or another dealer "takes" his asked price or "hits" his bid price.

"There is, of course, a lot of chicanery and gamesmanship between the dealers, especially in the brokers' market where dealers do a lot of business to mask their identity," says Mr. Rigg. "But the runs are essential for intelligence gathering because they reveal how other dealers feel about the market by whether the dealers are quoting prices above or below the market."

The pressure on Mr. Rigg and his fellow traders is enormous. The market constantly moves in reaction to the ever-changing flow of economic, market, and political news. On a typical day Mr. Rigg trades as much as $100 million of government securities. A trade of less than $1 million is considered an odd lot.

Traders can seldom afford to leave their posts, even for a moment. On a recent morning, just when one of Continental's agency traders was about to go to the washroom, a market rally caused his telephone console to light up like a Christmas tree. He finally took a break three hours later.

For all of this, the traders are generally better compensated than other bank employes of comparable age and status. Mr. Rigg declines to disclose his annual income. However, head government securities traders at banks can make $50,000 or more, depending on their performance.

The government securities market revolves around New York, where most of the major dealers are located. Normally there's a short trading lull at about 12:30 p.m. EDT, the time at which the New York traders traditionally gulp down their sandwiches at the trading desk. Mr. Rigg eats his lunch at 11:30 C.D.T. to synchronize with the New York traders. Veteran traders recall that the government securities market nearly ground to a halt during the 1969 World Series as the traders stopped to follow the fortunes of the New York Mets.

'Sneakers' and his pals

In the in-grown, fraternal world of trading, most of the traders are given nicknames. There's "Sneakers," a Merrill Lynch trader who got his name from his ability to get in and out of positions quickly. The origin of such other trader nicknames as "The Archer," "The Ghost," "Mr. Wonderful" and "Quixote" are

shrouded in obscurity. Mr. Rigg is called "Mo," because his first two initials are "M.O."

The dealers make profits in a variety of ways. In constantly turning over their inventories, they earn or lose the "spread," or the difference between what a certain issue costs and what it is sold for. But the spreads on actively traded issues are narrow, often totaling no more than $1/32$ of one percentage point, or $312.50 per $1 million trade. During some periods, dealers are able to earn "positive carry" on their inventories. In other words, the interest income from their inventories exceeds the cost of the money the dealers borrow from other banks or corporations to finance the inventories.

Most important, however, are the trading profits gained from selling from dealer inventories after government securities prices rise as a result of a drop in their interest rates. Dealers also can make profits from price declines in government securities by "selling short"— selling borrowed securities in hopes of replacing them later with lower-priced securities. But that strategy isn't as profitable because of the expense and difficulty of borrowing securities to sell.

To formulate Continental's trading strategy, Mr. Rigg analyzes a number of economic statistics such as industrial production, leading economic indicators, retail sales, and unemployment rates to get an idea of economic trends. He also keeps close tabs on government spending, Treasury borrowing needs, money supply, demand for government securities, and certain technical factors.

Fed's intervention

Most crucial, of course, are moves of the Fed, because it intervenes almost daily in the government market. Mr. Rigg and other government securities traders are the first to know of any Fed open-market operations because they are all contacted simultaneously in a telephone "go-around" whenever the Fed decides to buy or sell securities.

Yet the contact gives Mr. Rigg scant advantage in divining the Fed's current monetary policy. The minutes of the monthly meeting of the Fed Open Market Committee, at which targets for monetary growth and interest rate levels are set, are released publicly after a 45-day lag. On a daily basis, it is difficult to interpret the significance of open-market transactions because frequently they are done purely for technical reasons, such as temporarily boosting the money supply for the Christmas season.

Bad news is frequently good news in Mr. Rigg's world. Deterioration in the economy usually means an abatement in credit demand and a drop in interest rates and therefore a rise in the prices of government securities. Recessionary trends also prompt the Fed to ease monetary policy, which drives interest rates down.

Mr. Rigg, who lives with his wife in an apartment on Chicago's trendy North Side, brings useful credentials to his job. He has a master's degree in economics from the University of Missouri and worked three years as an economist at the Federal Reserve banks in St. Louis and Minneapolis. He joined Continental as an international economist in 1968 and switched to the government desk three years later. "I wanted to see whether I could use my economics to make money in the real world," he says.

The Rigg record

In recent months, Mr. Rigg has shown considerable market acumen. In September of last year, he decided that the economy was headed for a severe recession and that the Fed was in the process of easing monetary policy. So, at Mr. Rigg's recommendation, Continental's trading account bought heavily in government securities, boosting its position to more than $450 million.

The Treasury security market rallied sharply over the ensuing six months. Continental's government securities inventory accounted for the bulk of the $17 million six-month profits of the bank's trading account, which also includes municipal bonds, bankers' acceptances, and certificates of deposit.

By early spring, however, Mr. Rigg began to get nervous about the bank's large government securities inventory. He was concerned that the looming U.S. budget deficits and heavy Treasury financing needs would soon drive down market prices. Also, he felt that the economy might soon turn up, and with a corresponding resurgence in business credit demand, interest rates would inevitably climb.

As a result, Continental cut its government inventory to about $150 million at a time when most dealer inventories were bloated. It also shortened the average maturity, to eliminate much of the portfolio's price risk. Thus, the bank wasn't bloddied as much as many dealers when the government market tumbled in March and April, giving up more than half of the gains of the earlier rally.

SOURCE: Jonathan R. Liang, "The Trader: Treasury-Bond Dealer Finds Job More Hectic as the Market Gyrates," *The Wall Street Journal*, August 13, 1975.

CONCLUSION

This chapter has provided conceptual and institutional material necessary to an understanding of specific major markets within the overall market for borrowed funds. We have surveyed standard yields and contractual arrangements for a number of large-volume markets in the United States. There are many additional instruments, participants, and markets that would deserve mention in a more exhaustive survey. The purposes of this chapter, however, are principally to provide an introduction to the markets and to provide necessary background for our analysis of liquidity and interest-rate spreads in the next chapter.

PROBLEMS

1. Columns 1 and 2 of the following table show secondary market prices and yields for Treasury notes and bonds on August 20, 1981. Column 3 shows discount yields (bid and asked) and ITF-equivalent yields for Treasury bills (ITF yields are based on an average of each issue's bid and asked discount yields).
   a. If, on August 20, 1981, you had been comparing an investment in 1-year Treasury note., i.e., the $11\frac{1}{8}$s (coupon rate) maturing in August 1982, with an investment in 20-year Treasury bonds, i.e., the $13\frac{3}{8}$ of August 2001, and planned a one-year holding period, what selling price would you have had to anticipate for the 20-year bond, on August 20, 1982 to expect the same realized return as on the 1-year Treasury notes?
   b. Check the latest issue of *The Wall Street Journal* for the actual selling price of the $13\frac{3}{8}$ of August 2001 and calculate the actual realized return to date for an investor who had purchased these bonds on August 20, 1981.
   c. Explain why the bond-equivalent yield for Treasury bills maturing on August 27, 1981 was the same as the average of the bid and asked discount yields for these bills (15.61 percent) whereas the bond-equivalent yield for bills maturing on August 12, 1982 was 197 basis points higher than the average of their bid and asked discount yields (16.63 versus 14.66 percent.)

Treasury Issues

* * *

Bonds, Notes & Bills

Thursday, August 20, 1981

Mid-afternoon Over-the-Counter quotations; sources on request.

Decimals in bid-and-asked and bid changes represent 32nds; 101.1 means 101 1/32. a-Plus 1/64. b-Yield to call date. d-Minus 1/64. n-Treasury notes.

Treasury Bonds and Notes

Rate	Mat.	Date	Bid	Asked	Bid Chg.	Yld.
$9\frac{5}{8}$s,	1981	Aug n	99.24	99.28	...	15.51
$6\frac{3}{4}$s,	1981	Sep n	98.27	98.31	+ .2	16.68
$10\frac{1}{8}$s,	1981	Sep n	99.6	99.10	...	16.38
$12\frac{5}{8}$s,	1981	Oct n	99.1	99.5	+ .1	16.68
7s,	1981	Nov n	97.18	97.22	+ .1	17.32
$7\frac{3}{4}$s,	1981	Nov n	97.22	97.26	...	17.46
$12\frac{1}{8}$s,	1981	Nov n	98.18	98.22	...	16.78
$7\frac{1}{4}$s,	1981	Dec n	96.23	96.27	...	16.60
$11\frac{3}{8}$s,	1981	Dec n	98	98.4	...	16.75
$11\frac{1}{2}$s,	1982	Jan n	97.18	97.22	− .1	17.09
$6\frac{1}{8}$s,	1982	Feb n	95.4	95.8	− .1	16.89
$6\frac{3}{8}$s,	1982	Feb	95.5	95.9	− .1	17.08
$13\frac{7}{8}$s,	1982	Feb n	98.16	98.20	− .1	16.75
$7\frac{7}{8}$s,	1982	Mar n	94.30	95.2	...	16.80
15s,	1982	Mar n	98.29	99.1	...	16.75
$11\frac{3}{8}$s,	1982	Apr n	96.13	96.17	− .1	16.91
7s,	1982	May n	93.12	93.20	...	16.63
8s,	1982	May n	94	94.8	...	16.68
$9\frac{1}{4}$s,	1982	May n	94.24	94.28	+ .1	17.00
$9\frac{3}{8}$s,	1982	May n	94.18	94.22	...	17.00
$8\frac{1}{4}$s,	1982	Jun n	93.16	93.20	+ .1	16.55
$8\frac{5}{8}$s,	1982	Jun n	93.21	93.25	...	16.73
$8\frac{7}{8}$s,	1982	Jul n	93.12	93.16	− .2	16.65
$8\frac{1}{8}$s,	1982	Aug n	92.28	93.4	+ .1	16.01
9s,	1982	Aug n	93.18	93.22	...	16.25
$11\frac{1}{8}$s,	1982	Aug n	95.8	95.12	...	16.23
$9\frac{1}{4}$s,	1989	May n	75.1	75.17	− .14	14.63
$10\frac{3}{4}$s,	1989	Nov n	81.7	81.15	− .13	14.71
$3\frac{1}{2}$s,	1990	Feb	79.4	80.4	+ .2	6.60
$8\frac{1}{4}$s,	1990	May	70.22	71.22	− .23	13.96
$10\frac{3}{4}$s,	1990	Aug n	80.18	80.26	− .10	14.66
13s,	1990	Nov n	91.2	91.10	− .20	14.75
$14\frac{1}{2}$s,	1991	May n	98.5	98.13	− .21	14.82
$14\frac{7}{8}$s,	1991	Aug n	99.30	100.2	− .20	14.86
$4\frac{1}{4}$s,	1987-92	Aug	76.12	77.12	− .4	7.28
$7\frac{1}{4}$s,	1992	Aug	63.10	64.10	− .5	13.61
4s,	1988-93	Feb	78.4	79.4	− .3	6.63
$6\frac{3}{4}$s,	1993	Feb	59.28	60.28	− .7	13.58
$7\frac{7}{8}$s,	1993	Feb	64.4	64.20	− .28	14.20
$7\frac{1}{2}$s,	1988-93	Aug	63.8	64.8	+ .6	13.64
$8\frac{5}{8}$s,	1993	Aug	67.3	67.11	− .15	14.43
$8\frac{5}{8}$s,	1993	Nov	66.30	67.6	− .15	14.40
9s,	1994	Feb	68.17	68.25	− .23	14.47
$4\frac{1}{8}$s,	1989-94	May	78.14	79.14	− 1	6.53
$8\frac{3}{4}$s,	1994	Aug	66.22	66.30	− .20	14.46
$10\frac{1}{8}$s,	1994	Nov	74.20	75.4	− .20	14.38
3s,	1995	Feb	78.8	79.8	+ .2	5.16
$10\frac{1}{2}$s,	1995	Feb	76.16	76.24	− .22	14.46
$10\frac{3}{8}$s,	1995	May	75.14	75.30	− .29	14.44
$12\frac{5}{8}$s,	1995	May	89.18	89.26	− .10	14.34
$11\frac{1}{2}$s,	1995	Nov	82	82.8	− .22	14.47
7s,	1993-98	May	57.22	58.22	− .16	13.17
$3\frac{1}{2}$s,	1998	Nov	78.16	79.16	− .4	5.33
$8\frac{1}{2}$s,	1994-99	May	64.26	65.26	− .7	13.68
$7\frac{7}{8}$s,	1995-00	Feb	59.28	60.12	− .20	13.87
$8\frac{3}{8}$s,	1995-00	Aug	63.2	63.10	− .6	13.91
$11\frac{3}{4}$s,	2001	Feb	83.6	83.14	− .16	14.28
$13\frac{1}{8}$s,	2001	May	91.20	91.28	− .27	14.37
8s,	1996-01	Aug	61.4	61.20	− .12	13.64
$13\frac{3}{8}$s,	2001	Aug	93.4	93.12	− 1	14.39
$8\frac{1}{4}$s,	2000-05	May	61.26	62.10	− .17	13.62
$7\frac{5}{8}$s,	2002-07	Feb	58.16	59	− .26	13.29
$7\frac{7}{8}$s,	2002-07	Nov	61	61.16	− .12	13.10
$8\frac{3}{8}$s,	2003-08	Aug	62.16	63	− .25	13.52
$8\frac{3}{4}$s,	2003-08	Nov	64.22	64.30	− .24	13.67
$9\frac{1}{8}$s,	2004-09	May	67.1	67.9	− .22	13.73
$10\frac{3}{8}$s,	2004-09	Nov	75.4	75.12	− .24	13.88
$11\frac{3}{4}$s,	2005-10	Feb	84.13	84.21	− .26	13.94
10s,	2005-10	May	72.30	73.6	− .22	13.78
$12\frac{3}{4}$s,	2005-10	Nov	91.4	91.12	− .27	13.98
$13\frac{7}{8}$s,	2006-11	May	98.19	98.27	− .29	14.03

n- Treasury notes.

U.S. Treas. Bills

Mat. date	Bid Discount	Asked Discount	Yield
-1981-			
8-27	15.84	15.38	15.61
9- 3	15.83	15.49	15.77
9-10	15.58	15.14	15.46
9-17	15.20	14.84	15.20
9-24	15.21	14.89	15.29
10- 1	15.45	15.23	15.69
10- 8	15.54	15.30	15.82
10-15	15.47	15.23	15.79
10-22	15.50	15.24	15.85
10-29	15.56	15.32	15.98
11- 5	15.59	15.35	16.06
11-12	15.61	15.51	16.29
11-19	15.62	15.54	16.37
11-27	15.50	15.38	16.25
12- 3	15.59	15.43	16.35
12-10	15.59	15.43	16.40
12-17	15.50	15.34	16.35
12-24	15.50	15.34	16.41
12-31	15.54	15.38	16.50
-1982-			
1- 7	15.52	15.36	16.53
1-14	15.52	15.36	16.59
1-21	15.57	15.41	16.70
1-28	15.60	15.44	16.79
2- 4	15.63	15.49	16.90
2-11	15.63	15.49	16.95
2-18	15.59	15.51	17.03
2-25	15.51	15.39	16.92
3-25	15.22	15.12	16.64
4-22	15.22	15.10	16.69
5-20	15.15	15.03	16.72
6-17	14.93	14.83	16.60
7-15	14.84	14.72	16.60
8-12	14.70	14.62	16.63

2. Discuss the role of reserve requirements in the cost to depository institutions of time-deposit funds.

ADVANCED READINGS

Handbook of Securities of the United States Government and Federal Agencies. New York: First Boston Corporation, 28th ed. 1978.

Money Market Instruments. Federal Reserve Bank of Cleveland, 1971.

Zwick, Burton. "The Market for Corporate Bonds." Federal Reserve Bank of New York *Quarterly Review*, Autumn 1977, pp. 27–36.

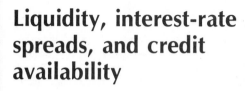

Liquidity, interest-rate spreads, and credit availability

7

In Chapter 2 liquidity was identified as one of the intrinsic characteristics of money. (Recall the liquid-store-of-value function.) But it was pointed out that assets other than checkable deposits and currency also serve as relatively liquid stores of value. Liquidity may be a very critical factor in the economy. In the first several sections of this chapter we examine the concept and its importance closely, explaining the role of financial intermediaries as suppliers of liquidity, the contribution of credit availability to liquidity, and the nature of a liquidity crisis. The second part of the chapter relates liquidity and other factors to interest-rate spreads in the credit markets. In the final part, the credit availability school and the effect of interest-rate ceilings on credit availability and liquidity at business-cycle peaks are explained.

THE DIMENSIONS OF LIQUIDITY

If you will pardon the pun, liquidity is an especially slippery concept to define. Distinctions must be made between the liquidity of an asset, the liquidity of an entity (firm, household, or government), and the aggregate liquidity of entities in the economy. Consider first the verbal gymnastics necessary to define asset liquidity.

Asset liquidity

The liquidity of an asset is a quality reflecting the perceived speed, ease, closeness, and certainty with which the asset can be exchanged for goods or services at a price such that the asset earns as high a return as that expected for it over a short-term period. This definition will be explained in the discussion that follows.

Since asset liquidity is a quality, it cannot be measured in absolute magnitudes; but it is often possible to rank assets according to the relative degree of liquidity they afford. To perform such a ranking it is helpful to identify the more concrete attributes of assets which enhance or detract from their liquidity. Three to which we will devote special attention are *marketability, risk of default,* and *maturity.*

Marketability is the one attribute most obviously related to liquidity; it is the speed, ease, and closeness with which an asset can be exchanged for other assets, goods, or services at the best price obtainable. Marketability is usually highest for homogeneous assets with organized secondary markets. In an organized secondary market there are firms or individuals who are always willing—indeed it is their business—to buy or sell reasonable quantities of specific assets at quoted prices. A secondary market can be crucial to an investor who may have to or want to sell an asset before maturity.[1] Without such a market, considerable price concessions may be required to dispose of the asset. Several financial assets with organized secondary markets were identified in Chapter 6.

Many real assets also have established secondary markets—oriental rugs and used cars, for example; but most real assets are less marketable and hence less liquid than financial assets because they are generally less homogeneous, divisible, and transportable than financial assets. We could further explore the factors which underlie the varying degrees of marketability among assets, but that would take us deeper into the complexities of market analysis than we can go here.[2]

Risk of default is a second important determinant of liquidity for credit-market assets because it affects the certainty of the interest and principal payments. The greater the risk of default, the greater the potential for a lower than expected realized return, and hence the lower the liquidity of a credit-market asset. Risk of default is often called *credit risk.*

The third major attribute we identified was maturity. This also affects the certainty of the realized return on an asset. As the mate-

Marketability

Risk of default

Maturity

---

[1]The degree of competition among those who "make" the secondary market is also an important factor determining liquidity because it affects the bid-ask price spread, and hence the closeness with which an investor can sell an asset at the highest price other investors are willing to pay.

[2]For advanced reading on this subject see H. Demsetz, "The Cost of Transacting," *The Quarterly Journal of Economics,* February 1968, 33–53.

rial in Chapter 6 emphasized, the maturity of a credit-market instrument in terms of repayment of principal determines the sensitivity of the asset's realized yield to market conditions, should the instrument have to be sold before it matures. This, in turn, has clear implications for the liquidity of a credit-market asset if market conditions are changeable because it increases the potential for a less-than-expected realized return. Several examples in Chapter 6 demonstrated variations in the market prices and realized yields for short- and long-term marketable debt instruments.[3]

INTRODUCTION TO ARTICLE

The article in Chapter 6 on government-securities dealers mentioned losses incurred by bond dealers in early 1974, as bond yields, and interest rates generally, rose unexpectedly. The article below from *The Wall Street Journal* (April 11, 1974) provides more information on this particular period and illustrates the risk of *unexpected* losses in the market value of bonds and hence their lower liquidity in comparison to assets of shorter maturity. Even sharper surges in bond yields took place six years later, in early 1980 and again late in that same year; but securities dealers were not caught off guard as badly in those episodes as they were in 1974.

Unexpected blow: Plunging Bond Prices Bring Added Problems to Securities Industry

NEW YORK—As if Wall Street hasn't had enough troubles with the slumping stock market, it has found still another way to lose potfuls of money—the bond market.

Prices of bonds—including corporate and municipal bonds and government-agency issues—have plummeted in the past month to three-year lows. Bond dealers, including both banks and securities firms, who loaded up at the beginning of the year in anticipation of rising prices have been caught with huge piles of debt issues in their inventories.

When they have been able to get rid of them, the losses have been tremendous. Street sources estimate that the combined losses during March of some two-dozen major dealers that report rate data to the Federal Reserve Bank of New York were $150 million. This was about equally divided between realized losses from bonds actually sold and paper losses on inventory still stuck on the shelves. Securities firms must include paper gains and losses in their net profit figures, under Securities and Exchange Commission rules, whereas banks don't.

Lots of red ink

"It's been a bloodbath," says Donald T. Regan, chairman of Merrill Lynch, Pierce, Fenner & Smith Inc., the nation's largest securi-

---

[3]In actual experience, short-term yields tend to fluctuate more than long-term yields so that the comparisons drawn in Chapter 6 overstate the actual relative downside price risk on long-term assets relative to short-term assets. Nevertheless, long-term asset prices do fluctuate considerably more than those for short-term assets because of the higher sensitivity of long-term asset prices to changes in long-term yields, the factor which was emphasized in Chapter 6.

ties firm and one of the major bond dealers. Mr. Regan says his firm suffered bond-market losses in the first quarter, although Merrill Lynch still expects to report an overall profit for the period.

Citicorp, the holding company that owns First National City Bank, reported yesterday that its first-quarter pretax profit in bond trading, including commissions, was only $17,000, compared to $1.4 million a year earlier. Chase Manhattan Corp. has told its stockholders that "substantial losses" in its bond-dealing operations will slow the pace of first-quarter earnings growth. Some other dealers may even post losses for the period. Indications will emerge in the next few days as publicly held dealers report results.

"This thing hit like a tornado in the Midwest," says Leon T. Kendall, president of the Securities Industry Association, a trade group of broker-dealers and commercial banks. "But it hit the first team, including a category of securities firms that have maintained an above-average level of profitability. That's what risk capital is for at those |organizations—for risks."

Most of the hard hit dealers are big outfits, and nobody expects the bond market to force any major financial institution to collapse. Nevertheless, for the securities industry, which is already concerned about low stock prices and volume and uncertain about such basic problems as its future structure, the bond-market reversals are like another kick to a man who is down.

A warning signal

Moreover, the reversals threaten repercussions far beyond the first quarter's earnings statements. They are another warning signal to already skittish potential contributors of fresh funds to capital-hungry securities firms.

According to New York Stock Exchange figures, the composite net worth of member firms shrank 13 percent in 1973 to $3.65 billion from $4.20 billion at the end of 1972. Only $40 million of the $550 million decline was attributable to operating losses; the rest was accounted for by shrinkage in the market value of capital (some of which was in the form of marketable

securities) and by the flight of capital as investors switched stakes to ventures that seemed less risky.

"The ability of the industry to raise subordinated debt or to borrow obviously is going to be impaired by the recognition (by investors) of the volatility of any business where (securities firms) act as principals," says Paul L. Miller, president of First Boston Corp., a major bond-market dealer that Mr. Miller admits didn't do particularly well in bonds the first quarter.

The reason for the nose dive in bond prices is no mystery. Bond prices normally move inversely to interest rates and bond yields—when rates and yields rise, bond prices fall, and vice versa. Because a bond carries a fixed interest rate, the only way it can compete with other bonds and securities is by its market price. Thus, if new bond issues carry higher rates and therefore are more attractive to investors, the prices of bonds issued previously at lower rates must be marked down to make them competitive.

The interest rates of new bonds have been rising to keep pace with higher interest rates elsewhere. For example, two months ago a Southern Bell Telephone issue reached the

"Do you mean to tell me you don't carry any cash at all – even for emergencies like this?"

market yielding 8.06 percent at a price of $992.87 for a $1,000 face-value bond. Yesterday, it sold at $937.50 to yield 8.55 percent.

The bond market's troubles stem from optimism at the end of 1973 that the cost of money, as measured by bank lending rates and other key indicators, would decline in 1974. Equally important, it was believed this low-cost money would come about by an easing of credit policy by the Federal Reserve System and by declining demand for loans.

Instead, interest rates climbed as loan demand soared and the Federal Reserve Board tightened the credit spigots. During the week ended Feb. 13, according to Federal Reserve Bank of New York figures, optimistic dealers built their bond holdings by 36 percent to $5.01 billion. By April 3 those holdings had been reduced to $3.5 billion as dealers sold in despair.

How long will the bond-market slump last? "Sooner or later rates are going to flow the other way, downward," says Mr. Kendall of the securities industry trade group. "But I guess the only one who can save the bond dealers is the Fed."

SOURCE: Richard E. Rustin, "Plunging Bond Prices Bring Added Problems, to Securities Industry, *The Wall Street Journal,* April 11, 1974.

A broad definition of maturity. We can broaden the concept of maturity here to permit comparisons for a wider range of assets. *In a most general sense, the maturity of an asset is the length of time before the asset is redeemable at a fixed price for more liquid or intrinsically valuable assets, goods, or services.* To provide contrast, consider a savings deposit in a commercial-bank passbook account which pays interest from date of deposit to date of withdrawal. Such an asset usually is redeemable in cash with stipulated interest virtually on presentation of the passbook at the bank. (The bank has the right to make the deposit owner wait 30 days, but in normal practice this right is not exercised.) Therefore, the maturity of this asset in cash usually is zero, and its money return always would be equal to that expected for it over the holding period. This contributes to a savings deposit's high liquidity. On the other hand, a government bond maturing in 20 years has a fairly uncertain realized money return over short-term holding periods. (An illustration of a lower market price and higher realized return for a 20-year bond was provided in Chapter 6; and the boxed article above describes an actual episode of an unanticipated decline in bond prices in 1974 which had a severe impact on realized returns for government-securities dealers.)

Combining attributes to determine liquidity. It may be useful at this point to show how two of the three characterisitcs we have discussed, marketability and maturity, combine to account for the relative liquidity of a variety of assets. In Figure 7–1 a number of assets are classed according to their marketability and maturity. Some real assets are included to help fill in the boxes with examples.

The classifications and most of the entries should be obvious, but a few asset entries bear comment.

Starting with U.S. currency in box A, we know this asset is extremely liquid. This is not because of its low maturity—neither the Treasury, the Federal Reserve, nor anyone else will redeem U.S. currency at a fixed price in terms of some other asset, good, or service. Low maturity is not necessary because of the extreme marketability of currency. General marketability based on law and confidence makes U.S. currency more liquid than any other asset in the economy. (Indeed, it is the low maturity in currency of the assets in box B which accounts in good measure for *their* high liquidity.)

Corporate stocks, gold, and diamonds also are assets which never

FIGURE 7–1
Assets classified by maturity, marketability, and liquidity

	High maturity	Low maturity
	A	B
High marketability	**Varying degress of liquidity:** a. U.S. currency b. U.S. Government long-term bonds c. Publicly issued corporate bonds d. Corporate stocks listed on stock exchanges e. Gold bullion f. Diamonds	**High liquidity:** a. Checkable deposits at commercial banks and thrifts b. Marketable Treasury bills c. Negotiable certificates of deposit d. Bankers' acceptances e. Repurchase agreements f. Eurodollar deposits
	C	D
Low marketability	**Relatively low liquidity:** a. Privately placed corporate bonds b. Long-term loans to developing countries c. Second mortgages d. Real estate e. Amplifiers and equipment for a rock band	**Varying degrees of liquidity:** a. Savings and short-term time deposits at commercial banks and thrifts b. Money-market mutual fund shares c. Non-marketable Treasury bills d. Commercial paper e. Non-negotiable certificates of deposit f. Business and personal loans

mature at a fixed price in terms of another, more liquid asset. Yet, because of their marketability and potential stability in *real return*, they are often ranked by investors as among the more liquid assets available.[4] In periods of extreme uncertainty about inflation or stability of the government, gold may become considered more liquid than currency.

As this discussion suggests, asset liquidity is related to a variety of characteristics. These characteristics combine in different degrees to account for the liquidity rankings of different assets. No one characteristic is crucial. Moreover, judgments about asset liquidity are subjective.

Despite these problems, it is desirable to have measures of the aggregate quantity of liquid assets in the economy. The Federal Reserves broad measures of money provide several alternatives.

Liquid assets in the Federal Reserve's broad measures of money. The Federal Reserve's measures are identified in terms of specific assets in Figure 7–2. As noted in Chapter 2, assets added to M-1B to arrive at the M-2 measure are mainly savings deposits and *small* time deposits at depository institutions. Large time deposits are excluded from M-2 because their size makes them less convenient as a source of quick cash for small (less than $100,000) transactions.

The M-2 measure also includes money-market mutual fund shares—a relatively recent and rapidly growing type of liquid asset, described briefly in Chapter 4. Money-market mutual funds invest in Treasury bills, short-term obligations of off-budget Federal agencies, commercial paper, bankers acceptances, RPs, and CDs; they fund these investments by accepting share deposits, usually in increments of $1,000. The interest earnings are paid out to the shareholders after deducting a management fee. Shareholders can withdraw funds on short notice; some funds even provide a check-writing privilege, though checks usually are restricted to a minimum value of $500.[5] Money-market mutual fund shares have become an attractive avenue for small savers to earn higher interest than available on savings accounts without apparent sacrifice of liquidity. (The principal reservation an investor might have with these funds is that their share deposits are not insured by a Federal agency; hence credit risk is higher for investments in money-market mutual fund shares than it is for deposits held in an insured depository institution.)

Money-market mutual funds

---

[4]Beginning in 1933 and ending only in 1975, it was against the law for American citizens to hold gold except in the form of jewelry or numismatically valuable coins.

[5]Because of this checkable feature, some analysts argue that money-market mutual funds should be included in the Federal Reserve's M-1B aggregate. In 1980 the Federal Reserve staff expressed the opinion, however, that the $500 minimum restriction on checks makes these funds more of a savings vehicle than a medium-of-exchange asset.

FIGURE 7-2
The Federal Reserve's broad measures of money

Aggregate	Component	Amount in billions of dollars (not seasonally adjusted) November 1979	share of total
M-2 =			
	M-1B assets* ....$ 387.9		25.7%
	+ Small time deposits at all depository institutions† 640.8		42.4
	+ Savings deposits at all depository institutions 420.0		27.8
	+ Money-market mutual fund shares 40.4		2.7
	+ Overnight RPs issued by commercial banks 20.3		1.3
	+ Overnight Eurodollar deposits held by U.S. nonbank residents at Caribbean branches of U.S. banks 3.2		0.2
	− M-2 consolidation component‡ ....− 2.7		− 0.2
	Total M-2 ....$1,510.0		100.0
M-3 =	M-2 assets...........................$1,510.0		85.8
	+ Large time deposits at all depository institutions 219.5		12.5
	+ Term RPs issued by commercial banks 21.5		1.2
	+ Term RPs issued by savings and loan associations 8.2		0.5
	Total M-3 ....$1,759.1		100.0
L =	M-3 assets...........................$1,759.1		82.8
	+ Liquid Treasury obligations 125.4		5.9
	+ Commercial paper 97.1		4.6
	+ Savings bonds 80.0		3.8
	+ Other Eurodollars of U.S. residents other than banks 34.5		1.6
	+ Bankers acceptances 27.6		1.3
	Total L	$2,123.8	100.0

Note: Components of M-2, M-3, and L measures generally exclude amounts held by domestic depository institutions, foreign commercial banks and official institutions, the U.S. government (including the Federal Reserve), and money-market mutual funds. Exceptions are bankers acceptances and commercial paper for which data sources permit the removal only of amounts held by money-market mutual funds and, in the case of bankers acceptances, amounts held by accepting banks, the Federal Reserve, and the Federal Home Loan Bank System.

*M-1B equals currency plus travelers checks plus checkable deposits held by the nonbank public. Data shown exclude travelers checks issued by nonbanks due to lack of data availability as of February, 1980.

†Time deposits issued in denominations of less than $100,000.

‡In order to avoid double counting of some deposits in M-2, those demand deposits owned by thrift institutions (a component of M-1B) which are estimated to be used for servicing their savings and small time-deposit liabilities in M-2 are removed.

§Time deposits issued in denominations of $100,000 or more.

SOURCE: Federal Reserve Bulletin, February 1980; M-1B definition amended by author to reflect change in June 1981.

The next largest component of M-2 is overnight RPs issued by commercial banks. This type of asset has grown rapidly in recent years in response to efforts by large firms to find ways to earn interest on day-to-day transactions balances, despite Federal prohibitions on such interest payments for ordinary demand deposits. New cash-management systems devised for business firms by commercial banks permit customers to exchange their demand-deposit balances for overnight RPs at the close of business each day. Since the overnight RP automatically returns funds to the customer's account the next morning, the customer is never without a transactions balance, and interest is earned overnight. These features make overnight RPs every bit as liquid as demand deposits.[6]

Lastly, M-2 includes overnight Eurodollar deposits held by U.S. nonbank residents at Caribbean branches of U.S. banks. Like overnight RPs, these deposits can automatically generate next-day money, whereas, because of time-zone differences, overnight Eurodollar deposits held at London banks normally are not available on as timely a basis.

Further down the liquidity scale come large time deposits of all depository institutions and term (larger than overnight) RPs issued by commercial banks and savings and loans. These assets are added to M-2 to arrive at M-3. Other Eurodollars held by U.S. nonbank residents, bankers acceptances, commercial paper, U.S. savings bonds, and short-term, marketable Treasury debt are added to M-3 to arrive at L.[7]

Which of these broad money-supply measures is the best gauge of total liquidity in terms of the supply of liquid assets in the economy? No a priori objective answer can be given to this question since these aggregates combine assets with different degrees of liquidity, and assessments of the degree of difference in the liquidity of components are at least partly subjective.

Before leaving the Federal Reserve's broad measures of the money supply, it may be noted that these measures include mainly obligations of depository institutions which are highly liquid for the reasons brought out in this section. Further reasons why the obligations of depository institutions are particularly important sources of liquidity will be brought out in a later section.

---

[6]As with money-market mutual fund shares, there are analysts who argue that overnight RPs at commercial banks should be included in the M-1B money supply. The argument for including overnight RPs at commercial banks is that they are virtually checkable balances which escape measurement in M-1B since M-1B deposits are measured on a close-of-business-day basis.

[7]The Fed staff has stated that term Eurodollars and overnight Eurodollars at centers other than the Caribbean logically belong in M-3 along with term RPs, but were not included in the February 1980 revised M-3 because of data reporting lags for these assets. See Thomas D. Simpson, "The Redefined Monetary Aggregates," *Federal Reserve Bulletin*, February 1980, 97–114.

Entity liquidity

The discussion of the Federal Reserve's broad measures of the money supply brings out the difficulty involved in identifying the liquidity of individual assets and combining assets with diverse char- *Balance-sheet* acteristics into a single measure of liquid assets for the economy. *and cash flow* The liquidity of an entity is even more difficult to identify. A total *perspectives* balance-sheet perspective is helpful since the relative values and the characteristics of assets *and liabilities* are important. Maturity is the most important characteristic for liabilities. In this respect, an entity is more liquid the longer the maturity of its liabilities. Longer-term debt has more certainty of cost. But this raises the point that balance sheets report only stocks of assets and liabilities— at historical values, usually. Flows are important too. Various ratios employing stocks and flows have been used to gauge the liquidity of firms: the ratio of short-term assets to short-term debt, the ratio of net income to debt maturing within one year, and the ratio of all debt to equity are examples.

The importance of entity liquidity, of course, is that it can deter- mine the ability of a firm, household, or local government to *The availability of* weather a difficult period during which income is temporarily down, *credit* expenses are high, or both. If an entity cannot make it through the short-run, the long-run may be academic. This directs attention to one more important aspect of liquidity at this level: *the availability of credit*. For example, if a firm is assured of borrowing ability through understandings or, if necessary, contractual arrangements and guarantees, it will consider itself more liquid and able to engage in risky endeavors. However, as important as it is, attempts are seldom made to measure the availability of credit; it is a variable which does not show up in balance sheets or income statements and, in any case, would be difficult to quantify.

Aggregate liquidity

The liquidity of the economy as a whole—an extension of entity liquidty—also is difficult to measure. Some measure of total liquid assets is often used but has the drawback just brought out in the previous section—it ignores balance-sheet considerations. The ratio of short-term financial assets to short-term debt will not do either because, in the aggregate, this ratio is always equal to one, neglect- ing federal short-term debt, foreign loans to U.S. entities, and loans abroad. The average debt/equity ratio may be useful for gauging the aggregate liquidity of most firms, but is not similarly applicable to households, governments, or the aggregate economy.

The ratio of gross debt to national income, or GNP, has some usefulness as an aggregate liquidity statisitic, however. As the ap- pendix to Chapter 4 described, net debt for the economy is approxi-

The gross debt/
income ratio for
the aggregate
economy

mately zero, but this does not detract from the value of comparing gross aggregate debt to national income. Interest and amortization payments on debt are usually paid out of current income. If debt rises relative to income, the ability of debtor entities to meet their contractual payments may be strained; moreover, if this occurs because income is falling, the ability of creditor entities to roll over debt and extend new funds to debtor entities diminishes and liquidity declines.

Figure 7–3 presents data for total debt and GNP. As the figure shows, the ratio of debt to GNP rises in major recessions (shaded areas); finer detail would show that it falls in the early stages of expansions and rises again in the later stage of expansions. This implies a fall in the liquidity of the economy in recessions, a rise in the early stage of expansions, and a fall in the later stage of expansions. In terms of components of the ratio, in a recession income falls, but debt remains relatively constant. In the early stage of an expansion, income rises rapidly, and debt rises less rapidly as debtor entities are more able to pay off debt and want to, remembering the burden of debt in the recession. At the later stage of an expansion, new debt is willingly incurred and at a more rapid rate

FIGURE 7–3
Debt in the United States
Debt, end of year; GNP annually

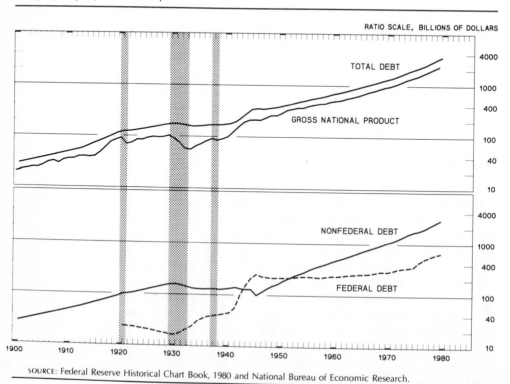

SOURCE: Federal Reserve Historical Chart Book, 1980 and National Bureau of Economic Research.

relative to income. In general, aggregate liquidity is inversely related to the ratio of debt to GNP.

It bears repeating that the ratio of debt to GNP does not present a complete picture of aggregate liquidity, however. And we should warn that this ratio can present a distorted picture when there are credit controls or other factors which curb the availability of credit. In such instances, liquidity in the economy and the ratio of debt to GNP would tend to fall at the same time. (Recall that entity liquidity was related to the availability of credit.)

A decline in liquidity in a recession is to be expected and normally is no cause for special alarm. However, if a recession is particularly severe or protracted, or if the general level of entity liquidity at the outset of a recession happens to be unusually low for some reason, liquidity may reach a critical level such that the threat to the solvency of firms, households, and state and local governments becomes widespread. In short, a liquidity crisis may develop. Financial intermediaries are a key sector determining whether such a crisis becomes self-reinforcing, for reasons suggested briefly in Chapter 1 and to be described in the next two sections.

THE ROLE OF FINANCIAL INTERMEDIARIES AS PROVIDERS OF LIQUIDITY

Financial intermediaries pool funds from surplus entities, providing them with interest and/or services, and pass these funds on to deficit entities. Pooling funds for investment in this way provides two principal advantages: it facilitates diversification and it yields economies of scale in information and management.

Diversification is valuable because it can reduce the risk of unexpected losses on the lending side.[8] Furthermore, for intermediaries, diversification reduces the risk of an unexpected, large net withdrawal of funds on the deposit side. Most importantly, diversification reduces a chance combination of losses and withdrawals which triggers insolvency.[9]

---

[8]This conclusion can be supported in part by an important theorem from statistics. The theorem states that the variance of the sum of n random variables is equal to the sum of their variances and covariances. Subjective estimates of the variance of a return may be taken as a proxy for risk, and diversification permits an entity to take advantage of any negative covariances among investments, thereby reducing total variance and risk of a portfolio. Suppose, for example, that the expected returns on two distinct assets were each $8 per $100, with a variance of $4, and suppose the covariances of the two returns were −$3. Counting the covariance twice as we should, the expected return on a portfolio comprised of equal proportions of the two assets would be $8 per $100 with a variance of $2—the same return with half the risk of the individual investments.

[9]There is another theorem from statistics which is applicable here, but is too complex to be explained in this text. For an application to the deposit side of the intermediary's balance sheet see D. Patinkin, *Money, Interest, and Prices*, 2d ed. (New York: Harper & Row, 1965), pp. 82–88;450–56.

Economies of scale and specialization in the management of funds enable financial intermediaries to asses the risk and expected return characteristics of deficit units better and at less cost than is possible for individual surplus units.

The result of these various benefits of aggregation is that financial intermediaries are able to offer surplus units a higher level of security and perhaps also higher realized returns than would be obtainable by placing funds directly with deficit units. Deficit units, on the other hand, may obtain funds at lower cost and/or with more stable availability than otherwise possible. Intermediaries therefore, when they function properly, improve the cost/return and liquidity characteristics of the debt/asset structures of deficit and surplus entities. This facilitates an increase in the degree of external finance in the economy, providing a more efficient allocation of resources, wider choices, and generally enchanced economic welfare.

The improvement in the liquidity of surplus- and deficit-entity balance sheets through intermediation is apparent if we examine the asset and liability entries of the depository institutions shown in Figure 7–4. Note that, in general, commercial banks, savings and loans, and mutual savings banks provide surplus entities with deposits or other assets of much shorter maturity than the maturity of claims on deficit entities held by these intermediaries. Hence these intermediaries effectively transform the maturity characteristics of assets which flow in the opposite direction to the flow of funds. The default risk associated with the assets supplied to surplus entities is also generally lower. We conclude, therefore, that financial intermediaries in general, and depository institutions in particular, play a major role in creating liquidity in the economy. This conclusion provides one further reason, promised in an earlier section, for an emphasis on the obligations of depository institutions in the Federal Reserve's broad money-supply measures.[10]

The special role of commercial banks

It bears noting also that, among the various types of intermediaries, commercial banks are of prime importance as providers of liquidity. This is partly because of their size and because their liabilities are so liquid, but there is another reason to single out commercial banks. Commercial banks are relied upon by nonfinancial firms, other financial intermediaries, local governments, and other entities (schools, for example) as a source of funds when other, normal sources become unavailable. In other words, commercial banks are the principal insurers of credit availability for many entities. Banks encourage and capitalize on this role by granting credit lines and loan commitments for which they charge separate fees.

---

[10]Still another reason is that most of these obligations are insured by an agency of the federal government.

FIGURE 7–4
Balance sheets for
three major types of financial intermediaries

ALL COMMERCIAL BANKING INSTITUTIONS
Balance Sheet
December 1978
($ billions)

Assets		*Liabilities*	
Currency ....$	15.5	Demand deposits ....$	418.9
Reserve deposits		Time deposits	630.0
at Federal Reserve	35.0	Borrowings	144.0
Other cash items	146.3	Other liabilities	81.2
U.S. Treasury		Total	
securities	94.5	liabilities $1,274.1	
Other securities	177.0		
Commercial and		Net Worth ....$	95.5
industrial loans	251.2		
Other loans	574.4		
Other assets	75.9		
Total assets $1,369.7			

SAVINGS AND LOAN ASSOCIATIONS
Balance Sheet
December 1978
($ billions)

Assets		*Liabilities*	
Cash and		Savings shares.............. .$	431.0
investment		Other	63.6
securities ....$	44.9	Total	
Mortgages	432.9	liabilities ....$	494.6
Other	45.9		
Total assets ....$	523.6	Net worth ....$	29.0

MUTUAL SAVINGS BANKS
Balance Sheet
December 1978
($ billions)

Assets		*Liabilities*	
Cash ....$	3.7	Deposits ....$	142.7
Securities	48.0	Other	
Mortgages	95.2	liabilities	4.6
Other loans	7.2	Total	
Other assets	4.1	liabilities ....$	147.3
Total assets ....$	158.2	Net worth ....$	10.9

SOURCE: Federal Reserve *Bulletin,* June 1979

The nature of a liquidity crisis

From the perspective of economic stability, the drawback to intermediation and external finance, of course, is that the process does
not always function smoothly and can break down in the absence of
adequate safeguards and management. The system becomes particularly strained when aggregate economic conditions are poorer

than expected. Nonfinancial firms, households, and state and local governments which have not provided adequately for adverse economic conditions (i.e., enough liquid assets to draw upon to cushion lower income) require additional external finance *if they can get it.* If additional finance is not available because banks and other intermediaries have inadequate reserves or are not able to raise enough new deposits, obligations of entities experiencing difficulty may not be met. This, in turn, can place a strain on creditors which have obligations or plans based on expectations of timely payment.

Financial intermediaries are highly leveraged creditors. Hence, in a general downturn, the solvency of many financial intermediaries, in turn, may become suspect. Unless holders of liquid claims on intermediaries are protected from loss by insurance or somehow legally prevented from exercising their claims, the laws of probability no longer sustain the intermediary—withdrawals or other exercise of claims become nonrandom, indeed a flood, and sources of new funds tend to disappear.

When intermediaries begin to fail and cut back on lending, there can be a considerable decrease in the supply of liquidity and credit at the very time when demand is at its greatest. The result is a severe shock to an economy which is already headed down. Commercial-bank failures are particularly serious because banks are key providers of liquidity and because failures of commercial banks are more disruptive to the payments process.

In today's economy, financial intermediaries are regulated, and the supply of liquidity can be augmented by a number of government agencies. Much of the regulation of intermediaries is designed to prevent the widespread failures which have occurred in the past. (The development of U.S. government regulation and control in the money and credit area will be described in Part 3.)

INTRODUCTION TO ARTICLE

In a period of buoyant growth and optimism, nonfinancial firms often borrow heavily to finance expansion of plant and equipment. Then, when a peak in economic activity arrives unexpectedly, firms can be excessively encumbered with debt and half-finished capital projects. At this stage of the business cycle, for various reasons including, often, tight monetary policy, short-term interest rates tend to move higher relative to long-term interest rates, and the availability of long-term credit dries up because of investors' concern about the risk of bankruptcies and higher inflation. This leaves some firms in particularly precarious low-liquidity positions as sales rates drop and firms are forced to turn to high-cost bank loans to bridge the cash-flow gap. The following *Business Week* article describes this situation which existed on a worldwide scale in the summer of 1974, about midway through the severe recession of 1973–75.

The Worldwide Liquidity Shortage

"You've got a situation in Europe and Japan parallel to what you have in the U.S.," says Thomas L. Chrystie, head of underwriting at Merrill Lynch, Pierce, Fenner & Smith. "Whether it's debt or equity, it's a very difficult market in which to get long-term money."

It takes capital in monumental quantities to feed the world economy, but today there is an increasingly critical shortage of long-term capital. With stock prices disappointingly low and short-term interest rates temptingly high, investors all over the world are wary about equities and chary about commitments to long-term debt. Inflation, racing faster in most countries than that in the U.S., contributes to investors' disillusion and keeps them out of long-term markets.

Investors—including the Arabs with their oil billions—are staying short or getting out of paper investments altogether, shifting into gold, for instance, and into real estate. This is true both in the national markets abroad and in the international markets that have grown vast over the past decade. Roy C. Smith, a vice president of Goldman, Sachs International, estimates the volume of Eurobond issues in the first half of 1974 at less than $1 billion versus nearly $3 billion in the first half of 1973.

The results of this lack of enthusiasm by investors are twofold. First, stock prices are sinking. In every major market around the world, equities are down significantly from their 1972 highs. In some countries, such as Britain, where the *Financial Times* index recently touched its lowest point in 15 years, they are down dramatically. Billions of dollars' worth of stock values have been wiped out, and each new jolt sends prices lower. The failure last week of Bankhaus I. D. Herstatt, the big German private bank, gave investors still more bad news to fret about.

The second consequence of investor disinterest is likely to be graver still over the long run. Since most companies are unable to finance long-term, the great majority are being obliged to finance short-term—generally with banks and at suffocatingly high rates. But no company can go very long borrowing short-

term to invest long-term. Even if companies wanted to do things this way, the state of the foreign markets is such today that no one can be certain that even short-term money will be available when needed.

The loan-money mirage

No bank has unlimited resources, and this is particularly true today when most nations are using increasingly tight monetary policy to cope with inflation. Enormous quantities of whatever money is available must go to pay those staggering oil bills. The oil-producing nations do have money, of course, but they are being very picky about where they place it. Most of the oil money that has been reinvested thus far—some $15 billion, according to Robert O. Blomquist, a senior vice president of Chase Manhattan Bank—has gone into Eurodollar deposits in a relatively small number of banks, mostly the London branches of the big U.S. banks. Moreover, the money is being invested for extremely short periods—often just overnight. Nor does Minos A. Zombanakis, managing director of First Boston (Europe), see evidence that the Arabs are about to start investing long, rather than short, in the economies of the developed world. "Arab governments," says Zombanakis, "simply shy away from environments where they cannot control the destiny of their investments. They have fears of nationalization in many countries."

So more and more would-be borrowers willing to settle for short-term money cannot get even that. In Italy, a U.S. financial executive reports: "The banks have long lines of clients waiting for the first available lire."

A few companies—Bowater is a recent example—have been able to obtain financing overseas through medium-term loans from international banking syndicates. Borrowers get the money for seven years or more, but the rate "floats" every six months in line with the London rate for Eurodollars. But this market, according to Blomquist of Chase, "has shifted from commercially oriented to government oriented," and the few companies able to borrow in it are "world class."

Some banks, particularly in London, are now restricting their international loan participations exclusively to corporate customers of the very highest credit quality. And some clearly wish they were not involved in making this sort of loan at all, since the available supply of money is becoming so tight. "Banks that have committed themselves to floating-rate loans may not be able to refinance their commitments," warns Zombanakis.

This is a potentially staggering development because so much of the world economy in recent years has been financed by these medium-term, floating-rate loans. The market provided $22 billion in 1973 and another $14 billion in the first quarter of this year. The banks in this market are household names: Chase, Manufacturers Hanover, First National City Bank, National Westminster of England, France's Société Générale. But even these titans must cut back on loan commitments because they cannot be sure of getting all the money they need.

The common denominator

If these giant international markets are tense, the domestic markets abroad are virtually hysterical. James J. Needham, chairman of the New York Stock Exchange, says that markets abroad are "filled with despair about capital-raising—every problem we have, the other exchanges share."

SOURCE: Reprinted from *Business Week,* July 6, 1974, by special permission. © 1974 by McGraw-Hill, Inc., All rights reserved.

INTRODUCTION TO ARTICLE

The severe recession which began in December of 1973 ended in February of 1975. By mid-1976 the economy was well into recovery and the previous precarious liquidity position of the economy, described in the *Business Week* article above, was replaced by a much improved environment. As the *Business Week* article below describes, however, too much liquidity can also be a cause for concern. It subsequently turned out that, excess liquidity did not fuel an outburst of excessive spending in 1976. As often happens, it took longer than expected for the economy to develop excesses. Spending, inflation, and interest rates did not really take off until 1978.

The Recovery Produces a Flood of Liquidity

As the nation enters its second year of economic recovery, consumers, businessmen, and bankers are paying off their debts and rebuilding their cash resources at a faster rate than in any upswing since World War II. As a result, there is much less pressure on the financial markets to finance the rebound, and the increased liquidity offers the promise of support for a durable recovery well into 1977, and perhaps beyond.

The fact that the economy is awash with liquidity may be a mixed blessing, however. In the first place, it stems in part from the lackluster performance of capital spending. And some economists are cautioning that if the new liquidity manages to spur too much spending, it could thereby re-ignite inflation.

Since late 1974 corporations and consumers have paid off short-term debt and boosted savings from greatly improved profits and personal incomes. Furthermore, some companies have reduced their short-term debt by borrowing in the bond market or selling equity. The tax cut of 1975, the rapid slowing of inflation, and cost-cutting by business also helped in the process. Now both business and consumers have plenty of cash or easily convertible assets, mostly short-term government securities, on hand to help them finance current expenditures without borrowing heavily. In 1975, commercial banks bought $30 billion worth of short-term government securities, and nonfinancial corporations bought $11 billion worth. Corporate cash flow has risen almost 30 percent over the past year, and personal savings increased $15 billion, or 17 percent.

This liquidity buildup is a major reason why bank loan demand has remained surprisingly weak and interest rates have risen very little even in the face of a vigorous economic recovery. And most economists are predicting that because there is so much liquidity in the economy, bank loan demand will remain relatively soft and interest rates will rise only moderately over the next year—even while the economy moves into an expansion phase and both inventory building and capital spending gather momentum.

More intense.

A recent report by Lionel D. Edie & Co. predicts that by mid-1977 the key federal funds rate, to which other short-term interest rates are pegged, will rise only about one percentage point from the current level of 5½ percent. "As the recovery continues this year, the expansion in cash flow will fairly well match the growth in capital spending and inventory investment," says Edie economist Carol A. Stone. "Next year the strengthening in plant and equipment outlays is expected to outstrip the growth in cash flow, and increasing amounts of external funds will be required." she continues. "But the ability of corporations to handle expanding business activity has been greatly enhanced by the rebuilding of corporate liquidity."

Allen Sinai, financial economist for Data Resources Inc., goes further: "Every sector will have the wherewithal in stored-up liquidity to keep expenditures going much longer than in previous postwar recoveries." Such "reliquification" is typical of economic recoveries, but according to Sinai, it has been much more intense this time, in part because the combination of inflation and recession ravaged balance sheets so badly. "The restructuring of balance sheets has been unprecedented, and the economy now has a solid financial base," he says. He notes that it is unique for companies still to be building liquidity and to finance spending almost solely from cash flow at this stage in the recovery.

Nobody disagrees that the strengthening of financial conditions in the past two years has been healthy, but at least one economist questions whether the financial foundation is really all that solid. "Liquidity has improved considerably, but you must view it in a historical perspective," says Henry Kaufman, chief economist and partner at Salomon Bros. "Compared to 10 or 20 years ago, the liquidity measures show that there is still substantial indebtedness," he says. Although Kaufman admits that there is "no magic formula" to determine what is an adequate amount of liquidity, he maintains that current levels are insufficient to support nominal economic growth, the combination of real growth and inflation, in "double digits."

Limitations.

Most economists think Kaufman is dead wrong. They are predicting that nominal economic growth will be in double digits for the next year, with real gross national product expanding at a rate of 5% to 6% and inflation rising at about the same pace. And the consensus view is that the economy will be able to sustain that growth without serious strains. Some economists, however, worry that because there is so much liquidity in the economy, it will be difficult to keep growth within those bounds.

"Liquidity is inherently expansionary; it energizes the economy," say Albert T. Sommers, an economist at the Conference Board and a member of Democratic Presidential nominee Jimmy Carter's economic advisory team. "The principal impact of liquidity is to increase the propensity to spend," he explains. "I am not worried about liquidity per se, but how much of the potential spending it represents is translated into inflation and how much becomes production," he adds. As Sommers sees it, the U.S., like other modern industrial societies, is inflation prone, and the recent buildup in liquidity could lead to "another round of cyclical inflation on top of secular inflation."

Limited powers

To complicate matters further, Sommers, like many other nonmonetarist economists, believes that the Federal Reserve's powers to control such a potential inflationary explosion are limited when the economy is very liquid.

"The cutting edge of Fed policy is blunted because it works through commercial banks, and their role is diminished when there is much less need to borrow," he says. A Federal Reserve Board official agrees: "The more liquid the economy, the more time it takes for monetary policy to bite."

For monetarist economists it is not a question of whether the Fed has the economic muscle to prevent the recovery from developing into a painfully familiar inflationary boom-or-bust pattern, but whether it has the political will to do so. "The improvement in liquidity helped defuse a potential conflict between rising interest rates and the Fed's monetary growth targets," says Jerry Jordan, chief economist for Pittsburgh National Bank. Clearly, the rebuilding of liquidity enabled the Treasury Department to float a record amount of debt without exerting upward pressure on interest rates.

As long as interest rates remain relatively stable, Fed Chairman Arthur Burns's numerous Democratic critics will not press him to adopt a more expansive policy. But Jordan and others fear that this could quickly change, especially in an election year, if interest rates now begin to rise rapidly as business and households use up their liquid assets. "To convert liquid assets into cash you have to induce someone not to spend, and you do that by raising yields on the assets," he says. "I am skeptical that you can have such a transfer from one sector to an-

other, especially if it is from the consumer sector to the business sector, without pushing up interest rates significantly." Jordan is predicting that the fed funds rate will rise by "more than two percentage points" by mid-1977.

Most economists do not see the Fed being squeezed by a policy dilemma because they believe there is enough capacity, both physical and financial, to prevent a reacceleration of inflation or a sharp rise in interest rates. "The arguments that inflation and interest rates will take off imply that we are operating much closer to full employment of men, machines, and financial resources than is actually the case," says Sinai. And while he agrees with Jordan that using up available liquidity means transferring assets from one sector to another, strong upward pressures on interest rates will occur only if everyone tries to sell off at once, which "based on the evidence is highly improbable," he notes.

"In past cycles, selling off assets was not synchronized," explains Sinai. Adds a Fed official: "A substantial part of the liquidity buildup has been for safety purposes, and there is no evidence that consumers, businessmen, or bankers are becoming less prudent with their dollars. On the contrary, inventory building and capital investment are still very moderate."

SOURCE: Reprinted from *Business Week*, July 26, 1976, by special permission. © 1976 by McGraw-Hill, Inc. All rights reserved.

INTEREST-RATE SPREADS

We have now developed enough explanation of financial relationships, the calculation of market interest rates, and the importance of liquidity to introduce the topic of interest-rate spreads. Why are some interest rates higher or lower than others, and why do differences change over time? There are seven principal factors which distinguish financial assets and affect the behavior of their yield differentials: method of yield calculation, taxability, risk of default, marketability, maturity, seasoning, and interest ceilings.

Method of yield calculation

As explained in Chapter 6, the method of calculating yields can make a difference in yield levels. For example, the market yield on commercial paper is usually below the yield on CDs of similar maturity and risk. This is simply because the commercial-paper rate is a discount yield and the CD yield is an interest-to-follow (ITF) yield. Because of the way the formulas work, this particular spread tends to be higher the higher market interest rates are. In general, one important step in making investment decisions is to adjust market yields for this type of difference in calculation before comparisons are drawn.

Taxability

Most financial investors are subject to income and capital gains taxes; hence, in general, it is after-tax returns which count. Differences in return taxability are especially important for high-income households and for corporations.[11] Other considerations aside, the most attractive assets from this standpoint are municipal bonds. Interest income from municipal bonds is exempt from federal taxes and often from state and local taxes in the state in which they are issued. The interest returns on U.S. government securities and some Federal financing agencies' debt are exempt from state and local taxes, but not from federal taxes. The tax advantage of these securities means that they do not have to offer as high a yield as otherwise would be necessary to attract investors. As Figure 7–5 shows, the municipal bond yield is usually lower than the yield on U.S. government bonds. The difference between these yields has fluctuated, however. One reason is a third consideration to which we now turn.

Risk of default

Investors must consider, in practically every case, the possibility that a debtor entity will not live up to its obligations. In the worst possible case the return and the investment are completely lost. This seldom happens, however. Usually debtor difficulty leads to stretched-out payments, implying a lower yield or partial loss on the investment. U.S. government securities are the only domestic securities considered virtually immune from such risk, mainly because the United States is stable politically and the federal government has, through the Federal Reserve, the power to create the money with which to meet its obligations, if necessary. State and municipal governments do not have this power and can encounter difficulties, as described in the article on New York City in Chapter 4.

Corporate obligations are, of course, very much subject to this risk. Figure 7–5 shows historical yields for corporate bonds rated Aaa, the highest credit rating, and Baa, three ranks below Aaa, by Moody's Investors Service. The difference in these yields is ac-

---

[11]When one allows for both income and capital-gains taxes, the after-tax money rate of interest, j, is

$$j = (1 - t_y) \, i_y + (1 - t_c) \, i_c$$

where t_y is the marginal income-tax rate, t_c the capital-gains tax rate for the entity in question, and i_y and i_c are the interest-income and capital-gains return rates on a taxable asset. The formula given in Chapter 6 for the after-tax, real rate of interest neglected the capital-gains tax rate because Treasury-bill capital gains are treated as income for tax purposes.

FIGURE 7–5
Long-term bond yields

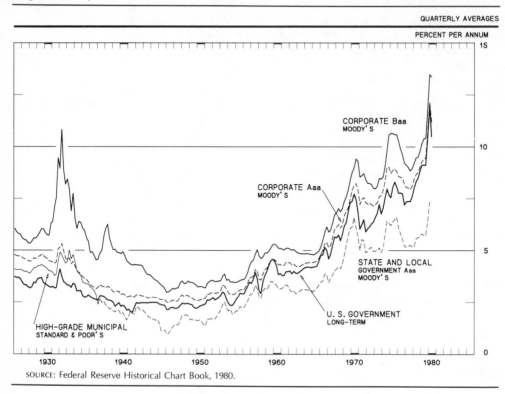

QUARTERLY AVERAGES

PERCENT PER ANNUM

CORPORATE Baa
MOODY'S

CORPORATE Aaa
MOODY'S

STATE AND LOCAL
GOVERNMENT Aaa
MOODY'S

U. S. GOVERNMENT
LONG-TERM

HIGH–GRADE MUNICIPAL
STANDARD & POOR'S

SOURCE: Federal Reserve Historical Chart Book, 1980.

counted for by risk of default. Risk of default, of course, was one of those characteristics of an asset which we identified as a determinant of asset liquidity.

INTRODUCTION TO ARTICLE

The credit ratings assigned to various debt securities by private investor-service companies are very important to firms and governments issuing debt, as well as to investors, since they affect the cost of credit to these entities. This *Wall Street Journal* article describes instances of pressure on these rating firms from borrowing entities and also provides a glimpse of the methods used for determining ratings as of October 1976.

The rating game: credit-grading firms wield greater power in public debt market

NEW YORK—The credit-rating business has come out of the closet, into the spotlight—and sometimes into battle.

Long important to professional investors in debt securities, the major credit-rating services—Moody's Investors Services Inc. and

Standard & Poor's Corp.—in the past few years have acquired considerable public visibility as well. Their evaluations of the creditworthiness of debt-issuing corporations and governmental bodies not only are strongly influencing investment decisions but also, in the case of municipal securities, are provoking headlines in newspapers and heartburn in politicians.

In publishing their ratings, the services often are largely determining the interest rate that a debt issuer must pay. Occasionally, they are, in effect, deciding who can or cannot raise capital in the public debt market and thus who can or cannot build a factory or a school building. Inevitably; such decisions are plunging the rating services into some heated disputes.

Changed environment

The heat has been most obviously generated by New York City's long-running flirtation with financial disaster. But interest in the activities of Moody's and Standard & Poor's has been increasing, not only in financial centers but also in small towns all across the country, for many other reasons, too. Bond specialists cite the following:

Increased trading in and out of bond issues by financial institutions, with some of that activity geared to the possibility of changes in the debt issuer's credit rating.

Increased participation in the market by unsophisticated investors, who have been attracted by the climb in bond interest rates in recent years but who themselves lack the expertise to evaluate bond issues.

Increased awareness of the threat of default.

At first glance, credit ratings have a disarming simplicity about them. The best bonds, carrying the least risk, are rated Aaa by Moody's and AAA by S&P; high quality is designated Aa (or AA by S&P); upper medium grade, A at both services; medium grade Baa (or BBB); and so on, down through various degrees of speculative risk to issues in default. Both services also show further gradations, such as S&P's pluses and minuses.

Yet the ratings really aren't simple at all. They are based on a welter of financial data supplied by the bond issuer, on various ledger ratios, on forecasts of such imponderables as

population trends, on guesses about the outcomes of lawsuits—in short, on a complicated morass of indications about whether the debtor will be able to repay the debt.

High Stakes

Furthermore, the stakes are high. Ratings have a direct impact on an issuer's borrowing costs—currently, a single A-rated corporation would have to pay about 0.25 percentage point more in annual interest on a new issue than a double-A borrower would, and within the past year the rate spread has ranged as high as a full percentage point. Because of the size of many issues, millions of dollars in interest payments are involved.

The stakes also are high for financial institutions. "Bond-market investors, particularly institutions, no longer buy a bond and then hold it until maturity," a senior bond trader observes. "They play with bonds in much the same way they play with stocks. They buy and sell and try to capitalize on certain situations—like rating changes—that may arise." Their efforts to squeeze out extra profits through trading in anticipation of rating changes have been facilitated by the greater number of such changes; in 1974, for example, about 750 corporate issues underwent rating changes of at least one full grade, against only about 200 in 1969.

And the stakes are high for individual investors. Salomon Brothers, a leading bond house, estimates that as of January 1 about $278 billion of bonds was held by individuals, up sharply from $227 billion two years before. These small buyers, generally knowing little about bonds or bond issuers, have to depend heavily on the agencies' ratings.

"The institutions have a great deal of their own research capability and may capitalize on a rating change," a senior retail salesman says. "But the individual doesn't have that capability and can suffer from a downgrading. Thus, there is more pressure exerted on Moody's and S&P to be accurate."

Threat of default

The ultimate threat to any bond buyer, large or small, is the possiblity that the borrower won't be able to pay interest and principal when due. The threat of default, long considered a hangover from the depression years, suddenly has seemed very real indeed in the wake of New York's woes, the Penn Central Transportation bankruptcy proceedings, and the W. T. Grant Company collapse.

In addition, the recent, lingering recession came on the heels of years of steadily rising debt and steadily deteriorating liquidity all through the economy. The deterioration can be seen clearly in the electric-utility industry; currently, only two utilities—Dallas Power & Light Company and Texas Power & Light Company, both owned by Texas Utilities Company—are rated triple-A by both rating agencies, compared with 17 in 1971.

At a time when more people than ever before are worried about the quality of bond issues, the credit-rating agencies have some problems of their own. Their rating methods are often attacked. So are their conclusions. They have difficulty holding on to competent personnel. And they face a threat of federal control over their operations.

But despite their problems, both agencies are prosperous. In 1975, pretax profit of Standard & Poor's, a subsidiary of McGraw-Hill Inc., surged to about $4 million from $2.9 million in 1974. Moody's figures aren't disclosed by Dun & Bradstreet, its parent company, but the parent's 1975 annual report said Moody's had chalked up record results for the third consecutive year.

Moody's and S&P have played the rating game for half a century. Both rate not only corporate and municipal bonds but also private placements, commercial paper, preferred stocks, and debt issued by foreign governments and companies. Last year Moody's rated 692 corporate issues and 1,250 municipals; S&P graded 470 corporates and 1,440 municipals. (A third service, Fitch Investors Service Inc., is smaller and best known for rating banks.)

Both Moody's and S&P derive their revenues from fees charged the debt issuers for the ratings and from various investment publications. Rating fees are based on the amount of work required and generally range from $500 to $15,000. S&P, whose operating revenue totaled $38.3 million last year began charging for municipal ratings in 1968 and for corporates in

1974. Moody's instituted charges in 1970.

Moody's is the older of the two; it began by rating corporates in 1909. Some wags think it still is only emerging from the Victorian era. Visitors to company headquarters in lower Manhattan must obtain passes to get past the guards, and in its rating area rows on rows of desks are staffed mostly by males dressed with unrelenting sobriety.

Two key officials

At S&P, the atmosphere is markedly more relaxed and, possibly, more publicity conscious. The pattern is set by S&P's 48-year-old president and chief executive officer, Brenton W. Harries, who appears to be perpetually at ease, is highly articulate, and has a knack for dominating without appearing pushy. During his 4½ years at the helm, Mr. Harries has greatly expanded S&P's operations, which had been far smaller than Moody's.

Aides say that when it comes to Mr. Harries, there isn't much middle ground. "You either love the guy or you hate his guts," an S&P executive says. "You either feel he is pushing you to better things or you feel he is pushing you . . . period."

Moody's most highly visible official recently has been Jackson Phillips, its 55-year-old vice president in charge of municipal ratings. (Its president, named last January, is John D. Lockton, 40, formerly executive vice president of Funk & Wagnalls Inc., a book publisher also owned by Dun & Bradstreet.) It was Mr. Phillips who caught the barrage of criticism leveled at Moody's last spring when the agency sharply downgraded the bonds of the Municipal Assistance Corporation, the New York State body set up to help rescue New York City

Mr. Phillips, a rather slight, soft-spoken former Texan who could easily pass as a high-school geometry teacher, refers to Mr. Harries as "flamboyant." He defends the formal atmosphere at Moody's and takes a subtle jab at Mr. Harries. "The nature of the job—studying income, cash flow, and things like that—demands that we operate in this manner," he says. "We deal in numbers and judgments of what those numbers mean. We can't function at our proper efficiency if we become too relaxed."

But a critic of Mr. Phillips jabs back. "If you lined up Phillips and Harries next to one another, you would think one of them was dead . . . and it sure as hell wouldn't be Harries," he says.

Working under the top people is the power-wielding core of the business, the rating analysts. Moody's has 58 and S&P 47. Most are relatively young "scholarly, student types," Mr. Phillips says. Moody's trainees all hold master's degrees in business administration; S&P hires some with only bachelor's degrees but trains them extensively.

In appraising a new issue, a rater scrutinizes the statistical and other information. Besides numbers on income and cash flow (for a corporation, cash flow is net income plus depreciation), such considerations as future borrowing plans are weighed. Some figures are combined to form significant ratios, like fixed-charge coverage (the number of times annual interest obligations are covered by after-tax income). Analysts say a coverage ratio of five or more usually would produce a triple-A rating, for example, and a ratio between four and five would produce a double A.

Another ratio closely watched by raters is the issuer's cash flow divided by long-term debt; they say a figure of about 65 percent would warrant a tripple-A, 45 percent a double-A, and so on down the line. When key ratios give conflicting signals, of course, the problems of reaching an evaluation become more difficult.

Besides looking at numbers, the rater may visit the issuing company or municipality and interview various financial officials. Or the rater himself may be visited by a top official pleading his case; well-known governors and mayors, including Jimmy Carter when he was governor of Georgia, have put in their pitches in hopes of getting higher ratings—and thus lower interest costs. Much of this interplay between raters and issuers is pure public relations, however. Mr. Harries says he has never heard of a bribe being offered to a rating analyst.

"Tips" often help

To keep tabs on issuers, raters subscribe to countless newspapers to learn of any local event that would affect a rating. And Hyman C. Grossman, S&P's vice president for municipal ratings, says: "Often we get help from an unexpected source. We'll get a call from a bond trader, a frustrated taxpayer, or a local-government official with a 'tip' which, of course, we check out."

The rater's initial evaluation of a new issue takes an average of 10 to 12 man-hours, Mr. Grossman estimates. In problem situations, however, much more extensive research is required. "On recent ratings for issues by Philadelphia and Detroit, for example," Mr. Grossman says, "I'd say that 20 man-hours were used on each. With issues like those, we want to stay very current on specific figures, like revenue-sharing, that can change very dramatically in a short time." If an existing issue is being reviewed—a task performed at least once a year—the analyst often is already familiar with the security, and much less time is involved.

The analyst presents his appraisal, whether of a new or existing issue, before a four-to-six-person rating committee, which makes the final decision. At Moody's, a unanimous vote is required before a rating is published. At S&P, a majority vote rules, but if junior staffers outvote the panel's senior members, a new group is likely to take over the rating job. To reach its decision, a committee may take anywhere from five minutes to all day.

Throughout the rating process, the agencies are heavily dependent on the judgment and quality of their raters—and the young analysts are constantly being lured away as soon as they learn the ropes. The problem has been aggravated by the movement of the big bond houses into their own research, because they pay far more than the $11,000 to $20,000 a year offered by the rating services. A striking example occurred about a year ago, when H. Russell Fraser, 3½-year-old chief of S&P's corporate department, was hired away by Paine, Webber, Jackson & Curtis Inc. to head its new fixed-income research department for $100,000 a year.

Another problem faced by the agencies is that they heavily depend on numbers tabulated by the debt issuers themselves, and it isn't always easy to pick out phony figures. This difficulty, coupled with the numbers of debt securities issued all across the country, leads some doubters to wonder how the rating agencies could possibly keep up with such a kaleidoscopic situation, particularly with small towns.

Replies Mr. Phillips: "Some small municipalities present very good figures, which are very professionally done. Others don't. If they don't, we don't rate them."

The agencies also sometimes get into hot water when they look at the same data and reach different conclusions. Such was the case when Moody's suddenly dropped "an absolute bombshell," as one trader puts it, by slashing the rating of the Municipal Assistance Corporation three grades in one day—and S&P didn't budge at all.

Announcing the downgrading, Moody's noted "the question as to whether MAC can carry out its agreements and the prospect of bankruptcy action by the city (which would certainly involve the MAC financing)."

However, S&P, in its publication, *The Fixed Income Investor,* said: "Our rating of these bonds is based on certain assumptions: . . . that tax revenue will not be attached in the event of a New York City bankruptcy . . . Legal opinions have been received from the state's attorney general and bond counsel that these are revenues of the state's and can't be attached in the event of a New York City bankruptcy."

Thus, the discrepancy was simple: One agency saw the tax revenues backing the MAC bonds being attached for some other purpose if the city went bankrupt, and the other didn't.

Threat in Congress

The resulting discrepancy in their MAC ratings—single B at Moody's and single A plus at S&P—is the sort of thing that critics of the rating agencies decry. Indeed, a bill was introduced in the recently ended session of Congress to allow the Securities and Exchange Commission to order a rating agency to issue a new rating for an issuer that the SEC thinks was rated incorrectly.

S&P's Mr. Harries has grave doubts about the proposal.

"Although this bill doesn't say it (is designed to help) issuers that are rated lower than

they think they should be, I assume that to be the intent," he says, "because I can't imagine an issuer complaining to the SEC for being rated higher than it thought it deserved."

Calling the bill "unworkable and potentially damaging to the issuer," Mr. Harries adds that "an SEC-directed rating would result in a rating that would have no credibility with investors. We (S&P) would not publish an SEC rating, and the bonds would become unrated. This would result in greatly restricted marketability."

The bill died, but rating specialists believe that the idea is quite alive. Basically, of course, much of the momentum behind the proposal comes from the fact that in rating municipalities, the agencies also, in large part, are rating politicians, and not all politicians enjoy the analysis.

Provoking the trouble?

Political leaders, indeed, often claim that the problems of their municipalites arise from a low credit rating itself. Do the agencies feel inhibited by the possibility that a bad rating can actually provoke trouble for a city?

Replies Mr. Harries: "Things like that can't enter into a rater's decision. It is up to an issuer to keep its house in order. All we do is evaluate their performance," Moody's Mr. Phillips agrees. "We aren't the causers of problems, we are the reporters of them." And, a securities trader says, "The rating change isn't likely to spur more troubles because somehow a bond will change in value a month or so before a rating change. The word gets out that this or that credit is improving or sliding, and the market reacts."

The raters also say they never have been bullied into assigning a desired rating, and they proudly cite the MAC downgrading. MAC threatened to sue Moody's and also sought to have the service disqualified from rating its securities. Neither event came to pass, and Mr. Phillips says, "There's no threat that can make me change my mind on the MAC downgrading."

Mr. Harries is equally adamant. What he calls the "two strongest assets" of a credit-rating agency, "independence and credibility," have never really been questioned, he says.

"Our independence was really tested in 1971," he recalls. "We had to reduce to triple B from single A the rating of a large company . . . and never hesitated."

The company was McGraw-Hill, which owns S&P.

SOURCE: Michael L. Geczi, "The Rating Game: Credit-Grading Firms Wield Greater Power in Public Debt Market," *The Wall Street Journal*, October 26, 1976.

Marketability

The influence of marketability is quite straight-forward. Since marketability is a desirable characteristic of assets, debtors who are able to offer obligations which are more marketable than others will be able to attract investors with a lower yield than otherwise necessary. On the other hand, for most publicly issued obligations, borrowers have to pay registration fees and make certain disclosures. Then the degree of public acceptance of an issue tends to be a function of whether the issue is rated and, additionally, whether the borrower is a well-known name in the market. In any case, highly marketable assets have a clear advantage over others, and this affects their comparative yields.

Maturity

The spread between yields on assets which are similar in all respects except maturity is the most important and difficult spread to explain. It is also the most fascinating. There are three principal theories that have been advanced on this spread by economists and credit-market analysts who have been interested in the pattern of interest rates over the maturity spectrum, or what is known as *the term structure of interest rates.* These theories go by a variety of names. Here, we will refer to them as *the pure-expectations hypothesis, the liquidity-premium hypothesis,* and *the preferred-habitat hypothesis.*

Before discussing these theories, let us first establish a few facts by reference to Figure 7–6 which shows the historical relationship between the yields on short-term and long-term obligations of prime corporate borrowers.[12] The obligations represented have had similar risks of default, degrees of marketability, and approximately the same degree of taxability.[13] Hence these yields are closely comparable in every respect except maturity.

---

[12]The short-term commercial paper rate has not been adjusted to an ITF basis. The adjustments necessary to bring a three-month discount instrument up to an ITF or bond-yield equivalent basis are relatively small—less than 10 basis points for most of the period shown. The adjustment would be greater for a longer-term discount instrument. (Recall that the example in Chapter 6 which required a 70 basis-point adjustment was for a one-year Treasury bill.)

[13]The tax rate on a corporate bond is lower if it is purchased at a discount and held for long-term capital gains.

FIGURE 7–6
Long- and short-term interest rates

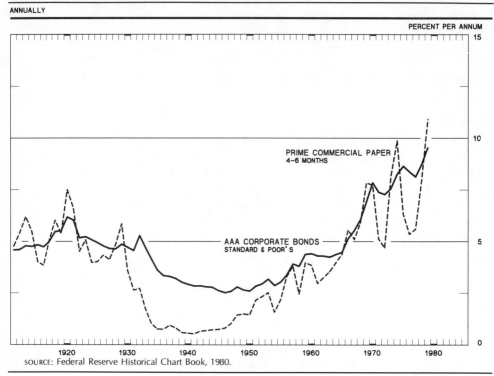

ANNUALLY

SOURCE: Federal Reserve Historical Chart Book, 1980.

Characteristics of
the history of
interest rates since
1910

There are several generalizations which can be made from the history shown and which are worth remembering: (1) the long-term bond yield tends to lie above the yield for the short-term instrument—certainly this is true on average. (2) The short-term yield has, on occasion, risen above the long-term yield; when this has happened, the long-term yield has usually been at a high level relative to its position in the immediately proceeding period and, often, following periods. (3) Both yields trended downward during the period 1920 to 1940 and trended upward during the period since World War II.

The pure-
expectations
hypothesis

The pure-expectations hypothesis explains the relationship between equivalent short-term and long-term yields at a particular moment in time by arguing that most investors—or at least a sufficiently large, well-financed class of investors—will move back and forth between short- and long-term assets according merely to which type of assets is expected to have the highest realized yield over a given holding period.

To develop the logic of this theory we will assume you are an investor who wishes to place funds in interest-bearing securities for one year. (The assumption of a one-year holding period is not necessary to the theory but is convenient for our explanation.) Consider the option of (1) buying a 1-year corporate note and holding it to maturity, or (2) buying a 20-year corporate bond, holding it for a year, and then selling it for whatever its market price is at the end of the year. Which do you choose? According to the pure expectations hypothesis, you will choose the second option if the bond's expected realized yield over one year (that is, after allowance for expected capital gain or loss between purchase and sale) is greater than the yield on the one-year note. You will choose the first option if, on the other hand, the note yield is higher than the expected realized yield on the bond.

Now, if this type of behavior characterizes a sufficiently large segment of securities investors and if investors as a group are not wedded to any particular holding period, relative demands for these securities in response to the highest expected realized return will cause note and bond market yields (which are yields to maturity) to adjust such that, in equilibrium, there is no difference in realized yields expected over any given holding period.

Suppose, for example, that the realized yield expected on long-term bonds held for a year. is higher than the market yield on one-year notes. Investors will tend to sell notes and buy bonds, driving up the note rate and bringing down the bond rate in the market. These adjustments will bring both the market rates and the expected rates over a one-year holding period closer; and, since movement out of notes and into bonds would continue as long as a differential in expected realized rates existed, expected realized rates would be brought into equality in equilibrium.

The next step in the theory maintains that securities markets adjust extremely rapidly to changes in expectations so it is not unreasonable to assume that these markets are always in equilibrium. This and the previous analysis mean that, *according to our first theory the expected realized yields over any holding period on securities of different maturities, but otherwise similar, are always equal.*

The equality of expected realized yields according to pure-expectations theorists

Now if expected realized yields over any holding period are always equal, what do the spreads between long- and short-term markets yields in Figure 7.6 imply? Well, if the long-term yield is higher than the short-term yield (after adjustment to a bond-yield equivalent basis), it must mean that investors expect capital losses on long-term bonds—at least over the short run. Otherwise, investors clearly would expect to be able to do better holding long-term bonds, and this would not be an equilibrium situation according to the pure-expectations hypothesis. Conversely, if the short-term yield is above the long-term yield, it must mean that investors expect capital gains on long-term assets. Moreover, the degree of difference in equivalent yields reveals the degree of expected capital gain or loss on long-term bonds.

Statement of the
pure-expectations
hypothesis

The above conclusions can be restated in a more useful way. First, recognize that since security yields and prices are inversely related, if a capital loss is expected on long-term bonds (a fall in bond prices), this means that the market yield on long-term bonds is expected to rise. The reverse also holds, an expected capital gain means an expected fall in bond yields. We can, therefore, state the pure-expectations hypothesis of the spread between long- and short-term interest rates as follows: *a positive spread between long- and short-term interest rates on otherwise equivalent assets is entirely accounted for by an expected rise in the long-term interest rate; a negative spread (the short rate above the long) is fully accounted for by an expected fall in the long-term interest rate.*

Yield curves

This statement of the pure-expectations hypothesis is extremely intriguing. If it is correct, we can tell what the market thinks will happen to interest rates in the future by examining the spread between long- and short-term interest rates on otherwise equivalent securities. Analysts who are interested in this possibility and the relationship between yields according to maturity, generally, fit "yield curves" to market yields by maturity to depict the term structure for specific dates.

FIGURE 7–7
Yield curves for U.S. Treasury obligations

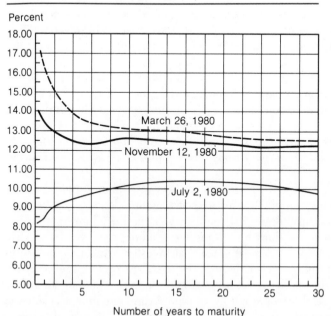

SOURCE: Federal Reserve Bank of New York.

Figure 7–7 shows yield curves for government securities for three specific dates during 1980, a year of extreme fluctuations in interest rates. According to the pure-expectations hypothesis, the market as of March 26, 1980 must have expected a fall in interest rates because short-term rates were far above the rates for longer maturity issues. In the second quarter of 1980, there was a brief, but sharp, contraction in the economy and an easing in inflation, leading, in fact, to a record fall in interest rates, as shown by the July 2 yield curve. The July 2 curve also shows, again according to our first theory, a change in market expectations regarding future interest-rate changes. As of July, the market appeared to be looking for higher interest rates, although the yield curve was not uniformly upward sloping. In the second half of the year, the economy began to recover, inflation reaccelerated, and the Fed moved to restrain bank reserves. As a result, by November 12, rates had retraced most of their earlier fall, so the market appeared to have been right about the direction of interest-rate changes once again. The forecast implicit in the November 12 yield curve did not pan out as well, however. Interest rates rose to new records in December. Whether the market was right or wrong in its expectations, the important point of these illustrations is the interpretation which can be given to yield curves by the pure-expectations theory.

We turn now to the next hypothesis. The liquidity premium hypothesis accepts the notion that expectations of changes in interest rates will affect the spread between long- and short-term yields. It maintains, however, that such expectations are not the *only* factor to be taken into account; in particular, there is a liquidity factor which explains part of this spread.   **The liquidity premium hypothesis**

Let us go back to your position as an investor who wants to place funds for one year. Even if your expected realized yield on 20-year AAA corporate bonds held for one year happened to be equal to the one-year yield on prime corporate notes there would be a remaining significant difference in these opportunities. You *know* what the realized yield on the note will be because it matures at the end of the year; the one-year realized yield on a 20-year bond, however, is an estimate based on your *anticipation* of market conditions one year from now. Your estimate could turn out wrong. In particular, the market price for long-term bonds could turn out to be much lower than you expect—resulting in an unexpected capital loss and low realized return. Consequently, *a long-term instrument involves the risk of a lower-than-expected realized return over short-term holding periods.* This risk can pursuade some investors to avoid long-term bonds unless the expected realized yield on long-term securities over the planned holding period is sufficiently higher than the return on short-term assets to compensate for such risk.

This much of the liquidity premium hypothesis is based on logic. The next part is based on an empirical judgment. The theory asserts that *the credit market is dominated by investors who are concerned about the uncertainty of realized returns over short-term holding periods.* This means that the realized yield expected on long-term assets held for short periods will tend to exceed the yield on short-term assets. This extra return is a *liquidity premium* required to induce investors to buy long-term assets.

Statement of the liquidity-premium hypothesis.

Because of the liquidity premium, the yield curve will have a positive slope even when market interest rates are not expected to rise. To be more specific, the liquidity-premium hypothesis asserts that: *a positive spread between long- and short-term interest rates may be accounted for by a liquidity premium (explained above) or by a combination of (1) a liquidity premium and expectations of a rise in the long-term interest rate, or (2) a liquidity premium and expectations of a decline in the long-term rate where the liquidity premium effect is stronger; a negative spread between long- and short-term interest rates is accounted for by expectations of a fall in the long-term interest rate sufficient to outweigh the liquidity premium.*

The theory is supported by, among other types of evidence, the fact that short-term interest rates were below long-term interest rates on average during 1920–1940 despite the downward trend of interest rates during that period. Either there was a liquidity premium, or the market rather consistently failed to anticipate that trend.

The preferred-habitat hypothesis

The third theory, the preferred-habitat hypothesis, recognizes the risk of an unexpected rise in market interest rates and low realized yields on long-term bonds for investors who may have, or plan, to sell these bonds before they mature. It also recognizes, however, a second group of investors who are major participants in the long-term segment of the market. These investors are not concerned about liquidity; they have long-term financial liabilities and seek long-term assets *because* these assets will not mature until a date far into the future. They are concerned about the potential for an unexpected *decline* in market interest rates should they invest in short-term assets on a recurring basis. Such a decline would reduce the realized yield on their assets over a long investing period.

The risk of lost income opportunities

The first group of investors, those concerned about the risk of an unexpected rise in interest rates, includes commercial banks and most households. The second group is comprised of life-insurance companies and pension funds. In general, each investor group has a preferred habitat along the maturity spectrum and must be offered a premium in terms of a higher expected realized yield to induce a movement away from that preferred maturity for investments.

Statement of the preferred-habitat hypothesis

The yield curve, according to this third theory, tends to have a slightly humped shape when market interest rates are not expected to change. Such a hump reflects the premium required in the intermediate range to induce the dominant investors away from their preferred habitats at opposite ends of the maturity spectrum. In general, however, *the preferred-habitat theory does not permit an interpretation of the relative levels of short- and long-term rates in terms of market expectations and persistent premiums at one end of the market; it is recognized that market expectations affect these relative levels, but so do relative supply and demand conditions in various segments of the market because these conditions can cause significant yield premiums and at either end of the market.* Consequently, interpretations of market expectations from yield curves require information about relative supply and demand conditions in different segments of the market, information which is often difficult to obtain and evaluate.

Each theory of the term structure has its advocates. Though judgments about majority opinions are always hazardous, it would seem that the preferred-habitat theory is the one with the widest acceptance among economists and market analysts.

Seasoning

When new debt instruments are issued, they usually offer higher yields than identical, but previously issued, or *seasoned*, debt instruments. New-issue yields tend to be higher than seasoned-issue yields, particularly when interest rates are rising cyclically; when interest rates are falling cyclically, this differential is less and may even be reversed. A higher yield for a new issue in a stable interest-rate environment reflects the premium required to induce the trading market to absorb a significant volume of new securities within a short period of time. In a rising interest-rate environment, investment bankers and dealers tend to have the expectation, or at least a greater sensitivity to the risk, that interest rates will rise during the marketing period; and new-issue premiums tend to be higher to compensate investment bankers in such an environment. Conversely, in a falling-rate environment, little or no premium is necessary because of expectations that rates will fall or that there is little risk that rates will rise.

INTRODUCTION TO ARTICLE

The following two articles from *Business Week* provide a description of the penchant of banks to invest in short-term obligations and of life insurance companies to invest in long-term obligations. They also illustrate, however, that even these habitual lenders at opposite ends of the maturity spectrum may, to a degree, "play the yield curve." In this case—the fall of 1976—banks were being attracted into longer-term assets and life insurance companies temporarily into short-term assets. Their expectations regarding the timing of an increase in loan demand and, hence, interest rates apparently were somewhat different. After this article was written, loan demand continued to be soft, and long-term interest rates fell for several months; then in mid-January 1977, the market turned around, and long-term yields rose sharply.

A Scramble for Borrowers

Life insurance companies still have $2 billion to $3 billion in uncommitted investable funds this year, and—with corporate borrowers still flush with cash—the insurers are finding it hard to put the money to work. Funds which normally would be invested in high-yielding, long-term private placements of corporate debt are instead being held in lower-yielding, short-term instruments waiting for a turnaround in loan demand, which probably will not show up until next year at the earliest.

By September such big investors as Prudential Insurance Co. of America have normally committed all their private placement money, but the Pru still has not invested about 10 percent of the $3.5 billion it plans to place directly this year. The big lenders are also scrambling for next year's deals. By this time of the year, according to Jerome T. Greene, a vice president at Salomon Bros., the life companies have normally committed 30 percent to 40 percent of the next year's private placement funds—but so far they've only committed 10 percent to 15 percent.

This year—thanks to strong insurance sales, raised premiums, new pension money lured away from commercial banks by guaranteed rate of return contracts, and the paydown of mortgage and policy loans—the life companies found themselves with nearly $40 billion to invest. Yet the demand for funds, despite the $12 billion done in private placements already this year and the $17.9 billion done publicly, falls far short of the supply. Nor are insurers willing to take up the slack by investing as heavily in mortgages as they once did. Total mortgage debt outstanding is up 9 percent from last year; the portion held by life companies is up barely 3 percent.

Fast deals

Competition is stiff for the few deals that are available. Says Paul Kelly, a partner in Cleveland banking house Prescott, Ball & Turben, "They've got to make their checks out very quickly. The deals are selling out in the first day." On one recent $25 million private offering, Kelly claims he had to turn away 11 insurance companies. "You try to close a deal as fast as you can," says Philip R. Reynolds, senior vice president of Travelers Insurance Co. "Borrowing gets deferred, or they haggle over rates, or they leave you for someone else," he says.

As a result, life insurance companies are giving ground. Their rate expectations are coming down. Where they were getting a heady 10¼ percent at the beginning of the year, lenders are now accepting 9 percent and even lower. And they are also stretching out maturities, lending for as much as five years longer than they would have 18 months ago.

"Investors are also putting more eggs in one basket," says Robert T. Madden, chairman of his own private placement specialist company. He observes that lenders are bidding for bigger chunks of the few deals that are available. "Historically, people would raise their eyebrows if an insurance company put more than 1 percent of admitted assets in any one company. Today, they're putting in 2 percent to 3 percent." In addition, lenders are relaxing some of their covenants.

Meager yields

While waiting for demand to rally, the life companies are putting their $3 billion or so in short-term instruments, such as commercial paper, Treasury bills, and bank certificates of deposit, though they are currently yielding a meager 5 percent to 5¼ percent. And the outlook is no brighter for the next year from the companies' view.

"I have more money for next year than I

almost know what to do with," admits Walter G. Ehlers, senior vice president of Teachers Insurance & Annuity Association of America.

Banks Change their Bond Mix

Some of the nation's biggest commercial banks, apparently convinced that loan demand is going to stay soft for some time to come, are trying to bolster disappointing earnings by shifting more of their money into longer-term Treasuries—those with maturities of five years or longer. They are also trying to make their investment portfolios more secure by buying only top-quality municipal bonds and by doing more of their own research into tax-exempt issues.

In an unannounced decision made only last week, New York's Chemical Bank joined the growing list of banks that are moving out on the yield curve, buying longer-term issues that yield more than short-term securities. In just the past two weeks, banks increased their holdings of Treasury issues with maturities of one year and more from 56 percent to 60 percent of their total government portfolios. The longer maturities do return more: Five-year governments are yielding about 7 percent today, compared with about 5 percent for a 90-day Treasury bill. But the farther banks go out on the yield curve, the less liquid their investments—and that could pose problems.

If loan demand picks up sooner than the banks expect, or if it booms rather than increases gradually, they could be caught in a liquidity bind. On one hand, they could be forced to raise cash in the money market in a big way for the first time since the crisis days of 1974. Or they could be forced to repeat their bitter experience of 1972: selling bonds in a market where prices would be falling because increasing demand for loans was driving rates upward.

Quite safe

Given the gradual recovery thus far, along with their predictions that it will continue at roughly the same pace, most economists think the banks are on solid enough ground. William N. Griggs, money-market economist for J. Henry Schroder Banking Corp. in New York, maintains, "I don't think loan demand is going to be that strong relative to the liquidity that banks have and the ability they have to go out and write certificates of deposit."

But Shuman, Agnew & Co., the San Francisco brokerage house, remains more skeptical. "Hopefully," it says, "the large banks are not diminishing the liquidity built up during this cycle, so loan demand can be funded profitably."

Meanwhile, Treasury issues may be popular with banks, but municipal bonds are not, because banks have found other ways to reduce their tax bills. Their growing activity in international banking, which provides tax credits, and leasing, which provides credit as well as the depreciation of the equipment, has permitted them to take an increasing part of their income in taxable form.

At Crocker National Bank in San Francisco, holdings of municipals went down to $666.1 million from $738.5 million, a decline of 12 percent in 18 months ended last June 30. Larry F. Clyde, Crocker senior vice president, explains that the bank built up tax credits from its international operations. That, coupled with an increasing leasing operation that provides tax credits and depreciation, means that Crocker has less need to shelter income with tax-exempt municipals, Clyde says.

Cutting municipals

Not only are banks cutting back on municipals, but they are also cutting back drastically on municipals that are not of high quality. Some 93 percent of the tax-exempt holdings of Republic National Bank of Dallas are rated A or better. And such big banks as Morgan Guaranty Trust Co. and Citizens & Southern National Bank in Atlanta are trusting less to the rating agencies and doing more of their own research.

Continental Illinois National Bank & Trust Co., meanwhile, has shortened the maturities of its municipals, and Donald C. Miller, vice chairman, stresses that "this represents a move toward conservatism, as we've become concerned about municipal credits." The average

maturity in Continental's municipal portfolio is 63 months, down from 75 months one year ago. The reduction comes mostly from cutbacks in holdings of 10-year and longer maturities.

Interest-rate ceilings

For a variety of reasons, federal and state governments have imposed ceilings on certain interest rates; and when these are effective they, of course, create interest-rate differentials. Mention has already been made of the interest-rate ceilings on certain deposit liabilities of commercial banks and thrifts which are being phased out. These ceilings were established for banks which are members of the Federal Reserve System by the Federal Reserve Board under its *Regulation Q.* [14] Although there have been federal ceilings for other types of market interest rates at times in the past, ceilings on deposit interest rates have been the only important federal restriction in recent years. [15]

At the state level, there are usury laws which set maximum levels for certain interest rates, principally those on mortgage, personal, and retail-credit loans. These ceilings often are intended to protect unsophisticated or destitute borrowers from unscrupulous lenders, but they usually cap prevailing interest rates for all customers for certain types of loans, mortgages in particular. [16]

Interest-rate ceilings are important because they can alter the interest-rate spreads we would otherwise expect to find based on the other factors described in this chapter. They are also important because they can have a significant restrictive impact on the availability of credit to certain borrowers during high interest-rate periods. Some economists favor such a mechanism for curbing the availability of credit, as explained in the next section.

---

[14] As will be described in Chapter 13, similar ceilings were set for most other banks by the Federal Deposit Insurance Corporation and for savings and loans by the Federal Home Loan Bank Board. The phasing out of these ceilings is being carried out by the Depository Institutions Deregulation Committee.

[15] FHA- and VA-guaranteed mortgage loans have ceiling interest rates, but these ceilings are adjusted frequently to reflect changes in unrestricted market rates.

[16] Federal legislation in 1979 and 1980 suspended state usury ceilings for mortgages, subject to state reinstatement of such ceilings in new legislation. (See Chapter 13.)

CREDIT AVAILABILITY

As indicated earlier in this chapter in the sections on liquidity, the availability of credit can be of considerable importance to the economy at particular times. The emphasis in those sections was on credit availability as one element of liquidity, and we indicated the importance of maintaining credit availability in an economy in deep recession. There is a significant school of economists, primarily in the business community, however, that places an emphasis on credit availability at other stages of the business cycle as well. In particular, these economists view excessive credit availability as a key element sustaining rapid business expansions, leading to unrealistic expectations of profits and to accelerating inflation. To restrain the economy in such circumstances, these economists believe credit availability per se must be curtailed by specific controls such as interest-rate ceilings.[17] It is argued that restrictive fiscal policy will not be very effective, and tight monetary policy, in terms of lower growth in the money supply or higher interest rates, will not "bite" as long as credit is available.[18]

The Theory

An analysis of the credit availability argument can be presented with the aid of Figure 7–8. The supply and demand curves in this figure represent the supply and demand for credit in a particular market, such as the market for mortgage funds. Whatever market we choose, the key feature of the analysis is the assumption of an inelastic demand curve.

Assume that monetary policy is tightened. This means that interest rates rise for banks' borrowed funds, and the rate of growth of the money supply is curtailed. With a rise in interest costs to banks and other intermediaries and with lower growth in deposits, the supply curves for credit in final markets tend to shift to the left. In our figure, this raises the relevant interest rate from i_1 to i_2. The quantity of credit demanded drops only a little, however, from L_1 to L_2, if the credit availability school is correct. Several reasons may account for this: (1) borrowers' expectations about future income may be so buoyant that interest costs are perceived to have negligible implications for future spending choices; (2) some borrowers are locked into certain levels of borrowing and spending by prior com-

[17]Other possible controls include minimum down payments and maximum quantities of credit.

[18]Students who have encountered the *credit availability doctrine* should not identify the arguments here as the essential points of that doctrine as promulgated in the 1950s. The ideas set out in this section, however, are similar to those of the credit availability doctrine in many respects, and they may be viewed as the intellectual descendants of the earlier doctrine which was geared to the special institutional setting of the early 1950s. See Thomas Mayer, *Monetary Policy in the United States* (New York: Random House, 1968), pp. 126–37.

FIGURE 7–8
Supply and demand for credit

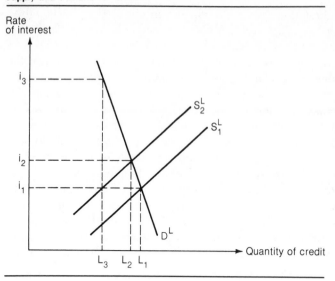

mitments regardless of the interest-rate cost; (3) even at higher interest rates, inflation expectations may be such that real, after-tax interest rates were not before and are not yet one of the important limiting variables for credit demands. Regardless of which reasons are correct, the result is that the quantity of credit and the spending which it finances are curbed little if at all by interest-rate increases. And liquidity is maintained because credit is still available, albeit at a higher cost.

How then can policymakers restrain spending? The answer, according to the credit availability school, lies in interest-rate ceilings or other selective credit controls. If, to use the case represented in Figure 7–8, the maximum rate of interest were constrained by law to i_1, the same shift in the supply curve in response to tight monetary policy would reduce the availability of credit more sharply, from L_1 to L_3, because few lenders would view i_1 as a profitable opportunity. Such a sharp reduction in credit, they argue, would place a great constraint on liquidity and spending.

Objections

One very obvious challenge to the credit availability school is that, if the demand for credit in certain key markets is, in fact, so inelastic in periods of high business activity, this simply means that policy-induced interest-rate increases must be larger to curb credit demands adequately. Still tighter monetary policy with an interest rate of i_3 would achieve the same result as the combination of an interest-rate ceiling at i_1 and moderately stringent reserve action.

Interest rates
should be raised

Another challenge concerns the assertion of extreme interest insensitivity of credit demands in major markets. Monetarists in particular stress that, provided real, after-tax interest rates are positive and are the focus of the analysis, credit demands are fairly sensitive to interest costs.

Credit demand may not be inelastic

The effectiveness of interest-rate ceilings or other controls in restraining *total* credit availability is also challenged. When interest ceilings become effective, they cause investors to seek other investments which are not constrained in yield. This augments the supply of credit in other areas and through other channels. When such a rerouting of funds affects commercial banks and thrifts it is called *disintermediation*. In several past periods when interest rates on marketable debt instruments such as Treasury bills have risen significantly above the interest rates available to small savers at banks and other financial intermediaries subject to controls, small savers have withdrawn deposits from these institutions and invested them in short-term debt instruments, particularly Treasury bills and Treasury notes. This tends to cause credit supplies from controlled intermediaries to shrivel—hurting housing especially—while at the same time the supply of funds through other channels tends to increase in an offsetting manner, though not necessarily ending up with the same final sectors receiving funds as previously.

Disintermediation and other effects may not curb total credit

Credit markets, it should be noted, are highly competitive and innovative. Each postwar episode of high interest rates and effective ceilings has witnessed the creation of new ways to effectively evade ceilings, and the international integration of credit markets has made ceilings almost meaningless for those entities which have access to foreign markets for the placement and raising of funds.

Another objection is that, when ceilings are effective in shutting down credit availability to certain sectors, these sectors—such as housing—are hit harder and sooner than other sectors by tight policies. The issue here is one of equity. Why should housing bear the brunt of the restraint? Concern for this and general political support for subsidies to housing have done much to encourage the liberalization of interest-rate ceilings and the development of special federal programs to blunt their effects.[19]

The equity issue

CONCLUSION

Our principal concern is this chapter has been liquidity: its definition for assets and entities, its importance in the economy, the

---

[19]In 1978, for example, the Federal Reserve and other federal regulatory agencies authorized banks and savings and loans to issue six-month savings certificates with yields tied to six-month Treasury bill yields. These certificates greatly reduced the degree of disintermediation in 1978–80 in comparison to past high-rate periods. Even so, housing construction dropped sharply in 1979 and 1980 due to high mortgage-interest rates.

role of financial intermediaries in providing liquidity, and the explanation of interest-rate spreads, in part by factors which are related to liquidity. We have also investigated a number of other elements accounting for interest-rate spreads. And we have discussed a school of thought which advocates interest-rate ceilings and other controls to curb credit availability and liquidity in inflationary periods.

The next chapter will shift our focus from strictly domestic financial relationships to international finance and the world economy. World economies and credit markets are becoming more and more interdependent. Exchange-rate changes, foreign interest-rate changes, and inflation and real-income growth in other countries all have an impact on our economy and our financial markets.

PROBLEMS

1. Discuss the major components of the Federal Reserve's M-2 measure of money, explaining those characteristics which add to or subtract from each asset's liquidity.

2. How do financial intermediaries supply liquidity to the economy?

3. The crowding-out effect was discussed in Chapter 5. According to the expectations hypothesis, what sort of yield curve is likely to occur when crowding out is anticipated by financial markets? Explain why.

4. Discuss, according to the liquidity-premium hypothesis, the likely effect on the yield curve of an increase in uncertainty as to the future level of long-term interest rates.

ADVANCED READINGS

Friedman, Milton, and Schwartz, Anna J. *Monetary Statistics of the United States.* New York: Columbia University Press for the National Bureau of Economic Research, 1970, pp.128–35.

McKean, Roland N. "Liquidity and a National Balance Sheet." *Journal of Political Economy* 57 (1949): 506–22.

Malkiel, Burton. *The Term Structure of Interest Rates: Theory, Empirical Evidence, and Applications.* New York: McCaleb-Seiler, 1970.

International finance

This chapter extends our analysis of the financial sector to the international arena. In the course of doing so, it provides a survey of much of the material that appears in intermediate-level texts on international finance. Topics include the foreign-exchange market, the balance of payments, institutional features of the international financial markets, and the issue of fixed versus flexible exchange rates.

THE MARKET BETWEEN MONIES AND THE FOREIGN-EXCHANGE VALUE OF MONEY

International financial relationships are more complex than domestic relationships, but most of the essentials are fairly straightforward extensions of concepts and analysis covered in earlier chapters. It will help to grasp the principal differences between international and domestic financial relationships if you imagine for a moment that each of the 50 states of the United States has its own money, that state governments have the power to print (create) their own state currencies and bank reserves, and that states also have the power to restrict external commercial and financial transac-

8

tions through taxes or direct controls. Certainly economic relations and our analysis in earlier chapters would be altered considerably under these circumstances. But how? Let us start with the fact that there would be a different money for each state.

A fictitious example

To be more specific, let us call each state's money the _____ (*name of the state*) dollar. Now assume that there are no restrictions on interstate commerce imposed by state governments and you are a New York resident interested in ordering a dulcimer from a musical instrument firm in North Carolina. The price is 500 North Carolina dollars payable in North Carolina dollars. You have a bank account of New York dollars. Where do you get a balance of North Carolina dollars? How many North Carolina dollars can you get for one New York dollar?

Suppose you can get a check for North Carolina dollars drawn on a New York bank at a price of 1.10 New York dollars per 1.00 North Carolina dollar ($1.10 N.Y./N.C.). The New York bank does not create North Carolina dollars in issuing this check; to honor the check, it will have to obtain the North Carolina dollars from some entity willing to exchange a balance of North Carolina dollars for New York dollars—possibly a North Carolina bank, which in turn needs New York dollars to supply to a North Carolina resident ordering merchandise from New York.

Exchanges of balances of different monies such as this constitute a market. We could analyze it as a market for North Carolina dollars and specify supply and demand functions for North Carolina dollars, or as a market for New York dollars, specifying supply and demand functions for New York dollars.

The existence of separate state monies would obviously complicate life in the United States. Aside from the additional transactions (between monies), the prices of goods and services from other states in terms of your own state's money would be determined by (1) the price of the item in the state of origin, and (2) the price of that state's money in terms of your state's money. In our example the price of the dulcimer in New York dollars is $550 N.Y. ($500 N.C. × $1.10 N.Y./N.C.).

The foreign-exchange market is the real-world counterpart to our fictitious market in state monies. International transactions for a tremendous variety of purposes lead to exchanges of one sovereign nation's money for another. These exchanges may be unrestricted by domestic laws for all holders of a domestic money, in which case the money is *fully and freely convertible,* or there may be a variety of restrictions on certain transactors and/or on certain transactions; restrictions may apply to the quantity, price, or the purpose of exchanges.

Recall that in Chapter 3 where we examined the supply and demand for the stock of checkable deposits, travelers checks, and currency in the United States, a central topic of interest was the value of U.S. money *in terms of domestic goods and services.* As indicated above, our central topic of interest here will be the value of U.S. money in another sense—*its value in terms of foreign monies.* Our analysis in this chapter will be different in two more ways: it will be developed using money flows instead of stocks, and it will examine an explicit market in money with explicit prices for money.

INTRODUCTION TO ARTICLE

The following article from *The Wall Street Journal* (August 24, 1976) describes some of the types of restrictions that were imposed on currency exchanges and the policing problems that went along with them in Britain during most of the 1960s and 1970s when the pound was falling in value. Aside from creating incentive for both petty and grand crime, exchange controls lead to a lower volume of world trade and reduced economic welfare. Still, governments often resort to them as one way to affect the quantity of their currency supplied in the foreign exchange market and, thusly, the value of their money in terms of other monies.

In 1978 and 1979, Britain gradually dropped its exchange controls as part of a shift toward more laissez-faire policies by the British Government and as North Sea oil discoveries and a restrictive monetary policy by the Bank of England strengthened the pound.

Britain's Currency Smugglers

LONDON—Americans tend to take a lot of freedoms for granted, sometimes seeing as inalienable human rights what foreign governments see as mere financial privileges. One such freedom is our freedom from exchange controls, the limits many countries impose on the ability to move money internationally.

An unappreciated freedom is the easiest kind to lose, and appreciation isn't apt to arise in time unless one happens to learn the hard way in a place where his home country privileges aren't portable. That's what happened a few years back with a West German couple observed at the airport in Nairobi, Kenya. Their attempt to buy a ticket shortly before flight time went smoothly, until the man plunked down cash, several hundred dollars worth of Kenyan currency.

Instead of accepting it, the airline agent demanded to know where they got it. At a bank downtown, they said, and he asked for proof. They vaguely recalled having been handed a slip of paper at the bank, but they hadn't saved it. Without it, the agent assumed they bought their money illegally on the local black market.

They couldn't use their Kenyan cash to buy a ticket, nor could they convert it back into any other currency at a legitimate bank, either. So they headed disconsolately back to town, presumably to purchase—at a highly unfavorable rate and with risk of being caught in a criminal act—foreign currency which they could then pretend to have brought in with them. Or maybe they're still there.

If that's the sort of thing one should be prepared for in developing and in Communist countries, it's scarcely the sort of thing one expects to encounter in this cradle of liberal democracy.

It's Britain's exchange controls which are causing a stir lately. One reason is the way they've been snagging individual travelers, innocent and otherwise. Some of the instances provide British newspaper columnists with comic relief, such as *The Sunday Telegraph's* recent account of an Arab asked by the customs man at Heathrow Airport how much sterling he had with him. "Fifty thousand pounds," he calmly responded.

The mood changed when the customs man informed him that the limit on British cash that can be carried out of the country is 25 pounds, or about $45. "A flea in a camel's ear" to a wealthy Arab, the *Telegraph* observed, but the limit nevertheless. As a non-resident, the Arab was doubtless allowed to cash in the other 49,975 pounds for a foreign currency, officials say, noting that there would have been no problem if he had had proof he'd brought it all with him from abroad.

Suitcases stuffed with pounds

Such mutual "embarrassment" is increasingly common, a British Treasury man says. In the same matter-of-fact spirit with which American newspapers report arrests for income tax evasion and heroin smuggling, British newspapers carry stories of secretaries arrested with suitcases stuffed full of their country's currency. In the most recently measured 12-month period, British customs seized 362,000 outbound pounds, and prosecuted 42 individuals. Since then, there've been cases involving vaster sums.

Why should anyone want to spirit sterling out of Britain? The pound sterling's shrinking value on the foreign exchange markets (around $1.80 lately, down from $2.60 several years ago) makes the offense more tempting rather than less. Chiefly there's the incentive to unload it for foreign currency before the pound goes down even more, and then there's the hope that investments abroad are more apt to prove profitable than those at home.

Human nature being what it is, the sheer existence of government constraints makes investing abroad seem more exotically alluring

to Britons. To control the tendency without making it impossible, the government has inadvertently created an extra temptation for illicit profit. This is the "investment currency pool," from which Britons must buy dollars, for instance, when they want to buy shares in an American company.

The pool is fed when Britons sell off foreign securities. Because demand for the limited supply of such special "investment dollars" varies constantly, there's a fluctuating premium price for them, often 50 percent above the ordinary exchange rate. That automatically increases the cost to Britons of buying foreign securities, a substantial deterrent. But when they later sell their foreign securities, 75 percent of their special dollars can be sold for pounds at a premium, too, whatever it happens to be at the moment.

Putting the system in the spotlight lately is the opportunity to receive a premium price without having paid one—by using smuggled pounds to buy securities more cheaply abroad. People have been charged with doing this to the tune of millions of dollars, a caper almost surely requiring the help of some of the thousands of bankers, brokers, and lawyers on whom the Bank of England mainly relies for enforcement, and possibly—the investigation is still pending—the connivance of a "bent" ("crooked") official in the Bank of England itself.

Now there is talk of beefing up the bank's own exchange-control staff, already some 750 people, and otherwise tightening up on the policing and paperwork. One possibility mentioned, despite the staggering burden it would place on the bureaucracy, is having officials peruse every import document, because one way of getting pounds out of Britain is to pad the amounts paid to suppliers abroad, who collaborate by putting the extra amount in a Swiss account.

Some British businessmen devote the same sort of mental energies to evading currency controls that some Americans devote to matching wits with the Internal Revenue Service. One otherwise solid citizen figures he could get plenty of pounds out by arranging to have himself sued by, and settling out of court with, a collaborating continental. Or, perhaps by carrying such a bulky bundle of traveller's checks that they'd be seized, whereupon he could be reimbursed by American Express elsewhere.

All that raises the question of whether it wouldn't be better to "decriminalize" currency movements by scrapping the whole system of controls. To British officials, though, it's out of the question to even think of that, except maybe for some far-distant day when everything is coming up roses for the British economy.

The main reason is that currency controls of some sort have been in force for so long, since early in World War II, that there may be a tremendous pent-up amount of capital which would surge out of England if that were allowed. Nobody hazards a guess on how much, but the risk of millions of Britons rushing their savings out of pounds is one officials clearly aren't willing to take. If there were only a little movement of that sort, they reason, it still might be enough to start a panicky pullout by those foreign governments which still keep reserves in sterling, thus depressing the pound to unplumbed depths.

More surprising than the attempts to breach the British controls is the way they're accepted as a matter of course. Concerned that some member firms were being driven out of business by one particular feature of the controls, the stock exchange here recently made a pitch to the treasury for relief. But only for relief on that particular point, which it suspected wouldn't get very far anyhow.

Correctly, it turns out. The relief sought was from the "temporary" 1965 rule that 25 percent of the proceeds of selling foreign securities must be sold for pounds at the market exchange rate, without the benefit of the premium. The practice, as the exchange was well aware, brings several hundred million dollars a year into Britain's reserves, now about $5.3 billion. And this, as the exchange figured the treasury would say, isn't the time to give up anything that helps the reserves even a little.

Small talk over sherry

That's recognized by executives of an eminent British multinational manufacturing company, too. Over their boardroom ports and

sherries, they often talk about transplanting the headquarters to America. "Our bright young executives could earn four times as much" there than British mores and tax rates permit, says a top official. But under the exchange control laws, the treasury would find ways to thwart it, he says resignedly, adding, "anyway, this is a very pleasant country to live in."

The acquiescent attitude is much the same towards the travel allowances. The 25 pounds cash limit per trip is seen as generous in comparison with the 15 pounds a year prevailing prior to 1970, and the current limit of 300 pounds worth of foreign currency traveler's checks per trip is widely generous against the previous ceiling of 50 pounds per year.

Businessmen don't grumble much because they can always get permission to carry out more traveler's checks by justifying their needs on a Bank of England form, officials note, and a British private economist says the simpler old limits were secretly popular with the country's husbands. "You could always tell your wife, sorry, that's all the government will allow you to spend" on a vacation trip, he recalls.

Britons take comfort in the fact that numerous other countries have exchange controls, too. Italy limits travelers to 35,000 lire (about $42) in or out, and the faltering franc has France tightening up its capital outflow rules; impoverished Pakistan permits its citizens 20 rupees (about $1.20) in cash.

Although they didn't touch the average traveler, even America has had its brushes with exchange controls, while carefully avoiding use of the term. The ending in early 1974 of restaints on large capital outflows wasn't much noticed outside of financial circles though, and the current requirement to merely tell the Treasury about carrying large amounts of cash across borders is far from being the same thing as a prohibition.

But people can't usually get very far without their money, so such curbs always have the potential of limiting the freedom of movement of human beings, too. And there's almost bound to be a "next time" when a declining dollar raises the question of whether the U.S. needs outright exchange controls. Experience abroad suggests that if the answer is "yes," the final result could be decades of burgeoning bureaucratization and declining civil liberty and morality.

SOURCE: Richard F. Janssen, "Britain's Currency Smugglers," *The Wall Street Journal*, August 24, 1976.

THE FOREIGN-EXCHANGE MARKET AND THE BALANCE OF PAYMENTS

If we divide the world into two parts—the United States and the rest of the world—we can examine systematically the principal sources of the demand and supply of dollars in exchange for other countries' currencies. Knowledge of these principal sources and of the variables which motivate them will permit us to explain the major determinants of the value of our money in relation to other countries' monies.

The balance of payments

The many transactions which give rise to exchanges of U.S. money for foreign money over a period of time are summarized in the U.S. balance of payments. Figure 8–1 presents the U.S. balance of payments for 1978. The balance of payments records transactions which lead to a purchase of U.S. money with foreign money as a credit, and transactions which usually involve a sale of U.S. money for foreign money are recorded as a debit. Credits and debits should balance since purchases must equal sales in any market.[1]

The trade balance

The balance of payments is divided into groups of entries. The first of these comprises foreign payments for our exports (our export receipts), item (1), and our payments for imports, item (2). Exporters ultimately are paid for their goods in U.S. dollars, so export receipts is a credit item. Foreigners offer foreign exchange for dollars in the foreign exchange market in order to pay for U.S. exports. Conversely, when we pay for our imports, we (or importing companies) in the U.S. supply dollars in the foreign exchange market in order to acquire the foreign currency that foreigners require as payment for their goods. The net of the dollar value of our exports

---

[1]In fact, the recorded transactions in the balance of payments rarely balance, and the account is brought into overall balance through an errors and omissions entry which is simply the difference between recorded credits and debits. This error in the records occurs because most of the entries that are made are not actually identified directly with purchases and sales in the foreign-exchange market. Most represent international transactions which are known to give rise to foreign-exchange purchases or sales and are recorded or estimated independently from the foreign-exchange transactions. In some cases substantial sources of demand and/or supply are incorrectly estimated or do not get accounted for at all. Also, there are some entries in the balance of payments which do not necessarily give rise to a supply or demand for dollars. Hence the balance-of-payments credit and debit entries should be viewed as merely rough estimates of the sources of the international supply and demand for dollars.

FIGURE 8–1

UNITED STATES
Balance of Payments, 1978
(millions of dollars)

Credits *(transactions leading to purchases of dollars)* **and Balances on** **International Accounts** *(memo items)*		**Debits** *(transactions leading to sales of dollars)*	
(1) Receipts for exports of goods	$141,884	(2) Payments for imports of goods	$176,071
(3) *Memo:* *Trade balance (item (1) less item (2))*	− 34,187		
(4) Services and other current account transactions, net	20,292		
(5) *Memo:* *Balance on current account (item (3) plus item (4))*	− 13,895		
(6) Foreign private investment in the United States	29,956	(7) U.S. private investment abroad	57,033
		(8) U.S. Government capital transactions other than official reserve transactions (outflow)	4,656
(9) *Memo:* *Balance on capital account (item (6) less items (7) and (8))*	− 31,733		
(10) *Memo:* *Balance of recorded autonomous pay- ments (item (5) plus item (9))*	− 45,628		
(11) Increase in foreign official assets in the United States	33,758		
(12) Decrease in U.S. official reserves of gold and foreign exchange	732		
(13) Discrepancy	11,139		
Total credits	$237,761	Total debits	$237,761

FIGURE 8–2
U.S. INTERNATIONAL TRANSACTIONS (Current account balances)

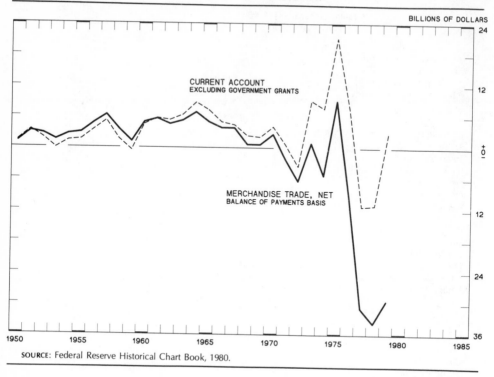

SOURCE: Federal Reserve Historical Chart Book, 1980.

**The current
account balance**

**The capital
account balance**

minus the dollar value of our imports is our balance of trade; item (3), and represents the net demand (+) or supply (−) of dollars as a result of these transactions.

Sales and purchases of services and private and public gifts of funds from the U.S. abroad or vice versa also represent sources of supply and demand for dollars in the foreign exchange market. When the net of these transactions, item (4), is added to the balance of trade, we have the balance on current account, item (5).

The next major block of transactions involves mainly investment (real or financial) in the U.S. by foreign residents, item (6) and investment abroad by U.S. residents, item (7). A decision either of a U.S. resident to purchase the stock of a British firm on the London stock exchange or of a U.S. firm to build a plant in France with profits from its U.S. operations will generate a supply of dollars in the foreign-exchange market to obtain the necessary foreign exchange with which to make the ultimate payments. The same relationship holds in reverse for foreign investment (real and financial) in the United States. A decision by Volkswagen in 1976 to establish a plant in New Stanton, PA meant that Volkswagen needed to buy substantial sums of dollars, or at least use dollars that it otherwise would have sold in the foreign-exchange market. The balance of these private capital (investment or loan) transactions is the balance on "capital" account, item (9).

Excluded from the capital account are financial transactions by the U.S. government which are considered "official reserve" trans- actions, item (12), and also excluded are foreign official government transactions involving U.S. assets—usually, but not always, of a "re- serve" nature, item (11). Reserve transactions add to or subtract from government holdings of gold and foreign exchange. They are of special interest because *they often have the express purpose of af- fecting the value of the dollar relative to foreign exchange* and thereby represent government intervention in the foreign-exchange market. All other transactions are "autonomous," that is, independ- ently motivated. The balance of autonomous payments, which is the combined balance of the current and capital accounts, is what is usually meant today by "the" balance of payments (surplus, deficit, or equilibrium).[2] It is clear from the payments statement in Figure 8–1 that most of the autonomous demand for dollars is accounted for by payments for our exports plus private foreign investment in the United States, and that the autonomous supply of dollars is ac- counted for by our payments for imports plus private U.S. invest- ment in other countries. We will turn now to an explanation of the major economic variables which influence each of these components of demand and supply.

Official reserve
changes

SOURCES OF THE DEMAND FOR DOLLARS: EXPORT RECEIPTS

Preliminary matters

It is important to recognize that the exports entry in the pay- ments statement is for the *dollar value* of our exports, not the physi- cal quantity. (This applies to the imports entry as well.) This dollar value can be thought of as equal to the average dollar price of our exports, $P^{\$X}$, times the quantity of our exports, X.

Dollar values

What determines the price and quantity of our exports? We know from supply and demand analysis that a complete answer to this question requires, as usual, careful development of a demand func- tion, a supply function, and an equilibrium condition. It turns out that the variables in this analysis and a similar analysis for imports can be related ultimately to the characteristic differences in domes- tic and foreign production possibilities and preferences. The twin principles of comparative advantage and the gains from trade ex- plain the motivations for world trade and the determination of the

---

[2]There have been several balance-of-payments concepts used in the past; the concept used above is what was called the *official settlements balance.*

prices and quantities of exports and imports in the absence of intervention. However, such a general-equilibrium analysis of world trade is a topic for courses in international economics, and our analysis here will have to be less complete.

Export supply

Although it may not be correct for all goods, export sales generally represent a small proportion of the total sales of most goods for U.S. firms. For simplicity we will assume that U.S. exports, therefore, can increase or decrease without any impact on their dollar prices; in other words, their supply is infinitely elastic. And we assume that the average price of U.S. exports is equal to the general and, for this analysis, exogenous price level for the domestic U.S. economy, P^{US}; in symbols $P^{\$X} = P^{US}$. This assumption enables us to relate the quantity of our exports entirely to foreign-demand considerations, ignoring any interferences such as government controls.

Export demand factors

The foreign demand for U.S. exports, X^D, is influenced principally by the level of foreign real income, the price of U.S. exports to foreigners *in terms of foreign money,* and the prices of foreign goods. There are also, of course, a variety of special factors which will have a bearing on the demand for U.S. exports from time to time; these include unusually poor or good harvests in other countries and war.

Foreign income

The influence of foreign real income is straight-forward. *The level of foreign real income, y^f, exerts a positive influence on the quantity of U.S. exports* for the same reason that higher real income increases the demand for goods in general. Foreign prosperity can be a very important factor for U.S. exports.

The foreign price of U.S. exports

Naturally the price of U.S. exports in terms of foreign money is the price that counts as far as foreign buyers are concerned—the dollar price is, in itself, of no direct interest to them. *The higher the foreign price of U.S. exports, the lower is the quantity demanded, ceteris paribus.* The foreign price is related to the dollar price by the exchange rate of the dollar, ER, that is, the value of the dollar in terms of foreign exchange. Export subsidies, implicit or explicit, provided by the U.S. government and foreign tariffs also have a bearing on the foreign price. Neglecting subsidies and tariffs, however, the foreign price of U.S. exports is equal to the dollar price of these exports times the exchange rate of the dollar. Recall the calculation of the New York dollar price of the dulcimer in our earlier example. (North Carolina was the exporting state.) *It is apparent, therefore, that the price of U.S. exports can go up to foreigners either through a rise in the dollar price of our exports, P^{US}, or through a rise in the value of the dollar in terms of foreign exchange, ER.*

It should also be noted that the dollar price of U.S. exports could rise without the price to foreigners rising, if the value of the dollar were to fall by just enough to provide an offset to any increase in P^{US} Suppose, to return to our earlier example, that the price of North Carolina dulcimers went to $518.87 N.C., but at the same time for some reason the price of N.C. dollars fell to $1.06 N.Y./N.C.; the price of N.C. dulcimers in N.Y. dollars would remain at $550 N.Y.

The level of foreign prices, P^f, is important to export demand   Foreign prices
since it represents the price of goods which compete with U.S. exports. *The higher foreign prices are, the greater the demand for U.S. exports will be, ceteris paribus.*

We can now summarize our export demand function, expressed in quantities, as follows:

$$X^D = X = f(P^{US}, ER, P^f, y^f, \ldots)$$

Influenced variable	Influencing variable	Direction of influence
X: the quantity of U.S. exports	P^{US}: the U.S. price level	Negative
	ER: the exchange rate for the dollar	Negative
	P^f: the price level in foreign countries trading with the United States	Positive
	y^f: real foreign income	Positive

This is not the end of the story as far as the demand for dollars arising from exports is concerned, however; for, you will recall, the entry in the balance of payments is the *dollar value* of exports or the quantity of *dollars* required to pay for the quantity of exports. To obtain this demand for dollars we simply multiply our equation above by P^{US}.

$$P^{US}X = P^{US} [f(P^{US}, ER, P^f, y^f, \ldots)]$$

Now the influence of each variable on the dollar value of the demand for our exports should be the same as for the real quantity, with the possible exception of P^{US}. An increase in U.S. prices will   The influence of
tend to decrease the real quantity of U.S. exports, ceteris paribus,   U.S. prices on the
because of a decline in foreign demand. However, because U.S.   dollar value of
exports now cost more, the quantity of dollars demanded for the   exports
purchase of our exports (price times quantity) *could* go up. In our
analysis, it all depends upon how price sensitive the foreign demand

for real exports is. If foreign demand is price elastic, the percentage fall in X will be greater than the percentage rise in P^{US}, and $P^{US}X$ will fall.[3] There are theories and evidence to support the view that the long-run price elasticity of the foreign demand for our exports is greater than unity. Consequently, we will accept the direction of influence of P^{US} on $P^{US}X$ as negative, even though it will not be as strongly negative as its influence on X alone.

SOURCES OF THE DEMAND FOR DOLLARS: FOREIGN INVESTMENT IN THE UNITED STATES

The second major component of the demand for dollars listed was foreign investment in the United States. This component is itself comprised of a variety of types of investment. We can distinguish between investment in real and equity assets and investment in credit-market assets. Among credit-market assets, we will distinguish short- from long-term assets. Investment by foreigners in real assets and equities in the United States, such as the purchase and expansion of an automobile plant in New Stanton, Pennsylvania, by Volkswagen in 1976, is motivated by expected future profits from these assets relative to alternative investments in other parts of the world. Many considerations enter into the formulation of these profit expectations, including labor costs, political stability, foreign-exchange restrictions, etc. Because the motivations for these investments are quite complex, and the volumes involved usually are not large relative to other transactions, we will not make this area an integral part of our analysis; foreign investment in real and equity assets in the United States is simply taken as given.

Foreign real and equity investment

Foreign investment in credit-market assets in the United States, on the other hand, does have to be dealt with in some detail. Let us return to our fictitious example of state currencies and consider a New York resident who is evaluating an investment in North Carolina state bonds versus New York state bonds. Under the assumptions we made originally, both states have the power to print their own money, so there should be no particular advantage between these assets as far as default risk is concerned. There may be tax considerations which favor the home state's obligation, but we will assume that away too. The assets also, let us say, have the same maturity—one year—and the same degree of marketability. In other words, the only difference between these assets is their denomination in different monies and, possibly, their yields. At the start we will set their yields equal at 6 percent with each asset selling at 100 percent of par.

Foreign investment in credit-market assets

---

[3]A more comprehensive analysis would take into account also the actual elasticity of the supply of exports, which we have assumed to be infinite.

The relevant yield to the N.Y. resident is the yield in N.Y. dollars —on either investment. He knows that this yield is 6 percent on the New York bond. But what about the N.C. bond? The yield on the North Carolina bond in North Carolina dollars, b^{NC}, is given by the usual formula:

$$P_B^{NC} = \frac{C^{NC} + \$100 \text{ N.C.}}{1 + b^{NC}}$$

or, solving for b^{NC},

$$b^{NC} = \frac{C^{NC} + \$100 \text{ N.C.}}{P_B^{NC}} - 1$$

where P_B^{NC} is the price of the bond in North Carolina dollars and C^{NC} is the coupon payment in North Carolina dollars.

The New York resident must make two exchange transactions between state monies when he invests in a North Carolina bond—at the time of purchase and at the time he receives the face value and coupon payment. This creates the following expression for b^{NC} in terms of New York dollars:

$$b^{NC} = \frac{C^{NC} (ER_1) + \$100 \text{ N.C. } (ER_1)}{P_B^{NC} (ER_0)} - 1$$

where ER_0 is the price of N.C. dollars in terms of N.Y. dollars at the present time, and ER_1 is this price one year from now. From what has already been assumed we know $P_B^{NC} = \$100$ N.C. and $C^{NC} = \$6.00$ N.C. Let us suppose ER_0 to be our original \$1.10 N.Y./N.C. What about ER_1? Well, our New York investor will not know ahead of time exactly what ER_1 will be (and this can be an important consideration as far as liquidity is concerned), but suppose he expects that it will be \$0.99 N.Y./N.C. In other words, he expects the value of N.C. dollars will fall over the year by 10 percent.

The formula, with our values entered and converted to New York dollars, is now

$$b^{NY} = \frac{\$5.94 \text{ N.Y.} + \$99.00 \text{ N.Y.}}{\$110 \text{ N.Y.}} - 1$$

which can be solved for

$$b^{NY} = -4.60\%$$

This is approximately equal to the yield on the North Carolina bond in North Carolina dollars, 6 percent, minus the expected fall in the value of North Carolina dollars, 10 percent. The result demonstrates that, in evaluating the expected returns on credit-market assets denominated in foreign money, investors should take into account possible and expected percentage changes in the value of foreign money.

Foreign investment in U.S. credit-market assets, therefore, will be positively related to current yields on these assets in U.S. dollars and negatively related to (1) the expected rate of fall in the value of the dollar, (2) the risk of a greater than anticipated fall in the value of the dollar, and (3) the current yields on debt assets denominated in other currencies. A variety of other influences may also be relevant. These include the incentive to evade taxes in home countries and the concern for political risk, as well as the more obvious considerations such as different tax rates and direct controls on foreign or domestic investment.

SOURCES OF THE SUPPLY OF DOLLARS: PAYMENTS FOR IMPORTS

The factors affecting the demand for imports

Our analysis of import payments corresponds closely to our analysis of export receipts. Because U.S. imports, in general, represent a small proportion of the rest of the world's production, we again take supply as perfectly elastic. This makes the price of U.S. imports in terms of foreign exchange a given, and we will also assume that this is equal to the general level of foreign prices, P^f. For the usual reasons, *the U.S. demand for imports, N^D, is inversely related to the level of the price of imports in terms of U.S. dollars, and positively related to the levels of real income and the price of competing goods in the U.S.*

The analysis of the dollar price of U.S. imports

The price of imports in terms of dollars requires the same sort of analysis accorded the foreign price of U.S. exports earlier. We go again to our two-state example where North Carolina is the home state. A North Carolinian ordering a camera from a New York firm may discover that the camera costs $220 N.Y. Earlier we assumed an exchange rate of $1.10 N.Y./N.C. Assuming this also represents the rate applicable to North Carolinians exchanging their money for New York money, the North Carolinian can obtain $220 N.Y. for merely $200 N.C. ($220 N.Y. divided by $1.10 N.Y./N.C.). The price, then, of the New York camera is $200 in North Carolina dollars. *In general, therefore, the price of U.S. imports will be equal to the level of foreign prices divided by the value of the dollar in terms of foreign exchange.* If this value rises, the dollar price of U.S. imports will tend to fall, ceteris paribus, because it will take fewer dollars to pay the same foreign price for imports. Also, note that it is possible for the foreign price of U.S. imports to rise without the price in dollars rising, if the value of the dollar has risen just enough to offset the rise in P^f.

The import-quantity function

Our import-quantity function may be summarized as:

$$N^D = N = f(P^f, ER, P^{US}, y, \ldots)$$

Influenced variable	Influencing variable	Direction of influence
N: the quantity of U.S. imports	P^f: the price level in foreign countries trading with the United States	Negative
	ER: the exchange rate (value) of the U.S. dollar	Positive
	y: the level of income in the United States	Positive
	P^{US}: the U.S. price level	Positive

We have one step remaining to convert this relationship to an import-payments function, just as we had another step going from our export-quantity function to our export-payments function to allow for P^{US}. In this case, the payment function involves *two* more variables because, as we have seen, the dollar price of our imports equals the foreign price of our imports divided by the exchange rate of the dollar. Therefore, the import-payments relationship is:

$$\frac{P^f}{ER}(N) = \frac{P^f}{ER} \, [f(P^f, \ ER, \ P^{US}, \ y, \ . \ . \ .)]$$

Note that the exchange rate shows up twice on the right-hand side of this relationship. (Contrast this to the export-receipts relationship discussed earlier.)

The same potential difficulty arises for import payments as for export payments in terms of uncertainty as to the direction of the influence of the price term. Keep in mind that in this case there are two elements, P^f and ER, to the relevant price term, $\dfrac{P^f}{ER}$. *Under the assumptions of our analysis, the influence of P^f on $\dfrac{P^f}{ER}(N)$ will be negative and the influence of ER will be positive, provided the U.S. demand for imports is elastic with respect to import prices.* [4]

There is not as strong a reason to expect the U.S. demand for imports to be price elastic as there is for the foreign demand for our exports. U.S. exports compete with a great many other countries' exports, and a slight price differential in favor of the United States

---

[4] A more comprehensive analysis takes the elasticity of the supply of imports into account as well.

may be enough to switch substantial demand from other countries' exports to U.S. exports. U.S. imports, on the other hand, compete only with domestic production, and, therefore, the possibilities in terms of substitutes are more limited. Nevertheless, we shall assume that the U.S. demand for imports is price elastic. Hence, all of the variables in our import-payments function have the same direction of influence as was listed for them under our import-quantity function.

SOURCES OF THE SUPPLY OF DOLLARS: U.S. INVESTMENT ABROAD

The similarities here to the analysis of foreign investment in the United States are close. Real investment abroad will be motivated by the same variables cited as factors affecting real investment in the United States. As described for U.S. instruments, investments in credit-market assets in other countries will take into account any expected change in the relevant exchange rates. In general, an expected *rise* in the value of the dollar in terms of foreign exchange subtracts from the realized yield in U.S. dollars of a given yield on foreign assets. *Therefore, U.S. investment in foreign credit-market assets will be positively related to the yield on these assets and nega-*

"If I only could remember the number of my secret bank account in Switzerland."

Reprinted by permission *The Wall Street Journal*

tively related to (1) an expected rise in the value in the dollar, (2) the risk of a greater than expected rise in the value of the dollar, and (3) the yield on U.S. financial assets.

INTRODUCTION TO ARTICLE

As consumers, most of us do not realize the impact exchange-rate changes have on the prices of things we buy. The reason, of course, is that, except when they travel abroad, consumers pay dollars for imports; it is the importers who must pay in foreign exchange and feel the impact most directly. The article below from *The Wall Street Journal*, April 7, 1977, illustrates how these changes affect importers and their pricing decisions. This story was repeated many times during the rest of 1977 and through 1978 as the dollar declined further and more sharply to below 180 yen to the dollar in October 1978, its low point against the yen in the 1970s.

Japan Car Firms Plan to Increase Their U.S. Prices

Prices for Japanese autos sold in the United States are beginning to rise as a result of the recent decline of the U.S. dollar against the yen.

Toyota Motor Sales Company, the sales arm of Toyota Motor Company and the biggest auto importer in the United States, said it's planning to raise retail prices in the U.S. market to make up for exchange losses from the drop in the dollar's value. Nissan Motor Company, the maker of Datsuns and the second largest importer, said it also is considering such a move. And sources said American Honda Company, the third largest importer, also is planning a price boost.

Toyota officials in Tokyo declined to give details of the planned increases. The Honda sources in the United States said, however, that they expected a rise in retail prices of about 5 percent will be announced next week.

Toyota said that prices for exporting passenger cars to the United States were pegged at a rate of 290 yen to the dollar. The dollar in Tokyo Wednesday was about 273 yen. Officials calculate that they must bear an exchange loss of $12 to $15 a car every time the dollar falls by one yen.

On a large-size passenger car such as the Celica GT, which retails for $4,599 in the United States, this means an exchange loss of more than $200 for each unit.

Last October, Toyota increased its U.S. retail prices an average of $112 a car. Toyota's automobile shipments to the United States totaled 40,700 units in January and 42,400 units in February. Shipments to the U.S. in 1976 were up 53 percent to 441,641 units.

In Torrance, CA, a spokesman for Toyota Motor Sales, said that "how the dollar valuation will affect the prices of Toyota vehicles hasn't been set." The company, he said, will be considering higher costs it has experienced for shipping, labor, and materials as well as the currency change when it reprices the autos.

Noting that some European auto makers have recently increased prices and that U.S. auto makers have raised prices on some optional equipment and certain popular models, he said he doesn't expect any price boost to hurt sales "to any significant degree."

Ironically, the rise of the three Japanese companies to the top ranks of U.S. auto importers has been attributed to the decline of Volkswagen. The West German import has been forced out of the low-priced end of the small-car market, partly because of the strength of the West German mark during the past five years.

Officials of Nissan in Tokyo said they expect their sales to the United States this year will level off at just about 1976's total of 42,456 cars which was up 38 percent from 1975.

SOURCE: "Japan Car Firms Plan to Increase their U.S. Prices," *The Wall Street Journal*, April 7, 1977.

THE MAJOR DETERMINANTS OF THE U.S.–DOLLAR EXCHANGE RATE

We are now in a position to focus on the dollar exchange rate. Recall that, under our assumptions, export payments are negatively related to the exchange rate of the dollar. As we have analyzed it, *The demand curve* the other major component of the demand for dollars, foreign investment in the United States, is related to the expected rate of change in the exchange rate, not to its level. Therefore, the downward slope of the demand-for-dollars curve in Figure 8–3, which includes both components, is due essentially to the negative influence of the exchange rate on export receipts.[5]

The supply curve and equilibrium The same reasoning underlies our supply curve in Figure 8–3. A rise in the exchange rate induces higher import payments, ceteris

FIGURE 8–3
Supply and demand for dollars

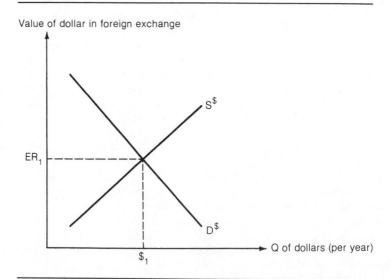

Value of dollar in foreign exchange

paribus, and hence, a higher total supply of dollars. For the moment, we will assume that the quantity of autonomous demand equals the quantity of autonomous supply (reserve transactions are

---

[5]This is a simplification. There is an influence of the level of the exchange rate on foreign real investment in the United States which has been ignored to simplify the discussion.

zero), and the exchange rate which establishes that equilibrium is ER_1. Now, of course, there is no single exchange rate for the dollar in the foreign-exchange market; in our analysis, ER_1 represents a weighted average of the exchange rates of the dollar in terms of trading- and investing-partner countries, with the weights reflecting the relative importance of those partners in U.S. international payments. However, to give ER_1 more concreteness, let us assume that it reflects, in part, an exchange rate of two West German marks to the dollar (2.00 DM/\$). Exchange-rate changes will be described in terms of the mark as a representative foreign currency, and West Germany will serve as a representative trade and investment partner.

Purchasing-power-parity pressure

A principal influence on the dollar exchange rate is the level of U.S. prices relative to prices abroad. With free trade there will be market pressure to establish *purchasing-power parity* (PPP) between monies. *Purchasing-power parity exists when the exchange rate between two currencies is such that the prices of similar goods in each of the respective countries are equal if expressed in terms of a common currency unit.* In other words, PPP holds when $P^{US} = \dfrac{P^f}{ER}$ or $ER = \dfrac{P^f}{P^{US}}$.

To see the origin of the pressure to establish PPP, suppose the price level in the U.S. rises by 11 percent and the West German price level remains constant. A rise in the U.S. price level makes U.S. exports less attractive to foreigners, and, at the same exchange rate, imports from foreigners appear more attractive to U.S. residents since import prices in U.S. dollars would remain constant while prices of domestic products are rising. In terms of the purchasing power of the dollar, the parity between domestic goods and West German goods has been disturbed. Using our supply and demand model, we know that the dollar-demand curve shifts to the left, and the dollar-supply curve shifts to the right, as shown in Figure 8–4. With no intervention in the foreign exchange market, the exchange rate of the dollar will fall. According to the *purchasing-power-parity doctrine*, the exchange rate will fall to the point where the dollar price of U.S. imports from West Germany has risen to the level of U.S. prices and the foreign exchange price of U.S. exports has fallen back to its original level. This would occur at an exchange rate of 1.80 West German marks to the dollar.[6] The end result

---

[6]Let $ER_1 = P_1^f/P_1^{US} = 2.00$ DM/\$ and $P_2^f/P_2^{US} = P_1^f/[P_1^{US} (1 + .11)]$. Then PPP requires that $ER_2 = P_2^f/P_2^{US} = (2.00$ DM/\$)/$(1 + .11) = 1.80$ DM/\$.

FIGURE 8–4
An increase in the U.S. price level

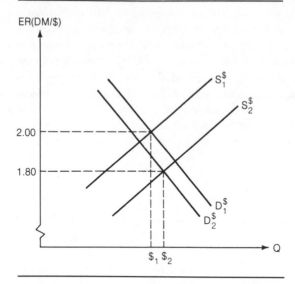

would be a return of the quantities of U.S. exports and imports to their original levels, but the dollar exchange rate would be permanently lower by approximately the same percentage amount as the rise in the U.S. price level. Purchasing-power parity for the dollar in terms of domestic and foreign goods would be restored.

In the post–World War II period price levels have risen worldwide, particularly during the 1970s. The purchasing-power parity effect implies that the equilibrium exchange rate between two monies will tend to adjust continually if the rates of inflation in the two corresponding countries are different; the exchange rate for the more inflationary country falls. During the 1970s the United States, for example, had a higher rate of inflation on average than West Germany, but a lower one than Italy, as shown by the price indexes in Figure 8–5. Consequently, as the chart in Figure 8–6 shows, relative to the dollar the value of the mark rose, and the value of the Italian lira fell.

The purchasing-power parity effect may take a very long time to fully assert itself. In the intervening period there are other, less permanent effects which can cause significant movements in exchange rates.

International business cycles

There are two different real-income variables, you will recall, which are involved in our analysis of import payments and export receipts: U.S. real income and foreign real income. As U.S. real

FIGURE 8–5
Price level changes

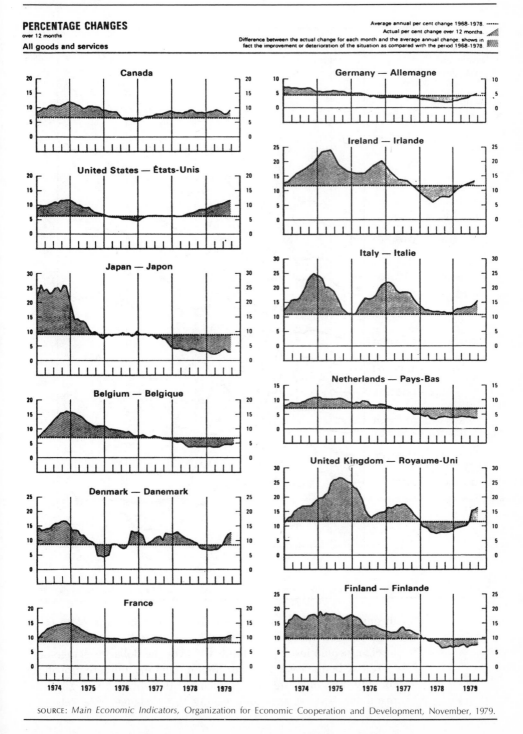

PERCENTAGE CHANGES
over 12 months
All goods and services

Average annual per cent change 1968-1978. ......
Actual per cent change over 12 months.
Difference between the actual change for each month and the average annual change; shows in fact the improvement or deterioration of the situation as compared with the period 1968-1978

Canada

United States — États-Unis

Japan — Japon

Belgium — Belgique

Denmark — Danemark

France

Germany — Allemagne

Ireland — Irlande

Italy — Italie

Netherlands — Pays-Bas

United Kingdom — Royaume-Uni

Finland — Finlande

SOURCE: *Main Economic Indicators,* Organization for Economic Cooperation and Development, November, 1979.

FIGURE 8–6
Exchange rates; dollars per local currency units

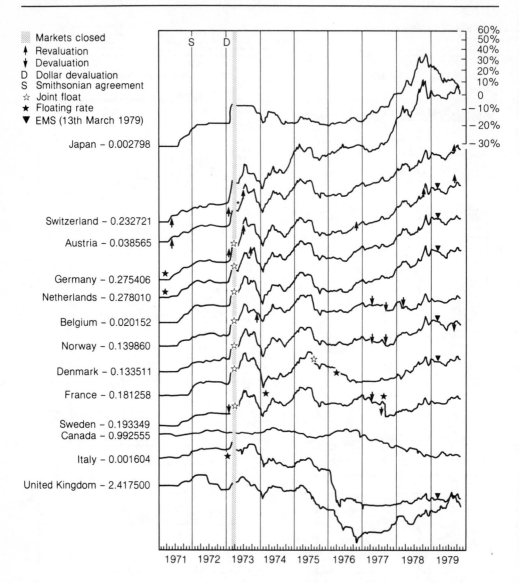

SOURCE: *Main Economic Indicators,* Organization for Economic Cooperation and Development, November, 1979.

income grows, the U.S. demand for imports and, therefore, U.S. import payments increase. Other things being the same, including foreign income levels, this tends to lower the dollar exchange rate.

It may be the case, however, that foreign incomes are growing at roughly the same rate as U.S. income, thereby increasing the demand for U.S. exports and leaving the exchange rate relatively unchanged.[7] One reason foreign incomes might increase is the stimulus to foreign economies of increased demand in the United States for foreign products, though some lag would ordinarily occur in the effect of this stimulus. Another reason could be an internationally coordinated program of expansionary monetary and fiscal policies. This, in fact, has been an objective of meetings among the leaders of major industrial countries from time to time. In practice, however, it is difficult to coordinate these policies because of the inflationary impact of expansionary policies and because of the different weights attached to policy goals in different countries. Consequently, some correspondence does exist between business cycles among major trading partners; but the correspondence is not close, and there remains an influence of different income growth rates on exchange rates.

Pressure toward adjusted interest-rate parity

Purchasing-power parity and business-cycle influences pertain mainly to the current-account elements in the balance of payments. We turn now to the capital-account entries. These, you recall, are not affected in our analysis by the level of the exchange rate, but the reverse does not hold. Capital-account changes can affect the level of the exchange rate because they lead to purchases and sales of dollars in the foreign-exchange market.

Our analysis of private capital-account entries emphasized the importance of interest rates and expected changes in exchange rates. Wherever there are not overriding considerations imposed by tax or risk factors or controls, sophisticated financial investors often move vast sums of funds among credit-market assets denominated in different currencies. They seek investments for which market yields are highest after allowing for the expected rate of change in the relevant exchange rate. Such a flow of funds can be large enough to drive market interest rates down in "strong-currency" countries and raise interest rates in "weak-currency" countries. *Over time, interest rates may adjust to the point that rates in all countries are equal after allowing for expected changes in their exchange rates and after allowing for risk and tax considerations.* If so, a type of *adjusted interest-rate parity* is eventually established, and the capital flows which were induced by the original interest-rate differences diminish. Though this state is seldom ever completely reached, there is normally pressure toward adjusted interest-rate parity.

---

[7]In order for the exchange rate not to be affected *at all* by income changes, it would also have to be the case that the income elasticities of the demands for imports are the same across trading partners.

FIGURE 8–7
Effect of tight monetary policy in the U.S.

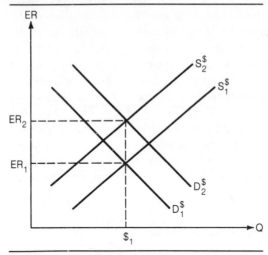

The effects of monetary policy via interest rates and expected exchange-rate changes

During a period when monetary policies are changing, there are effects on supply and demand relationships in the foreign-exchange market. Suppose, for example, that the Federal Reserve imposes a tight monetary policy on the U.S. economy which, in the course of events, raises the level of interest rates in the United States relative to interest rates in West Germany. This will induce an increase in investment in U.S. financial assets by West Germans and a decrease in U.S. private investment in West German assets. The demand for dollars shifts to the right and the supply shifts to the left, as shown in Figure 8–7. As a result, the equilibrium exchange rate of the dollar tends to rise, ceteris paribus.

A similar effect occurs if changes in monetary policy alter market expectations about the long-run trend in the exchange rate. Consider the United States and West Germany again, and suppose that monetary policy moves suggest that the future rate of inflation is likely to be lower in the United States than previously thought whereas expectations of German inflation are unchanged. Market participants will tend to infer from this that the dollar exchange rate will be higher in the future than previously expected in terms of the mark because purchasing-power parity pressure will be changed. Given current interest rates in the United States and West Germany, financial assets in the United States will appear more attractive, and a capital flow into U.S.–dollar-denominated assets will occur. This will shift the demand curve for dollars in the foreign exchange market to the right, and the supply curve will shift to the left, raising the exchange rate of the dollar *in advance* of the purchasing-power parity effect.

Official reserve transactions

Thus far we have totally ignored intervention in the foreign exchange market by the U.S. or a foreign government in order to influence market exchange rates for the U.S. dollar and other monies. There have been several motives behind *official reserve transactions* and other government actions designed to influence exchange rates in recent years.

To explain one of these motives, let us return to the immediately preceding example where expectations of a future fall in the value of the dollar led to capital flows which induced a near-term fall. Expectations of a future fall in the dollar stemmed from anticipated changes in the inflation rates of the two economies. But the near-term fall induced by capital flows could cause its own, self-perpetuating downward influence on the exchange rate if this fall is a surprise and creates expectations of a greater fall in the exchange rate than anticipated earlier. Another round of capital outflows from the United States might result, perhaps with enough impact to cause expectations of a still greater fall in the dollar. This process could continue with a severe overshooting, downward adjustment in the exchange rate—a decline beyond any reasonable level in terms of purchasing-power parity and long-run equilibrium.

Such an overshooting of an exchange rate disturbs trade relationships in an undesirable way. Moreover, wild swings in exchange rates introduce great uncertainty to international economic relationships. If the U.S. government enters the foreign-exchange market and buys dollars with reserves of foreign exchange on hand, how-

Motives for intervention

The motive to prevent destabilizing capital flows

FIGURE 8–8
Intervention in the exchange market

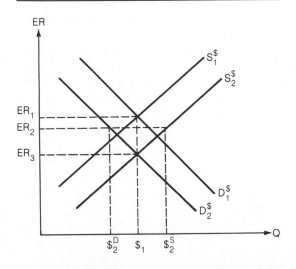

ever, the extreme fall in the exchange rate might be prevented. The result is shown in Figure 8–8 where the exchange rate falls from ER_1 to only ER_2 instead of to ER_3 and possibly lower in future periods in response to destabilizing capital flows. The dollar value of the U.S. reserves of foreign exchange sold is approximately the amount $\$_2^S - \$_2^D$, which reflects the excess supply of dollars at the exchange rate ER_2. As this example illustrates, an important motivation for government intervention in the foreign-exchange market has been to prevent wide, self-reinforcing swings in the exchange rate due to short-term capital flows.

The counter-inflation motive   A second motive stems from the impact exchange-rate changes have on domestic inflation rates. Consider the decline in the value of the dollar by roughly 25 percent against the West German mark and 30 percent against the Japanese yen during 1977–78. These exchange-rate changes raised U.S. import prices for cars, steel, televisions, and other products from these countries. Such price increases added directly to the U.S. inflation rate and encouraged increases in the prices of domestically produced goods which otherwise would have had to compete with low-priced imports.

One policy response to such a situation is to allow the exchange rate to fall but curb the demand for domestic goods and imports through restrictive monetary and fiscal policies. Demand restraint can stem the depreciation of the dollar in the foreign-exchange market and keep domestic prices from rising. Another approach is to coordinate restrictive macroeconomic policies with direct intervention in the foreign-exchange market to keep the exchange rate from falling and putting upward pressure on import prices. Intervention of this sort must be combined with restrictive demand policies to be successful in the long run, however. With or without restrictive policies, a desire to curb the effects of exchange-rate depreciation on domestic inflation is often the motive behind government intervention in the foreign-exchange market.[8]

Trade motives   Other motivations for intervention include (1) a desire to protect domestic and export industries from the competition of foreign goods, made cheaper by appreciation of the exchange rate, and (2) a desire to protect certain consumers of import goods from price increases caused by a depreciating exchange rate.

---

[8]Discussion of an important argument against the use of intervention without restrictive demand policies is left out of the text, for it would take us away from our immediate concern which is simply the motives—wise or unwise—for government intervention in the foreign-exchange market.

Very briefly, the argument is that the root cause of a depreciating currency is likely to be excessively expansionary monetary and fiscal policies. As long as such policies are maintained, intervention will only postpone an inevitable decline in the exchange rate to achieve purchasing-power parity. If these expansionary policies are reversed, intervention probably would not be necessary.

Intervention and exchange rates from a global perspective

It should be noted that the disequilibrium exchange rate, ER_2, could be the result of reserve intervention by a foreign government instead of that of the United States. The excess supply of dollars, $\$_2^S - \$_2^D$, could be taken off the market by purchases of dollars (additions to reserves) by foreign governments. From their point of view, $\$_2^S - \$_2^D$ implies a corresponding excess *demand* for their currencies. Their central banks may simply create more of their money with which to make purchases of dollars, thereby accommodating the excess supply of dollars and the excess demand for their monies at ER_2. This raises an important point: exchange rates are not independent prices, established in a vacuum with respect to each other. For each two-currency exchange rate, there is one other two-currency exchange rate which is its reciprocal. A decision by the Japanese government to "manage" its exchange rate vis-a-vis the dollar, the yen/dollar rate, therefore, means that the dollar/yen exchange rate is also being managed. For this reason, the United States may be very much affected by intervention of foreign governments in the foreign-exchange market, and other countries are affected by U.S. intervention.

Many governments in the past, and some today, have agreed to pursue *fixed exchange rates*. Under a policy of fixed exchange rates, virtually *any* excess supply of a country's money at some floor exchange rate is offset by selling official reserves of foreign exchange or other assets such as gold; and *any* excess demand at a narrowly higher ceiling exchange rate is offset by buying foreign exchange or other reserve assets with domestic money.

Fixed exchange rates

Purchases of foreign exchange, of course, build official reserves and sales deplete them. If the official band for the exchange rate is realistic in terms of long-run purchasing-power parity and similar permanent forces, reserves should build and fall within reasonable limits over periods encompassing business-cycle and other short-term influences. This is the ideal world of fixed exchange rates. Problems arise because of difficulty in knowing what level is realistic for the exchange rate, and more fundamentally, as we shall see later, what currency or other standard to adopt for exchange-rate fixing.

At the end of World War II a fixed exchange-rate system was negotiated among the major industrial countries of the developed West at Bretton Woods, NH. Under this system, which lasted until 1973, most currencies were pegged to the dollar. The dollar was, in turn, pegged loosely and ineffectually to gold. The system was subject to periodic crises and eventually broke down in 1973, mainly because of (1) a persistent rise in U.S. inflation, and (2) substantially different inflation rates and policy priorities among Western industrial countries. The system that has prevailed since has

The Bretton Woods system of fixed rates

been a mixture of flexible (floating) and semifixed exchange rates. Intervention occurs, especially in countries participating in "currency blocks," but even among these countries exchange rates are allowed to adjust to market forces fairly frequently. The arguments for fixed versus flexible exchange rates are summarized in a later section in this chapter.

"I see where the value of the dollar has started to go up everywhere except in the United States."

Reprinted by permission *The Wall Street Journal*

INSTITUTIONAL FEATURES OF THE INTERNATIONAL FINANCIAL MARKETS

The forward exchange market

In a world of fluctuating exchange rates, international transactions involve a degree of foreign-exchange risk. Suppose, for example, that you are an importer contracting today for goods from West Germany which will require you to pay one million marks three months from now. Say the current (spot) price of the mark is 50 U.S. cents (2.00 DM/$). If the mark rises unexpectedly by 1 percent over the next three months, you will have to pay $5,000 more for your West German imports than you expected. This type of loss is a cause for concern among firms engaged in international trade. Fortunately, there is a readily available way for many international transactors to avoid such unexpected losses through the forward exchange market.

The forward exchange market is a market in contracts for foreign exchange at some date in the future at a price agreed upon today. As the U.S. importer in our previous example, you could obtain a contract from a bank for one million marks at a prespecified price in terms of dollars three months from now. If you have an established relationship with the bank, it may not be necessary for you to commit any funds in advance of the contract date.

The exchange rate agreed upon for this future transaction might be a little less favorable than the rate for a current (spot) transaction, depending upon current market conditions, but you will, at least, avoid an unexpected loss. The three-month forward rate for marks, for example, might be 50.1 U.S. cents. This would make the purchase price of your imported goods $501,000—$1,000 higher than they would be at the current spot exchange rate of 50¢, but $4,000 less than in our example earlier where the mark rate rose unexpectedly by 1 percent.[9]

Just as the forward exchange market allows a U.S. importer to hedge against an unexpected rise in the value of the mark, it also allows a West German importer to hedge against an unexpected rise in the value of the dollar. In fact, the other ultimate party involved in the contract described above could be a West German importer ordering approximately $500,000 worth of U.S. goods. Part of the total market for forward contracts in foreign exchange is comprised of such trade hedgers. Another part is accounted for by investment hedgers. The remaining activity is mainly due to speculators—those assuming foreign-exchange risk intentionally in expectation of profit from future foreign-exchange-rate prices at variance with prices in the forward exchange market.

The forward exchange market has grown in volume and importance since the advent of flexible exchange rates. According to one theory, the forward rate for a given currency should tend to equal the spot rate that the market anticipates in the future for that currency. If this relationship holds, it is possible to compare the forward rate for a certain currency with the spot rate that actually occurred to determine how accurate the market was in its past forecasts of future exchange rates. The evidence from recent history reveals a great deal of discrepancy between forward rates and subsequent spot exchange rates.

The predictive accuracy of forward-market prices

The Eurocurrency market

Another market important in the world of international finance is

---

[9]You may ask yourself at this point why an importer would not simply obtain the marks at the current exchange rate and invest them in Germany for three months. It would seem possible to save $1,000 by doing so. This is certainly a viable option for an importer who wants to hedge, but it is unlikely to save him much money if interest rates are lower in Germany, as they are apt to be.

the so-called Eurocurrency market. The Eurocurrency market originated with dollar-denominated bank deposits and loans in Europe, particularly in London, following World War II. (Eurodollar deposits were described in Chapter 6.) Dollar time deposits were acquired by British and other foreign banks, including foreign branches of U.S. banks, from foreign governments and various firms and individuals who, for different reasons, wanted to hold dollars (a foreign currency to them) outside the U.S. Banks based in Europe accepted dollar-denominated deposits and made dollar-denominated loans to a variety of customers.

This type of foreign-currency-denominated financing has grown tremendously, now encompasses loans denominated in many more currencies than the dollar, and takes place in several countries outside of Europe. Regardless of where they occur, *most credit-market financings denominated in foreign currency vis-a-vis the country where the financings take place are part of what is known as the Eurocurrency market.* These include, for example, a loan of yen by a Japanese bank in Nassau to an importer in South Africa, despite the fact that in this case neither the currency of denomination, the intermediary, the borrower, nor the locale has anything to do with a European country.[10]

One advantage to obtaining and placing loans outside the country of the currency of denomination often is that it is possible to avoid many governmental regulations and restrictions by doing so. You will recall, for example, that in the United States the interest rates payable on time deposits have been constrained at times by the Federal Reserve's Regulation Q and other regulations. Interest rates on deposits of dollars and other currencies in the London branches of U.S. banks are not subject to such ceilings, however. As a result, in the past, deposits have tended to move from the United States to the Eurodollar market when Regulation Q ceilings became effective on rates payable on large CDs in the United States. As owners of time deposits in the United States transferred balances to Eurodollar accounts at higher interest rates, U.S. banks turned to their foreign branches and other foreign-based banks and borrowed these dollars back at higher interest rates than those allowed on U.S. time deposits. In this manner, the ceilings were circumvented to a degree. As a result, Regulation Q ceilings on large CDs were removed in 1973.

The Eurocurrency market has become an important addition to the conventional methods of engaging in external finance around the world. It does not change any of our previous analysis of the determinants of exchange rates. It does, however, influence the

---

[10]It may be noted, however, that in recent years a few Asian cities have developed as centers for dollar-denominated deposits and loans, and this market, with Singapore as the center, is sometimes given separate identification as the Asian dollar market.

success with which governments can influence the exchange rate for their currency by imposing restrictions on capital movements into or out of their country. And, it also reduces to a degree the effectiveness of restrictions on domestic credit, as the Regulation Q example testifies.

The International Monetary Fund

The International Monetary Fund (IMF) is an organization which was created by 44 Western countries following World War II, partly to facilitate the operation of a fixed exchange-rate system. It has served as an intermediary for reserve loans to countries experiencing downward pressure on their exchange rates, and it has been a valuable forum for international monetary discussions and agreements. Funds for reserve loans come from loans and contributions of gold and foreign exchange from participating governments. The role of the IMF as an intermediary in reserve loans between governments has diminished somewhat in recent years with the demise of the Bretton Woods fixed-exchange-rate system. Nevertheless, the fund remains an important international institution for balance-of-payments loans and, as always, a valuable source of information on world economies and international monetary issues.

In 1967, the IMF created a special unit of account and medium for reserve loans called the "special drawing right" or SDR. The institutional arrangements involved with SDRs are not important to the purposes of this text. They are mentioned here partly because they will come up again in Chapter 14 in connection with the Federal Reserve's mechanism of control for the money supply.

The SDR

FIXED VERSUS FLEXIBLE EXCHANGE RATES

Exchange rates between convertible monies may be maintained within a narrow range of "official" or target levels by government sales or purchases of reserves, as described earlier. In addition to preventing possibly destabilizing speculative pressures on exchange rates, a fixed exchange-rate system is often advocated as conducive to world trade and, consequently, efficient organization of worldwide production. It is argued that, under fixed rates, foreign traders do not have to worry about unexpected exchange-rate changes, and this is favorable to more trade.

How fixed rates are meant to function

In theory, for most countries a fixed exchange-rate system would function as depicted in Figure 8–9. In periods when, without reserve intervention, the exchange rate would tend to be lower than a certain floor rate, intervention occurs to keep the exchange rate at

FIGURE 8–9
Fixed exchange rates

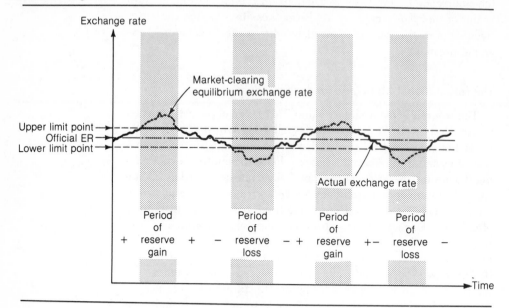

or above the floor rate, and home country reserves fall. Reserves rise during periods when the exchange rate would tend to be higher. If things work out right, these periods of reserve ebb and flow reflect mainly seasonal and cyclical influences on autonomous demands for and supplies of foreign exchange. They may also be caused by natural disasters, poor harvest years, and perhaps market instability—all *temporary* influences—at home or abroad.

With fixed exchange rates, there may be one country whose currency is chosen as a standard of value and a preferred reserve asset for intervention operations. This was the case for the United States and, to a lesser extent, Britain during the postwar, fixed-rate period. Such reserve-currency countries do not necessarily need to respond to any slack in demand or supply for their currency, as shown in Figure 8–8. Since *other* countries set their intervention points in terms of a reserve currency and automatically buy up this currency when it is in excess supply and sell it when it is in excess demand, there may be little or no intervention by a reserve-currency country under fixed exchange rates.[11]

The tendency of a country's long-run equilibrium exchange rate

Reserve-currency countries

[11]Complete freedom from pressure to intervene may not exist, however, if the reserve currency is, in turn, pegged to gold or another commodity-reserve asset. In the Bretton Woods fixed-rate system, market exchange rates were allowed to vary 1 percent on either side of the official, or par, exchange rates under the IMF rules prevailing until 1971. Official rates for other currencies were set in terms of the U.S. dollar, and reserves of other countries were comprised mainly of dollars held by foreign official agencies, that is, central banks. These reserve dollars were exchange-

to always stay within the intervention points around an official exchange rate cannot be assumed, of course. Changes in the long-run
equilibrium rate might occur for a variety of reasons: excessive inflation at home, a lag in technological improvements relative to other
countries, changes in the organizational structure of the world supply of some imports (e.g., the formation of OPEC), depletion of
domestic supplies of limited resources, and permanent changes in
world or domestic demand preferences, to name a few.

Countries faced with changing long-run equilibrium exchange   Fundamental dis-
equilibrium
rates would find themselves in positions similar to those depicted in
Figures 8–10 and 8–11. Periods of reserve losses and deficits in the
balance of payments are not matched by periods during which reserves are adequately replenished in Figure 8–10. The reverse occurs in Figure 8–11. These are often described as situations of *fundamental disequilibrium*. The situation shown in Figure 8–10 could
be handled by a downward adjustment of the official exchange rate—
that is, an official *devaluation*—to the neighborhood of the lower
long-run equilibrium rate. Where the long-run equilibrium rate is
rising, as in Figure 8–11, the official exchange rate could be raised—
a *revaluation*.

FIGURE 8–10
Balance-of-Payment deficits with fixed exchange rates

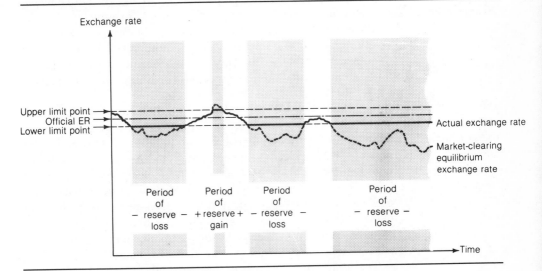

able for gold from the U.S. Treasury at a fixed rate. Due to a fundamental disequilibrium in the balance of payments of the United States (described next in the text),
foreign central banks accumulated large amounts of dollars in the 1960s through
intervention, and significant amounts of these dollars were exchanged for U.S. gold.
Finally, in August 1971, the U.S. gold window was closed, effectively devaluing the
dollar.

FIGURE 8–11
Balance-of-Payment surpluses with fixed exchange rates

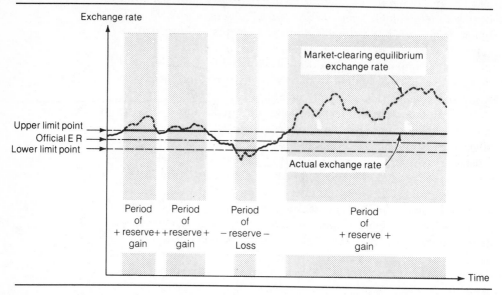

The role of
monetary and
fiscal policies

One other way to respond to the trend shown in Figure 8–10 might be to impose a program of austerity, that is, restrictive monetary and fiscal policies. These policies would eventually raise the long-run equilibrium rate by reducing the home country's rate of inflation relative to other countries' inflation rates. If the cause of the downward trend in the equilibrium exchange rate were higher home-country inflation, this latter answer would seem particularly appropriate.

The discipline
argument for
fixed exchange
rates

Tight policies, of course, also will tend to cause real income to decline, at least for a while; consequently, austerity is not always politically attractive, and governments tend to avoid it as long as possible. This fact leads some economists to advocate fixed exchange rates to force governments that are not sufficiently concerned about inflation to act "responsibly." The point they stress is that a fixed exchange-rate system is valuable because potential reserve losses under this system force governments to pursue price stability. A corollary to this argument is that devaluations should not be undertaken except under very exceptional circumstances.[12]

There are, therefore, three principal advantages to a fixed exchange-rate regime according to its advocates: *(1) the potential for*

---

[12]There are other arguments against devaluations or intentional depreciations of a currency which have been debated in the past and which we cannot develop in detail here. They include (1) a concern for "competitive" devaluations by countries, each vying for a larger share of world exports, and (2) a concern for perverse effects whereby a devaluation creates a still greater excess supply of a currency because the currency supply curve (the quantity supplied as a function of the exchange rate) is negatively sloped and flatter than the demand curve.

destabilizing speculation is avoided; (2) world trade is encouraged; and (3) governments are forced to pursue price stability through responsible monetary and fiscal policies.

The arguments for flexible rates

All of these points in favor of fixed exchange rates are arguable, according to the advocates of flexible exchange rates, a group which probably includes the majority of economists today. Regarding point (1), advocates of flexible rates assert that fixed exchange rates tend to be defended too long in the face of fundamental disequilibriums. It is difficult to identify a true fundamental disequilibrium; and even once such a situation is identified, national prestige and domestic politics often interfere with a needed devaluation. As speculators become aware of policy foot-dragging and the likelihood of eventual devaluation, they dump large quantities of a "weak" currency on the market, creating a still more severe drain on the defending government's reserves. This can lead to a crisis situation involving temporary suspension of market trading in a currency, a devaluation, doubt about the adequacy of the devaluation, and possibly more speculative pressure, further devaluation, and crisis.

It is argued that such crises, accompanied and abetted by speculative activity, are a characteristic of fixed exchange rates. Destabilizing speculation under flexible exchange rates, on the other hand, is unlikely because speculators will lose money if they are wrong, and the chances of losing money are greater under flexible rates. When speculators are right, speculation *helps* to move exchange rates to long-run equilibrium values and keep them there.

Flexible-rate advocates maintain that point (2) made under the fixed-rate case also is not valid. Foreign traders must worry about the risk of devaluations under fixed exchange rates; devaluations can involve large, if infrequent, losses to traders. There are also risks arising from erratic, balance-of-payments-induced changes in fiscal and monetary policy. Moreover, governments often respond to balance-of-payments deficits by imposing exchange controls, placing quota or tariff restrictions on imports, and limiting investment abroad. Finally, it is asserted that the exchange-rate risk involved under flexible rates need not deter trade because it can be avoided by hedging operations in the forward-exchange market. The conclusion of these arguments is that the international trade and capital flows which are a boon to world economic welfare are in fact more inhibited under a fixed exchange-rate system than they are under a system of flexible rates.

The third point made by fixed-rate advocates is attacked obliquely. *Fixed rates create pressure on countries to conform not to zero inflation, but to the rate of inflation of the reserve-currency*

Discipline of
fixed rates limited
to the self-
discipline of
reserve-currency
country

country; this rate will not necessarily be zero and may be significantly higher than other countries want to permit.

The United States is an obvious example. During the late 1960s
and early 1970s, the U.S. inflation rate increased considerably, due
principally to sharply higher government expenditures on the war
in Vietnam and social programs and to the financing of these expenditures through money creation. Higher inflation in the United
States created wide deficits in our balance of payments. For other
countries participating in the fixed-rate system, such deficits would
have created a severe loss in reserves forcing a devaluation or restrictive policies as described earlier. Because the U.S. dollar was
the major currency used for reserves and for setting intervention
points for reserve actions by other countries, there resulted large
accumulations of dollars by foreign central banks. (Our deficit was
reflected in their balance-of-payments accounts as a surplus, and
from their perspective in the foreign exchange market as an excess
demand for their currency.) For reasons that will be covered in
Chapter 11, these accumulations of reserves of dollars led to an
expansion of domestic money supplies in these countries. A surge in
inflation abroad soon followed. Consequently, U.S. inflation by the
early 70s was spread around the world through the fixed exchange-
rate system. The stable price-level discipline of fixed exchange rates
was not effective in restraining the United States and, therefore,
much of the rest of the world under the system as it operated during
the 1960s and early 1970s.

Flexible exchange rates, it is argued, might have prevented or at
least tempered the spread of U.S. inflation to other countries in the
1967–72 period. The dollar would have fallen in value in terms of
foreign exchange as our prices rose, keeping the prices of our goods
abroad relatively stable in foreign exchange and the prices of foreign
goods in line with ours in terms of dollars. More important, foreign
governments would have avoided the expansion in their money supplies forced on them by our large balance-of-payments deficits.

The case for flexible exchange rates is summarized as follows: *(1)
international monetary crises are avoided; (2) foreign trade volume
is at least as high, and perhaps higher, under flexible rates; and (3)
countries are free to pursue their own inflation and employment
objectives with monetary and fiscal policy independently of the policies of reserve-currency countries.*

Recent experience

The current system of managed flexibility in exchange rates has
itself experienced considerable strain in recent years. This strain
was associated partly with the resurgence of inflation in the United
States and the sharp decline in the value of the dollar during 1977–78
—sharper against many currencies than would be suggested by pur-

chasing-power parity considerations alone—and its subsequent recovery in 1980–81. Such overshooting and volatility has caused some disenchantment with flexible exchange rates. However, there seems little prospect of a return soon to anything approaching the old fixed exchange-rate system. One important reason is that inflation rates have continued to vary considerably among the major industrial countries; a fixed-rate system could not survive in this environment. Another reason is that world traders have been able to adjust fairly well to flexible exchange rates through forward-exchange contracts and other hedging operations. Finally, a number of industrial countries have benefitted from having national monetary and fiscal policies that are more independent than those possible with fixed exchange rates.

INTRODUCTION TO ARTICLES

Despite the demise in 1973 of the broad postwar fixed-rate system, there have continued to be situations in which certain countries individually or in small groups have pegged their exchange rates to another country's currency. One of these situations involved a continuation by Mexico, after 1973, of a fixed exchange rate between the Mexican peso and the dollar, despite a fundamental imbalance in Mexico's international accounts. Finally, in a move which surprised many, as described in the first *Wall Street Journal* article below, the Mexican peso was devalued and allowed to float against the dollar in late August 1976.

Another type of a fixed-rate system has been organized among several Western European countries. Under the European arrangement, these countries' currencies are fixed essentially in terms of the West German mark. They fluctuate within a narrow range against the mark and, with the mark, they float more freely against most other currencies, including the dollar. The time pattern of their values in terms of the dollar tends to look like a snake with a width no greater than the permitted range of fluctuation against each other; consequently, the arrangement as it existed prior to 1979 was nicknamed the European snake. Subsequent to March 1979, the arrangement has been more formal and is now known as the European Monetary System. From time to time devaluations or revaluations become necessary within this arrangement, as with other fixed-rate systems; also, members leave and join the system at different times. The second *Wall Street Journal* article (April 4, 1977) reports a realignment of pegged values for several currencies in the spring of 1977.

Mexican Peso Declines as Much as 20 Percent Against Dollar Following Float Decision

In limited trading, the Mexican peso dropped as much as 20 percent against the U.S. dollar in the wake of the Mexican government's surprise decision Tuesday night to float the currency, abandoning 22 years of fixed parity.

On New York markets, the value of the peso fell to between 6.4 cents and 6.9 cents from 8 cents. But foreign-exchange observers said the rate could change substantially, either up or down, when the Banco de Mexico, the government central bank, reopens today and announces the price at which it will convert pesos to dollars.

All Mexican banks were closed yesterday in a traditional bank holiday established for the president's annual state of the union message. President Luis Echeverria said in his speech the government will uphold free exchange of the peso and won't impose any restrictions.

Mr. Echeverria said he had rejected exchange controls proposed by some financial experts. "With the establishment of exchange controls, a foreign exchange black market would appear with the consequent corruption that this class of market generates," he said.

As recently as April, Finance Secretary Mario Ramon Beteta had said there wasn't any need to float or devalue the peso. But since then, he said Tuesday night, there has been a heavy flight of capital from the country and continuing high inflation has severely cut its all-important tourism.

He said the float is a temporary measure and that the government probably will reestablish an official parity with the dollar, but he didn't say when that might be done.

Central bank intervention

Mr. Beteta said the Mexican central bank will intervene in dealings from time to time to maintain an orderly market, but he said the bank wouldn't attempt to establish long-term parity with the dollar at a predetermined level.

He said the government plans to continue the traditionally free exchange of the peso and won't try to control currency movements across its borders.

He said the government will take special measures to minimize the expected inflationary impact of the peso float. "There will be a tax on excess profits and export goods," Mr. Beteta said.

He added that an unspecified compensa-tion would be provided to retired persons and others who depend on fixed-income investments, to partly offset the effects of the float.

In New York, G. A. Costanzo, vice chairman of Citibank, one of Mexico's largest creditors and the only U.S. bank with branches in the country, hailed the float as "very positive and timely."

"It bodes well for the economy," he said. "It would have been costly if held off."

In theory, the peso float should be a three-fold aid to the Mexican economy, boosting exports and tourism by making its goods and services cheaper in relation to other currencies, and cutting imports by making them more expensive.

Economic benefits in doubt

But many economic observers doubt that such benefits actually will result. They say the nation's imports, mostly capital goods such as drilling rigs and machine tools to expand its industrial base and develop natural resources, can't be reduced without hampering economic growth. And they contend Mexico already is exporting at full capacity.

Whatever the float's impact on the economy, however, it will clearly hurt the thousands of U.S. investors who in recent years have put large sums into peso time deposits at Mexican banks to take advantage of interest rates that run as high as 12 percent annually. When the certificates mature, or whenever the money is withdrawn, the dollar value of these deposits will have dropped in proportion to the effective devaluation.

Those Americans with dollar deposits in Mexican banks will be unhurt.

Less clear is the float's long-term effect on American owners of Mexican common stocks. The nation's stock exchange, the Bolsa de Valores, was closed yesterday because of the bank holiday. When it reopens today, trading is expected to be hectic.

Dollar value of stocks

Initially, the dollar value of all stocks will be down substantially from Tuesday's closing level. But market observers expect that the prices of many Mexican securities will quickly soar, and some may rise more than enough to offset the change in peso parity, depending on how the float is expected to affect the industry involved.

Merrill Lynch, Pierce, Fenner & Smith Inc., manager of a pending $50 million Mexican bond issue, said the peso float could delay the offer temporarily, but at this point only because it will require filing of an amended prospectus with the U.S. Securities and Exchange commission. The issue was tentatively scheduled for mid-September.

The float hasn't caused any defections among underwriters for the issue, a Merrill Lynch spokesman said, or large declines in existing Mexican bond issues. The 9½ percent bonds due 1981 dropped $2.50 to $1,005 for each $1,000 face amount. The 10 percent bonds of 1980 fell $3.75 to $1,027.50.

SOURCE: "Mexican Peso Declines as much as 20% against Dollar Following Float Decision," *The Wall Street Journal,* September 2, 1976.

Sweden to Cut Krona's Value 6 Percent Today: Denmark, Norway Post 3 Percent Devaluations

The European "snake" has been reshaped again, this time by its Scandinavian tail.

Effective today, Sweden trimmed the value of its krona 6 percent against its six sister funds in the European joint currency float, usually dubbed the snake. Denmark and Norway devalued their currencies 3 percent.

Moreover, Finland, which isn't linked with the snake but has considerable trade with Sweden, halted its currency markets for today to assess whether it should follow the lead of the other Scandinavian countries.

Sweden insisted on the currency realignment at an unheralded meeting of European finance ministers and central bankers in Brussels Friday.

Thorbjorn Falldin, the leader of Sweden's center-right coalition government, had pushed for the cheaper krona to spur Swedish exports to foreign lands.

Such sales have been lagging in recent months. Swedish iron ore has been piling up in the Norwegian port of Narvik, sales of Swedish autos are off, and Sweden's wood-products industries have been plagued by sluggish demand for their wares. Sweden has been forced to borrow to finance its international trade accounts.

Could only incite inflation

Devaluation, however, wasn't universally held as a solution to Sweden's woes. West German Chancellor Helmut Schmidt warned that a cheaper krona could only incite inflation in Sweden.

But Norwegian shipbuilders applauded the devaluations and wished that Norway had gone as far as Sweden and also cut its krone 6 percent.

The European snake was created by the Common Market countries to keep their currencies from moving too far apart from each other while they all floated against the U.S. dollar and other non-European funds.

A number of Common Market countries have pulled out of the joint float, but the main participants at present are West Germany, Belgium, the Netherlands, Luxembourg, and Denmark. Sweden and Norway aren't Common Market countries, but they joined in the float anyway because of their close links with Denmark.

Under the rules, each participating country is obliged to hold its currency within a band 2.25 percent above and below its assigned rate against other funds in the joint float. Thus, when the German mark is especially strong and the Swedish krona is particularly weak, one or the other governments has to intervene in trading to keep the funds within their assigned total spread of 4.5 percent.

Second in six months

The latest realignment in the snake configuration is the second in six months. On October 17, the members agreed to raise the value of the mark 2 percent, cut the values of the Norwegian krone and Swedish krona 3 percent, and reduce the Danish krone 6 percent.

Today's reductions have the effect of boosting the value of the U.S. dollar against the Scandinavian funds. In late Friday trading in New York, the Swedish krona was worth about 23 cents, the Norwegian krone was 19 cents, and the Danish krone was almost 17 cents.

In other currency trading Friday, the U.S. dollar was mixed against major funds.

In London, the British pound slipped to $1.7196 from $1.7201 Thursday.

The dollar edged up in Frankfurt to 2.3928 West German marks from 2.3907, and in Paris to 4.9725 French francs from 4.9705. But in Zurich the U.S. fund inched down to 2.5440 Swiss francs from 2.5460.

The Canadian dollar fluctuated widely Fri-day before dropping in Montreal to 94.54 U.S. cents from 94.89 cents the day before.

Dealers said the Canadian fund rose on trader satisfaction with the Canadian budget announced Thursday night, but then slipped on concern about Canadian government policy concerning intervention on foreign-exchange markets. Canadian officials said they didn't see any switch. Canada has allowed the Canadian dollar to float and has intervened only to maintain orderly markets.

Gold's price dropped 60 cents an ounce. The five major London bullion dealers lowered their common quote 65 cents at their morning meeting but restored five cents in the afternoon, to $148.30 an ounce.

SOURCE: "Sweden to Cut Krona's Value 6% Today; Denmark, Norway Post 3% Devaluations," *The Wall Street Journal*, April 4, 1977.

CONCLUSION

This chapter has provided a survey of the international financial relationships which are necessary to an understanding of current and recent money and credit developments involving the United States and most of our trading partners. This completes Part 2. Part 3 returns to a more concentrated focus on money—money supply and money demand as introduced in Chapter 3. The next few chapters will set out concepts and relationships which have been important to monetary developments in the past as well as those of the recent period.

PROBLEMS

1. Discuss the elements in the U.S. balance of payments which give rise to a demand for dollars. Which elements are influenced by the exchange rate? How and why?

2. Define purchasing-power parity and adjusted interest-rate parity. Could these conditions be mutually existent?

3. Describe the principal ways the Federal Reserve can act to encourage a stronger dollar in the exchange markets.

ADVANCED READINGS

Herrin, J.; Lindbeck, A.; and Myhrman, J., eds. *Flexible Exchange Rates and Stabilization Policy.* Boulder: Westview Press, 1977.

Putnam, Bluford H., and Wilford, D. Sykes, eds. *The Monetary Approach to International Adjustment.* New York: Praeger Publishers, 1979.

Mundell, R. A., and Polak, J. J. *The New International Monetary System.* New York: Columbia University Press, 1977.

Quinn, B.S. *The New Euromarkets.* New York: John Wiley & Sons, 1975.

Riehl, Heinz and Rodriguez, Rita M. *Foreign Exchange Markets: A Guide to Foreign Currency Operations.* New York: McGraw-Hill, 1977.

Yeager, Leland B. *International Monetary Relations: Theory, History, and Policy.* 2nd ed. New York: Harper & Row, 1976.

Analysis of money and monetary systems

Further conceptual background for money supply and demand analysis

In Chapter 2 we covered the three principal functions of money in the economy and several definitions of money related to these functions. These topics were preparatory to our analysis of money and credit in Parts 1 and 2. This chapter presents more conceptual and definitional material on money necessary to the analysis in Part 3 of the determinants of the money supply in different monetary systems.

There are four topics covered in this chapter. First, certain associations between the physical forms and the operational qualities of money are set out; second, several conditions supporting acceptance of a money are identified; third, a few key types of money are distinguished and explained; and, finally, we define four basic monetary systems in terms of the key types of money they include.

PHYSICAL FORMS AND OPERATIONAL QUALITIES OF MONEY

As illustrated by the examples of different monies already mentioned in this book, money may take a great variety of physical forms, such as: checkable deposits, paper notes, and coins in our

9

current system; cigarettes in Radford's P.O.W. camp (see the article in Chapter 2); and cattle in ancient pastoral societies. Perhaps the most bizzare form in recorded experience is the huge stone money of the Island of Yap, which is described in an article later in this chapter. Gold as coins, as dust, or as bullion has been one of the most widely used, lauded, and recurrent forms through history; and for many individuals and institutions gold still does perform monetary services, mostly as a liquid store of value but also, in some cases, as a payments medium as well.

Aside from satisfying intellectual curiosity, attention to the physical forms of money is worthwhile because the operational qualities of a money—the factors affecting the efficiency with which it functions in the payments system—can depend to an important degree on its physical form. The distinct operational qualities of different forms, in turn, have been an important factor in the evolution of money and a determinant of the composition of mixed money stocks—the composition of the current U.S. money stock in terms of checkable deposits, travelers checks, and currency, for example.

The operational qualities of money

The important operational qualities of money are: (1) the ability to be readily recognized and agreed upon as to exchange value, (2) the ability to be stored securely and inexpensively, (3) the ability to be transferred securely and at low cost, (4) the ability to be combined in small or large values so as to be usable conveniently in a wide range of transactions, (5) stability in purchasing power, and (6) wide acceptability.

The first quality, the quality of readily recognized exchange value, partly explains the adoption of certain widely traded commodities as money in simple societies—for example, the use of weapons in hunting societies and of cattle in pastoral civilizations. A severe drawback of such monies, however, is their heterogeneity. Weapons and cows come in many variations of quality, making it impractical to quote prices in standard units. In the evolution of money, it was found that metals in a basic form were superior to most other articles, particularly in their ability to be standardized and, hence, agreed upon as to value. It was also discovered that the minting of metal coins by or under the control of the government or some trusted private entity was an advantageous method of standardizing metals for use as circulating money.

Even circulating coins of minted valuable metal are not a fully satisfactory money form from the standpoint of homogeneous and readily recognized value, however. Once in circulation, these coins are subject to wear and, usually, to clipping and sweating, methods of removing some of the valuable metal for profit. Moreover,

Readily recognized exchange value

debased, lower-valued coins tend to be passed on while new, full-valued coins are hoarded.[1]

If paper money representing claims to valuable metal is substituted for coins as a circulating medium, the problem of public debasement and hoarding can be eliminated. Another solution is to make coins of lower intrinsic value than their face value, such as is done presently in the United States. In a sense, debasement still occurs in this case—it is accomplished officially by the government—but at least the uniformity of the circulating medium is maintained.[2]

Partly because our money has little intrinsic value and because of standardization, recognition of exchange value is not a serious problem for the forms of money in use in the United States today. Our coins and paper currency are homogeneous. Most travelers-check and deposit money can be considered homogeneous also.

Conveniently stored, transferred, and combined in different values

The second advantage of being able to store money cheaply and the third advantage of being able to transfer money easily are rather self-evident; and the fourth advantage, the ability to combine a money conveniently in different values, is as well. Checkable deposit balances have an obvious edge over currency in all of these qualities and this explains to a great extent the greater share of deposits (roughly 80 percent) in the U.S. money supply today. Deposits are stored fairly safely and inexpensively in financial intermediaries. Also, title to checkable deposits can be transferred simply and safely. Finally, transfers by check are made for desired amounts without encountering the problems of bulk and change often involved with currency. Of course, currency has its advantages for many transactions. Currency is more suitable for small-value transactions. Since transactions in currency are most easily kept secret—an attractive advantage in the "underground economy"—it can be preferred for large-value transactions as well.[3]

Stability in purchasing power

The fifth quality, stability in purchasing power, is a quality which can be an element of distinction among alternative physical forms of money. Historically, it has sometimes accounted for the choice of one specific form over others by a society. For example, the choice of gold over other metals or commodities in certain historical periods has been based on an alleged superiority of gold in this regard, and the choice, in general, of commodity over paper or deposit

---

[1]The tendency for the public to hoard valuable coins and circulate coins of lesser value is an example of Gresham's law. This law is usually stated as "bad money drives out good money." A careful definition and full explanation of the conditions necessary for it to apply are postponed until Chapter 10.

[2]Later in this chapter coinage of lower intrinsic value than face value will be identified as part of a money type called fiat money.

[3]The "underground economy" refers to transactions or production which are illicit or are not reported as legally required for taxation.

monies has been advocated often for the same reason. However, as we shall see, the stability in purchasing power of a money is not uniquely related to its physical form. The money type, the broader monetary system which may encompass it, and, where relevant, the monetary policies of the government are more fundamental to the stability or instability in purchasing power of a money than is its particular physical form, be it metal, paper, or checkable deposits. (The role of government policies in our current monetary system has been described at a preliminary level in earlier chapters.)

The last quality, wide acceptability, is of considerable importance. To a degree, it tends to be a function of all the previous qualities listed—the more a money has of these qualities, the more widely used and accepted it will tend to be. With respect to stability in purchasing power, it is *confidence* in this quality which counts for wide acceptance. A money may have a history of stability in real value and yet, for some reason related to confidence in future stability, lose a certain amount of its general acceptance.

Wide acceptance

While the operational qualities of money and confidence in its purchasing power are important general conditions for wide acceptability, there are also specific economic or institutional conditions conducive to wide acceptability which are addressed in the next section.

FOUR CONDITIONS CONDUCIVE TO ACCEPTANCE OF A MONEY

One or more of the following conditions support confidence in and acceptance of a money: (1) the money has *intrinsic value* comparable to its offered value in transactions; (2) the money is *legal tender,* that is, it is designated by the government as lawful money for settling specific or general transactions; (3) the money is *backed by (that is, redeemable in terms of) valuable goods, money of intrinsic value, or legal tender;* (4) the money is *institutionalized in the economy.*

Any one of the first three conditions will help to establish at least initial acceptance and confidence in a money. If money has intrinsic value comparable to its offered value in general transactions, it will be perceived that those valuing it for alternative uses constitute a ready, fall-back market and support for its value. (Recall the cigarette money used in the P.O.W. camp described in the article in Chapter 2. Prisoners and guards who were smokers provided such a ready market. Would cigarettes at the outset have been confidently accepted as money in trades by nonsmokers without this fall-back?) If a money has legal-tender status, our second condition, transactors know that they have recourse to the courts to force acceptance of such a medium in payment. The third condition works because a money which is redeemable for goods or more acceptable money provides that very recourse for the holder.

Finally, to turn to the fourth condition, regardless of the reason for its initial acceptance, an institutionalized money will tend to enjoy continued acceptance to a certain extent simply because of familiarity with it and established reliance upon it.

In the next section, the above four conditions are used together with certain supply conditions to define four money types which have distinctive supply characteristics in the economy.

KEY TYPES OF MONEY CLASSIFIED BY CONDITIONS SUPPORTING ACCEPTANCE AND CONDITIONS OF SUPPLY

Commodity
money

The key types of money are: commodity money, traditional money, fiat money, and debt money. The first type, *commodity money, is naturally associated with the first condition related to acceptance—intrinsic value comparable to exchange value.* The cigarettes of Radford's P.O.W. camp are one example. Gold and silver coins circulating at close to intrinsic value—and known in their time as specie—are another.

Commodity money may be standardized and issued through a government, as with official specie, or its supply may be organized entirely privately. The money commodity need not itself circulate; paper certificates with 100 percent backing of commodity reserves may take its place in circulation.[4] Such a substitute in circulation preserves the essential characteristics of the money type under discussion and therefore falls under our heading of commodity money *as long as there are 100 percent commodity reserves supporting it.*

Whether the money commodity itself circulates or not, *it is essential for the preservation of the intrinsic-value condition that (1) conversion of the money commodity to money or reserves and conversion of the commodity money to other uses be determined by market forces, and (2) there always be an available supply of the money commodity from new production or from the diversion of the commodity from other uses.* These are our conditions of supply for commodity money. The analysis in the next chapter will show why these requirements for supply are necessary to preserve the compa-

---

[4]The intended meaning of the term "money commodity" in this sentence should be clear from its context, but for clarity here and in later discussions it is worthwhile to note explicitly that the *money commodity* is the relevant commodity however it is used—gold coins and gold jewelry, for example. Commodity money is the money commodity exclusively in its particular form as money—gold coins but not jewelry, for example.

rability for the intrinsic value of the money with its exchange value, the hallmark of this type of money as defined here.[5]

The second type, *traditional money, enjoys confidence and acceptance primarily because it has become institutionalized in the economy.* As a type of money distinct from commodity money and other types, it has significantly less intrinsic value than its exchange value, it is not legal tender, and it is not contractually redeemable for assets having another source of value.

Traditional money

Over the long run, the supply of traditional money must be constrained somehow to a rate of increase lower than or equal to the rate of increase in the demand for it stemming from real growth in the economy. Otherwise, its exchange value will tend to fall until that value reaches the intrinsic value of the money form, at which point it becomes a commodity money.

The stone money of the Island of Yap provides an example of traditional money. See the article below.[6]

INTRODUCTION TO ARTICLE

The stone money of the Island of Yap has long intrigued economists. The reasons for its initial acceptance as money are not revealed by the author of this passage. It is clear from his discussion, however, that the stone money of Yap fits our category of traditional money in terms of both its condition for continued acceptance and its condition of supply.

The Stone Money of the Isle of Yap

That precious metal or other useful materials are not needed to maintain the value of money is illustrated by the stone money of the Isle of Yap or Uap, one of the Caroline Islands in the Pacific Ocean now under Japanese mandate. The principal money in this island consists of large stones, shaped like grindstones, which are good for nothing except to use as money. A person's wealth depends upon the number and size of the "rocks" that he owns. A stone about four feet in diameter is sufficient to purchase a wife. The larger stones are too big to move so that, when they change hands with each purchase, their physical location is not changed. The mere acknowledgement of transfer of ownership of the stone from one native to another is sufficient: no signatures or endorsements are necessary. In fact, the richest family on the isle holds that rank because it is the acknowledged owner of a huge stone, which was accidentally sunk in transport and has for several generations been lying on the

---

[5]Some texts use the term *full-bodied* commodity money for this money type. The adjective full-bodied is meant to distinguish this money from monies such as the U.S. nickel coin which contains a metal commodity but has a significantly lower intrinsic value than exchange value. In most cases less than full-bodied commodity monies fall into our category of fiat money.

[6]Traditional money is the least important of those covered here and will not be analyzed in detail in later chapters. It is included to make our classification of money types complete and to facilitate explanations in following chapters of the evolution of debt and fiat types of money. Also, recognition of its existence in certain societies is worthwhile to underscore the remarkable variety of recorded monetary experience.

bottom of the ocean. No one living has ever seen it, but nobody questions that this family is the richest on the island.

What "backing" or "security" has this stone money, which serves to transact the business of Yap? None. Yet it is far from worthless. To the natives it is worth more than gold or silver coins.

Before the World War the Germans, then in possession of the island, wished to have the natives repair the highways, which were in a bad condition. The German authorities were at a loss to know how to induce the natives to do the work, until finally they hit upon the happy thought of confiscating some of the stone money by painting the black German cross on it. This device worked like a charm, and those natives who had lost all their money through confiscation by the German authorities were quite willing to repair the highways in order to

earn it back again. When they had done so by working on the roads, the German crosses were erased from the stone money, and the natives were wealthy once more.

The inhabitants of the Island of Yap have an economical money, which will not wear out very quickly, and its value remains relatively stable, since no new money is being mined, minted, produced, or printed. What would cause the stone money of Yap to depreciate? Lack of good security? No, only an increase in the amount of stone money on the island or a decrease in the demand for its use as money because, say, the natives began to use some other money in its place.

SOURCE: Richard A. Lester. *Monetary Experiments* (Princeton NJ: Princeton University Press, 1939), pp. 30—31.

Fiat money

Fiat money is so named because it garners confidence in acceptance primarily through government fiat making it legal tender. As a distinct type, fiat money has far less intrinsic value than its value in circulation and is not redeemable in valuable assets.

The supply of fiat money must be at the discretion of government authorities. If it were supplied privately at private discretion, its exchange value would tend to fall to zero. Our analysis in Chapter 11 will suggest why.

The currency of the United States today is fiat money and so are the currencies of most countries. A paper $100 bill issued by the Federal Reserve is legal tender and worth $100 in exchange for goods at their quoted dollar prices; but it is virtually worthless for any use other than as money and is not redeemable at the Federal Reserve for any fixed quantity of real assets. Our coins have a higher intrinsic value than paper currency bills but also, with a few exceptions, circulate at a value considerably in excess of their value in alternative uses.[7]

---

[7]In 1968, the value of the silver content of the silver dimes, quarters, half-dollars, and dollars that had been minted for more than a century in the United States rose above the value of these coins in circulation. Subsequently, almost all silver coins have been removed from circulation by the public or the government. (The copper penny appeared to be on the verge of a similar fate in 1973 but was saved by the collapse of copper prices over the next few years.) The hoarding of U.S. silver coinage is another example of Gresham's law, as explained in Chapter 10.

The last type of money, debt money, is also in wide use today.   Debt money
In fact, debt money represents by far the greatest proportion of
the money supplies of the advanced Western countries. *Debt money
is a debt instrument or deposit balance redeemable on demand in
another asset of value—usually commodity money or fiat money—
and backed less than 100 percent by reserves of the other asset.* It
is not accepted in transactions because of intrinsic value or legal-
tender status but because transactors are confident, despite fractional reserves behind it, that it can be exchanged for other assets of
value. *Debt money has unique supply characteristics which stem
from the fact that it is backed less than 100 percent by reserves;
these will be explained in Chapter 10.*

In modern industrial economies, most debt money is issued by
commercial banks and other intermediaries in the form of checkable
deposits. Prior to the Civil War, the dominant form of debt money
in the United States was paper notes issued by private commercial
banks and redeemable in specie. Paper debt monies redeemable on
demand in specie or other assets of intrinsic value, with reserves of
less than 100 percent, have also been issued by governments. Government issues of subsidiary coins (that is, low face-value coins,
usually of low intrinsic value relative to face value) redeemable in
coins of full value are a form of debt money.

Debt money is important not only because of its dominant proportion in our money supply today and because of its own supply
characteristics, but also because *debt-money creation represents a
credit-market transaction resulting in a net addition to financial
resources available to the debt-money issuer.* (Recall that your
checkable deposit balance was cited in Chapter 4 as an extension of
credit by you to a depository institution.) As this type of money
increases in quantity so does credit, at least in this form.

The supply characteristics of three of the money types identified
in this section—commodity, fiat, and debt types—will be explained
in the chapters ahead. The analysis will be developed within the
framework of four basic monetary systems which capture the essential characteristics of most present and past actual systems. These
basic systems are defined in the next section.

BASIC MONETARY SYSTEMS AND MONETARY STANDARDS

The basic systems

Our four basic monetary systems are: (1) the primary commodity-money system, (2) the secondary commodity-money system, (3)

Primary
commodity-
money system

the primary fiat-money system, and (4) the secondary fiat-money system.[8] A primary commodity-money system simply consists of one or more commodity monies. The cigarette currency system of Radford's P.O.W. camp provides a useful example once again. As our analysis will show in Chapter 10, the determinants of the supply of money in this system are not as simple as they might seem. The analysis requires an examination of the market for the money commodity.

Secondary
commodity-
money system

A secondary commodity-money system is a combination of commodity and debt monies. Naturally, such a system is even more complex in operation and behavior than the primary commodity-money system. Credit and, usually, banks and other depository institutions are involved; and government debt money and government regulations such as reserve requirements for depository institutions may be, as well.

Primary fiat-
money system

The primary fiat-money system is similar to the primary commodity-money system in that a single type of money is involved—fiat money. Since fiat money necessarily introduces government control of the money supply, the analysis of a primary fiat-money system must focus largely on monetary policy and the behavior of government authorities.

Secondary fiat-
money system

The last system identified, the secondary fiat-money system, is the predominant system in the Western world today and the one existing in the United States since the Great Depression. It combines fiat and debt money. The money supply is determined by government policy and by the behavior of private financial intermediaries and the public.

Monetary standards

Although we have identified and will analyze four different *systems*, there are only two general *monetary standards* among these systems: a commodity-money standard and a fiat-money standard. A monetary standard is the standard that is chosen by a society for its ultimate standard of value and which also, usually, serves as an asset of value promised on demand by debt-money issuers. There will be some discussion of specific standards, such as the gold standard, in the chapters that follow.

---

[8]Students should be warned that these particular categories and labels of monetary systems are not a part of conventional textbook descriptions or the economic literature and have been adopted here to facilitate the analysis in the following chapters.

CONCLUSION

This chapter has set out the operational qualities of money and the key types of money which have unique supply characteristics in the economy. We have also designated certain monetary systems which will be used to organize our analysis of the supply characteristics of different types of money in the next two chapters. Chapter 10 analyzes the two systems having a commodity standard. The primary and secondary fiat-money systems are covered in Chapter 11.

PROBLEMS

1. Identify the operational qualities of checkable deposits which are superior to those of currency.
2. Discuss the distinction between a commodity money and a money commodity.
3. What factors give rise to confidence in a money?

ADVANCED READINGS

Breckinridge, S.P. *Legal Tender.* Chicago: University of Chicago Press, 1903.

Burns, Arthur F. *Money and Monetary Policy in Early Times.* New York: Alfred A. Knopf, 1927.

Crowther, G. *An Outline of Money.* Revised Edition. London: Thomas Nelson and Sons, 1948.

Einzig, Paul. *Primitive Money.* Second Edition. Oxford: Pergamon Press, 1966.

Mason, W.E. *Clarification of the Monetary Standard.* University Park: Pennsylvania State University Press, 1963.

Robertson, D.H. *Money.* London: James Nisbet and Co., 1948.

Primary and secondary commodity-money systems

This chapter develops models to explain the major determinants of money in two systems with a commodity standard. The emphasis will be on conceptual analysis, with occasional reference to historical and current events. Conclusions here will be helpful background for later, more detailed discussions of U.S. monetary experience and of the current U.S. system.

The first section begins with the market for a *money commodity* in a *closed economy*. Next there is a description of the *money-supply process* in the primary commodity-money system which was defined in the last chapter. Sections follow on the *international gold standard*, and *multiple-commodity standards and Gresham's law*.[1]

The secondary commodity-money system is introduced with a section describing the evolution of debt money and *banks of issue*. Then the expansion of bank loans and bank money on a given *reserve base* is explained. The concepts of the *monetary base* and the *money-stock multiplier* are defined and used to analyze the operation of the overall money-supply mechanism in the secondary commodity-

10

---

[1]Key terms in this and the next paragraph are defined later in this chapter and in the glossary at the end of the text.

money system. Particular attention is given to the behavior of money in this system over the business cycle.

THE MARKET FOR A MONEY COMMODITY

If a money is commodity money, there is a demand for it for one or more uses *other* than as money. This other demand competes with the demand for the commodity as money. To deal with this we must postpone a direct analysis of the supply and demand for commodity money, and begin instead with the supply and demand for the *money commodity—that commodity which is serving both monetary and other uses.*

The supply of a money commodity in a *closed* economy—that is, an economy closed to foreign trade—is determined essentially by the same factors that determine the supply of any commodity. Those analyzed here are the price of the commodity and the costs of producing the commodity. Costs of production reflect wage rates for labor, unit costs of capital, and the technological base of society.

A fictitious example

The kingdom of Oros will be our fictitious example. Suppose that the king of Oros, on the advice of his sorcerer, establishes the *glitter* as the unit of account and medium of exchange for the Oros economy. The glitter's gold content is set at one-half ounce of gold. Effectively then, all goods are priced in one-half-ounce units of gold. This also has the effect of setting the unit-of-account value of one ounce of gold in Oros at two glitters.

To produce the glitter, the king establishes a royal mint with an initial stock of gold and gives instructions to the royal mint to buy all the gold offered to it at a price of two glitters in coin per ounce of raw gold. All gold so purchased and some previously stocked by the royal treasury is minted into coins.

Now, it should be apparent that under these conditions, the glitter price of gold will never change in the Oros economy; it will always be two glitters and it is, therefore, in itself uninteresting. (Recall that the unit-of-account price of our money today is always unity and was rejected as uninteresting in Chapter 3.) For our purposes, it is the value of glitters or gold in terms of all other goods and services which is the useful focus for our analysis.

The real value of the money commodity

Suppose initially that all goods and services in Oros have a unit-of-account price of one quarter of a glitter. Then the value of an ounce of gold would be eight units of anything else. For convenience we will call a unit of anything else a "uoot." So one ounce of gold initially trades for eight uoots.

Now consider a gold-mining firm, the Heavy Lode, which has produced in the past at a rate of as much as 100 ounces of gold per year but which is not in operation currently. A competitive, profit-maximizing firm will produce only if long-run profits are positive. The output rate will tend to be where marginal cost is constant or rising and equal to the price of the product. But, as shown in Figure 10–1, the Heavy Lode finds that its lowest marginal and average

FIGURE 10–1
Costs of gold production

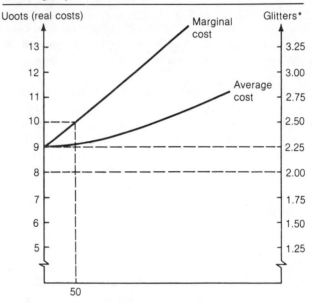

Ounces of gold per year

*This scale is a valid reference only for a price level of 1/4 of a glitter per uoot. A change in the price level to 1/5 glitter per uoot, as assumed later, shifts the glitter scale up and makes it narrower. Only the uoot scale will be used in subsequent analysis and graphs.

Supply without production

cost per ounce of gold is 2.25 in terms of glitters (right scale) or 9 in terms of uoots (left scale). It would be an unprofitable proposition to operate at any positive rate of output when the price of gold is below nine uoots, as it is in our diagram and example. If this cost and price configuration is representative of the entire gold-mining industry, no gold is being produced in Oros, and we assume no other sources of new gold exist currently. The supply or stock of gold, therefore, in our initial situation in Oros amounts simply to the accumulated amount of gold garnered from production and other sources in the past. The initial supply curve for the stock of gold below a price of nine uoots is vertical at the existing stock of gold, which we assume to be 20,000 ounces, as shown in Figure 10–2.

Increases in the gold stock with production

Suppose the value of gold rises to 10 uoots (this implies that the average glitter price of other goods and services falls to one fifth of a glitter). At this price, the Heavy Lode will start up and produce at a rate of 50 ounces per year. Other mines also will begin operating

FIGURE 10–2
The supply of gold

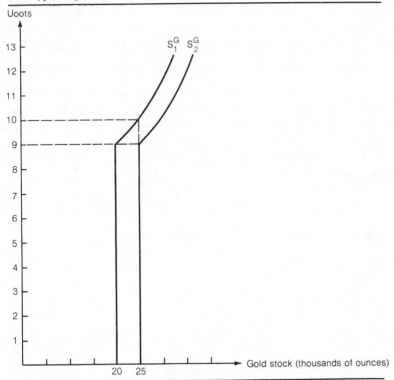

such that, we assume, total production comes to 5,000 ounces per year. (Imagine there are 100 identical mines.) After one year of operations, the stock of gold will rise by 5,000 ounces. If the price were still higher, the amount of increase in one year would be still greater.

As long as the price of gold remains above nine uoots, the stock of gold will continue to rise *each year*. Demand for the stock of gold, about which we have so far been silent, will have to rise by an equal amount each year or the price of gold will tend to fall to or below nine uoots once more. At a price equal to or below nine uoots, the supply curve for gold is again vertical, but this time at a higher stock level.

Our injection of demand considerations above takes us a little ahead of the story. We should stop to summarize our discussion of the determinants of the stock supply of gold, our money commodity, with the following equations. First,

$$G_t^S = G_{t-1}^S + \Delta G^S \tag{1}$$

This simply says that the gold stock in period t is identical to the gold stock in period t−1 plus the change in the gold stock between these periods.

Second,

$$\Delta G^S = f\left(\left(\frac{N}{P}\right)_t, C_t, T_t, \ldots\right); \Delta G^S \geq 0 \tag{2}$$

This says that the change in the gold stock between t and t−1 is a function of (1) the real price of gold, $\left(\frac{N}{P}\right)_t$ (explained further in the box below the next expression); (2) the real opportunity cost of producing gold, C_t; and (3) the technological and resource base, T_t. The part to the right of the semicolon in the equation above states that the change in the gold stock can only be zero or positive.

Finally, substitute the first equation into the second and rearrange terms to get

$$G^S_t = G^S_{t-1} + f\left(\left(\frac{N}{P}\right)_t, C_t, T_t, \ldots\right); G^S_t \geq G^S_{t-1} \tag{3}$$

which is explained in the following box.

Influenced variable	Influencing variables	Direction of influence
G^S_t: the stock of gold supplied in period t	G^S_{t-1}: the stock of gold supplied in the previous period	Positive; G^S_t will not be less than G^S_{t-1}
	$\left(\frac{N}{P}\right)_t$: the number of units of account per ounce of gold divided by the price level for all other goods in terms of the unit of account (uoots in our example); in other words, the real value of an ounce of gold	Positive
	C_t: real marginal costs (of producing an ounce of gold) per unit of labor and capital inputs	Negative
	T_t: the technological and resourse base for gold production	Positive

Let us turn now to the demand for the money commodity.

As indicated earlier, the total demand for a money commodity is comprised of two demands: a demand for the commodity to be used as money—the demand for glitters in our fictitious economy—and a separate demand for the commodity for other uses. (Because of other uses of gold you might say, "All that gold is not glitters" in Oros.) We will analyze these demands individually.

First, consider the demand for the commodity as money. The demand for money where the money is a commodity money, such as the gold glitter, is affected by the same variables as the demand for any other type of money. In fact, to express this demand in terms of the quantity of glitters, we can use the same demand-for-money function we developed in Chapter 3:

The monetary demand for the commodity

$$M^D = f\left(\frac{1}{P}, \; y, \; i, \; \ldots\right)$$

To show this demand in terms of an ounce of gold, we simply adjust for N, the number of glitters per ounce of gold, as follows:[2]

$$\frac{M^D}{N} = f\left(\frac{N}{P}, \; y, \; i, \; \ldots\right)$$

The second demand—the non-monetary demand for gold—is similar to the demand for any good. In the case of the demand for gold to be used in jewelry, for example, relevant variables include the real value (price) of gold, real income, and the prices of related goods such as silver and other competing jewelry metals.

The demand for nonmonetary uses

Our demand function for these uses is:

$$J^D = f\left(\frac{N}{P}, \; y, \; P^R, \; \ldots\right)$$

Influenced variable	Influencing variable	Direction of influence
J^D: the quantity of gold demanded (stock demand in ounces) for jewelry and other nonmonetary uses	$\frac{N}{P}$: the real value of gold	Negative; not necessarily proportional
	y: real income	Positive
	P^R: prices of related goods	Positive for substitutes (competing goods); negative for complements

---

[2]The mathematics of this adjustment have not been shown above so as not to distract the reader from the central story. We include them in this footnote.

If the demand for nominal glitter balances is inversely proportional to 1/P, it is proportional to P. This means we may legitimately restate the demand-for-money function from Chapter 3 as follows:

$$M^D = P \; (f(y, \; i, \; \ldots))$$

If both sides of this equation then are divided by N, we have,

(*continued on next page*)

The total demand for gold, G^D, is the sum of the two parts just explained,

$$G^D = \frac{M^D}{N} + J^D$$

The demand curve for each component demand (dashed lines) and for the total demand (a solid line) is shown in Figure 10–3. Note that the curve representing the monetary demand for gold is a rectangular hyperbola, just as the curve representing the demand for money was in Chapter 3, and for the same reason. If the value of gold falls by one half, the demand for it for use as money will rise two-fold, because it takes twice as much to engage in the same transactions, ceteris paribus.

The commodity demand curves

Proportionality does not necessarily apply to the other component demand curve, however. The demand for gold for jewelry, for example, may be highly price elastic or inelastic—there is no particular reason why it should exhibit a constant elasticity.

The curve representing the total demand for gold is the horizontal sum of the two component demand curves. The value for gold at the intersection of the total demand curve with the supply curve, $\left(\dfrac{N}{P}\right)_1$, is the equilibrium value—the value the market will tend to establish and where

$$G^D = G^S$$

We could at this point introduce some changes in the variables determining the positions of our supply and demand curves for gold to illustrate their implications for the value of gold in equilibrium, but our real purpose in this analysis is to reveal the implications of such changes for the supply and demand for money. We are now at a point where we can shift the focus of the analysis to the market for the stock of glitters and consider changes in variables in that context.

THE MARKET FOR A COMMODITY MONEY

Let us first concentrate on the supply of gold available for glitters and what that, in turn, implies for the supply of money. Ignore the $D^{M/N}$ demand curve in Figure 10–3 for a moment. Note that the quantity of gold demanded for nonmonetary uses in Figure 10–3 is

$$\frac{M^D}{N} = \frac{P}{N} \, (f(y, \, i, \, . \, . \, .))$$

In words, M^D/N is proportional to P/N. Alternatively, M^D/N is inversely proportional to N/P. Going back to our original, more general, expression we can, therefore, say:

$$\frac{M^D}{N} = f\left(\frac{N}{P}, \, y, \, i, \, . \, . \, .\right)$$

where it is understood that M^D/N is inversely proportional to N/P.

FIGURE 10–3
The supply and demand for gold

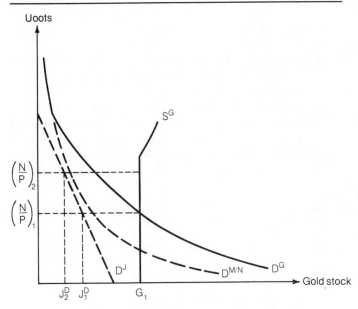

The supply and demand for gold

J_1^D when the price or value of gold is $\left(\dfrac{N}{P}\right)_1$. The difference between the total stock of gold, G_1, and this quantity, J_1^D, obviously represents the supply of gold available for glitters when the price of gold is $\left(\dfrac{N}{P}\right)_1$.

Now consider a higher price for gold, $\left(\dfrac{N}{P}\right)_2$. At this price, the quantity of gold demanded for nonmonetary uses falls to J_2^D, and the total supply of gold remains the same at this price. (The price of gold has not yet reached the point where new gold is profitably mined.) Therefore, the quantity of gold available for glitters would rise to $G_1 - J_2^D$. Considering other prices above and below $\left(\dfrac{N}{P}\right)_1$, we can find other quantities, higher and lower than $G_1 - J_1^D$, of gold available for coinage into glitters.[3]

The quantity of gold supplied for money, then, is always given by the horizontal distance between the D^J curve and the S^G curve.

---

[3]The analysis in the text ignores the fact that there are costs of fabricating jewelry and coins from gold. These costs mean that the gold stock is not quite as flexibly adjustable between jewelry and coins as our analysis suggests. Price movements would have to be large enough to overcome the costs of fabrication before the adjustments we have described would take place.

More to our point, this distance multiplied by N provides us with the quantity of glitters that will be supplied through market interactions.

It can be seen from our analysis above that the quantity of monetary gold supplied clearly is positively related to the real value of gold. The higher the price of gold, the lower the quantity demanded

The supply curve for glitters

for nonmonetary uses and, at some point, the greater the production of new gold. Since N is a constant, the value of a glitter, $1/P$, changes in proportion to changes in the value of gold; so *the same positive relationship holds between the quantity of glitters supplied and the real value of a glitter.* Our supply curve for the stock of glitters, derived from Figure 10–3, is presented in Figure 10–4.

FIGURE 10–4
Supply of glitters

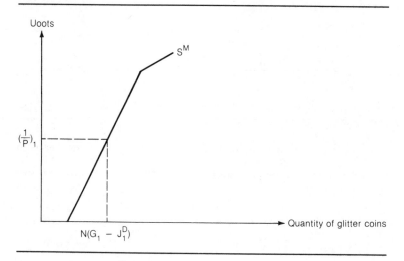

This supply curve will, of course, shift in response to factors operating so as to shift the D^J and S^G curves in Figure 10–3. It would take more space than we can devote here to trace through changes in each of the relevant variables by shifting curves first in Figure 10–3 and then in Figure 10–4. The analysis should be sufficiently well established at this point for the reader to be able to do this (and it would be a good exercise to work it through for several variables).

The money-supply function

We will simply summarize the results in the following money-supply function for a primary commodity-money system

$$M^S = f\left(\frac{1}{P},\ y,\ P^R;\ C,\ T\ .\ .\ .\right)$$

Influenced variable	Influencing variable	Direction of influence
M^S: the stock of commodity money	$\dfrac{1}{P}$: the value of one unit of the commodity money in terms of other goods and services (that is, in our example, other than gold)	Positive. (This influence is stronger if $1/P$ is high enough to induce production of the money commodity.)
	y: real income	Negative because it increases the nonmonetary demand for the money commodity
	P^R: the prices of goods related to the money commodity in non-monetary uses	Negative for substitutes; positive for complements
	C: real unit costs of labor and capital relevant to the production of the money commodity	Negative. (This variable is set off by a semicolon in the equation because it is operative only when production becomes profitable.)
	T: the technological and resource base for the production of the money commodity	Positive. (This variable also is operative only if production becomes profitable.)

Now to complete a market model of commodity money we need merely to assume $M^D = M^S$ and reintroduce our familiar demand-for-money function in its original form,

$$M^D = f\left(\frac{1}{P}, \; y, \; i, \; \ldots \right)$$

(Since our analysis is now focused on quantities of glitters in place of ounces of gold, there is no need to adjust this function by N.) The usual demand curve is depicted along with our supply curve in Figure 10–5.

The equilibrium price for money, $\left(\dfrac{1}{P}\right)_1$, in this graph represents implicitly the same price for gold as $\left(\dfrac{N}{P}\right)_1$ in Figure 10–3. The two graphs incorporate the same relationships and produce the same conclusions. Our choice of one or the other for analytical exposition is simply a matter of convenience based on the focus and purpose of our analysis. Note that either of the two approaches implies that the value of gold will tend to be the same in both monetary and non-monetary uses. This is the hallmark of a commodity money as defined in Chapter 9. A necessary condition for it to hold is that the money commodity must be freely convertible from one type of use to the other. This completes the development of our primary com-

The market equilibrium for money

FIGURE 10–5
Supply and demand for glitters

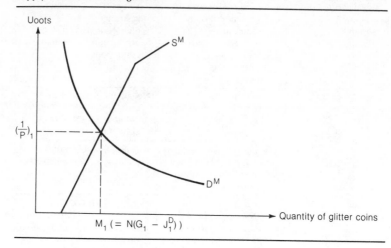

$M_1 (= N(G_1 - J_1^D))$

modity-money model, and we are now prepared to consider some variable changes.

First, suppose real income rises because of growth in the labor force and/or the stock of capital in the economy. From our analysis of Chapter 3 we know that this tends to increase the demand for money, shifting the demand-for-money curve to the right as shown in Figure 10–6.

The effect of a change in real income

At the same time, an increase in real income will tend to raise the nonmonetary demand for gold, shifting the money supply curve to the left, also shown in Figure 10–6. Both of these shifts tend to raise the value of money and combine to determine a new equilibrium value at $(1/P)_2$. Since a rise in the value of money means a fall in the

FIGURE 10–6
Effect of growth in real income

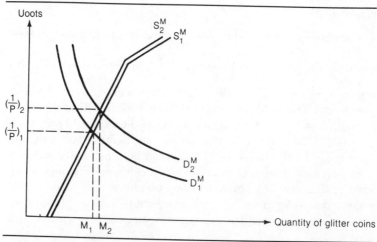

general level of prices, we conclude that *real income growth tends to cause deflation in a primary commodity-money system, ceteris paribus.*[4]

Next, suppose there is a new gold discovery in a remote region of Oros. This causes a shift down and perhaps also a flattening of the average and marginal cost curves for the gold industry, causing, in turn, the money-supply curve to shift as shown in Figure 10–7. As a result, the value of gold glitter coins (and of gold in general) falls, meaning higher glitter prices for other goods and services. *Discoveries of new and cheaper sources of a money commodity are inflationary in a primary commodity-money system, ceteris paribus.*

The effect of a gold discovery

FIGURE 10–7
Effect of a gold discovery

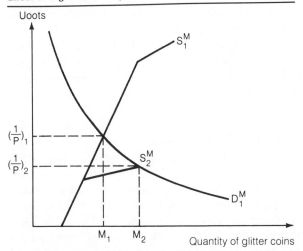

INTERNATIONAL EFFECTS WITH A GOLD STANDARD

All of the foregoing analysis assumed a closed economy. Although it was not labeled as such, the system developed in earlier sections as an example of a commodity-money system qualified as a *gold-standard system* for a single country. As we shall see, more complex systems also may qualify as gold-standard systems, but for now we will keep the analysis as simple as possible with the primary commodity system and extend it to two countries. Both of these countries are on a gold standard and impose no restrictions on international trade.

Our second country is Staron whose medium of exchange and unit of account is the flek. The gold content of a flek is set at one ounce which means that the Staron mint will take all gold offered to

---

[4]This conclusion assumes that gold production is not taking place, as implied in Figure 10–6, or at least that production is not adequate to overcome the effects described.

it at a price of one flek per ounce, using one ounce of gold to make one-flek coins.

Oros and Staron open their borders for trade, and a foreign-exchange market develops immediately among intermediaries servicing importers and exporters. What will be the exchange rate between the glitter and the flek? The answer is one-half flek per glitter, of course—provided transportation and processing costs for gold are ignored. If the exchange rate of the glitter were higher than this, say one flek per glitter, it would pay to sell glitters for fleks in the foreign exchange market, melt down the flek coins for gold, and sell the gold to the Oros mint at a profit—a profit of 100 percent in this case. The reverse would hold at an exchange rate lower than one-half flek per glitter. The exchange rate, therefore, will tend to stay fixed at one-half flek because there is an excess supply of glitters above that rate and an excess demand below it.

You should recall from Chapter 8 that in the absence of intervention, the exchange rate for a money was determined by the supply and demand for that money in the foreign-exchange market arising from imports and exports and other sources of autonomous international payments. Is our analysis different here?

The answer is yes and no. Our monies in Chapter 8 were fiat monies, not commodity monies. With no intrinsic value to a paper dollar or a paper mark, there is no profit to physically converting them into anything else; and neither dollars nor marks can be redeemed at a fixed rate for anything else of significant intrinsic value. The same is true for most other media in use today. The exchange rate between two commodity monies with the same fungible commodity base and free exchange, on the other hand, will remain relatively constant because of international flows of the commodity used as money in response to any imbalance in autonomous international payments. Such flows of the money commodity eventually have opposite effects on the price levels in each country. Price-level adjustments in turn feed back to autonomous payments, bringing them into balance *automatically* at the gold-standard exchange rate.[5] As a result, the exchange rate in the international gold-standard system is consistent with equality in autonomous payments as in Chapter 8; but this is a long-run result here, and autonomous payments adjust more to the exchange rate than the other way around.

To explain the gold-standard adjustment mechanism further, suppose Oros and Staron have an imbalance in their international payments because Oros is importing more in glitter value from

---

[5]Actually, it may be argued that flows of gold should be counted as part of trade, then there never is any imbalance in autonomous payments in this system. But treating flows of gold this way distracts attention from the monetary role of gold in each country and the gold-standard adjustment mechanism.

Staron, its sole trading partner, than it is exporting. More glitters than before are being offered for available fleks in the exchange market, where trades were taking place before at a rate of two glitters for one flek. The value of the glitter weakens slightly in response. The story does not end here because this causes glitter coins to be melted down and offered to the Staron mint. This means a decline in the stock of glitters in Oros, and an increase in the stock of fleks in Staron. As a result, the price level in Oros will tend to fall, and the price level in Staron will tend to rise. We know from Chapter 8 that a fall in the price level in Oros will tend to increase export receipts and decrease import payments for Oros. A rise in Staron's price level has the same effect on Oros' payments. Hence, eventually, through opposite price-level adjustments in each economy, balance will tend to be restored to trade payments between the two countries—at the original exchange rate.

The gold-standard adjustment mechanism

This is the mechanism of adjustment of payments that occurs among countries when each country's money supply is linked to gold and gold is freely traded among participating countries. In a sense a pure international gold standard gives the participating countries a single unit of account and medium of exchange in gold. An increase in the aggregate gold supply among these countries, regardless of its distribution, means that the price levels in all participating countries tend to rise proportionately.

Viewed from the perspective of an individual country, a gold flow in response to a balance-of-payments imbalance constitutes an additional factor affecting the supply of gold and money in that country. From a broader perspective, if the system performs flawlessly, a gold flow simply reflects the effects of price levels that are out of alignment. Gold tends to flow to that country having the highest price of gold (or lowest price level). In a pure international gold system our money-supply variable, $1/P$, already introduced, explains much of the influence on the money supply of the balance of payments as well as some of the influence of domestic factors described earlier.

Our analysis of the pure gold-standard system ignored many of the complications and slippages in the gold standard as it worked historically. Transportation costs for gold and lags in communication about market conditions were hindrances in the 19th century. More important, however, was the fact that, in historical periods under the gold standard, the money supply in each country was only loosely linked to gold. This was the case, for example, for the United States and several major countries in Europe during much of the 19th century and the first third of the 20th century. Nevertheless, during this period the money supplies in these economies were interdependent; consequently, the inflationary effects of gold dis-

Slippages in the system

"Remember when a piece of eight really bought something?"

Reprinted by permission *The Wall Street Journal.*

coveries in the United States and other developing areas spread to Europe under the international gold-standard mechanism.

There were several reasons why money supplies during the reign of the international gold standard were only loosely tied to gold. Gold was used as a medium of exchange but also as a reserve asset for debt money issued by governments and by banks in a secondary commodity-money system (to be explained shortly). Moreover, during some periods there were *two* commodity monies in general use and freely minted by governments. The dollar, for example, was for periods in the 19th century fixed in terms of a certain quantity of gold and *also* a certain quantity of silver. In other words, either gold or silver could be sold at a fixed-dollar price to the U.S. mint for coinage. The prices were different for each metal and were intended to reflect the relative market prices of the metals at the time the standards were set. The ratio of the prices of the two metals at the

The bimetallic standard

mint was called the *mint ratio*. Prices for goods in general were quoted simply in dollars as they are today. Payment was made in gold or silver dollars or in debt money redeemable in either form of specie. This arrangement, which existed as well in major countries of Europe at times, is known as *a bimetallic standard* or *bimetallism*.

MULTIPLE-COMMODITY MONIES AND GRESHAM'S LAW

When governments or societies establish a commodity-money system based on two or more commodities, it is often the case that eventually one of the money commodities is hoarded or converted to other uses and fails to circulate as part of the money supply. This tends to occur when market values of the different money commodities move significantly out of line with the mint ratio originally established for them.

Suppose, for example, that the king of Oros decides to adopt a bimetallic standard and establishes the glitter's content at one-half ounce in terms of gold *and* ten ounces in terms of silver. This makes one ounce of silver exchangeable for one tenth of a glitter and one twentieth of an ounce of gold—a mint ratio of 20:1, silver for gold. (Over long historical periods the ratio of the price of an ounce of gold to the price of an ounce of silver has varied between roughly 10:1 and 40:1.) Now you might say, "All that's glitters is not gold!" But you might be wrong. It all depends upon what happens to the relative supplies and demands for the two metals.

Suppose a new gold discovery in Oros greatly increases the supply of gold. Some of this increased gold will be made available for jewelry and some will be shipped to the mint, swelling the money supply. The value of gold will fall; and the value of silver *as money* also will fall, because of a rise in the general price level. At a lower value as money, some monetary silver will be diverted for nonmonetary uses. (We assume no additional supply of silver is available from new silver discoveries. The greater quantity of silver devoted to nonmonetary uses comes from a reduction in the quantity of circulating silver glitters. A decline in the quantity of circulating silver can happen and will proceed without a tendency for the general price level to return to its original level because silver glitters are being replaced in circulation by the increased supply of gold glitters.)

The process may develop to the point at which the quantity of circulating silver glitters becomes very small and the market price of silver begins to reflect dominant nonmonetary supply and demand factors, causing the price of silver to rise significantly above its old relationship to the price of gold. At this point, whatever remaining silver glitters there are may tend to be hoarded as a better store of value than gold.

To turn to a real-world example, in the 1840s the United States and one of its major trading partners, France, were on a bimetallic standard. Both silver and gold were used for coins in these countries. In the early 1850s, however, gold discoveries in California and Australia caused the world's supply of gold to grow substantially, increasing the money supplies in these countries and reducing the value of gold and silver as money. As a result, silver fell out of general circulation in France and the United States, and these countries were de facto, if not de jure, on a gold standard.

Gresham's law

This episode and the previous example are illustrations of Gresham's law, which is usually stated as *"bad money drives out good money,"* meaning *that less valuable money tends to replace more valuable money in circulation.* It was originally propounded in the 16th century by Sir Thomas Gresham, a financial minister of the British government, as a generalization of the tendency in those times for new coins which were high in metal content and intrinsic value to be hoarded while worn, clipped, and sweated coins circulated freely.

This phenomenon—certain money forms failing to circulate because they are intrinsically more valuable than other forms of money—still arises from time to time. However, specific conditions must be satisfied for it to occur:

Necessary conditions for Gresham's law

1. *The money which is intrinsically more valuable than other money must also be more valuable in other uses than it is as money in circulation.*
2. *The more intrinsically valuable money must be relatively fixed by law or custom in its parity with another money*—fixed, that is, in the rate at which it can be exchanged for another money or used as money in the same transactions as another money.

The failure of the first condition to apply explains the fact that our coin currency today circulates as freely as paper currency despite its higher intrinsic value.

The second condition is more subtle but also important. Gresham's law may not hold where one commodity money becomes more intrinsically valuable than another money (at the old parity) if the parity changes. Suppose, for example, that the dollar's content in the United States in the 1850s had been fixed only in terms of silver, with coins of gold also minted but adjustable in gold content. Under this arrangement, the U.S. mint could have responded to new gold discoveries by reducing the government's offer price for gold and raising the gold content of the dollar. This would have stemmed the rise in the money supply and kept the price level from rising significantly. As a result, relative values of raw gold and silver would have changed in all uses—silver becoming more valuable—and silver coins would have remained in circulation. Another, actual example of Gresham's law not applying for the same reason is provided in the following article.

INTRODUCTION TO ARTICLE

The article below is a second excerpt of passages from Radford's "The Economic Organization of a P.O.W. Camp." (The first excerpt appeared in Chapter 2.) These passages illustrate two cases in which Gresham's law operated because the necessary conditions were fulfilled—first, better cigarettes (Churchman's No. 1), and then manufactured cigarettes ceased to circulate. They also illustrate a case in which Gresham's law failed to operate because the second necessary condition cited in this text was not fulfilled; cigarettes and Bully Marks both continued to circulate prior to the August disaster despite changes in their relative values because prices were quoted in each *and the rate of exchange between them was flexible.*

Finally, Radford describes the operation of several factors which influenced the price level in the camp's commodity-money system, most operating on the supply of the money commodity. Fluctuations in the money supply caused periodic deflations and inflations. The descriptions given by Radford are applications of the principles presented in this chapter. (Note, however, that the money commodities in Radford's camp were consumable and the stocks could decline, whereas the money commodity in our fictitious country of Oros could not decline.)

The economic organisation of a P.O.W. camp

The cigarette currency

Although cigarettes as currency exhibited certain peculiarities, they performed all the functions of a metallic currency as a unit of account, as a measure of value, and as a store of value, and shared most of its characteristics. They were homogeneous, reasonably durable, and of convenient size for the smallest or, in packets, for the largest transactions. Incidentally, they could be clipped or sweated by rolling them between the fingers so that tobacco fell out.

Cigarettes were also subject to the working of Gresham's law. Certain brands were more popular than others as smokes, but for currency purposes a cigarette was a cigarette. Consequently buyers used the poorer qualities and the shop rarely saw the more popular brands: cigarettes such as Churchman's No. 1 were rarely used for trading. At one time ciga-

rettes hand rolled from pipe tobacco began to circulate. Pipe tobacco was issued in lieu of cigarettes by the Red Cross at a rate of 25 cigarettes to the ounce and this rate was standard in exchanges, but an ounce would produce 30 homemade cigarettes. Naturally, people with machine-made cigarettes broke them down and re-rolled the tobacco, and the real cigarette virtually disappeared from the market. Handrolled cigarettes were not homogeneous and prices could no longer be quoted in them with safety: each cigarette was examined before it was accepted and thin ones were rejected, or extra demanded as a makeweight. For a time we suffered all the inconveniences of a debased currency.

Machine-made cigarettes were always universally acceptable, both for what they would buy and for themselves. It was this intrinsic value which gave rise to their principal disadvantage as currency, a disadvantage which exists, but to a far smaller extent in the case of metallic currency; that is, a strong demand for nonmonetary purposes. Consequently our economy was repeatedly subject to deflation and to periods of monetary stringency. While the Red Cross issue of 50 to 25 cigarettes per man per week came in regularly, and while there were fair stocks held, the cigarette currency suited its purpose admirably. But when the issue was interrupted, stocks soon ran out, prices fell, trading declined in volume and became increasingly a matter of barter. This deflationary tendency was periodically offset by the sudden injection of new currency. Private cigarette parcels arrived in a trickle throughout the year, but the big numbers came in quarterly when the Red Cross received its allocation of transport. Several hundred thousand cigarettes might arrive in the space of a fortnight. Prices soared, and then began to fall, slowly at first but with increasing rapidity as stocks ran out, until the next big delivery. Most of our economic troubles could be attributed to this fundamental instability.

Price movements

Many factors affected prices, the strongest and most noticeable being the periodical currency inflation and deflation described in the last paragraphs. The periodicity of this price cycle depended on cigarette and, to a far lesser extent, on food deliveries. At one time in the early days, before any private parcels had arrived and when there were no individual stocks, the weekly issue of cigarettes and food parcels occurred on a Monday. The nonmonetary demand for cigarettes was great, and less elastic than the demand for food: consequently prices fluctuated weekly, falling towards Sunday night and rising sharply on Monday morning. Later, when many people held reserves, the weekly issue had no such effect, being too small a portion of the total available. Credit allowed people with no reserves to meet their nonmonetary demand over the weekend.

The general price level was affected by other factors. An influx of new prisoners, proverbially hungry, raised it. Heavy air raids in the vicinity of the camp probably increased the nonmonetary demand for cigarettes and accentuated deflation. Good and bad war news certainly had its effect, and the general waves of optimism and pessimism which swept the camp were reflected in prices. Before breakfast one morning in March of this year, a rumour of the arrival of parcels and cigarettes was circulated. Within 10 minutes I sold a treacle ration for four cigarettes (hitherto offered in vain for three), and many similar deals went through. By 10 o'clock the rumour was denied, and treacle that day found no more buyers even at two cigarettes.

Paper currency—Bully Marks

Around D day, food and cigarettes were plentiful, business was brisk, and the camp in an optimistic mood. Consequently the Entertainments Committee felt the moment opportune to launch a restaurant, where food and hot drinks were sold while a band and variety turns performed. Earlier experiments, both public and private, had pointed the way, and the scheme was a great success. Food was bought at market prices to provide the meals and the small profits were devoted to a reserve fund and used to bribe Germans to provide grease paints and other necessities for the camp theatre. Originally meals were sold for cigarettes but this meant that the whole scheme was vulnerable to the periodic deflationary waves, and furthermore heavy smokers were unlikely to attend much. The whole success of the scheme depended on an adequate amount of food being offered for sale in the normal manner.

To increase and facilitate trade, and to stimulate supplies and customers therefore, and secondarily to avoid the worst effects of deflation when it should come, a paper currency was organised by the restaurant and the shop. The shop bought food on behalf of the restaurant with paper notes and the paper was accepted equally with the cigarettes in the restaurant or shop, and passed back to the shop to purchase more food. The shop acted as a bank of issue. The paper money was backed 100 percent, by food; hence its name, the Bully Mark. The BMk was backed 100 percent, by food: there could be no over issues, as is permissible with a normal bank of issue, since the eventual dispersal of the camp and consequent redemption of all BMk's was anticipated in the near future.

Originally one BMk was worth one cigarette and for a short time both circulated freely inside and outside the restaurant. Prices were quoted in BMk's and cigarettes with equal freedom—and for a short time the BMk showed signs of replacing the cigarette as currency. The BMk was tied to food, but not to cigarettes. As it was issued against food, say 45 for a tin of milk and so on, any reduction in the BMk prices of food would have meant that there were unbacked BMk's in circulation. But the price of both food and BMk's could and did fluctuate with the supply of cigarettes.

While the restaurant flourished, the scheme was a success: the restaurant bought heavily, all foods were saleable and prices were stable.

In August parcels and cigarettes were halved and the camp was bombed. The restaurant closed for a short while and sales of food became difficult. Even when the restaurant reopened, the food and cigarette shortage became increasingly acute and people were unwilling to convert such valuable goods into paper and to hold them for luxuries like snacks and tea. Less of the right kinds of food for the restaurant were sold, and the shop became glutted with dried fruit, chocolate, sugar, etc., which the restaurant could not buy. The price level and the price structure changed. The BMk fell to four-fifths of a cigarette and eventually farther still, and it became unacceptable save in the restaurant. There was a flight from the BMk, no longer convertible into cigarettes or popular foods. The cigarette reestablished itself.

But the BMk was sound! The restaurant closed in the New Year with a progressive food shortage and the long evenings without lights due to intensified Allied air raids, and the BMk's could only be spent in the coffee bar—

relict of the restaurant—or on the few unpopular foods in the shop, the owners of which were prepared to accept them. In the end all holders of BMk's were paid in full, in cups of coffee or in prunes. People who had bought BMk's, for cigarettes or valuable jam or biscuits in their heyday were aggrieved that they should have stood the loss involved in their restricted choice, but they suffered no actual loss of market value.

Conclusion

The economic organisation described was both elaborate and smooth working in the summer of 1944. Then came the August cuts and deflation. Prices fell, rallied with deliveries of cigarette parcels in September and December, and fell again. In January 1945, supplies of Red Cross cigarettes ran out, and prices slumped still further; in February the supplies of food parcels were exhausted and the depression became a blizzard. Food, itself scarce, was almost given away in order to meet the nonmonetary demand for cigarettes. The restaurant was a memory and the BMk a joke. The shop was empty and the exchange and mart notices were full of unaccepted offers for cigarettes. Barter increased in volume, becoming a larger proportion of a smaller volume of trade.

By April, 1945, chaos had replaced order in the economic sphere; sales were difficult, prices lacked stability. Economics has been defined as the science of distributing limited means among unlimited and competing ends. On 12th April, with the arrival of elements of the 30th U.S. Infantry Division, the ushering in of an age of plenty demonstrated the hypothesis that with infinite means economic organisation and activity would be redundant, as every want could be satisfied without effort.

SOURCE: R. A. Radford, "The Economic Organisation of a P.O.W. Camp," Economica 12 (1945).

This completes our analysis of the primary commodity-money system. We turn next to the secondary commodity-money system.

THE EVOLUTION OF EARLY DEBT MONEY AND
BANKS OF ISSUE

As described in Chapter 9, the evolution of money often can be explained in terms of the operational qualities of different physical forms of money and of the tendency of an established money to acquire institutionalized acceptance. It was found as long ago as the ninth century in China that several operational drawbacks to a circulating commodity money can be overcome with a substitute circulating medium such as paper notes backed by reserves of commodity money. In time, in various societies it was discovered that circulating paper money acquired institutionalized acceptance such that less than 100 percent reserves were necessary to sustain confidence in it. In this manner debt money—money pledged to be redeemable in other assets of value and backed by fractional reserves—evolved.

Debt monies issued by governments have been identified for many early societies. Usually issues were made by the government treasury. Later, government-run central banks developed in countries on a commodity standard; these banks naturally issued debt money on reserves of commodity money. Whichever type of agency is involved, in these situations the government agency's reserve is an important factor determining the money supply, as explained in a later section of this chapter.

Early forms of debt money issued through private entities have been identified by historians for a number of countries and societies. One of these which led directly to the development of an advanced banking system was the issue activity of goldsmiths in England during the 17th century. Deposits of gold coins and other valuables were accepted by goldsmiths for safekeeping. Depositors found that title to these deposits could be transferred by writing bearer certificates of ownership or by drawing up orders to a goldsmith to transfer ownership. Either type of document enabled specific claims on goldsmiths to be used as money.

In time, goldsmiths discovered that depositors exercising claims did not require return of the very coins left for security; coins of equivalent value were sufficient. General claims on goldsmiths in the forms of deposits and of paper notes in convenient, standard denominations gradually replaced specific claims and acquired institutionalized acceptance. With the circulation of their representative money from second- to third-party holders without claims being presented for gold, goldsmiths found that claims on a day-to-day basis were far less than the volumes of gold on deposit with them. Therefore, a certain proportion of the gold on hand was redundant and could be loaned out at interest.

Why lend excess gold and not spend it? Goldsmiths were accustomed to extending loans, and it no doubt occurred to them that one

*Government
agencies*

*English
goldsmiths*

way to minimize the risk that claims could not be met was to employ excess gold in short-term, secure loans. If specie became needed to meet an accumulation of claims, it could be recovered—at least within a short period of time, assuming the loans were in fact secure. Over time, then, and in this way there evolved "banks of issue," meaning banks which issued notes and deposit balances in exchange for specie and as loans.

Banks of issue

Banks of issue which were conservatively and responsibly managed became recognized as beneficial to commerce not only because they provided a more convenient form of money for most transactions, but also because they allowed a desirable expansion of the money supply and because they were more reliable and cheaper sources of credit to business than alternative sources. By their nature, they were able to lend at interest funds obtained at virtually zero cost—an almost certain profitable venture. Even though these "gold mine" operations often were overly exploited, early banks played a significant role in expanding monetization, augmenting liquidity, and improving the volume and allocation of savings in the economy.

Without government restraint, it was very tempting for private banks to issue large volumes of debt money on tiny reserves. In the early part of the 19th century in the United States, as described later in Chapter 12, there were particularly widespread abuses by banks of the issue power, resulting in an excessive supply of money, suspensions of redemption of notes into specie, loan defaults, and bankruptcies.

To restrain commercial banks and other depository institutions —our modern descendants of the early banks of issue—to responsible policies today, federal and state governments impose restrictions for charters for these institutions and limit their issue activity with regulations such as reserve requirements. The role of issue banks' reserve decisions in the money-supply process is brought out in the next section. Reserve requirements are introduced in a later part of this chapter.

ISSUE BANKS' RESERVE DECISIONS AND THE SUPPLY OF DEBT MONEY

Return to our fictitious country of Oros now and assume the king charters a single bank, the Midas Bank, which issues deposit balances and its own paper notes in exchange for deposits of glitter coins and as loans. This bank must decide on the appropriate relationship between its reserves and its monetary liabilities. Suppose that the relationship chosen is one glitter of reserves to four glitters of monetary liabilities. Balance sheets for the nonbank public in Oros and for the Midas Bank, the only issue bank in Oros, look as follows (relevant entries only):

The single-bank case

The Midas Bank (thousands of glitters)				The Oros Nonbank Public (thousands of glitters)			
Assets		Liabilities		Assets		Liabilities	
Reserves of		Bank notes	20	Specie	30	Loans	
specie	10	Demand		Bank notes	20	from banks	30
Loans	30	deposits	20	Demand			
		Total debt		deposits	20	Total lia-	
Total assets	40	money	40	Total		bilities	30
				assets	70		

The public, we assume, has decided to exchange 10,000 glitters in specie with the Midas Bank in return for debt money, retaining 30,000 glitters in specie. The Midas Bank has found that it can safely issue 40,000 glitters in monetary liabilities against these reserves, 10,000 in exchange for the 10,000 in specie and 30,000 loaned out (the mixture of these liabilities between notes and deposits is unimportant in our example). The supply of debt money as a result is four times the quantity of reserves in the Midas Bank.

Suppose the Oros public were to exchange 10,000 more glitters in specie for debt money from the Midas Bank. Based on the relationship we assumed between reserves and monetary liabilities and the fact that there are no other banks in Oros, the Midas Bank would feel safe in doubling its loans and issues of debt money as shown below.[6]

The Midas Bank (thousands of glitters)				The Oros Nonbank Public (thousands of glitters)			
Assets		Liabilities		Assets		Liabilities	
Reserves of		Bank notes	40	Specie	20	Loans	
specie	20	Demand		Bank notes	40	from banks	60
Loans	60	deposits	40	Demand			
		Total debt		deposits	40	Total lia-	
Total assets	80	money	80	Total		bilities	60
				assets	100		

The supply of debt money in Oros clearly depends upon the volume of reserves in the Midas Bank. If the Midas Bank maintains a constant ratio, r, between reserves, R, and its supply of debt money, N^S, the relationship is quite simple,

$$N^S = \frac{1}{r} R$$

In our Midas Bank example, r equals .25; consequently, a one-glitter rise in reserves produces a four-glitter rise in debt money.

---

[6]We have not yet introduced complications which have to do with the public's preferences for commodity money relative to debt money. Later we will allow for the fact that an increase in the volume of debt money such as shown here is likely to feed back to a rise in the public's desired holdings of specie, leading to some offsetting drain in reserves from the bank.

Now, ordinarily, we would not expect the ratio of reserves to debt money to remain constant at all times for the Midas Bank. There are several economic factors relevant to the Midas Bank's decision regarding r. Before considering these, however, we should extend the analysis to allow for the case of more than one bank in Oros.

Suppose a second bank, the Advance Bank, is chartered by the king and attracts, at first, 10,000 glitters worth of specie from the public in exchange for notes and deposit balances. The Midas Bank, we assume, has its original levels of reserves, money liabilities, and loans. The initial balance sheets are as follows:

The two-bank case

The Midas Bank (thousands of glitters)				The Advance Bank (thousands of glitters)				The Oros Nonbank Public (thousands of glitters)			
Assets		Liabilities		Assets		Liabilities		Assets		Liabilities	
Reserves of specie	10	Debt money	40	Reserves of specie	10	Debt money	10	Specie	20	Loans from banks	30
Loans	30			Loans	0			Debt money	50		
Total assets	40			Total assets	10			Total assets	70	Total liabilities	30

Assume the Advance Bank also wants to keep a ratio of reserves to debt money of .25. The Advance Bank realizes, however, that it cannot make loans too aggressively because the Midas Bank is likely to acquire some Advance Bank notes from Midas Bank customers as Advance Bank borrowers spend their funds. The Midas Bank will present these notes to the Advance Bank for specie, causing a drain of reserves. As a result it lends 12,000 glitters of new debt money to borrowers, figuring that even if half of all this new debt money is collected by the Midas Bank and presented for specie, enough reserves will remain in the Advance Bank to support its remaining liabilities at a ratio of .25.

As a next step, we assume that the Advance Bank was duly prudent; half of the new debt money issued by the Advance Bank ends up being presented for redemption by the Midas Bank. After this occurs our balance sheets show:

The Midas Bank (thousands of glitters)				The Advance Bank (thousands of glitters)				The Oros Nonbank Public (thousands of glitters)			
Assets		Liabilities		Assets		Liabilities		Assets		Liabilities	
Reserves of specie	16	Debt money	46	Reserves of specie	4	Debt money	16	Specie	20	Loans from banks	42
Loans	30			Loans	12			Debt money	62		
Total assets	46			Total assets	16			Total assets	82	Total liabilities	42

The Midas Bank now has more reserves than it needs to support its monetary liabilities. It determines that additional loans of 7,200 glitters in debt money could be made provided that no more than half of this new debt money is collected by the Advance Bank. This is done, and half of the new issues by the Midas Bank are collected and presented by the Advance Bank.

The pattern of our story is sufficiently well developed now to move rapidly to a conclusion. Loans by each bank are always made with a realization that some reserves will be lost to the other bank as the loaned funds are spent. The additions to loans and debt money continue but grow smaller and smaller on each round. Twenty rounds are summarized in Figure 10–8.

FIGURE 10–8

	(1)	(2)	(3)	(4)	(5)	(6)
	The Midas bank (glitters)			The Advance bank (glitters)		
Round	Changes to reserves	Changes to loans	Changes to debt money	Changes to reserves	Changes to loans	Changes to debt money
0	0	0	0	10,000	0	10,000
1	6,000	0	6,000	− 6,000	12,000	6,000
2	− 3,600	7,200	3,600	3,600	0	3,600
3	2,160	0	2,160	− 2,160	4,320	2,160
4	− 1,296	2,592	1,996	1,296	0	1,296
5	778	0	778	− 778	1,555	778
6	− 466	933	466	466	0	466
7	278	0	778	− 278	560	278
8	− 168	336	168	168	0	168
9	101	0	101	− 101	201	101
10	− 60	121	60	60	0	60
11	36	0	36	36	73	36
12	− 22	44	22	22	0	22
13	13	0	13	− 13	26	13
14	− 8	16	8	8	0	8
15	5	0	5	− 5	9	5
16	− 3	6	3	3	0	3
17	2	0	2	− 2	3	2
18	− 1	2	1	1	0	1
19	1	0	1	− 1	1	1
20	− 0	1	0	0	0	0
Total	3,750	11,250	14,999	6,250	18,749	24,999

Rounds 1 and 2 were developed in the preceding T-accounts. Note the totals at the bottom. The volume of new debt money issued by the two banks together after 20 rounds, the sum of columns (3) and (6), comes to virtually 40,000 glitters, the same as the added volume issued by the Midas Bank alone when it received an additional 10,000 glitters in specie as a single, monopoly bank. The volume of new specie reserves of the two banks always remains 10,000 glitters, the same as the volume of new reserves for the Midas Bank alone in the earlier case. The conclusion we draw from this exercise is that, although in a system with multiple banks each bank may view itself as being able to lend less than its reserve ratio would permit, the end result for all banks taken together will be the same as it was in the case of a monopoly bank. The volume of debt money will be a multiple of reserves held by banks, with that multiple given by the inverse of the reserve ratio.

Determinants of the reserve ratio

Now we turn to consider the determinants of the reserve ratio. It is important to recognize that, as developed so far, r is a *desired* reserve ratio without government restraints. Nothing has been discussed yet about required reserves or a required reserve ratio, though this will be done shortly. In the system that we have described, reserves are held only because it is prudent to do so. Our desired reserve ratio, therefore, is not an institutionally given number. It can change and, in fact, will tend to change in response to economic conditions. Small changes in the r ratio, moreover, can have a major impact on the supply of debt money. If, for example, our two banks in Oros were to reduce their desired ratios from .25 to .20, the supply of debt money—without considering complications introduced by the public's portfolio preferences—would rise from 80,000 glitters to 100,000 glitters.

The first variable we consider is the level of interest rates on bank loans. The higher the rate of interest on bank loans, the greater the incentive for a bank to expand loans on a given reserve base. This incentive exists even if it is perceived that an increase in loans means a loss in reserves. There is an opportunity cost to holding reserves of specie because specie yields no interest. A bank will realize that, if its reserves can be reduced by one glitter, loans can be increased by at least one glitter. This increases a bank's risk that it cannot meet a note or deposit claim, but the higher the rate of interest the more it pays a bank to take added risk. Therefore, *the higher the rate of interest, the lower is the desired reserve ratio.*

The interest rate

The state of economic activity will affect confidence in banks and banks' reserve decisions. As described in Chapter 7, if times are bad, some borrowers are likely to default. If defaults exceed a bank's net worth, the bank will become insolvent. Fearing this, debt-money holders may tend to convert debt money to specie in hard times. In other words, a run on banks may develop. (More will be said shortly about the effects of this on the money supply.) To avoid any sign of weakness which would encourage a run and to help in the event of a run, banks will try to build up reserves, boosting the r ratio. When economic conditions are good and there is no threat of a run, lower reserves are held. Therefore, *the desired reserve ratio will tend to rise and fall in opposite phase to the rise and fall in real economic activity over the business cycle.*

Real economic activity

The final factor which may affect the r ratio is government regulation. Suppose that the king of Oros grows concerned that banks in Oros are not holding adequate reserves and imposes a minimum required reserve ratio of .33 for chartered banks, with severe penal-

Government regulation

ties if the ratio slips below this level. If the banks in our two-bank case respond by boosting the ratio from .25 only to .33, the supply of debt money would decline from 80,000 glitters to 60,000 glitters.

Actually, because of the penalties for the r ratio slipping below .33, it would be wise for the banks to raise the r ratio further—say to .40. This would cut the volume of debt money down to 50,000 glitters. The r ratio in this situation is comprised of a required reserve ratio, r^r, equal to .33, and an excess reserve ratio, r^e equal to .07. In symbols

$$r = r^r + r^e$$

This completes an initial analysis of the banks' reserve ratio and its impact on the supply of debt money in Oros. We turn now to a framework which will facilitate an analysis of the total money supply—debt money plus commodity money in circulation—and complications introduced by likely variations in the public's holdings of commodity money.

MONEY SUPPLY ANALYSIS USING THE MONETARY BASE AND THE MONEY-STOCK MULTIPLIER

Definition of the base and the mulitplier

It is convenient at this point to introduce some terminology and a framework which will be useful throughout the remainder of the book for analysis of the money supply in secondary monetary systems (those including debt money). *The monetary base, B, is the aggregate quantity of money which is used or can be used as primary reserve money for banks.*[7]

The monetary base

Ordinarily a certain amount of the monetary base is held by the public outside of the banking system (specie held by the public in Oros, for example); consequently,

$$B = K + R$$

where K is the part of the monetary base outside of the banks and R, defined before as reserves, is the part of the monetary base held by banks.

The money-stock multiplier

The money-stock multiplier, m, is the ratio of the total money stock to the monetary base:

$$\frac{M^S}{B} = m$$

Rearranging this relationship, we have

$$M^S = m \times B$$

---

[7]The monetary base is also known as high-powered money.

The quantity of money supplied in the economy is equal to the money-stock multiplier times the monetary base.

Note in passing that the total money supply is equal to the part of the monetary base outside the banks plus the quantity of debt money supplied by the banks

$$M^S = K + N^S$$

In our examples in this chapter up to this point, the monetary base equals the total quantity of specie: specie held by the banks as reserves *plus* specie held by the public. The multiplier for *debt money* on the reserve base, R, was equal to 1/r. We did not develop a multiplier for the total money stock earlier. In fact, our analysis of the money supply was not complete because we examined the supply of money under artificial conditions in which the reserve base did not interact with other variables.

We will correct this deficiency now. Recall that our analysis in the previous section did show how a decision by the public to exchange more specie for bank money was capable of affecting the supply of debt money by changing the quantity of reserves available to banks. Left out of the analysis was the fact that changes in the supply of debt money, in turn, are likely to feed back to the public's demand for specie and thereby alter the quantity of reserves available to banks from the level assumed earlier.

The relevance of the public's behavior

To be more specific, a rise in the quantity of debt money supplied will induce a rise in the quantity of specie demanded by the public. This may occur for several reasons. A rise in the supply of debt money may, because of an associated rise in the total money supply, induce a rise in the price level. A rise in the general price level will increase the public's demand for money of *both* types, specie and debt money. Any effects of the expansion in debt money on real income or interest rates would have the same type of feedback effect. Another reason is that debt money from banks may be viewed as risky by cash-balance holders; other things being the same, a rise in debt money will induce a rise in the demand for specie to keep portfolio risk from rising.

The influence of the volume of debt money

The currency ratio

These considerations lead us to posit a positive relationship between the public's demand for specie, K^D, and its holdings of debt money, other things being the same. This relationship is not necessarily proportional, but we will assume it is for convenience. Recognizing that the public is easily able to satisfy its demand for specie by presenting debt-money claims to banks, we also assume that $K = K^D$, i.e., the actual quantity of specie in circulation equals the desired quantity. Our basic behavioral relationship for the public, therefore, is:

$$K = k \times N^s$$

where the k variable in this expression is simply the ratio of K to N^s and is called the *currency ratio*.

Real economic activity

We will shortly combine the currency ratio and the reserve ratio in an analysis of the money-stock multiplier, but first we must consider two influences on the currency ratio. The first one was recognized earlier in connection with the r ratio. Since general economic conditions affect confidence in banks and debt money, the k ratio (as well as the r ratio) will tend to vary over the business cycle in our system. In periods of recession, confidence in banks will be low, making the demand for specie high relative to bank money and raising the k ratio. Conversely, in periods of prosperity, the k ratio will tend to be low when confidence in banks is high.

Seasonal factors

The second influence will be of less concern to us but deserves mention. This is the impact that seasons, especially the Christmas and summer holidays, have on the currency ratio. The currency ratio tends to rise in holiday seasons.[8]

The multiplier in terms of ratios

We have finally reached a point now where our behavioral relationships can be integrated into a complete money-supply model. This integration utilizes the following definitions and ratios already introduced:

$$m = \frac{M^s}{B} \tag{1}$$

$$M^s = K + N^s \tag{2}$$

$$B = R + K \tag{3}$$

$$r = \frac{R}{N^s} \tag{4}$$

$$k = \frac{K}{N^s} \tag{5}$$

We are interested in how the ratios r and k combine to determine the value of the money-stock multiplier. Our five equations together constitute a system of equations which can be used to solve for m in terms of the ratios k and r. To do this, first substitute Equations (2) and (3) into (1) to get:

$$m = \frac{K + N^s}{K + R}$$

Next solve (4) for R and (5) for K and substitute the results into the equation above to find

---

[8]Today, standard monetary data are seasonally adjusted so that the tendency for the currency ratio to fluctuate seasonally is not evident unless care is taken to refer to nonseasonally adjusted data.

$$m = \frac{k(N^S) + N^S}{k(N^S) + r(N^S)}$$

Finally, divide through by N^S and we obtain

$$m = \frac{k + 1}{k + r}$$

The money-stock
multiplier in
terms of ratios

This shows how the values of our k and r ratios combine to determine the value of the money-stock multiplier.

Let us use some actual values to indicate the nature of this result. Suppose the r ratio is equal to .25 as some of our previous examples have assumed, and let the k ratio equal .15, which is reasonable. The money-stock multiplier equation then may be solved to find a value for the multiplier of 2.875. This means that a monetary base of 10,000 glitters would support a total money stock of 28,750 glitters. A higher base will support a higher money stock by a multiple of 2.875.

Influences on the money-stock multiplier

But the multiplier can change also. Recall that the r and k ratios are affected by certain economic variables, and the r ratio can be changed by a change in the required reserve ratio, if there is a required reserve ratio. A rise in real economic activity will tend to decrease both the k and r ratios as described previously. (Why? Check your understanding of these effects.) It is apparent that a fall in the r ratio will raise the money-stock multiplier. It is less obvious that the same effect follows from a decline in the k ratio, but it does. (The k ratio enters both the numerator and the denominator of the mutliplier expression; however, as long as the r ratio is less than unity, a rise in the k ratio must reduce the multiplier.[9]) Therefore, *a rise in real income will tend to increase the money-stock multiplier, ceteris paribus.*

Real income

A rise in the interest rate, you should recall, will reduce the r ratio, which, to repeat, raises the multiplier. Hence, *a rise in the interest rate increases the multiplier.*

The interest rate

If reserve requirements are raised, the value of the r ratio will rise, reducing the multiplier.

Reserve requirements

During holiday periods, the k ratio will tend to rise, reducing the multiplier.

Seasonal factors

---

[9]This can be verified indirectly by trial or directly using calculus. The partial derivative of m with respect to k is negative if $r < 1$:

$$\frac{\partial m}{\partial k} = \frac{r - 1}{(r + k)^2}$$

Influences on the monetary base

Of course, the monetary base also may be affected by economic variables in the secondary commodity-money system we have analyzed so far. The monetary base is equal to the stock of commodity money in the system; therefore, the economic factors identified in the first part of this chapter as the determinants of the money supply in a primary commodity-money system apply here to the monetary base. We want to recognize the relevance of all these economic factors as well as those impinging on the money-stock multiplier. However, in order to keep our analysis of the secondary commodity-money system from becoming excessively encumbered with effects which are weaker than others or not of central concern, we will carry over only one economic variable from our earlier analysis of a primary commodity-money system to our analysis here. This is the value of the commodity money, 1/P.

The complete model

We may therefore summarize all of the analysis in this section with the following functions for a secondary commodity-money system with private debt money:

$$B = f\left(\frac{1}{P}, \ldots\right)$$

$$m = f(i, y, A, s, \ldots)$$

therefore,

$$M^S = f\left(\frac{1}{P}, i, y, A, s, \ldots\right)$$

Influenced variable	Influencing variable	Direction of influence
M^S: the total stock of money in a secondary commodity-money system	$\frac{1}{P}$: the value of one unit of money in terms of other goods and services	Positive on the base, hence on the money stock
	y: real income	Positive on the multiplier, hence on the money stock
	i: the rate of interest	Positive on the multiplier, hence on the money stock
	A: monetary policy	Positive or negative on the multiplier, hence on the money stock, according to whether reserve requirements are lowered or raised
	s: seasonal factors	Negative on the multiplier at holiday seasons, hence on the money stock

DETERMINANTS OF THE MONETARY BASE WITH GOVERNMENT DEBT MONEY

As stressed at a few points in the previous analysis, we have assumed so far that the monetary base was comprised entirely of commodity money. However, in several important periods of U.S. monetary history, the federal government issued debt money redeemable in gold. This debt money circulated and qualified as reserves for banks along with specie; consequently, the monetary base was comprised of specie plus federal government debt money.

It was necessary for U.S. government agencies to maintain reserves of gold in order to be able to redeem government debt money and in order to conform to statutory minimum reserve requirements imposed by Congress. The public, including banks, held balances of both gold specie and federal debt money in accordance with the public's preferences.

It is not difficult to recognize that, in such a system, the determinants of the monetary base are similar in some respects to the determinants of the money supply just outlined in the previous section. In fact we can duplicate that analysis in terms of a multiplier and relevant ratios,

$$B = b \times G$$

$$b = \frac{k^b + 1}{k^b + r^b}$$

where b is the multiplier showing the relationship between the monetary base and G, the stock of monetary gold k^b is the public's preference ratio for gold specie relative to government debt money, and r^b is the ratio of the government's reserves of gold relative to its debt money.

The determinants of the ratios k^b and r^b are somewhat different in this analysis from the determinants of k and r in the money-stock multiplier analysis. Confidence in the U.S. government's ability or willingness to redeem its debt money was sensitive mainly to political conditions which supported or threatened continuation of the gold standard. If political conditions are supportive of a commodity standard, the k^b ratio is likely to be relatively low and stable. If it appears that the commodity standard may be dropped by a government, a run on the government's reserves might develop, with the k^b ratio rising as a result.

The r^b ratio may be fixed by law. If not, it is available as a government policy variable. During the gold-standard years of the Federal Reserve, 1914–33, there was a minimum reserve ratio of 40 percent for gold relative to the major portion of Federal Reserve debt money, but the Fed could vary r^b above the minimum level. Consequently, changes in the quantity of gold in the economy could be offset by changes in the r^b ratio within the lower bound of the minimum statutory level of 40 percent and an upper bound close to 100 percent.[10]

Operations by a central bank or government treasury which alter r^b so as to offset the effects of changes in the stock of commodity money on the monetary base are known as *sterilization actions*. Use of sterilization actions by the Fed was one of the reasons the pure gold-standard adjustment mechanism described above was not fully operative for the United States during the period 1914—33.

THE NATURAL BEHAVIOR OF THE MONEY SUPPLY DURING THE BUSINESS CYCLE IN A SECONDARY COMMODITY-MONEY SYSTEM

We will draw on our analysis of the money supply and particularly r and k now to examine some factors which can cause natural variations in the money supply over the business cycle in a secondary commodity-money system. The top panel of Figure 10–9 traces representative business-cycle patterns for real economic activity and the level of interest rates. They move in phase, mainly because of the income effect on interest rates. The middle panel indicates the associated movements in k and in r assuming reserve requirements do not exist or are left unchanged. The r ratio moves in opposite phase to real income and the level of interest rates, for reasons given earlier, and the k ratio moves in opposite phase to real income due to associated changes in the state of confidence in the banking sector.

The bottom panel shows the pattern of the money supply that results from the counter-cyclical patterns of r and k. Since the money supply is inversely related to r and k, it will tend to move *in phase* with real income, provided the monetary base does not change sufficiently over the cycle in a way and to a degree that would offset these influences.[11]

The cyclical money supply phenomenon depicted in the bottom panel was once of considerable importance, and it played a major role in certain severe recessions in U.S. history. As described in Chapter 1, for example, there was a sharp decline in the money supply during the Great Depression. This was caused in large part

---

[10]Since its beginning, the Federal Reserve has paid its own expenses. A certain minimum level of interest-bearing assets was necessary for this during the gold-standard years. Hence the r^b ratio could not be raised as high as 100 percent.

The minimum gold reserve ratio of 40 percent applied to Federal Reserve notes, which represented the major portion of the Fed's monetary liabilities. A ratio of 35 percent was required for the Fed's deposit liabilities.

[11]The base may fall if prices rise significantly with real income. Also, if the system is linked to others through an international commodity standard, a rise in real income may induce a rise in imports, causing an outflow of the money commodity and a decline in the base. In practice these effects on the base were not as important for the money supply as those operating on the multiplier described above.

FIGURE 10–9
Business-cycle relationships

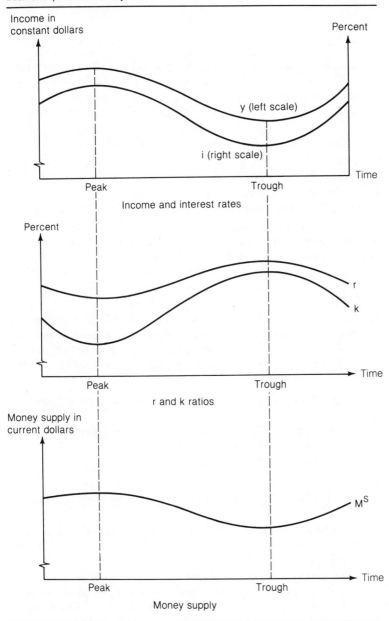

Income in
constant dollars   Percent

y (left scale)

i (right scale)

Time

Peak   Trough

Income and interest rates

Percent

r

k

Time

Peak   Trough

r and k ratios

Money supply in
current dollars

M^S

Time

Peak   Trough

Money supply

by increases in the r and k ratios. A rise in the k^b ratio was a factor
also in the bank holiday crisis of 1933 as doubt arose regarding the
government's resolve to remain on the gold standard. The decline in
the money supply in these years was unfortunate, of course, be-

cause it curbed spending further and kept downward pressure on prices.[12]

CONCLUSION

This chapter has developed an analysis of money-supply determination in two stylized monetary systems—the primary and secondary commodity-money systems. Both of these systems have existed, with various special institutional characteristics, through important periods of history for the United States and for other societies. They are important for this reason, for the reason that our present system has evolved from them, and for the reason that a system based on a commodity-money standard always represents an alternative to, and basis of comparison with, our present system.

The next chapter turns to fiat money, describes its evolution and analyzes the supply of money within our two stylized systems based on fiat money. Some comparisons are drawn among our four basic systems in the conclusion to that chapter.

PROBLEMS

1. Suppose the United States adopted the gold standard once more by imposing a fixed gold-reserve requirement on the Federal Reserve and establishing the price of gold at which the Fed will have to buy or sell gold for dollars. What would tend to happen to the quantity of money in the economy if:

   a. the Fed's price for gold is set considerably above the existing market price?
   b. significant new industrial uses are developed for gold?
   c. the public's preferences shift radically in favor of currency backed by gold and away from deposit money?

2. Explain why Gresham's law operated for different grades of cigarettes in Radford's P.O.W. camp and did not operate for Bully Marks versus cigarettes.

3. If the number of banks expands in a secondary commodity-money system, does the money supply tend to expand, contract, or stay the same? Explain.

4. Examine the various factors which influence the supply of money in the secondary commodity-money system and identify the extent and direction of influence of these same factors on the supply of bank credit, assuming banks' sole type of liabilities is bank notes and demand deposits.

---

[12]Procyclical behavior of the money supply has continued to be a problem in recent years for the U.S. economy, though the major cause of such a pattern today is different. This is a topic which will receive further attention later.

ADVANCED READINGS

Friedman, Milton, and Schwartz, Anna S. *A Monetary History of the United States.* Princeton, N.J.: Princeton University Press, 1963.

Hawtrey, R.G. *The Gold Standard in Theory and Practice.* 5th Ed. London: Longmans and Green, 1947.

Keynes, John Maynard. *A Treatise on Money.* London: Macmillan, 1930.

Walker, F.A. *International Bimetallism.* New York: Henry Holt, 1896.

Fiat-money systems and central-bank operations

Fiat money was identified in Chapter 9 as money which has significantly less intrinsic value than its face value, is accepted in transactions at face value because it has legal-tender status, and is supplied or controlled at the discretion of government authorities. This chapter describes how fiat money evolved and how it greatly enhances the powers of the government to garner revenue from money creation and to control the total money supply. Central-bank operations which lead to the creation of fiat money are analyzed in sections on the secondary fiat-money system.

THE EVOLUTION OF FIAT MONEY

Debasement of coins and seigniorage

Fiat money evolved from commodity and debt monies in a variety of circumstances. In cases prior to the commercial revolution of the 1600s, fiat money often replaced a commodity money as a result of government efforts to obtain profits from the minting of coins. Debasement of legal-tender coinage was an obvious way for governments to obtain revenue in feudal societies, and the net revenue

11

272

obtained from minting coins is still called *seigniorage*, originally a designation for the rights of the king or the feudal lord.[1] Debasement of the coinage expanded the money supply, and severe debasement drove up prices, of course.

Later, it was discovered that issues of paper fiat money were even more profitable than the debasement of coins. It appears that the first issues of paper fiat money in Western civilization were a response to financing requirements for the French and Indian Wars in the American colonies. In the later 1600s the colonial government of Massachusetts paid its troops in paper notes with a promise that the notes would be redeemed in specie at some unspecified date in the future. These paper notes were made legal tender, and they circulated without depreciating but also without being redeemed by the Massachusetts government for several years. Later, excessive issues caused a substantial depreciation in the value of these notes and eventually they were retired through redemption in specie at a small fraction of their face value.

Colonial paper money issues for government finance

The benefits of paper money issues, both as a medium of exchange and as a means of government finance, were quickly realized by other colonies, and at various times all of the colonies had paper issues. Some were debt money, redeemable on demand in specie—British silver shillings or Spanish silver dollars—but in many cases they were irredeemable fiat money. The values of these monies fluctuated in terms of each other and in terms of specie in response to relative supplies and demands.[2]

Government finance was not the only reason for colonial issues of paper money. Several colonies issued it to make up for a dearth of specie and to stimulate the economy. Specie was scarce in the colonies because of a lack of indigenous supplies of gold and silver and because Britain had imposed mercantilist restrictions on the export of specie from the British Isles. Pennsylvania and a few other mid-Atlantic colonies issued modest quantities of paper fiat money expressly to combat the depressing effect of money scarcity on colonial economic activity in the early 1700s. The strategem was amazingly successful—domestic trade rebounded in these colonies.

Colonial paper issues to overcome a dearth of specie

With the outset of the American Revolution, the financing capacities of the American governments were severely strained again. This was particularly true for the new Continental Congress which lacked taxing authority. To pay for troops and supplies, the Continental Congress issued paper continental dollars. Not surprisingly, the issues were very large relative to the demand for money, and

The revolution and continental dollars

---

[1]Sometimes the term seigniorage is applied generically to all government revenue from fiat-money creation.

[2]Rhode Island and several other New England colonies were the most prone to excessive issues of irredeemable paper money. The mid-Atlantic and Southern colonies were more restrained.

Examples of colonial paper money

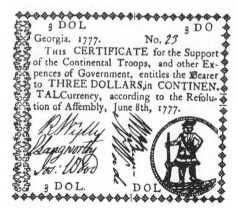

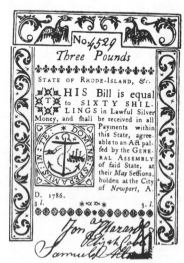

the continental dollar depreciated rapidly during the war, imposing a severe hardship on soldiers and other patriots.

This experience with continental dollars gave rise to the expression, "Not worth a continental!" More significantly, it helped to form a natural distaste for government-issued paper money in the early history of the United States. Nevertheless, the fundamental forces which led to the paper fiat-money issues in our colonial history—the need to augment government revenues, especially in time of war, and the need to control the money supply more effectively—gave rise later to other adoptions of fiat money and led, ultimately, to the establishment of our present monetary system based on a fiat-money standard. Most other countries have adopted fiat-money standards for similar reasons.

THE SUPPLY OF MONEY IN A PRIMARY FIAT-MONEY SYSTEM

First, it should be explained that fiat money may be issued in a variety of ways in a primary fiat-money system. The easiest to implement and understand is the printing of paper notes to be spent directly by the government on goods and services, as in the case of the Continental Congress and continental dollars. Alternatively, the government treasury may issue fiat money in the form of loans. In this case, the new money enters circulation as it is passed on in trade by the borrowers. Interest payments on the loans are available to the government for expenditure financing. Other arrangements are possible. In at least one case, a government has explicitly given paper money away as a sort of tax rebate or social dividend.[3]

Methods of issuing fiat money in a primary system

Whatever the mechanism by which fiat money reaches circulation in a primary fiat-money system, the supply is virtually at the discretion of the government authorities or, ultimately, society—if society is able and willing to exert its influence. Corresponding to the two motives for the adoption of a fiat money described in the previous section—revenue from money creation and monetary control—there are two general ends to which societies or governments have applied their power to create fiat money and which determine how the supply of money will tend to behave: the revenue objective and the stabilization objective.

The general objectives of government authorities

The revenue objective and the supply of money

To examine the revenue objective and its impact, return once more to our fictitious example developed in the previous chapter, the kingdom of Oros. Suppose the king of Oros, on the advice of his sorcerer, rescinds the royal decree tying the glitter to gold, and

---

[3]In 1733, the colonial government of Maryland distributed a new issue of paper money by giving 30 shillings in new notes to each resident on the tax rolls.

orders instead the printing of irredeemable paper glitter notes to help finance a new, expensive foreign war. The paper notes are declared legal tender for all debts, public and private.[4] The sorcerer has informed the king that each one-glitter note costs the royal treasury of Oros an insignificant amount to print and garners in money terms the equivalent of one glitter in resources for the government as it is spent into circulation by the treasury. The sorcerer figures that the nominal revenue from money creation in each period is equivalent to the increase in the money supply, ΔM^S.

The king is shrewd though and knows that, if he depends upon a continuous increase in the money supply for revenue as the sorcerer recommends, inflation will follow. He reminds the sorcerer of this and asks how much of an increase in the money supply and inflation will be necessary if the war is financed by money creation. To arrive at an answer the sorcerer first reasons that the king's nominal revenue requirements are likely to rise with the price level in Oros. It is best, therefore, to think in terms of the level of *real* revenue required from money creation.

The real revenue from the creation of fiat money

The real revenue from a given increase in the money supply each period depends upon the price level in Oros. If the money supply is increased by 1,000 glitters over a year, this will enable the king to purchase 800 units of real goods and services, or 800 "uoots," if the average price of these real purchases is 1.25 glitters. At a higher price level, the real revenue from 1,000 glitters will be less. The sorcerer determines, therefore, that, in general, *the real revenue from the creation of fiat money, E, is equal to the increase in the fiat-money supply divided by the price level.*

$$E = \frac{\Delta M^S}{P}$$

By performing a very simple manipulation, the sorcerer transforms the term on the right-hand side of this equation to a more convenient form:

$$E = \frac{\Delta M^S}{P} \times \frac{M^S}{M^S}$$

$$= \frac{\Delta M^S}{M^S} \times \frac{M^S}{P}$$

The two terms on the right-hand side of this last expression are, respectively, the rate of growth of the money supply, $\frac{\Delta M^S}{M^S}$, and the

----

[4]You may wonder what would happen to the gold glitters in circulation following announcement of the king's decision and distribution of the paper currency. The analysis of Gresham's law in the previous chapter should suggest a quick answer to this question.

level of real balances in the economy, $\dfrac{M^S}{P}$. In words, these terms express *the real revenue from the creation of fiat money as the rate of growth of the money supply times the level of real balances of fiat money.*

Based on this analysis, on estimates of the level of real balances in the economy, and on the king's revenue requirements, the sorcerer believes he can make a calculation as to how fast the money supply must grow and how high inflation must be to finance the war entirely from money creation. The sorcerer estimates that aggregate real balances are worth 50,000 uoots and that the king needs 5,000 uoots per year to wage war. He reasons, therefore, that the money supply would have to increase by 10 percent per year. And he finds that a 10 percent annual growth rate of the money supply will, other things being the same, cause 10 percent inflation. Inflation will be 10 percent, the sorcerer reasons, because prices will have to rise at that rate in order for the demand for nominal money balances to rise enough to remain in equilibrium with increases in the money supply. (See Chapter 3.)[5]

The sorcerer's first solution

Proud of his ingenious work, the sorcerer reports these results to the king. The king is impressed but not fully satisfied. He notes that the sorcerer's solution assumes real balances remain at their original level of 50,000 uoots. The king asks the sorcerer whether this is likely following a sustained rise in inflation from zero to 10 percent. "Won't the level of real balances in Oros tend to decline to a lower level because 10 percent inflation will become an expected cost of holding money?"

To see the king's point consider your own money balance. The higher the rate of inflation, the greater is the rate of loss in the purchasing power of your money. To put it differently, think of inflation as a tax on your money balances—an analogy which has been used by John Maynard Keynes and Milton Friedman, alike.[6] The greater the expected level of this tax, the greater the incentives for money-balance holders to cut down on their real balances.[7]

Inflation as a tax on real balances

---

[5]Our analysis excludes the continuous effect of rising real income on the demand for money in a growing economy. If this were allowed for, inflation would be slightly less than the rate of growth of the money supply. See Chapter 15.

[6]See John Maynard Keynes, *Tract on Monetary Reform* (New York: Harcourt Brace, 1924); and Milton Friedman, "Discussion of Inflationary Gap," in Milton Friedman, *Essays in Positive Economics* (Chicago: University of Chicago Press, 1953).

[7]The influence of expected inflation on the demand for money was accounted for indirectly in Chapter 3. Recall that our demand-for-money function in Chapter 3 included an inverse relationship between the demand for nominal balances and the nominal rate of interest—the cost of holding money. Also recall that the nominal rate of interest was expressed in terms of expected inflation and expected real interest rate components in Chapter 5. (See the analysis of the Fisher effect.) As expected inflation rises, the nominal rate of interest rises, reducing the demand for nominal balances relative to the price level. The analysis in this chapter focuses directly on the expected-inflation element in the cost of holding real balances and implicitly assumes a constant expected real rate of interest element. See the sorcerer's analysis in the paragraphs below.

The demand for
real balances

The king is correct that this reaction of the public to expected inflation should be included in the sorcerer's calculations. On reflection, the sorcerer decides that a direct supply and demand analysis of real balances would be the best approach to arriving at a more accurate conclusion regarding the inflationary consequences of the king's war and the monetary creation necessary to finance it. He starts with the demand-for-money function we developed in Chapter 3:

$$M^D = f\left(\frac{1}{P}, \ y, \ i, \ \ldots\right) \tag{1}$$

To convert this to a demand for real balances relationship, he multiplies through by the inverse of the price level to get[8]

$$\frac{M^D}{P} = f(y, \ i, \ \ldots) \tag{2}$$

Next the sorcerer makes use of the Fisher-effect equation presented in Chapter 5:

$$i = z^* + r^* \tag{3}$$

which expresses the nominal interest rate in terms of the expected rate of inflation, z^*, and the expected real rate of interest, r^*. Substituting this equation into Equation (2), the sorcerer obtains a relationship which expresses what the king suspected intuitively:

$$\frac{M^D}{P} = f(y, \ z^* + r^*, \ \ldots) \tag{4}$$

The demand for real balances is inversely related to the expected rate of inflation.

This relationship is shown as the $D^{M/P}$ curve in Figure 11–1. It is drawn so as to be inelastic in the region below 31.25 percent for the expected rate of inflation.[9]

If the expected rate of inflation equals the actual rate of inflation, we can interpret the vertical axis on the graph as the actual rate of inflation or, also useful to our purposes, the rate of monetary expansion.[10]

---

[8]Dividing through by P eliminates this variable from the right-hand side of the equation because of the inverse proportionality of the relationship between M^D and $1/P$.

[9]It turns out that, in the region where the demand for real balances curve is inelastic, the government garners more revenue in equilibrium by *raising* the rate of monetary expansion. In the region above 31.25 percent for the expected rate of inflation, where the demand curve is elastic, the government increases its equilibrium revenue take by *lowering* the rate of monetary expansion.

An assumption that the demand curve is inelastic in a range extending at least from zero to 31.25 percent is consistent with the results of most empirical studies, some of which are reviewed in Chapter 15.

[10]See footnote 5 in this chapter.

FIGURE 11-1
Demand for real balances

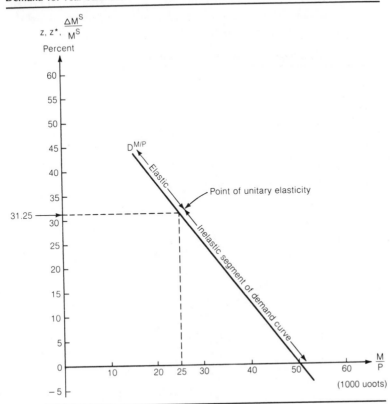

Now, to find a supply of real balances relationship, the sorcerer returns to his earlier analysis of the real revenue from money creation. First, he assumes that the king's revenue requirements remain fixed, and writes the real revenue equation as last shown

$$E_1 = \frac{\Delta M^S}{M^S} \times \frac{M^S}{P} \tag{5}$$

where E_1 is the fixed level of real revenue. Next, he solves for $\frac{M^S}{P}$

$$\frac{M^S}{P} = \frac{E_1}{\Delta M^S/M^S} \tag{6}$$

This says that *the supply of real balances will be inversely proportional to the rate of growth of the money supply when the government varies the rate of growth of the money supply so as to keep the real revenue from money creation constant.*[11] This relationship is depicted by the $S^{M/P}$ curve in Figure 11–2. Note that it is a rectangular hyperbola, the same type of relationship as our standard de-

FIGURE 11–2
Supply of real balances with constant real revenue

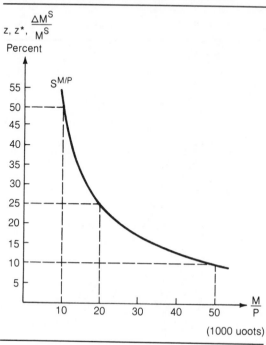

(1000 uoots)

mand-for-nominal-money/value-of-money curve developed in Chapter 3. (They both are inverse, proportional relationships.)

Another important thing to note about the $S^{M/P}$ relationship in Figure 11–2 is that its distance from the origin is determined by the size of E. The higher the revenue requirements of the king, the further northeast the $S^{M/P}$ curve will be from the origin. This is evident once it is realized that the real revenue from money creation is represented by the area of any rectangle subtended by the $S^{M/P}$ curve. (This must be since $E = \dfrac{\Delta M^S}{M^S} \times \dfrac{M^S}{P}$.)

To complete his analysis, the sorcerer assumes that the quantities of real balances supplied and demanded are equal in equilibrium and overlays the supply and demand curves for real balances, as in Figure 11–3, to observe where this solution occurs.

---

[11] Some care must be exercised in the interpretation of expression (6). In a sense, the government does not really determine the supply of real or nominal balances in this analysis. It only determines the revenue requirement E. The interaction of this objective with the public's reactions will determine $\dfrac{M^S}{P}$ and $\dfrac{\Delta M^S}{M}$ in equilibrium.

FIGURE 11–3
Supply and demand for real balances

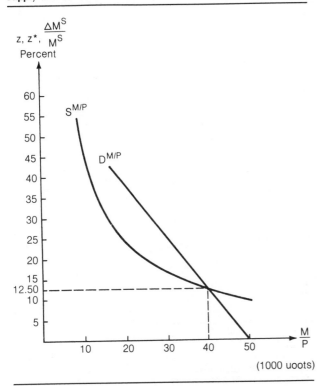

In our illustration, the equilibrium rate of monetary expansion and the equilibrium rate of inflation are 12.5 percent per year, and the equilibrium level of real balances is 40,000 uoots. A tax rate of 12.5 percent on 40,000 uoots of real balances will yield 5,000 uoots per year in tax revenues. The same yield is not obtainable in equilibrium with a tax rate of 10 percent on 50,000 uoots of real balances due to the effect of the expected rate of inflation on the demand for real balances.

Suppose now that the king's war turns out to be 7,500 uoots, more expensive than the sorcerer assumed. A higher level for E shifts the $S^{M/P}$ curve to the northeast as shown in Figure 11–4. As a result the equilibrium rates of monetary expansion, inflation, and expected inflation are higher at 25 percent, and the level of real balances is lower at 30,000 uoots.

The effect of a higher revenue requirement

To consider another effect on our solution, it should be evident that the lower the slope, d, of the demand-for-real-balances relationship, the higher the money growth and inflation rates necessary to reach the king's original revenue objective.[12] This is shown in Fig-

The effect of a lower slope to the demand curve

---

[12]Such a result holds as long as the demand curve remains inelastic in the relevant range—a condition implicitly assumed in the paragraph above, as well.

FIGURE 11–4
Effect of higher real revenue

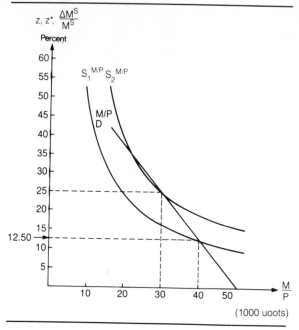

(1000 uoots)

FIGURE 11–5
Effect of lower slope of the demand curve

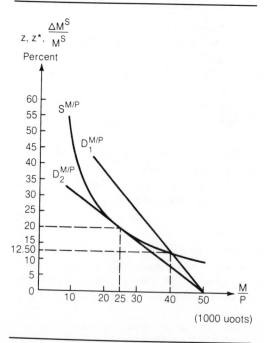

(1000 uoots)

ure 11–5 by the $D_2^{M/P}$ demand curve. As shown, the equilibrium
rates of inflation and monetary expansion are 20 percent, versus
12.5 percent with the $D_1^{M/P}$ curve.

The two preceding exercises illustrate two of the fundamental
determinants of the equilibrium rate of growth of the money supply
in a primary fiat-money system when the government is pursuing
monetary expansion to finance a given amount of real expenditure.
These determinants are (1) the level of the real-revenue requirement, and (2) the value of the slope of the demand-for-real-balances
curve. Other determinants not brought out in the foregoing examples include any factors in addition to d which are relevant to the
demand for real balances, factors such as the level of real income.

We may summarize our determinants now as follows:

$$\frac{\Delta M^S}{M^S} = f(E, \ d, \ y, \ \ldots)$$

Influenced variable	Influencing variable	Direction of influence
$\frac{\Delta M^S}{M^S}$: the rate of growth of the fiat money supply when the government has a revenue objective	E: the real level of government expenditure financed by the creation of fiat money	Positive
	d: the slope of the demand for real balances curve	Negative; the higher this slope the lower the sensitivity of the demand for real balances to expected inflation; hence $\frac{\Delta M^S}{M^S}$ is lower for a given E
	y: the level of real income	Negative; as real income grows it raises the demand for real balances, hence $\frac{\Delta M^S}{M^S}$ is lower for a given E

From the real-world perspective of government authorities and
the political process, the resort to an inflation tax on real balances
may be viewed as having two advantages. First, it is a hidden tax
which, once fiat money has been adopted, usually can be imposed
without any authorizing legislation. Second, the inflation tax is collected automatically—no reporting, processing, or policing of taxes
due is necessary. Of course, governments seldom identify these
advantages of inflationary finance explicitly. Usually the creation of
fiat money is chosen as a source of finance by default because other
forms of finance—normal taxation or borrowing—are unattractive

The benefits and costs of inflationary finance

politcally or not feasible for practical reasons; in other words, they do not possess the attributes identified above for inflationary finance. Less developed countries and nations at war in particular have relied on inflationary finance as an expedient.

The costs of inflationary finance to government authorities are usually delayed and often minor. They involve the politcal costs of inflation to the extent that the public identifies government authorities as responsible for inflation.

From the perspective of society's general welfare, however, the costs of inflationary finance can be substantial. The efficiency of this tax as a means of raising revenue for the government must be compared to the efficiency of alternative sources of revenue after allowing for the hidden costs of inflationary finance to society. The hidden costs include the disruptive effects of inflation on plans and markets when inflation is unanticipated. There is also an arbitrary redistribution of wealth as a result of unanticipated inflation because most contracts for goods and services are set in nominal terms and do not provide for ex-post inflation adjustments. Finally, even if inflation is anticipated or allowed for ex post in contracts, there is a cost to society in terms of the inconvenience and inefficiency associated with a lower level of real cash balances in the economy, a cost identical to that associated with lower utilization of any good or service subject to tax.[13]

The stabilization objective and the supply of money

The other general end to which the government may devote its power to create money in a primary fiat-money system is the stabilization of the supply of money and/or the business cycle. Usually the government would like to accomplish stabilization of the money supply, of income, and of the price level.

As the colony of Pennsylvania discovered in the early 1700s, fiat money can make up for a dearth of commodity money and add at least a temporary stimulus to real income. If policy is directed only toward stabilizing the money supply, it is *defensive*. If it is directed further toward varying the money supply so as to moderate other

Defensive and activist policies

[13]Because there is a loss to society of some of the potential services of money when there is a reduced level of real balances, and because the true cost of real balances of fiat money to society is virtually zero—in the sense that no real resources are diverted by them from other uses—some economists have argued that governments actually should pursue a steady rate of *falling* prices. This could be done by continually reducing the money supply in a stationary economy or by holding the money supply constant in a growing economy. The object in either case would be to reduce the nominal interest rate and induce larger holdings of real balances.

If there were a steady rate of deflation in the economy equal to the expected real rate of interest, the nominal interest rate would tend to fall to zero, making the opportunity cost of real balances zero. Real balances would increase to the "optimum" level, as a result. This outcome would be 54,000 uoots in real balances for a real interest rate of 5 percent and inflation of −5 percent in Figure 11–1. See Milton Friedman, "The Optimum Quantity of Money," in Milton Friedman, *The Optimum Quantity of Money and Other Essays* (Chicago: Aldine, 1969).

influences accounting for fluctuations in real income and prices, it is offensive, or *activist*. Ideally for an activist monetary policy over the business cycle, the supply of money should grow more rapidly to add stimulus when economic conditions are depressed, and it should grow less rapidly to restrain the economy when real activity is "overheating" and prices rising. The activist approach has become known as "leaning against the wind." If followed successfully, an activist policy would lead to the following money-supply relationship:

$$M^S = f(P, y, \ldots)$$

Influenced variable	Influencing variables	Direction of influence
M^S: the money supply in a primary flat-money system with a successful activist policy	P: the price level	Negative
	y: real income	Negative for income fluctuations relative to the long-run trend

In practice, because of information problems and lags in the effects of money on real income, it is very difficult to engage in activist monetary policy successfully—that is, to key the timing of monetary expansion and restraint appropriately to the business cycle. Furthermore, because of the more delayed impact of money-supply changes on inflation, it appears to be an especially difficult, if not impossible, task to pursue income and price-level stabilization simultaneously over sustained periods of time. Since the 1960s in particular, high inflation has persisted well into recessions due to supply shocks and resilient expectations of inflation. As later chapters will bring out more clearly, stimulating income with monetary expansion under such conditions may not be a constructive policy.

The topic of price- and income-stabilization policy will receive more attention later in this chapter and in subsequent chapters. Our discussion in this section will end now because its main purpose has been to point out the greater latitude fiat money provides for government action in this area. In commodity-money systems, the money supply is less subject to government control. Gold discoveries, you will recall, were inflationary in Oros under a gold standard. Growth in the economy, on the other hand, led to deflation. Recall also that money-supply behavior was procyclical in the secondary commodity-money system. One might imagine the sorcerer recommending to the king of Oros that, with the adoption of a fiat-money system, Oros could avoid such disturbances to the economy.

The important considerations in a society's or a king's choice among systems will be summarized in the last section of this chapter. We have one last system to cover, however, before moving on to a general discussion of the advantages and disadvantages of the different systems.

THE SECONDARY FIAT-MONEY SYSTEM AND CENTRAL BANKING

A fiat money system is not often as simple in operation or development as we have depicted it so far, of course. Most monetary systems in the developed world today are secondary fiat-money systems. This type of system replaced the secondary commodity-money system as the dominant type after World War I and the Great Depression. Usually the shift from a commodity-based system to a secondary fiat-money system involves not only the substitution of a fiat-money standard for a commodity-money standard, but also some institutional change such as the establishment of a central bank or the vesting of a new power to create fiat money in an existing central bank.

The central bank and forms of fiat money

Typically, fiat money supplied by a central bank is in either or both of two forms: (1) paper currency held by the public and banks, and (2) deposits at the central bank held by banks as reserves. The central bank issues these forms of fiat money in exchange for securities or as direct loans. No reserves need be held by the central bank to back its liabilities since these are fiat money and, as such, not redeemable for any other assets of value.

The balance-sheet effects

Suppose a fiat-money standard and a central bank are established in Oros to replace the secondary commodity-money system described in the previous chapter. The decree goes out that henceforth paper glitter notes issued by the central bank are legal tender for all transactions. Also, all banks must maintain reserves of either paper glitter notes issued by the central bank or of demand deposits with the central bank. These assets are obtainable at the central bank in exchange for government debt. Simultaneously, paper notes issued by banks are banned by the king to achieve a uniform currency and a wider circulation for the new notes. Finally, the sorcerer, as the country's most eminent and accomplished financial wizard, is made chairman of the Central Bank of Oros.

After a brief transition period, balance sheets for the central bank, the banking system, and the general public appear as follows:

The Central Bank of Oros (thousand glitters)				Consolidated Account of Oros Banks (thousand glitters)				The Oros Nonbank Public (thousand glitters)			
Assets		**Liabilities**		**Assets**		**Liabilities**		**Assets**		**Liabilities**	
Oros government securities	35	Central bank paper notes	35	Central bank paper notes	5	Demand deposits	40	Central bank paper notes	30	Loans from banks	25
Loans of reserve deposits to banks	5	Demand deposits of banks	5	Demand deposits with central bank	5	Borrowings from central bank	5	Demand deposits with banks	40	Total liabilities	25
Total assets	40	Total fiat money	40	Total reserves	10	Total liabilities	45	Oros government securities	10		
				Loans	25			Total assets	80		
				Oros government securities	10						
				Total assets	45						

The Central Bank of Oros has purchased 35,000 glitters worth of Oros government securities and made 5,000 glitters worth of loans to Oros banks, creating 40,000 glitters of bank reserves and currency in circulation in the process. The balance sheets for the Oros banks and the nonbank public above may be compared to the balance sheets for the Midas Bank and the public in Chapter 10. The important differences are: (1) the replacement of central-bank liabilities for specie as the reserve assets of the banking system, and (2) the replacement of central bank notes for specie as base money in the balance sheet for the nonbank public.

The organization of the supply of fiat money through a central bank obscures but, usually, does not change the essential nature of fiat money as a revenue source for the government. The profits from a central bank's money-issuing operations are equal to the interest on its loans and investments less its expenses. Invariably these profits are turned over to the government treasury.

Revenue from money creation in a secondary money system

Usually a central bank's assets will be dominated by holdings of government debt as shown above.[14] To the extent that the central bank does hold government debt, the government is effectively borrowing at a reduced or zero rate of interest because, after deducting expenses, interest paid to the central bank by the treasury is simply recycled to the treasury in the form of central-bank profits.[15] Therefore, from a revenue perspective, the treasury and central bank should be viewed as one unit. If the balance sheet for the Oros treasury, not shown above, is combined with the accounts of the central bank, the net position of the Oros government vis-a-vis the bank and nonbank public is revealed.

Royal Treasury of Oros (thousand glitters)		The Central Bank of Oros (thousand glitters)		Consolidated Government Account (thousand glitters)	
Assets	**Liabilities**	**Assets**	**Liabilities**	**Assets**	**Liabilities**
	Oros government securities 60	Oros government securities 35	Fiat money 40	Loans of reserve deposits to banks 5	Oros government securities 25
		Loans of reserve deposits to banks 5			Fiat money 40

As shown, the introduction of fiat money and a central bank has permitted the government of Oros effectively to replace a substantial portion of its outstanding debt with fiat money, usually noninterest-bearing liabilities.[16]

---

[14]Even if the central bank buys private debt, the government benefits in a manner similar to that described in the text. See if you can discern how.

[15]Central-bank expenses could, but normally do not, include interest payments on reserve deposits. Such interest payments could significantly reduce the profits of the central bank.

[16]As mentioned briefly in Chapter 4, by convention, the fiat monetary issues of governments and central banks are carried on their balance sheets as liabilities even though they normally cannot be exercised as effective claims on government or central-bank resources.

Debt
monetization

Such acquisitions of interest-bearing assets by a central bank are called *debt monetization*—the modern process by which governments garner spendable funds without legislating new taxes or borrowing from the public. As existing debt is monetized, interest payments to the public are reduced. New debt bought by the central bank can provide almost an equivalent amount of funds to the treasury interest-free.

Of course, as government debt is monetized, the money supply tends to increase. The mechanism determining the total money supply on a given monetary base is the same as the mechanism described for monetary expansion and the money-stock multiplier in the secondary commodity-money system in Chapter 10. The essential difference between the two secondary monetary systems is the composition of the monetary base. In the system under analysis here, the base consists of government fiat money, i.e., irredeemable currency and bank deposits with the central bank.

Control of the
monetary base

In a secondary fiat-money system the central bank usually has the ability to exercise substantial control of the monetary base.[17] *Control of the monetary base is effected through (1) changes in the central bank's lending rate on loans of reserves to banks, and (2) by central-bank purchases or sales of government securities or other assets.*

Consider the central bank's lending rate first. If the central bank lowers its lending rate significantly below market interest rates, banks will tend to increase their borrowings of reserves in order to make loans at higher interest. This adds to the total supply of reserves, the monetary base and, ultimately, the supply of money.

Suppose, for example, that the Central Bank of Oros lowers its lending rate by 50 basis points such that it is 100 basis points below the prime bank rate. This, say, encourages 10,000 glitters in new borrowings by Oros commercial banks from the central bank, permitting the banks to expand loans. Based on a reserve ratio of .25 at banks and ignoring interactions with the k ratio, the following balance-sheet changes can be shown:

The Central Bank of Oros (thousand glitters)		The Consolidated Account of Oros Banks (thousand glitters)		The Oros Nonbank Public (thousand glitters)	
Changes in Assets	Changes in Liabilities	Changes in Assets	Changes in Liabilities	Changes in Assets	Changes in Liabilities
Loans of reserve deposits to banks +10	Demand deposits of banks +10	Demand deposits with central bank +10	Demand deposits +40	Demand deposits +40	Loans from banks +40
		Loans +40	Borrowings from central bank +10		

[17]The ability of the central bank to exercise discretionary control of the monetary base might be constrained, however, by legal or other institutional limits on its behavior. Binding rules have been advocated for central-bank behavior, for example. Several of these are described in later chapters.

As a result of the creation of 10,000 glitters in new bank reserves via a loan of central bank funds, bank loans and deposits expand by 40,000 glitters.

Next, consider a purchase of 10,000 glitters in government securities by the central bank from commercial banks. This equally means an increase in the monetary base and results in a fourfold expansion of bank loans and deposit balances, shown as follows:

The Central Bank of Oros (thousand glitters)		Consolidated Account of Oros Banks (thousand glitters)		The Oros Nonbank Public (thousand glitters)	
Changes in Assets	Changes in Liabilities	Changes in Assets	Changes in Liabilities	Changes in Assets	Changes in Liabilities
Oros government securities +10	Demand deposits of banks +10	Demand deposits with central bank +10 Loans +40 Oros government securities −10	Demand deposits +40	Demand deposits +40	Loans from banks +40

The foregoing changes demonstrate the central bank's influence on the monetary base in a secondary fiat-money system. There is one additional influence on the monetary base in this system which bears analysis here. *The level of market interest rates will tend to affect the monetary base as market rates rise and fall relative to the central bank's lending rate.* A rise in market interest rates relative to the central bank's lending rate makes it more attractive for banks to borrow reserves from the central bank and use these funds to make loans at higher interest. As long as the central bank does not follow a rise in market interest rates with an increase in its lending rate, higher borrowings of reserves, a higher monetary base, and a higher money stock will tend to result.

The effect of changes in market interest rates

This completes our analysis of new factors introduced by the secondary fiat-money system. No new analysis of the behavior of the public and banks as reflected in the k and r ratios is necessary. Our analysis of the money-stock multiplier for the secondary commodity-money system in Chapter 10 applies here as well. Consequently, the determinants of the money supply in a secondary fiat-money system may be summarized as follows:

$$B = f (A, i, \ldots)$$
$$m = f (i, y, A, \ldots)$$

therefore

$$M^S = f (A, i, y, \ldots)$$

Influenced variable	Influencing variable	Direction of influence
M^S: the total stock of money in a secondary fiat-money system	A: central-bank monetary actions	Positive or negative on the monetary base and the multiplier and, hence, on the money stock, according to the overall thrust of central-bank actions—expansionary or restrictive—that is, the net effect of the central bank's specific tools (changes in the central-bank lending rate, purchases or sales of assets, and changes in reserve requirements)
	i: the rate of interest	Positive on the monetary base and on the multiplier and, hence, positive on the money stock
	y: real income	Positive on the multiplier and, hence, on the money stock

THE GENERAL OBJECTIVES OF GOVERNMENT AUTHORITIES IN SECONDARY FIAT-MONEY SYSTEMS

What have been the general objectives of government authorities in secondary fiat-money systems? They can be identified as being the same as they were under the primary fiat-money system: (1) revenue and (2) stabilization. There is little to add with regard to revenue. The revenue potential from money creation is considerably

Revenue

less than it is in a primary fiat-money system because the base for the inflation tax in a secondary fiat-money system is the real level of the monetary base—not the total money stock. It should also be observed that, outside of war periods, monetary policy in the present U.S. system has been tuned far more to stabilization objectives than to providing a source of government finance.

Under the objective of stabilization above we include money supply, income, and price stabilization, as before, and also financial and exchange-rate stabilization. Prior comments on income and price stabilization in the section on the primary fiat-money system apply here. Further comments are integrated with a discussion of financial stabilization.

Financial stabilization

Financial stabilization refers to actions by the central bank to prevent extreme fluctuations in credit- and equity-market conditions and, especially, to insure against collapse of the financial sector. A central bank with the powers described in this section is well equipped to perform this function. In the event of a loss of confidence in banks, open-market purchases of securities by the central

[18]There may, however, be legal limits or technical constraints such as a dearth of "qualified" securities or other assets which the central bank can buy or accept as security for loans.

bank can infuse reserves into the banking system. Loans to banks in difficulty also may be helpful. Since the central bank's notes are legal tender and involve no promise of redemption in other assets of value, the central bank usually has the ability to expand the monetary base virtually without limit if necessary and if central bank officials are willing.[18] If banks have plentiful reserves and lending capability, confidence in the financial sector should follow.

In an effort to stabilize financial markets and the economy, central banks operating within a secondary fiat-money system have often elected to focus their actions on market interest rates. For example, open-market operations may be geared such that a tendency for market interest rates to rise is met with aggressive purchases of government securities, thereby expanding bank reserves and the supply of money and credit. As a result, the rise in market interest rates is prevented or at least attenuated. Conversely, under this approach, a tendency for market interest rates to fall is met with sales of government securities, contracting the supply of money and credit. The result of such a focus for monetary actions is shown in Figure 11–6.

The dangerous practice of interest-rate stabilization

FIGURE 11–6
Effect of interest-rate pegging

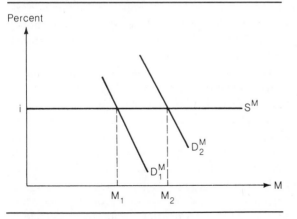

The money supply curve becomes perfectly elastic at the rate of interest pegged by the central bank. Any increase or decrease in the demand for money at that interest rate is accommodated by the central bank.

As indicated, the central bank's intention is to stabilize financial markets and the economy, but experience has shown that a policy of pegging the interest rate is likely to have the opposite effect. Note that a shift to the right of the demand-for-money curve from D_1^M to D_2^M in Figure 11–6 elicits an increase in the quantity of money supplied from M_1 to M_2. If such an increase in the demand for money is attributable to inflationary pressures in the economy, the central bank is accommodating inflation. The same positive association occurs between the supply of money and fluctuations in real income.

In other words, *central-bank reserve actions geared to pegging the interest rate tend to create procyclical movements in the money supply, often exacerbating the business cycle, price movements, and, ultimately, interest-rate adjustments, as well, if money-supply changes become cumulative.* The central bank effectively surrenders its control of the money supply when it pegs interest rates.

In less extreme cases than the one just described, the central bank may merely attempt to attenuate interest-rate movements. Though less severe than in the case of rigid interest-rate pegging, procyclical movements in the money supply still tend to occur under such a policy.

As a result of bad experiences with policies focused on interest rates, in recent years, central banks have shifted their attention increasingly to achieving specified targets for the rate of growth of the money supply. Interest rates still receive attention, but they are permitted to adjust more flexibly, and, in fact, sharp changes are often sought to gain better control of the money supply. An explanation of the exact control techniques effective in the United States in recent years, including the role of interest-rate adjustments and the problems involved therein, must await the development of more institutional background on the Federal Reserve in Chapters 13 and 14. Suffice it to say that as recently as October 1979, the Federal Reserve embarked on a new approach to controlling the money supply—one which was intended to place less reliance on interest rates as a guide to Federal Reserve actions.

Exchange-rate
stabilization

Exchange-rate stabilization can be pursued by a central bank in two ways.[19] First, the central bank can respond to downward pressure on the exchange rate with tight monetary policy. This raises interest rates, thereby attracting capital inflows, and restrains real income and inflation, thereby curbing the demand for imports and boosting exports. Upward pressure on the exchange rate can be fought with an expansionary monetary policy.

A second method of exchange-rate stabilization involves direct intervention in the foreign-exchange market by the central bank. This means selling some of its own holdings of foreign exchange or gold (an internationally accepted asset), if it has such holdings, when there is downward pressure on the exchange rate and buying for-

---

[19]Students may wish to review Chapter 8 in connection with the following discussion of exchange-rate stabilization.

[20]Many central banks today have significant foreign exchange and/or gold holdings and substantial authority to buy and sell these assets for their own account. The Federal Reserve has limited capabilities in this area. As will be described in more detail in Chapter 13, most foreign-exchange and gold holdings of the U.S. government are carried on accounts of the Exchange Stabilization Fund and other divisions of the U.S. Treasury, and significant intervention by the Fed must be coordinated with the U.S. Treasury. The Federal Reserve can borrow foreign exchange from another central bank to sell, but such borrowings also normally entail coordination with the Treasury.

[21]To see this, retitle the "Oros government securities" entries in the balance sheets given earlier "foreign-exchange holdings." The analysis is the same.

eign exchange or gold for its own account, if it has the authority to do so, when the exchange rate is under upward pressure.[20]

When purchases and sales of foreign exchange are made for a central bank's own account they have the same monetary effects as purchases and sales of government securities.[21] They are virtually open-market operations—though not quite the sort we are accustomed to discussing. Consequently, other things being the same, sales of foreign exchange by the central bank for its own account tend to support an exchange rate under downward pressure in two ways: (1) the intervention itself provides a temporary offset to the excess supply of a currency on the foreign-exchange market, and (2) the intervention automatically reduces the monetary base and imposes a tight monetary policy which will tend to remove the downward pressure on the exchange rate permanently. The reverse effects apply, of course, in the case of foreign-exchange purchases.

"Other things being the same" in the paragraph above includes an assumption that the foreign-exchange sales or purchases by the central bank are not offset by other central-bank actions having an opposite effect on the monetary base. If offsetting actions are taken— say a purchase of government securities—so as to leave the base unchanged, the monetary effects of the foreign-exchange operation are said to be *sterilized*.[22] A special case of sterilization occurs when foreign-exchange operations are conducted for a government account other than the central bank's; here, the foreign-exchange operations are automatically sterilized since no central-bank assets or liabilities are permanently involved.[23]

Sterilization in a fiat money system

CONCLUSION: ADVANTAGES AND DISADVANTAGES OF FOUR SYSTEMS

This completes our discussion of the four basic monetary systems. Each system has its own particular supply characteristics and, from the points of view of government authorities and society, which may be distinguished, potential advantages and disadvantages.

From society's point of view, the primary commodity-money system usually involves less efficient physical forms of money in circulation, though this need not be the case since paper or deposit forms can take the place of the money commodity in circulation if backed 100 percent by reserves of the money commodity. The primary commodity-money system, on the other hand, *may* be more conducive to greater stability in the price level and real income than the other systems are. Much depends upon the kind of variations in the supply of and in the nonmonetary demand for the monetary com-

The primary commodity-money system

---

[22]This is effectively the same phenomenon as the sterilization of gold flows described in Chapter 10.

[23]This type of automatic sterilization applies to U.S. foreign-exchange intervention via the U.S. Treasury's Exchange Stabilization Fund. See footnote 20.

modity. Periodic gluts and dearths in supply were a problem with cigarettes in Radford's P.O.W. camp, as described in the preceding chapter. Much depends also on the nature of the other systems, including, where relevant, how well they are managed by government authorities.

The secondary commodity-money system

Our analysis of the secondary commodity-money system included a discussion of the procyclical behavior of the money supply due to cyclical changes in the r and k ratios. This money-supply pattern developed when there were no offsetting actions by monetary authorities such as a change in reserve requirements for commercial banks or in a central bank's gold reserve ratio. Often government actions to offset such fluctuations were nonexistent or inadequate during the United States experience with this system. This was due in some respects to the government having inadequate powers to take action; there was no power to vary reserve requirements before the 1930s, for example. On the positive side, a secondary commodity-money system as a secondary system provides a stimulus to the development of a financial sector and constitutes, in itself, a valuable mechanism for augmenting and allocating savings.

The primary fiat-money system

As suggested by the analysis in this chapter, from the point of view of government authorities, the primary fiat-money system is attractive in two ways. First, this system provides the greatest potential for government revenue from money creation. Second, it provides the government with maximum control of the money supply for stabilization purposes. From society's point of view, there are hidden costs to inflationary finance in either of the two fiat-money systems, costs which can be severe and which probably make this practice, on balance, detrimental to economic growth. Stabilization of the money supply and of the economy are beneficial to society, though the question remains as to how well the latter can be accomplished in the face of information and lag problems.

The secondary fiat-money system

The secondary fiat-money system carries the same advantage as the secondary commodity-money system in terms of the encouragement it provides to the development of the financial sector. It provides the further advantage of the potential for better stabilization, though it is clear that much remains to be accomplished before the secondary fiat-money system can lay claim to being able to realize this potential. As suggested by earlier discussion, experience with secondary fiat-money systems has been mixed. For an extended period in the 1950s and early 1960s, after the United States had abandoned the gold standard in the Great Depression and after World War II, fluctuations in U.S. real economic activity were less severe than earlier and inflation was 1 to 3 percent per year—quite low and reasonable, especially by recent standards. Since the late 1960s, however, fluctuations in real output have become more severe and high inflation has become a persistent problem. Some of this deterioration in the later period was attributable, no doubt, to

Federal Reserve actions being keyed too closely to stabilizing market interest rates.

The performance of each of the four basic monetary systems in different periods of U.S. history will be described in more detail in Chapter 12. The evidence summarized there suggests that significant progress has been made in the evolution of the monetary system and the development of related institutions, but much still remains to be accomplished.

PROBLEMS

1. Define the revenue from money creation and how it would be measured in a primary fiat-money system.
2. What are the advantages to the government of taxation by inflation?
3. What are the usual stabilization goals of a central bank and how are these goals easier or harder to achieve with a fiat-money standard versus a commodity-money standard?
4. Explain how, for a country with a secondary fiat-money system, intervention in the foreign exchange market by the central bank can influence the money supply of that country. How can such an influence be thwarted?

ADVANCED READINGS

Bailey, Martin J. "The Welfare Cost of Inflationary Finance." *Journal of Political Economy*, April 1956, pp. 93–110.

Cagan, Phillip. "The Monetary Dynamics of Hyperinflation." In *Studies in the Quantity Theory of Money*, edited by M. Friedman. Chicago: University of Chicago Press, 1956.

Carlile, W. W. *The Evolution of Modern Money.* London: Macmillan, 1901.

Cathcart, Charles D. "Monetary Dynamics, Growth, and the Efficiency of Inflationary Finance." *Journal of Money, Credit and Banking* 6 (May 1974): 169–90.

Friedman, Milton. "The Optimum Quantity of Money." In M. Friedman *The Optimum Quantity of Money and Other Essays.* Chicago: Aldine, 1969.

_____. "Government Revenue from Inflation." *Journal of Politcal Economy* 79 (July/August 1971): 846–56.

Galbraith, J. K. *Money: Whence It Came, Where It Went.* Boston: Houghton Mifflin Co., 1975.

Keynes, John M. *Tract on Monetary Reform.* New York: Harcourt Brace, 1924. Chapters I and II.

Willms, M. "Controlling Money in an Open Economy: The German Case." Federal Reserve Bank of St. Louis *Monthly Review*, (April 1971): 10-27.

The development of U.S. monetary institutions and policies

Study of U.S. monetary history is useful because our present financial institutions and approach to monetary policy have been shaped by our past experience and by efforts to correct deficiencies perceived in earlier periods. Despite major reforms in several important periods, there are still serious needs for change. Indeed, some current reforms in progress involve undoing earlier reforms. To understand our present system better and to evaluate current reform proposals effectively, it is necessary to know how our monetary systems have performed in the past and why earlier reforms were instituted.

The first section of this chapter describes U.S. monetary history prior to the Civil War and the National Bank Acts of 1863 and 1864. The second section reviews important developments during the 50-year period, 1863–1913, when the National Bank Acts shaped the money-supply mechanism. Experience since the creation of the Federal Reserve in 1913, including sweeping reforms of the banking system and the demise of the gold standard in the 1930s, is detailed in the final section.

12

296

U.S. MONETARY HISTORY PRIOR TO THE CIVIL WAR

In the first 50 years or so of U.S. Colonial history, there were virtually no native monetary or financial institutions of note. Barter was common. But the development of even rudimentary commerce created the need for a medium of exchange and unit of account. An English unit of account, the shilling, was the first to be widely used. It would have been natural for English coinage to be adopted also. However, as mentioned in Chapter 11, English coinage was difficult to obtain because of mercantilist restrictions on the export of coins from the mother country.

The Colonial period

One effect of England's policy was to force colonists to rely on wampum, the Indian medium of exchange, and on widely traded goods in the colonies—tobacco, beaver pelts, and liquor. Gresham's law operated whenever these commodities were accepted in payment at the same price regardless of differences in intrinisic values; those of the poorest quality circulated, and the higher quality medium-of-exchange goods were consumed or exported.

Another effect of England's policy was to induce the colony of Massachusetts to establish its own mint and coinage in 1652. The mint operated for 34 years before English objections to it as a usurpation of the sovereign government's rights forced it to close.

Some of the void left by the absence of English coins was filled by other European coins, particularly Spanish silver dollars, known as pieces of eight.[1] These coins were obtained mainly through trade with the West Indies and as privateer booty. Heavy reliance on Spanish coins later led to the adoption of the dollar as the name for the U.S. unit of account.

Under these circumstances of generally inadequate and inefficient means of payment and, additionally, of great difficulties experienced by colonial governments in raising revenue, it is not surprising that the first issues of fiat paper money in the western world occurred in the American colonies, with innovative Massachusetts leading the way in 1690. These issues of paper money, described earlier in Chapter 11, were a great boon to commerce and helped to extend the measure of monetary independence experienced with the Massachusetts mint. As with coins, however, England opposed issues of paper money in America, and ultimately they were banned for all the colonies.

Private issues of paper bank notes began in the late 17th century in the colonies. Early banks operated on a small, local scale, issuing notes in exchange for mortgages on land. In 1781, the Bank of North America, the first bank of substantial size and commercial orientation, was organized by Robert Morris in Philadelphia under a state charter.

The Bank of North America

[1]The subsidiary unit to the Spanish dollar was called the bit, and there were eight bits to the dollar. Today, in some parts of the United States a quarter of a dollar is still referred to as two bits.

Morris' intention was to use his bank to help finance the Revolution as well as private commerce. Massive issues of continental dollars by the Continental Congress had undermined confidence in the ability of the fledgling U.S. government to manage its finances and survive the war. Morris' bank issued paper notes payable in foreign specie and made loans to the government and private borrowers. It was immensely successful and served as a model for the establishment of additional commercial banks in Pennsylvania and other states.

The establishment of the U.S. mint and a bimetallic standard

With fiat money discredited, the monetary system evolved toward a secondary commodity-money system based on specie. Under the Constitution, Congress was given the power to coin and regulate the value of money. In 1792, Congress established the United States mint to produce a national coinage, and the valuable metal content of U.S. specie was set at 24.75 grains of gold per dollar and at 371.25 grains of silver per dollar. This placed the nation officially on a bimetallic standard with a mint ratio of 15 units of silver to 1 of gold ($371.25/24.75 = 15/1$).[2]

The mint was not effective in establishing a national circulating medium during its first 30 years or so. There were two defects in the original legislation which accounted for this: first, Congress failed to appropriate enough funds to finance an initial inventory of gold and silver for the mint; and second, foreign coins were permitted to continue to serve along with domestic coins as legal tender at face value. As a result of the latter factor, badly clipped and sweated foreign coins persisted for many years as the dominant circulating specie in America while new U.S. coins, which contained more in valuable metal, slipped into hoards or were exported abroad.

Gradually the mint gained in capacity and the legal-tender status of foreign coins was restricted so that a national coinage became established by the mid-1830s. Prior to this, most U.S. coinage was predominantly silver because the mint ratio of 15:1 set by Congress in 1792 turned out to be too low; that is, it undervalued gold relative to silver in comparison to the market prices of the two metals. Consequently, in conformity with Gresham's law, very little gold was presented to the mint for coining until 1834 when the mint ratio was changed. During this period, 1792–1834, the de facto U.S. standard was a combination of foreign specie and domestic silver specie.

The First Bank of the United States

In 1791, Alexander Hamilton persuaded Congress and President Washington to charter a quasi-central bank, the Bank of the United States. It was the first of two such banks having the same name and lasting separate spans of 20 years in the pre-Civil War period. The purposes of the first Bank of the United States were: (1) to serve as

---

[2]One grain equals 1/480 troy ounce of metal. Therefore, the U.S. dollar was fixed at roughly .77 (371.25 grains per dollar/480 grains per ounce) ounces of silver and .05 (24.75/480)ounces of gold. Alternatively, one can say that the price of silver was fixed at $1.29 (480/371.25) per ounce and the price of gold at $19.39 (480/24.75) per ounce.

a fiscal agent of the U.S. Treasury in the handling of both disbursements and tax receipts, (2) to provide a reliable source of loans to the government, and (3) to finance the growth of real private investment. The bank was opposed by Thomas Jefferson and other anti-Federalists who mistrusted banks in general as of doubtful usefulness and any sort of central bank in particular as a dangerous concentration of power.

The first Bank of the United States was a central bank in only a limited sense as such banks are usually organized and empowered today. It was not exclusively a banker's bank; it did not have the power to create fiat money since the nation was on a commodity-money standard; and, finally, it did not have any legal or intended power to control the activities of other banks through reserve requirements or other regulations. It did have a unifying and stabilizing influence on the monetary system, however.

Unification of the monetary system was helped by the establishment of eight branches of the bank in major cities around the country. This encouraged nationwide circulation of the bank's notes and facilitated money transfers among the states. Stability was enhanced by the bank's own conservative policies and by the pressure the bank applied on state banks to hold more reserves of specie and restrain loans more than they would have otherwise. State banks were pressured to follow more restrained policies because the Bank of the United States made a practice of collecting large blocks of notes of the less responsible banks and presenting these to the issuing banks for redemption without warning. State banks had to keep larger quantities of reserves on hand to be able to meet such redemptions.

Opposition to the first Bank of the United States was increased by the bank's successes, especially as a competitor to and restraining influence on state-chartered banks. Foreign ownership of a significant proportion of its stock was another point of criticism. Unfortunately, its unifying and stabilizing influences on the monetary system were not appreciated enough to offset this opposition. Consequently, a move in 1811 to renew the bank's 20-year charter failed in Congress by one vote, and the bank was dissolved. This ended a period of relatively low inflation and tranquil financial conditions.

The number of state banks increased sharply in the absence of the restraining influence of the Bank of the United States and in response to liberalized requirements for bank charters in many states. The number of banks almost tripled in the five-year period 1811–16. This happened also to be a period encompassing the War of 1812, and the government turned to state banks for loans to finance the war. State banks responded by issuing more and more notes without adequate reserves of specie. The result was a three-fold increase in the money supply, widespread suspensions of the

The 1811–1816 expansion of state banks

convertability of bank notes into specie, and a burst of inflation during the war. The rise in prices is evident from the chart in Figure 12–1.

FIGURE 12–1
Wholesale prices (log scale, 1967=100) 1810–1973

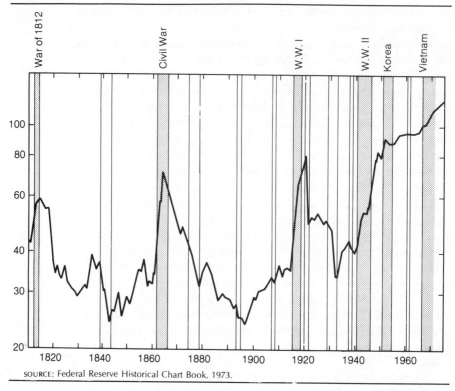

SOURCE: Federal Reserve Historical Chart Book, 1973.

The Second Bank of the United States

In response to inflation and the chaotic state the monetary system had reached by 1815, the Madison administration proposed a second quasi-central bank. The second Bank of the United States received a 20-year charter in 1816. It was quite similar to its predecessor, except that it was much larger in size and had one additional *intended* purpose: to curb inflationary issues of state-bank notes. Unfortunately, the second Bank of the United States was poorly managed under its first president, who resigned after three years. No effective progress was made in restricting the supply of state-bank notes during the first two years of his tenure. Belatedly, in 1818 the bank began to reign in its own loans and note issues and brought strong pressure on the state banks to build their reserves. The result was a rash of bank failures and a sharp two-year decline in the money supply. Reeling from this and other factors contributing to a weak economy, the United States plunged into a severe two-year recession.

Following the recession of 1818–20, the second Bank of the United States performed its central-banking responsibilities with more success, but opposition developed similar to that experienced by the first bank. In 1832, Andrew Jackson vetoed an early bill to renew the bank's charter. The bank's president, Nicholas Biddle, responded with a "scorched-earth" policy. The bank's loans and note issues were contracted sharply, causing a bank panic and a mild recession. This turned the public against the bank all the more, however. And Jackson weakened the bank's power by switching the Treasury's deposits to "pet"state banks. By 1934, the second bank's fate was sealed. After its national charter ran out in 1836, Biddle attempted to operate the bank as an influential state bank but without success, and it failed in 1841.

With the curtailment of the second bank's influence after 1832, the country entered a new period of monetary expansion and chaos. State banks exploded in number, encouraged once again by permissive banking legislation in a number of states. Abuses were particularly acute among banks in the frontier areas. So-called "wildcat" banks issued notes on paltry reserves of specie, taking advantage of the fact that some borrowers would spend these notes in far away Eastern cities where the notes would stay and circulate. When wildcat banks failed, as many did, note holders in the cities were left with worthless paper.

1832–1863 expansion of state banks

Similar tendencies to irresponsible practices existed in lesser degree among country banks close to large commercial cities. In the New England area, however, the Suffolk Bank of Boston had developed into a sort of regional central bank, providing considerable protection from excessive monetary expansion. In 1818, the Suffolk Bank began restraining issues of state-bank notes regionally, much as the first Bank of the United States had done nationally. The notes of country banks surrounding Boston were collected and country banks were threatened with redemptions in large quantities unless these banks kept specie reserves on deposit with the Suffolk Bank. To a certain extent, this practice enabled the Suffolk Bank to grow at the expense of other banks in its region, but the benefits were not all one-sided. In return for deposits of specie, the Suffolk Bank redeemed the notes of other banks at par, making these notes more acceptable to the public. Principally as a result of the Suffolk Bank's influence during the 1832–63 period of rapid growth in state banking, monetary expansion in New England was far more moderate and the payments mechanism was much more efficient than in the rest of the nation.

The Suffolk Bank of Boston

Another noteworthy institution operating during this period was the New York Safety Fund which had been established by New York State in 1829 to insure the note issues of banks in the state. The New York Safety Fund lacked adequate regulatory powers or authority to vary fees, however, and this precursor to the Federal

The New York Safety Fund

Deposit Insurance Corporation was swamped with claims stemming from numerous bank failures. Because the irresponsible practices of state banks persisted without effective restraints, insurance of bank note issues was not a viable operation.

The change to a de facto gold standard in 1834

During the period of state banking, 1832 to 1863, in the United States the de jure monetary standard was still a bimetallic standard. As already described, for 40 years or so the de facto standard was a monometallic, silver standard, however, because the mint ratio of 15:1 set by Congress in 1792 undervalued gold relative to silver. In 1834, the dollar was devalued in terms of gold from 24.75 grains set in 1792 to 23.22 grains, increasing the mint ratio to almost 16:1 and raising the price the mint could pay for gold by roughly $1.28 per ounce.[3] This change in the mint ratio overvalued gold slightly relative to silver, and encouraged sales of gold to the mint for coinage. Subsequently, the discovery of gold in California in 1848 tipped the balance decidedly in favor of gold and resulted in the establishment of a de facto gold standard. (See the discussion in Chapter 10.)

Bank panics in the 1832–1863 period

The period 1832–63 was marked by several widespread bank panics. The panic of 1833, precipitated by Nicholas Biddle's feud with Andrew Jackson, was mentioned earlier. A far more severe panic erupted in 1837 following a poor harvest in 1836. Farmers defaulted on loans, causing banks to contract, and decreased export earnings caused a drain of specie through the balance of payments. Runs on banks eventually forced virtually every bank to suspend specie payments, and large numbers of banks failed. In terms of the analytical framework developed in Chapter 10, both the money-stock multiplier and the monetary base contracted sharply. Consequently, the stock of money dropped by roughly 40 percent between 1837 and 1843, contributing to the most severe depression of the 19th century in the United States.

As described in the next section, the Civil War brought on some major institutional changes, most of which were beneficial. The war closed a period of rampant growth and acute abuses in banking, a period of a confusing array of more than 5,000 different paper monies, and a period of minimal federal involvement in the monetary process.

FROM THE CIVIL WAR TO THE FEDERAL RESERVE

The outbreak of hostilities between the North and the South in 1861 brought on a panic and recession in the North, partly because of losses Northern banks sustained on existing loans to Southern businesses. However, prosperity soon returned to the North as the

---

[3]As explained in an earlier footnote, initially an ounce of gold (480 grains) was valued at $19.39 (480 grains per ounce/24.75 grains per dollar = $19.39 per ounce). After the devaluation, an ounce of gold was worth $20.67 (480/23.22 = $20.67), a price increase of $1.28 per ounce.

effects of Union government war expenditures were felt and the United States resorted once more to fiat-money issues for war finance.

With the first issue of irredeemable greenback notes in 1862, the Union went off the gold standard, and the familiar pattern of rapid monetary expansion and inflation to finance a war was repeated once again.[4] The South also resorted to inflationary finance and by one measure at least outperformed the North by a factor of two to one; by the time the war was over approximately $1 billion in Confederate notes had been issued by the South versus only about $450 million in issues of United States notes (greenbacks) by the Union.

Fiat-money issues to finance the war

In addition to greenback issues, the North attempted to tap its developing capital market for war finance, but the market was not very receptive to Union securities at the interest rates the government was willing to pay. Partly to create a more favorable market for its debt and partly to correct some of the obvious deficiencies of the existing banking system, Congress passed the National Bank Act of 1863 and amended it with a second National Bank Act in 1864.

The National Bank Acts

These acts set out the following authorizations and requirements for any banks having a national bank charter:

National bank notes.　Each national bank could issue national bank notes for its own financing in an amount up to 90 percent of the value of U.S. government bonds placed on deposit as security with the Treasury. (This amounted to a 111 percent "security deposit" requirement.) National bank notes were redeemable at national banks or the Treasury for greenbacks and later, after resumption of the gold standard, for specie.

Reserve Requirements.　For purposes of setting reserve requirements, national banks were categorized as central-reserve city banks, reserve city banks, or country banks according to the importance of their location as financial centers. (Until 1887, New York City was the only city designated as a "central-reserve" city.) Central-reserve city banks were required to maintain a reserve ratio of .25 against their deposit and note liabilities; and only legal-tender money—U.S. greenbacks or specie—qualified as reserves. Reserve city banks also had a required reserve ratio of .25, but half of their reserves could be in the form of deposits with central-reserve city

---

[4]While the United States was off the gold standard in the 1860s and 1870s, most business and commerce in the East and Midwest used the greenback dollar effectively as the unit of account; that is, prices were quoted in "greenback dollars" or just "dollars," which made greenbacks acceptable payment at face value. Prices in greenback dollars rose rapidly during the war. However, most commerce on the West Coast and some in the East specified prices in "gold dollars." Little inflation occurred in these prices. Because of this dual-pricing practice and a flexible rate of exchange between greenback dollars and gold dollars, specie continued in circulation, particularly on the West Coast, in defiance of Gresham's law. See Milton Friedman and Anna Schwartz, *A Monetary History of the United States*, 1867-1960 (Princeton, N.J.: Princeton University Press, 1963), p.27.

banks. Finally, country banks had a reserve ratio of .15, but deposits with reserve or central-reserve city banks could qualify for up to 60 percent of their reserves.

Capital Requirements.   Capital requirements were set for each bank according to the number of residents of that bank's city.

Examinations.   The national banks were to be monitored and examined by a new agency under the executive branch, the *Office of the Comptroller of the Currency*. (This agency still reviews the activities of and grants charters to national banks today.)

The dual system of banking

In the first few years following the National Bank Acts, few banks applied for national-bank charters because the one significant advantage of a national charter, the ability to issue national bank notes, was not enough to outweigh the costs imposed by the requirements for a charter. A state charter which imposed less restraint on note issues was more profitable. But in 1865, the federal government imposed a 10 percent annual tax on state bank notes, and this shifted the balance substantially in favor of national banking for a number of years. Subsequently, in the 1870s, the public's preference turned increasingly to deposit money, shifting the competitive advantage for many banks back once again to a state bank charter. As a result, state banking staged a comeback, and since that time the United States has maintained a fairly stable dual system of state and nationally chartered banks with state banks in the majority.

The accomplishments of the National Bank Acts

There were three important functional accomplishments of the National Bank Acts. First, a uniform currency was established in place of the myriad issues of the state banks. Second, the money-stock multiplier was reduced and stabilized by the imposition of reserve requirements on national banks' monetary liabilities and the tax on state-bank notes.[5] Third, the federal government created a market for its securities which helped to finance the Civil War.

The resumption of the gold standard

Following the war, the government intermittently pursued a policy of retiring greenbacks from circulation by running budget surpluses. The objective was to raise the value of the greenback dollar to the old prewar parity with gold specie. This was achieved over a 15-year period, and in January 1879, the United States returned to a gold standard by pledging to redeem greenbacks on demand in gold specie and by the resumption of specie issues at the prewar rates.[6]

Of course, raising the value of the greenback meant putting most of the country through a period of deflation with attendant losses in

---

[5]Reserve requirements for national bank notes were lifted in 1874. However, the quantity of these notes was still restrained by the 111 percent security-deposit requirement described earlier.

[6]Greenbacks became debt money once the government pledged to redeem them in gold since the government's reserves of gold were less than 100 percent of the outstanding quantity of greenbacks. They remained legal tender and legal reserves for national banks, however, and, consequently, they continued as part of the monetary base.

real output and employment during much of the adjustment period. There was a period of particularly acute contraction in economic activity and falling prices from 1873 to 1879, just prior to the resumption of the gold standard.

The de jure bimetallic standard before the war had been de facto a gold standard because of Gresham's law, and when the United States restored the dollar to its prewar parity with gold, the country returned to a de facto gold standard. Silver was not abandoned as a standard, but several bills passed in the 1870s and 1880s weakened the link between silver and the dollar so that Gresham's law and an undervaluation of silver were no longer necessary to keep the United States effectively on a gold standard. Consequently, silver discoveries in these years and falling silver prices resulted in only a modest expansion of the money supply.

The demonetization of silver

Under the gold standard and the banking system shaped by the National Bank Acts, prices tended to fall gradually during the 1880s and early 1890s despite moderate growth in the money supply. Deflation resulted from a rapid rate of growth in the demand for real money balances which in turn was attributable to a rapid rate of economic growth for the United States. In other words, downward pressure on prices developed because the money supply did not increase rapidly enough to keep up with the increased demand for money induced by economic growth. (Review the sections of Chapter 10 dealing with this phenomenon.)

1879–1895 deflation and the free silver movement

Falling prices created hardship for debtors by increasing the real value of their debt. Rising real debt burdens were particularly severe and caused rancor in the new agricultural areas of the South and West. Another factor causing agitation in the West was the discovery of significant new sources of silver which caused the price of silver to fall sharply. Western and southern politicians recognized their common interests and joined forces to press for removal of the restraints on the monetization of silver. They realized that such action would result in profits for silver interests and relief from deflation through expansion of the money supply.

The free silver movement was opposed by northeastern financial and industrial interests, however. Northeasterners resisted the monetization of silver because England and several other major trading partners of the United States were on a gold standard. It was feared that if the United States remonetized silver, the value of the dollar would fall relative to the English pound and capital inflows beneficial to the financial markets of the Northeast would be jeopardized.

The free silver movement gained momentum in the early 1890s, achieving the nomination of William Jennings Bryan as the Democratic presidential candidate in 1896. Bryan captured the Democratic convention with his famous "Cross of Gold" speech. The silver interests were undercut in the campaign, however, by a rise in the supply of gold and a moderate inflation in 1895–96. McKinley was elected over Bryan, and four years later, with the Currency Act of 1900, the gold standard finally was officially affirmed as the solitary U.S. monetary standard.

Bank panics in the post-Civil War period

During the post-Civil War years, 1865–1913, the United States continued to experience banking panics despite the considerable improvements to the monetary and financial system introduced by the National Bank Acts. Bank panics were, in fact, an inherent characteristic of the business cycle, in some cases precipitating and in other cases precipitated by declines in economic activity. The reasons should be familiar from previous chapters. A decline in economic activity, from crop failures, for example, would cause borrowers to default on bank loans. These defaults would cause some banks to fail with substantial losses to depositors. Fears of further failures led to runs on banks, causing banks to suspend specie payments on deposits and to contract loans and the money supply. (Review the section on the rise in the k and r ratios in a business downturn in Chapter 10.) A drain of specie reserves from the country as a result of a deficit in the balance of payments would tend to set off a similar sequence of events.

Institutional deficiencies of the monetary system: 1865–1913

Bank panics were one symptom of several important institutional deficiencies of the monetary system as it operated under the National Bank Acts and the gold standard. First, the required reserve ratios for national banks were not variable. This meant that the government had no capacity to respond to a bank panic by lowering reserve requirements.

Fixed required-reserve ratios

No lender of last resort with vast reserves

Second, the structure of the system and of the reserve requirements for national banks meant that central-reserve city banks had to shoulder too much of the reserve needs of the entire system. During periods of stress, country banks drew on their deposits with reserve city banks which, in turn, drew on their deposits with central-reserve city banks. Central-reserve city banks were at the end of the reserve chain and had nowhere else to turn. Hence, once the central-reserve city banks' resources were depleted, the system was forced to suspend payments on deposits, thereby disrupting the payments process and depressing the economy. A lender of last resort with adequate resources to sustain the financial system through a severe liquidity crisis was needed.

No deposit insurance

Third, there was no insurance available for national-bank depositors such as provided for state-bank notes in New York before the Civil War by the New York Safety Fund. The absence of deposit insurance made the k ratio more volatile than it otherwise would have been. If depositors had had insurance, they would have been less inclined to withdraw currency from their bank at the least sign of weakness.

Fourth, the supply of currency was not responsive to seasonal and cyclical fluctuations in the demand for it or to secular increases in the demand for currency as the economy grew. Currency consisted of national bank notes, specie, greenbacks, and assorted minor government issues. National bank notes were limited in supply by the requirement for security deposits of government obligations. Over most of the period under review, the supply of national bank notes was restricted and declined mechanically because the government persistently ran budget surpluses which decreased the quantity of outstanding government debt and available security.[7] The quantity of specie in circulation was determined and limited by the market forces described in Chapter 10. This meant that a temporary deficit or surplus in the balance of payments could whipsaw the specie component of the monetary base. In addition, the supply of greenbacks was capped by a statutory ceiling on the quantity outstanding. In sum, the quantity of currency was, as characterized at the time, "inelastic," that is, inflexible with respect to changes in the demand for currency consistent with a stable price level and a stable financial sector.

Inflexible currency supply

Fifth, although national banks were subject to examinations, reserve requirements, and other restrictions, many state banks were not so restrained. Regulations for state banks varied greatly among the states, and still do. In addition, there emerged some new financial institutions which were relatively unconstrained by federal and state regulations. The most important of these were trust companies, flourishing particularly in New York.

Inadequate regulation

Lastly, the check-clearing system which existed during this period was cumbersome. Clearings for most banks were conducted through a complex structure of correspondent relationships among banks. Checks took weeks and, often, months to clear through this system. Large banks in some cities established clearinghouse associations which speeded transactions considerably, but these facilities were of little value for checks drawn on out-of-town banks.

Inefficient check-clearing system

Despite recognition of most of these problems in the 19th century, no meaningful reforms were instituted. The silver issue dominated the monetary scene until the mid-1890s, and the increased supplies of gold in the late 1890s helped to bring on a period of prosperity which lasted for over 10 years with only minor setbacks and no major bank panics.

The Panic of 1907

In 1907, however, the country experienced a gold drain through the balance of payments, and a massive bank panic set in after a

---

[7]The original 111 percent security deposit requirement for National Bank notes was reduced to 100 percent by the Currency Act of 1900. A substantial increase in the quantity of these notes followed over the next few years, but this palliative was temporary.

large trust company in New York failed. Many banks failed, others suspended currency payments, and output and prices nose-dived. New York banks were particularly affected. The contraction was brief, but it focused attention on the deficiencies of the monetary system under the National Bank Acts.

Temporary reform legislation in 1908 provided for emergency issues of additional national bank notes. At the same time, a special commission of Congressmen was formed to study and recommend permanent reforms. The commission, chaired by Senator Nelson Aldrich, submitted its recommendations in 1912, and in the following year these recommendations, with minor alterations, were adopted in the Federal Reserve Act.

FROM THE CREATION OF THE FEDERAL RESERVE THROUGH 1980

Institutional provisions of the Federal Reserve Act

The Federal Reserve Act of 1913 provided for the establishment of a central bank consisting of the following entities: (1) 12 regional Federal Reserve Banks to serve and represent the local needs of specific regions of the country, (2) a Federal Reserve Board, comprised of eight members including the Secretary of the Treasury and the Comptroller of the Currency, to give central policy direction to the system and to supervise banks in the system, and (3) a Federal Advisory Council, comprised of private bank officials and businessmen from each district, to advise the board.

The Federal Reserve banks were established in Atlanta, Boston, Chicago, Cleveland, Dallas, Kansas City, Minneapolis, New York, Philadelphia, Richmond, St. Louis, and San Francisco; and districts were designated to include economic regions served by each of these cities. The decision to establish 12 semi-independent, regional reserve banks was designed to alleviate concern that policies directed by a single central bank would not recognize and serve the special needs of the disparate economic sections of the country. Each reserve bank was to be directed by a board of nine individuals, six selected by the member banks of the district and three selected by the Federal Reserve Board.

Operational provisions of the Federal Reserve Act

The important operational provisions of the Federal Reserve Act were:

1. National banks were required to be members of the system while state banks were given the option of becoming members.
2. Each member bank was required to hold reserves, with distinctions for required reserve ratios among banks according to their location, as under the National Bank Act, and with currency held by member banks and member banks' deposits at the Federal Reserve banks qualifying as legal reserves.[8]

---

[8]The qualification of currency held by member banks as legal reserves was suspended in 1917, but gradually reinstated in the late 1950s.

3. The Federal Reserve banks were given the power to issue a paper currency, Federal Reserve notes, which member banks could obtain by drawing on their deposit accounts at the reserve banks.

4. Federal Reserve banks were required to maintain reserves of gold equal to 40 percent or more of their notes outstanding and 35 percent of their deposits, and to redeem Federal Reserve notes and deposit liabilities in gold on demand. In addition, Federal Reserve banks were required to hold reserves of commercial paper equal to 100 percent of their note liabilities.

5. Federal Reserve banks were to operate as bankers' banks and create reserve deposits for member banks through loans by rediscounting eligible commercial paper or government securities submitted by member banks to the discount window of their Federal Reserve bank.

6. Federal Reserve banks also were authorized to make purchases of government securities at their own discretion, making payment with newly created deposits.

7. Federal Reserve banks were to act as the fiscal agents of the U.S. government, handling borrowings and transfers of funds.

8. Finally, the Federal Reserve was directed to establish a free check-clearing system for all banks in order to improve the efficiency of the national payments mechanism.

Accomplishments of the Federal Reserve Act

The Federal Reserve Act's original provisions accomplished five major changes in the monetary system. First, by providing for and obtaining voluntary membership from many state banks, considerably more of the nation's banks and money stock came under more stringent and uniform government regulation.   **Better regulation**

Second, by specifying that the reserves of member banks were to be held at Federal Reserve banks where they could be exchanged for Federal Reserve notes, the excessive burden placed on the currency reserves of central-reserve city national banks was alleviated. And, with the establishment of the discount window, lender-of-last-resort facilities were made available for member banks caught in a liquidity squeeze.   **Improved lender-of-last-resort facilities**

Third, as intended, the discount window also provided a way to exercise some discretionary control of bank reserves and the monetary base. This could be done, of course, by raising or lowering the discount rate relative to market interest rates. (See Chapter 11.) Though not planned or anticipated as a tool of monetary policy, open-market purchases and sales of government securities eventually were found to be even more effective in controlling member-bank reserves.   **More discretionary control of the money supply**

Fourth, the Federal Reserve Act retained but weakened the gold standard. As just described, the Federal Reserve could influence   **Weakened gold standard** the quantity of money in the economy through the monetary base. However, since the Fed had minimum gold reserve ratios, an upper bound to expansionary actions was encountered when the minimum legal level of gold relative to notes and reserve deposits was reached. A lower bound to restrictive actions was reached when the Federal Reserve possessed inadequate supplies of securities in its portfolio to sell to offset, or "sterilize," an increase in the quantity of gold entering the economy.[9] Within these bounds, the gold-standard mechanism could be made inoperative.

The real-bills doctrine and other deficiencies

Although the degree of discretionary control of the supply of currency and bank reserves accomplished by these changes was an important potential improvement of the monetary system, its actual contribution to monetary stability was to depend, of course, upon Federal Reserve behavior, i.e., how wisely discretionary monetary policy was used. The Federal Reserve Act itself suggested that the Fed should pursue a policy which has become known as the *real-bills doctrine*. Unfortunately, as explained below, central-bank policy based on the real-bills doctrine is likely to destabilize the economy, leading to inflation and boom followed by deflation and bust.

According to the real-bills doctrine, a central bank should provide enough reserves to support all the bank financing demanded by business for goods in the process of production or in inventory. Credit-market instruments associated with such financing were called real bills because they were secured by "real" goods. Real bills were considered a desirable investment for banks because of their safety; and it was considered desirable for the central bank to key its supply of reserves to the quantity of real bills presented to banks for discount because it was thought this would ensure enough money and credit to service the "needs of trade" without, at the same time, creating an inflationary condition of "too much money chasing too few goods." Inflation was precluded because the quantity of money and bank credit was tied to the quantity of goods—or so it seemed.

The pitfall in the real-bills doctrine is that, despite its title and the surface appeal of its logic, it does not really tie the quantity of money and bank credit to the real value of goods in production and inventory. The tie, in fact, is to the *nominal* value of these goods. To see this, it is necessary only to recall from Chapter 5 that the quantity of credit demanded to finance goods rises with increases in

The real-bills doctrine

---

[9]Sterilization by a central bank in a secondary commodity-money system was explained in Chapter 10. It involves the use of the discount rate or open-market operations in securities to offset the effects on the monetary base of increases or decreases in the quantity of gold held by banks and the public. Such offsetting operations alter the gold reserve ratio of the central bank.

prices in the economy as well as with increases in the quantity of goods. If any increase in the demand for credit in the form of real bills presented for discounting is accommodated, the central bank will tend to validate inflation in goods prices. Higher goods prices validated by an expansion in money and credit will tend to feed through to higher wage demands and other input prices, further boosting credit demands, which the central bank will accommodate, and so on. Once started, inflation tends to be self-reinforcing under the real-bills doctrine, at least for a while.

To see how the process can lead to a bust following a boom, consider the advanced stage of a business expansion when costs of production and business credit demands tend to rise. If the central bank expands reserves in response to higher credit demands, and inflation gains momentum, firms will begin to build inventories in anticipation of future price increases. (Anticipated price increases mean expected profits on inventories for firms.) The process feeds on itself. At some point, however, inflation is likely to become severe enough to cause the central bank to alter its real-bills policy and clamp down on the supply of bank reserves. Banks respond by restraining credit and the money supply falls. This reduces the demand for goods, placing firms with high inventories in a double bind—higher interest costs and lower sales. Defaults and a full-fledged panic may ensue.

In this situation, it is clear that the real-bills doctrine does not provide as reliable a guide to low-risk commercial-bank lending as it sounds, either. Goods in production or inventory provide solid security for loans only if they can be sold at prices equal to or higher than cost. If demand conditions weaken, this security can evaporate.

The Federal Reserve Act was deficient, therefore, in suggesting a real-bills rule for Federal Reserve actions. Following the real-bills doctrine would have created severe instability in the economy. For a variety of reasons, the Federal Reserve never followed the real-bills doctrine as an automatic rule. However, as will be seen later, it has operated under other equally flawed guides to policy in various periods.

In addition to providing wrong direction for monetary policy, the Federal Reserve Act was deficient in the following areas: there was no provision for deposit insurance for banks; the Federal Reserve was not given the power to vary reserve requirements for member banks; the locus of ultimate control as between the board and the district reserve banks was not adequately defined; the independence of the Federal Reserve from the Treasury, and from political pressures in general, was not strong enough; and, finally, there were insufficient incentives for membership in the system to attract and hold as large a proportion of the state banks as desirable. As we shall see, these deficiencies just listed have been largely removed through subsequent legislation.

Other deficiencies of the Federal Reserve Act

The World War I period

World War I broke out in Europe in 1914, the same year the Federal Reserve began its operations. As a result of the war, there was a considerable inflow of gold. This inflow could not be sterilized by the new Fed because it lacked an adequate volume of loans or securities to reduce as an offset. Consequently, between 1914 and 1917, the monetary base and the money supply expanded at average annual rates of roughly 12 and 14 percent, respectively. Average inflation in wholesale prices for the same period was 18 percent per year.

After the United States entered the war, the inflow of gold from abroad slowed, but by this time the Federal Reserve had begun to buy government securities to help the Treasury finance the war. Federal Reserve purchases of government debt helped the Treasury directly by monetizing some of the debt and indirectly by expanding bank reserves which made banks better able to take on government debt. In the process, interest-rate increases were moderated. The monetary base grew more rapidly in this period, but the rate of growth of the money supply and inflation slowed somewhat due to a decline in the money-stock multiplier associated with the war.

When the war ended in late 1918, there was a brief recession, and inflation abated further; but monetary expansion continued at a rapid pace, and inflation picked up again within the next year. Monetary expansion continued because, in response to Treasury influence, the Fed persisted in supporting market prices for government debt and commercial paper. This was done by keeping the discount rate significantly below market interest rates, giving banks an incentive to borrow funds from the Federal Reserve for investments in securities and paper.

The contraction of 1920–1921

As a result of resurgent inflation, a deficit developed in the balance of payments, and the Federal Reserve began to lose gold reserves at an alarming rate during the second half of 1919. Finally, in January 1920, the discount rate was jumped by 125 basis points, from 4.75 to 6 percent. Unfortunately, this rate increase coincided with other factors tending to weaken the economy. Economic activity declined a bit and monetary expansion slowed for several months until midyear. At this time, the New York Federal Reserve responded to a still-falling gold-reserve ratio by raising its discount rate another 100 basis points. At that point, the money supply began to fall more rapidly, and output and prices experienced a sharp collapse which persisted until mid-1921. Despite declines in prices and output, a steady rise in bank failures, and an easing of the gold drain, the Federal Reserve kept its discount rate high. Over a period of a year and a half, industrial production fell by one-third and prices fell by one half.

With the benefit of hindsight, it is clear that the new Federal Reserve performed poorly in its first real opportunity to stabilize the economy without the interference of war or other special circumstances. If tight money policies had been adopted sooner, the inflation and gold drain of 1919 probably could have been avoided. Though it would seem that the Federal Reserve's mistakes in the 1919–21 period were partly due to inexperience and to excessive Treasury influence, the pattern of waiting too long to impose restraint and then imposing excessive restraint at a most sensitive point for the economy has been repeated often during the Fed's history. This pattern, experienced most recently in 1977–81, is often attributable to shifting political priorities and pressures on the Federal Reserve—first to sustain a business expansion and later to squelch inflation.

The lessons of 1919–1921

The stable 1920s

The next period, extending from 1921 to mid 1929 and the onset of the Great Depression, stands out as a period of considerable success for Federal Reserve policy. The money stock changed little over these eight years. Gold inflows were sterilized, and seasonal fluctuations in the needs for money and credit were met with muted fluctuations in interest rates. Real economic activity expanded vigorously over the period; yet prices declined mildly. Through most of this period, Federal Reserve policy was substantially influenced by the Federal Reserve Bank of New York, partly because of the importance of New York as the nation's financial center and partly because of the personal stature of Benjamin Strong, the president of the New York Fed.

Background to the Great Depression

Despite the prosperity and stability of the 1920s there were, nevertheless, three important developments which in one way or another contributed to the collapse of the financial sector in the Great Depression. The first of these was a wave of hyperinflations which swept Central Europe following World War I. (Recall the article in Chapter 3 on the 1923 German hyperinflation.) Although the United States was not a victim of this type of trauma during the 1920s, the experiences of European countries shocked U.S. officials, and the spectre of hyperinflation was partly responsible for a later reluctance of the Fed to adopt aggressive reflationary measures once the Great Depression began. Fear of hyperinflation also partly accounted for extreme reactions in the international financial markets in the early 1930s to any hint that the United States might abandon the gold standard—reactions which induced the Federal Reserve to tighten monetary policy several times after economic activity had collapsed.

The second factor was the growing use of bank credit to finance speculative, highly leveraged stock purchases in 1927–29. The Federal Reserve had no tools to deal directly with this problem.

A third development was the death in 1928 of Benjamin Strong, the influential head of the Federal Reserve Bank of New York and a principal architect of the successful policies of the 1921–28 period. After Strong's death, the Federal Reserve Board began to assert a greater influence on policy relative to the Federal Reserve Bank of New York and the other Federal Reserve banks; but the locus of dominant power remained an unsettled issue until 1933, and this contributed to indecision among Federal Reserve officials.

The Great Depression

In early 1929, the Federal Reserve Bank of New York wanted to raise its discount rate from 5 to 6 percent to curb credit going to finance stock market speculation, but the Federal Reserve Board, which had to approve any discount-rate changes, denied the request. The board was concerned about criticism that the Fed had overdone discount-rate increases in 1920. The economy was not overheating, and a measure with as broad an impact as an increase in the discount rate did not seem appropriate for the special problem of excessive speculation in stocks. Instead, the Federal Reserve Board wanted the New York Fed to use persuasion with its member banks to get them to cut back on credit supporting stock purchases. But the New York Fed felt that this tactic would not be successful, and it was not pursued seriously. Finally, in August 1929, the board approved an increase in the New York bank's discount rate. It so happened that August also was the business-cycle peak.

The stock market crash

Once again, a tightening move by the Fed coincided with a weakening in the economy. The stock market rose sharply and defiantly for a month after the Federal Reserve action. However, a moderate decline in stock prices set in over a six-week period beginning in early September. Gradually, investors who had borrowed to the hilt began to have second thoughts. Each price decline brought more margin calls.[10] Then, in late October 1929, panic erupted; stocks were dumped on the market, and the Great Crash ensued. By the

---

[10]Margin is the "down payment" or "good money" put up by an investor purchasing a stock on credit. Brokerage houses or other lenders provide the credit. When stock prices fall, the loss in capital value on the stock is charged against the investor's margin, and there is a margin call, which means that the investor must replenish the margin or the brokerage house will sell the stock at the current market price.

end of October, popular stock-price indexes stood at less than half their peak levels of early September.

The stock market crash had a profound psychological impact on most individuals, for a great many small investors had gotten into the market and lost their life savings. A number of banks failed because of defaults on loans, but widespread runs did not develop for a year.

Economic decline in the first year after the August 1929 peak was severe—about 25 percent in industrial production, 13 percent in employment, and 12 percent in commodity prices. The money supply declined by a small amount, less than 5 percent; even so, this decline, which was due to a reduction in the monetary base supplied by the Federal Reserve, was counterproductive to a revival of the economy. The Federal Reserve cut the discount rate in steps, to 2.5 percent by mid-1930, but market interest rates fell just as fast. Banks were reluctant to borrow, and the Fed was reluctant to pursue open-market purchases vigorously. Banks were reluctant to borrow at the discount window both because of low market interest rates relative to the discount rate and because borrowing was a sign of weakness. The Federal Reserve, on the other hand, failed to make aggressive open-market purchases, partly because of indecision and partly because of concern that such actions would be inflationary.

In October 1930, a bank panic developed, and more than 500 banks failed in a span of just a few months. A brief respite from panic and declining production occurred in early 1931, but a fresh crisis erupted in March of that year. The public rushed to convert deposits to currency, and the rate of decline in the money supply accelerated.

The bank panics of 1930 and 1931

The chaotic and depressed state of affairs of the United States in 1930–31 was shared by countries abroad, including Britain, and in the summer of 1931 doubts arose about the ability or willingness of Britain and the United States to remain on the gold standard. A run on the pound and the dollar developed in September 1931, with foreigners converting these currencies to gold. Britain abandoned the gold standard that month. But the United States remained "on gold," and the Federal Reserve fought off the attack by raising the discount rate 200 basis points.[11] The price of this defense was severe, however. Both the gold drain and the discount-rate rise accentuated the decline in the U.S. money supply. Bank failures accelerated, and the depression deepened. Employment in 1931 declined 15 percent on top of the 13 percent decline in 1930.

The gold drain and monetary tightening in 1931

---

[11]By putting upward pressure on other interest rates, a discount-rate rise helped to stem the capital outflow from the United States which, in turn, tended to improve the balance of payments and preserve the Federal Reserve's gold supply.

In early 1932, several emergency acts initiated by Congress and the Hoover administration helped to stem bank failures and stabilize the economy; the Federal Reserve assisted in the spring with aggressive open-market purchases. However, Federal Reserve action was sufficient only to stop the money supply from falling further. The Federal Reserve was inhibited once again by fears of inflation—despite the fact that prices had fallen drastically—and by disagreement among the centers of power within the Fed as to the proper course of action. Industrial production and commodity prices rose for several months. Then commodity prices sagged anew, and a fresh wave of bank failures began in agricultural states in late 1932.

The bank panic of 1932–1933

Unfortunately, this return of bank failures coincided with a lame duck period for the Republican administration. Hoover and Congress were biding time, waiting for Franklin Roosevelt and the Democrats to assume office in March 1933. Consequently, no new remedial actions were initiated by Congress or Hoover, and the bank panic spread. Runs on banks caused a sharp rise in the currency ratio and pressed the money supply down drastically.

The money-supply decline was due also to new fears that the United States would leave gold. Roosevelt's campaign had promised a "new deal" without identifying specific changes planned. As a result, hopes for recovery were raised but so was uncertainty about monetary policy. There was considerable speculation that one of Roosevelt's actions would be to take the United States off the gold standard. Both domestic and foreign holders of dollar-denominated assets rushed to convert to gold or foreign currency. The Federal Reserve's gold stock fell sharply, and, in response, the Federal Reserve raised the discount rate in February 1933 as it had in October 1931. Still the gold drain continued, and a few days before Roosevelt's March 4 inauguration, the gold reserve ratio of the Federal Reserve Bank of New York fell below the minimum required level.

By March 4th, most banks in the country, including the New York Fed, were closed by state-declared bank holidays. On March 4, 1933, Roosevelt attempted to calm the nation in his inaugural address with assurances that "the only thing we have to fear is fear itself." As described in Chapter 1, Roosevelt then proceeded to order all banks closed until they could be examined and certified as sound. Simultaneously, the United States abandoned the gold standard as an effective influence on the U.S. money supply.[12] Over the next few years, New Deal legislation introduced vast economic reforms.

---

[12]Roosevelt took the United States off the gold standard first as an emergency measure. Later the dollar was devalued. Though formally still linked to gold through a gold-reserve ratio, the dollar was effectively tied to gold only for purposes of international settlements—an arrangement called a gold-exchange standard. U.S. residents and banks were prohibited from holding gold for monetary purposes. The gold-exchange standard, which was finally abandoned in 1971, never operated as a direct influence on the U.S. money supply.

The important reforms of the monetary system, incorporated mainly in the Banking Acts of 1933 and 1935, were as follows:

1. The Federal Deposit Insurance Corporation (FDIC) was created to provide limited insurance for deposits of all banks which were members of the Federal Reserve system and of other banks which applied and were approved for insurance.

2. The power of individual Federal Reserve banks to conduct open-market purchases and sales of government securities on their own authority was rescinded, and control of these operations for the 12 banks' accounts was formally vested in a Federal Open Market Committee (FOMC).[13] Its membership included the seven members of the board and five Federal Reserve bank presidents, one always from the Federal Reserve Bank of New York and four on a rotating basis from the other Federal Reserve banks.

3. The Federal Reserve Board was renamed the Board of Governors of the Federal Reserve System and strengthened by the structuring of the FOMC to give the board a dominant voice, by granting the board power to vary member-bank reserve requirements, and by establishing with the board authority to set margin requirements for stocks bought on credit. Also, the Secretary of the Treasury and the Comptroller of the Currency were removed as ex officio members of the board in order to accord the board more independence.

4. The payment of interest on demand deposits was prohibited and maximum interest rates on time deposits were to be set for member banks by the Board of Governors (Regulation Q ceilings) and by the FDIC for nonmember, insured banks. These interest-rate restrictions were designed to strengthen the banking system. The notion was that banks had an inherent tendency to weaken themselves by competing too vigorously with each other for deposits. High interest rates on deposits, it was believed, reduced bank profitability below safe levels and induced banks to seek higher yielding, riskier investments than desirable.

The post-1933 period

Following the Bank Holiday Crisis of 1933 and Roosevelt's emergency actions in March of that year, the financial system and the economy entered a four-year period of recovery. The money supply grew and economic activity increased rapidly in percentage terms,

---

[13]Predecessors of the FOMC had been introduced at the Fed as early as 1923 as the system grew more cognizant of the importance of open-market operations, and committee power had increased during the early years of the Great Depression as the board asserted itself over the influence of the New York Fed.

but each from such low levels that conditions remained quite depressed. Before recovery was complete, a sharp one-year setback began in the spring of 1937.

The contraction
of 1937–1938

One factor in the recession of 1937–38 was an increase in reserve requirements by the Federal Reserve in 1936–37.[14] The Fed became concerned about a high level of excess reserves which had built up in the banking system as the recovery proceeded. (See Figure 12–2.) This reserve buildup probably was due both to an extraordinarily low level of short-term interest rates—three-month Treasury bill yields were less than .5 percent during this period—and to a desire on the part of banks to provide for better protection from the liquidity strains which had occurred during the contraction of 1929–33. However, the Federal Reserve viewed these excess reserves as a weakening of its control of money and credit. Still fearing inflation, the Fed was concerned that banks might suddenly mobilize their excess reserves to expand loans and the money supply. To preclude this from happening, the Federal Reserve moved to double reserve requirements in several steps. In response to this and to a decline in the monetary base, banks cut back on their loans, and the money supply started falling in March 1937. Several months later, real output began to fall sharply.

FIGURE 12–2
Excess reserves and borrowings of member banks ($billion)

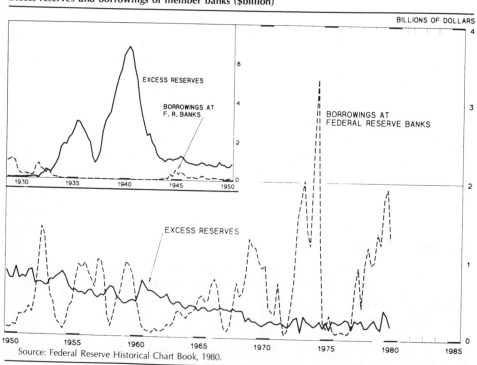

Source: Federal Reserve Historical Chart Book, 1980.

[14]Another factor was a substantial rise in Social Security taxes in 1937.

Although the drop in output in 1937–38 was sharp—about one third—it was over within one year; and the financial system was spared a major panic which had been a customary feature of similar recessions in the past. One reason was that bank deposits were considered safer. In fact, the critical k ratio in the money-stock multiplier remained stable. This episode demonstrated, however, that the new tool of variable reserve requirements necessitated more careful application and that the problem of ill-timed or inappropriate Federal Reserve policy had not been solved by the reforms of 1933–35.

Reserve requirements were reduced, and the monetary base began rising in early 1938, causing the previous downward trend of the money supply to reverse. A recovery ensued at midyear. The next year World War II broke out in Europe and shortly became the dominant influence on the U.S. economy, even though the United States remained neutral for two years. The Federal Reserve assumed the same role in the government debt market as it had during World War I. By supporting the price of government securities, the Fed monetized about one third of the government's debt issues. This was not unusual; in most of the belligerent nations there was a shift in the priorities of the central bank from stabilization to providing revenue. The U.S. money supply rose at an average annual rate of 13.5 percent during the war. Though efforts were made to contain inflation through wage and price controls and with the use of special Federal Reserve powers to limit consumer credit, inflation in consumer prices averaged 6.3 percent per year between 1939 and 1948.

World War II inflation

Following World War II, the Federal Reserve continued to support market prices for government securities in response to the same type of political pressure which had operated after World War I. The Fed finally grew sufficiently concerned about inflation after the Korean War began in 1950 to challenge the Treasury; and it reached an agreement with the Treasury in March 1951 to end its automatic support of government debt. This agreement, known as the *Accord*, marked a return to stabilization as the primary policy objective of the Federal Reserve.

The Accord

Monetary policy and the economy enjoyed a period of relative stability during the 1950s and early 1960s, much as had occurred during most of the 1920s. There were no external shocks to the economy, and the Federal Reserve was not subjected to significant political pressure to pursue either too expansionary or too contractional a policy.

A stable period: 1950s to early 1960s

The ideas of John Maynard Keynes dominated analysis and prescriptions for policy during this period. As described in Chapter 1, in 1936, Keynes had argued in his book, *The General Theory of Employment, Interest and Money*, that expansionary fiscal policy was of primary importance to the restoration of full employment in Britain and in the United States. It took time for these ideas to take hold. Keynes' advocacy of an activist fiscal policy and management of the business cycle ran counter to established philosophies of conservative government finance, including balanced budgets and general laissez-faire (noninterference in the private sector). Marking a new era, in 1946, Congress passed the Employment Act which committed the government to the pursuit of full employment and price stability through the use of fiscal and monetary policy.

The ascendency of Keynesianism

But aggressive, activist policy was not actually tried until 1964. In that year, the Kennedy administration persuaded Congress to cut taxes to stimulate the economy, which was below capacity output and full employment. Although monetary policy was not a central focus of attention, the Federal Reserve complemented the stimulus of the tax cut with expansionary monetary actions. By 1966, unemployment had declined to a 4 percent rate, which was associated at that time with a state of full employment.

The Vietnam war and inflation

Success in achieving full employment appeared to herald a new day for economic policy and the government's ability to fine tune the economy. The clouds of inflation began to gather in 1966, however, partly because of the stimulus begun in 1964 and partly because of a pickup in military expenditures for the Vietnam war. Economic advisors in the Johnson administration advocated a tax increase to pay for the war and to prevent inflation from rising, but Johnson was reluctant to push a tax increase through Congress. Military expenditures continued to escalate. The Federal Reserve tightened monetary policy briefly in 1966 but returned to an expansionary policy in 1967. Inflation in consumer prices worsened from 2.9 percent in 1967 to 4.2 percent in 1968.

1968–1970 setbacks to Keynesianism

Finally, in 1968, Congress passed a tax increase, and policymakers braced themselves for a recession. The Federal Reserve intended for monetary policy to be moderately complementary to the fiscal restraint imposed by the tax increase. Interest rates were rising mildly, and, due to the influence of Keynesian analysis, the Federal Reserve viewed this as evidence that its policy posture of moderate restraint was on track. Early Keynesian analysis, as later chapters explain, argued that monetary policy works through changes in the level of interest rates. In fact, as measured by the rate of growth of the money supply, monetary policy was highly expansionary in 1968.[15] The growth rate of the money supply accelerated from 6.6 percent in 1967 to 8 percent in 1968. Interest rates rose, but by less than the rise in the rate of inflation. Consequently

---

[15]Within its own framework, there were two important omissions in the early Keynesian analysis. First, there was an inadequate treatment of wealth in the analysis of the determinants of spending. Second, the treatment of interest rates failed to distinguish between real and nominal rates of interest. A more complete explanation of Keynesian analysis must be postponed to later chapters in Part 4.

real interest rates fell, the economy picked up momentum despite an increase in taxes, and inflation continued on a rising trend into 1969.[16]

In mid-1969, after the Nixon administration took office, the Federal Reserve finally imposed meaningful restraint. Money-supply growth dropped sharply, and the economy slipped into a recession late in the year. Due to the long lag of prices behind money-supply changes, however, inflation remained stubbornly high at 5 to 6 percent.

The 1968–70 period presented Keynesians with two setbacks. First, the failure of the 1968 tax increase to curb spending cast serious doubt on the effectiveness of fiscal policy—at least as a means of restraint in a state of full employment. Second, the persistence of high inflation during 1970, a year of recession, ran counter to a key conclusion of Keynesian analysis that inflation is a condition associated only with excess demand at capacity output in the economy.

As a result of the 1968–69 experience with fiscal policy, monetarism gained credibility. That credibility was tarnished slightly by the persistence of high inflation in late 1970, more than a year after tight monetary policy had been imposed; but on the whole the 1968–70 period marked a turning point in the debate between Keynesians and monetarists and in the attention devoted to monetary policy. The 1968–70 period was important also because it demonstrated the fallacy of the assumption that interest rates were a useful indicator of the actual thrust of monetary policy.

The decline in the economy terminated toward the end of 1970, and inflation began to wind down in early 1971. Even so, unemployment remained high and the administration grew concerned that economic conditions would not be favorable to a Nixon reelection in 1972. Nixon's economic advisers were of semimonetarist persuasion, and the Nixon program in 1971 called for the Federal Reserve to expand the money supply vigorously.[17] Either coincidentally or consequently, money-supply growth picked up sharply. Then, in

Nixon's inflationary drive for re-election

---

[16]In September 1968, the Federal Reserve changed the accounting period for member-bank reserves from the week contemporaneous with deposits subject to reserve requirements to the week two weeks later. In other words, after September 1968, member banks were required to maintain a certain level of reserves each week in accordance with their deposit levels two weeks prior to the current week. Some economists believe that this practice, known as lagged-reserve accounting, weakens the Fed's ability to control the money supply and may have played a role in the 1968–69 surge in monetary expansion and inflation. This issue is mentioned in the text later in this chapter and is analyzed in Chapter 14, following a more complete description of the Federal Reserve's monetary tools and practices.

[17]Nixon's economic advisors were of monetarist persuasion in terms of their evaluation of the relative importance of monetary and fiscal policy. Monetarists advocate

(continued on next page)

the summer of 1971, a wage-price freeze was imposed to curb inflation.

The combination of wage and price controls and an expansionary
monetary policy had a pressure-cooker effect on the economy. Unemployment declined from 5.9 percent in January 1972 to 5.2 percent in October 1972, just before the election, and to 5 percent by
January 1973. Because of controls, inflation in consumer prices remained at 3 to 3.5 percent. But this policy combination achieved
short-run benefits at considerable long-run cost. As described in
Chapter 3, even elementary supply and demand analysis can predict that controls on prices and wages will cause shortages and encourage black markets when these controls are actively suppressing
prices and wages. Severe shortages and market distortions began to
appear in 1972. Buyers became so acutely concerned with the availability of goods that, at one point, rumors of an impending shortage
in toilet paper cleared grocery store shelves of this item in a matter
of days. Simultaneously, price increases accelerated for wholesale
commodities for which controls were not feasible. (Wholesale price
increases were due both to strong demand and to a worldwide scarcity of food in 1972–73.)

In early 1973, controls were relaxed somewhat to alleviate distortions and shortages, and inflation in consumer prices surged to the
double-digit level. In the summer of 1973, the Federal Reserve
finally tightened monetary policy. If economic events had followed
their normal course from that point, the economy probably would
have experienced a mild recession, ending by mid-1974.

However, in October 1973, war broke out in the Middle East.
Oil shipments to the United States were embargoed for several
months, and the Organization of Petroleum Exporting Countries
(OPEC) began an almost fourfold escalation of oil prices. The Federal Reserve's immediate response was one of concern for the im-

**The severe
contraction of
1973–1975**

---

steady growth of monetary aggregates, however, and this Nixon's advisers did not do
in 1971. Sherman Maisel, then a member of the Board of Governors of the Federal
Reserve, wrote later:

> ...both economic and political problems had become serious...the results of
> the 1970 congressional elections had been disappointing from the Administra-
> tion's point of view. If the forecast was correct, the 1972 elections would take
> place with unemployment close to 6 percent.... It was clear that last-minute
> fiscal changes would not bring about the projected additional $18 billion in
> spending. It was also clear to the White House where the new expansionary
> pressures ought to be generated. The finger pointed right at the Federal
> Reserve....
>
> The rule of gradualism no longer satisfied George Schultz, director of the
> Office of Management and Budget and the strongest economic voice in the
> Administration. He now espoused an activist monetary policy. Money would
> determine spending. If an election were to be won, the Federal Reserve
> would have to increase the money supply at far more than the 4.2 percent
> average of 1969–70. In his words, the 'real juice' for the expanding economy
> had to come from monetary policy.

Sherman J. Maisel, *Managing the Dollar*, (New York: W. W. Norton & Co., 1973),
pp. 267–68.

pact of the oil shock on real output and employment. Consequently, the tight-money policy imposed in the summer of 1973 was quickly reversed in the fall. Business activity reached a peak in November 1973, but for three quarters the decline was moderate because of stimulative monetary policy and because firms built high levels of inventories despite a decline in demand. Inventories were accumulated in order to profit from inflation and to avoid shortages at product and retail levels.

Inflation accelerated further in the spring of 1974, business credit demands grew rapidly to finance inventories, and the dollar weakened in the foreign-exchange market. Once again, the Federal Reserve reversed; this time it tightened sharply, propelling some major short-term interest rates up by more than 200 basis points in the course of three months. The rate of economic decline accelerated sharply in the second half of 1974. By the time of the trough of the cycle (March 1975), the United States had experienced its worst contraction since the 1937–38 recession. Industrial production fell by more than 13.5 percent.

Of course, the severity of the recession in 1973–75 was only partly attributable to the unfortunate pattern of monetary policy. The shock of the oil price rise in 1973–74 was bound to have a strong negative impact on the economy. Nevertheless, the Federal Reserve's policy switches were hardly conducive to an orderly adjustment to this shock and clearly exacerbated strains in the financial sector. For the first time since the Great Depression, financial strains were severe enough to raise doubts about the solvency of many major banks; these contributed to the failure of the nation's 20th largest bank, the Franklin National Bank.

A strong recovery got underway in early 1975, aided by a substantial tax cut and a turn toward more expansionary monetary policy by the Fed. Inflation continued to wind down through most of 1976. Then, in 1977, the dollar weakened and price increases began to pick up again. The Federal Reserve responded by raising interest rates moderately in 1977 and through mid-1979, but, except for brief interludes, the growth rate of the money supply continued to rise at a faster rate than the Federal Reserve's target ceilings.

The 1975–79 recovery and return to double-digit inflation

Analysts debate the reasons for faster growth in the money supply in the 1975–79 period. The following, not mutually exclusive, reasons are most frequently cited. First, a technical procedure for reserve accounting known as *lagged-reserve accounting* forced the Fed automatically to accommodate increases in the demand for money, at least over two-week periods and possibly longer. With lagged-reserve accounting, which was adopted in September 1968, member banks' reserve requirements each week were based on deposits and certain other reservable liabilities which were outstanding two weeks prior to the current week. Before September

1968, reserve requirements were contemporaneous with reservable liabilities. An analysis of the issues involved with lagged-reserve accounting is provided in Chapter 14.

Second, the Federal Reserve maintained an accommodative posture in the late 1970s by establishing a narrow target range for the federal funds rate, usually for the duration of the periods between monthly meetings of the FOMC. This meant that when increases in the growth rate of the money supply occurred, it was often several weeks or more before any action was taken to encourage the federal funds rate to trade higher.

Third, when the Federal Reserve did raise interest rates, it did not move aggressively enough because of excessive concern for the risk of a recession. This concern was shared by the Federal Reserve and by the Carter administration which proceeded with tax cuts in 1977 and 1978 despite rising inflation.

The Federal Reserve may have hesitated to act aggressively also due to concern for declining membership in the Federal Reserve System. Banks were leaving the system due to the high opportunity cost of reserves to member banks. Most state nonmember banks could hold interest-bearing assets as part or all of their reserves, whereas member banks had to hold noninterest-bearing reserve deposits or currency. Each rise in market interest rates and reserve requirements caused more banks to leave the system.

In response to rising inflation and money growth in 1978, there was a sharp decline in the dollar in the foreign-exchange markets. Finally, in November 1978, to stabilize the dollar and to curb inflation, the Federal Reserve raised reserve requirements on member banks' certificate-of-deposit liabilities and increased the discount and federal funds rates sharply. The growth rate of the money supply slowed afterward.

Economic growth slowed in early 1979, but inflation accelerated because of past monetary expansion and because OPEC began to accelerate oil-price increases. Low money-supply growth persisted through March 1979. Then monetary expansion resumed at a high rate in the spring and summer, adding to inflationary expectations and rekindling selling pressure on the dollar. Although the Federal Reserve had not sought higher growth in the money supply, critics asserted that a pickup in monetary expansion was accommodated by the Federal Reserve's reserve-accounting and federal-funds-rate targeting procedures, noted earlier; and the Fed was reluctant to respond vigorously over the summer because the economy appeared to be in the early stages of a recession.

The October 1979 policy measures

Finally, in October 1979, pressure on the dollar once again forced the Federal Reserve to take the aggressive action it had avoided in the summer. The Fed announced another round of higher reserve requirements, sharply higher interest rates, and, of particular significance, a change in the Fed's approach to targeting the federal funds rate. It was decided to drop the use of a narrow target range for the federal funds rate, permit this important rate to vary more on a day-to-day and week-to-week basis, and focus more attention on the growth rate of various reserve aggregates, such as total bank reserves and the monetary base, in determining appropriate actions.

Money growth slowed for several months, but inflationary expectations continued to increase in response to four factors. First, oil-price increases imposed by OPEC accelerated. Second, Russia invaded Afghanistan, raising the threat of a world war. Third, President Carter presented budget proposals for wider federal deficits in 1980 and 1981 than previously expected. Fourth, the Federal Reserve's newly declared resolve to control the money supply via reserves began to be doubted.

The rate of growth of bank reserves accelerated in December and January without evoking any response by the Fed. The discount rate remained at 12 percent, the rate set in October, despite heavy borrowing at the discount window, and the federal funds rate stabilized at approximately 13.5 percent, little changed from the level in October. The effect of these events on expectations of inflation was dramatic. Within a span of six weeks, from early December to mid-January, the price of gold rose from $428 to $843 an ounce, and long-term government bond yields climbed 200 basis points between early December and mid-February.

As a result of higher inflation expectations, sharp oil-price increases, and previous monetary expansion, inflation in consumer prices accelerated from 13 percent in November to 16 percent in December and then to 18 percent in January and February. The reaction of policymakers over the next two months was significant. In mid-February, the Federal Reserve raised the discount rate to 13 percent and announced lower targets for the monetary aggregates. Over the next six weeks, the federal funds rate was permitted to soar 650 basis points to more than 20 percent. The Carter administration decided to revise its budget plans to provide for a budget surplus in 1981, and emergency legislation, the Credit Control Act of 1969, was invoked to give the Federal Reserve sweeping powers to curb the growth of consumer and business credit. Finally, Congress passed the Depository Institutions Deregulation and Monetary Control Act, which provided for phasing out federal interest-rate ceilings on deposits over a period of six years, suspended state-imposed usury ceilings on mortgage interest rates, and scheduled all depository institutions to meet Federal Reserve reserve requirements. The latter order provided for all depository institutions to reach specific, uniform required reserve ratios on checkable deposits and nonpersonal time deposits at the end of an eight-year transition period and effectively ended the erosion of membership in the Federal Reserve system.

Inflation and policy measures in early 1980

The effect of this combination of restrictive policies was predictable in direction, if not in degree. The money supply dropped sharply, and real GNP declined at an annual rate of almost 10 percent in the second quarter of 1980—a record for the post-World War II period. But, as severe as the decline in the economy was, it was also the briefest on record. True to its new approach to monetary control, the Fed permitted interest rates to plummet; the federal funds rate fell from 20 percent to 8.5 percent in the course of only 12 weeks. Also, the Federal Reserve moved quickly to dismantle the special credit controls imposed at the end of the first quarter. Money growth rebounded and the economy began a recovery in the second half of the year. Inflationary expectations also rebounded, however, and money growth became excessive, moving above the Fed's targets. As a result, the Federal Reserve moved aggressively to restrain money growth once again. Interest rates surged to new records, raising doubts about the prospects for continued recovery. As the year ended, the wisdom of the Federal Reserve's policies and new approach to monetary control were actively questioned by many analysts in view of the wild gyrations in interest rates and money growth during the year; but there was also considerable support for the Federal Reserve's apparent new commitment to adhere to its anti-inflation objective.

The details of the 1979–80 change in Federal Reserve policy and in legislation affecting depository institutions will be described and analyzed in the two chapters which follow. A principal conclusion of that analysis is already largely evident from this chapter: despite the contributions of monetary reforms over the years and the benefits future reforms may bring, the key to lower inflation and more stable policies in the future rests primarily with the decisions of policymakers and, ultimately, with the public. There must be a resolve to keep money growth from getting out of hand, even in the face of ever-present risks of recession. If such a policy is followed at earlier stages of business expansions, the chances are better that later difficulties with rising inflation and risks of greater recessions can be avoided.

CONCLUSION

This chapter has outlined the development of U.S. monetary institutions and policies from the colonial period through 1980. Much has been neglected in surveying such a vast period in one chapter. Yet many key lessons have been covered. They range from the advantages of a national, uniform currency to the danger of using interest rates as an indicator of the level of the degree of ease or tightness in monetary policy.

The section on experience since the creation of Federal Reserve included criticism of Fed policy in certain periods. Much of this criticism has been acknowledged as valid in the Federal Reserve's own staff studies and in the writings and speeches of Federal Reserve officials. The purpose of reviewing Fed policy critically is to identify the nature of past errors, not to pillory public officials. Postmortem examinations of past business cycles and policy measures are a necessary step toward improved performance in the future.

From the broader perspective of the monetary system as a whole, many of the reforms instituted in the past, including the creation of the Federal Reserve, have led to key improvements in the performance of the U.S. payments system and in the financial sector. Reforms currently in progress and under discussion will be described in subsequent chapters.

PROBLEMS

1. Explain why the United States was unsuccessful in establishing its own currency as the dominant form of base money prior to the mid-1830s.

2. Compare the current dollar price of gold to the dollar price of gold established by Congress in 1792, and calculate the decline in the value of the dollar implicit in these gold prices. Perform the same comparison for silver. What does this suggest the current de facto standard would be if the United States reverted to a bimetallic standard with the original mint ratio of 15:1 adopted in 1792?

3. Explain why the price level fell over the second half of the 19th century—a period of high average economic growth for the United States.

4. Discuss the accomplishments and deficiencies of the original Federal Reserve Act.

5. Review the results of interest-rate targeting by the Federal Reserve in the 1960s and 1970s.

ADVANCED READINGS

Angell, Norman. *The Story of Money*. New York: Frederick A. Stokes, 1929.

Friedman, Milton, and Schwartz, Anna J. *A Monetary History of the United States*. Princeton, N.J.: Princeton University Press, 1963.

Hammond, B. *Banks and Politics in America*. Princeton, N.J.: Princeton University Press, 1957.

Maisel, Sherman J. *Managing the Dollar*. New York: W.W. Norton & Co., 1973.

Mints, L.W. *A History of Banking Theory in Great Britain and the United States*. Chicago: University of Chicago Press, 1945.

Studenski, P., and Krooss, H.E. *Financial History of the United States*. New York: McGraw-Hill, 1952.

Temin, P. *Did Monetary Forces Cause the Great Depression?* New York: W.W. Norton & Co., 1976.

Government monetary agencies, regulations, and the structure of the current U.S. monetary system

Some of the regulatory structure of the current U.S. monetary system has been described in previous chapters. This chapter pulls together and expands upon this earlier information to provide a more comprehensive picture of the framework of government agencies and regulations affecting the system. Much of this material is necessary background for the chapter which follows on the money-supply process and the implementation of monetary policy in the current system.

The first several sections of this chapter describe the organization and powers of the Federal Reserve, the monetary functions of the Treasury, and the operations of the Federal Deposit Insurance Corporation. Two sections follow on other federal agencies and on state regulations. The last section outlines the distribution of control of private financial institutions.

THE FEDERAL RESERVE

As the nation's central bank, the Federal Reserve is the key monetary authority in the economy. Powers granted in the original Federal Reserve Act of 1913 and expanded in subsequent legislation,

13

328

give the Fed control over most of the currency and reserves of depository institutions and enable it to influence directly or indirectly the vast majority of these institutions through Fed regulatory decisions.

The Federal Reserve is comprised of a central headquarters unit, several policymaking and advisory committees, and 12 regional banks. The Board of Governors of the Federal Reserve, located in Washington D.C., is the headquarters unit. Seven governors of the board participate in policy and regulatory decisions, and they oversee research and statistical operations at the headquarters facility.[1]

The Board of Governors

Each governor of the board is appointed by the President and confirmed by the Senate for a 14-year term. The same appointment-approval process applies to the designation of one governor as Chairman of the Board for a period of four years.[2]

Among its normal specific duties, the board:

1. Supplies the majority membership (seven twelfths) of the important Federal Open Market Committee, explained below, and hosts the location for Federal Open Market Committee meetings.
2. Sets reserve requirements (within limits specified by Congress) for the checkable deposits of all depository institutions and for certain other liabilities of banks.
3. Approves applications for discount-rate changes from the Federal Reserve's 12 regional banks and regulates the administration of reserve banks' discount windows.
4. Sets ceilings under its Regulation Q power for interest rates member banks can pay on time deposits.
5. Establishes margin requirements for stock purchases.
6. Supervises member banks and bank holding companies by reviewing mergers, acquisitions, lending activities, capital ratios, and other aspects of these firms' practices.

In addition, from time to time the board has been granted special credit control powers. The latest instance of the granting of special powers occurred in March 1980, when President Carter invoked the Credit Control Act of 1969 to provide the Fed with the power to impose temporary reserve requirements on consumer credit, money-market mutual funds, and the managed liabilities of nonmember banks.

---

[1]Many of the studies and data produced by the board staff are made available to the public in the monthly Federal Reserve *Bulletin*, in the quarterly Federal Reserve *Flow of Funds*, and in various special reports and releases.

[2]The four-year term for the Chairman of the Board expires midway through the four-year term of the nation's President. From time to time there have been proposals to shift the Fed Chairman's term of office so that it coincides with that of the President. The arguments for and against this proposal will be considered in Chapter 20.

The Chairman of
the Board of
Governors

In conformance with requirements of the 1978 Full Employment and Balanced Growth Act (known as the Humphrey–Hawkins Act), the Chairman of the Federal Reserve Board reports to Congress twice a year on the performance and objectives of monetary policy. As the Federal Reserve's chief spokesman and representative in policy consultations with other government agencies, the administration, Congress, and foreign central banks, the Chairman of the Board of Governors is the most important government official in the monetary area. Normally, Federal Reserve actions are strongly influenced by the opinions and leadership of the Chairman of the Federal Reserve Board.

The Federal
Open Market
Committee

The Federal Open Market Committee (FOMC) is the principal policy-making unit of the Federal Reserve. Its nominal purpose is to establish guidelines and authorizations only for open-market operations (purchases and sales of securities) and for foreign-exchange operations undertaken by the Federal Reserve Bank of New York.[3] However, because of the primacy of open-market operations as a policy tool and because of the need for coordination between open-market operations and the Federal Reserve's other principal monetary tools—changes in the discount rate and in reserve requirements—the FOMC is really the unit that decides on the overall thrust of monetary policy.

The FOMC is comprised of the seven governors of the Board of Governors, the President of the Federal Reserve Bank of New York, and, on a rotating basis, four presidents from the other 11 Federal Reserve banks. The Chairman of the Board of Governors is automatically Chairman of the FOMC. The president of the New York Fed is a permanent member and traditionally is elected the Vice Chairman of the FOMC because of the New York Fed's role as the bank which implements open-market operations.

Regular meetings of the FOMC are held each month. (Occasionally the February and July meetings are not held due to the Federal Reserve's semiannual reports to Congress in those months.) At each FOMC meeting, there is a review of recent developments in the economy and of the economic outlook based on forecasts prepared by board staff economists. The key areas which draw attention are inflation, unemployment, growth in real output, the stability of the financial markets, the exchange rate of the dollar, and, not least, the growth rates of the monetary and credit aggregates.

Following this review, policy options are discussed and a course of action is framed, including a *directive* to the *Manager of the System Open Market Account.* The manager of the system account is the officer of the New York Fed in charge of open-market opera-

---

[3]The Federal Reserve Bank of New York conducts open-market operations on behalf of the entire system. The centralization of such operations at the New York Fed developed as a result of the location of the nation's largest financial markets in New York City.

tions. The directive sets guidelines for day-to-day purchases and sales in securities markets. Votes for and against the directive are published along with a record of policy actions after the next regular meeting of the committee.[4]

In addition to participating in policy formation via the FOMC, the officers and staff of the Federal Reserve banks manage the Fed's provision of banking services for banks and for the federal government in each respective regional district. (A map of the 12 districts is shown in Figure 13–1.) Reserve bank officers also participate in the Federal Reserve's regulatory decisions.

The Federal Reserve banks

FIGURE 13–1
The Federal Reserve system: Boundaries of Federal Reserve districts and their branch territories

SOURCE: Federal Reserve *Bulletin,* March 1978.

---

[4]The record of policy actions for the FOMC meeting held in October 1979 is printed in an appendix to the next chapter. Published records appear in the Federal Reserve *Bulletin.*

Specific banking services provided by the Federal Reserve banks include:

1. The extension of loans to depository institutions via each Federal Reserve bank's discount window.
2. The transportation and clearing of checks among commercial banks in different Federal Reserve districts.
3. The processing of transfers of funds (federal funds) among depository institutions via a Federal Reserve wire system, resulting in same-day credits and debits to the demand-deposit accounts (reserve accounts) of depository institutions at Federal Reserve banks.
4. The issuance of Federal Reserve notes and Treasury coin to depository institutions on request and in exchange for reserve deposit funds.
5. The extension of credit to the Treasury and off-budget federal agencies by participation in Federal Reserve purchases of their debt.
6. The performance of fiscal and banking services for the Treasury, including retail sales of new debt issues, placement of short-term surplus funds, provision of checking-account services, and agent services for foreign-exchange operations.

The Federal Reserve banks are incorporated. Each has nine directors: three are chosen by member banks from the banking community in the bank's district, three are chosen by member banks from the nonbank business community, and three, including a chairman, are chosen by the Board of Governors. The president of each reserve bank is chosen by that bank's directors, with the approval of the Board of Governors. Each reserve bank has its own staff of economists, statisticians, and bank examiners.[5]

The foregoing constitutes the operating units of the Federal Reserve. There are also several Federal Reserve advisory committees, including the Federal Advisory Council which was created by the Federal Reserve Act. The council is comprised of 12 private individuals, one from each of the Federal Reserve districts, who meet periodically and provide the Fed with outside commentary on matters related to Federal Reserve concerns.

The Fed's tools for controlling the money supply

To summarize the Fed's tools for controlling the money supply, *open-market operations* are used by the Fed to expand and contract the quantity of reserves in the monetary system. Open-market purchases of Treasury bills or other instruments expand reserves and, thereby, facilitate an expansion of the money stock. Open-market

---

[5]Studies and statistics prepared by the staffs of the reserve banks appear in reserve bank publications which are available free of charge. The Federal Reserve Bank of Philadelphia provides a free bibliography of all these studies and studies appearing in the Federal Reserve *Bulletin*. The bibliography, which is called *The Fed in Print*, is updated quarterly.

sales from the Fed's portfolio of securities contract the supply of reserves and curb money growth.

Changes in the *discount rate* also influence the quantity of reserves in the system. A rise in the discount rate discourages borrowings from the Fed and thus reduces reserves. A reduction in the discount rate encourages discount-window borrowings and hence an increase in reserves and the money supply.

Adjustments in *reserve requirements* are the third major device at the Fed's disposal for controlling money. A rise in reserve requirements locks up funds in the system, thereby tending to reduce the money supply. A reduction in reserve requirements frees up funds for lending and deposit expansion.

Detail on how these tools affect the money supply in the present system is provided in the next chapter.

THE TREASURY

The U.S. Treasury has three monetary functions: (1) debt management, (2) exchange-rate policy, and (3) Treasury currency operations.

The Treasury determines the maturities of the total outstanding debt of the government, and the Treasury and Federal Reserve jointly determine the maturities of the Treasury debt held by the public. If the Treasury issues exclusively short-term, liquid debt to finance a current deficit or to refinance maturing long-term debt, the average maturity of Treasury debt held by the public will tend to shorten, and liquidity will tend to rise. The Federal Reserve can effect the same change by simultaneously purchasing long-term Treasury bonds and selling short-term government debt from its portfolio. Decisions relating to the maturity of Treasury debt held by the public are known as *debt management*. Treasury debt management is usually set so as to establish a desired refinancing schedule for the government. It has also been directed toward minimizing the expected interest costs of the government's debt, and, from time to time, the Fed and the government have attempted to use it to influence the total supply of liquid assets in the economy and the term structure of interest rates, thereby providing an occasional, supplementary tool of monetary policy.[6]

Debt management

The second area of the Treasury's monetary functions involves government intervention in the foreign-exchange market. Actual

[6]The best known instance of an attempt to influence interest rates via debt management occurred in 1961. The objective of "operation twist," as the plan was called, was to raise short-term interest rates and lower long-term interest rates by shortening the maturity structure of outstanding Treasury debt held by the public. Operation twist was not implemented effectively, however, due to inconsistent operations by the Treasury and the Federal Reserve. See Franco Modigliani and Richard Sutch, "Innovations in Interest Rate Policy." "*American Economic Review*, May 1966, pp. 178–97.

Exchange-Rate policy

intervention operations are carried out by the Federal Reserve, but normally intervention activity is done only after consultation with the Treasury. To support the dollar, the Treasury can authorize the Fed to draw upon its own holdings of foreign exchange, foreign exchange borrowed from foreign central banks under "swap" arrangements, and foreign exchange provided by the Exchange Stabilization Fund of the U.S. Treasury.[7]

The Federal Reserve's own holdings of foreign exchange usually are small (on the order of $1.5 billion) in proportion to the volume of intervention which has occurred during certain periods. In contrast, the Treasury has considerable reserves of gold, foreign exchange, and special drawing rights (SDRs) issued by the International Monetary Fund. Consequently, the Treasury often assumes a dominant role in intervention decisions. The Secretary of the Treasury and the Under Secretary for Monetary Affairs of the Treasury are the key officials setting Treasury policy in this area.

The third monetary function of the Treasury involves U.S. currency. The U.S. Treasury operates the Bureau of the Mint, which

Treasury currency operations

produces U.S. coinage, and the Bureau of Engraving and Printing, which prints U.S. paper currency—now almost exclusively Federal Reserve notes. Coins and a small amount of paper currency are carried as liabilities on the accounts of the U.S. Treasury. They provide a direct source of funds to the Treasury as they are distributed to the public via the Federal Reserve and private depository institutions. (Federal Reserve notes are treated as a liability of the Federal Reserve and provide funding to the Treasury indirectly.)

Once the dominant type of currency, most Treasury paper currency has now been retired from circulation, and coins issued exclusively by the Treasury constitute only 10 percent or so of U.S. currency outstanding. Hence the contribution of Treasury liabilities to the money supply is very small. And, as brought out in the next chapter, even this element is supplied passively. Therefore, the Treasury has no significant influence on the money supply as a result of its currency operations.

THE FEDERAL DEPOSIT INSURANCE CORPORATION

The Federal Deposit Insurance Corporation (FDIC) was formed in the 1930's. It has the following specific functions:

---

[7]A swap borrowing by the Federal Reserve involves a simultaneous spot purchase and forward sale of foreign exchange—both usually arranged with a foreign central bank. (See Chapter 8 for a description of forward sales and purchases of foreign exchange.) The Federal Reserve has the use of the purchased foreign exchange for intervention or for reserves until the forward contract matures, usually three months or so later. The Exchange Stabilization Fund also has used swap borrowings to obtain intervention funds.

1. Management of fees and disbursements for federal insurance for bank deposits.
2. Management of failed, insured banks.
3. Examinations of insured banks (with occasional issuance of an order for changes in a bank's practices).
4. Regulation of ceilings for interest rates insured banks can pay on time deposits.

As of April 1980, federal deposit insurance covered the deposit funds of the accounts of individuals and businesses up to an amount of $100,000 total per depositor entity per insured bank. Both commercial banks and mutual savings banks may apply for FDIC insurance. The $100,000 ceiling for ordinary accounts is not a concern for most households, but it can be for firms. Where more coverage is desired it can be obtained by splitting deposits funds among several insured banks or registering accounts in the names of different family members or firm subsidiaries.

Coverage of FDIC insurance

Actually, effective protection from FDIC insurance is normally greater than the $100,000 ceiling implies for two reasons; first, FDIC bank examiners monitor insured banks and usually order corrective actions at "problem" banks before these banks reach a critical stage, thereby protecting all deposits; second, when an insured bank fails, the FDIC takes complete charge of the bank's affairs, often working out an arrangement for assumption of all the failed bank's deposits by other banks. As a result, few depositors have lost funds because of ceilings on insurance coverage.

"'You approved my loan? No wonder you're on the list of potential trouble banks!'"

Reprinted by permission *The Wall Street Journal.*

Between 1934, when the FDIC began operations, and 1978 there were 548 cases of failures of insured banks requiring disbursements of FDIC funds. The total deposits of those banks came to $7.35 billion. Of that amount, better than 99 percent was returned to depositors. Losses absorbed by the FDIC over the same period came to $349.5 million.[8]

FDIC fees and reserves

The FDIC is financed by assessments levied on insured banks and by interest earnings on its accumulated reserves. The effective net assessment rate in recent years has been about .038 percent per year on each bank's assessable deposits, or $380 per year per $1 million of deposits. The FDIC's reserves came to $8.8 billion in 1978, equal to roughly 1.2 percent of insured deposits. An additional $3 billion in funds can be borrowed from the U.S. Treasury, if needed, and the Federal Reserve has the power to lend to the FDIC or directly to any private intermediary in an "emergency."

FDIC administration

The FDIC is administered by a board of directors comprised of two regular directors appointed by the President to six-year terms and one ex officio director, the Comptroller of the Currency. (The Office of the Comptroller of the Currency is explained in the next section below.) Normally, one of the regular directors serves as Chairman of the FDIC. The headquarters of the FDIC is located in Washington, D.C., and regional offices are located throughout the U.S.

OTHER FEDERAL GOVERNMENT AGENCIES AND REGULATIONS

The Office of the Comptroller of the Currency

The Office of the Comptroller of the Currency was originally established during the Civil War to monitor the issuance of national bank notes and to administer regulations and approve charter applications for national banks. Virtually all national bank notes have been retired from circulation, but the Comptroller still supervises national banks. Also, as mentioned above, the Comptroller is an ex officio director of the FDIC. The President appoints the Comptroller to a five-year term, with the Senate's approval.

The Federal Home Loan Board and Bank System

The Federal Home Loan Board and Bank system is a regulatory and reserve-bank system for savings and loans and mutual savings banks. It was created by New Deal legislation during the Great Depression to parallel the functions of the Comptroller's office, the Federal Reserve, and the FDIC. The Federal Home Loan Bank Board charters and regulates federal savings and loan associations; it supervises the Federal Home Loan Bank system; and it manages

---

[8]As these figures testify, up to 1978 the FDIC has bore all but a tiny amount of the losses on deposits of insured banks. The Federal Savings and Loan Insurance Corporation (FSLIC) compiled a similar record—until 1981, when high interest rates bankrupted an unusually large number of insured savings and loans.

the Federal Savings and Loan Insurance Corporation and the Federal Home Loan Mortgage Corporation.[9] Regulatory functions include the imposition of interest-rate ceilings on deposit-type accounts, restrictions on the types of accounts institutions which are members of the Home Loan Bank system may offer, and the establishment of minimum liquidity (reserve) ratios for member institutions. The board consists of three members appointed to four-year terms by the President with Senate approval.

There are 12 regional Federal Home Loan banks with districts similar to those of the Federal Reserve banks. Their principal purpose is to advance loans to member institutions, especially during high interest-rate periods when thrifts tend to lose deposits due to interest-rate ceilings. Home Loan banks also have supervisory functions.

The National Credit Union Administration is another federal agency created by the New Deal in the 1930s to parallel the functions of the agencies already described. It charters and regulates federal credit unions, extends funds to members, and administers the National Credit Union Share Insurance Fund.

The National
Credit Union
Administration

STATE REGULATIONS AND AGENCIES

All of the foregoing sections described regulations and official agencies at the federal level. There are also important state regulations and agencies in the monetary and credit areas. The key state regulations fall into four categories: (1) regulations limiting the markets of federal- and state-chartered depository institutions, (2) regulations restricting interest rates depository institutions may charge on certain loans (usury laws), (3) supervisory controls administered by state agencies, and (4) reserve requirements imposed on some state-chartered institutions.

With regard to the first type of regulations, those limiting institutions' markets, most states have statutes prohibiting or restricting the number and/or location of branches depository institutions may establish.[10] One purpose of such restraints is to prevent the growth of excessively large and monopolistic institutions. Another objective is to encourage the use of local savings for local investment.

Restraints on
markets

Many economists question the effectiveness of branch limitations as a device for encouraging competition among intermediaries. It can be argued that this practice actually enhances monopoly power

---

[9]The Federal Savings and Loan Insurance Corporation performs functions similar to those of the FDIC. The Federal Home Loan Mortgage Corporation uses Federal borrowing power and subsidies to channel funds into mortgages, as Federal Home Loan Banks do also.

[10]States actually have power over only state-chartered institutions, but, as a matter of practice, federal authorities usually hold federally chartered institutions to these state regulations.

by eliminating the competition branching might bring to markets too small to support several independent financial firms. Generally, economists also support the broadest feasible integration of financial markets in order to provide the most efficient distribution of savings and investment in the economy. As a result, many states have liberalized their restraints on intrastate branching in recent years, and there have been tentative steps at both the federal and state level toward permitting branching across state lines. Eventually the United States may have nationwide branching for financial intermediaries.[11]

Usury laws

Usury laws were described in Chapter 7 in connection with the factors affecting the spreads between specific interest rates. Prior to late 1979, state-imposed interest-rate ceilings on mortgage loans were binding on state-chartered institutions and were honored usually by federal authorities in their regulation of federally chartered intermediaries.[12] Usury ceilings for mortgages and other loans are usually intended to protect unsophisticated borrowers from exorbitant interest charges; but when interest rates rose generally in the 1970s due to inflation, ceilings tended to curb the availability of credit to all borrowers. As mentioned in Chapter 7, in December 1979, following a sharp increase in interest rates, Congress acted to suspend all state usury ceilings on mortgage loans to free up the availability of funds for the housing sector, but some states have overridden that suspension by passing new legislation.

Supervisory controls

State-chartered depository institutions usually are subject to state supervisory regulations, including examinations, capital requirements, and limitations on lending and investment activities. If the liabilities of a state-chartered institution are insured by a federal agency such as the Federal Deposit Insurance Corporation—and in most cases they are—the institution will be subject to federal supervisory controls as well. State and federal agencies coordinate their supervisory activities for these institutions.

Reserve requirements

Until 1980, depository institutions which were not members of the Federal Reserve system, The Home Loan Bank system, or the National Credit Union system were subject to state-imposed reserve requirements; institutions in Illinois were an exception in that no reserves were required by the State of Illinois. Requirements have varied considerably among states in terms of both required reserve ratios and the assets which qualify as reserves. Vermont has

---

[11]Concern that large institutions exercise monopoly power and concern that broad branching leads to undesirable geographical redistribution of savings have been stronger and more traditional in the United States than in other countries. Consequently, the U.S. system of restricted markets for financial intermediaries is unusual. The systems of most other countries are characterized by proportionately fewer and larger financial intermediaries with nationwide branches.

[12]However, national banks were permitted to put their lending rate on mortgages one percentage point above the Federal Reserve's discount rate regardless of state usury ceilings.

had the highest required reserve ratio for banks at 27 percent for demand deposits. In comparison, the Federal Reserve's highest required reserve ratio for member banks at the end of 1979 was 16.25 percent for demand deposits.[13]

Most states' reserve requirements could be satisfied in some degree by holdings of interest-bearing U.S. government securities. Member banks, however, have had to hold their reserves entirely in the form of assets which do not bear interest—demand deposits with their Federal Reserve bank and vault cash. As a result, nonmember state banks generally had and still have less of a drain on their profits from reserve requirements than member banks. This was a key factor contributing to the Federal Reserve's "membership problem," which is discussed at the end of the next section.

THE EFFECTIVE INCIDENCE OF GOVERNMENT REGULATORY CONTROLS IN KEY AREAS RELATED TO MONEY AND CREDIT

The preceding sections have provided the details of government controls affecting the monetary system, while omitting the perspective of the relative incidence of these controls. Now that the foregoing institutional details have been covered on an agency-by-agency basis, we can reorganize some of this information to describe the effective domains of the various agencies and regulations in three areas: (1) supervision of depository institutions, (2) selective credit controls such as Regulation Q ceilings, and (3) reserve requirements on checkable deposits and other sources of funds to depository institutions.

It is evident from the description of the supervisory powers of federal and state regulatory authorities in this chapter, that considerable overlaps exist. In terms of the de facto divisions of principal responsibility for segments of the banking system and of banks' assets, the breakdowns as of mid-1978 were as follows.

Supervision

The Office of the Comptroller of the Currency supervised 30.4 percent of the total number of banks (national banks as a share of total commercial and mutual savings banks), and these banks accounted for 49 percent, the largest share, of total bank assets.

The FDIC supervised the largest share of total banks, 59.9 percent; but these banks held the second largest proportion of total bank assets, 30.9 percent, since the FDIC has principal responsibility for insured, state-chartered nonmember banks which tend to be smaller than national banks.

The Federal Reserve had principal responsibility for the supervision of 6.6 percent of all banks; these were state-chartered member banks which accounted for 15.7 percent of bank assets.

---

[13]This ratio applied to banks' aggregate demand deposits in excess of $400 million. The complete schedule of Federal Reserve requirement ratios is provided in Chapter 14.

Finally, state authorities were sole supervisors of state-chartered, noninsured banks which comprised 3.1 percent of total banks and held 4.4 percent of total bank assets.

The breakdowns for supervision of other depository institutions are less complex.

As of September 1979, 42.3 percent of all savings and loans, holding 56.4 percent of total savings and loan assets, were federally chartered. Another 43.4 percent, holding 41.6 percent of total assets, were state-chartered, federally insured savings and loans, making a total 85.7 percent of all savings and loan institutions and 98 percent of the industry's assets under the direct or indirect supervision of the Federal Home Loan Bank Board. The remaining proportion fell under the sole supervision of state authorities.

At the end of the year 1979, 48.2 percent of all credit unions were federally chartered and 16.5 percent were federally insured and state chartered, giving the National Credit Union Administration supervisory power over 64.7 percent of all credit unions. State agencies had sole responsibility for the rest. Credit union assets were distributed in like proportions.

As these data attest, the great majority of depository institutions and of these institutions' assets are subject to the supervision of federal authorities. There has been concern in Congress and among private economists, however, that federal supervision is too fractured and that the existing overlaps of authority lead to excessive bureaucracy, red tape, and potential conflicts or lapses in supervisory functions.

The present system is defended by those who feel that the existing level of diversity and redundancy is manageable and actually healthy because it keeps the regulators on their toes. Agencies are more alert because they know that their actions will be reviewed by other agencies.

Partly because of this latter argument, and partly because, for all its costs, the present system appears to work, reform legislation in the area of supervision has had less momentum in recent years than legislation affecting other aspects of the financial system.[14]

Selective credit controls

Under various federal laws and regulations, such as the Federal Reserve's Regulation Q, interest-rate ceilings may be imposed on all deposits at federally supervised banks, savings and loans, and credit unions. Additionally, under the Credit Controls Act of 1969, the President can give the Federal Reserve power to establish controls

[14]Criticism did spur the establishment of an Interagency Supervisory Committee in 1977, however. This committee, which includes all of the federal supervisory agencies for banks, savings and loans, and credit unions, sets uniform guidelines for the evaluation of the soundness of depository institutions and works toward reducing duplication in the activities of the federal agencies. Beginning in 1980, this committee has been supplemented by the Depository Institutions Deregulation Committee, which oversees implementation of the deregulation provisions of the Depository Institutions Deregulation and Monetary Control Act of 1980.

such as special reserve requirements, minimum down payments, maximum maturities, and interest-rate ceilings on a broad spectrum of credit transactions.

As described in Chapter 7, interest-rate ceilings on deposits can result in substantial disintermediation of funds from depository institutions during periods of high interest rates. In the 1950s and 1960s, interest-rate ceilings on deposits were viewed as a valuable adjunct tool of monetary policy, and they were purposely maintained at levels which tended to curb deposits and credit supplied by depository institutions at later stages of business expansions. However, in the 1970s financial innovations made interest-rate ceilings less effective as a restraint on the total supply of credit, and public policy-makers and private economists began to question their merit on grounds both of usefulness and of equity. As a result, in 1978, federal supervisory agencies approved new deposit instruments with high, flexible ceilings, and in 1980, Congress passed legislation providing for interest-rate ceilings on deposits to be phased out over a period of six years.

Despite fundamental support for a relaxation of interest-rate ceilings and other selective credit controls in recent years, sentiment for their use persists among some economists, and, as shown by the imposition of special controls in 1980, there is always a possibility of an "emergency" use of controls, particularly in an inflationary period. Hence federal interest-rate ceilings and other selective credit controls are less important today than they were in the past, but they are always a potential adjunct tool of monetary policy.

As was described briefly in earlier chapters and as will be explained in more detail in the next chapter, reserve requirements levied by the Federal Reserve are a key part of the mechanism by which the Fed presently controls the supply of money and credit in the economy. As a result, the proportion of the deposits in the monetary system subject to Federal Reserve reserve requirements carries implications for the degree of the Federal Reserve's control of money and credit. For a number of years prior to recent legislation, the proportion of banks in the Federal Reserve system was declining due to the costs of belonging to the system, and this trend had been a cause of concern to the Federal Reserve and to Congress. At the end of 1979, membership had declined to 36.8 percent of all banking institutions versus 42.1 percent in 1970. Deposits of member banks were a majority proportion of total deposits of banking institutions, 69.1 percent in 1979, but this share was down from 80 percent in 1970.

Costs associated with membership related partly to the extensive data reporting requirements imposed on member banks and to capital contributions member banks are required to make to the Federal Reserve banks. But the largest cost for most member banks was the

Reserve requirements and the membership problem

opportunity cost associated with reserve requirements imposed by the Federal Reserve.

Declining membership in the Federal Reserve system was a problem in two senses. As already suggested, *past* losses of members weakened the degree of control the Federal Reserve could exert over the supply of money and credit. In addition, the fear of *future* losses of members probably restrained the degree of control the Federal Reserve was *willing* to exercise when there were inflationary situations requiring aggressive tightening actions. Tightening actions tended to raise the costs of membership.

The membership problem has probably been largely remedied with the passage of the Depository Institutions Deregulation and Monetary Control Act of 1980. Among other provisions, including the phased deregulation of federal deposit interest-rate ceilings, this act gradually imposes Federal Reserve reserve requirements on checkable deposits held by almost all nonmember depository institutions. It also stipulates that all banks which left the system after June 30, 1979 must hold the same reserves as required for member banks. As a result of this act, the decline of membership in the system almost certainly has been stopped and may tend to reverse in the years ahead. Even if membership in the Federal Reserve system were to continue to decline, however, there should be no loss of control of checkable deposits, since the checkable deposits of all depository institutions will remain subject to Federal Reserve reserve requirements under the 1980 legislation.

CONCLUSION

This chapter has provided a description of the key regulatory features of the current U.S. monetary system. Our next chapter draws on much of this material in developing an analysis of the money-supply process.

PROBLEMS

1. Identify the composition and function of the Federal Open Market Committee.
2. Explain the advantages and disadvantages of consolidating the various regulatory agencies for the depository institutions into a single agency.
3. Would liberalization of restrictions on interstate and intrastate activities of depository institutions tend to enhance or retard competition among financial institutions? Explain.

ADVANCED READINGS

"An Analysis of Federal Reserve System Attrition Since 1960." Federal Reserve *Bulletin*, January 1978. 12-13.

Annual Report of the National Credit Union Administration. Washington, D.C.: National Credit Union Administration, 1977.

Annual Report of Operations of the Federal Deposit Insurance Corporation. Washington, D.C.: Federal Deposit Insurance Corporation, 1978.

The Federal Reserve System: Purposes and Functions. Washington, D.C.: Board of Governors of the Federal Reserve System, 1974.

"The McFadden Act: Is Change in the Making?" Federal Reserve Bank of Philadelphia *Business Review*, July 1979 3-7.

"1978 Annual Report." *Federal Home Loan Bank Board Journal*, April 1979.

"Usury Ceilings: Shield or Scourge?" *Economic Review*, Federal Reserve Bank of Atlanta, September 1979 111-15.

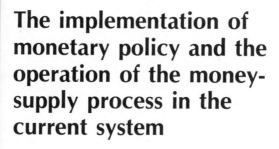

The implementation of monetary policy and the operation of the money-supply process in the current system

Several earlier chapters have provided summary descriptions of the operation of monetary policy and of the money-supply process in the current system. (See Chapters 11 and 12.) The first section of this chapter gives a general description of the use of *indicators* and *targets* by the Federal Reserve and identifies two classes of these policy variables, including the *M-1B money supply* and the *monetary base*.

The monetary base and a slightly modified form of the monetary base, the *adjusted monetary base*, are explained in terms of sources and uses in separate sections which follow. Then the *money-stock multiplier* for the current system is developed. Finally, in the last section, there is a discussion of two different points of view regarding the Federal Reserve's practice of *lagged-reserve accounting* as it affects the basic control mechanism for the money supply.

344

FEDERAL RESERVE POLICY VARIABLES

Class I policy variables:

As already described at various points in this book, the Federal Reserve monitors various measures of money and credit and a number of interest rates. Some of these variables are considered to be key *leading indicators of the thrust of monetary policy, controllable by the Federal Reserve, and proximate influences on spending decisions.* These constitute what we will call class I policy variables for the Federal Reserve. The second class of policy variables is identified later below.

Policy variables proximate to spending decisions

The class I variable which has absorbed our attention in Part 3 is the narrowly defined money supply—measured by M-1A or M-1B in the present system (or perhaps by the time this book reaches you, just plain M-1 again). We noted in Chapter 2, however, that economists are not unanimous in their preferences for a narrow definition of the money supply. Many believe that, whether less important than the M-1 measures or not, some of the broader monetary aggregates are of considerable interest in their own right as measures of liquidity which are, in varying degrees, subject to Federal Reserve control. (The role of liquid assets and liquidity in the economy was explained in Chapter 7.) As a result, along with M-1A and M-1B, several broader measures of money are followed by policymakers and private economists as key indicators of monetary policy.

There are also schools of thought (one was outlined in Chapter 7) which ascribe primary importance to the supply and cost of credit as key variables affecting spending decisions. Consequently, in gauging the thrust of its policy, the Federal Reserve has also monitored credit aggregates and interest rates subject, in some degree, to its control.

The same factors which make the variables described above of interest as policy *indicators* also make them candidates as *targets* in Federal Reserve planning for its actions. If these variables are in fact proximate, leading influences on spending decisions and controllable by policy actions, it would seem that the best approach for the Federal Reserve to follow in trying to achieve its inflation and unemployment objectives would be to establish in advance explicit targets for these policy indicators. Such an approach evolved in the early 1970s for short-run objectives, and in 1975, as requested in a congressional joint resolution, the Federal Reserve began establishing and announcing long-run (year ahead) targets for several measures of the money supply.

Indicators as targets

Class II policy variables

Though policy indicators and targets proximate to spending decisions are chosen partly because they are susceptable to Federal Reserve influence, it is recognized by the Fed that none is completely controlled by Federal Reserve actions, and there are lags before such actions take effect on most of the class I policy variables. To gauge the effects of its actions and set objectives at an earlier stage of the process, the Fed relies upon a number of *intermediate indicators and targets,* including the federal funds rate and several measures of bank reserves. These comprise our class II policy variables. *Useful indicators and targets at the intermediate level provide a stable reading of the relationship between specific Federal Reserve actions and the money supply or other policy variables proximate to spending decisions.*

To summarize, in setting its plans, the Federal Reserve monitors and sets targets for two classes of policy variables: those which are proximate to spending decisions and those which are more intermediate in the transmission process of Federal Reserve influence. The next section describes the major variables included in the first class.

POLICY VARIABLES PROXIMATE TO SPENDING DECISIONS

The M-1 money supply measures

The policy variables most closely followed by the majority of economists and policymakers are the M-1 money-supply measures. Interest in these variables is based partly upon theoretical analysis such as that described in Chapter 3 and partly upon empirical analysis showing a close correlation between growth of narrow definitions of money and subsequent spending and inflation. The relationship between the narrowly defined money supply and inflation has been described for various inflationary episodes in earlier chapters, and it is illustrated again in the graph in Figure 14–1.

Recall that the M-1A money supply is defined as currency plus commercial-bank demand deposits held by the nonbank public, and the M-1B money supply adds other checkable deposits and travelers checks to M-1A. Estimates for these aggregates are reported by the Federal Reserve on a weekly basis with a one-week lag.

It should be noted that errors in weekly estimates for the M-1 aggregates can be substantial; in fact, following-week revisions in the M-1 data occasionally are larger than the changes first reported. Even so, the Federal Reserve and participants in the financial markets often react sensitively to weekly data which appear to signal a change in the trend of the M-1 data. A speed-up in the rate of growth of M-1B could mean that the Federal Reserve will have to rein-in bank reserves to keep this M-1 aggregate within its target range. Such a tightening normally would imply higher interest rates for a period of time. Anticipating future tightening actions by the Fed, market participants often push interest rates higher immediately following the announcement of a large, unexpected increase in the money supply. Correspondingly, news of an unexpectedly small

FIGURE 14–1
Money and price changes in the long run

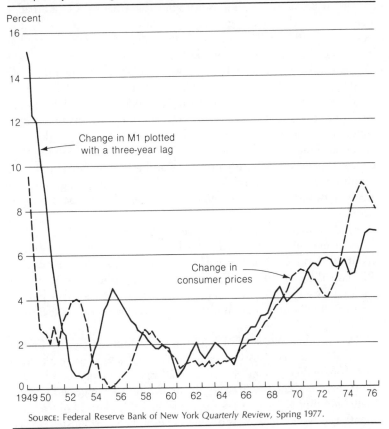

Percent

SOURCE: Federal Reserve Bank of New York *Quarterly Review*, Spring 1977.

increase or large decline in an M-1 aggregate can cause interest rates to fall. Therefore, *when a central bank is following a money-supply target in planning its reserve actions, sensitive market interest rates tend to rise in response to faster money-supply growth and fall in response to slower money-supply growth.*[1]

---

[1]This positive relationship between money growth and interest rates seems contradictory to our analysis in Chapter 3 which posited an inverse relationship between changes in the money supply and interest rates. Recall, however, that the Chapter 3 relationship held in a ceteris-paribus context. The apparent contradiction between the relationship above and the Chapter 3 relationship can be explained by the fact that, when the central bank is setting policy in terms of a money-supply target, the Chapter 3 ceteris-paribus assumption is invalid. With a target-oriented policy, higher money-supply growth in the present implies lower money-supply growth in the future—if the Fed is to achieve its target. *Early* Federal Reserve restraining actions and *expectations* of future Federal Reserve restraining actions can move sensitive interest rates *before* money-supply growth slows.

Another reason market interest rates may respond not inversely, but positively, to changes in the trend of money-supply growth is that inflationary expectations may be very sensitive to money-supply growth—another invalidation of the ceteris-paribus assumption in Chapter 3. In the last 10 years or so the financial markets have become highly sensitive to the inflationary implications of rapid growth in the money supply so that this latter relationship has become a common one.

Broad money aggregates and credit

The M-2 money
supply

The M-2 money supply was introduced in Chapter 2 as a broader concept than the M-1 aggregates. As shown in Figure 14–2, it is comprised of the M-1B assets plus savings deposits, small-denomination time deposits, money-market mutual fund shares, overnight RPs issued by commercial banks, and overnight Eurodollar deposits held by U.S. nonbank entities at Caribbean branches of U.S. banks.

The liquidity characteristics of the assets added to M-1B to get M-2 were described in Chapter 7. These assets are considered by a number of economists to be virtually the same as checkable deposits in terms of their liquidity and, therefore, also in terms of their influence on spending. Monthly estimates of the M-2 money supply are published by the Federal Reserve with a one-month lag, and the Federal Reserve establishes long-run targets for the M-2 money supply.

The M-3 money
supply

As described in Chapter 2, the M-3 money supply is a still broader measure of money. It adds large-denomination time deposits at all depository institutions and term (longer than overnight) RPs issued by commercial banks and savings and loans to M-2. The Federal Reserve publishes monthly estimates of the M-3 money supply with about a one-month lag and establishes long-run targets for M-3 growth.

The liquid-assets
aggregate

The broadest measure of liquid assets computed by the Fed is L, which adds term Eurodollar deposits held by U.S. nonbank entities, bankers' acceptances, commercial paper, savings bonds, and short-term marketable Treasury debt to the M-3 aggregate. Estimates for this aggregate are available monthly with about a two-month lag. No Federal Reserve targets have been established for L.

Total bank credit

Lastly, the Federal Reserve constructs estimates for total bank credit as a policy indicator. Total bank credit is defined as total loans and investments plus loans sold by domestically chartered banks. Data are available monthly with a one-month lag. The Fed publishes long-run projections for this aggregate consistent with its targets for the money-supply aggregates.[2]

The foregoing are the key class-I policy variables monitored by the Federal Reserve as of mid-1981. It should be noted that the Federal Reserve is continually reviewing its approach to implementing monetary policy, and the specific variables in this class and the Federal Reserve's measurement of them change from time to time. The most current practice should be discernable from the latest available minutes of the Federal Open Market Committee meetings or from data published in the Federal Reserve *Bulletin*.

[2]Weekly data are available for the balance sheets of large banks with a one-week lag. The Federal Reserve does not publish projections of credit aggregates for the large banks, but the financial markets and the Fed do monitor commercial and industrial loans and other items in these weekly reports to gain more current information on the trend and composition of total bank credit than the more comprehensive monthly data permit.

FIGURE 14–2
Federal Reserve measures of money and liquid assets

Aggregate		*Amount in billions of dollars (not seasonally adjusted) November 1979*
M-1A		$ 372.2
	Currency	106.6
	Demand deposits*	265.6
M-1B		387.9
	M-1A	72.2
	Other checkable deposits†	15.7
M-2		1510.0
	M-1B	387.9
	Overnight RPs issued by commercial banks	20.3
	Overnight Eurodollar deposits held by U.S. nonbank residents at Caribbean branches of U.S. banks	3.2
	Money-market mutual fund shares ...	40.4
	Savings deposits at all depositary institutions	420.0
	Small time deposits at all depositary institutions‡	640.8
	M-2 consolidation component§	−2.7
M-3		1759.1
	M-2	1510.0
	Large time deposits at all depositary institutions[11]	219.5
	Term RPs issued by commercial banks	21.5
	Term RPs issued by savings and loan associations	8.2
L		2123.8
	M-3	1759.1
	Other Eurodollars of U.S. residents other than banks	34.5
	Bankers acceptances	27.6
	Commercial paper	97.1
	Savings bonds	80.0
	Liquid Treasury obligations	125.4

Note: Components of M-2, M-3 and L measures generally exclude amounts held by domestic depository institutions, foreign commercial banks and official institutions, the U.S. government (including the Federal Reserve), and money-market mutual funds. Exceptions are bankers acceptances and commercial paper for which data sources permit the removal only of amounts held by money-market mutual funds and, in the case of bankers acceptances, amounts held be accepting banks, the Federal Reserve, and the Federal Home Loan Bank System.

*Net of demand deposits due to foreign commercial banks and official institutions.

†Includes NOW, ATS and credit union share draft balances, and demand deposits at thrift institutions. M-1B definition was later revised (in June 1981) to include travelers checks.

‡Time deposits issued in denominations of less than $100,000.

§In order to avoid double counting of some deposits in M-2, those demand deposits owned by thrift institutions (a component of M-1B) which are estimated to be used for servicing their savings and small time deposit liabilities in M-2 are removed.

[11]Time deposits issued in denominations of $100,000 or more.

SOURCE: Federal Reserve *Bulletin*, February 1980

The level of market interest rates

Before closing this section it is worthwhile to draw attention once again to one variable which was closely followed in the 1960s as the key policy indicator proximate to spending decisions, but which is now generally recognized as an unsatisfactory guide to the thrust of policy actions. This variable is the level of market interest rates. (Earlier discussion of the drawbacks to the use of this variable as an indicator or target was included in Chapter 12.)

The notion that the level of market interest rates, as measured by the commercial-paper rate or the prime bank rate, for example, is a key indicator of the thrust of monetary policy can be explained by two observations: (1) Federal Reserve actions can affect market interest rates strongly; and (2) market interest rates are an important factor in spending decisions.

In the 1950s and early 1960s more sophisticated analysis, based for the most part on early Keynesian theory, supported the notion that the impact of monetary policy could be measured by the level of market interest rates. In fact, early Keynesian theory viewed monetary policy as affecting spending decisions *only* through market interest rates. The unqualified conclusion was that high market interest rates imply tight monetary policy, and low market interest rates imply expansionary monetary policy.

This notion was so accepted that market interest rates became the dominant indicator and target for monetary policy by the early 1960s. As described in Chapter 12, in the mid-1960s, inflation began to accelerate in response to increased government spending and monetary expansion associated with the Vietnam war. Finally, in 1968, taxes were raised and the Federal Reserve implemented what it believed to be a moderately tight monetary policy. Interest rates rose, with the prime rate averaging 6.3 percent in 1968 versus 5.61 percent in 1967. However, real economic activity and inflation continued to increase, propelled by high consumer spending. What happened? Were monetary and fiscal policy incapable of restraining spending?

Postmortem analyses of the 1968–69 period conclude that the economy continued to expand because *monetary policy in fact was highly expansionary in 1968 as measured by the rate of growth of the money supply.*[3] The M-1 money supply grew at a rate of 7 percent in 1968 versus 4 percent in 1967. Interest rates were an invalid indicator of the thrust of monetary policy because expected inflation was rising and because a strong level of real spending was pushing

---

[3]Fiscal policy was tight, however, since the tax increase was contractionary. The effects of the tax increase were probably muted, though, by the fact that the increase was announced as a temporary one. According to a theory called the *permanent-income hypothesis* (covered in most intermediate macroeconomics courses), households are more likely to reduce their savings to pay for higher taxes if they know the loss in spendable income is temporary.

up credit demands. In other words, interest rates rose due to positive Fisher and income effects not due to a restraining liquidity effect (see Chapter 5) as the Federal Reserve presumed.[4]

The Federal Reserve shifted its attention to the monetary aggregates following the 1968–69 experience, but interest rates did not fade out of the picture entirely. Over the next decade, concern for interest-rate stability in the interests of the financial sector, a concern dating back to the beginning of the Fed, remained, and political resistance to Federal Reserve actions tending to raise interest rates was little diminished by the 1968–69 experience. Also, in developing its strategy for controlling the money supply, the Federal Reserve came to rely upon the federal funds rate as its key intermediate indicator and target.

This last point takes us to our next topic—a description of the Federal Reserve's intermediate indicators and targets.

INTERMEDIATE INDICATORS AND TARGETS

The tentative nature of the Federal Reserve's selection and measurement of class I indicators and targets was noted in the previous section. The same comment applies with more emphasis to intermediate indicators and targets. In fact, as of mid-1981, the Federal Reserve's post-October 1979 approach to intermediate indicators and targets still remained in a state of active experimentation and flux.[5] Our discussion describes the principal variables which have been used or are under consideration by the Fed and those which have been urged upon the Fed by its critics. Recent history is provided to give perspective.

The federal funds rate

Following a period of experimentation in the early 1970s and up until recently, the Federal Reserve focused almost exclusively on the federal funds rate as its intermediate indicator and target.[6] The federal funds rate was identified in Chapter 5 as the interest rate on federal funds—unsecured loans of immediately available funds traded among banks and other financial firms. (It may be helpful at this point to reread the sections on federal funds, RPs, CDs, and

---

[4]One alternative to using a market-interest-rate indicator is to construct and follow a real-interest-rate indicator. There are two drawbacks to this approach, however: (1) the pace of real economic activity affects the level of real interest rates, causing even a real-interest-rate indicator to give occasional false signals about the thrust of policy; and (2) technically, the interest-rate variable which affects spending decisions is the *expected, after-tax,* real rate of interest—a measure which could not be constructed with any reasonable degree of precision because it requires judgments about investors' and borrowers' *expectations* regarding inflation and effective tax rates.

[5]On October 6, 1979, the Federal Reserve announced that it would institute a change in its approach to intermediate targets. See Chapter 12.

[6]In the early 1970s the Fed tried using a reserve aggregate it called *reserves available to support private deposits.* After a few years of unsatisfactory experience with this variable, it was dropped in favor of the federal funds rate.

C&I loans in Chapter 6.) Although participation in the federal funds market by firms other than banks has grown rapidly and become significant in recent years, the market is still dominated by banks, and the federal funds rate may be analyzed in terms of just the supply and demand for interbank loans.[7]

Bank activity in the federal funds market

In certain respects, banks' demands for and supplies of federal funds are similar to their demands for and supplies of other "managed liabilities," such as Eurodollars, RPs, and CDs. The demand for these funds originates with banks desiring to expand their customer loans or their investments relative to their base of passive deposits. Passive deposits are deposits which banks can not or do not bid for aggressively with competitive interest rates (because of regulatory restraints or market conditions); examples are demand deposits and savings deposits. Banks with larger volumes of passive deposits or other sources of funds than they care to use for customer loans and term investments often supply funds to other banks via loans of federal funds, Eurodollars, and RPs.

Federal funds are an important type of interbank loan in that they generate "immediately" available funds with no collateral requirement. These features make the federal funds market a convenient vehicle for banks wishing to fine tune their reserve balances. A bank which is short of reserve funds can phone a broker in the federal funds market and arrange for a same-day credit to the bank's account with the Fed. The broker accomplishes this by advising an offering bank that its offer to lend federal funds has been accepted. The offering bank then instructs the Fed by wire to transfer the funds from its account to the account of the borrowing bank. In the same manner, a bank which has an unexpected supply of excess reserves which earn no interest can immediately place these funds at interest through the federal funds market.

As a result of a growing reliance of banks on the federal funds market as a mechanism for adjusting reserve balances in the late 1960s, the Fed came to view this market and the federal funds rate as barometers of the degree of tightness or ease in the total supply of reserves among banks. It was apparent to the Fed that its reserve actions had a direct, observable impact on the federal funds rate. Actions supplying or freeing-up reserves tend to augment the supply of funds in the federal funds market and reduce the federal funds rate, while actions absorbing available reserves tend to have a reverse effect on the supply of federal funds and raise the federal funds rate. The federal funds rate, therefore, seemed a natural indicator and target for Fed actions.

Fed uses of the federal funds rate in the 1970s

The federal funds rate came to be used as an indicator and target in two ways: as a guide to Federal Reserve actions necessary to correct for "technical factors," and as an instrument to achieve the

---

[7]A complete analysis would deal with supply and demand relationships for all participants.

Federal Reserve's money-supply targets. Each of these uses will be explained in turn.

For a variety of reasons made explicit later in this chapter, there can be changes in the relative supply and demand for reserves which are independent of Federal Reserve actions or of changes in the demand for money. The Fed attempts to anticipate these technical factors and offset them by adding or draining reserves as warranted. The purpose of correcting for such technical factors is to prevent them from creating unnecessary disturbances in the financial markets and/or the money supply. It is easy to miss in these operations, however, and herein lies the potential value of the federal funds rate. If the Fed miscalculates, and the net effect of technical influences and Fed actions is to create an unintended tighter reserve condition in the system, the federal funds rate will tend to rise. A miscalculation in the other direction will tend to drive the federal funds rate to lower levels. By monitoring the federal funds rate, the Fed believed it could be alert to any unexpected tightness or ease in reserves due to technical factors. An unencouraged rise or fall in the federal funds rate was thus viewed as a valuable signal that corrective Federal Reserve actions were warranted.

There are several steps to the analysis of why the federal funds rate also came to be viewed as a valuable device for controlling the rate of growth of the money supply. First, note that because the federal funds market is one of the competing markets available to banks for investing funds and for borrowing, if the Fed encourages the federal funds rate to rise, rates on competing sources and uses of bank funds tend to rise, including, with a lag, the prime bank rate. In this manner, the general level of short-term interest rates tends to rise. Second, recall from Chapter 3 that higher interest rates tend to curb the demand for money. That is to say, as market interest rates rise, individuals and firms tend to cut down on the quantity of currency and checkable deposits they hold. Third, due to certain conditions existent in our current monetary system and to be explained in the last section of this chapter, a reduction in the demand for money tends to result in a reduction in the money supply.[8] This is the logic of the mechanism linking the federal funds rate to the money supply. A rise in the federal funds rate tends to curb the rate of growth of the money supply, ceteris paribus. The process may be viewed as reversible. A sustained reduction in the federal funds rate tends to boost the money supply.

According to one point of view, this, in fact, was the mechanism through which the Federal Reserve controlled the money supply during the 1970s. Narrow target ranges were established for the federal funds rate between meetings of the Federal Open Market Committee. If, at the next FOMC meeting, the monetary aggre-

---

[8]The conditions referenced here make the Fed and the banking system passive suppliers of whatever quantity of currency and checkable deposits the public demands, given the current level of interest rates.

FIGURE 14–3

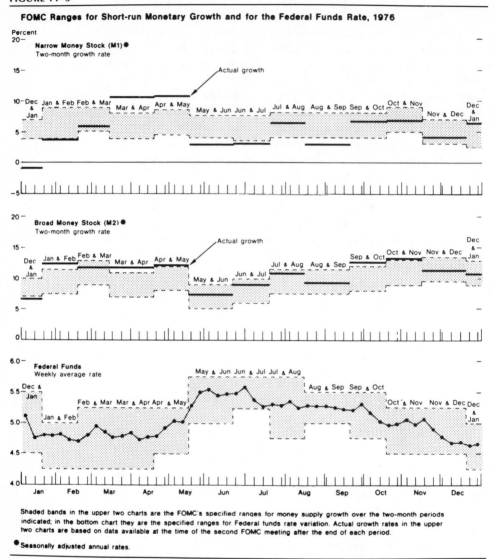

FOMC Ranges for Short-run Monetary Growth and for the Federal Funds Rate, 1976

Shaded bands in the upper two charts are the FOMC's specified ranges for money supply growth over the two-month periods indicated; in the bottom chart they are the specified ranges for Federal funds rate variation. Actual growth rates in the upper two charts are based on data available at the time of the second FOMC meeting after the end of each period.

* Seasonally adjusted annual rates.

gates appeared to be growing excessively relative to the Fed's targets, the federal-funds-rate target was adjusted upward. If the aggregates were growing slowly, the federal-funds-rate target was adjusted downward.[9] Sometimes adjustments were made in the federal-funds-rate target between FOMC meetings in accordance with prearranged instructions to the manager of the account or following a telephone conference among the committee members. Eventu-

[9]Usually the short-run monetary targets were also adjusted at these meetings. If excessive money growth were judged to be attributable partly to unanticipated, temporary influences, the short-run monetary targets might be raised at the same time that the federal-funds-rate target was raised. Correspondingly, monetary and funds-rate targets often were lowered simultaneously. See Figure 14–3.

ally, with a lag of from one to three months, money growth would respond to aggressive interest-rate changes. The record of the actual paths of the M-1 and M-2 aggregates (old definitions), of the federal funds rate, and of the corresponding short-run target ranges is shown for the year 1976 in Figure 14–3.

There were two criticisms of the Federal Reserve's use of the federal funds rate as an intermediate target and indicator during the 1970s. One criticism was that, as a normal practice, the Fed was not aggressive enough in its adjustments of the federal-funds-rate target when money-supply growth was excessive. Small adjustments of 1/4 and 1/2 percentage points in the federal-funds-rate target were the usual response to money growth that was off target. The more appropriate response, according to this point of view, would have been changes of one full percentage point or more, particularly in 1977 and 1978. As it turned out, these types of adjustments were eventually forced on the Fed in late 1978 and again in late 1979 as the dollar came under severe downward pressure in the foreign-exchange markets, but not before money growth had accelerated high and long enough to push the inflation rate into double digits.

Criticisms of a federal-funds-rate target

Another criticism of the Federal Reserve's management of the money supply via a federal-funds-rate target was more basic. According to this point of view, the federal funds rate is an invalid indicator of the thrust of the Federal Reserve's influence on the available supply of reserves and on the future rate of growth of the money supply. This line of criticism, which is associated with, but is not limited to, monetarists, holds that various measures of the quantity of reserves, including the monetary base, are better indicators and more appropriate targets for monetary control. If the quantity of bank reserves is growing rapidly, the growth rate of the money supply will tend to pick up in subsequent weeks or months. To forestall such a development, the Fed should have keyed its actions to the growth rate of one of the reserve aggregates.

In response to the second line of criticism and to the all too apparent difficulties in maintaining a lid on money growth, the Federal Reserve announced, on October 6, 1979, that, simultaneously with a tightening move, it was changing its approach to monetary control. In the future it would devote more attention to the growth rates of the reserve aggregates. The federal funds rate would not be dropped completely, but it would be permitted to trade in a much wider range. The initial range was 4 percentage points versus a range of one percentage point or less common to the earlier period.[10]

We will return to the criticisms described in the paragraphs above and different points of view regarding the money-supply process in the current system in the last section of this chapter. At this point, we turn our attention to a description of the reserve

---

[10]The minutes of the October 1979 meeting of the FOMC are reproduced as an appendix to this chapter.

aggregates which have been proposed as replacements for the federal funds rate in Fed targeting at the intermediate level.

Total reserves

One obvious intermediate target would be *total reserves,* which are defined as *reserve deposits plus currency held by depository institutions as reserves to satisfy Federal Reserve reserve requirements.* The argument for this target is based on the familiar, standard notion that, as the quantity of reserves held by depository institutions rises (falls), the total quantity of deposits and credit issued by depository institutions tends to rise (fall) by some multiple of the rise (fall) in total reserves.

Adjusted total reserves

Another candidate is *adjusted total reserves. Adjusted total reserves are a refined version of total reserves which incorporate the effect of changes in reserve requirements on the quantity of reserves available to support an increase in deposits.* To see why adjusted total reserves are useful, suppose there are simultaneously an increase in reserve requirements and an increase in total reserves. The net effect on deposits might be neutral, yet the increase in total reserves would suggest that the money supply was on the verge of higher growth. Focusing on adjusted reserves as an intermediate indicator and target avoids false signals and/or the necessity of changing the reserve-aggregate target each time reserve requirements are changed.[11]

Nonborrowed reserves

Another reserve aggregate which has been proposed as a target is *nonborrowed reserves.* Nonborrowed reserves are equal to *total reserves less borrowings of depository institutions from the Federal Reserve.* According to advocates of the use of nonborrowed reserves, there are two reasons for focusing on this aggregate as opposed to, say, total reserves. One reason given is that the Fed does not control borrowed reserves as closely as it does nonborrowed reserves. Depository institutions borrow at the discount window at their own initiative, and although the Fed can always close the window to persistent borrowers or raise the discount rate to discourage borrowers, the degree of control is less than it is for nonborrowed reserves.

---

[11]Total reserves are only one among several reserve aggregates for which there are adjusted versions to reflect changes in reserve requirements. Later in this chapter we will examine the adjusted monetary base constructed by the Federal Reserve Bank of St. Louis.

Another reason given is that borrowed reserves are best excluded from a reserve target to preserve them as a safety valve and buffer in the system. When the Fed moves to curb money-supply growth, it runs the risk of being too stringent. If the system is "whipsawed" by a sudden cut in available reserves, some depository institutions might be caught off balance, and unnecessary disturbances, including the failure of a number of institutions, might result. If non-borrowed reserves are the target aggregate, so the reasoning goes, such a development is less likely. Actions to restrain the supply of nonborrowed reserves will still curb money growth because they will drive some institutions to the discount window, which can be slowly closed. Total reserves will not be curbed as sharply as non-borrowed reserves at first, but after a few weeks, as the Fed becomes an unwilling lender to institutions using the discount window persistently, the growth rate of total bank reserves will converge with the rate of increase in the nonborrowed reserves; within a month or so the money supply will respond, reaching a lower growth path. In this manner, it is argued, the Fed can wield a "gentle whip" without surrendering effective control.

Free reserves and net borrowed reserves

Free reserves are a reserve-aggregate concept which has a long history in the annals of the Fed's search for a useful intermediate indicator and target, and, despite rather convincing criticism (described after net borrowed reserves below), they have retained a following among some officials and private economists. *Free reserves are excess reserves less borrowed reserves.* The notion underlying this concept is that both excess reserves and borrowed reserves are good indicators (with opposite signs) of the degree of ease or tightness in the supply of reserves in the depository system. If excess reserves are high and borrowed reserves are low, reserves are plentiful and likely to support higher growth in the money supply. If excess reserves are low and borrowed reserves high, the supply of reserves is tight and likely to restrain money growth. Free reserves combine excess reserves and borrowed reserves into one indicator.

Net borrowed reserves are another variable which represent the same concept and, in fact, the same magnitude, with a change of sign, as free reserves. They are defined as *borrowed reserves less excess reserves.* Net borrowed reserves are usually used in discussions in place of free reserves whenever free reserves are negative.

The critics of the use of free reserves and net borrowed reserves cite the fact that both excess reserves and borrowed reserves are at least as responsive to the level of interest rates as they are to Federal Reserve actions. Hence they are poor policy indicators individually or combined in a single variable. As interest rates rise, the opportunity cost of excess reserves rises, and depository institutions

Criticism of free reserves

tend to devote more resources to managing their reserve levels to a minimum degree over the required level. Higher interest rates also encourage depository institutions to borrow from the Federal Reserve as long as the discount rate lags increases in market interest rates, as it has in the past under Fed policy. When economic activity is booming, market interest rates tend to rise and free reserves tend to fall, suggesting tighter reserve policy by the Fed based on the free-reserves indicator. Yet total reserves will have risen, because of higher borrowed reserves, and excess reserves will have been put to work supporting more deposits. As a result, money-supply growth will tend to rise. In summary, free reserves, according to the critics, can give false signals and should never be the basis for gauging or targeting policy actions.

It should be noted that the same criticism leveled at free reserves applies as well in some degree to nonborrowed reserves since these implicitly also treat high borrowings of reserves as a sign of monetary restraint. Those who stress the response of borrowed reserves to market interest rates and the need for Federal Reserve actions to offset this effect tend to prefer a more inclusive reserve aggregate such as total reserves or the monetary base.

The monetary base

The concept of the *monetary base* was introduced in Chapter 10. An appropriate definition of the monetary base for the current system is *total reserves held by depository institutions plus currency held by the nonbank public*. The arguments supporting the adoption of this indicator in preference to total reserves alone are twofold. First, currency held by the rest of the public is part of the money supply provided directly by the Fed and the Treasury. Total reserves is too narrow a concept because it is related solely to deposits. Second, currency held by the rest of the public constitutes high-powered money. It qualifies as reserves when deposits are made, and in planning its reserve actions the Fed must allow for changes in the public's preferences which result in deposits or withdrawals of currency from depository institutions. The monetary base and the money-stock multiplier concepts draw attention to and facilitate planning for this complication.

This completes our identification of the merits of the various intermediate indicators and targets for now. Further comparative discussion will be provided in the last section of the chapter. Before we reach that section, there are two analytical sections on the monetary base and the money-stock multiplier to be presented.

TECHNICAL FACTORS AND SOURCES OF THE MONETARY BASE

In an earlier section of this chapter and in Chapter 4, there was mention of technical factors which cause changes in the available supply of reserves in the depository system independently of Federal Reserve actions. For convenience, we will focus on the monetary base and use a sources-of-the-monetary-base/money-stock-multiplier framework to explain these technical factors and how they affect the system. This section sets out the sources of the monetary base and related technical factors.[12]

The definition of the monetary base provided earlier was a definition by *uses*. The monetary base, B, has two uses: R, reserves held by depository institutions, and PC, currency held by the rest of the public.

$$B = R + PC \qquad (1)$$

In order to set out the determinants of the monetary base in terms of Federal Reserve actions and independent technical factors, we will work from the definition above to a definition of the base by its *sources*.

Recall that reserves are comprised of reserve deposits with the Federal Reserve, RD, and currency held as reserves by depository institutions, RC.

$$R = RD + RC \qquad (2)$$

By substituting Equation (2) into (1), we can identify the monetary base as

$$B = RD + RC + PC \qquad (3)$$

The sum of our two currency items, RC and PC, equals C, total currency outside of the Federal Reserve and the Treasury.

$$C = RC + PC \qquad (4)$$

This currency total, C, can also be identified as comprised of Federal Reserve notes outstanding, FRN, plus Treasury coin and notes outstanding, TC, less Treasury cash holdings, tch:

$$C = FRN + TC - tch \qquad (5)$$

Working back now by substituting (5) into (4) and the results into (3), we have

$$B = RD + FRN + TC - tch \qquad (6)$$

The first two items on the right-hand side of this expression, reserve deposits and Federal Reserve notes outstanding, are monetary liabilities of the Federal Reserve banks. The third item, Treasury currency outstanding, is a monetary liability of the U.S. Treasury. The fourth item, Treasury cash holdings, is a small consolidation adjust-

---

[12]The sources-of-the-monetary-base framework presented in this section draws heavily on Leonall C. Andersen and Jerry L. Jordan, "The Monetary Base: Explanation and Analytical Use," Federal Reserve Bank of St. Louis *Monthly Review*, August 1968, 7-14. Changes have been made in their analysis and definition of the monetary base to adjust for institutional and regulatory changes in recent years.

FIGURE 14–4

FEDERAL RESERVE BANKS
Condition Statement
($ millions)

Account	Wednesday					End of month		
	1980					1979		1980
	Jan. 2	Jan. 9	Jan. 16	Jan. 23	Jan. 30	Nov.	Dec.	Jan.
	Consolidated condition statement							
Assets								
1 Gold certificate account	11,112	11,172	11,172	11,172	11,172	11,112	11,112	11,172
2 Special drawing rights certificate account	1,800	1,800	1,800	1,800	2,968	1,800	1,800	2,968
3 Coin	408	405	427	441	462	415	403	469
Loans								
†4 Member bank borrowings . .	2,060	1,250	1,740	1,116	924	2,034	1,454	828
†5 Other	0	0	0	0	0	0	0	0
Acceptances								
†6 Bought outright	0	0	0	0	0	0	0	0
†7 Held under repurchase agreements	1,078	0	0	327	0	269	704	0
Federal agency obligations								
†8 Bought outright	8,216	8,216	8,216	8,216	8,216	8,221	8,216	8,216
†9 Held under repurchase agreements	1,122	0	0	907	0	973	493	0
U.S. government securities Bought outright								
†10 Bills	45,359	46,592	43,727	43,903	41,431	47,101	45,244	45,264
†11 Certificates—Special	0	0	0	0	0	0	0	0
†12 Notes	56,494	56,494	56,494	56,494	56,494	55,928	56,494	56,494
†13 Bonds	14,553	14,553	14,553	14,553	14,553	14,499	14,553	14,553
†14 Total[1]	116,406	117,639	114,774	116,950	112,478	117,528	116,291	116,311
†15 Held under repurchase agreement	2,664	0	0	1,660	0	559	1,167	0
†16 Total U.S. government securities	119,070	117,639	114,774	118,610	112,478	118,087	117,458	116,311
†17 Total loans and securities	131,546	127,105	124,730	129,176	121,618	129,584	128,325	125,355
18 Cash items in process of collection	15,957	14,748	14,454	12,696	10,905	10,137	13,571	10,050
19 Bank premises	407	408	409	411	410	403	408	411
20 Denominated in foreign currencies[2]	2,483	2,310	2,338	2,276	2,376	2,607	2,483	2,192
21 All other	2,847	2,587	2,550	2,692	2,800	1,685	2,722	2,634
22 Total assets	166,560	160,535	157,880	160,664	152,711	157,743	160,824	155,251

ment necessary to obtain an accurate statement of net currency balances outside of government accounts. Hence expression (6) identifies the monetary base entirely in terms of the net monetary liabilities of two government entities, the Federal Reserve and the Treasury.

Our next step is to go to the consolidated balance sheet of the Federal Reserve Banks, locate entries corresponding to RD and FRN, and replace them with other entries from that account. This can be done because any balance sheet is an identity and can be

Account	Wednesday					End of month		
	1980					1979		1980
	Jan. 2	Jan. 9	Jan. 16	Jan. 23	Jan. 30	Nov.	Dec.	Jan.
	Consolidated condition statement							
Liabilities								
*23 Federal Reserve notes	113,477	112,155	110,845	109,681	109,095	109,908	113,355	108,927
Deposits								
Reserve accounts								
*24 Member banks	34,525	31,876	29,517	34,538	27,864	32,280	29,520	31,232
*25 Edge Act Corporations . . .	304	316	418	293	355	296	265	244
*26 U.S. agencies and branches								
of foreign banks	8	15	28	34	50	41	7	16
*27 Total	34,837	32,207	29,963	34,865	28,269	32,617	29,792	31,492
28 U.S. Treasury—General								
account	3,961	3,472	3,468	3,309	3,051	2,590	4,075	2,931
29 Foreign—Official accounts	379	299	250	242	249	490	429	440
30 Other	1,821	324	307	357	261	352	1,412	339
31 Total deposits	40,998	36,302	33,988	38,773	31,830	36,049	35,708	35,202
32 Deferred availability cash items	7,180	7,171	8,061	6,865	6,437	6,408	6,804	5,440
33 Other liabilities and accrued								
dividends[3]	2,564	2,345	2,209	2,353	2,147	2,313	2,667	2,425
34 Total liabilities	164,219	157,973	155,103	157,672	149,509	154,678	158,534	151,994
Capital Accounts								
35 Capital paid in	1,146	1,146	1,150	1,152	1,153	1,142	1,145	1,153
36 Surplus	1,145	1,145	1,145	1,145	1,145	1,078	1,145	1,145
37 Other capital accounts	50	271	482	695	904	845	0	959
38 Total liabilities and								
capital accounts	166,560	160,535	157,880	160,664	152,711	157,743	160,824	155,251
39 Memo: Marketable U.S. govern-								
ment securities held in								
custody for foreign and inter-								
national account	80,963	80,715	79,426	80,192	80,799	74,403	80,828	81,039

SOURCE: Federal Reserve *Bulletin,* February, 1980.

1. *Includes* securities loaned—fully guaranteed by U.S. government securities pledged with Federal Reserve Banks—and *excludes* (if any) securities sold and scheduled to be bought back under matched sale-purchase transactions.

2. Beginning December 29, 1978, such assets are revalued monthly at market exchange rates.

3. Includes exchange-translation account reflecting, beginning December 29, 1978, the monthly revaluation at market exchange rates of foreign-exchange commitments.

*Monetary-based liabilities.

†Under Federal Reserve control.

written in the form of an equation, such as A − L = NW. In words, assets, A, minus liabilities, L, equal net worth, NW. We want to use such an equation to make balance-sheet substitutions because the Federal Reserve does not control the quantity of its monetary-base liabilities, RD + FRN, directly. Control is exercised indirectly and less than perfectly through the asset side of the balance sheet. To see this, consider the consolidated balance sheet (condition statement) for the 12 Federal Reserve banks shown in Figure 14–4.

The items in the balance sheet marked with an asterisk are totals or components of the Fed's monetary-base liabilities; the items marked with a dagger are totals and components under varying degrees of Federal Reserve control; and the remaining items may affect the monetary base but are not entries which the Fed can or is likely to manipulate to control the base.

Suppose the Federal Reserve purchases $10 million worth of U.S. government securities from a nonbank securities dealer. Asset item 16 will rise by $10 million, and liabilities item 30, other deposits, will rise by $10 million as the Federal Reserve creates additional deposits in favor of the nonbank securities dealer to pay for the government securities. Thus far, no change has occurred in the Fed's monetary-base liabilities and will not as long as the securities dealer retains these deposits.

The securities dealer is not likely to hold these deposits very long, however, for they earn no interest. One way to employ them is to lend them to a bank via the federal funds market. Following such a transaction, item 30 is debited $10 million; and item 24, bank reserve deposits, is credited $10 million. In this manner, the monetary base is indirectly increased by $10 million, the Federal Reserve's original open-market purchase of government securities.

Consider one more sequence of transactions before we move on with our identities. Item 28, U.S. Treasury general account, is the demand deposit account of the U.S. government with the Federal Reserve, the account on which most government checks are written. Suppose the government mails $3 billion in Social Security checks. As these checks are deposited with depository institutions and then presented to Federal Reserve banks, debits are made to item 28, and credits are made to item 24, raising the monetary base. The Federal Reserve has no control over the U.S. Treasury account balance, but a decrease in this balance tends to add to the monetary base, other things being the same.

A regrouping of Fed balance-sheet items

Now the same principle at work in the cases of the open-market purchase and of the checks drawn on the U.S. Treasury general account applies to all of the other entries in the consolidated balance sheet not marked by an asterisk. An increase in any asset item tends to add to the monetary base, other things being the same; an increase in any liability or capital item tends to decrease the monetary base. To capture these effects in a framework convenient to further discussion, the asset, liability, and capital entries of the Fed's consolidated balance sheet can be grouped and arranged as follows:

	Grouped term	Items from composite balance sheet
1.	FRI: .... Federal Reserve investment in U.S. government securities and other purchased assets	Items 6 + 7 + 8 + 9 + 16
2.	LDI: .... Federal Reserve loans to depository institutions through the discount "window"	Item 4

3. FLO: .... Item 18 − Item 32
   Federal Reserve
   float
4. G&SC: .... Items 1 + 2
   Gold and SDR certi-
   ficates
5. FE: .... Item 20
   Foreign exchange
6. OA: .... Items 3 + 5 + 19 + 21
   Other assets not else-
   where specified
7. USD: .... Item 28
   U.S. Treasury
   general account
8. OL&C: .... Items 29 + 30 + 33 +
   Other liabilities not   35 + 36 + 37
   elsewhere accounted for
   plus capital items
9. RD + FRN: .... Items 23 + 27
   Monetary base
   liabilities of the
   Federal Reserve

Before we explain each of these terms and their importance, note that by relating each term back to the consolidated balance sheet and using the balance sheet identity we can find

$$RD + FRN = FRI + LDI + FLO + G\&SC \qquad (7)$$
$$+ FE + OA - USD - OL\&C$$

In general, an increase in any of the first six terms on the right-hand side of the equation tends to cause an increase in the Federal Reserve's monetary-base liabilities; an increase in either of the last two terms tends to decrease the monetary base. Each right-hand term is now explained further.

FRI (Federal Reserve investments).   This represents primarily interest-bearing assets obtained in the past through open-market purchases. At the end of December 1979 this term totaled $126.9 billion and included U.S. government securities of $117.5 billion, federal agency obligations of $8.7 billion, and a small amount—$0.7 billion—of bankers' acceptances. Because sizable changes in FRI are easily managed by the Fed through open-market operations, this term represents the key control point of reserves and the monetary base for the Federal Reserve. Open-market purchases directly increase FRI, and open-market sales decrease it.

LDI (Loans to depository institutions).   Through the discount window there were $1.5 billion LDIs at the end of December 1979.[13] These loans are virtually loans of reserves which carry an interest cost, the discount rate. Depository institutions will tend to borrow at the discount window as a last source of funds when under stress, and they will tend to borrow for profit when the discount rate is significantly below the federal funds rate.[14] If the Fed raises the

---

[13]Prior to April 1980, these loans were restricted to member banks. Subsequently, all depository institutions have had access to the discount window.

[14]Also some banks in agricultural areas are encouraged to borrow from the Fed to help meet seasonal demands for credit in their areas.

FIGURE 14–5
LDI and interest rates.

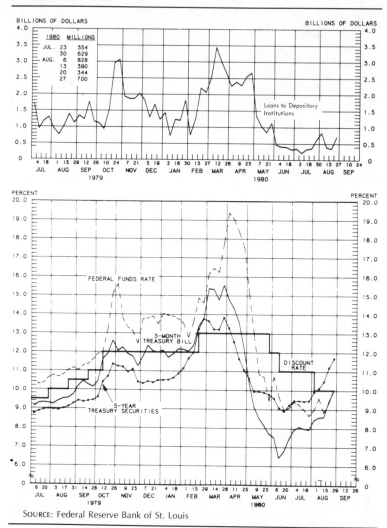

SOURCE: Federal Reserve Bank of St. Louis

discount rate relative to the federal funds rate, borrowed reserves will tend to fall, lowering the monetary base, ceteris paribus. A lower discount rate relative to the federal funds rate encourages borrowing and raises the monetary base. Hence the Federal Reserve influences loans to depository institutions, a source of the monetary base, through changes in the discount rate.

As mentioned earlier in this chapter, the normal practice of the Fed has been to adjust the discount rate with a lag following changes in market interest rates, and normally there is a positive spread between the federal funds rate, and the discount rate of 25 basis points or more. This means that for certain periods of time in a rising interest rate environment, reserve borrowings have often been allowed to rise to high levels, effectively surrendering some degree of control over the monetary base through this source—at least in the short run. (See Figure 14–5.)

Infrequent changes in the discount rate have been defended as having valuable "announcement effects" about the intention of monetary policy, and, as mentioned before, according to some economists, temporary increases in reserve borrowings following a rise in the federal funds rate should be tolerated as a necessary safety valve and an integral part of the gentle whip mechanism of money-supply control.

FLO (Federal Reserve float).   This is a source of interest-free credit to the banking system from the Federal Reserve, which arises as a result of the Federal Reserve's check-clearing operations.

To see how float works, suppose a check is drawn on a bank in California and deposited in a bank in New York. Both banks have reserve accounts with their respective Federal Reserve bank. The bank in New York will present the check to the New York Fed for clearing and credit to its reserve account. When the New York Fed receives the check, it is not credited right away to the New York bank's reserve account. There is a set delay to allow for the time it takes for the check to arrive in San Francisco and be debited from the California bank's reserve account with the San Francisco Fed. Normally this set delay is less than the actual time it takes to process the check. Consequently, for a brief period of time after the set delay, the reserves of the presenting bank are increased without a corresponding decrease in the reserves of the bank upon which the check is drawn. As a result, there is a net addition to total reserves, an addition which represents an extension of interest-free credit from the Fed to those banks presenting checks for clearing. This source of reserves to banks and other depository institutions is called Federal Reserve float. At any single point in time, there are always some checks in the process of clearing which have already been credited to depository institutions' reserve accounts. Hence there is always some aggregate level of float in the system—normally from \$1 billion to \$9 billion.

Float is important as a sizable source of reserves and the monetary base, but of utmost concern to the Fed is the fact that float is highly variable and unpredictable. Severe weather in one or another section of the country can delay checks moving from one Federal Reserve district to another, causing float to balloon by several billion dollars. As a result, float represents the most difficult short-run technical factor the Federal Reserve must contend with in managing a reserve target.

When bundles of checks are first presented by a bank to the Fed for clearing and during the delay period for the presenting bank, the checks as a group are credited to a special liability account in the Fed's balance sheet called *deferred availability cash items,* item 32 in Figure 14–4. On the asset side of the Fed's balance sheet, they are carried as *cash items in the process of collection,* item 18, until

Measuring float

they actually clear. The value of Federal Reserve float, therefore, can be found by subtracting deferred availability cash items from cash items in the process of collection in the Fed's consolidated balance sheet. Based on the data in Figure 14–4, float came to $6.8 billion at the end of December 1979.

It would seem that float could be eliminated. If the set delay in crediting individual checks to presenting banks' accounts were perfectly timed with the actual delay before the accounts of the banks drawn upon are debited, total reserves would be unaffected by check clearing, and no float would occur. It is not practical to keep track of each individual check in this manner, however. More than 10-billion checks clear through the Federal Reserve each year.

G&SC (Gold and Special Drawing Right (SDR) Certificates). These are entries which had more significance in past gold-standard and gold-exchange-standard periods. The Federal Reserve is no longer required to maintain gold-certificate reserves against Federal Reserve notes as it once was. Nevertheless, there can be changes in this term as the Treasury sells or buys gold.

When the Treasury buys gold, gold certificates may be issued by the Treasury and "sold" to the Federal Reserve in exchange for credits to the U.S. Treasury general account. The "security" for the gold certificates is the inventory value of the Treasury's gold stock. Consequently, more gold certificates may be issued to the Federal Reserve when the Treasury buys gold or when the inventory value of the Treasury's existing gold stock rises through a rise in its accounting price. In this manner, the Treasury is able to "monetize" the U.S. gold stock. Such a monetization tends to raise the monetary base. There were $11.1 billion in gold certificates held by the Fed at the end of December 1979.

SDR certificates are similar to gold certificates in that they represent monetized assets of the Treasury. Mentioned briefly in Chapter 8, SDRs are fiat-money assets issued by the International Monetary Fund and distributed on a pro rata basis to governments which are members of the IMF. The monetary base rises as they are monetized. There was $1.8 billion in monetized SDRs at the end of September 1979.

FE (foreign exchange). The Federal Reserve normally holds a "working balance" of foreign-exchange assets including deposits in accounts with foreign central banks. This balance, worth $2.5 billion at the end of December 1979, can be drawn upon in conducting intervention operations in the foreign-exchange market. Sales of foreign exchange decrease FE and, hence, the monetary base, ceteris paribus. Purchases tend to increase the base in the same manner that open-market purchases of government securities do. As a normal matter of practice, however, this effect of a foreign-exchange market operation is sterilized by an offsetting open-market operation in government securities.

OA (Other assets in the Federal Reserve's accounts). These are not of significant concern to us. When increasing, they do add to the monetary base in a ceteris-paribus sense, but are not likely to because other liabilities or capital are likely to change automatically in an offsetting manner.

USD (The U.S. Treasury general account). This account was explained earlier. Changes in this account can be substantial, and the Federal Reserve has no real control here. But the Federal Reserve usually has advance notice about prospective fluctuations in this account and can engage in open-market operations to neutralize most of its effects on total reserves and the monetary base.

OL&C (Other liabilities and capital accounts). This is another term, like OA, that is not noteworthy for monetary control and is included here essentially for accuracy in expression (7).

This completes our analysis of the sources of the monetary base from the Federal Reserve's balance sheet. There remains the monetary-base term TC in expression (6) and a description of the determinants of the breakdown of the Fed's monetary liabilities between RD and FRN.

The term TC, Treasury currency outstanding, is comprised almost entirely of coin. In exchange for a credit to the U.S. Treasury general account, the Treasury issues coins on demand to Federal Reserve banks which in turn distribute coins and Federal Reserve notes to depository institutions requesting them. These institutions pay for coins and paper currency by drawing on their reserve deposit accounts with the Fed. Hence when currency is distributed to depository institutions by the Fed, the total monetary base, RD + FRN + TC − tch, is unchanged. The TC term, therefore, is not a source of the monetary base which is functionally independent of sources derived from the Federal Reserve's balance sheet.

Treasury currency

All of our sources terms can be brought together now on the right-hand side of the following expression:

Deriving the complete sources and uses statement

$$RD + FRN + TC - tch = FRI + LDI + FLO + G\&SC \quad (8)$$
$$+ FE + OA - USD - OL\&C$$
$$+ TC - tch$$

This is simply expression (7) with the addition of TC − tch to the left- and right-hand sides.

Substituting (1), our original definition of the base in terms of uses, into (8), we have a complete uses and sources statement for the monetary base, shown in the following equation and in the table on page 368

$$B = R + PC = FRI + LDI + FLO + G\&SC + FE \quad (9)$$
$$+ OA - USD - OL\&C + TC - tch$$

To summarize this section, the Federal Reserve does not influence reserves or the monetary base directly. Influence is exercised primarily through additions to (or subtractions from) Federal Reserve investments, which tend to add to (or subtract from) the base indirectly. A secondary avenue of indirect influence operates through the discount rate and loans to depository institutions. In addition to these Federal Reserve actions, there are a number of other influences which show up as changes in other source entries for the base. These influences are "technical factors" which the Federal Reserve must anticipate and adjust for in planning its actions if the monetary base is the intermediate-target objective.

MONETARY BASE
Sources and Uses
(billions of dollars)
Year ended December 1979

Sources:		Uses:	
Federal Reserve investments (FRI)	$126.9	Reserves	$ 44.1
Loans to depository institutions (LDI)	1.5	Currency held by the rest of the public	111.6
Federal reserve float (FLO)	6.8		155.7
Gold and SDR certificates (G&SC)	12.9		
Foreign exchange (FE)	2.5		
Other Assets, n.e.s. (OA)	3.5		
U.S. Treasury general account (USD)	−4.1		
Other liabilities and capital account, n.e.s. (OL&C)	−6.8		
Treasury currency outstanding (TC)	12.9		
Treasury cash holdings (tch)	−0.4		
Total sources	155.7		

THE ADJUSTED MONETARY BASE AND THE MONEY-STOCK MULTIPLIER

As complex as it is, the foregoing analysis of the sources of the monetary base does not take into account all of the factors relevant to achieving a desired rate of growth for the money supply via a monetary-base target. One important tool of monetary policy—changes in reserve requirements—is missing, and there are additional technical factors. The influences of reserve-requirement changes and the remaining technical factors can be analyzed in the context of the money-stock multiplier for the monetary base, as was done for the secondary commodity-money system in Chapter 10. Alternatively, changes in reserve requirements can be reflected in an adjustment to the monetary base, as described earlier in this chapter for adjusted total reserves. The resulting aggregate, the adjusted monetary base, will rise when reserve requirements are reduced and fall when reserve requirements are raised, ceteris paribus.

As it happens, there are two published versions of the adjusted monetary base, one constructed by the Federal Reserve board staff and one constructed by the research staff of the Federal Reserve Bank of St. Louis. The St. Louis version has been available for a longer time and is the most widely followed; consequently, it will be the one upon which our analysis is based. The essential difference between the two published versions is that the board version adjusts the base only for changes in the required reserve ratios, whereas the St. Louis version adjusts for other factors affecting the average required reserve ratio, as explained below. (Slight differences exist between our measure of the adjusted monetary base and the St. Louis measure, but these differences are of no analytical consequence.)

The St. Louis adjusted base

The various Federal Reserve required reserve ratios in effect in June 1980 are shown in Figure 14–6. As of that date, the Fed had different required reserve ratios for different types of deposits, sizes of banks, and base versus marginal levels of banks' managed liabilities. The average of these ratios weighted by their respective relative contributions to total reserves is called *the average required reserve ratio*. The average required reserve ratio may be expressed and calculated more simply as total required reserves divided by total deposits and managed liabilities subject to reserve requirements, but the former definition is more useful for explaining changes in the ratio.

The average required reserve ratio

The average required reserve ratio may change because the Federal Reserve changes one or more of the required reserve ratios shown in Figure 14–6. The average required reserve ratio also may change because of changes in the composition of deposits and managed liabilities of depository institutions. For example, a shift of checkable deposits from small to large institutions will tend to raise the average required reserve ratio because, as shown in Figure 14–6, there is a higher required reserve ratio applicable to higher levels of deposits. Other composition changes which will change the average required reserve ratio include changes among types of deposits and managed liabilities and changes in the location of deposits and managed liabilities as between member banks and other depository institutions.

The St. Louis Fed allows for changes in the average required reserve ratio through its *reserve adjustment magnitude* (ram) which is calculated such that it adds (subtracts) a dollar amount to (from) the monetary base equal to the cumulative effect of the decrease (increase) in the average required reserve ratio from a base period in the past. The effect captured by the ram is the change in the quantity of reserves required to support the current level of deposits and managed liabilities as a result of changes in the average required reserve ratio.

The St. Louis reserve adjustment magnitude

When the reserve adjustment magnitude is added to the monetary base, we have adjusted monetary base, AB:

$$AB = B + ram$$

FIGURE 14–6 Member bank reserve requirements, percent of deposits (requirements in effect June 30, 1980)

Type of deposit and deposit interval ($ millions)	Percent
Demand deposits*	
0–2	7
2–10	9½
10–100	11¾
100–400	12¾
Over 400	16¼
Time and savings**	
Savings	3
Time:	
0–5, by maturity;	
30–179 days.....................................	3
180 days to 4 years.............................	2½
4 years or more	1
Over 5, by maturity;	
30–179 days.....................................	6
180 days to 4 years.............................	2½
4 years or more	1

	Legal limits	
	Minimum	Maximum
Demand deposits:		
Reserve city banks	10	22
Other banks	7	14
Time	3	10
Borrowings from foreign banks	0	22

Note: Required reserves must be held in the form of deposits with Federal reserve banks or vault cash.

*Requirement schedules are graduated, and each deposit interval applies to that part of the deposits of each bank. Demand deposits subject to reserve requirements are gross demand deposits minus cash items in process of collection and demand balances from domestic banks.

**Negotiable orders of withdrawal (NOW) accounts and time deposits, such as Christmas and vacation club accounts, were subject to the same requirements as savings deposits.

The average reserve requirement on savings and other time deposits must be at least 3 percent, the minimum specified by law.

Effective November 2, 1978, a supplementary reserve requirement of 2 percent was imposed on large time deposits of $100,000 or more, obligations of affiliates, and ineligible acceptances.

Effective with the reserve maintenance period beginning October 25, 1979, a marginal reserve requirement of 8 percent was added to managed liabilities in excess of a base amount, with the maintenance period beginning April 3, 1980, the requirement was increased to 10 percent, and with the maintenance period beginning June 12, 1980, it was decreased to 5 percent. In general, the base for the marginal reserve requirement was originally the greater of (a) $100 million or (b) the average amount of the managed liabilities held by a member bank, Edge corporation, or family of U.S. branches and agencies of a foreign bank for the two statement weeks ending September 26, 1979. For the computation period beginning March 20, 1980, the base was lowered by (a) 7 percent or (b) the decrease in an institution's U.S. office gross loans to foreigners and gross balances due from the foreign offices of other institutions between the base period (September 13–26, 1979) and the week ending March 12, whichever is greater. For the computation period beginning May 29, 1980, the base was increased by 7.5 percent above the base used to calculate the marginal reserve in the statement week of May 14–21, 1980. In addition, beginning March 19, 1980, the base was reduced to the extent that foreign loans and balances declined. The minimum base remained $100 million.

SOURCE: Federal Reserve *Bulletin,* July 1980.

Suppose that the Federal Reserve raises certain reserve requirement ratios, and suppose also that the monetary base rises by just the amount necessary to support depository institutions with the increased level of required reserves resulting from the increases in required reserve ratios. The unadjusted monetary base would rise, suggesting that monetary policy had eased. The adjusted monetary base would remain constant, however, reflecting the true thrust of monetary policy more accurately according to advocates of this indicator/target. Similarly, a change in the composition of bank deposits or of bank managed liabilities might counterbalance a change in the monetary base such that the adjusted monetary base and the thrust of monetary policy were unaffected.

Summarizing the analysis of this section so far, the advantages of the adjusted monetary base over the simple base are two-fold: (1) the net effect of all of the Federal Reserve's principal tools, open-market operations, changes in the discount rate, and changes in reserve requirements are reflected in the adjusted monetary base; and (2) one important additional technical factor affecting reserves available to support deposits and the money supply is allowed for, namely, changes in the average required reserve ratio due to changes in the composition of deposits and managed liabilities.

The remaining technical factors relevant to the relationship between Federal Reserve actions and the money supply are summarized in the money-stock multiplier for the adjusted monetary base, am:

The money-stock multiplier

$$am = \frac{M^S}{AB}$$

In principle, the money stock in this expression could be defined as any one of the Federal Reserve's monetary aggregates, but in our analysis it is defined as M-1B.

For historical values, the money-stock multiplier can be calculated simply as the ratio of the M-1B money stock to the adjusted monetary base as indicated by the equation above and as shown in Figure 14–7 along with the adjusted monetary base and the multiplier for M-1A. For purposes of explaining these past values and projecting future values, however, it is useful to decompose the money-stock multiplier into elements reflecting specific technical factors, as done for the simpler system and multiplier in Chapter 10. The technical factors pertinent to the secondary system in Chapter 10 were expressed in terms of several key behavioral ratios, and our approach here will be the same.[15]

Our first ratio for the current system is defined as:

The ar ratio

$$ar = \frac{AR}{TRL} \qquad (1)$$

The ar ratio is equal to AR, adjusted total reserves, divided by TRL, total reservable liabilities of depository institutions. The adjustment to total reserves used to arrive at AR is the St. Louis reserve adjustment magnitude. As a result, changes in the ar ratio reflect only changes in the ratio of excess reserves to total reservable liabilities.

---

[15]The analysis which follows is adapted from Jerry L. Jordan, "Elements of Money Stock Determination," Federal Reserve Bank of St. Louis *Monthly Review*, October 1969, 10-19.

FIGURE 14–7
Adjusted monetary base (averages of daily figures seasonally adjusted by this bank)

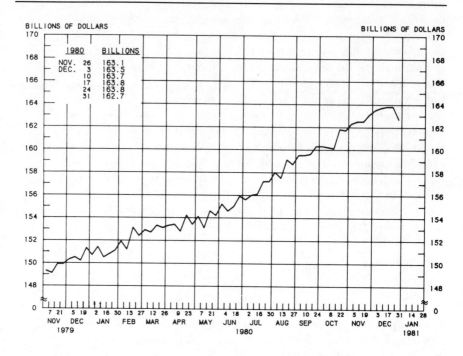

BILLIONS OF DOLLARS

1980	BILLIONS
NOV. 26	163.1
DEC. 3	163.5
10	163.7
17	163.8
24	163.8
31	162.7

Multipliers* (averages of daily figures seasonally adjusted)

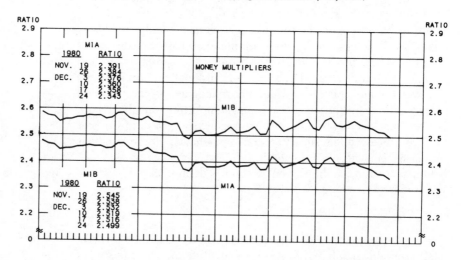

M1A 1980	RATIO
NOV. 19	2.391
26	2.384
DEC. 3	2.376
10	2.360
17	2.358
24	2.343

M1B 1980	RATIO
NOV. 19	2.545
26	2.538
DEC. 3	2.532
10	2.519
17	2.516
24	2.499

MONEY MULTIPLIERS

Changes in the average required reserve ratio have already been taken into account in the reserve adjustment magnitude. Total reservable liabilities include checkable deposits and nonpersonal time deposits of all depository institutions and certain managed liabilities at member banks, as explained below.

Our second ratio is k:

The k ratio

$$k = \frac{PC}{D} \tag{2}$$

The k ratio is equal to PC, total currency held by the public outside of depository institutions, divided by D, the checkable-deposit and travelers-checks component of M-1B. The behavior of the k ratio was explained for earlier periods in Chapter 10. Recent behavior will be explained shortly in this section.

The two ratios introduced so far are similar to ratios defined in Chapter 10. The third ratio, orl, is new:

The orl ratio

$$orl = \frac{ORL}{D} \tag{3}$$

The orl ratio is equal to ORL, other reservable liabilities of depository institutions, divided by D. Other reservable liabilities are simply total reservable liabilities less D.

Deriving the multipler in terms of ratios

This completes our list of ratios. A few simple identities are required now to permit a solution of the system to show the multiplier in terms of our three ratios.

The first identity is

$$M^S = D + PC \tag{4}$$

This defines the money supply, as measured by M-1B, in terms of its checkable-deposit-plus-travelers-check and currency components.

Our second identity defines the adjusted monetary base in terms of two components

$$AB = AR + PC \tag{5}$$

The adjusted base equals adjusted reserves plus the currency component of the M-1B money supply.

The third identity is

$$TRL = D + ORL \tag{6}$$

Total reservable liabilities are comprised of checkable deposits and travelers checks plus other reservable liabilities.

The complete set of equations is as follows:

$$ar = \frac{AR}{TRL} \tag{1}$$

$$k = \frac{PC}{D} \tag{2}$$

$$orl = \frac{ORL}{D} \tag{3}$$

$$M^S = D + PC \tag{4}$$

$$AB = AR + PC \tag{5}$$

$$TRL = D + ORL \tag{6}$$

To solve for the multiplier, substitute (6) into (1), solve for AR and substitute the result into (5) to find

$$AB = ar\,(D + ORL) + PC \tag{7}$$

Next solve (2) and (3) for PC and ORL, respectively, and substitute the results into (7) and simplify to get

$$AB = (ar\,(1 + orl) + k)\,D \tag{8}$$

Finally solve (8) for D and (2) for PC, substitute the results into (4), and simplify as follows

$$M^S = \frac{1 + k}{ar\,(1 + orl) + k} \cdot AB \tag{9}$$

This expression permits us to identify the money-stock multiplier for the M-1B money supply and the adjusted monetary base as

$$am = \frac{1 + k}{ar\,(1 + orl) + k} \tag{10}$$

The effect of a change in the k ratio

Expression (10) reveals how our ratios affect the value of the money-stock multiplier. Suppose, for example, that the k ratio rises. Even though the k ratio enters both the numerator and denominator of the multiplier, a higher value for the k ratio tends to reduce the multiplier as long as $ar\,(1 + orl)$ is less than one—as it almost certainly always will be—because this makes any value added in the denominator larger as a proportion of the initial value than the proportional change for an equal value added in the numerator.[16]

The above is the mechanical explanation of the effect of a change in k. For a more intuitive explanation, we can point to the fact that a rise in the k ratio may imply that the public is withdrawing currency from depository institutions. This drains reserves from these institutions and, ceteris paribus, tends to cause a multiple reduction in checkable deposits. The result of these changes is a rise in the PC component of the money supply, but a larger fall in the D component.

---

[16]See footnote 9 in Chapter 10 for an explanation of a similar result using calculus.

FIGURE 14–8
Money multiplier and related ratios

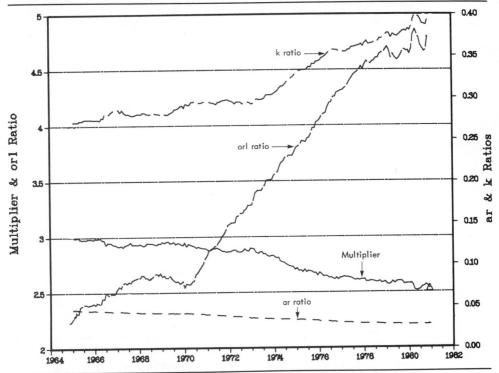

The k ratio has had a positive trend in recent years and a slight cyclical pattern, shown in Figure 14–8. The positive trend may reflect growth in the proportion of economic activity accounted for by the underground economy.[17] The cyclical pattern may be a mild reflection of the same influences which caused severe cyclical fluctuations in the k ratio before the introduction of deposit insurance. It is certainly possible that in a recession, some depositors still become uneasy about the safety of their deposits and prefer currency.

A rise in the ar ratio clearly tends to cause the multiplier to fall. If depository institutions raise their excess reserves relative to total reservable liabilities, there will be fewer checkable deposits outstanding, ceteris paribus.

The ar ratio has been relatively steady in recent years, mainly because, since 1968, the Fed has used lagged-reserve accounting. As explained briefly in Chapter 12, lagged-reserve accounting sets required reserve levels for depository institutions based upon their reservable liabilities two weeks prior to the current week. Since individual institutions thus know in advance the exact level of required reserves they must achieve each week, there is no need to carry excess reserves with the Fed as a precaution against unexpected changes in the level of required reserves. The decline in the

The effect of a change in the ar ratio

[17]See the discussion in Chapter 9.

FIGURE 14–9
Excess reserves

	(1) Excess Reserves	(2)
Average of period	Millions of dollars	Percent of required reserves
1960	$547	3.0%
1961	599	3.2
1962	522	2.7
1963	445	2.3
1964	396	2.0
1965	379	1.8
1966	359	1.6
1967	367	1.6
1968	356	1.4
1969	230	0.9
1970	187	0.7
1971	205	0.7
1972	193	0.6
1973	221	0.7
1974	193	0.5
1975	183	0.5
1976	219	0.6
1977	209	0.6
1978	193	0.5
1960–68	441	2.0
1969–78	204	0.6

ratio of excess reserves to required reserves after 1968 is shown in Figure 14–9. As a result, fluctuations in the ar ratio due to interest-rate changes and other influences have been very small in recent years.

The effect of changes in the orl ratio

A rise in the orl ratio tends to lower the money-stock multiplier because, as other reservable liabilities rise relative to the checkable-deposit and travelers-check component of the money supply, reserves are absorbed to support these other reservable liabilities, leaving less to support D, ceteris paribus. The orl ratio has tended to rise over the long run. Around its long-run positive trend, the orl ratio tends to rise during business expansions and fall during recessions. The long-run rise reflects continuing improvements in the cash management techniques of businesses and individuals, the extention of Federal Reserve requirements to new types of managed liabilities, and increased reliance of depository institutions on managed liabilities. The cyclical pattern of the orl ratio reflects the strong cyclical pattern of bank credit, which is financed at the margin by managed liabilities such as CDs and federal funds.[18]

---

[18] Other reservable liabilities include interbank deposits, U.S. government deposits at banks (known as tax and loan accounts), savings and small time deposits, and certain managed liabilities. The behavior of each of these liabilities could be examined separately and accounted for with individual ratios in our multiplier analysis. We have chosen not to do this not only to simplify the analysis but also because it probably is not a meaningful exercise in the current system.

Prior to the relaxation of Regulation Q ceilings on large CDs in the early 1970s, such a fine analysis was necessary because banks were more limited in their ability to

As the foregoing discussion reveals, the value of the money-stock multiplier in the current system depends upon a number of complex variables in the economy. Variations in its value cannot be traced to interest-rate and real-income changes as strongly or for the same reasons as applied to earlier periods, covered by the analysis in Chapter 10. Institutional changes such as lagged-reserve accounting and federal deposit insurance account for the differences. Also, because reserve requirements in the present system are applied to managed liabilities of member banks as well as to checkable deposits, there is now a cyclical influence on the multiplier which tends to reduce it at business-cycle peaks and increase it at business-cycle troughs, as described earlier in the paragraph on the orl ratio.

Getting the intermediate target

If the Federal Reserve were to focus on the adjusted monetary base as an intermediate target and on M-1B as a money-supply target, the money-stock multiplier described in this section would be the one pertinent to the establishment of an appropriate target range for the adjusted monetary base, and projections for the multiplier would be made based on the factors identified in this section. To see how this would work, suppose that, on the basis of an analysis of our three ratios, it is projected that the multiplier is likely to rise by 2 percent over the next year, and suppose the midpoint of the target range for M-1B were 5 percent, then the appropriate midpoint of a target range for the adjusted monetary base would be roughly 3 percent. As this example illustrates, the basic relationship between the growth rates of the M-1B money supply, the multiplier, and the adjusted monetary base is[19]

---

raise funds and disintermediation was an important factor affecting the multiplier. (See discussion in Jerry L. Jordan, "Elements of Money Stock Determination," Federal Reserve Bank of St. Louis *Monthly Review*, October 1969, 10-19.) In the recent period, banks have tended to offset losses of savings and small time deposits during high interest-rate periods with increased issues of CDs and other managed liabilities. Effects on the money supply due to differences in required reserve ratios remain, but are accounted for in the reserve adjustment magnitude.

[19]The relationship on the next page can be derived from the equation, $M^S = am \cdot AB$, by taking logarithms and the time derivative of the result as follows:

$$\ln (M^S) = \ln (am) + \ln (AB)$$
$$\frac{d \ln (M^S)}{dt} = \frac{d \ln (am)}{dt} + \frac{d \ln (AB)}{dt}$$

which is the continuous-time version of the relationship in the text.

Alternatively, using the delta operation to get

$$\Delta M^S = \Delta am (AB) + \Delta AB (am)$$

and dividing by M^S, we find

$$\frac{\Delta M^S}{M^S} = \frac{\Delta am (AB)}{M^S} + \frac{\Delta AB (am)}{M^S}$$

which can be converted to the same expression as the one in the text by substituting $am \cdot AB$ for M^S in each term on the right-hand side and clearing.

$$\frac{\Delta M^S}{M^S} = \frac{\Delta am}{am} + \frac{\Delta AB}{AB}$$

For a given target growth rate for the money supply, the target growth rate for the adjusted monetary base will be higher or lower according to projected changes in the multiplier.

Other intermediate targets and multipliers

If the Federal Reserve uses a narrower reserve aggregate such as total reserves for an intermediate target, a slightly modified version of the am multiplier—one incorporating some of the technical factors allowed for in the construction of the adjusted monetary base— would have to be projected. The projection for this multiplier and the target for M-1B would establish the appropriate target range for the narrower aggregate, as described for the adjusted monetary base.

TWO VIEWS OF THE MONEY-SUPPLY PROCESS AND LAGGED-RESERVE ACCOUNTING

The analysis of this chapter so far has skirted a fundamental issue which will be taken up in this last section.[20] Earlier sections described the Federal Reserve's use of the federal funds rate as an intermediate indicator and target during the 1970s and its shift to a reserve-aggregate approach to monetary control in October, 1979.

According to one point of view, the 1979 shift in the Federal Reserve's approach was an appropriate and highly promising move, for, whether the Fed used them or not, the reserve aggregates have always been better intermediate indicators, the effective locus of control, and hence preferable targets for Federal Reserve actions. Another point of view is that, subsequent to the seemingly innocuous change from contemporaneous accounting to lagged accounting for reserves in 1968, the reserve aggregates have not been meaningful indicators or appropriate targets for Federal Reserve actions. As long as lagged-reserve accounting is retained (and as of mid-1981 it was still), the effective control mechanism for the money supply will remain, as it has been since 1968, short-term interest rates in general and the federal funds rate in particular. To make its recent conversion to reserve-aggregate targeting complete, the Fed must revert to contemporaneous-reserve accounting.

The view of the critics of lagged-reserve accounting

To understand the reasoning behind the second point of view, it is important to recognize that, because of lagged accounting, depository institutions are locked into a certain level of required reserves each week. They cannot change the level of their reservable liabili-

_____

[20]Lagged-reserve accounting may have been dropped by the time you read this book. If so, this section will be of less interest from a current perspective, but should still be valuable for recent history and for insight into the money-supply process.

ties two weeks in the past, upon which their current required reserves depend. The Federal Reserve knows this, it knows the total
level of reserves required, and it usually plans its open-market operations accordingly. Indeed, the original purpose of lagged-reserve
accounting was to facilitate such planning. Even if the Fed plans
poorly, depository institutions have access to the discount window.
Hence, one way or another, the Fed will supply the required level
of reserves. To do otherwise would eventually force some depository institutions into a penalty situation and/or drive the federal
funds rate to ridiculous levels.

This means that the money supply drives the reserve aggregates,
not the other way around. Put differently, the relationship that
would normally exist between the reserve aggregates and the
money supply is reversed under lagged-reserve accounting, and the
reserve aggregates cannot be used as a control mechanism for the
money supply.[21]

It would seem that the above analysis implies that the money
supply is completely uncontrolled under lagged-reserve accounting,
but this is not so. According to the critics of lagged-reserve accounting, the Fed still controls the money supply but the control mechanism operates through interest rates instead of the reserve aggregates. Each week, depository institutions willingly supply whatever
level of checkable deposits the public demands because these deposits are a bargain basement source of funding and because these
institutions know without a doubt that reserves will be available two
weeks later. The demand for money, therefore, controls the supply.
In order to control the supply of money, the Federal Reserve must
control the demand for money, and it does this, whether it recognizes it or not, through interest rates.

The interest-rate control mechanism

Though the depository system is locked into a set level of required reserves each week, and the Fed is locked into supplying

---

[21]In terms of the adjusted monetary base, for example, and equations allowing for
lags, the normal relationship between the money supply and the base would be
represented as follows:

$$M_t^s = \sum_{i=1}^{n} b_i (AB_{t-i})$$

$$ame = \sum_{i=1}^{n} b_i$$

where ame is an "equilibrium" multiplier. The first equation says that the money
supply in the current period is a function of the monetary base in the current period
and in previous periods (up to the nth previous period). The second equation says
that the equilibrium multiplier, ame, measures the total influence over time of the
base on the money stock.

Due to lagged-reserve accounting, the above relationships are replaced by

$$AB_t = \frac{1}{ame} (M_{t-2}^s)$$

where t denotes weekly periods. This says that each week the monetary base is a
simple function of the money stock two weeks ago.

those reserves, the Fed can vary the opportunity cost of reserves by waiting for the federal funds rate to trade up or down before making the necessary additions or subtractions to reserves. As described earlier in this chapter, significant changes in the federal funds rate translate into changes in the general level of short-term interest rates, and the demand for money is inversely related to the level of short-term interest rates. The control mechanism, therefore, is such that a rise in the federal funds rate is the appropriate action to take to curb the rate of growth of the money supply, and a decline in the federal funds rate is the most fruitful way to encourage faster money growth under lagged-reserve accounting.[22]

To support their position, critics of lagged-reserve accounting point to an absence of any correlation between the growth rates of the reserve aggregates and subsequent growth in the money supply during the post-1968 period.[23] They also cite the high variability of money growth rates in the post–1968 period and particularly during 1980–81—a symptom, they assert, of the way the money supply tends to perform when interest rates are the control device. Finally, they cite the tendency for changes in adjusted total reserves to follow changes in the money supply with a two-week lag, as shown in Figure 14-10.

Defense of the 1980–1981 approach

Those who believe that lagged-reserve accounting does not interfere with the Fed's new approach cite the Federal Reserve's narrow target range for the federal funds rate as the reason for exceptional

---

[22]Reserve requirements on managed liabilities are another potential control device since reserve requirements influence the effective cost of managed liabilities to member banks. See footnote 16 in Chapter 6. The discount rate is also effective to the extent that borrowed reserves are or become an important source of funds to depository institutions.

[23]The following regression results for pre– and post–September 1968 periods illustrate the evidence noted above.
1.   Period: January 1957 to September 1968:

$$\dot{M}_t^s = 1.79 + .22\ \dot{A}B_t + .15\ \dot{A}B_{t-1}$$
$$(4.10)\quad (4.33)\qquad\quad (3.02)$$
$$R^2 = .14 \quad F = 11.4 \quad DW = 1.65$$

2.   Period: October 1968 to December 1979:

$$\dot{M}_t^s = 3.27 + .42\ \dot{A}B_t + .06\ \dot{A}B_{t-1}$$
$$(2.70)\quad (4.67)\qquad\quad (0.68)$$
$$R^2 = .14 \quad F = 10.7 \quad DW = 1.89$$

Monthly data were used. Students t statistics are reported in parentheses. As the first regression shows, for the pre–September 1968 period, M^s, the rate of growth of M-1 (old definition), is significantly related to AB, the rate of growth of the monetary base, in the same month *and to AB lagged one month*. In the post–September 1968 period, covered by the second regression, however, $\dot{M}^s$ is no longer significantly related to $\dot{A}B$ lagged one month.

See also David A. Pierce, "Money Supply Control: Reserves as the Instrument Under Lagged Accounting," *Journal of Finance*, (June 1976): 845–52.

FIGURE 14-10
Adjusted bank reserves* money stock (M1B) (averages of daily figures seasonally adjusted)

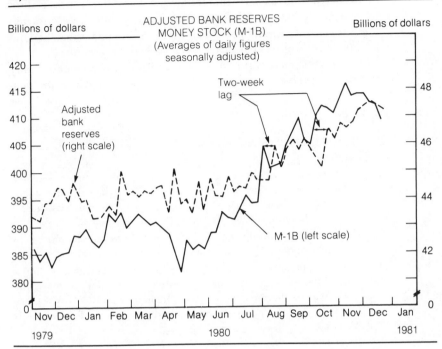

variability in money growth rates during the 1970s. It is argued that despite lagged-reserve accounting, the Federal Reserve can assert control over nonborrowed reserves and, ultimately, the money supply via this reserve aggregate and the discount window. These analysts rely upon the "gentle whip" mechanism explained earlier in the discussion of nonborrowed reserves. The high variability of money growth during 1980–81 is explained by Fed inexperience with the new approach, the on and off effects of credit controls in 1980, and high and variable inflation.

The debate on lagged-reserve accounting may be resolved soon by a reversion to contemporaneous accounting since the Fed has indicated that it is studying the issue. Even so, this topic will remain an interesting example of how small institutional changes may have big, unanticipated implications for the performance of monetary policy—implications that take years to become generally recognized and still more years to be corrected.

CONCLUSION

This chapter has outlined the operation of the money-supply process and the implementation of monetary policy in the recent period. The material included a description of the significant change in Federal Reserve control procedures in 1979 in response to difficulties in monetary control and unsatisfactory experience with inflation in the 1970s. It is too early to tell how successful the new procedure which focuses on the reserve aggregates will be, but, as described in the last section, doubts remain in the minds of some that Federal Reserve's control problems have been adequately resolved.

The next chapter turns to the other blade of the money supply and demand scissors, the demand for money. This will be the final chapter in Part 3.

PROBLEMS

1. Discuss the Federal Reserve's need for targets and indicators. Provide examples.

2. In Chapter 3 it was stated that a rise in the rate of growth of the money supply tends to reduce interest rates initially. In this chapter it was stated that a rise in the rate of growth of the money supply may cause a quick rise in interest rates. Reconcile these statements.

3. What is the value in adjusting various reserve aggregates for changes in required reserves, e.g., adjusted nonborrowed reserves?

4. The first column of the following clipping provides key items from the Federal Reserve's and Treasury's balance sheets relevant to the supply of reserves in the monetary system. Identify those items which are under the Federal Reserve's control and explain how that control is exercised.

Federal Reserve Data

MEMBER BANK RESERVE CHANGES
Changes in weekly averages of member bank reserves and related items during the week and year ended May 27, 1981 were as follows (in millions of dollars)-b

		Chg fm wk end	
	May 27 1981	May 20 1981	May 28 1980
Reserve bank credit:			
U.S. Gov't securities:			
Bought outright	120,112	− 1,475	− 13
Held under repurch agreemt	....	....	− 726
Federal agency issues:			
Bought outright	8,720	....	− 157
Held under repurch agreemt	....	....	− 211
Acceptances−bought outright			
Held under repurch agreemt	....	....	− 119
Borrowings from Fed	2,923	+ 948	+ 1,799
Seasonal borrowings	309	+ 38	+ 280
Float	2,497	− 547	− 1,009
Other Federal Reserve Assets	9,869	+ 18	+ 4,960
Total Reserve Bank credit	144,121	− 1,057	+ 4,523
Gold stock	11,154	....	− 18
SDR certificates	2,818	....	− 150
Treasury currency outstanding	13,551	+ 8	+ 284
Total	171,643	− 1,050	+ 4,638
Currency in circulation	135,945	+ 203	+ 10,758
Treasury cash holdings	506	− 3	− 60
Treasury dpts with F.R. Bnks	2,830	− 289	+ 216
Foreign deposits with F.R. Bnks	258	− 16	− 97
Other deposits with F.R. Bnks	241	− 35	− 537
Other F.R. liabilities & capital	4,885	− 53	− 158
Total	144,664	− 195	+ 10,120
Reserves			
With F.R. Banks	26,979	− 855	− 5,482
Total inc. cash	40,393	− 167	− 3,207
Required reserves	39,810	− 546	− 3,804
Excess reserves	583	+ 379	+ 597
Free reserves	− 2,031	− 531	

b-The figures reflect adjustment for new Federal Reserve rules that impose reserve requirements on most deposit-taking institutions, including non-member commercial banks, mutual savings banks and savings and loan associations.

MONETARY AND RESERVE AGGREGATES
(daily average in billions)

	One week ended:	
	May 20	May 13
Money supply (M1-A) sa	363.9	364.9
Money supply (M1-B) sa	427.4	428.6
	May 27	May 20
Monetary base	164.03	163.63
Total Reserves	40.49	40.42
Nonborrowed Reserves	37.56	38.47
Required Reserves	39.90	40.22
	Four weeks ended:	
	May 20	Apr. 22
Money supply (M1-A) sa	364.8	365.2
Money supply (M1-B) sa	428.7	428.4

sa-Seasonally adjusted. nsa-Not seasonally adjusted.

KEY INTEREST RATES
(weekly average)

	May 27	May 20
Federal funds	18.71	18.89
Treasury bill (90 day)	16.41	16.52
Commercial paper (dealer, 90 day)	17.52	17.80
Certfs of Deposit (resale, 90 day)	18.28	18.56
Eurodollars (90 days)	19.16	19.08

SOURCE: The Wall Street Journal, June 1, 1981.

5. Is the federal funds rate a good indicator of the thrust of Federal Reserve policy? Explain.

ADVANCED READINGS

Andersen, Leonall C., and Jordan, Jerry L. "The Monetary Base—Explanation and Analytical Use." Federal Reserve Bank of St. Louis *Monthly Review*, August, 1968.

Burger, Albert. *The Money Supply Process*. Belmont, Ca.: Wadsworth, 1971.

Cathcart, Charles D. "A View of Monetary Control and Lagged-Reserve Accounting." *The Money Manager*, March 10, 1980.

Controlling Monetary Aggregates. Boston: Federal Reserve Bank of Boston, 1969.

Controlling Monetary Aggregates II: The Implementation. Boston: Federal Reserve Bank of Boston, 1972.

Davis, R.G. "Broad Credit Measures as Targets for Monetary Policy." Federal Reserve Bank of New York *Quarterly Review*, Summer 1979.

"The Depository Institutions Deregulation and Monetary Control Act of 1980." Federal Reserve *Bulletin*, June 1980.

Hayes, A. "Prospects and Problems for Monetary Policy." Federal Reserve Bank of New York *Monthly Review*, February 1973.

Jordan, Jerry L. "Elements of Money Stock Determination." Federal Reserve Bank of St. Louis *Monthly Review*, October, 1979.

Mayer, T. "The Federal Reserve's Policy Procedures." *Journal of Money, Credit, and Banking* 4 (August 1972).

Monetary Policy Report to Congress. Washington, D.C.: Board of Governors of the Federal Reserve System, February 19, 1980.

Pierce, D.A. "Money Supply Control: Reserves as the Instrument Under Lagged Accounting." *Journal of Finance*, June 1976, 845–52.

APPENDIX

RECORD OF POLICY ACTIONS OF THE FEDERAL OPEN MARKET COMMITTEE: Meeting held on October 6, 1979

Domestic policy directive. This meeting of the Committee was called by the Chairman to consider actions that might be taken, in conjunction with actions being contemplated by the Board of Governors, to improve control over the expansion of money and bank credit in the light of developing speculative excesses in financial and commodity markets and additional evidence of strong inflationary forces in the economy. Special attention was given to the conduct of open market operations in order to contain growth in the monetary aggregates within the ranges previously adopted by the Committee for the year ending in the fourth quarter of 1979.

The information available at the time of the meeting suggested somewhat stronger economic activity in the third quarter than had been indicated at the time of the Committee's meeting on September 18, and real output of goods and services was estimated to have recovered a significant part of the second-quarter decline. According to staff projections, however, a decline in activity in the fourth quarter still appeared probable. Prices on the average were continuing to rise somewhat more rapidly than anticipated earlier, in part because of additional large increases in energy items and renewed upward pressures on foods. Moreover, developments in spot and futures markets for a number of commodities were indicative of an intensification of speculative activity and of the possibility of a further surge in prices.

In foreign exchange markets the weighted average value of the dollar against major foreign currencies had declined substantially since the Committee's meeting in mid-September, and monetary authorities had purchased, net, a large amount of dollars. Over the last few days dollar exchange rates had strengthened somewhat and gold prices had fallen considerably from record highs, apparently in anticipation of official actions to support the dollar. However, the atmosphere in the exchange markets remained sensitive and unsettled.

In accordance with the Committee's decision at its meeting on September 18, open market operations initially were directed toward a slight increase in the federal funds rate to about 11 1/2 percent. On September 18, moreover, the Board of Governors announced an increase in Federal Reserve Bank discount rates from 10 1/2 to 11 percent. Subsequently, open market operations were aimed at maintaining the funds rate at about 11 1/2 percent, although the rate generally was somewhat higher during the week preceding this meeting. Interest rates had remained under considerable upward pressure since mid-September, and most yields had risen to new highs for the year.

The monetary aggregates—M–1 and M–2—continued to expand at rapid rates in September, and growth in bank credit appeared to have accelerated appreciably from its pace in the prior two months. Banks were reported to have financed a substantial portion of their loan growth through sizable increases in the outstanding volume of large-denomination certificates of deposit and through continued large borrowings in the Eurodollar market.

At its meeting on July 11, 1979, the Committee reaffirmed the ranges for monetary growth in 1979 that it had established in February. Thus the Committee agreed that from the fourth quarter of 1978 to the fourth quarter of 1979, average rates of growth in the monetary aggregates within the following ranges appeared to be consistent with broad economic aims: M–1, 1 1/2 to 4 1/2 percent; M–2, 5 to 8 percent; and M–3, 6 to 9 percent. The associated range for commercial bank credit was 7 1/2 to 10 1/2 percent. Having established the range for M–1 in February on the assumption that expansion of ATS and NOW accounts would dampen growth by about 3 percentage points over the year, the Committee also agreed that actual growth of M–1 might vary in relation to its range to the extent of any deviation from that estimate. It now appeared that expansion of such accounts would reduce measured growth of M–1 over the year by about 1 1/2 percentage points. After allowance for the deviation from the earlier estimate, the equivalent range for M–1 was 3 to 6 percent.

Over the first three quarters of the year, growth in M–1, M–2, and M–3 was within the ranges for 1979 set by the Committee. However, growth in all three monetary aggregates became increasingly rapid after the first quarter. Thus M–1 grew at annual rates of about 7 1/2 and 9 1/2 percent in the second and third quarters respectively, after a decline at a rate of about 2 percent in the first quarter. Growth in M–2 and M–3 accelerated to annual rates of about 12 percent and 10 1/4 percent, respectively, in the third quarter. For bank credit, growth exceeded its 1979 range in each of the first three quarters. In order that growth of the monetary aggregates fall within the Committee's ranges for the whole of 1979, expansion during the final quarter of the year would have to slow substantially from the rapid rates of recent months.

In the Committee's discussion of policy for the period immediately ahead, the members agreed that the current situation called for additional measures to restrain growth of the monetary aggregates over the months ahead. The members felt that growth of the aggregates at rates within the ranges previously established for 1979 remained a reasonable and feasible objective in the light of the available information and the business outlook. Given that objective, most members strongly support a shift in the conduct of open market operations to an approach placing emphasis on supplying the volume of bank reserves estimated to be consistent with the desired rates of growth in monetary aggregates, while permitting much greater fluctuations in the federal funds rate than heretofore. A few members, while urging strong action to restrain monetary growth, expressed some preference for continuing to direct daily open market operations toward maintenance of levels of the federal funds rate and other short-term interest rates that appeared to be consistent with the Committee's objectives for growth in the monetary aggregates. The advantages and disadvantages of the different approaches were discussed.

The principal reason advanced for shifting to an operating procedure aimed at controlling the supply of bank reserves more directly was that it would provide greater assurance that the Committee's objectives for monetary growth could be achieved. In the present environment of rapid inflation, estimates of the relationship among interest rates, monetary growth, and economic activity had become less reliable than before, and monetary growth since the first quarter of 1979 had exceeded the rates expected despite substantial increases in short-term interest rates. Committee members recognized that for a number of reasons the relationship between growth of various reserve measures and growth of the monetary aggregates was not precise; thus the shift in emphasis to controlling reserves improved prospects for achievement of the Committee's objectives for monetary growth over the next few months but did not assure it.

Committee members suggested that the shift in operating techniques, along with the other actions being comtemplated by the Board of Governors, would tend to increase confidence at home and abroad in the System's determination to achieve its objectives for monetary growth and to avoid further deterioration in the inflationary outlook. Partly because it would increase uncertainty about the near-term course of interest rates, the new operating technique should induce banks to exercise greater caution in extending credit and might dampen speculative behavior by increasing its risks and costs. Altogether, the System's action would tend to moderate inflationary expectations, thereby exerting a constructive influence over time on decisions affecting wages and prices in domestic markets and on the value of the dollar in foreign exchange markets.

The observation was made that the new emphasis in open market operations might be accompanied by larger increases in interest rates in the immediate future than would otherwise occur. On the other hand, the emphasis on reserves also could be expected to produce a shift toward easier conditions in money markets more promptly whenever the demand for money and credit abated significantly in response to a weakening in economic activity. The point was made that an easing in money market conditions under circumstances in which growth of monetary aggregates was restrained, economic activity was weakening, and the rise in prices was moderating should not adversely affect inflationary expectations and the value of the dollar in foreign exchange markets.

At the conclusion of the discussion and after full consideration of the advantages and disadvantages of alternative courses of action, the committee agreed that in the conduct of open market operations over the remainder of 1979 the Manager for Domestic Operations should place primary emphasis on restraining expansion of bank reserves in pursuit of the Committee's objective of decelerating growth of M–1, M–2, and M–3 to rates that would hold growth of these monetary aggregates over the year from the fourth quarter of 1978 to the fourth quarter of 1979 within the Committee's ranges for that period. Specifically, the Committee instructed the Manager to restrain expansion of bank reserves to a pace consistent with growth from September to December at an annual rate on the order of 4 1/2 percent in M–1 and about 7 1/2 percent in M–2 and M–3, provided that in the period before the next regular meeting the federal funds rate remained generally within a range of 11 1/2 to 15 1/2 percent. Because such rates of expansion would result in growth of the monetary aggregates in the upper part of their ranges for the year, the Committee also agreed that over the three-month period somewhat slower growth would be acceptable.

The Committee anticipated that the shift to an operating approach that placed primary emphasis on the volume of reserves would result in both a prompt increase and greater fluctuations in the federal funds rate. It was recognized that on particular days, or for several days, the federal funds rate might rise above or fall below the general limits established, and those limits were interpreted to apply to weekly averages. The Committee also agreed that it would consider whether supplementary instructions were needed if it appeared that operations to achieve the necessary restraint in expansion of reserves would tend to maintain the federal funds rate within 1 percentage point of the upper limit of its range of 11 1/2 to 15 1/2 percent. It was understood, moreover, that the Committee's decisions with respect to open market operations in the period immediately ahead had implications for Federal Reserve Bank discount rates.

The following domestic policy directive was issued to the Federal Reserve Bank of New York:

Taking account of past and prospective developments in employment, unemployment, production, investment, real income, productivity, international trade and payments, and prices, the Federal Open Market Committee seeks to foster monetary and financial conditions that will resist inflationary pressures while encouraging moderate economic expansion and contributing to a sustainable pattern of international transactions. At its meeting on July 11, 1979, the Committee agreed that these objectives would be furthered by growth of M–1, M–2, and M–3 from the fourth quarter of 1978 to the fourth quarter of 1979 within ranges of 1 1/2 to 4 1/2 percent, 5 to 8 percent, and 6 to 9 percent respectively, the same ranges that had been established in February. The range for M–1 had been established on the basis of an assumption that expansion of ATS and NOW accounts would dampen growth by about 3 percentage points over the year. It now appears that expansion of such accounts will dampen growth by about 1 1/2 percentage points over the year; thus, the equivalent range for M–1 is now 3 to 6 percent. The associated range for bank credit is 7 1/2 to 10 1/2 percent. The Committee anticipates that for the period from the fourth quarter of 1979 to the fourth quarter of 1980, growth may be within the same ranges, depending upon emerging economic conditions and appropriate adjustments that may be required by legislation or judicial developments affecting interest-bearing transactions accounts. These ranges will be reconsidered at any time as conditions warrant.

In the short run, the Committee seeks to restrain expansion of reserve aggregates to a pace consistent with deceleration in growth of M–1, M–2, and M–3 in the fourth quarter of 1979 to rates that would hold growth of these monetary aggregates over the whole period from the fourth quarter of 1978 to the fourth quarter of 1979 within the Committee's longer-run ranges, provided that in the period before the next regular meeting the weekly average federal funds rate remains within a range of 11 1/2 to 15 1/2 percent. The Committee will consider the need for supplementary instructions if it appears that operations to restrain expansion of reserve aggregates would maintain the federal funds rate near the upper limit of its range.

Votes for this action: Messrs. Volcker, Balles, Black, Coldwell, Kimbrel, Mayo, Partee, Rice, Schultz, Mrs. Teeters, Messrs. Wallich, and Timlen. Votes against this action: None. (Mr. Timlen voted as an alternate member.)

On October 6, after the meeting of the Committee, the Board of Governors unanimously approved complementary actions also directed toward assuring better control over the expansion of money and bank credit and toward curbing speculative excesses in financial and commodity markets. Specifically, the Board approved an increase in Federal Reserve Bank discount rates from 11 percent to 12 percent and established a marginal reserve requirement of 8 percent on increases in the total of managed liabilities of member banks, Edge corporations, and U.S. agencies and branches of foreign banks. (Managed liabilities include large-denomination time deposits with maturities of less than one year, Eurodollar borrowings, repurchase agreements against U.S. Government and federal agency securities, and borrowings of federal funds from institutions other than members of the Federal Reserve System.)

Subsequently, on October 22, 1979, the Committee held a telephone conference to review the situation and to consider whether supplementary instructions to the Manager were needed. Since October 6, expansion of total reserves had exceeded the pace consistent with the Committee's objective for growth of the monetary aggregates during the fourth quarter. At the same time, the federal funds rate had begun fluctuating close to the upper limit of the 11 1/2 to 15 1/2 percent range established by the Committee. It was recognized that the desired restraint in the expansion of total reserves might involve continued pressure on money market conditions, including higher levels of member bank borrowings from the Federal Reserve than had been anticipated, as banks made orderly adjustments that would in time slow monetary growth. It was not clear, however, that retention of the 15 1/2 percent upper limit of the range for the federal funds rate would be inconsistent with the

desired restraint on monetary growth. Moreover, unsettled conditions in financial markets also suggested no change in the upper
limit of the range for the federal funds rate. Consequently, no
change was proposed in the domestic policy directive issued at the
meeting on October 6.

SOURCE: Federal Reserve *Bulletin,* December 1979.

The demand for money: Alternative approaches, major theories, and evidence

The importance of the demand for money is clear from previous chapters. Just the preliminary analysis of the demand for money in Chapter 3 permitted us to draw conclusions about the causal relationship between the money supply and the price level, for example. Economists do not always use an explicit demand-for-money function in analyzing the relationships between money and major economic variables, however. The first section of this chapter describes two alternative approaches based on classical monetary theory and shows how these approaches can be interpreted in terms of our earlier analysis of the demand for money. The second section extends the analysis of Chapter 3 to examine the major postclassical theories of the demand for money. The last section presents a summary of the evidence on the sensitivity of the demand for money to key economic variables.

ALTERNATIVE APPROACHES

Economists have long studied the relationship between money and other economic variables, but it has only been relatively recently, in the last 40 years or so, that they have developed their

15

analysis in terms of the explicit supply- and demand-for-money functions we have presented in previous chapters.

Fisher's approach

One earlier approach is associated with the work of Irving Fisher, an American economist who, you will recall, developed the Fisher interest-rate, expected-inflation equation presented in Chapter 5.[1]

Fisher's monetary analysis utilized the following *equation of exchange:*

$$M^S V^T = P^T T$$

The equation of exchange and transactions velocity

where M^S is, as always in this text, the money supply, V^T is the transactions velocity of money, explained further below, P^T is the average price of all items transacted in the economy over a set period of time, usually a year, and T is the total physical quantity of items exchanged for money over that same period of time.

The transactions velocity of money is the average number of times per period that a dollar of the money supply turns over or changes hands. When this is multiplied by the total money stock, as on the left-hand side of Fisher's equation, the result is the total value of money expenditures in all transactions (i.e., market exchanges) in the economy. The right-hand side, $P^T T$, can be said to represent the total market value of all items sold in the economy. This explains the name of Fisher's equation, the equation of exchange.

At one level, the equation of exchange can be treated as an identity with actual values for each of the variables involved

$$M^S V^T \equiv P^T T$$

This expression may be termed the *identity of exchange*. The identity sign, $\equiv$, means that the relationship described is *true by definition,* as opposed to the equals sign in the previous expression, which means that the relationship may be true only as a tendency or in *an equilibrium situation*. Obviously, the use of *actual* values for the variables in the equation of exchange makes it an identity because the actual total value of all money expenditures always equals the actual total value of all items sold. In contrast, if the left-hand side represents *desired* expenditures and the right-hand side is *desired* receipts, we have a description of an equilibrium condition, the usual meaning of the equation of exchange.

The identity of exchange

A convenient property of the identity of exchange is that it can be solved for V^T,

---

[1]Irving Fisher, *The Purchasing Power of Money* (New York: Macmillan, 1911).

$$V^T \equiv \frac{P^T \ T}{M^S}$$

and used to find measured values for V^T by using values obtained for P^T, T, and M^S, instead of finding V^T by estimating it directly.[2]

Aside from its use in measuring actual V^T, the identity of exchange is of limited value, however. It simply states that, if the money supply rises, either transactions velocity must fall, the prices of items transacted must rise, or the number of items transacted must rise, ceteris paribus. If the ceteris-paribus assumption is dropped, there are many more possibilities. Clearly, restrictions on, or theories of the behavior of some of these variables in an equilibrium, equation-of-exchange context are necessary in order to obtain more useful conclusions.

The long-run value of V^T

Fisher, in fact, had some specific notions regarding the behavior of two of these variables, V^T and T, in a long-run equilibrium. He recognized that transactions velocity might change significantly and interact with other variables in the equation of exchange within short-run periods of a few years or less; but, he reasoned, over an extended period of 5 or 10 years the rate at which the money supply turns over should be independent of other key variables in the economy and relatively stable because it is related to the institutional structure of the economy's payments system. In other words, Fisher viewed the long-run value of transactions velocity as determined by such things as the frequency with which the labor force is paid (weekly, biweekly, or monthly, for example), the frequency with which bills are customarily rendered and the speed with which they are paid, and the efficiency with which the banking system processes checks. These characteristics of the payments system were viewed as likely to change only slowly, if at all, over time; it was believed, therefore, that transactions velocity would tend to keep a constant value in the long run.

The long-run behavior of T

The other variable treated as independently determined by Fisher was T, the total quantity of items transacted in the economy. Fisher recognized that T is related to the level of real activity in the economy, that is, to the level of production and employment. In the long run, real activity, in turn, is related to nonmonetary variables such as the economy's stock of basic resources (population, natural resources, and the manufactured capital stock) and technology. Though these nonmonetary factors do tend to change over time, usually leading to long-run growth in the economy, Fisher assumed them to be constant as a matter of convenience for his analysis. This permitted him to assume that T is constant.

---

[2] In principle, V^T could be measured directly by monitoring individual transactions in the economy. Normally, it is much easier, however, to obtain estimates of the aggregate volume of all sales and of the total money stock, permitting a calculation of actual transactions velocity from the identity of exchange.

With these notions about V^T and T, Fisher was able to draw a specific conclusion from the equation of exchange regarding the money supply and the price level: *in the long run changes in the money supply tend to cause proportional changes in the price level.*

Fisher and the proportionality of prices to the money stock

To see how this conclusion follows from Fisher's analysis, first solve the equation of exchange for the price-level variable, P^T

$$P^T = \frac{V^T}{T} \times M^S$$

Next, note that if V^T and T are both constant in the long run, then their ratio, V^T/T, must also be constant. It follows that any change in the money supply will lead to a proportional change in the price level in the long run.[3]

For further insight, consider an equivalent explanation in terms of the equation of exchange in its original form. Note that a rise in the money supply ultimately causes a rise in money expenditures, $M^S V^T$, since V^T is constant in the long run. A rise in money expenditures must generate an equal rise in the value of total sales P^T T. This rise in total sales must be entirely accounted for by a rise in P^T since T is constant in the long run.

More generally, Fisher concluded that, in the long run, the price level is essentially a monetary phenomenon; that is, over an extended period of several years, the level of prices is determined more by the quantity of money in the economy than by any other factor. This idea had been developed and was widely, if not universally, held long before Fisher's analysis. It was known in Fisher's time as the *quantity theory of money.* Today it is known as the *"classical" quantity theory of money.*[4]

The classical quantity theory of money

Fisher was not the first economist to utilize the equation of exchange and the concept of velocity. Nevertheless, Fisher developed this approach to a much more refined state than his predecessors had and used it to organize strong empirical arguments in support of the classical quantity theory of money. As a result, the equation of exchange and transactions velocity became associated more with Fisher than with any other economist.

---

[3]Consider initial values of 100, 0.01, and \$10,000 for a P^T index, V^T/T, and M^S, respectively. Let M^S rise by 10 percent to \$11,000, then P^T also rises by 10 percent to 110.

[4]The meaning of the term "the quantity theory of money" has changed over the years. As noted above, in the 19th century and the early part of this century, the quantity theory of money referred to the theory that changes in the price level are caused almost entirely by prior changes in the money supply. (Unfortunately the theory was not described well by its name; a better name would have been "the quantity of money theory of the price level.")

Later in this chapter we will identify a *modern quantity theory of money* which refers to a particular approach and a particular set of empirical judgments regarding the demand for money. It is also a term used almost synonymously with monetarism because the empirical judgments associated with the modern quantity theory are among those stressed and embraced by monetarists, as described later in this chapter.

As described, Fisher's approach focused on the physical use of money in transactions and on spending on the total of all items transacted, T. The spending total in his analysis includes spending for intermediate goods such as crude materials, intermediate services such as production labor, secondhand goods such as used cars, and financial assets such as common stocks—which are excluded from GNP to avoid double counting and simple exchanges of ownership. In recognition of its association with a broader concept than GNP and physical turnover of money, Fisher's definition of velocity is usually identified as *transactions* velocity and given a special symbol, such as V^T here. Correspondingly, the price level in Fisher's analysis is a special price level, the average price of all items transacted, P^T.

The income-velocity version of Fisher's equation

Our usual focus throughout this book is slightly different from Fisher's. Our concern normally centers on money as a factor affecting spending only on *final* goods and services (GNP) and as a determinant of the price level associated with real final output—output of final goods such as new cars and final services such as medical care—and income which is derived from final output. Shifting to this perspective, we can identify an analogous equation to Fisher's as

$$M^S V^y = P \, y$$

where V^Y is the *income velocity* of money, P is the price level, and y is real final output (or real income), as defined throughout this book.

A drawback to this latter version of Fisher's equation is that income velocity does not have the concrete, physical meaning that transactions velocity does. It does not measure the turnover rate for money in the economy, since money is used in many transactions other than those for final goods and services. An advantage of the income-velocity version of Fisher's equation, on the other hand, is its orientation to variables of more fundamental interest than P^T and T. For example, it can be manipulated in the same manner as the equation of exchange to find

$$P = \frac{V^y}{y} \times M^S$$

which implies that the price level for final output will be proportional to the money supply, *provided V^y/y is constant.*

Will V^y/y tend to be constant? We might reason that V^y will be related to transactions velocity and so ascribe some long-run value to it, as Fisher did to transactions velocity. Also, in line with Fisher's analysis, we might assume that y is constant in the long run. Then V^y/y is constant in the long run. In this manner we could extend Fisher's analysis of P^T to P, the price level for final output.

However, in point of fact, often V^y and normally y are not constant—even in the long run. (Nor, it may be noted, are V^T and T constant in the long run.) To facilitate an analysis of situations where

V^y and y are changing, let us consider a growth-rate form for the income-velocity equation[5]

$$\left(\frac{\Delta M^S}{\Delta t} \times \frac{1}{M^S}\right) + \left(\frac{\Delta V^y}{\Delta t} \times \frac{1}{V^y}\right) = \left(\frac{\Delta P}{\Delta t} \times \frac{1}{P}\right) + \left(\frac{\Delta y}{\Delta t} \times \frac{1}{y}\right)$$

This relationship states that the rate of growth of the money supply, $\frac{\Delta M^S}{\Delta t} \times \frac{1}{M^S}$, plus the rate of growth of velocity, $\frac{\Delta V^y}{\Delta t} \times \frac{1}{V^y}$, equals the rate of inflation, $\frac{\Delta P}{\Delta t} \times \frac{1}{P}$, plus the rate of growth of real income, $\frac{\Delta y}{\Delta t} \times \frac{1}{y}$. It is a valuable relationship for two reasons. First, as noted above, the income velocity of the money supply often has not been constant, even in the long run. In recent years, the velocity of the M-1B money supply has tended to rise at a rate of roughly 3.5 percent per year, for example. Second, the long-run average growth rate of real income is usually positive. Over the 1970s, the average growth rate of real personal income was roughly 3 percent per year. Holding such *rates of change* constant (instead of holding V^y and y constant as Fisher's analysis would suggest), we can find that, in the long run, a given steady rate of growth of the M-1B money supply implies a given steady rate of inflation. For example, based on the numbers above for velocity and real income growth rates, 6.5 percent growth for M-1B implies a 7 percent inflation rate.

M-1B money growth of		M-1B velocity growth of		Inflation of		Real income growth of
6.5%	+	3.5%	=	7.0%	+	3.0%

The Federal Reserve's target ceiling for the M-1B money supply in 1980 was 6.5 percent. If recent history for M-1B velocity growth and real-income growth hold in the future, success in achieving 6.5 percent or less growth for M-1B in 1980 and subsequent years implies that inflation in the United States should gradually wind down

Velocity growth and monetary targets

---

[5]To find this relationship, use the delta operator on the income velocity version of Fisher's equation to get

$$\Delta M^S (V^y) + \Delta V^y (M^S) = \Delta P(y) + \Delta y(P)$$

and divide the right- and left-hand sides of this equation by Δt and by the right- and left-hand sides, respectively, of the income velocity equation as follows:

$$\frac{\Delta M^S (V^y) + \Delta V^y (M^S)}{\Delta t(M^S \ V^y)} = \frac{\Delta P(y) + \Delta y(P)}{\Delta t(P \ y)}$$

This reduces to the growth-rate equation in the text.

The continuous version of this growth-rate relationship may be found by taking the time derivative of the log of the income velocity equation to get

$$\frac{d \ln M^S}{dt} + \frac{d \ln V^Y}{dt} = \frac{d \ln P}{dt} + \frac{d \ln y}{dt}$$

to 7 percent or less as a long-run average. This calculation is not an esoteric textbook illustration; it is just this sort of math which underlies the Federal Reserve's long-run targets for the monetary aggregates.

FIGURE 15–1
Velocities of new and old M-1 measures (quarterly, seasonally adjusted at annual rates)

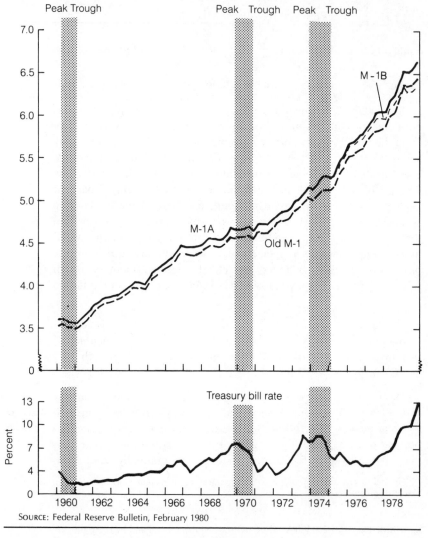

SOURCE: Federal Reserve Bulletin, February 1980

Explaining changes in income velocity

Why has income velocity been rising so rapidly in recent years, as shown in Figure 15–1? Fisher's analysis would point directly to institutional changes in the payments system, changes such as the spread in the use of credit cards among households and the adoption of sophisticated cash management methods by business firms.

These changes obviously have accelerated the rate of turnover of the money stock.

Another, less direct, explanation is based on a reconciliation between the velocity approach and the supply and demand for money approach to monetary analysis developed in Chapter 3. We start with the income-velocity equation,

$$M^S \; V^y = P \; y \tag{1}$$

and assume, as we did in Chapter 3, that the quantity of money supplied equals the quantity of money demanded in equilibrium

$$M^S = M^D \tag{2}$$

Next substitute Equation (2) into Equation (1) and solve for V^y to get

$$V^y = \frac{P \; y}{M^D} \tag{3}$$

In words, in equilibrium, income velocity can be viewed as equal to the nominal value of total output (or income) divided by the demand for money.

Now consider a slightly modified version of our demand-for-money function in Chapter 3

$$M^D = f(P, \; y, \; i, \; . \; . \; . \; .) \tag{4}$$

where P is substituted for 1/P in our Chapter 3 demand-for-money function. A rise in P causes a proportional rise in M^D since, you recall, a fall in 1/P causes a proportional rise in M^D.

What are the likely effects of a change in P, y, and i, respectively, on income velocity? First, a rise in the price level will tend to increase the quantity of money demanded proportionately, increasing the denominator on the right-hand side of expression (3). But note also that there will be a precisely offsetting proportional change in the numerator of expression (3) as a result of the rise in P. Consequently, *a one-time change in the price level should not have any effect on the level of the income velocity of money.*[6] This is an interesting result because it lends support to Fisher's conclusion that velocity tends to be constant in the long run. We have two more variables to consider, however.

The price level

If real income rises, the quantity of money demanded, the denominator of expression (3), will rise, and so will the numerator of expression (3). Will these changes offset each other precisely? The rise in the numerator will be proportional to the rise in real income. The rise in the denominator will not necessarily be proportional to the rise in real income, however. (Recall that it was stated in Chapter 3 that we could not say the quantity of money demanded would

Real income

---

[6]The modifier "one-time" is used to distinguish this price-level change from an inflation-rate change, covered later.

respond proportionately to changes in real income.) If the rise in the denominator is less than proportional, income velocity will tend to rise with a rise in real income. If the rise in the denominator is more than proportional, income velocity will tend to fall with a rise in real income.

Hence the income sensitivity, i.e., the value of the income elasticity of the demand for money, is critical to the relationship between real income and income velocity. *If the income elasticity of the demand for money is less than unity, a rise in real income will tend to increase the income velocity of money; if the income elasticity of the demand for money is unity, a rise in real income will have no effect on the income velocity of money; and if the income elasticity of the demand for money is greater than unity, a rise in real income will reduce the income velocity of money.* Therefore, in order for velocity to tend to a long-run constant, as Fisher's analysis assumed, either (1) the income elasticity of the demand for money must be unity, or (2) real income must be constant. Constant real income is, of course, the other key assumption in Fisher's analysis, one adopted by Fisher as a matter of convenience; but it is clearly not consistent with the experience of most economies, including that of the United States, in the recent decade. *We conclude that the rising trend to the income velocity of the M-1B money supply in recent years might be attributable, at least in part, to rising real income in the United States and to a less than unitary elastic relationship between the demand for M-1B money and real income.*[7]

The level of market interest rates

The remaining variable we need to consider now is the level of market interest rates, i. If the level of market interest rates rises, ceteris paribus, the demand for money will fall. Since interest rates do not enter the numerator of the velocity equation and this is a ceteris paribus change as far as P and y are concerned, income velocity must rise. Consequently, *a rise in market interest rates causes a rise in the income velocity of money, ceteris paribus.*

This result is clearly inconsistent with Fisher's assumption regarding velocity, unless interest rates are constant in the long run.

---

[7]Estimates of the actual income elasticity of the demand for money will be described in the last section of this chapter.

To see the effects described above, let velocity in period 1 be identified as

$$V_1^y = \frac{P_1\, y_1}{M_1^D}$$

Assume that the income elasticity of demand for money equals 0.5 and that real income rises by 5 percent. Then the demand for money will rise by 2.5 percent $(0.5 \times 5.0\%)$, and velocity in period 2 will be

$$V_2^y = \frac{P_1\, y_1\, (1 + .05)}{M_1^D\, (1 + .025)} = V_1^y\, (1 + .024)$$

Hence velocity will rise by 2.4 percent.

As this example illustrates, the rate of change in income velocity caused by rising real income is equal to $[(1 + y)/(1 + y \times e)] - 1$, where y is the rate of growth of real income and e is the income elasticity of the demand for money.

Though there was not a marked trend to interest rates, up or down, in Fisher's time, in recent years there has been a distinct, rising long-run trend to U.S. interest rates (See Figure 15–1.) *Hence the relatively high positive trend to income velocity in the United States in the 1970s was probably partly attributable to the rising level of interest rates over this period.*

These influences can be summarized in a general way by the following velocity function.

$$V^y = f(y, i, \ldots)$$

Influenced variable	Influencing variable	Direction of influence
V^y: the income velocity of money	y: real income	Positive if the income elasticity of the demand for money is less than unity; zero if the income elasticity of the demand for money is unity; and negative if the income elasticity of the demand for money is greater than unity
	i: the level of market interest rates	Positive

One last point should be made before leaving Fisher's approach. Since the level of market interest rates rises with expected inflation, there is a positive relationship between velocity and expected inflation which is implicit in the velocity function above. We could also say more directly that inflation is obviously a cost to holding money, so a rise in expected inflation should lead to a rise in velocity.

Memo: Expected inflation and velocity

The classical Cambridge approach

During approximately the same period that Fisher was developing his analysis based on velocity and the equation of exchange, Alfred Marshall, A.C. Pigou, and several other prominent English economists at Cambridge University developed the classical Cambridge cash-balance approach to monetary analysis. Their work laid the foundation for the modern supply and demand framework.

In one of the clearest statements of the Cambridge approach, Pigou posited that individuals desire to hold cash balances for the services that these balances provide and choose the desired level of their money balances in some direct proportion to their total real "resources" (or wealth) and in indirect proportion to the value of money expressed in terms of some representative good such as wheat.[8] In symbols

---

[8] A.C. Pigou, "The Value of Money," *The Quarterly Journal of Economics* 32(1917–18); 38–65.

$$M^D = \frac{k\,w}{1/P^b} \tag{1}$$

where k is that proportion of their real wealth which individuals choose to keep in the form of money, w represents individuals' real wealth valued in bushels of wheat, and $1/P^b$ is the value of money in terms of a bushel of wheat.

The quantity of money demanded can be set equal to the quantity of money supplied in equilibrium, and equation (1) then can be solved to find the value of money, $1/P^b$, in terms of k, w, and M^S

$$\frac{1}{P^b} = \frac{k\,w}{M^S} \tag{2}$$

This says that the value of money (in bushels of wheat) equals the Cambridge cash-balance proportionality factor, k, times individuals' real wealth, w, divided by the money supply, M^S. Alternatively, to put this result in more familiar terms, Equation (2) can be solved for its reciprocal

$$P^b = \frac{M^S}{k\,w} \tag{3}$$

which says that the price level (as measured by the price of a bushel of wheat) is directly proportional to the money supply and indirectly proportional to k and real wealth.

Determinants of Cambridge k

Cambridge economists recognized that, in general, k should not be viewed as a constant. In fact, it was explicitly stated to be inversely related to "the loss of real income involved through the diversion to [the use as money] of resources that might have been devoted to the production of future commodities..." And it was also recognized that "...any expectation that general prices are going to fall increases people's desire to hold [cash balances relative to their real wealth]; and any expectation that they are going to rise has the contrary effect."[9] These statements can be interpreted to mean that k was viewed as inversely related to (1) the real rate of interest, and (2) the expected rate of inflation. Alternatively, they imply that k is inversely related to i, the sum of the real rate of interest and the expected rate of inflation:

$$k = f(i, \ldots)$$

Determinants of wealth

In addition, it was recognized that individuals' real wealth is variable and hence a potential source of influence on the demand for money and the price level. Real wealth was viewed as determined by factors such as accumulated real savings and the rate of growth of the economy. The money supply, it should be noted, was not viewed as a factor influencing real wealth in the long run.

---

[9]Pigou, "The Value of Money," 43–44.

This explains the general framework of the Cambridge approach. The process of adjustment of the value of money to a rise in the money supply can be described now. A rise in the money supply without any prior adjustment in P^b or w means that actual k, in all likelihood, has risen relative to desired (or equilibrium) k. Individuals now possess more cash balances than they desire relative to their other resources. In response, they attempt to spend down their cash balances and augment their holdings of other forms of wealth. Of course, the total money supply cannot be reduced in this manner, but, as transactions take place and ownership of the excess cash balances is redistributed, there is a stimulus to the production of real goods, so that w rises, and prices in general are bid up, including P^b, the price of the representative good. In response to changes in these factors, the demand for money rises and equilibrium is restored.

The process of adjustment in the Cambridge approach

Since real wealth is determined in the long run mainly by nonmonetary factors, the long-run result of changes in the money supply is predominantly a rise in the price level. Hence though coming at it from a different approach, the Cambridge school drew the same conclusion as Fisher: the price level is essentially determined by the money supply.

Pigou, in fact, identified a direct correspondence between the Cambridge and Fisher approaches as follows. Let the two price indexes, P^b and P^T, be the same

Pigou's comparison of the two approaches

$$P^b = P^T \qquad (5)$$

Then substitute Equation (3) for P^b on the left of Equation (5), and also substitute the price-level solution of the equation of exchange for P^T on the right of Equation (5) to get

$$\frac{k\,w}{M^S} = \frac{T}{M^S\,V^T} \qquad (6)$$

or, rearranging terms,

$$k\,V^T = \frac{T}{w} \qquad (7)$$

Now it may be reasonable to assume that the ratio of transactions to real wealth T/w, is a constant; it follows that the Cambridge k ratio is inversely proportional to V^T. Thus, according to Pigou, Cambridge k and V^T play essentially identical roles in each respective framework.

For another comparison, the Cambridge approach can be interpreted in an income version, just as we did for Fisher's approach.[10] Suppose individuals adjust their desired cash balances so as to keep them in some proportion to their nominal income

A comparison based on income versions

---

[10]The Cambridge analysis is often presented only in the income format which follows in the text. Our wealth rendition, just completed, is based on Pigou's article

(continued on next page)

$$M^D = k(P \ y) \tag{8}$$

Now solve Equation (8) for k, and recognize the result as the reciprocal of income velocity:

$$k = \frac{M^D}{P \ y} = \frac{1}{V^y} \tag{9}$$

In words, *when the Cambridge approach is interpreted in an income format, the Cambridge k variable is precisely the reciprocal of income velocity*. Hence all of our earlier analysis of income velocity holds for the income version of Cambridge k, with the independent variables, y and i, having influences on k opposite to those influences described for V^y.

One should not get the impression from these reconciliations of the velocity and Cambridge cash-balance approaches that the two are virtually identical. For one thing, each approach reveals valuable insights not directly or readily revealed by the other. Fisher's transactions-velocity approach focuses on *the rate at which money is spent* and draws attention to *institutional factors* which bear on this nexus between money and spending. The Cambridge cash-balance approach analyzes *desired holdings of money balances* and their interaction with *key economic variables* which adjust to bring desired balances into alignment with the money supply. Moreover, both the velocity and the Cambridge approaches in their different formats remain very much a part of modern monetary economics. Students should be reassured, therefore, that it is worthwhile mastering both analytical frameworks.

INTRODUCTION TO ARTICLE

The importance of changes in velocity in discussions of monetary policy, particularly since the Federal Reserve began to focus on growth rates for the monetary aggregates in the early 1970's, is brought out in the following article from *The Wall Street Journal*. The article, which is obviously editorial and monetarist in tone, also illustrates the fact that, just as there is debate regarding the appropriate definition of

---

cited in footnote 8. The distinction between wealth and income, and hence the difference in these formats, can be important.

Most elements of the distinction between wealth and income should be apparent from the appendix to Chapter 4. One element is that wealth is a stock whereas income is a flow. More important, wealth can rise independently of current income—through the discovery of new natural resources, for example. They are, on the other hand, related concepts in that wealth can be viewed as the capitalized value of expected *future* income, and individuals' expectations of future income are, no doubt, influenced by current income.

money, there is a corresponding debate regarding the appropriate measure of velocity.

Speedy Money

One of the simplest concepts in economics is also one of the least understood: the velocity of money. Everyone knows that the dollar he spends today is likely to be spent later by someone else. The velocity of money is nothing more than a measure of the speed at which dollars change hands.

Velocity is important because it determines how much work a given quantity of money can do. If there is a sharp rise in velocity, even a modest increase in the money supply can result in strong upward pressure on prices. A sharp drop in velocity, on the other hand, can lead to deflation even if the money stock, defined as currency and bank checking accounts, keeps on growing.

The monetarists, led by Milton Friedman of the University of Chicago, long have argued that changes in the rate of growth of the money stock exert major influence on short-run economic trends. There is still ample controversy in this area, but most economists now agree that the monetary growth rate is at least highly important.

Some economists, however, contend that unexpected changes in velocity can offset conscientious efforts to stabilize the economy by promoting a steady and moderate growth of the money stock. Last year, in a letter to Sen. William Proxmire of the Joint Economic Committee, Chairman Arthur Burns of the Federal Reserve Board put it this way:

"Changes in the rate of turnover, of money have historically played a large role in economic fluctuations, and they continue to do so. For example, the narrowly defined money stock—that is, demand deposits plus currency in circulation—grew by 5.7% between the fourth quarter of 1969 and the fourth quarter of 1970. But the turnover of money declined during that year, and the dollar value of the gross national product rose by only 4.5%.

"In the following year the growth rate of the money supply increased to 6.9%, but the turnover of money picked up briskly, and the dollar value of GNP accelerated to 9.3%. The movement out of recession in 1970 into recovery in 1971 was thus closely related to the greater intensity in the use of money."

Mr. Burns used this example to explain why, in his view, the Federal Reserve cannot concentrate solely on promoting a steady and moderate growth of the money stock but must instead use "a blend of forecasting techniques," including econometric models.

One trouble with this argument is that the Fed can neither control velocity nor anticipate its movements with precision. Nor is it really necessary to do so.

There are several ways to measure velocity, but a common one is to divide the gross national product for a given period by the average money stock during that period. It's true that this GNP velocity in terms of the narrowly defined money stock (M-1) has risen quite a lot over the past two decades—from less than 3.0 in the early 1950s to around 5.0 now, with brief ups and downs, such as Chairman Burns mentions.

Lately, however, velocity appears to have leveled off. Argus Research Corp. economists predict that the rate, which was 4.95 in the second quarter, will move up gradually during the rest of this year and 1975, but only to 5.16 in the final quarter of next year.

The velocity of the broadly defined money stock (M-2), which includes not only currency and checking accounts but bank time deposits, has been stable for a much longer time. In a study for the National Bureau of Economic Research, Milton Friedman and Anna J. Schwartz showed that M-2 velocity reached a peak in 1962 and remained extraordinarily constant through 1972. There has also been little change since then. Partly for that reason, Professor Friedman thinks that monetary policy should focus on M-2; the changes in velocity can be largely neglected.

Professor Friedman does not argue that M-2 velocity will be forever flat. He has theorized that the recent stability of the M-2 rate is a product of countervailing forces. Increasing inflation and rising interest rates encourage the public to hold smaller money balances and thus tend to increase velocity. At the same time there are factors working to encourage the public to hold larger balances and thus reduce velocity—especially, the long-term trend of rising real income.

Lately, of course, inflation has produced an actual decline in disposable personal income— in terms of constant-value dollars. If, however, inflation is reduced and interest rates decline, Professor Friedman would expect M-2 velocity to decline.

There are a number of other factors that can influence velocity over either short or long periods. One of the simplest is that a speedup in the rate of money growth will, in the very short run, lead to a decline in velocity.

As Argus Research notes, the growth rate, of M-1 jumped from 4.6% in last year's fourth quarter to 6.9% in this year's first quarter and then to 8.8% in the second quarter. M-1 velocity declined from 4.99 in the fourth quarter to 4.97 in the first quarter and then to 4.95 in the April-June period. The money supply was sim-

ply growing faster than the public could increase its use.

On a longer-range basis economists have pondered the steady rise in velocity that came after World War II. Milton Friedman and Anna Schwartz considered this period in their monumental study, "A Monetary History of the United States, 1867–1960." Much of the rise, they said, was a normal reaction to the wartime decline in velocity. During the war there was little to spend money for, so the public's money balances rose considerably.

As a major additional factor, they suggested that the public's expectations about economic stability were changing. Memories of the 1930s were gradually receding, and the public was deciding that it was prudent to hold smaller money balances.

Long term trends in velocity are important, but the trends lately—especially for M-2—have been remarkably stable. If monetary growth were equally stable there could be quite a gain in economic stability.

SOURCE: Lindley H. Clark, Jr., "Speaking of Business," *The Wall Street Journal*, August 26, 1974. Reprinted by permission *The Wall Street Journal*.

POSTCLASSICAL MONETARY THEORY: CONTROVERSY, SHORT-RUN ANALYSIS, AND NEW INSIGHT INTO THE DEMAND FOR MONEY

Keynes' criticism of the long-run focus of classical theory

The classical quantity theory of money, expressed in terms of both the Fisher and the Cambridge approaches, dominated monetary economics prior to the Great Depression. Total spending in the economy was viewed as determined principally by the money supply. As described in the last section, the focus of the theory was on the long run, and monetary economists in general tended to restrict their concern and prescriptions for monetary policy to the long run. Hence the classical view was that the monetary authorities should strive to gear the money supply to the desired price level or value of money in the long run. However, the protracted and severe unemployment brought on by the worldwide Great Depression of the 1930s caused a reevaluation of classical ideas by John Maynard Keynes, a prominent Cambridge economist and student of Marshall.[11] Keynes brushed aside the relevance of long-run equilib-

[11]Keynes' analysis was presented in his book, *The General Theory of Employment, Interest, and Money* (New York: Harcourt Brace Jovanovich, 1936).

rium analysis and a long-run focus for policy with the remark, "In the long run, we are all dead." He set out strong criticisms of several classical theories, particularly the Cambridge analysis of the demand for money, to make the case that these theories were not applicable to the short run, and he went so far as to suggest that they were wrong even for the long run.

The core of Keynes' attack on classical monetary theory was a criticism of the notion implicit in the theory that the demand for money is not highly sensitive to the rate of interest. The classical Cambridge analysis, you will recall, recognized that the demand for money (and hence the Cambridge k factor) is related to the rate of interest. But this relationship was not viewed as a critical part of the analysis, and it was ignored in the context of policy recommendations. The reason was partly that classical economists tended to restrict their attention to the medium-of-exchange, or transactions, function of money, which was viewed as relatively interest inelastic. Keynes agreed that there is reason to believe that the demand for money for transactions purposes is not very sensitive to interest rates, but he identified a total of three motives for holding money:

Keynes' three motives for holding money

1. *The Transactions Motive: the demand for money for day-to-day use as a medium of exchange.*
2. *The Precautionary Motive: the demand for money as a liquid store value to be available when unexpected needs or opportunities arise, held, in other words, to avoid risk.* An example would be a $50 bill kept in the hidden fold of your wallet to be used in case of an emergency. This motive was recognized but not stressed by classical Cambridge economists. Keynes cited this motive as a potential source of instability in the demand for money but not as a motive which increases the interest sensitivity of the demand for money.
3. *The Speculative Motive: the demand for money to avoid expected losses on assets with variable prices such as long-term bonds.* (Examples and further explanation will be provided below.) This motive had not been identified by classical economists. Keynes placed great emphasis upon it, however, and used it to argue that the demand for money is highly sensitive to interest rates, expecially when the economy is in a severe slump such as the Great Depression. (The importance of the interest sensitivity of the demand for money will be brought out in the discussion which follows.)

The speculative demand for money can be readily explained by reference to Chapters 6 and 7. (You may wish to review both of them at this point.) Recall from Chapter 6 that the realized return on a long-term bond over a short-term holding period is comprised of a coupon return plus (less) the rate of capital gain˙ (loss) on the bond over the holding period. Under circumstances in which inves-

Explanation of speculative demand

tors anticipate a capital loss on bonds (i.e., a rise in the long-term interest rate), the expected realized return may be negative. If the expected realized return is negative, investors will find it attractive to hold cash balances in preference to bonds. In other words, they will have a preference for liquidity in their investments. The demand for money in response to expected capital losses on bonds constitutes Keynes' *speculative,* or *"liquidity preference,"* demand for money.

The existence of a speculative demand for money does not by itself make the total demand for money highly sensitive to the level of market interest rates. However, Keynes theorized that expected capital losses on bonds are influenced by the level of interest rates in a way which makes the speculative demand for money, and hence the total demand for money, respond very strongly to market interest rates.

Keynes argued that, at times, market participants have definite notions about future interest rates relative to current interest rates. If the rate of interest is low at present, relative to what has prevailed in the past, for example, market participants may expect a rise in the rate of interest in the future back toward its "normal" value. The lower the rate of interest falls, the greater the rise expected subsequently. Hence the greater the expected capital loss on bonds will be, and the greater liquidity preference will be.

FIGURE 15–2
The speculative demand for money and the rate of interest

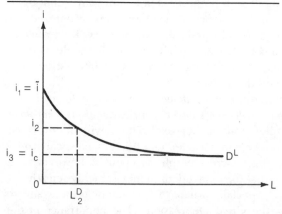

The relationship envisioned by Keynes is interpreted in Figure 15–2 by the D^L curve. When the current level of market interest rates, i_1, equals the normal level, $\tilde{i}$, the speculative demand for money, L^D, is zero. If the current market rate falls below $\tilde{i}$, say to i_2, a number of market participants will conclude that the interest rate will rise in the future and that cash is now more attractive to hold than bonds. Consequently, the speculative demand for money rises to L_2^D. The lower the interest rate, the larger will be the number of market participants who become convinced that cash is preferable to bonds and who alter the placement of their funds accordingly.

At some point, virtually all market participants are willing to exchange bonds for cash at any interest rate lower (bond price higher) than the prevailing rate (price). This implies that the speculative demand for money becomes perfectly elastic at some "critical" interest rate, represented by i_c in Figure 15–2.

The relationship we have described can be summarized as follows:

$$L^D = f(i)$$

where it is understood that L^D is highly sensitive (inversely) to levels of the rate of interest below $\tilde{i}$, the normal level, and becomes increasingly so as the interest rate approaches i_c, the critical level.

As noted earlier, Keynes also incorporated the transactions and precautionary demands for money in his analysis. He accepted the classical notion that the transactions demand is not very sensitive to the rate of interest; in fact, for analytical convenience, Keynes assumed that both the transactions and the precautionary demands for money are completely unresponsive to the interest rate, a relationship depicted by the vertical D^N curve in Figure 15–3.

The other demands for money

FIGURE 15–3
The transactions-precautionary demand for money and the rate of interest

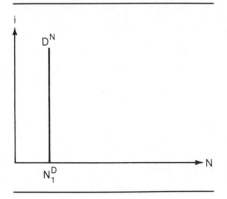

The demands for money for transactions and precautionary purposes are, of course, a function of real income and the price level, however. Consequently, the function representing the sum of the transactions and precautionary motives in Keynes' analysis can be summarized as follows:

$$N^D = f(y, P) \tag{2}$$

where N^D is the quantity of money demanded for transactions and precautionary purposes, and the influences of y and P on N^D are positive.

Now we can add the speculative function and transactions-precautionary function to get the total demand-for-money function.

$$M^D = L^D + N^D = f(i, y, P) \tag{3}$$

And the key relationship between the total demand for money and the rate of interest can be shown in Figure 15–4 as the horizontal sum of the relationships in Figures 15–2 and 15–3.

FIGURE 15–4
The Keynesian total demand for money

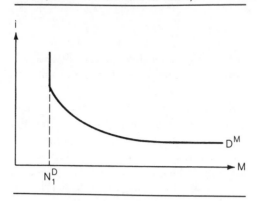

The importance of the interest sensitivity of the demand for money

This total demand function can be used to explain the importance of the interest sensitivity of the demand for money. First, assume that the supply of money is completely exogenous and determined by the Federal Reserve, as shown in Figure 15–5.

FIGURE 15–5
The money supply

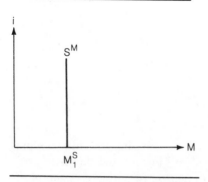

Second, combine this relationship and Keynes' demand-for-money function as in Figure 15–6.

Next, consider a shift to the right of the money-supply curve from S_1^M, to S_2^M, shown in Figure 15–7. As a result of this shift, the interest rate falls from i_1 to i_2.

A lower interest rate stimulates spending, and this is beneficial, of course, in a severe depression. In fact, according to Keynes, unless monetary policy is successful in reducing the interest rate, the

FIGURE 15–6
The supply and demand for money

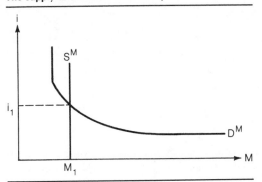

monetary authorities cannot stimulate the spending necessary to extricate the economy from a slump. But the greater the interest sensitivity of the demand for money, the smaller will be the fall in the rate of interest subsequent to a given rise in the money supply. This can be seen in Figure 15–7 where the interest rate declines by a smaller amount, from i_2 to i_3 (versus i_1 to i_2 before) following a second, equal rightward shift in the money supply curve from S_2^M to S_3^M.

FIGURE 15–7
An increase in the money supply

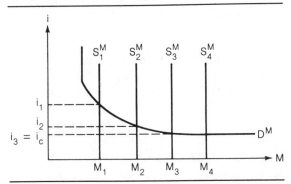

The figure also shows that, at some point, further expansion of the money supply is not successful in reducing the interest rate at all. This is the point at which the demand for money becomes perfectly elastic due to pervasive expectations that there will be substantial capital losses on bonds. No interest-rate decline results from the shift from S_3^M to S_4^M in Figure 15–7. As a result, at the critical interest rate, i_c, the economy becomes entrenched in what Keynes called a *liquidity trap*, a situation in which monetary policy is totally impotent as a counter-recessionary tool.

The liquidity trap

Unfortunately a liquidity trap, according to Keynes, is most likely to develop in a state of severe economic collapse, though even then it should be regarded as a special case. Keynes' recommended

A velocity
interpretation

solution in such a predicament, and in recessions in general, was expansionary fiscal policy—a solution which will be examined in Parts IV and V of this book.

To recapitulate Keynes' analysis, we will shift to the income velocity framework. Recall two equations presented in the first section of this chapter:

$$(1) \qquad\qquad M^S \ V^y = P \ y$$

$$(2) \qquad\qquad V^y = \frac{P \ y}{M^D}$$

These equations are the income velocity version of the equation of exchange and income velocity as it is related to the demand for money. Now consider a rise in the money supply. According to the classical quantity-theory school, a rise in M^S in Equation (1) will cause a rise in spending and total nominal output, $P \ y$; but such a result presumes that V^y does not move inversely to M^S by an amount sufficient to completely offset the rise in money. Keynes argued that any rise in spending following a rise in the money supply requires a fall in the rate of interest. However, a fall in the rate of interest tends to increase the demand for money and, as implied by Equation (2), depress V^y, at least partly offsetting a rise in M^S. In the special case of a liquidity trap, the offsetting movement of V^y is complete so that:

$$\uparrow M^S \ \downarrow V^y = \overline{P \ y}$$

where the bar over $P \ y$ indicates that total nominal output remains constant. In support of this argument, Keynesians cite the procyclical behavior of velocity, illustrated in Figure 15–1 (note the slowdown in velocity growth during recessions), and particularly the sharp decline in velocity during the Great Depression, shown in Figure 15–8.

FIGURE 15–8
Income velocity of money, seasonally adjusted, quarterly ratio scale, turnover rate

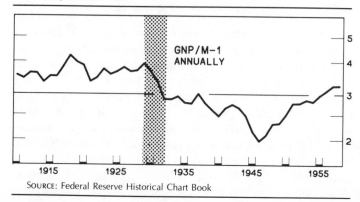

SOURCE: Federal Reserve Historical Chart Book

The essential points of Keynes' attack on classical monetary economics, therefore, were that (1) the orientation of the theory and of classical policy recommendations was too long run; (2) classical monetary theory neglected the speculative demand for money; (3) as a result of not recognizing the speculative demand for money, the classical school underestimated the interest sensitivity of the demand for money; and (4) as a result of underestimating the interest sensitivity of the demand for money, classical economists overestimated the ability of monetary policy to stimulate spending in a depression.

The experience of the Great Depression and Keynes' assault on classical ideas discredited the quantity theory and demoted monetary policy to a status decidedly inferior to fiscal policy in the view of most economists by the mid-1940s. As a result, for the next few decades, research was concentrated on formalizations and extensions of Keynes' ideas in the area of fiscal policy.

A notable advance in monetary theory within the new, Keynesian orthodoxy, however, was the development of models elaborating on the transactions and precautionary motives for holding money. Among the pioneering studies in this area were one by William Baumol and one by James Tobin.[12] Baumol developed a formal algebraic model of transactions balances at the level of the micro unit (individual, firm, or government). A real-balances version of Baumol's formula is as follows:

Baumol's transactions demand model

$$\frac{C^*}{P} = \sqrt{\frac{b\,T}{2\,i}}$$

where C^*/P is the optimum average level of real cash balances for transactions purposes for the micro unit to hold; b is the real cost expended in switching funds from interest-bearing investments to non-interest-bearing cash (real "brokerage fee" in Baumol's terms, but implying time as well as explicit costs); T is the number of items purchased per period between receipts of new funds (e.g., between paydays for individuals); and P and i are, as always in this text, the price level and the rate of interest, respectively.[13]

---

[12]William J. Baumol, "The Transactions Demand for Cash—An Inventory Theoretic Approach," *Quarterly Journal of Economics* 66 (November 1952), 545–56; and James Tobin, "Liquidity Preference as Behavior Towards Risk," *Review of Economic Studies* 25 (February 1958), 65–86.

[13]Baumol's model assumed that expenditures occur as a continuous flow while receipts just sufficient to cover total expenditures occur at periodic "payday" intervals. When a receipt occurs, the funds are invested in an interest-bearing asset and cashed out periodically, in fixed amounts, to replenish a non-interest-bearing cash balance from which expenditure payments are made.

During one pay period the total number of cash-outs from interest-bearing investments is equal to T/W, where T is defined as in the text above and W is the real value of a cash-out. Each cash-out has a real cost, b, and non-interest-bearing cash held has an opportunity cost, i. On average, there is P(W/2) in funds tied up in

Several interesting results emerge from Baumol's formula when it is converted to a form recognizable as a demand-for-money function,

$$C^D = C^* = (2)^{-1/2} \, P \, (b)^{1/2} \, (T)^{1/2} \, (i)^{-1/2}$$

This demand function implies that the elasticity of the demand for cash for transactions purposes with respect to the price level is positive unity; the elasticity with respect to b, the real cost of converting funds to cash from interest-bearing assets, is positive ½; the elasticity with respect to T, the number of items purchased, is positive ½; and the elasticity with respect to the rate of interest is negative ½.[14]

The first result, unitary elasticity for the price level, is no surprise, but it is comforting since we have stressed from Chapter 3 on that the demand for money is inversely proportional to the value of money. The second result, elasticity of ½ with respect to b, is

---

non-interest-bearing cash. Total real costs associated with the use of cash for transactions, therefore, are defined by X:

$$X = b \, \frac{T}{W} + i \, \frac{W}{2} \tag{1}$$

Now to find W*, the real size of a cash-out which minimizes X, take the derivative of X with respect to W and set it equal to zero to get

$$\frac{\partial X}{\partial W} = - \frac{b \, T}{W^2} + \frac{i}{2} = 0 \tag{2}$$

or

$$W^* = \sqrt{\frac{2 \, b \, T}{i}} \tag{3}$$

Finally, since $\frac{C}{P}$, the average real value of holdings of non-interest-bearing cash, equals W/2

$$\frac{C^*}{P} = \frac{W^*}{2} = \sqrt{\frac{b \, T}{2 \, i}} \tag{4}$$

[14]Elasticities are easily read from this demand function because it is a first-order multiplicative function. In such cases, the exponent of each independent variable is the elasticity of the dependent variable with respect to that independent variable. To see this result for the function above, take the logarithm of the function to get

$$\ln C^D = -\tfrac{1}{2} \ln 2 + \ln P + \tfrac{1}{2} \ln T - \tfrac{1}{2} \ln i$$

Then take the partial derivative of $\ln C^D$ with respect to each of the independent variables to obtain the elasticities,

$$\frac{\partial \ln C^D}{\partial \ln P} = 1$$

$$\frac{\partial \ln C^D}{\partial \ln b} = \tfrac{1}{2}$$

$$\frac{\partial \ln C^D}{\partial \ln T} = \tfrac{1}{2}$$

$$\frac{\partial \ln C^D}{\partial \ln i} = -\tfrac{1}{2}$$

interesting because it suggests the nature of the response of the demand for money to innovations in the financial system which reduce the cost of converting interest-bearing assets to cash.[15]

The third result, an income elasticity of ½, implies that there are economies of scale in the use of money for transactions. To put this in the context of the income-velocity framework, Baumol's model says that income velocity should tend to rise over time with real income, unless other influences are of overriding importance.

The final result derived from Baumol's model provides ammunition for both sides of the issue regarding the interest sensitivity of the demand for money. Many Keynesians regard an interest elasticity of −½ as a significant degree of sensitivity for transactions balances, adding to the interest sensitivity of the total demand for money. Many of those less sympathetic to Keynes' theory of the speculative demand for money, including many monetarists, regard Baumol's model as suggestive of the interest elasticity of the *total* demand for money. This would mean that the interest elasticity of the total demand for money is relatively low and does not rise in absolute value as the rate of interest falls.

As mentioned earlier, James Tobin also has contributed to monetary theory in an important way. Among other contributions, Tobin introduced the idea that the demand for money might be highly sensitive to the rate of interest even if bond-market participants do not have a firm notion that the rate of interest is likely to rise. In effect, Tobin presented a case for an interest-sensitive precautionary demand for money.

To see the logic of Tobin's analysis, recall the discussion of the liquidity-premium hypothesis of the term structure of interest rates presented in Chapter 7. As described there, investors who are considering bonds for short-term holding periods will be concerned about the risk of an *unexpected* rise in interest rates. In response to the perceived risk of an unexpected loss on long-term investments, market participants will tend to prefer short-term assets, including cash balances, unless the return on bonds is sufficient to compensate them for the disutility of bearing risk. Tobin concluded that *the lower the rate of return on bonds, the smaller the proportion of their portfolios investors will devote to bonds and the greater the proportion they will commit to cash, purely as a matter of risk avoidance.* He also concluded, as Keynes had earlier, that *an increase in uncertainty regarding the level of future interest rates*

Tobin's analysis of liquidity preference

---

[15]Of course, these innovations have also blurred the distinction between cash for transactions and funds placed for interest earnings. NOW accounts and money-market mutual fund shares are two important examples. (See Chapters 2 and 7.) Baumol's model is limited in its applicability to non-interest-bearing transactions balances, though modifications can be made to extend it to a broader class of transactions balances.

tends to increase the demand for money because it raises the perceived risk on long-term investments. [16]

The modern quantity theory

Despite the rather sweeping victory of Keynes' ideas in the 1940s, there remained a few defenders of classical economics and the quantity theory of money. These defenders were concentrated at the University of Chicago, and Milton Friedman, who was appointed to the faculty of Chicago in the early 1950s, soon assumed leadership in the development of a *modern quantity theory of money* and the monetarist school. The modern quantity theory was launched with a set of studies published by Friedman and his students in 1956 and has developed further in numerous articles and books in subsequent years. [17]

Friedman's demand function

As enunciated by Friedman, the modern quantity theory posits simply that money is a type of capital good which is held for the services it provides, whatever these may be. Starting from this basis, the theory incorporates insights from the classical economists, from Friedman's work in other fields, and, to a degree, from Keynes to formulate a demand for money function along the following lines.

$$M^D = f(P, \ w, \ z^*, \ i^s, \ \dots \ )$$

where w is real wealth or "permanent income" (explained below); z^* is, as elsewhere in this text, expected inflation; and i^s is the rate of interest on short-term assets (or the expected realized rate of return on long-term assets held for short-term periods). [18]

The first point to note about this demand function is that it is not based upon any notions about specific motives for holding money. A second point stressed by Friedman is that the demand-for-money function is regarded by quantity theorists as a stable relationship. Both of these are points of difference between Keynesian and monetarist approaches to the demand for money.

The price-level variable

With regard to individual variables in the demand-for-money function, Friedman redirected attention to the price level as a key variable; indeed, according to monetarists, the price level is the single most important variable in the demand-for-money function because it provides and explains the link between money and inflation. Keynes and his early followers did not stress the price level in their analysis and often neglected to include it at all in the demand-

---

[16]Tobin's formal model is too complex to summarize here. The essential features of the model included an assumption that investors' preferences with regard to return and risk avoidance fit certain conventional requirements. There is also an implicit assumption that investors have a preference for short-term assets.

[17]The initial studies were included in Milton Friedman, ed., *Studies in the Quantity Theory of Money*, (Chicago: University of Chicago Press, 1956).

[18]This demand function is an abridgement and synthesis of several ideas and demand formulations presented by Friedman.

for-money function. Inflation was viewed by Keynesians as attributable either to excess demand at capacity output and capable of being contained by restrictive fiscal policy, or to cost-push factors such as union wage demands which wage quidelines or "income policies" can restain. Monetarists argue that such a view overlooks the essential nature of the price level as the reciprocal of the value of money and the role that the price level plays in bringing the supply and demand for money into balance.

The real wealth variable in Friedman's demand-for-money function identifies his approach as part of the Cambridge tradition. Friedman added one important twist in this area, however, by suggesting that permanent income, a concept developed by Friedman in a separate line of research, can be substituted for wealth in the demand-for-money function. Permanent income refers to the expected trend of future income. In a key study, Friedman argued that procyclical movements in income velocity are attributable to procyclical movements of current income relative to permanent income and not to procyclical movements in interest rates as Keynesians assert.[19] Friedman's idea is that, during periods of prosperity, the demand for money rises proportionately with permanent income but less than proportionately with a rise in current income because permanent income rises less than current income in a business expansion. This implies that income velocity rises in prosperity since income velocity is defined as a *current* income concept, i.e., $V^y = (P\ y)/M^D$ where y is, as usual, current real income. Likewise, during a depression, permanent income and the demand for money decline proportionately in relation to each other but less than proportionately in relation to current income, and income velocity falls.

Real wealth and permanent income

The expected rate of inflation is another key variable neglected by Keynesians in their early studies. Under Friedman's direction, monetarists at the University of Chicago developed some pioneering work on hyperinflations and on the stability of the monetary system based on the effects of expected inflation on the demand for money.[20]

The expected rate of inflation

Finally, Friedman recognized the rate of interest as a variable in the demand-for-money function, either as a nominal rate or as an expected real rate, and even conceded the theoretical relevance of the expected capital loss on bonds if the yield on long-term bonds was used as the interest-rate variable. However, the rate of interest, and particularly expected capital losses on bonds, have often been

The interest rate

[19]Milton Friedman, "The Demand for Money: Some Theoretical and Empirical Results," *Journal of Political Economy* 67 (August 1959);327–51. For the original application of the permanent-income concept as a key variable in economic behavior, see Milton Friedman, *A Theory of the Consumption Function* (Princeton, N.J.: Princeton University Press, for the National Bureau of Economic Research, 1957).

[20]See in particular Phillip Cagan, "The Monetary Dynamics of Hyperinflation," in *Studies in the Quantity Theory of Money*, ed. Milton Friedman (Chicago: University of Chicago Press, 1956).

discounted by Friedman as having so little empirical influence on the demand for money that, for policy purposes, they can be neglected. It is probably fair to say that Friedman's position on this point is an extreme one, even among monetarists. Most monetarists view the interest sensitivity of the demand for money as relatively low, but not low enough to be ignored.

In summary, as a theory of the demand for money, the modern quantity of theory asserts (1) the value of analyzing the demand for money as a whole instead of examining it in terms of specific motives, (2) the stability of the demand-for-money function, (3) the key role of the price level in the demand-for-money function, (4) the role of cyclical movements of current income relative to permanent income as the cause of cyclical movements in income velocity, (5) the importance of expected inflation as a variable affecting the demand for money (inversely) in cases of rapid inflation, and (6) the low elasticity of the demand for money with regard to the rate of interest.

There are still other aspects of the Keynesian-monetarist controversy to be covered in later chapters. At this point, it is time to close this section on theories of the demand for money and turn to a summary of the empirical evidence on the demand-for-money function.

RESULTS OF EMPIRICAL STUDIES

Subsequent to the Keynesian revolution in the 1940s and simultaneous with the emergence of the monetarist counter-attack in the 1950s and 1960s, empirical economics came into its own with the development of computers and sophisticated econometric techniques. Empirical tools soon were employed by both schools to estimate the key characteristics of the demand-for-money function.

Major findings in the 1960s

The empirical studies were diverse in the techniques used and in the assumptions made about the form of the demand function (linear, log-linear, etc.). Even broad as well as narrow definitions of money were tried. Yet the results of the studies were fairly uniform:[21]

1. The interest elasticity of the demand for money was found to be significant but low (about -0.15 using a short-term interest rate and -0.70 using a long-term interest rate) and stable.
2. Most studies found no evidence of a liquidity trap or even of a tendency for a rise in the interest sensitivity of the demand for money during the Great Depression.
3. No evidence was found to suggest that the risk of capital losses on long-term bonds affects the demand for money.

---

[21]See David E. W. Laidler, *The Demand for Money: Theories and Evidence*, 2d ed. (Scranton, PA: Dun-Donnelly, 1977), for similar conclusions. Also see Thomas Mayer, *Monetary Policy in the United States* (New York: Random House, 1968).

4.   The demand for money appears to be more a function of wealth, permanent income, or lagged income (a proxy for permanent income) than of current income. Studies which investigated the elasticity of the demand for money with respect to an income or wealth variable found an elasticity greater than unity for the years prior to World War II and an elasticity less than unity for the years after World War II.

5.   It was a uniform finding that the response of the demand for money to the price level is proportional.

These results did much to quiet the debate between Keynesians and monetarists regarding the demand for money. The interest rate was established as an important variable in the money-demand function, but not so important or volatile an influence as to suggest that, on this basis alone, monetary policy is an ineffectual device for stabilizing the economy.[22]

Research in more recent years has refined and basically confirmed results obtained in the 1960s. A major concern of recent research has centered on an apparent downward shift in the demand   Recent research for money in the early 1970s. Several explanations involving the impact of financial innovations and regulatory change have been advanced. Aside from this structural shift, however, the evidence still suggests that the demand-for-money function is a remarkably stable relationship.[23]

CONCLUSION

This chapter has described the classical frameworks for monetary analysis, the major theories of the demand for money, and empirical evidence regarding the stability and sensitivity of the demand for money in relation to key variables. The Keynesian/quantity-theory controversy was a major topic running through the chapter because the development of monetary theory has been so much influenced by this debate. Despite more agreement in this area in recent years, differences persist. There are differences, for example, with regard to preferences for an approach to money demand in terms of motives versus services in general. And, even though the view that the economy reached a liquidity trap for the demand for money in the Great Depression is no longer widely held, debate regarding the theoretical possibility of such an occurrence will no doubt remain a part of monetary economics for years to come.

---

[22]Keynesians have also questioned the effectiveness of monetary policy on the basis that the response of total spending to a decline in the rate of interest is likely to be weak. See the discussion in Chapter 17.

[23]See Jared Enzler, Lewis Johnson, and John Paulus, "Some Problems of Money Demand," *Brookings Papers on Economic Activity* 1: 1976, 261–79; and R.W. Hafer and Scott E. Hein, "Evidence on the Temporal Stability of the Demand for Money Relationship in the United States," Federal Reserve Bank of St. Louis *Monthly Review*, (December 1979), 3–14.

This chapter completes Part 3 of the book which has focused on money. The next part covers the standard Keynesian analytical framework which incorporates the influence of non-monetary as well as monetary factors on the economy.

PROBLEMS

1. If some way could be found to pay interest on currency and the government did in fact begin making such interest payments, what would be the likely effect on income velocity?
2. Use the equation of exchange to show how an increase in the growth of real income can lead to lower inflation.
3. What assumptions are necessary in order for Fisher's equation of exchange and the Cambridge cash-balance equation to be equivalent?
4. Explain Keynes' theory of the speculative demand for money.
5. Why is the interest elasticity of the demand for money an important issue for monetary policy?
6. What does Baumol's model of the transactions demand for money suggest the long-run trend of income velocity should be? Why? (Hint: what is the income elasticity of the demand for money in Baumol's model?)
7. What have empirical studies found regarding the interest elasticity of the demand for money?

ADVANCED READINGS

Baumol, W.J. "The Transactions Demand for Cash—An Inventory Theoretic Approach." *Quarterly Journal of Economics* 66 (November 1952): 545–56

Fisher, Irving. *"The Purchasing Power of Money."* New York: Macmillan, 1911.

Friedman, Milton. "The Demand for Money: Some Theoretical and Empirical Results." *Journal of Political Economy* 67 (August 1959).

————."The Quantity Theory of Money—A Restatement."In *Studies in the Quantity Theory of Money.* Edited by Milton Friedman. Chicago: University of Chicago Press, 1956.

Keynes, J.M. *The General Theory of Employment, Interest and Money.* New York: Harcourt Brace Jovanovich, 1936. Chapter 15.

Laidler, David. *The Demand for Money: Theories and Evidence.* 2d ed. Scranton, Pa.: Dunn-Donnelly, 1977.

Poole, William. "Whither Money Demand?" *Brooking Papers on Economic Activity* 3:(1970), 485–500.

Pigou, A.C. "The Value of Money." *The Quarterly Journal of Economics* 32 (1917–18); 38–65.

Tobin, J. "Liquidity Preference as Behavior Towards Risk." *Review of Economic Studies* 25 (February 1958); 65–86.

Aggregate supply and demand analysis

The aggregate supply and demand model of output and the price level: Summary and applications

In earlier parts of this book we have traced the effects of money on the economy indirectly by describing the adjustments of economic variables likely to bring money demand and money supply into equilibrium. The advantage of this approach was that it kept our focus on money and avoided complications introduced by independent, nonmonetary factors. A disadvantage was that other important factors affecting the economy were neglected and a detailed linkage between money and specific types of spending was not provided. This chapter and the two chapters which follow lay out a general model, encompassing a number of influences in an integrated framework.

AGGREGATE DEMAND AND SUPPLY

Aggregate demand factors

Consider first a broad, simplified model of aggregate demand and aggregate supply for final output in the economy. Aggregate demand, y^D, measures total desired purchases of real goods and serv-

16

420

ices.[1] Our specification of the aggregate demand function incorporates the following key factors influencing y^D: the price level, the money supply, fiscal policy (government spending and taxes), and the current level of real output. The influence of each of these factors will be explained in brief, general terms below and then developed along with other factors as part of a structural model of aggregate demand in Chapter 17.

Ceteris paribus, the demand for real output tends to be inversely related to the price level for several reasons. First, a rise in the price level reduces the value of real cash balances held by individuals and firms. Such a loss in real wealth can be expected to curb spending. Second, under our ceteris-paribus condition, a rise in the price level means that current prices are high relative to expected future prices, so buyers will tend to postpone purchases. Third, also under our ceteris-paribus condition, a rise in the price level means that prices are high relative to wages, a situation which usually implies a redistribution of spending power from high spenders to low spenders.[2]

The price level

A rise in the money supply stimulates spending on real output by reducing interest rates on financial assets (the standard Keynesian mechanism) and by adding to real wealth in the form of real money balances (since prices are constant under our usual ceteris-paribus condition). Monetarists assert that there are other, less measurable ways that a money-supply increase stimulates spending. For example, an increase in the money supply alters the portfolio balance between financial and real assets for households, inducing households to acquire real assets without any necessary fall in interest rates.

The money supply

Higher government spending tends to boost total spending directly since it is a component of total spending.[3] An increase in government taxes absorbs disposable income and hence discourages spending.[4]

Fiscal policy

The higher the level of current output, the higher are individuals' incomes and, hence, the higher is consumer spending. Higher output and sales levels also spur desired inventory accumulation,

Current output

---

[1]Not all desired real GNP flows through markets. Desired increases in business inventories do not, for example. But it will be convenient for our exposition to term desired real GNP as desired purchases; the analysis is not affected.

[2]Only the first of these reasons is usually incorporated in textbook Keynesian analysis. The others are often part of large sophisticated models and have been added here to give additional support for a downward-sloping aggregate demand curve, described later.

[3]There also may be a secondary positive effect as the first-round rise in current output stimulates private income and spending, but this effect is subsumed under our later discussion of current output. On the other hand, there may be a negative second-round effect if the increase in government spending is financed by borrowing and raises interest rates sharply. This effect is ignored in the present analysis, but will be dealt with in Chapter 17.

[4]The comment in the previous footnote about second-round effects applies here as well.

and fixed investment spending by business rises as capacity levels are reached for existing plant and equipment.

The simplified aggregate demand function can be summarized now as follows:

$$y^D = f(P, M^S, F, y, \ldots)$$

Influenced variable	Influencing variable	Direction of influence
y^d: the demand for final output	P: the price level	Negative
	M^S: the money stock	Positive
	F: fiscal policy	Positive for a rise in government spending; negative for a rise in government taxes
	y: the level of real final output (real income)	Positive

Aggregate supply factors

Aggregate supply, y^S, measures the total quantity of final output firms wish to produce. The variables influencing aggregate supply include: the price level, the average wage rate for labor, costs per unit for the other production inputs, the technological base, and effective tax rates. As with aggregate demand, our discussion of these variables in this chapter will summarize more detailed analysis in a later chapter.

The price level

The aggregate quantity firms wish to produce is positively related to the price level. Ceteris paribus, as prices rise, the profit-maximizing rate of output rises for firms as long as marginal cost curves are upward sloping.

The average wage rate

Wages are a major variable cost of production. As the average wage rate rises, marginal cost curves shift upward and profit-maximizing rates of output decline for firms.

Other input costs

Other major input costs for firms include energy and capital expenses. Although not normally thought of as an input, the environment is another factor of production which, due to government regulation, may entail costs to the firm in the form of effluent charges and/or expenditures to curb pollution. As these costs rise, desired output and sales rates decline.

The technological base

The technological base for industry is an important determinant of aggregate supply because it sets the feasible rates of output for given quantities and combinations of factors of production. As technological advance takes place, costs per unit of output fall and profit-maximizing rates of output rise.

Taxes tend to affect the supply side as well as the demand side of the economy. A rise in business taxes for Social Security, for example, represents a rise in variable costs of production. The effective tax rate

Our aggregate supply function in symbols is

$$y^S = f(P, W, P^0, B, t, \ldots)$$

Influenced variable	Influencing variables	Direction of influence
y^S: the quantity of output supplied	P: the price level	Positive
	W: the wage rate	Negative
	P^0: other input costs such as energy and capital expenses	Negative
	B: the technological base for industry	Positive
	t: effective tax rates on business	Negative

The aggregate demand curve

Aggregate supply and demand curves can be obtained now from these functions. First, note that for the aggregate demand function, the quantity of output demanded is a function of both the price level *and the level of actual output*. This dependence of desired output on actual output requires a modification of our normal practice of deriving a ceteris paribus demand curve from the demand function. To see the modification necessary, consider the ceteris paribus demand curve, $D^{y|y_1}$ in Figure 16–1.

FIGURE 16–1
The ceteris-paribus demand curve

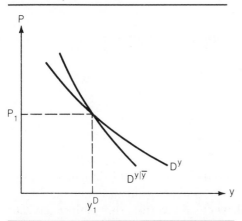

The superscript $y|\bar{y}_1$ denotes this relationship as the demand for final output in relation to the price level *assuming the actual level of final output remains constant at a level of* y_1.

The actual level of final output will change in the course of our analysis and this will feed back to the desired level of final output, shifting the $D^{y|\bar{y}_1}$ curve to the left or right following a change in the price level. A more useful demand curve, therefore, is one which is drawn under the assumption that the actual level of output equals the desired level. This assumption need not hold true at every point in time, but it will be true in equilibrium. The demand curve which incorporates this assumption is the D^y curve in Figure 16–1. It is more elastic than the $D^{y|\bar{y}_1}$ curve because, as the price level falls, the demand for final output rises both because of the fall in the price level and because of the rise in actual output in line with the initial rise in demand.

The aggregate supply curve can be treated as a conventional supply curve and combined with our modified aggregate demand curve as in Figure 16–2. The intersection of these curves determines output and the price level in equilibrium. Changes in one or more of the variables fixed by our remaining ceteris-paribus assumptions can be traced through with shifts of the curves to show how the economy responds to various events. Several examples are provided in the next section which uses the model to distinguish different types of inflation.

FIGURE 16–2
Aggregate demand and aggregate supply

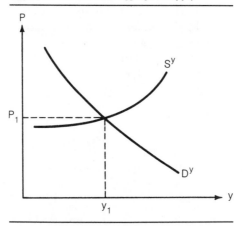

TYPES OF INFLATION

Demand-pull inflation

According to our aggregate demand function, an increase in the money supply and higher government spending tend to boost aggregate demand. This is shown by the vertical shift of the aggregate demand curve in Figure 16–3. In this figure, both output and the price level tend to rise. Any demand-induced rise in the price level such as this is called *demand-pull inflation*.

FIGURE 16–3
Demand-pull inflation

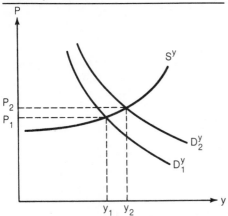

The relative degrees of increase in the price level and output in this example depend upon the slopes of the aggregate demand and supply functions. *The price increase will be smaller and the output increase larger, the flatter are the aggregate demand and supply curves. Conversely, the price increase will be larger and the output increase smaller, the more vertical are the two curves.* This result is noteworthy because the aggregate supply curve tends to become more vertical as capacity output is approached. As shown in Figure 16–4, increases in demand cause more inflation and smaller gains in output at higher rates of capacity utilization in the economy.

FIGURE 16–4
Demand-pull inflation

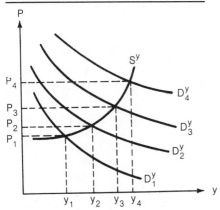

Cost-push inflation

Increases in wage rates, energy costs, and business taxes all contribute to *cost-push inflation,* shown in Figure 16–5. These factors tend to cause a vertical shift of the aggregate supply curve, leading to a fall in output and a rise in the price level.

FIGURE 16–5
Cost-push inflation

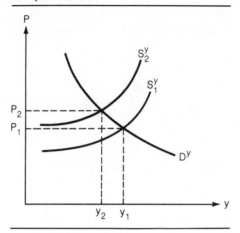

Balanced inflation

Inflationary episodes are seldom pure demand-pull or cost-push situations. One intermediate case (which is itself special) is *balanced inflation,* depicted in Figure 16–6. In a purely balanced inflation situation, both curves shift upward by the same amount, raising the price level and leaving output constant.

FIGURE 16–6
Balanced inflation

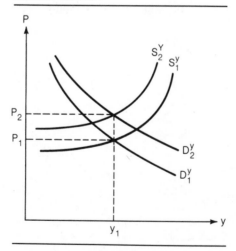

A balanced
inflation scenario
initiated by
demand-pull

An interesting scenario which leads to balanced inflation starts with a rise in the money supply intended to bring the economy up to capacity output. This creates demand-pull inflation as the economy moves closer to capacity output. As the price level and real output rise, workers seek and employers grant wage increases, partly in compensation for the price level increase, and the costs of other inputs tend to rise, shifting the aggregate supply curve up in catch-up fashion. Prices rise further, and real output tends to fall back toward a more normal level, as shown in Figure 16–7.

FIGURE 16–7
Demand-pull followed by balanced inflation

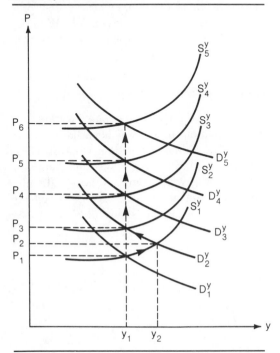

In subsequent periods, the money supply continues to rise, boosting aggregate demand persistently as the monetary authorities attempt to sustain real output; but aggregate supply rises equally because of established expectations of inflation on the part of workers and businesses.

Balanced inflation could continue indefinitely with the money supply rising at a steady rate. Suppose the monetary authorities shift priorities, however, and act to curb money growth with the objective of bringing inflation down. This, we assume, freezes the aggregate demand curve, but the aggregate supply curve is likely to keep rising due to entrenched expectations of continued inflation. The result is a difficult period of pure cost-push inflation, shown earlier in Figure 16–5. Inflation continues while output falls. Eventually, inflation expectations should abate and output should return to higher levels. But it may be necessary to keep policy restrained in the face of lower output over a protracted period to ensure this result.

A shift from balanced to cost-push inflation

WAGE AND PRICE CONTROLS

The scenarios just sketched illustrate recurrent, similar dilemmas faced by policymakers: how can output and employment be stimulated without igniting inflation? And, once started, how can endemic inflation be curbed without losses in output and higher unemployment? One answer to these dilemmas which is often proposed and occasionally adopted is wage and price controls. With the possible exception of a war emergency, this is usually a poor answer, however.

Controls with demand-pull pressures

For various reasons, controls tend to exacerbate inflation and curb output, particularly in situations in which policymakers wish to stimulate the economy without inducing inflation. Controls combined with stimulative policies lead to shortages, black markets with still higher prices than would otherwise occur, and heavy administrative costs for the government and the private sector. The effects on output and prices for an extreme case are shown in Figure 16–8.

FIGURE 16–8
Controls with demand-pull pressure

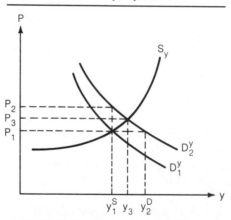

Aggregate demand rises with the stimulative policies adopted by the government. Though some rise in output would be likely at first since all prices could not be controlled and some firms would expand output without raising prices, our diagram assumes that all prices are frozen and that this puts a cap on the quantity producers wish to sell. The results are a general condition of shortages, reflected by the excess demand gap, $y_2^D - y_1^S$, and a blossoming of black markets, with the effective price at the lofty level shown by P_2. In the absence of controls, output would have expanded to y_3 and prices would have risen only to P_3.

To the extent that output does expand and/or that inflation expectations take hold despite price controls, wage controls produce similar shortages and black markets for labor. This pushes up the aggregate supply curve, exacerbating shortage and black-market conditions in product markets.

Finally, controls interfere with the signals and dynamic adjustments necessary for growth and development in a market economy. Relative prices and wages are the nerves which coordinate and induce appropriate responses by firms and individuals to normal change and progress. When prices are frozen, these nerve signals are interrupted, robbing the economy of much of its vitality.[5]

Controls in a cost-push inflation

The opposite and more appealing situation in which wage and price controls are often considered is as an adjunct to a program to curb an established inflation with restrictive policies. As described earlier, the process of winding down inflationary expectations can be protracted, causing output losses which *might* be avoidable. The idea is that wage and price controls can prevent the upward rise of the aggregate supply curve by outlawing wage increases and puncturing inflationary expectations.

There are several drawbacks to controls even in this situation, however. First, controls may not curb inflation expectations; if they do not, the aggregate supply curve will still tend to rise, leading to a greater loss in output, compounded by shortages and black markets, shown in Figure 16–9.

Second, by freezing *reported* prices and wages and thereby creating a sense of having more power than they do, wage and price controls may create an illusion among policymakers that inflation can be licked by controls alone so that restraint on monetary and fiscal policy is no longer required. If, as a result, stimulative policies are cranked up once more, conditions similar to those described for the first case will develop.

Finally, even in the most favorable situation, controls still impose a severe administrative burden and stifling effect on the economy. Most of these costs, and distributional losses as well, are borne by those who make every effort to comply with a controls program, while those who work to get around the program may actually benefit. Consequently, controls are inequitable and destructive to the public spirit.

---

[5]Controls programs often attempt to alleviate this effect by establishing guidelines for relative price adjustments within a framework designed to stabilize the general price level. In practice, such guidelines are an administrative nightmare, however. Either a stifling of relative price adjustments or ineffectual aggregate restraint tends to result.

FIGURE 16–9
Controls with cost-push pressure

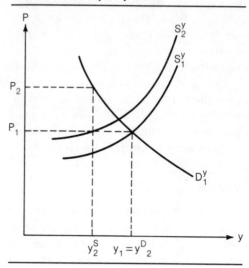

INFLATION AND UNEMPLOYMENT: A CRUEL TRADE-OFF?

Do the dynamics of aggregate demand and aggregate supply and the failures of wage and price controls imply that the economy faces a fundamental and inescapable trade-off between inflation and unemployment? In other words, is there some higher rate of inflation which goes hand in hand with lower rates of unemployment, as suggested in Figure 16–10? In the 1950s and 1960s there was considerable agreement that such a stable, enduring trade-off existed.

FIGURE 16–10
The Phillips curve

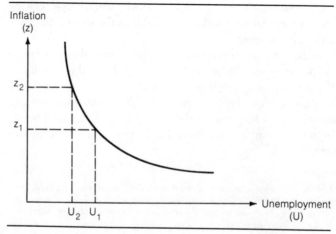

The Phillips curve

The idea was given particular impetus in a 1958 study by A.W. Phillips which examined the relationship between unemployment and the rate of increase in wage rates in the United Kingdom.[6] As a result of Phillips' study, any graphical relationship depicting a trade-off between inflation and unemployment, as in Figure 16–10, is conventionally called a Phillips curve. Phillips' original curve is shown in Figure 16–11, in which the dots represent individual years.

FIGURE 16–11
The original Phillips curve

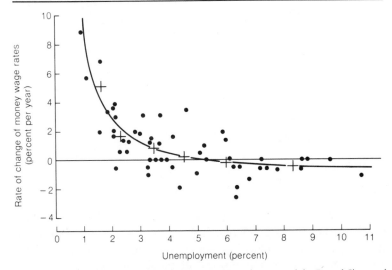

SOURCE: A.W. Phillips, "The Relationship Between Unemployment and the Rate of Change of Money Wage Rates in the United Kingdom, 1861–1957," *Economica* 25 (November 1958); p. 285.

Phillips' explanation of this curve was that the rate of change in wage rates in the United Kingdom was almost entirely determined by excess-demand and excess-supply conditions in the labor market, as measured by the unemployment rate and changes in the unemployment rate.[7] Inflation, of course, is another possible factor affecting wage increases via cost-of-living adjustments, but this was discounted by Phillips. Wage increases due to excess demand fuel inflation, however, as firms increase prices to pass on the costs of wage increases—hence the relationship shown in Figure 16–10.

---

[6]A.W. Phillips, "The Relationship Between Unemployment and the Rate of Change of Money Wage Rates in the United Kingdom, 1861–1957," *Economica* 25 (November 1958); 283–99.

[7]Changes in the unemployment rate were used to explain points above and below the solid line in Figure 16–11. When unemployment is falling, the excess demand for labor is particularly high and points tend to be above the line. When unemployment is rising, the excess demand for labor is particularly low or negative and points tend to be below the line.

"Yes, Farber—You wished to speak to me?"

Reprinted by permission *The Wall Street Journal.*

The effect of expected inflation

Suppose Phillips is wrong, however, and actual inflation does feed back to expected inflation and cost-of-living increases in wage rates. The result would be a shift upward of the curve in Figure 16–11, leading to a shift upward of the Phillips curve in Figure 16–10. This effect is extremely important for it means that, though there may be some relationship in the short run, chances are there is very little or no trade-off between inflation and unemployment in the long run. For example, stimulative government policies might be capable of moving the economy to the left along the bottom curve in Figure 16–12, reducing the unemployment rate from U_1 to U_2 at some tolerable cost in terms of inflation, z_1 to z_2—as long as inflation expectations do not rise and feed into a still higher rate of wage increases. Persistent inflation will cause inflation expectations to rise, however, and so raise wage demands. Such a rise in wage demands pushes the Phillips curve up vertically, increasing the inflation rate *and* unemployment. If this effect is severe enough, unemployment rises back to its original level so that ultimately there is no reduction in unemployment associated with higher inflation.

U.S. experience

Experience in the United States in the 1960s seemed to conform to the stable curve shown in Figure 16–10. In fact, every year from 1960 to 1969 can be placed on or close to a smooth curve, as shown

FIGURE 16–12
The effect of expected inflation

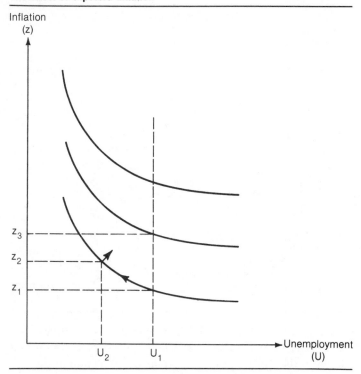

in Figure 16–13. Beginning in 1970, the relationship began to break down, however. The Phillips curve clearly shifted upward in 1970–71. Wage and price controls were imposed by the Nixon administration in the summer of 1971, and at first this appeared to help curb inflation expectations, shifting the curve down somewhat in 1972. Then shortages, renewed domestic inflation, and the quadrupling of prices for imported oil sent the curve upward to new heights in 1974–75. Further gyrations followed. In short, the notion of a stable, negatively sloped Phillips curve was destroyed by obviously contradictory events in the 1970s.

Although economists no longer debate the idea of a single Phillips curve which applies to both the short run and the long run, differences of opinion persist regarding the nature of the long-run trade-off in terms of whether there is virtually ńo trade-off, or a slight inverse trade-off (i.e., similar to, though steeper than, the curve in Figure 16–10). Keynesians tend to hold to the view that there is a slight inverse trade-off in the long run. Most monetarists, on the other hand, contend that the long-run relationship is either vertical or positive. Friedman contends, for example, that the economy always tends toward a "natural" rate of unemployment, U^n, which is determined by factors other than the inflation rate, as

The long-run
Phillips curve

FIGURE 16–13
Inflation and unemployment in the United States (1960–1980)

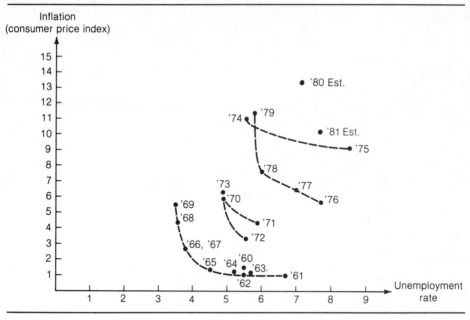

shown by the vertical curve at U^n in Figure 16–14.[8] Still another point of view is that, if society is willing to accept a continuing acceleration in the inflation rate, a permanent reduction in the unemployment rate below U^n is possible.

FIGURE 16–14
The long-run Phillips curve—two views

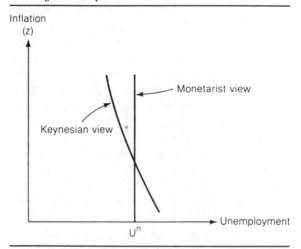

[8]Milton Friedman, "The Role of Monetary Policy," *The American Economic Review* 58 (March, 1968); 1–17.

HOW ARE EXPECTATIONS FORMED?

Expectations of inflation are obviously a key element in the ability of government policymakers to effect meaningful reductions in unemployment via stimulative policies. Somehow expansionary policies apparently were able to have more lasting effects on unemployment in the 1960s than in the 1970s. Perhaps the principal factor which accounts for this is the speed with which expectations adjusted or the way expectations were formed in the 1960s versus the behavior of expectations in more recent years.

Adaptive expectations

There are two basic models of expectations formation which economists have applied to different periods and behavioral relationships. One of these is the *adaptive expectations model*. In the most common version of this model, individuals adapt their expectations to surprises as follows

$$\Delta z^*_t = b(z_t - z^*_t)$$

This says that the change in the expected rate of inflation is proportional to the difference between the level of the actual rate of inflation and the level of the expected rate of inflation. The coefficient b is a measure of the speed with which expectations adjust and has a value between zero and unity. The model implies that, if inflation is higher than in the past but constant, expected inflation will adjust toward the actual rate, as illustrated in Figure 16–15.

FIGURE 16–15
Adaptive expectations (Coefficient b=.5)

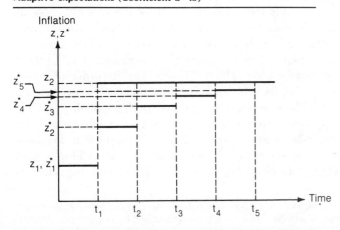

If the adaptive expectations model is a reasonably accurate representation of reality, the more rapid vertical shifts of the Phillips curve in the 1970s might reflect, in part, a higher value for b in the

1970s as individuals became more "adaptable" to the prospect of higher inflation.[9] If this is a valid explanation of expectations formation in the 1970s versus the 1960s, and if the adaptive expectations model still holds true in the 1980s, the government can pursue lower unemployment rates through expansionary policies, but society must be willing to put up with ever-increasing inflation rates.[10]

Rational expectations

The other model posits that individuals are "rational" in the sense that they look beyond the actual rate of inflation to the causes of inflation in forming expectations. Suppose, for example, that individuals attribute inflation to expansionary monetary and fiscal policies. The *rational expectations model* might be specified as follows

$$z^*_t = a\left(\frac{\Delta M^S}{M^S}\right)^*_t + b \; F^*_t$$

where $\left(\frac{\Delta M^S}{M^S}\right)^*_t$ is the expected rate of growth of the money supply, F^*_t is expected fiscal policy (as represented, say, by the government's budget deficit as a proportion of GNP), and a and b are coefficients which indicate the impacts expected money-supply growth and fiscal stimulus have on the public's expected rate of inflation.

Perhaps the Phillips curve shifted up more rapidly in the 1970s because individuals learned to key their expectations to the predictable impact of government policies on inflation. If this is a more accurate view of the public's behavior and state of knowledge today, it suggests that expansionary monetary and fiscal policies may have lost their capability to engineer more than fleeting reductions in unemployment. This indeed is the thesis of the *rational expectations school*. Economists who adhere to this school, which represents essentially a branch of monetarism, assert that *monetary and fiscal policy cannot influence real economic activity so long as these policies are predictable*. The only way the government could achieve continuing success would be if it could continually fool the public—not a likely prospect in the view of this school.

Not many economists adhere to the strong conclusions of the rational expectations school. Yet most probably agree that, in recent years, the public has come to associate inflation more closely with government expansionary policies, that inflationary expectations

---

[9]Phillip Cagan, in his study which introduced the adaptive expectations model, found evidence of a similar shift in the value of b for several European hyperinflations. See Phillip Cagan, "The Monetary Dynamics of Hyperinflation," in Studies in the Quantity Theory of Money, edited by M. Friedman (Chicago: University of Chicago Press, 1956).

[10]If inflation is ever rising, adaptive expectations are ever rising also, but always lag behind the actual inflation rate.

have become more volatile, and that these developments have undermined the ability of expansionary policies to achieve significant reductions in unemployment. The conclusion that many draw from this analysis is that government monetary and fiscal policies in the 1980s should be geared more to achieving stable and lower inflation rates and less to reducing the unemployment rate. Supply-side policies such as changes in the tax structure to improve incentives to work and the return to investment may be more successful in stimulating growth and reducing unemployment than demand-management (monetary and fiscal) policies.

CONCLUSION

This chapter has developed a summary analysis of the aggregate supply and demand model; described the major types of inflation; and discussed wage and price controls, the Phillips curve, and two models of expectations formation. The next two chapters provide more detailed material on aggregate demand and aggregate supply.

PROBLEMS

1. Explain the major factors affecting the aggregate demand function.
2. Analyze the current state of the economy in terms of whether it is characterized more by demand-pull, cost-push, or balanced inflation.
3. In what ways can wage and price controls tend to exacerbate inflation?
4. What is the key variable which tends to shift the short-run Phillips curve? Why does it have this effect?
5. Examine the two major models of expectations formation in terms of their implications for the likely success of government efforts to stabilize the business cycle.

ADVANCED READINGS

Alchian, A.A. "Information Costs, Pricing, and Resource Unemployment." *Western Economic Journal* 7 (June, 1969);˙109–28.

Friedman, Milton. "The Role of Monetary Policy." *American Economic Review*, March, 1968; 1–17.

————— "What Price Guideposts?" In *Guidelines, Informal Controls and the Market Place*, edited by G.P. Shultz and R.Z. Aliber. Chicago: University of Chicago Press, 1966; 17–37.

Hansen, A.H. *A Guide to Keynes*. New York: McGraw-Hill, 1953.

Humphrey, Thomas M. "Changing Views of the Phillips Curve," Federal Reserve Bank of Richmond *Monthly Review*, July 1973; 2–13.

Johnson, H.G. *Macroeconomics and Monetary Theory*. Chicago: Aldine, 1972.

Rasche, Robert H. "A Comparative Static Analysis of Some Monetarist Propositions." Federal Reserve Bank of St. Louis *Monthly Review*, December 1973.

Samuelson, Paul A., and Solow, R.M. "Analytical Aspects of Anti-Inflation Policy." *American Economic Review*, May 1960; 177–94.

Sargent, T.J., and Wallace, N. "Rational Expectations and the Theory of Economic Policy." *Journal of Monetary Economics*, April 1976.

Tobin, James. "Inflation and Unemployment." *American Economic Review*, March 1972; 1–18.

The determinants of aggregate demand

This chapter develops an abreviated version of the standard, simplified Keynesian analysis of aggregate demand as it is presented in most intermediate macroeconomics texts.

KEYNES' CONTRIBUTION

The essential structure of John Maynard Keynes' *General Theory of Employment, Interest, and Money* was a detailed and penetrating analysis of aggregate demand. Keynes' view was that a collapse of aggregate demand was the key cause of the depressed state of the 1930s. The collapse in aggregate demand in turn was attributed to certain nonmonetary, structural causes, explained in this chapter.

As suggested by the material in Chapter 15, classical economists viewed aggregate demand as stably related to the money supply. Consequently, before Keynes, there was little research or interest in the structural components of aggregate demand. If demand was depressed, it was either attributable to an insufficiency in the money supply or it was a temporary, self-correcting state of affairs.

Economists are still debating the cause of the Great Depression—whether it is traceable to a decline in the money supply, which in fact did drop sharply between 1929 and 1933, or to real structural

17

439

factors elucidated by Keynes' analysis. But there is no debate regarding Keynes' vast contribution to macroeconomics. He identified the major behavioral relationships which come together in the aggregate demand function and provided remarkable insight regarding the key determinants of the component demands.

The analysis divides the economy into two parts—the real sector and the monetary sector.

THE REAL SECTOR

Preliminary assumptions and definitions

Aggregate supply and the price level

In order to keep our analysis simpler at first, we will assume that the economy is operating along a flat segment of the aggregate supply curve, as depicted in Figure 17–1.

FIGURE 17–1
The aggregate supply curve

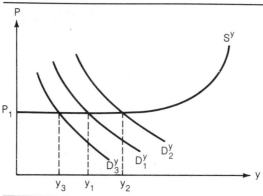

Shifts in aggregate demand elicit changes in real output without causing changes in the price level. This assumption is tantamount, therefore, to assuming a fixed price level.

Components of aggregate demand

Aggregate demand has the following components: C^D, desired *real personal consumption expenditures* (consumption demand); I^D, *desired real business investment spending* (investment demand); NX^D, *desired net exports* (net foreign demand); and G, *government spending*.[1] For brevity, our analysis will ignore net exports. Essentially then we will consider only a closed economy, where

$$y^D = C^D + I^D + G \tag{1}$$

Parallel to our components of total desired output are components of total actual output: C, actual consumption, I, actual investment,

---

[1]No distinction is made between desired and actual government spending, nor between federal government and state and local government spending in our simple model here.

and G, as before, so that

$$y = C + I + G \qquad (2)$$

Components of
actual output

The National Income Accounts (NIA) provide estimates of actual output and its components. The historical behavior of these components is shown in Figure 17–2. Note the declines or weakening in consumption, and particularly in investment spending, during recessions. We will examine Keynes' explanation for this behavior later.

No comparable direct estimates exist for desired values, but in equilibrium $C^D = C$, and $I^D = I$, making

$$y^D = y \qquad (3)$$

The equilibrium
condition for
demand

Consequently, over more than a quarter or so (over a year, say) the NIA data probably represent reasonable estimates of desired values as well.

This completes our list of preliminary assumptions and definitions. Our objective in the next two parts of this section will be to set out the principal determinants of the consumption-demand and investment-demand components.

FIGURE 17–2
Major Components of gross national product (seasonally adjusted annual rates, quarterly)

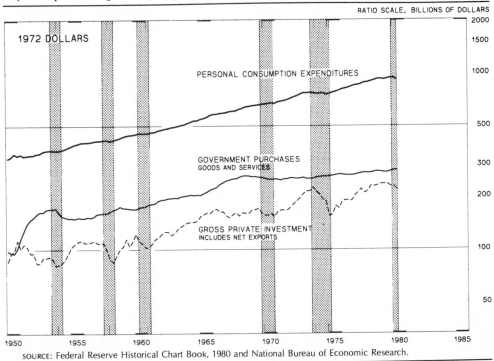

SOURCE: Federal Reserve Historical Chart Book, 1980 and National Bureau of Economic Research.

The consumption function

The consumption function is a key relationship in the economy because, although percentage changes are much smaller for consumer spending than for investment spending over the business cycle, consumer spending represents the lion's share of GNP (roughly two thirds in recent years). It is appropriate, therefore, that we begin our analysis of aggregate demand with this component.

The disposable income relationship

The single determinant of desired consumption in the simplified Keynesian model is *real disposable personal income,* y^n—that is, household real income after taxes. Disposable income is obviously a positive influence on consumer spending and Keynes emphasized this factor above any other.[2] In our formal analysis, the relationship takes the following specific form

$$C^D = a + b\, y^n \tag{4}$$

where a is *autonomous desired consumption,* a component of consumption demand which is not influenced by disposable income, and b is the *marginal propensity to consume,* a coefficient which indicates the strength of the influence of disposable income on consumption demand. The coefficient b times y^n represents *induced consumption,* that part of consumption demand which is influenced by disposable income.

The value of b is assumed to be greater than zero and less than unity. This results in a consumption relationship which slopes upward at less than a 45-degree angle, as shown in Figure 17–3.

FIGURE 17–3
The consumption function

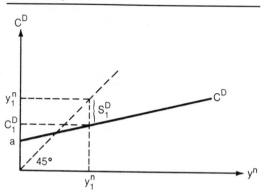

---

[2]Today most economists agree that the consumption function is more complex than Keynes perceived. We will reserve comment on the additional factors and considerations relevant to the consumption function until later in this chapter.

The 45-degree line is drawn in Figure 17–3 both to show the lower angle for the consumption function and to permit a visual calculation of the difference between consumption and disposable income.[3] Aside for two minor items which we shall ignore, this difference equals S^D, desired personal saving.[4] In symbols

The saving function

$$y^n - C^D = S^D \qquad (5)$$

This last expression can be used to find a *saving function* simply by solving it for C^D, substituting the result for C^D in Equation (4), and solving the result for S^D to get

$$S^D = -a + (1-b)y^n \qquad (6)$$

The saving function is shown in Figure 17–4. The slope of this function (coefficient on y^n) is the *marginal propensity to save*. Note that the marginal propensity to consume and the marginal propensity to save add to unity

$$b + (1-b) = 1$$

As long as the marginal propensity to consume is less than unity, the marginal propensity to save is greater than zero and saving will tend to rise with disposable income.

FIGURE 17–4
The savings function

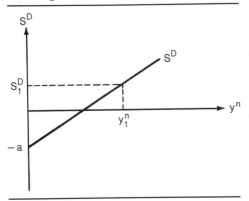

---

[3] A 45-degree line acts as a prism, reflecting values from the horizontal axis onto the vertical axis (or vice versa). When this property is used to project values for disposable income on the vertical axis, the difference between disposable income and desired consumption can be identified on the vertical axis and carried over and shown as the vertical difference between the 45-degree line and the consumption function, as in Figure 17–3.

[4] In the NIA, the difference between real disposable personal income and consumption spending equals household saving, net interest paid to business, and transfers to foreigners. The last two items here, net interest paid to business and transfers to foreigners, are normally small, in total less than 2.5 percent of real disposable income.

The final output
relationships

It will be useful for later analysis to express desired consumption and desired saving in terms of real final output. We assume

$$y^n = y - T \qquad (7)$$

where T represents net real tax receipts. In actuality, tax receipts vary with the level of final output, but T will be held constant in our analysis. Hence, when (7) is substituted into Equations (4) and (6), we have

$$C^D = a - b\,T + b\,y \qquad (8)$$

and

$$S^D = -a - (1-b)T + (1-b)y \qquad (9)$$

which are shown in Figures 17–5 and 17–6.

FIGURE 17–5
Consumption and real final output

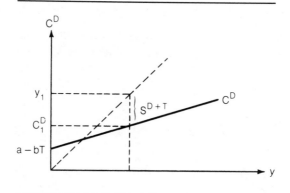

FIGURE 17–6
Savings and real final output

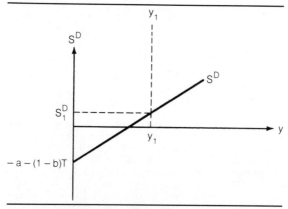

This completes our analysis of consumption demand and savings for now. We turn next to investment demand.

The investment function

As mentioned earlier, investment is a more volatile component of GNP than consumption. Keynes identified desired investment as dependent upon (1) business's expectations regarding the rate of return on additions to capital—*the marginal efficiency of investment*, (2) business's perceptions of risk, and (3) the rate of interest.

The marginal efficiency of investment.   Business investment is positively related to the marginal efficiency of investment, of course. The marginal efficiency of investment, in turn, is positively affected by the expected future demand for private output relative to the existing capital stock, and negatively affected by taxes on business profits and the price of capital goods relative to the general price level.

Risk.   Although the business community's perception of risk is difficult to quantify and hence is often neglected in formal models, Keynes placed great stress upon it. Elements of business risk include demand risk, i.e., the risk that the demand for future output will fall short of expectations; performance risk, the risk that contractual obligations will not be fulfilled by other parties necessary to the success of a venture; and political risk, the risk of unexpected government interference or expropriation.

The rate of interest.   The rate of interest represents an explicit cost of borrowed funds for the firm which finances investment by borrowing and an implicit opportunity cost for the firm which finances investment with internal funds. The higher the rate of interest, the lower is the level of desired investment, ceteris paribus.

The influence of these three principal factors are incorporated in the following simple relationship in our model

$$I^D = d - e\, i \tag{10}$$

where e is the slope of the relationship between investment demand and the rate of interest and d is a "shift" coefficient which incorporates the net effect of other influences identified in the paragraphs above. Our investment demand curve in terms of the rate of interest is shown in Figure 17–7.[5]

For analytical convenience, d is assumed to be independent of the current level of final output in our analysis. Consequently, investment demand in relation to final output is a horizontal line, as shown in Figure 17–8.

Equilibrium in the real sector

The last component of our aggregate demand function is government spending, and this is taken as fixed by fiscal policy, that is

Factors affecting investment demand

The investment relationship

---

[5]This relationship is often referred to as the marginal efficiency of investment schedule.

FIGURE 17–7
Investment demand and the rate of interest

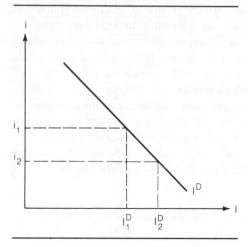

FIGURE 17–8
Investment demand and real final output

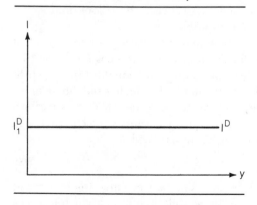

$$G = G_1 \tag{11}$$

Hence we have the following equations which, taken together, comprise aggregate demand

$$C^D = a - b\,T + b\,y \tag{8}$$
$$I^D = d - e\,i \tag{10}$$
$$G = G_1 \tag{11}$$

Equilibrium at a given interest rate

If we assume a constant interest rate, say i_1, which fixes investment at I_1, the components of aggregate demand and their total can be drawn as in Figure 17–9. The aggregate demand curve, y^D, which represents aggregate demand as a function of real final output in this figure, is the vertical sum of the curves in Figures 17–5 and 17–8 plus government spending, G_1. The intersection of this curve with the 45-degree line defines the point of equilibrium for final

FIGURE 17–9
Aggregate demand and real final output

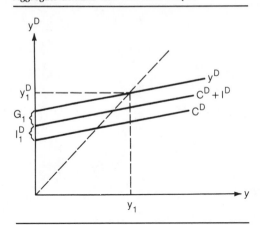

output, i.e., where $y^D = y$ for an interest rate i_1. Equilibrium occurs at y_1.

Equilibrium real output can also be found algebraically by substituting Equations (8), (10), and (11) into the identity for aggregate demand, (1), and the result into the equilibrium condition, (3), to get

$$a - b\,T + b\,y + d - e\,i + G_1 = y \qquad (12)$$

which with $i = i_1$ solves for

$$y_1 = \frac{a - b\,T + d - e\,i_1 + G_1}{1 - b} \qquad (13)$$

Now consider changes in several key determinants of aggregate demand. Suppose government spending rises from G_1 to G_2. The result is shown graphically in Figure 17–10. Aggregate demand shifts vertically by $G_2 - G_1$, and equilibrium output rises from y_1 to y_2. As shown visually, the rise in real output is greater than the increase in government spending.

The exact rise in real output can be found by solving Equation (12) for y_2.

$$y_2 = \frac{a - b\,T + d - e\,i_1 + G_2}{1 - b} \qquad (14)$$

and subtracting Equation (13) from Equation (14) to get

$$y_2 - y_1 = \frac{1}{1 - b}\,(G_2 - G_1) \qquad (15)$$

Because b, the marginal propensity to consume, is less than unity, the term $1/(1-b)$ is greater than unity. This term, therefore, provides and measures a *multiplier* effect. Other multipliers may be

FIGURE 17–10
Effect of an increase in government spending

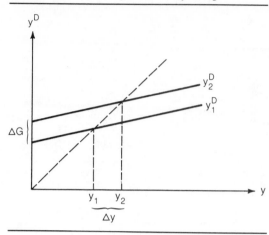

The simple
Keynesian
multiplier

calculated from the Keynesian model, and $1/(1-b)$ merely represents the basic multiplier of the simple model and under relatively restrictive conditions.

The same multiplier may be found for any change in autonomous private spending, that is, any change in a or d. The multiplier for government taxes is opposite in sign and of lower value, $-b/(1-b)$. (The derivation of this multiplier is left as an exercise for the reader.)

Why does a change in government spending or autonomous private spending have a multiplier effect on total spending and output? The answer is that, by raising income, a rise in government spending induces a rise in consumption spending which raises income further and induces still more consumption spending. The process has a limit as long as $b < 1$, and the multiplier calculates the total effect.

It was partly on the basis of this sort of algebra that Keynes viewed fiscal policy as a powerful tool for pulling an economy out of a depression. The cause of a depression according to Keynes was that the private sources of demand were insufficient to push the economy toward a state of full employment. Put differently, desired savings were too great relative to investment demand.

Equilibrium in
terms of saving
and investment

This last statement can be explained by restating our basic equilibrium condition, $y^D = y$, as follows.

First substitute Equation (1) into the basic equilibrium condition, Equation (3), to get

$$C^D + I^D + G = y \qquad (16)$$

Then substitute (7) for y^n in (5) and the result for C^D in (16) to find

$$S^D + T = I^D + G \qquad (17)$$

In equilibrium, therefore, desired saving plus taxes equal desired investment plus government spending.

This result can be shown graphically by adding taxes to the savings function in Figure 17–6 and separately plotting the sum of the investment curve in Figure 17–8 plus government spending, as shown in Figure 17–11.

FIGURE 17–11
Withdrawals and injections

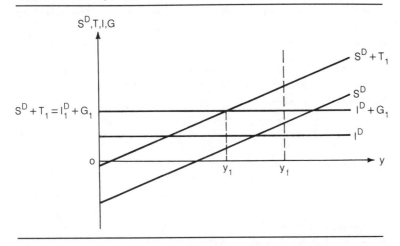

The intersection of the $S^D + T_1$ curve and the $I^D + G_1$ curve determines equilibrium real output. This equivalent way of analyzing equilibrium real output focuses on the fact that, in order for the economy to be in equilibrium, *withdrawals* from the spending stream, $S^D + T$, must equal *injections*, $I^D + G$. According to Keynes, the S^D function was too high and steeply sloped relative to the I^D function in the Great Depression to generate a full-employment level of output without deficit spending $(G > T)$ by the government.

THE MONETARY SECTOR

The foregoing analysis of equilibrium in the real sector was based upon, among other assumptions, a fixed interest rate—at a level of i_1. A lower interest rate would boost investment spending, helping a depressed economy to move back in the direction of full employment. You should recall that the interest rate in Keynes' analysis is determined by the supply and demand for money. (Review Chapter 15.) In this section on the monetary sector we will identify an equilibrium interest rate, assuming a fixed level of real income, as we did in Chapter 15. Then, in the next section, the real and monetary sectors will be combined to find a joint equilibrium, providing a more comprehensive analysis of the determination of aggregate demand.

The demand function

In Chapter 15 we identified Keynes' demand-for-money function as follows

$$M^D = L^D + N^D \tag{18}$$

or, dividing this by P,

$$\frac{M^D}{P} = \frac{L^D}{P} + \frac{N^D}{P} \tag{19}$$

where $\frac{N^D}{P}$ is the sum of the real transactions and precautionary demands for money, each of which depend upon real income; and $\frac{L^D}{P}$ is the speculative demand for money—that element of money demand which depends upon the rate of interest.[6] Specifically, we assume first

$$\frac{N^D}{P} = f(y) \tag{20}$$

and second

$$\frac{L^D}{P} = f(i) \tag{21}$$

FIGURE 17–12
Transactions-precautionary demand for money

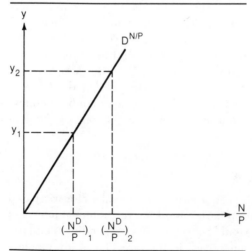

---

[6]Evidence presented at the end of Chapter 15 cast doubt on the existence of a speculative demand for money. The standard Keynesian model still incorporates a speculative demand-for-money relationship, however, with the understanding that it represents the interest-sensitive element of total money demand—be it derived from speculative, precautionary, or transactions demands.

These two relationships are shown in Figures 17–12 and 17–13.

FIGURE 17–13
Speculative demand for money

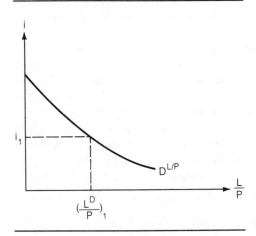

The curve representing the total demand for money in relation to the rate of interest is found by taking $\dfrac{N^D}{P}$ at a specific level of real income, say y_1, from Figure 17–12 and adding it horizontally to the speculative demand-for-money curve in Figure 17–13. The result is shown in Figure 17–14.

FIGURE 17–14
Determination of the interest rate

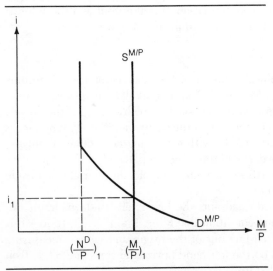

Equilibrium at a
given level of real
income

When this curve is confronted with the money supply divided by
the price level, which we assume is fixed because the economy is
operating on the flat segment of the aggregate supply curve (which
fixes the price level) and the money supply is fixed by the monetary
authorities, the equilibrium rate of interest, i_1, results.

Market
interactions
following a
change in an
exogenous
variable

Now consider the effect of an increase in the money supply on
each of our markets. An increase in the nominal money supply increases the real money supply and reduces the rate of interest, provided the speculative demand for money is not perfectly elastic. A
lower interest rate then stimulates an increase in investment demand, as implied in Figure 17–7. A higher level of investment demand shifts the aggregate demand curve upward in Figure 17–9,
leading to a rise in real output (just as a rise in government spending
did in our earlier exercise). These are the basic mechanics of monetary influence in the simple Keynesian model. But this is not the
end of the story, for a rise in real output, say to y_2, feeds back to the
monetary sector through an induced increase in $\dfrac{N^D}{P}$, as shown in
will shift the total money demand curve in Figure 17–14 to the
right, provoking a rise in the interest rate. This causes income to
change, and so on. Clearly the two sectors should be integrated to
find a joint equilibrium where such interactions have been fully
reflected.

IS-LM ANALYSIS:
THE JOINT EQUILIBRIUM OF THE REAL AND MONETARY
SECTORS

The two sectors can be integrated by solving each for all those
combinations of real output and the interest rate which satisfy the
requirement for equilibrium, ceteris paribus, in that sector. Then
we can find that single combination of real output and the interest
rate which is consistent with equilibrium in both sectors.

The IS curve

Consider a graphical solution of the real sector first. The four-
quadrant diagram in Figure 17–15 provides all of the necessary relationships. We begin with the fourth quadrant, i.e., the lower,
right-hand portion. In the fourth quadrant the $S^D + T_1$ function, is
repeated from Figure 17–11 with a 180 degree rotation about the
horizontal axis. The curve in this diagram plots $S^D + T$ on the lower
stem of the vertical axis for a given value of y on the right-hand side
of the horizontal stem.

The curve in third quadrant, the lower left-hand quadrant, imposes the equilibrium condition that $S^D + T = I^D + G$. It does this
since it is a 45-degree line out of the origin and we are measuring
the level of $I^D + G$ on the left-hand horizontal stem and $S^D + T$ on
the bottom vertical stem.

FIGURE 17–15
Derivation of the IS curve

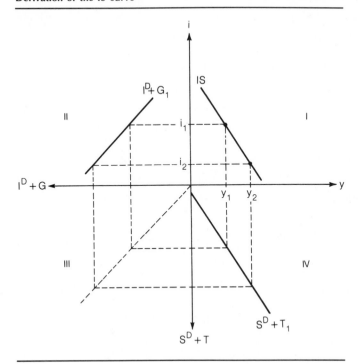

The curve in the second quadrant is derived by taking the investment demand curve from Figure 17–7, adding government spending to it, and rotating the result 180 degrees about the vertical axis. It shows, for a given level of $I^D + G$ injections, the interest rate which is required to induce that level of injections.

The required interest rate and the original level of real output come together in the first quadrant and define a point on a curve tracing all combinations of the interest rate and real output which are consistent with equilibrium in the real sector. This curve, which is downward sloping to the right, is called the IS curve.

The LM curve

Now we turn to the monetary sector. The necessary relationships are combined in the four-quadrant diagram in Figure 17–16.

The curve in the fourth quadrant is simply the D^{NP} curve from Figure 17–12 with the appropriate rotation. For a given real output level, it plots a given value for $\dfrac{N^D}{P}$ on the lower stem of the vertical axis.

The curve in the third quadrant imposes the equilibrium condition that the sum of the two demand components, $\dfrac{N^D}{P}$ and $\dfrac{L^D}{P}$ equal

FIGURE 17–16
Derivation of the LM curve

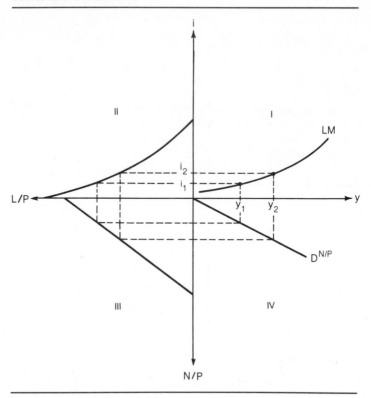

$\dfrac{M^S}{P}$. This occurs because the curve traces all those points where the
sum of the values on the two axes of the third quadrant equals a
fixed quantity. That fixed quantity can be measured as equal to each
of the intercepts of the curve. Hence, if the money supply increases
with the price level remaining constant, the curve in this quadrant
shifts outward from the origin and parallel to itself. (We will return
to trace through the effects of such a change later.) Given a fixed
price level, a fixed money supply, and a certain value for $\dfrac{N^D}{P}$, however, the curve in this quadrant defines the level of $\dfrac{L^D}{P}$ required for
equilibrium in the monetary sector.

The second quadrant shows the $D^{L/P}$ curve of Figure 17–13, ro-
tated 180 degrees about the vertical axis. In this diagram, it shows
the interest rate required to induce a given level of the demand for
real speculative balances.

The interest rate and real output come together in the first quadrant as they did for the real sector. This time they trace out those

combinations which are consistent with equilibrium in the monetary sector. This is the LM curve, which is upward sloping to the right.

The IS and LM curves can be brought together now in Figure 17–17 to solve for a joint equilibrium of our two sectors.

The joint equilibrium

FIGURE 17–17
The joint equilibrium

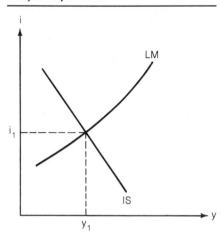

As shown, there is one interest rate, i_1, and one level of real output, y_1, consistent with equilibrium in both sectors *provided all of the assumptions which were invoked to establish the IS and LM relationships hold.*

Two changes can be considered to illustrate the mechanics of IS-LM analysis and the relative influence of fiscal and monetary policy within this framework. Suppose government spending rises from G_1 to G_2. This will shift the $I^D + G$ curve outward in our four-quadrant real sector diagram as shown in Figure 17–18.
As a result, the IS curve shifts to the right, raising the equilibrium level of real output by our simple multiplier, $1/(1-b)$, times the increase in government spending, *provided the interest rate is constant.*

A rise in government spending

To find the new joint equilibrium, we confront the shift in the IS curve with our LM curve in Figure 17–19. As described, in the new joint equilibrium the interest rate is higher and real output rises, but by less than suggested by the simple multiplier, $1/(1-b)$. The reason for a smaller rise in y is that the rise in the rate of interest has discouraged some private investment. Government spending has effectively crowded out some private spending. This is one among several mechanisms by which a *crowding out* of private spending by government fiscal actions can occur, reducing the Keynesian multi-

Crowding out

FIGURE 17–18
Effect of higher government spending

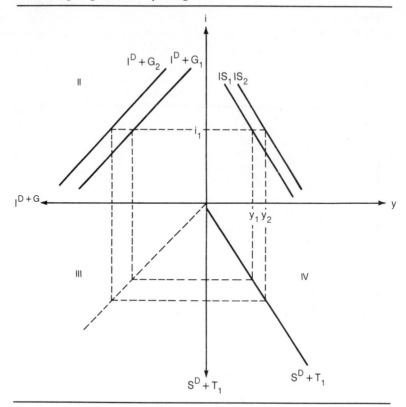

FIGURE 17–19
The new joint equilibrium with higher government spending

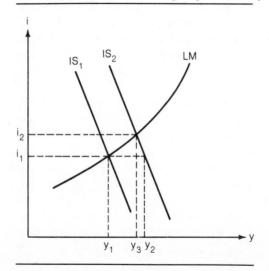

plier. Another was described in Chapter 5 and a third is described later in this chapter.[7]

The amount of crowding out in our IS-LM analysis is shown by the difference $y_2 - y_3$ in Figure 17–19. It can be found that *the degree of crowding out will be greater the flatter is the IS curve and the more vertical the LM curve*. The IS curve, in turn, will be flatter the greater is the interest sensitivity of investment demand; and the LM curve will be more vertical the lower is the interest sensitivity of the demand for money. In Chapter 15 we reviewed studies of the demand for money which suggest rather uniformly that the demand for money is inelastic with respect to the rate of interest. Studies of investment demand are less conclusive, leaving more room for disagreement. Keynesians tend to support the view that investment demand is relatively insensitive to the rate of interest, suggesting that crowding out via this avenue is not significant. Monetarists view investment demand as highly interest sensitive and consider crowding out through this and other channels to be severe.

The other change we will describe before closing this section is an increase in the money supply. The effect on the LM curve is shown in Figure 17–20.

A rise in the money supply

FIGURE 17–20
Effect of a rise in the money supply

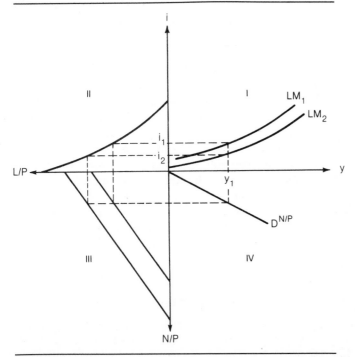

---

[7]The other mechanism described in this chapter involves the effect on private-sector demand of any rise in the price level associated with a rise in government spending and total demand. For still others see K.M. Carlson and R. Spencer, "Crowding-Out and Its Critics," Federal Reserve Bank of St. Louis *Monthly Review* (December 1975).

As noted earlier, with a fixed price level, a rise in the money supply shifts the curve in the third quadrant outward. This permits a lower interest rate at a given level of real output and causes a downward or rightward shift of the LM curve.

The shift of the LM curve is combined with our original IS curve in Figure 17–21. The result is a lower rate of interest and a rise in

FIGURE 17–21
The new joint equilibrium with a higher money supply

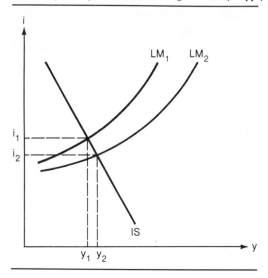

real output. Once again, the interest sensitivities of the demand for money and of investment demand are critical to the outcome. Eliminating the demand-for-money relationship as a source of disagreement, differences among Keynesians and monetarists come down once again, in part, to the interest sensitivity of investment demand. If investment demand is relatively insensitive to the rate of interest, as Keynesians maintain, the IS curve is relatively vertical, and the shift of the LM curve to the right will result in a relatively small increase in real output. If monetarists are correct, and investment demand is highly interest sensitive, the IS curve will be relatively flat and the rise in real income following a rise in the money supply via the interest-rate channel will be relatively large, ceteris paribus.

The effect of changes in the price level

Thus far we have held the price level constant by assuming the economy moves along a flat segment of the aggregate supply curve. This assumption can be relaxed now to show the effects of price-level changes on aggregate demand in the simple Keynesian model.

Recall that the price level was incorporated in our model of the monetary sector. For a given money supply, a rise in the price level reduces M^S/P, and this effect is shown now in Figure 17–22.

FIGURE 17–22
Effect of an increase in the price level

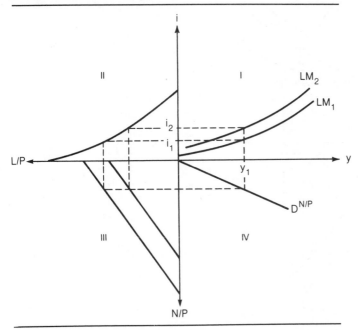

The curve in the third quadrant shifts in with a rise in the price level and this shifts the LM curve upward or to the left. The effect of a leftward shift of the LM curve is a rise in the rate of interest and a fall in real output, shown in the top portion of Figure 17–23.

We can use this effect to explain the possibility of another type of crowding out, referred to earlier. If an increase in government spending, which shifts the IS curve to the right, results in upward pressure on the price level, this will tend to shift the LM curve to the left, offsetting some of the expansionary influence of the rise in government spending. Note also that this effect means that expansionary monetary policy tends to be ineffective in expanding real output once money-supply increases induce proportional increases in the price level.

Crowding out as a result of increases in the price level

Figure 17–23 shows a series of upward shifts of the LM curve with successive increases in the price level. This permits us to trace out a downward-sloping curve below the IS-LM diagram showing an inverse relationship between the price level and real output, similar to the aggregate demand curve we used in Chapter 16.

Derivation of the aggregate demand curve

FIGURE 17–23
Derivation of the aggregate demand curve

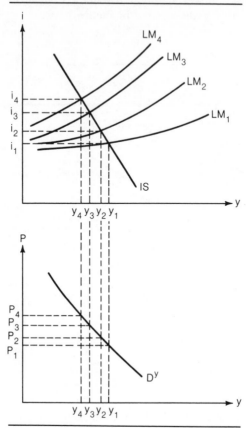

CONCLUSION

The Keynesian analysis of aggregate demand permits the specification of very exact linkages between policy instruments and major economic variables. The detail that this provides and the interdependencies in the economy that the model reveals are instructive. It should be acknowledged, however, that in the interest of simplicity and manageability, the model as we have presented it here incorporates only a few of the essential characteristics of aggregate demand and the monetary sector. Modifications or additional features found in more sophisticated models include:

1. Desired consumption is specified as a function of permanent income and/or wealth, instead of as a simple function of current income.[8]

---

[8]Permanent income was defined in Chapter 15 as the expected trend of future income. The expected trend of future income may depend *in part* upon current income. See the section on "Real Wealth and Permanent Income" and footnote 19 in Chapter 15.

2. Investment demand is related to current output through the accelerator mechanism, $I^D = f(\Delta y)$; and expected inflation should be incorporated in the investment demand function, or the interest rate which affects investment demand should be specified as the expected real rate of interest, r^*, not the nominal rate, i.
3. Government spending and tax receipts are specified to be a function of the level of real output, both because of automatic stabilizer adjustments and because of normal changes in discretionary fiscal policy over the business cycle. Real tax receipts are also affected by the price level (positively) due to the progressive tax structure for personal income.
4. Monetary policy is partly endogenous due to normal Federal Reserve responses to the business cycle and due to lagged-reserve accounting (explained in Chapter 14).

The next chapter develops a structural analysis of aggregate supply.

PROBLEMS

1. Explain the connection between the aggregate demand curve which relates real output demanded to the price level, and the Keynesian aggregate demand curve which relates real output demanded to the actual level of real output.
2. What determines the value of the ultimate Keynesian government-spending multiplier in the IS-LM model?
3. What determines the importance of money supply changes in the IS-LM model?
4. Explain two types of crowding out using IS-LM and/or aggregate-demand, aggregate-supply analysis.

ADVANCED READINGS

Carlson, K.M., and Spencer, R. "Crowding-Out and Its Critics." Federal Reserve Bank of St. Louis *Monthly Review*, December 1975.

Leijonhufvud, A. *On Keynesian Economics and the Economics of Keynes.* New York: Oxford University Press, 1968.

Samuelson, Paul A. "Interactions Between the Multiplier Analysis and the Principle of Acceleration." *Review of Economic Statistics* 21 (1939); 75–78.

Spencer, R.W. "Channels of Monetary Influence: A Survey," Federal Reserve Bank of St. Louis *Monthly Review* (November 1974); 8–26.

————, and Yohe, William P. "The Crowding Out of Private Expenditures by Fiscal Policy Actions." Federal Reserve Bank of St. Louis *Monthly Review*, (October 1979).

Teigen, R.L. "A Critical Look at Monetarist Economics." Federal Reserve Bank of St. Louis *Monthly Review*, (January 1972).

The determinants of aggregate supply

The underlying relationships which come together in the aggregate supply function are analyzed in this chapter. The first section describes the *production function* which defines the physical relationships between real output and employed resources. The next section develops an analysis of supply-side equilibrium in terms of *the supply and demand for variable inputs*. These relationships are then integrated in the final section to derive the aggregate supply function.

THE PRODUCTION FUNCTION

In a *physical* sense, output is always determined by employed resources or inputs and the effective technological base. Resources include: the capital stock, such as real plant and equipment; labor, both skilled and unskilled; and other resources such as energy and the environment. The effective technological base represents the state of society's knowledge and the ability of management to apply that knowledge to achieve the most efficient combination of resources and the optimum organization of the production process.

Determinants of production

The capital stock, K, includes fixed natural resources such as land and society's past investment in capital goods net of the depreciation or destruction of those goods over time. Since net new investment (total current investment less depreciation) is normally small relative to the existing level of the capital stock and the focus of our analysis is relatively short run, in most cases in this chapter we will assume the capital stock is fixed.

The capital stock

Employed labor is a factor of production which changes significantly in the short run. Variations are accomplished either by changes in the number of workers employed, E, or by changes in the average workweek, that is, the number of hours per worker per week. It will be convenient for our purposes to assume that the average workweek remains constant so that changes in labor employed can be identified as changes in the number of workers employed.

Labor

Other resources employed by the firm, O, are also normally variable in the short run. The use of energy ordinarily rises with a rise in output in the short run. The environment is another resource which is "employed" more as output rises in the sense that more wastes are discharged into rivers and the air, which have a limited capacity to dispose of wastes without imposing costs on society. The extent to which use of the environment imposes costs upon individual firms disposing of wastes depends upon regulations and restraints in this area, but environmental costs are being increasingly felt by firms.

Other resources

The effective technological base of society, B, advances over time, adding to the economy's output capacity. The advance of knowledge can constitute an extremely important contribution to the economy's long-run growth rate. In the short run, however, this influence is usually small relative to the influence of other factors. Consequently, we will hold the effective technological base constant in most of our analysis.

The effective
technological base

The general aggregate production function can be summarized as follows:

$$y = f(K, E, O, B, \ldots)$$

Influenced variable	Influencing variable	Direction of influence
y: the quantity of real output	K: the capital stock	Positive in the long run; no influence in the short run due to no changes in K, by assumption
	E: employed workers	Positive
	O: other resources such as energy and the environment	Positive
	B: the effective technological base	Positive in the long run; no influence on changes in the short run

Total and marginal product curves

The short run
with fixed
proportions
between labor
and other
variable resources

Focusing on the short run, how will output respond to greater applications of labor and other variable resources? Let us assume initially that, although labor, E, and other resources, O, are both variable, they are always combined in fixed proportions in a "basket" we will call R. As this basket of variable inputs rises, the level of output rises, but the additions to output will tend to be smaller and smaller for equal increments in R. In other words, the marginal product of R declines. This follows from our assumptions of a fixed capital stock and a fixed technological base in the short run. At higher output rates, larger quantities of R must be combined with the same quantity of plant and equipment and using the same tech-

FIGURE 18–1
Total and marginal product curves for variable resources

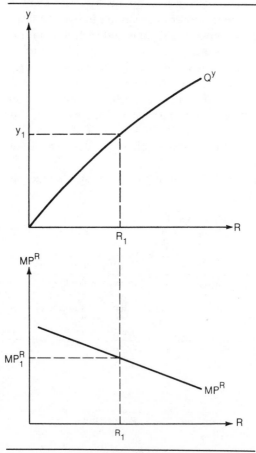

nology. As output rises in the short run, there is a dilution of capital per unit of R, thereby reducing the contribution of additional quantities of R to y. This is simply the application of the *law of diminishing returns*, a familiar principle covered in introductory and intermediate courses in microeconomics, to the aggregate economy.

The relationships just described are shown in Figure 18–1. The top panel shows the short-run production curve, Q^y, where y is plotted in relation to the employment of R, that is, of E and O combined in a certain fixed proportion. Note that the positive slope of this relationship declines at higher rates of output, due to the declining marginal productivity of our basket of variable resources. To identify this explicitly, the slope of the curve in the top panel, i.e., the marginal productivity of R, is plotted as MP^R in the bottom panel.

Now, to highlight the *separate* contributions of E and O, assume that the proportion in which labor and other resources are combined can vary and that, initially, the quantity of other resources, O, is fixed. In other words, suppose firms add to output only by adding workers. The slope of the short-run output curve now falls more sharply than in our earlier case where the employment of labor and other variable resources rose proportionally, as shown in Figure 18–2.

A case with variable proportions between labor and all other resources.

Although this case is less realistic as a representation of the actual behavior of output and the utilization of resources in the short run than is our first case, it is useful because it permits us to show the curve for MP^E, the marginal product of labor alone, depicted in the bottom panel of Figure 18–2. (Later the marginal product of labor curve will be shown to be equivalent to a demand-for-labor curve and used for this in an analysis of the labor market.)

The alternative extreme case in which labor is held constant and other resources are varied, can be described by similar relationships to those shown in Figure 18–2, with appropriate substitutions of the symbol O for the symbol E and MP^O for MP^E. Obviously, many other cases involving variable proportions between labor and other resources are possible. The essential relationships we need have been established by those cases we have covered, however.

SUPPLY-SIDE EQUILIBRIUM

The behavior of firms

All of the foregoing analysis describes physical relationships and possibilities without determining a supply-side equilibrium rate of output and an equilibrium mix between labor and other variable resources. The supply-side equilibrium conditions will depend

FIGURE 18–2
Total and marginal product curves for labor

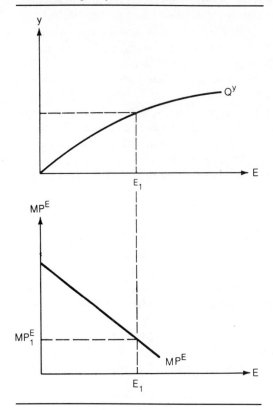

upon decisions by firms (owners of capital), workers, and the owners of other means of production as to their desired rates of output or input, as the case may be. Firms, we assume, will seek to maximize profits and will determine their desired rates of output accordingly. Standard theory of the competitive firm shows that profits are maximized where the marginal cost of output equals the price of output.[1] The marginal cost of output, in turn, can be analyzed in terms of the marginal costs of variable inputs and their marginal products.

Suppose, for example, that labor is the only input which is variable in the short run—a case considered in the previous section. The marginal cost of output then equals the incremental cost of the labor required to produce an incremental unit of output. If the wage rate of labor is fixed from the firm's point of view for small changes in employment, the incremental cost of labor for an incremental unit

---

[1]Our analysis will cover outcomes only for competitive markets for output and labor. Competitive conditions are assumed to prevail in sufficient degree in enough markets to make the competitive model a reasonably accurate characterization of the aggregate economy. Note that this does not exclude the existence of monopoly power in some markets, however.

of output equals the wage rate divided by the marginal product of labor.[2] This means that a profit-maximizing competitive firm will tend to hire labor and expand output up to the point where

$$P = \frac{W}{MP^E}$$

The result above can be rearranged to a more convenient form

$$MP^E = \frac{W}{P}$$

For the aggregate economy this implies that firms will tend to expand output and employment up the point where the marginal product of labor equals the real wage rate. The relationship between the marginal product of labor and the level of employment was shown earlier in the lower panel of Figure 18–2. That relationship is repeated in the bottom panel of Figure 18–3 with the real wage rate indicated on the vertical axis along with MP^E. As shown, for a given real wage rate, $(W/P)_1$, firms' desired employment of labor will be E^1 and desired output will be y_1. At levels of employment under E_1 (and output under y_1) the marginal product of labor is greater than the real wage rate. If firms expand output, profits are increased since labor's incremental contribution to output is greater than real wage costs. At employment levels (output rates) greater than E_1 (y_1), firms increase profits by reducing output since the loss in output is less than the real wage costs saved.

The labor market

This does not yet establish an equilibrium rate of output, however, since the real wage has been taken as given. We require a supply and demand for labor analysis which will establish the equilibrium real wage rate.

Return to the lower panel of Figure 18–3 for a moment and suppose the real wage falls from $(W/P)_1$ to a lower level. Firms will respond by expanding employment and output until the marginal product of labor falls to reach the new, lower real wage rate. We can find the new employment level from the marginal product of labor curve. Consequently, the marginal product of labor curve can be interpreted equivalently as a demand-for-labor curve.

The demand-for-labor curve

---

[2]This can be shown readily using calculus, where the variable cost, C^v, is given by

$$C^v = W \cdot E$$

$$\text{Then } \frac{\partial C^v}{\partial Q} = W \cdot \frac{\partial E}{\partial Q} = \frac{W}{\partial Q/\partial E} = \frac{W}{MP^E}$$

where Q is output and $\partial Q/\partial E$ or MP^E is the marginal product of labor.

FIGURE 18–3
Derivation of the demand for labor

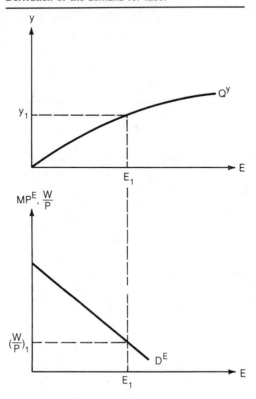

The supply-of-
labor curve

Workers are assumed to supply labor in relation to the perceived or *expected* real wage rate $(W/P)^*$. The higher expected real wages, the higher are the expected rewards to labor. Our labor-supply relationship is shown with the demand curve for labor in Figure 18–4. If the actual real wage equals the expected real wage, equilibrium is at $(W/P)_1$ and E_1, with output at y_1, as shown earlier.

Actual versus
expected real
wages

The distinction between actual real wages, which we have identified as the relevant variable for the demand for labor, and expected real wages, which determines the supply of labor, is important when workers' expectations of inflation lag behind actual inflation. Suppose the price level rises unexpectedly, for example. At the existing level of the money wage, the actual real wage falls, and, as a result, firms desire to add workers. Workers do not perceive the increase in the price level—at least they do not fully perceive the actual rise—hence they will willingly supply more labor at an actual money wage rate greater than before but not high enough to keep the actual real wage from falling.

FIGURE 18–4
Supply and demand for labor

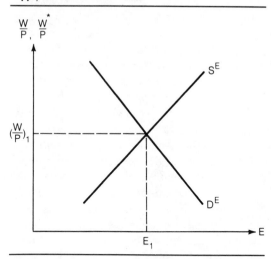

This effect can be shown in Figure 18–5 which plots both the supply of and the demand for labor in terms of the actual real wage rate. A rise in money wages subsequent to a rise in the price level fools workers into thinking that real wages have risen when, in fact, they have fallen. As a result, the supply of labor as a function of the actual real wage shifts to the right from S_1^E to S_2^E, as shown. The effect is a rise in employment and output until workers' expectations catch up with reality. When expectations catch up, the labor supply curve falls back to S_1^E and employment returns to E_1. Such a se-

FIGURE 18–5
Effect of a surprise rise in the price level

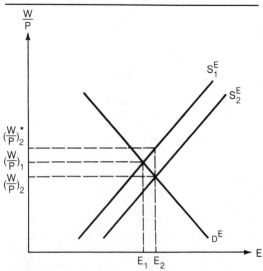

quence of adjustments was described before, in chapter 16, in terms of movements along and shifts in the aggregate supply curve following a rise in inflation initiated by a vertical shift in the aggregate demand function (demand-pull inflation). It was also described in terms of a movement along and a subsequent shift up in the short-run Phillips curve. Later in this chapter the curves and shifts just described will be related explicitly to the aggregate supply curve.

The effects of variable quantities of other resources

We cannot leave our analysis of the supply and demand for labor yet because the demand-for-labor curve has been developed so far only for the extreme case in which variations in the use of other resources are not permitted. Relaxation of this assumption will have two effects. First, it will tend to make the demand-for-labor curve more elastic. Consider a fall in the real wage rate. At a lower real wage rate, firms will tend to expand output and employment. As they do, the marginal product of labor will fall. If other resources complementary to labor can be added at the same time that labor is added, however, the fall in the marginal product of labor will tend to be less than we have shown previously in this section. Consequently, the quantity of labor can be expanded further before a new position is reached at which the marginal product of labor equals the

FIGURE 18–6
Effect of a rise in the price of complementary resources

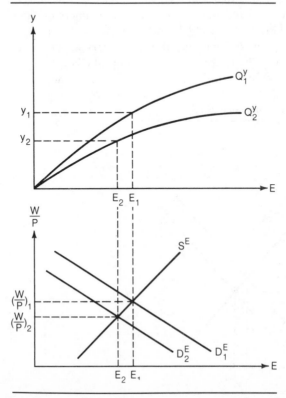

lower real wage rate. Correspondingly, the short-run production curve relating production to labor will tend to have a less sharply falling slope in this case.

The second effect of permissible variations in the use of other resources stems from any changes in the prices of other resources. If the prices of resources highly complementary to labor rise, the demand-for-labor curve will shift to the left because these resources will be conserved, reducing the marginal productivity of labor at every level of employment. Likewise, the short-run curve relating production to labor employment will exhibit a more rapidly declining slope, as shown by Q_2^y in Figure 18–6. Note that the production curve also shifts down. If the prices of resources for which labor is highly substitutable rise, the demand-for-labor curve will tend to shift to the right. The short-run production curve still shifts down, however, as shown in Figure 18–7, since labor is not likely to be a perfect substitute for these resources.

FIGURE 18–7
Effect of a rise in the price of substitute resources

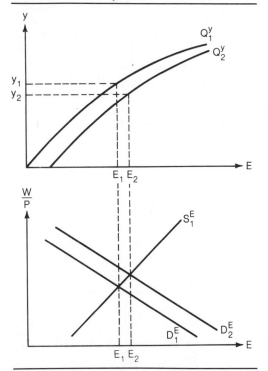

The same analysis we have developed in this section can be set out for other resources variable in the short-run. For example, the demand for energy resources such as crude oil can be derived just as we derived the demand for labor. Our analysis of the supply of crude oil would be different in one important respect. Since the existence of OPEC makes our assumption that all markets are competitive starkly invalid in this case, attention would have to be devoted to OPEC behavior and related factors affecting energy prices. We will end our analysis of input markets at this point, though, because all the important principles we need have been covered. The next section links the input markets and the short-run production curve to the aggregate supply curve presented in Chapter 16.

THE SHORT-RUN AGGREGATE SUPPLY CURVE

The short-run aggregate supply curve will be developed under the following assumptions: (1) the capital stock is assumed to be fixed; (2) the effective technological base is assumed to be constant; (3) the prices of all variable inputs with the exception of labor are held constant (the money wage rate can change); and (4) labor's expectations with regard to the price level are that it will not change.

The aggregate supply curve will be derived in the first quadrant of the four-quadrant diagram in Figure 18–8. Each of the other quadrants must be explained first.

The short-run production curve is shown in the fourth quadrant. Output rises with higher levels of employed labor, shown on the lower stem of the vertical axis. Changes in the utilization of other variable resources occur along this curve, in line with profit-maximi-

FIGURE 18–8
Derivation of the short-run aggregate supply curve

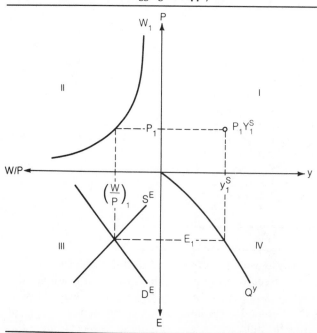

zing adjustments in input proportions by firms and the assumptions we have made about input prices.

The supply and demand for labor in relation to the *actual* real wage rate are shown in the third quadrant. At $(W/P)_1$ the actual real wage rate equals the expected real wage rate. Any discrepancy between the actual real wage rate and the expected real wage rate will result in an appropriate shift of the labor-supply curve. The second quadrant merely depicts the algebraic relationship between the real wage rate and the price level if the money wage rate is constant—a useful relationship for showing adjustments in the money wage rate necessary to derive the short-run aggregate supply curve. If the money wage rate rises, the curve in the third quadrant, which is a rectangular hyperbola, shifts outward.

The effect of a rise in the price level

We begin from an equilibrium situation where P_1, y_1^S, E_1, and $(W/P)_1$ are at levels consistent with the relationships shown. In other words, $P_1\ y_1^S$ represents a point on the short-run aggregate supply curve we wish to derive in the first quadrant. Now consider a higher price level, P_2, as a result, say, of a rise in aggregate demand. A higher price level at the same level of money wages, quadrant II in Figure 18–9, implies a lower level of real wages, and this, in turn,

FIGURE 18–9
Effect of an unexpected rise in the price level

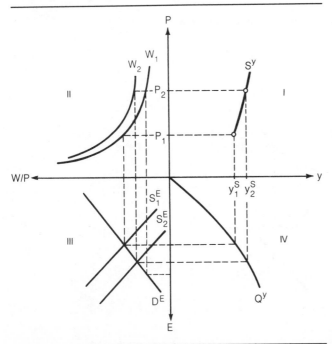

creates a higher level of desired labor employment by firms, shown by the lowest dashed line in quadrant III. This creates an excess demand for labor however, resulting in some increases in the money wage rate and an outward shift of the rectangular hyperbola in quadrant II.

Workers respond to any increase in the money wage rate as though it were a rise in the real wage rate. Consequently, the expected real wage rate rises even though the actual real wage rate has fallen, and the supply-of-labor curve in quadrant III shifts toward the bottom of the page (outward from the origin). Employment and output expand, creating a new point, $P_2\, y_2^S$, on our aggregate supply curve.

The effect of a fall in the price level

It will be instructive to consider a lower price level than P_1 (fall in aggregate demand) as well. With a constant money wage rate, a lower price level implies a rise in the real wage rate, creating an excess supply of labor condition and putting downward pressure on the money wage rate. The money wage rate may be less flexible downwards than it is upwards, however, due to labor's resistance to any apparent decline in the real wage rate and due also possibly to institutional constraints such as labor union contracts and the minimum wage. If the money wage rate is totally inflexible down-wards,

FIGURE 18–10
Effect of an unexpected fall in the price level

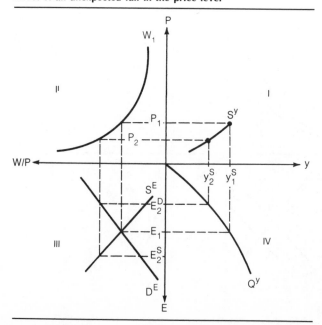

the excess supply of labor remains at $E_2^S - E_2^D$, shown in Figure
18–10. This represents a rise in the unemployment rate, of course.
Actual employment drops sharply to E_2^D since firms will hire no
more than E_2^D workers, and output drops to y_2^S.

Keynes was convinced that money wages are inflexible down-
wards and stressed the unemployment implications of a fall in aggregate demand partly for this reason. If money wages were flexible
downwards, the fall in employment and output would be far less
than that shown in Figure 18–10. (The derivation of this result is left
as an exercise for the reader.)

The points on the short-run aggregate supply curve derived in
Figure 18–9 and 18–10 are representative of further points that can
be derived on either side of $P_1 y_1$. The full short-run aggregate supply curve so derived is shown in Figure 18–11. Note that the short-
run aggregate supply curve is flatter to the left of $P_1 y_1$ due to the
downward inflexibility of money wages. The point $P_1 y_1$ is considered a point corresponding to a condition of full employment. Points
on S^y to the lower left of $P_1 y_1$ correspond to conditions of less than
full employment, and points to the upper right of $P_1 y_1$ correspond
to conditions of more than full employment. The flatness of the
short-run aggregate supply curve to the left of $P_1 y_1$ explains the
notion of Keynesian and even some monetarist economists that *an
increase in aggregate demand is likely to have a relatively strong
impact on real output and a relatively weak impact on prices when
the economy is operating at a pace which corresponds to less than
full employment.*

FIGURE 18–11
The full short-run aggregate supply curve

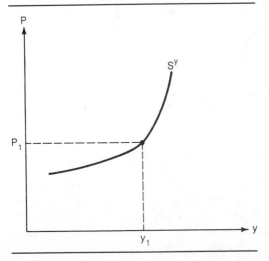

Changes in the expected price level

Our analysis of the labor market in the previous section suggested that a rise in employment associated with a rise in the price level above P_1 would be temporary in that labor would eventually realize that the actual real wage rate has fallen. This eventual adjustment causes the labor supply curve in the third quadrant of our model here to shift back to its original position, creating an excess demand for labor and a further shift out in the money wage curve, as shown in Figure 18–12. Effectively, the entire short-run aggregate supply curve shifts upward, as shown in quadrant I, since the original curve, S_1^y, was derived under the assumption that the expected price level equals P_1. The original output level, y_1, becomes associated with a higher price level, P_2. Hence, in general, *the model suggests that, if workers expect price increases, this will cause actual price increases and a reduction in output supplied.*

FIGURE 18–12
Effect of changes in the expected price level

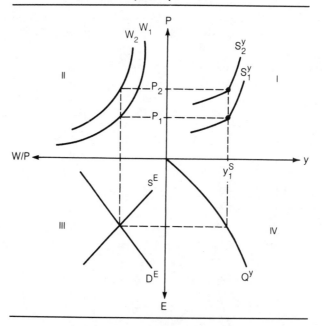

A change in the price of energy

The model can handle many other changes, most of which are left for the reader to explore. One more we will explain before closing this chapter is the effect of a change in the price of energy. As described in the previous section, a rise in the price of another variable input can shift the demand for labor in or out from the origin, depending upon whether labor and the other input are complements or substitiutes for each other.

The substitutability of labor and energy resources is partly a matter of time. Given the short-run focus of our analysis, including assumptions that the capital stock and the technological base are fixed, labor and energy resources are probably more complements than they are substitutes. Consequently, we show the demand-for-labor curve shifting in toward the origin in the third quadrant of Figure 18–13 in response to a rise in the price of energy. At the same time, the production curve shifts to the left, reflecting a lower feasible rate of output at each level of employment. The result is lower employment and a lower rate of output at the original price level. This means a shift upward of the short-run aggregate supply curve. When an aggregate demand curve is included, as was done in Figure 18–13, we can see that the implication of higher energy prices for the overall equilibrium is a higher price level and a still greater fall in output and employment. *Hence a rise in energy prices is both inflationary and contractionary for the economy,* a condition experienced in the U.S. in 1973–74 and again in 1979–80.

FIGURE 18–13
Effect of an increase in the price of energy

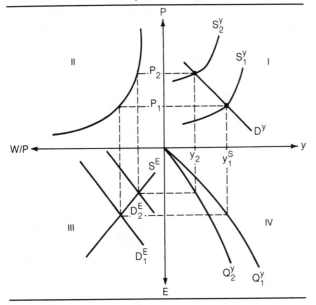

CONCLUSION

This chapter completes our analysis of the structural components of aggregate demand and aggregate supply and closes Part IV of the book. The next and final part returns to topics more directly related to money and credit.

PROBLEMS

1. Explain the principal assumptions which underlie the short-run aggregate production function.

2. An increase in output in the short-run aggregate supply model occurs when:
   a. the actual real wage rate rises
   b. the expected real wage rate rises
   c. the capital stock rises
   d. none of the above.

3. Use the aggregate supply model to describe the likely effects on prices, output, employment, and the real wage rate of a rise in the price of energy, *assuming labor and energy are substitutes.*

ADVANCED READINGS

Evans, Michael R. *Macroeconomic Activity: Theory, Forecasting and Control.* New York: Harper & Row, 1969. Chapter 10.

Gordon, R. J. "Recent Developments in the Theory of Inflation and Unemployment," *Journal of Monetary Economics*, April 1976.

Glahe, Fred R. *Macroeconomics: Theory and Policy* 2d ed. New York: Harcourt Brace Jovanovich, 1977. Chapter 2.

Leijonhufvud, Axel. *Keynes and the Classics.* London: The Institute of Economic Affairs, 1969.

Issues and Prospects

The relative strength of monetary and fiscal policies and other issues related to policy choice

As Chapters 15, 16, and 17 have brought out, the relative importance of fiscal and monetary policies has been a matter of considerable debate among economists since Keynes' *General Theory* was published. This issue is fundamental, of course, to the design and choice of appropriate economic policies, and it is important to those concerned with forecasts for the economy.

The first section of this chapter reviews empirical research which bears directly on the issue. The second section describes the problems introduced by lags in the implementation and in the effects of monetary and fiscal policies. Another issue, the relative importance to society of unemployment versus inflation and appropriate policy in this area, is discussed in the third section. Finally, the last section addresses appropriate policies for the attainment of internal (domestic) and external (international) economic stability.

EMPIRICAL STUDIES OF THE RELATIVE STRENGTH OF MONETARY AND FISCAL POLICIES

As the last section of Chapter 15 described, the empirical evidence on the demand-for-money function suggests that the demand for money is not highly sensitive to interest rates. The implication is that, contrary to Keynes' assertion, monetary policy is not weak on this account. But, as noted in Chapter 17, after this evidence became available, many Keynesians still questioned the importance of monetary policy based on their view that aggregate demand is relatively insensitive to a change in the rate of interest. (Chapter 17 showed explicitly how Keynesians view the principal mechanism by which a change in the money supply affects aggregate demand, that is, through a change in the interest rate.) Monetarists tend to reject the structual approach to analyzing the influence of money on the economy in general on the ground that this approach cannot properly include *all* of the channels of monetary influence; and they object specifically to the Keynesian notion that the influence of money through interest rates is weak. As another major point of contrast, monetarists view fiscal policy as weak due to crowding-out effects.

In the 1950s, Keynesians developed structural macro-econometric (statistical) models of the U.S. economy for the dual purposes of policy simulation and general forecasting. Early structural models represented the Keynesian view in the sense that monetary policy was linked to economic activity mainly through changes in the interest rate; indeed, in some models the only indicator of monetary policy was the level of some representative market interest rate. Despite evidence to the contrary in models which allowed for more than the pure interest-rate channel alone, authors of these models persisted in viewing monetary policy as weak relative to fiscal policy.[1]

The Friedman-Meiselman study

In 1963, Milton Friedman and David Meiselman published an econometric study which took a different approach from the structural statistical model and arrived at quite different conclusions from those of the Keynesian consensus.[2] Friedman and Meiselman argued that Keynesian and monetarist points of view could be reduced to a disagreement regarding the stability of velocity and the stability and size of the Keynesian multiplier: monetarists view velocity as "stable" (in the sense of low variability and/or high predictability), if not constant, and the Keynesian autonomous spending multiplier as unstable and low (less than unity) in value; Keynesians view velocity as unstable, often moving in a direction

[1]See Leonall C. Andersen, "The State of the Monetarist Debate," Federal Reserve Bank of St. Louis *Monthly Review*, (September 1973), 2–8; and Lawrence R. Klein, "Commentary on 'The State of the Monetarist Debate,'" Federal Reserve Bank of St. Louis *Monthly Review*, (September, 1973), 9–12.

[2]Milton Friedman and David Meiselman, "The Relative Stability of Monetary Velocity and the Investment Multiplier in the United States, 1897–1958," in *Stabilization Policies*, (Englewood Cliffs, N.J.: Prentice-Hall and the Commission on Money and Credit, 1963).

opposite to changes in the money supply, and the autonomous spending multiplier as stable and relatively high in value—on the order of two or three.

The test

To test these opposing views, Friedman and Meiselman examined (1) a simple direct statistical relationship between consumption spending and autonomous spending, using investment spending as a measure of autonomous spending; and (2) a simple direct statistical relationship between consumption spending; and the money supply. They claimed the results of their analysis strongly supported monetarist conclusions.

Objections

Keynesian economists rejected Friedman and Meiselman's claim on two general grounds. One was that the tests used were deficient in important technical respects. Keynesians also objected to the direct, "reduced-form" approach of the Friedman-Meiselman study.[3] Even so, the Friedman-Meiselman study as well as results obtained with their own structural models began to pursuade Keynesians in the 1960s to adopt a more moderate position that monetary policy is of significant importance. But it was still viewed as secondary to fiscal policy in *potence*. Monetarists held to a position that monetary policy is of vastly greater influence than fiscal policy.[4]

The St. Louis studies

The debate centered on the Friedman-Meiselman study for several years. Then the first of several studies on this issue by the staff of the Federal Reserve Bank of St. Louis appeared in 1968. Coming from a monetarist perspective, Leonall Andersen and Jerry Jordan set out to test a reduced-form, quarterly equation explaining changes in nominal GNP using variables and statistical methods which overcame some of the pitfalls of Friedman and Meiselman's test.[5] The general form of the Andersen-Jordan equation, which has become known as the St. Louis equation, is as follows:

The St. Louis equation

$$\Delta(P\ y) = a + b \cdot \Delta A + c \cdot \Delta F$$

where, as usual in this text, P y is nominal GNP, A is monetary

---

[3]A structural model, such as the Keynesian aggregate-demand model outlined in Chapter 17, often can be reduced to a single equation expressing a single dependent variable in terms of one or more independent variables. The reduced-form equation includes the relevant parameters from the individual structural equations in a single composite term which then can be estimated as to its size and stability. See Equation (12) in Chapter 17, for an example of a reduced-form equation.

[4]Also important in the progress of the debate was Milton Friedman and Anna J. Schwartz, *A Monetary History of the United States* (Princeton, N.J.: Princeton University Press, 1963); Milton Friedman and Anna J. Schwartz, "Money and Business Cycles," *Review of Economics and Statistics* 45 (February 1963); and Keynesian responses to these studies, for example, James Tobin, "The Monetary Interpretation of History," *The American Economic Review* 55 (June 1965); 646–685.

[5]Leonall C. Andersen and Jerry L. Jordan, "Monetary and Fiscal Actions: A Test of Their Relative Importance in Economic Stabilization," Federal Reserve Bank of St. Louis *Monthly Review*, (November 1968).

policy, and F is fiscal policy. A variety of specific forms of this equation were tested with similar results. One of the specific forms was the following:

$$\Delta(P\ y)_t = a + \sum_{i=0}^{4} m_i \cdot \Delta M_{t-i}^s + \sum_{i=0}^{4} e_i \cdot \Delta E_{t-i} +$$

$$\sum_{i=0}^{4} h_i \times \Delta H_{t-i}$$

where a is a constant term; the m_i (i = 1, 2, 3, 4) are the impact multipliers for changes in the money supply in the current quarter, t, in the previous quarter, t − 1, and so on, on changes in nominal GNP in the current quarter; the e_i (i = 1, 2, 3, 4) are the impact multipliers for changes in "high-employment" government spending over four quarters; and the h_i (i = 1, 2, 3, 4) are the impact multipliers for "high-employment" tax receipts over four quarters.

High-employment measures of government spending and tax receipts are measures of what the values of these variables would be if the economy were at a state of high or "full" employment. It was necessary for Andersen and Jordan to use such measures of fiscal variables in order to capture the effects of purely discretionary policy changes, as opposed to automatic-stabilizer changes, and, more important, to avoid confounding the influence of nominal GNP on these variables with the influence of these variables on nominal GNP. (This latter phenomenon, which is called *reverse causation*, is a common problem in statistical studies such as Andersen and Jordan's; we shall return to it later.)

Andersen and Jordan's estimates for impact multipliers over the period from the first quarter of 1952 to the second quarter of 1968 are shown in Figure 19–1.

High-employment variables

The results

FIGURE 19–1

	St. Louis impact multipliers*	
m_1 = \$1.51**	e_1 = \$0.36	h_1 = \$0.16
m_2 = 1.59**	e_2 = 0.53**	h_2 = −0.01
m_3 = 1.47**	e_3 = −0.05	h_3 = −0.03
m_4 = 1.27	e_4 = −0.78**	h_4 = 0.11
Σm_i = \$5.84**	Σe_i = \$0.07	Σh_i = \$0.23

*Results for equation 1.2 in Table 1 of Leonall Andersen and Jerry Jordan, "Monetary and Fiscal Actions: A Test of Their Relative Importance in Economic Stabilization," Federal Reserve Bank of St. Louis *Monthly Review* 50 (November 1978).

**Statistically significant.

These results imply that an increase of \$1.00 in the money supply creates a \$1.51 increase in nominal GNP in the same quarter, a \$1.59 increase in nominal GNP one quarter later, a \$1.47 increase two quarters later, and a \$1.27 increase three quarters later, for a total increase of \$5.84 in GNP over a full year. In contrast, a \$1.00 increase in high-employment government spending generates a 36¢

increase in GNP in the contemporaneous quarter, a 53¢ increase in
the next quarter, a 5¢ *decrease* in the following quarter, and a 78¢
decrease in the third quarter following the rise in goverment spending, for a total positive impact over a year of only 7¢. Finally, a $1.00
increase in high-employment tax receipts leads to a 16¢ *increase* in
GNP in the current quarter, a 1¢ decrease in GNP in the next
quarter, a 3¢ decrease in GNP in the following quarter, and an 11¢
increase in GNP in the last quarter, for a total 23¢ *positive* effect
over one year.

A positive cumulative influence for an increase in tax receipts is
completely inconsistent with the Keynesian model, but it should be
noted that only those impact multipliers marked with asterisks were
found to be "statistically significant" by the usual standard.[6] Since
none of the tax multipliers was statistically significant, the only conclusion which the equation suggests with regard to high-employment tax receipts is that this policy variable has no significant impact
on nominal GNP.

A rise in high-employment government spending has a statistically significant positive impact on GNP one quarter later and a
statistically significant negative impact on GNP three quarters later.
The net impact of high-employment government spending over a
full year is not significantly different from zero, however.

An increase in the money supply (measured by the old M-1
measure) has a significant impact on GNP in the current quarter, for
two more quarters, and for the full period of one year. The impact in
the final quarter is not statistically significant.

These results were startling and controversial because they appeared to provide strong support for an extreme monetarist point of
view. As Andersen and Jordan concluded, they are consistent with a
view that monetary actions have a stronger, more predictable, and
faster impact on GNP than fiscal actions have. Even in an absolute
sense, fiscal actions, particularly tax changes, were shown to be
weak indeed—presumably due to crowding-out effects.

The Keynesian
critique

The Keynesian response to Andersen and Jordan was very similar
to the Keynesian response to Friedman and Meiselman. Even
though many of the specific criticisms of Friedman and Meiselman's
study had been overcome by Andersen and Jordan's approach, sev-

[6]Statistically significant coefficients in a regression equation, by the usual standard, are those for which the 90 percent confidence band about the estimated value
does not include zero. Statistical significance can be determined from the standard
errors or "t" scores for each of the estimated coefficients. The t scores for the coefficients shown were 2.03, 2.85, 2.69, 1.82, and 6.57 for m_1, m_2, m_3, m_4 and Σm_i;
respectively. For the same multipliers for e, they were 1.15, 2.15, 0.19, 2.82, and
0.19; and for h, they were 0.53, 0.03, 0.10, 0.32, and 0.32. A t score of 1.98 or higher
satisfies the standard requirement for statistical significance.

Three other statistics of interest for Andersen and Jordan's equation above are the
R^2 = .58, the standard error of the estimate = 4.11, and the Durban-Watson
statistic = 1.80. The lag coefficients on the independent variables were estimated by
the Almon method.

eral objections carried over. First, Keynesians still objected to the monetarist single-equation approach which crams the entire mechanisms linking independent variables with the dependent variables into a "black box." This approach provides no insight regarding why the money supply matters so much and why fiscal variables matter so little. Without this type of information, which only structural models can provide, Keynesians have been inclined to remain skeptical of results such as those obtained by Andersen and Jordan.

Second, Keynesians questioned Andersen and Jordan's results on the ground that their equation was not indicative of the influence of money on GNP, but of the influence of GNP on money. The idea is that the banking system and the Fed typically are accommodative to changes in the demand for money which are, in turn, largely reflective of changes in GNP. To the extent that this is true, the m coefficients estimated by Andersen and Jordan measure the causal relationship running from GNP to the money supply, the reverse of the relationship presumed by Andersen and Jordan. This possible problem, known as *reverse causation*, persuaded many Keynesians to discount the Andersen and Jordan results.

Other criticisms of a more technical nature were made by Keynesians. Yet, despite all these objections, the St. Louis equation gained a measure of credibility for the monetarist position among many Keynesians for several reasons. First, the reverse causation argument was recognized to apply only to the current-quarter money coefficient, m_1, since a change in GNP in the current quarter could hardly cause a change in the money supply in one or more quarters in the past. Second, the St. Louis equation held up remarkably well when applied to different periods and when subjected to more refined and rigorous tests.[7] As one early Keynesian critic put it, "At the moment, I find it very difficult to believe in the St. Louis equation: I just don't quite see how things could work that way. On the other hand, I am ready to concede at least the possibility that proper allowance for various secondary wealth effects, credit availability effects, and a broader treatment of interest rates *might*, in principle, be able to make the St. Louis world seem plausible."[8]

The FRB–MIT model

At the same time that monetarists at the Federal Reserve Bank of St. Louis were developing their single-equation approach, research-

[7]The St. Louis equation was applied to earlier periods, including the Great Depression, by Michael W. Keran, "Monetary and Fiscal Influences on Economic Activity—The Historical Evidence," Federal Reserve Bank of St. Louis *Monthly Review*, (November 1969). The reverse causation argument was treated in Richard G. Davis, "How Much Does Money Matter? A Look at Some Recent Evidence," Federal Reserve Bank of New York *Monthly Review*, (June 1969); 119–31 and in Christopher A. Sims, "Money, Income, and Causality," *American Economic Review*, 62 (September 1972); 540–52.

[8]Richard G. Davis, "How Much Does Money Matter? A Look at Some Recent Evidence," Federal Reserve Bank of New York, *Monthly Review*, (June 1969); 31.

ers at MIT and the Federal Reserve Board were proceeding to explore the channels of influence of monetary policy within a structural model in a more elaborate and careful way than was characteristic of earlier Keynesian efforts. The early result of their efforts, the FRB–MIT model, had three principal channels: (1) a cost-of-capital channel—essentially the effect of the rate of interest on investment decisions; (2) the wealth-effect channel—an allowance for an effect of money on consumption spending via changes in stock-market prices; and (3) a credit-availability channel—the effect that tight monetary policy has on the availability of credit to various sectors, particularly housing.[9]

Three channels of influence

Simulations of the FRB–MIT model in 1969 produced the results for cumulative multipliers shown in Figure 19–2. A $1.0 billion

FIGURE 19–2
Effects of three expansionary policies: Initial conditions of 1964, Q1
(in percentage points unless otherwise indicated)

Quarter	Real GNP (billions of 1958 dollars)			GNP deflator			Money GNP (billions of current dollars)			Corporate Aaa bond rate			Unemployment rate		
	A	B	C	A	B	C	A	B	C	A	B	C	A	B	C
1	.7	6.6	1.4	—	—	—	.8	7.3	1.6	−.27	.06	.03	—	−.2	—
2	2.0	8.3	2.9	—	—	—	2.3	9.4	3.4	−.14	.05	.02	−.1	−.5	−.2
3	3.6	8.7	3.6	.1	.2	.1	4.3	10.3	4.4	−.12	.05	.02	−.2	−.6	−.2
4	5.4	8.9	4.0	.1	.2	.1	6.6	11.2	5.2	−.16	.06	.03	−.3	−.6	−.3
5	7.0	9.0	4.5	.2	.4	.2	8.9	12.0	6.1	−.19	.08	.04	−.4	−.6	−.3
6	8.3	8.7	4.8	.3	.4	.2	11.1	12.4	6.8	−.22	.09	.05	−.5	−.6	−.3
7	9.3	8.0	5.0	.4	.6	.3	13.2	12.6	7.6	−.23	.10	.06	−.6	−.6	−.3
8	10.0	7.9	5.2	.6	.7	.4	15.1	13.5	8.5	−.24	.12	.07	−.6	−.6	−.3
9	10.4	7.6	5.3	.8	.9	.5	16.9	14.1	9.3	−.25	.14	.09	−.7	−.5	−.4
10	10.7	6.8	5.4	.9	1.0	.6	18.6	14.3	10.1	−.26	.16	.10	−.7	−.5	−.4
11	10.3	6.1	5.4	1.2	1.1	.7	19.9	14.5	10.9	−.24	.17	.12	−.7	−.4	−.4
12	9.4	5.6	5.2	1.4	1.3	.8	20.6	15.2	11.6	−.25	.19	.14	−.6	−.4	−.3
13	7.9	5.8	4.7	1.7	1.4	.9	20.6	16.5	11.8	−.25	.20	.14	−.6	−.4	−.3
14	6.1	6.2	3.9	1.9	1.6	1.1	20.1	18.2	11.7	−.23	.22	.15	−.5	−.4	−.3
15	3.9	5.7	2.8	2.1	1.8	1.2	19.0	18.8	11.3	−.23	.24	.16	−.3	−.4	−.2
16	1.4	5.0	1.6	2.2	1.9	1.2	17.2	19.2	10.6	−.23	.25	.18	−.2	−.3	−.2

NOTE: A indicates step increase in unborrowed reserves of $1.0 billion; B indicates step increase in real federal wage payments of $5.0 billion; and C indicates step decrease in personal tax rate of .02 (about $4.5 billion in revenue).

SOURCE: Frank de Leeuw and Edward M. Gramlich, "The Channels of Monetary Policy," Federal Reserve *Bulletin* 55 (June, 1969); 472–91.

increase in nonborrowed reserves, the measure of monetary policy used in the FRB–MIT model, produces a total increase of $5.4 billion in real GNP and $6.6 billion increase in nominal GNP at the end of one year, as shown under the first A column. The maximum impact of monetary policy on real GNP is reached at the end of two-and-a-half years, at $10.7 billion. The effect on the price level, measured by the GNP deflator, keeps building through four years, the length of the simulation, to 2.2 percentage points. The effect on nominal GNP peaks at $20.6 billion at the end of three years.

---

[9]These channels and the results of the FRB–MIT model used here are described in Frank de Leeuw and Edward M. Gramlich, "The Channels of Monetary Policy," Federal Reserve *Bulletin* 55 (June 1969); 472–91.

Needless to say, the lags for monetary policy in Figure 19–2 are all much longer than the lag shown for monetary policy in the St. Louis nominal GNP equation, even after allowing for a reasonable lag of the money supply behind changes in nonborrowed reserves. When one adjusts for the multiplier between nonborrowed reserves and the money supply, a multiplier of roughly 10, the size of the cumulative multiplier for monetary policy in the FRB–MIT model can be seen to be substantial at about 2; but this is quite a bit less than the cumulative multiplier of 5.8 found with the St. Louis equation [10]

Comparisons with the St. Louis results

More dramatic contrasts are found for the multipliers for fiscal actions. As shown in the first B column, the cumulative effect of a permanent $5 billion increase in real federal wage payments on real GNP peaks at almost $9 billion, a multiplier of 1.8, after one year, and drops to $5 billion, a multiplier value of 1.0, but only at the end of four years. The effect on nominal GNP builds continuously, reaching $19.2 billion at the end of four years. Though a precise comparison cannot be drawn with the St. Louis equation because of the different variables used, i.e., a change in nominal government spending in the St. Louis model versus a change in real government spending in the FRB–MIT model, an unadjusted comparison is adequate for our purposes. At the end of one year, the multiplier between government spending and nominal GNP is roughly 1.3 in the FRB–MIT model versus .07 in the St. Louis model.

A comparison of multipliers for tax actions is also rough but suggestive. In the FRB–MIT model a cut in taxes of about $4.5 billion via a .2 reduction in personal tax rates ($4.5 billion cut in tax receipts) boosts real GNP $4 billion at the end of one year (see first C column), a multiplier of −.89 on the $4.5 billion cut, versus no significant impact in the St. Louis equation. The effect of a tax cut peaks at $5.4 billion at the end of two-and-a-half years in the FRB–MIT model, for a maximum multiplier of −1.2, and then drops to $1.6 billion at the end of the four-year simulation. The cumulative effect on nominal GNP peaks at $11.8 billion, just after three years, and declines to only $10.6 billion at the end of four years.

Discussions and empirical findings in subsequent years have encouraged some movement toward a middle ground by each side, but not a consensus. Monetarists have recognized the need to define the detailed transmission mechanism for monetary policy which underlies the results of their single-equation models; and Keynesians have adjusted their econometric models to provide for a greater role for money. At the same time, considerable disagreement persists regarding the importance of fiscal policy, with many monetar-

Subsequent developments

---

[10]The value of 10 for the multiplier relating the money supply to nonborrowed reserves above was calculated simply by dividing the money supply by nonborrowed reserves. A more accurate estimate would be based on the functional relationship between the money supply and non-borrowed reserves for the period studied.

ists holding to a firm view that fiscal policy effects are fleeting and small. Keynesian models now suggest that fiscal variables have zero multipliers for real output in the long run, i.e., over 5 to 10 years, but not for nominal output.[11] Meanwhile a recent version of the St. Louis model still turns up nonsignificant coefficients for high-employment government spending.[12]

INSIDE LAGS, OUTSIDE LAGS, AND POLICY INSTABILITY

The inside lag

The monetarist-Keynesian disputes regarding the influences of monetary and fiscal policies underscore the uncertain atmosphere confronting policymakers. Policymakers encounter uncertainty regarding the effects of their own actions, the influence of other factors, and the inherent momentum of the economy. In addition, policymakers are subject to political pressures which can hinder the adoption of optimal policies. All of these factors contribute to the *inside lag: the lag between the need for a specific policy action and the adoption of the policy action.*

The inside lag for monetary policy tends to be shorter than it is for fiscal policy partly because of the greater independence of the Federal Reserve from political pressures and its isolation from the distraction of other concerns which absorb Congress and the administration. Also, monetary policy is more flexible in the sense that changes in policy can be decided by a small committee on short notice—over the telephone, if necessary. Even so, the inside lag for monetary policy can be significant. The business-cycle peak of January 1980, for example, was not recognized until May; and monetary policy continued to tighten into the second quarter of that year as economic activity plunged.

The outside lag

The lag between the time policy action is taken and the timing of its effects is called the outside lag. The St. Louis equation suggests that the outside lag for monetary policy is relatively short—strong effects occur in the current quarter. Yet Friedman maintains that

---

[11]See Ettore F. Infante and Jerome L. Stein, "Does Fiscal Policy Matter?"; and Alan S. Blinder and Robert M. Solow, "Does Fiscal Policy Still Matter—A Reply," *Journal of Monetary Economics* 2 (November 1976); 473–510.

[12]Keith M. Carlson, "Money, Inflation, and Economic Growth: Some Updated Reduced Form Results and Their Implications," Federal Reserve Bank of St. Louis *Monthly Review*, (April 1980); 13–19. See also Benjamin M. Friedman, "Even the St. Louis Model Now Believes in Fiscal Policy," *Journal of Money, Credit, and Banking* 9 (May 1977); 365–67; and Keith M. Carlson, "Does the St. Louis Equation Now Believe in Fiscal Policy?" Federal Reserve Bank of St. Louis *Monthly Review*, (February 1979); 13–19.

the outside lag for monetary policy is long and variable. And most Keynesian models find long lags of two quarters or so for monetary policy.

Policy instability

These estimates suggest that the total policy lag is from one half to a full year, long enough to create significant problems. The obvious problem is that desirable policy actions are late in coming. Less obvious, but more important, is the possibility that shifts in the thrust of policy actions will be so out of tune with appropriate timing that they create greater fluctuations in economic activity than would have occurred without any effort to steady the cycle. Many economists believe that this latter situation is, in fact, a valid description of the way policy has performed in the past.[13]

Over the years there have been two types of responses to this assessment of policy performance. One response is that there is hope for better discretionary policy in the future as a result of improved forecasting techniques and/or policy formation practices. As a result, efforts should be directed toward making the advances which will do the job. This is the *activist* response.

The activist response

The other response is *passivist*. It holds that improvements in the ability of economists to forecast the economy and of policymakers to act appropriately are unlikely to occur. According to this view, the economy is too dynamic and shocks to the system are too unpredictable for forecasts to ever have the requisite accuracy. And because of uncertainty and political pressures, policymakers are always going to tend to wait too long before taking appropriate action. There is a natural bias in favor of waiting for just one more month's data, until the evidence that a certain policy action is needed is overwhelming and the political climate has become receptive to that action. Then, when aggressive policy action finally comes, there is a natural tendency for policymakers to overreact simply because the apparent need has become so great.

The passivist response

Economists who hold to this latter view tend to favor a rigid rule for monetary policy. The rule most often favored by monetarists is a constant rate of growth of the money supply.[14] Keynesians tend to prefer to leave some room for discretion in monetary policy in terms of a range of growth rates or a rule which would key the Fed's targets for the monetary aggregates to one or more key economic variables, such as inflation and/or unemployment, in a formula. A rise of one percentage point in inflation together with a decline of one-half percentage point in unemployment might call for an auto-

Rules versus discretion

[13]See, for example, Michael Evans, *Macroeconomic Activity: Theory, Forecasting and Control*, (New York: Harper & Row, 1969); 421–29.
[14]See Milton Friedman, *A Program for Monetary Stability* (New York: Fordham University Press, 1959).

matic one-point reduction in the targets for M-1A and M-1B, for
example.

Return to the gold
standard?

Disappointment with recent experience has lead also to renewed
interest in the gold standard. The case for a gold standard is based,
of course, upon the automatic discipline that this standard imposes
on the monetary authorities. A major drawback is the deflationary
effects that a gold standard can impose on the economy. As described in Chapter 12, such episodes of deflation under the gold
standard have occurred over protracted periods in response to rapid
economic growth and over briefer periods in response to financial
panic. Despite this drawback, the gold standard has recently received increased consideration by economists and policymakers.

UNEMPLOYMENT VERSUS INFLATION

The section on the Phillips curve in Chapter 16 described the
long-run trade-off between inflation and unemployment as far
weaker and perhaps nonexistent in comparison to the short-run
trade-off, which may be substantial. Assuming there is discretionary
monetary policy, or at least discretion in setting rules for policy,
how do policymakers and, ultimately, how does society choose between inflation and unemployment objectives under the conditions
described by these Phillips-curve relationships?

If anti-inflation policies are pursued vigorously, the result tends
to be higher unemployment—at least in the short run. What rise in
unemployment over what period, albeit "short run," is it worth suffering in order to reduce the long-run rate of inflation by one percentage point? Economists cannot offer a clear-cut answer to this
question, partly because it is a matter of personal opinion but also
because inflation and unemployment affect different segments of
the economy in different ways, making it a problem of social choice.

The costs of inflation

Inflation hurts those who are on fixed or relatively "inflexible"
incomes. This applies to many elderly persons; however, indexing
of Social Security payments and the advent of Medicare, Medicaid,
and food stamps programs have done much to insulate the elderly
from the effects of inflation.[15] Workers who have long-term wage
contracts without full cost-of-living adjustments are disadvantaged if
the inflation rate turns out to be higher than that anticipated at the
time of the contract negotiations. Inflation hurts others who enter

---

[15]Some economists argue that, in fact, low-income elderly persons now tend to
benefit from inflation because of the institutional changes cited above. Social Security
and many other retirement benefits are tied to the consumer price index, which is
not an index measuring prices paid specifically by the elderly. With Medicare, Medicaid, and food stamps, prices paid by the elderly in recent years have tended to rise
less rapidly than those paid by the average consumer.

similar long-term contracts— bondholders, suppliers of natural resources at fixed prices, etc.

Due to contractual, intitutional, or circumstantial rigidities in some prices, inflation tends to distort the relative price structure and the allocation of resources in the economy. The prices of goods and services of regulated industries tend to be held back by the lag in the approval process for price increases, for example. Savings are discouraged by ceilings on savings-deposit interest rates and taxes on nominal interest earnings. Also, inflation tends to encourage the growth of the public sector by providing the government with more real tax revenues as nominal incomes rise and push individuals into higher marginal tax brackets.

Finally, inflation reduces the efficiency with which money performs its basic functions by making it less useful as a standard of value and curbing the demand for real cash balances. (The effect of inflation as a tax and curbing influence on real cash balances was explained in Chapter 11.)

To reduce the cost of inflation, some economists have advocated wider applications of indexing formulas and the removal of government restraints on prices and interest ceilings. Other economists oppose indexing on the grounds that it reduces the public's opposition to inflation and tends to make the inflation rate subject to wider variations. This latter point refers to the rapid effect a surge in the prices of one sector such as agriculture, due, say, to a drought, would have on all prices and wages as indexing automatically spread higher food prices to other sectors.

Indexing as a palliative

The costs of unemployment

Unemployment obviously hurts those who lose their jobs, but there are wider effects than this. As the economy falls to below capacity output, hourly workers who keep their jobs work fewer hours, profits fall, and investment lags. Other costs of unemployment and recession include: a reduced tax base and pressure for higher government spending; disruption of careers and other long-run plans; and, of course, output lost as a result of the downturn. Some argue that these costs should be balanced against inefficiencies which get weeded out during economic downturns as well as against the benefits of reduced inflation.

As painful as unemployment and recession are, structural and institutional changes over the years since the Great Depression have greatly reduced the agony and suffering associated with a given unemployment rate. Today, a much greater share of the labor force is second-income earners. When there are two sources of labor income in a family, layoffs are likely to cause less of a shock to family income. Unemployment insurance and welfare programs also cush-

Palliatives for unemployment

ion affected families. And many labor contracts provide for supplemental or severance payments.

Palliatives for unemployment should tend to lessen society's resistance to anti-inflation programs. However, they also tend to extend the length of a downturn necessary to effect a given reduction in the inflation rate. This becomes an impediment to effecting a lasting reduction in inflation unless society is patient and trusting that, in fact, there will be a payoff in the future.

The net conclusion for policy concerning all of these considerations (and others we have no doubt neglected to mention here) cannot be determined on the basis of objective economic analysis. Policymakers must make normative decisions, in the interest of the public's general welfare as they perceive it, weighing the benefits and costs to different segments of society. But intelligent decisions by policymakers and by society in its choice of policymakers and positions on broad issues require a sound understanding of the basic principles elucidated by objective economics.

INTERNAL VERSUS EXTERNAL STABILITY

The foregoing discussion focused on policy choices involving exclusively "internal" variables, namely inflation and unemployment, without concern for "external" variables, such as the balance of payments and the exchange rate. This was appropriate since society's concern for the stability and performance of external variables is naturally less and, indeed, stems from the implications of external variables, eventually, for the stability and performance of internal variables. Nevertheless, at times there appears to be a trade-off or conflict between internal and external objectives. For example, at times policy-makers may desire to stimulate the economy toward higher levels of capacity ultilization but feel constrained by balance-of-payments deficits and downward pressure on the exchange rate that are likely to result.

Mundell's strategy

One strategy which has been proposed to deal with the predicament described above is to target monetary and fiscal policy to different objectives. The idea, which is attributable to Robert Mundell, is to use expansionary fiscal policy to move the domestic economy ahead and tight monetary policy to keep interest rates high, thereby attracting the capital inflows necessary to keep the balance of payments in equilibrium without depressing the exchange rate.[16] The

---

[16]See Robert A. Mundell, *The Appropriate Use of Monetary and Fiscal Policy for Internal and External Stability,* International Monetary Fund Staff Papers, vol. 9 (March 1962) pp. 70–77.

critical assumption underlying this approach, of course, is that an expansionary fiscal policy will be able to more than offset the restrictive effects on the domestic economy of the tight monetary policy required to keep an external equilibrium at the existing exchange rate.

Studies of the relative influence of monetary and fiscal policy, which were published after Mundell's original work and which were reviewed earlier in this chapter, and studies of import propensities suggest that it might be difficult to achieve internal and external stability with the strategy proposed by Mundell. Higher deficit spending might stimulate the demand for imports while domestic output languishes due to the depressing effect of high interest rates on real investment.

The global expansion approach

Another approach to the external-internal problem is to arrange for coordinated expansionary policies in the major Western industrial countries, leading to "global expansion." If most countries expand simultaneously, pressure should not develop to a significant degree on any one country's exchange rate. Efforts by the United States to arrange just such a coordinated expansion foundered in 1977–78 due to different inflation and unemployment objectives among the major Western countries, however. West Germany, Japan, and most other trading partners of the United States preferred to pursue more restrained policies in order to keep inflationary pressures from resurfacing following the price surges of 1973–75.

As a result of stronger concern for inflation and more restrained policies abroad, sharp downward pressure on the U.S. dollar developed in 1978 and 1979, forcing several tightening moves by the Fed. Policymakers in the United States could have chosen to ignore downward pressure on the dollar in the 1978–79 period, focusing exclusively on internal objectives and letting the dollar fall freely; indeed, this was close to the actual approach the Carter administration took during much of 1977 and 1978. Rapid downward adjustments of the dollar were a major source of concern to foreign governments if not to that of United States, however, due to the destabilizing effects of a weak dollar on their economies and internal capital markets.

It was pressure from foreign governments and concern over inflationary implications for the United States of a weak dollar that eventually induced a more active response of U.S. policy to external considerations in the late 1970s.

CONCLUSION

This chapter has described the major issues and considerations related to the appropriate use of fiscal and, particularly, monetary policies. The relative strength of these policies no doubt will continue to be a focus of study for economists for years to come. Yet it is clear that much progress has been made in the debate and in understanding in recent years.

The optimal approaches to the business cycle and monetary discipline are other areas which will continue to be studied. Monetary rules versus a gold standard is likely to be a focus of discussion.

The choices involved in the dynamics of the Phillips curve are a matter for the public to decide via the ballot box. A successful assault on inflation can be made if the public is willing to suffer the protracted, if temporary, unemployment and below-capacity output rates that are likely to be necessary. Alternatively, more palliatives for inflation can be designed and adopted.

Following our experience of the late 1970s external stability is likely to continue to be a constraint on U.S. monetary policy from time to time. We have found that flexible exchange rates can bring only limited freedom for policies in a reserve-currency country.

The next and final chapter discusses further issues in money and credit that are likely to be important in the years ahead.

PROBLEMS

1. Compare the Andersen and Carlson St. Louis equation with the FRB-MIT model of the channels of monetary policy.
    a. What variables were used to measure monetary and fiscal policies in each model?
    b. How long were the lags between policy changes and their effects?
    c. Which policy variables came out as most important?
    d. How can the results of these studies be reconciled?
2. Should efforts be made to improve the timing of changes in monetary policy relative to business fluctuations? Explain.
3. Compare the costs of inflation and unemployment.
4. Explain the potential conflict between internal and external stability.

ADVANCED READINGS

Andersen, Leonall C. *"The State of the Monetarist Debate."* Federal Reserve Bank of St. Louis *Monthly Review*, September 1973.

———, and Jordan, J.L. "Monetary and Fiscal Actions: A Test of Their Relative Importance in Economic Stabilization." Federal Reserve Bank of St. Louis *Monthly Review,* November 1968.

Blinder, A.S., and Solow, R.M. "Analytical Foundations of Fiscal Policy." In *The Economics of Public Finance*, Brookings Institution, 1974, pp. 3–115

Blinder, A.S., and Solow, R.M. "Does Fiscal Policy Still Matter? A Reply." *Journal of Monetary Economics* 2 (November 1976).

Davis, R. "How Much Does Money Matter?" Federal Reserve Bank of New York *Monthly Review*, June 1969, pp. 120–31.

de Leeuw, Frank, and Gramlich, Edward M. "The Channels of Monetary Policy." *Federal Reserve Bulletin* 55 (June 1969): 472–91.

Friedman, M. "The Effects of a Full-Employment Policy on Economic Stability: A Formal Analysis." *Essays in Positive Economics*, 117–132.

_____ and Meiselman, D. "The Relative Stability of Monetary Velocity and the Investment Multiplier in the United States." In *Stabilization Policies*, Commission on Money and Credit, Englewood Cliffs: Prentice-Hall, (1963), pp. 168–268.

Klein, L., and Brunner, K. "Commentary on The State of the Monetarist Debate." Federal Reserve Bank of St. Louis *Monthly Review*, September 1973, pp. 9–12.

Tobin, J. "Money and Income: Post Hoc Ergo Propter Hoc?" *Quarterly Journal of Economics* 84 (May 1970): 301–17.

_____ and Buiter, W.H. "Long-run Effects of Fiscal and Monetary Policy on Aggregate Demand." In *Monetarism*, edited by J.L. Stein. Amsterdam, North-Holland: pp. 273–309.

Further issues and prospects for the future

How is the financial system likely to evolve in the years ahead and what major institutional reforms are in store or advisable? The first section of this chapter examines issues related to innovations in progress or on the drawing boards for the financial system. The second section describes regulatory changes which have been programmed for the future, mostly under the Depository Institutions Deregulation and Monetary Control Act of 1980. The last section examines proposals for further change and summarizes prospects for the future.

INNOVATIONS IN THE FINANCIAL SYSTEM

There are five general areas in which financial innovations are likely to take place at a rapid pace in the years ahead: (1) the means of payment, (2) mortgage instruments, (3) consumer credit and savings instruments, (4) the international integration of credit markets, and (5) the pricing of intermediary services and loans to business.

496

The means of payment

Day-to-day transactions by business and the consumer are likely to shift toward increased use of electronic funds transfer (EFT) in the future. EFT refers to the transfer of funds among individual accounts by remote electronic signal, directly from the location of a transaction in some applications. In contrast to checks and credit-card charges, there is no paper, except possibly as a record of the transaction, and there is no delay involved in making transfers. EFT will probably be conducted via bank-computer-linked cash registers in stores for retail sales and via electronic "safes" in firms' treasury departments for wholesale, payroll, and other transactions.

Two developments which have been a spur to EFT are the rapid advances in microelectronics and the high interest rates experienced in recent years. Technological innovations have reduced the expense and improved the convenience of EFT. And high interest rates have increased the incentive to adopt EFT because it cuts down on reverse float for firms, i.e., the time between the receipt of a payment order (a check or credit-card charge) and the credit to the firm's account. Reverse float costs firms interest, of course, because funds received earlier could be placed at interest or used to pay off loans.

As EFT is introduced it tends to reduce the demand for money because it permits easier transfers from transactions accounts to higher-yielding assets when funds are needed (Baumol's b coefficient is smaller); and there is greater certainty as to actual cash-balance levels.

Alternatively, we can say the velocity of money tends to rise with the introduction of EFT. If this causes a speed up in the growth of velocity from its recent rate of 3.5 percent or so per year, the Federal Reserve should lower its monetary targets to keep inflation from rising.

The prospect of a continued, and perhaps accelerated, rise of velocity as a result of EFT and other innovations has created alarm among some analysts that the money supply will become too small in relation to GNP to represent a viable instrument for conducting monetary policy. Other analysts argue that the relevant issue is the stability of the rate of growth of velocity, and that EFT will not introduce any permanent instability in that growth rate.

Electronic funds transfer (EFT)

Implications of EFT

Mortgage instruments

Mortgage arrangements are likely to change further, shifting more of the risk of higher interest rates from the lender to the borrower. Variable-rate mortgages have already been introduced in a number of states. Under a variable-rate arrangement, the rate of interest on the mortgage is adjusted periodically, down or up, to reflect changes in the prevailing level of interest rates. Monthly payments of the borrower need not change; the lender may simply extend the maturity of the mortgage, thereby reducing the borrower's equity. In return for assuming the risk of a rise in interest rates, borrowers should be able to acquire funds at a lower cost over the long run if their expectations about future interest rates are accurate.

The movement to shift interest-rate risk to mortgagors is attributable to rising and more variable interest rates and to the relaxation of interest-rate ceilings on savings instruments available at regulated financial institutions. These developments have had a severe impact on the earnings of thrift institutions, particularly in recent high interest-rate periods.

Consumer credit and savings instruments

Higher and more variable interest rates have also accelerated innovations and change in the consumer-credit area and in the types of savings instruments available to consumers. Consumers may soon find their interest costs on revolving charge accounts fluctuating with market interest rates, whereas now the interest rates on these accounts rarely change. Overdraft facilities on checking accounts and five-year auto loans are likely to spread.[1] The recent popularity of money-market mutual fund shares is likely to continue, and other ways to give households access to potentially higher-yielding credit-market investments, including locally originated instruments denominated in foreign exchange, may be expected, regulatory conditions permitting.

The international integration of credit markets

Financial intermediaries have become highly innovative, aggressive, and successful in overcoming barriers to international capital flows; as a result, the trend toward the international integration of world credit markets is likely to continue. This trend is also fostered by the microelectronics revolution which is speeding communications and information processing. Credit is rapidly becoming a world-priced commodity, much as wheat or gold are. The Eurocurrency market, which is the most visible evidence of this movement, will probably continue to grow relative to domestic credit markets and elude the efforts of governments to regulate it.

The pricing of intermediary services and loans to business

Financial intermediaries, and even the Federal Reserve, are moving in the direction of charging explicit fees reflective of actual

---

[1]Recent liberalizations in bankruptcy legislation may slow this trend, however.

costs for services rendered to customers. This means, for example, that wire transfer, currency exchange, and other departments of banks will be expected to earn profits whereas now they are often unprofitable areas maintained to attract commercial and industrial borrowers; bank customers will therefore have more incentive to shop around for least-cost suppliers of these services.

Loans to commercial and industrial borrowers will be based increasingly on intermediaries' marginal cost of funds, at narrower spreads than are customarily reflected by the prime rate. This latter trend is due to stronger competition among domestic intermediaries, to competition from foreign banks, and to the increased sophistication of borrowers.

PROGRAMMED REGULATORY CHANGES

The Depository Institutions Deregulation and Monetary Control Act of 1980 has established a timetable for major changes in the financial system over the years 1981–88. The key changes programmed for the future (and identified in part in Chapter 13) include:

1. A gradual elimination of Regulation Q–type ceilings for interest payable on deposits and share accounts; this is scheduled to be completed by March 31, 1986.
2. Imposition of "uniform" reserve requirements on transactions accounts, "nonpersonal" time deposits, and Eurodollar liabilities at virtually all depository instititutions not covered by Federal Reserve reserve requirements as of June 30, 1979; these are to be phased in over the eight-year period 1980–88.
3. A reduction and simplification, over the three-and-a-half year period November 13, 1980 to March 30, 1984, of old reserve requirements applying to member banks in 1979–80. The new, uniform reserve requirements will apply to virtually all depository institutions after 1988.
4. Explicit, cost-based pricing of services provided to depository institutions by the Federal Reserve and other federal regulatory agencies; this was scheduled to take effect September 1, 1981.

Gradual elimination of Regulation Q

The elimination of Regulation Q ceilings will result in more competitive interest rates on savings and time deposits at commercial banks and thrifts. This will benefit the small saver, especially in high interest-rate periods, and result in higher mortgage interest rates for home buyers as financial institutions pass on higher costs for funds. On balance, the economy should benefit through higher savings in response to higher returns to savers and a more efficient allocation of savings among borrowers. Also, the cyclical pattern of savings outflows (disintermediation) and inflows at thrifts, which occurs with rising and falling interest rates, should moderate, leading to improved stability in the housing sector.

The phased elimination of interest-rate ceilings is being administered by a Depository Institutions Deregulation Committee, comprised of the head officials of the Treasury and each of the federal regulatory agencies for depository institutions. This committee will cease to exist after the complete elimination of ceilings in 1986.

Reserve requirements for nonmember depository institutions

The imposition of reserve requirements on certain deposits and accounts at nonmember depository institutions is designed to improve control of the money supply and stem the loss of member banks from the Federal Reserve system. The required reserve ratio for a small base volume of transactions accounts, called "the low-reserve-requirement tranche," will be phased in, reaching 3 percent in 1988.[2] For transactions account volumes above the first (low-reserve-requirement) tranche, the eventual reserve requirement ratio is planned to be 12 percent, with possible variations by the Federal Reserve Board of this ratio within a range of 8 to 14 percent. On nonpersonal time deposits and Eurodollar liabilities, the eventual reserve requirement ratio is set to be 3 percent, with changes possible within a range of zero to 9 percent, depending upon Federal Reserve policy.

Transactions accounts refer to the same types of deposits and accounts we call checkable deposits in this text. Nonpersonal time deposits are negotiable time deposits and/or deposits held by "a party other than a natural person." For purposes of reserve requirements Eurodollar liabilities are net borrowings from related foreign offices, borrowings from unrelated foreign depository institutions, loans to U.S. residents made by overseas branches of U.S.–chartered depository institutions, and sales of foreign and domestic assets by depository institutions in the United States to their overseas offices.

Adjustments to member-bank reserve requirements

The phased adjustment of member banks' requirements down to the new ultimate uniform requirements will establish more equity among depository institutions in terms of the reserve burdens they bear and should lead to improved monetary control. Uniform reserve requirements will help monetary control by eliminating the

---

[2]The initial ceiling of the 3 percent tranche was specified to be $25 million. Beginning on December 31, 1981, this $25 million is to be adjusted upward or downward according to a formula related to changes in the total volume of transactions accounts of all depository institutions.

changes in the average required reserve ratio that presently occur when the distribution of deposits shifts from member to nonmember institutions; and the simplified structure of the new reserve requirements should help to reduce fluctuations in the average required reserve ratio attributable to changes in the composition of deposits by deposit type.

Pricing of federal agency services

The pricing of services provided by the Federal Reserve and other federal regulatory agencies is intended to promote efficiency in the provision and use of these services. Such services include: (a) currency and coin handling services; (b) check clearing and collection; (c) wire transfer; (d) automated clearing-house; (e) settlements; (f) securities safekeeping; (g) Federal Reserve float; and (h) new services that the Federal Reserve system may offer such as services related to electronic funds transfers.[3] All depository institutions are to have the same access to Federal Reserve services that member banks have.

A likely effect of the introduction of explicit pricing will be increased reliance by member banks on private-sector sources for some services now provided mostly by the Fed. Competition among federal agencies for the business of servicing depository institutions is also a possibility.

OTHER PROPOSALS AND PROSPECTS

Changes in the financial system which have been proposed and not yet adopted or programmed as of the writing of this text include: (1) a shift from lagged-reserve accounting to contemporaneous-reserve accounting; (2) maintenance of the discount rate at a penalty level, i.e., above the federal funds rate; (3) imposition of reserve requirements on money-market mutual funds; (4) payment of interest to depository institutions on their reserve funds; (5) wider latitude on asset mixes for thrifts; and (6) nationwide branching for depository institutions.

As described in Chapter 14, a number of analysts have recommended that the Federal Reserve revert to contemporaneous-reserve accounting. Lagged-reserve accounting, in effect since September 1968, has no doubt caused some degree of loss of control of the money supply. In June 1980, the Federal Reserve announced that it was considering a change back to contemporaneous accounting and invited comments on such a move.

Change in the reserve accounting period

---

[3]Federal Reserve float is included in this list because it represents a source of credit to depository institutions using the Federal Reserve's clearing facilities. Interest charges will be effected by requiring interest payments at the federal funds rate on cash items credited prior to collections.

Discount-Rate policy

Discussion of discount-rate policy in Chapters 12 and 14 indicated that the Fed's normal practice in the past has been to keep the discount rate below the federal funds rate, providing a cheap source of funds to member banks. Economists have recommended for some time that this practice be changed to remove the built-in incentive it creates for banks to borrow reserves from the Fed. If the discount rate were kept at some positive spread over the federal funds rate, bank borrowing could be kept to a lower, more stable level, and the discount window could still provide lender-of-last-resort services.

Although the Depository Institutions Act of 1980 did not address discount-rate policy, it did extend discount-window privileges to virtually all depository institutions, and it removed the threat of further defections from the Federal Reserve system if the Fed toughened up on its discount-rate policy. These two changes may have made it more likely that the Fed will adopt a penalty-rate stance on the discount rate in the future. With wider access to the discount window, the Fed may become more concerned about greater abuse of the window; and, with the threat of defections from the system virtually removed, there is no incentive for the Fed to keep the discount rate at subsidy levels. The possibility remains, of course, that no policy change will be forthcoming.

Reserve requirements for money-market mutual funds

Earlier chapters have described the rapid growth of money-market mutual funds in recent years as a result of the high interest returns these funds offer investors. One reason higher returns can be paid is that there have been no reserve requirements on their deposits or shares. (See Chapter 7 for a description of the cost to banks of reserve requirements on CDs.) Other financial intermediaries have complained that this represents an unfair competitive advantage for the mutual funds. Economists and some regulators have become concerned that it has caused a loss in monetary control since money-market mutual funds are close substitutes for narrow money and perhaps even ought to be included in the narrow definition of money. As a result, there have been proposals to impose reserve requirements on money-market mutual funds, and legislation in this area may be forthcoming.

Interest on reserves

It is not necessarily desirable that reserve requirements impose a cost on depository institutions, reducing their earnings and creating an incentive for them to seek alternative sources of funds and other ways to minimize opportunity costs on reserve funds. It can even be argued that reserve requirements reduce liquidity by encouraging direct financings of deficit entities by surplus entities, instead of indirect financings through depository institutions which enhance liquidity for both savers and borrowers.

One way to avoid or reduce these drawbacks to reserve requirements would be for the Fed to pay interest on reserves. The principal impediment to doing this is the cost to the federal government since such interest payments would come out of Federal Reserve earnings presently turned over to the Treasury each year. If, at some future date, the government becomes less sensitive to the budgetary consequences of paying interest on reserves, this solution may be adopted.[4]

The Depository Institutions Act of 1980 liberalized the restraints on allowable investments of federally chartered thrift institutions. Federal savings and loan institutions, for example, were permitted for the first time to invest a significant share (up to 20 percent) of their assets in consumer loans, commercial paper, and corporate debt securities, and they can now offer credit-card services and exercise trust and fiduciary powers. These changes and others have blurred the distinction between commercial banks and other depository institutions. Competition among the various types of institutions and pressure on the earnings of thrifts as a result of the dismantling of interest-rate ceilings are likely to lead to further liberalizations in restrictions on the asset mixes of thrifts. The implications are that these institutions will become indistinguishable from commercial banks and that the preferential rates available on mortgages in the past will fade further from the scene.

Changing asset mix for thrifts

As described in Chapter 13, U.S. regulatory authorities traditionally have been fearful that multiple units and geographical expansion of depository institutions are conducive to monopoly practices and undesirable distributions of savings flows. These notions are undergoing change, however. There is growing recognition that limited branching can be anticompetitive, and that geographical redistributions of savings flows are desirable from an efficient allocation of resources point of view. Another argument in favor of a more liberal approach to branching is that foreign banks have been allowed to branch across states, providing these banks with a competitive advantage over domestically chartered institutions.

Nationwide branching

Nationwide branching could be implemented quickly at the federal level, by permitting all federally chartered institutions to branch across states. Or it could come slowly as states negotiate reciprocity agreements on branching in one state by banks chartered in another state.

Nationwide branching would result in a much smaller number of banks in the United States. The largest banks would become considerably larger. However, competition might persist at an even higher level than at present, and the system should operate more efficiently.

---

[4]Under present law, the Fed can levy and pay interest on special supplemental required reserves up to 4 percent of institutions' transactions accounts provided that, among other restraints, the supplemental reserve requirement is imposed only for the conduct of monetary policy and "not for the purpose of reducing the cost burdens resulting from basic reserve requirements." See "The Depository Institutions Deregulation and Monetary Control Act of 1980," *Federal Reserve Bulletin* (June 1980); 445.

CONCLUSION

This chapter concludes the text. As stated in Chapter 1, the study of money and credit is an especially important field in economics. Problems and controversies are bound to persist in the future as they have in the past; and study in this area is a never-ending process for those who wish to remain current.

The reader is invited to explore the topics we have covered further by turning to the recommended readings at the end of each chapter. To remain current on new developments, subscriptions to major business publications such as the *Wall Street Journal* and *Business Week* are recommended. The publications of the Federal Reserve Board and the 12 district banks are extremely valuable; these and, for students interested in advanced academic research, the latest issues of the major economic journals, are available in most college libraries.

PROBLEMS

1. Identify from the Federal Reserve *Bulletin* the current structure of reserve requirements and compare these to the eventual requirements mandated by the Depository Institutions Deregulation and Monetary Control Act of 1980. Will the average required reserve ratio tend to be higher or lower once the new ratios are fully implemented?

2. What effect will electronic funds transfer tend to have on velocity? Is this necessarily the case?

3. If contemporaneous-reserve accounting is, in fact, preferable to lagged-reserve accounting, would advanced-reserve accounting, i.e., where higher reserves must be set aside in advance of deposit increases, be even more preferable? Explain.

4. What are the advantages and disadvantages of nationwide branching for depository institutions?

APPENDIX

WALL STREET JOURNAL GUIDE FOR STUDENTS

As suggested by the frequent appearance of its articles in this text, *The Wall Street Journal* is an excellent source of current information (and test questions) on the economics and institutions relating to money and credit. The format of the paper appears forbidding to the uninitiated, but is actually quite efficient and easy to follow with a little guidance and exposure. Most articles are easily comprehended by those who have had an introductory sequence of economics courses. This appendix discusses the paper in two parts: *A. Front page* and *B. The rest of the paper.*

A. Front page

The front page has six columns which are organized as follows. *Columns 1 and 6* contain newsworthy feature articles on economics, politics, business, and so on. Often one or both of these columns will contain an article related to money and credit.

Columns 2 and 3 are comprised of short paragraphs summarizing "What's News." Column 2 covers "Business and Finance" and Column 3 is "World Wide." You should scan Column 2 for items related to money and credit, that is, those mentioning the Federal Reserve, interest rates, commercial banks, and so forth. In most cases, paragraphs in this column summarize and direct you to a full-length article inside the paper. The index for regular articles and information within the paper is located at the bottom of Column 2. Regular articles of special interest listed in the index will be discussed under *B* on the next page.

The top of *Column 4* has a chart of some economic variable for which new information has become available recently; the unemployment rate, for example. Often a note to the chart will direct you to a story on the new data inside the paper. Below the chart there is a feature article, which is usually on some light or whimsical subject totally unrelated to business or economics. (Economics professors and businessmen usually read this article first.)

Column 5 has a rotating title and content. Monday's Column 5 features "The Outlook," a short article on prospects for the economy, often of interest for a student of money and credit. Tuesday's Column 5 is titled "Labor Letter," short blurbs on union activities, the labor market, offbeat jobs, etc. Once in a while, one of these labor items will relate to the state of the economy. Most are interesting to read if only because we all are involved in the labor market in one way or another.

Wednesday's Column 5 features the "Tax Report" and contains short pieces on recent tax legislation, tax court and IRS decisions, etc. Most are interesting but seldom directly related to the material in this book. Thursday's Column 5 is headlined "Business Bulletin" and varies in content from articles similar to Monday's "The Outlook" to short paragraphs on new products, business practices, etc. It sometimes contains information on the state of the economy. Finally, in Friday's Column 5 you will find "Washington Wire," which features news items on political personalities, rumored changes in federal government policies, and gossipy information of interest to business and the public. Occasionally these will relate to monetary policy.

B. The rest of the paper

The key to the rest of the paper is found in the index at the bottom of Column 2 on the front page. You will find referenced there "Credit Markets," "Editorials," and "International News". These should be checked for content.

Check the credit markets articles for information on changes in interest rates and on Federal Reserve actions. On Mondays one of the credit market's articles will usually refer to the "Federal Reserve Report" on some nearby page. This "Federal Reserve Report" in each Monday's paper carries important information which is explained in Chapter 14.

On the editorial page, check the editorials on the left-hand side, the center column, and the right-hand side, which is usually a guest commentary. The editorials usually present politically conservative positions. Liberal positions may show up in the guest article or in "Letters to the Editor" on the page facing the editorial page. The guest commentary on the right-hand side of the editorial page is occasionally by a prominent economist who holds or has held an important advisory position in government.

The articles on international news typically cover developments involving foreign economies and the foreign-exchange markets. Look for items on monetary policies and credit market conditions abroad, as well as for ones on exchange-rate changes.

GLOSSARY

adaptive expectations model makes the change in the expected rate of inflation proportional to the difference between the level of the actual rate of inflation and the level of the expected rate of inflation.

adjusted monetary base the monetary base adjusted for changes in the average required reserve ratio.

adjusted total reserves total reserves adjusted for changes in the average required reserve ratio.

aggregate demand total demand for final output.

aggregate supply measures the total quantity of final output producers wish to sell or add to inventory.

ATS accounts automatic-transfer-savings accounts; savings accounts which permit funds to be switched to and from checking accounts automatically, for a fee; except for the fee, the ATS accounts are essentially the same as NOW accounts.

automatic stabilizers changes in government spending and taxes which occur automatically as real GNP changes and which tend to stabilize real GNP by stabilizing aggregate demand.

autonomous desired consumption component of consumption demand which is not influenced by disposable income.

average required reserve ratio total reserves divided by total reservable liabilities.

bank holiday holiday or other period where banks are legally closed; special bank holidays, such as the Bank Holiday of 1933, were called during the Great Depression in order to stem runs on banks.

banks of issue banks which issue notes.

basis point 1/100 of a percentage point.

barter direct exchange of one good or service for another good or service, without use of money as a means of payment.

bearer instrument debt instrument for which mere possession of the instrument confers to the holder the right to payment.

bimetalism commodity money standard ex-

507

pressed in terms of two metals as alternatives.

borrowed reserves borrowings of depository institutions from the Federal Reserve.

business cycle one cycle from peak to peak in the periodic expansions and contractions of the economy; usually averages around four years.

Cambridge k the proportionality factor between the demand for money and individuals' real resources in the original Cambridge approach to the quantity theory; in modern analysis, the ratio of the demand for money to current-dollar GNP.

capacity output real output at "full" employment of the economy's resources; alternatively, maximum sustainable rate of output.

ceteris paribus from Latin; other things the same.

certificates of deposit (CDs) "time-deposit" debt instruments issued by depository institutions; may be negotiable or nonnegotiable, large ($100,000 and over) or small (under $100,000).

closed economy economy closed to foreign trade.

commercial paper unsecured promissory notes issued both by large nonfinancial firms and financial companies with high credit ratings.

commodity money medium of exchange for which its intrinsic value is equal to its exchange value.

consumption function relationship between desired real personal consumption expenditures and independent variables, such as real disposable personal income.

corporate bonds long-term ITF obligations issued by private corporations in the public market or via private placement; some are convertible to stock.

CPI consumer price index, a monthly price index constructed by the Bureau of Labor Statistics; designed to measure changes in prices of goods and services purchased by urban wage earners and clerical workers.

credit major form of external finance used by households, firms, and governments in the economy; encompasses any financing which requires unconditional payment on demand or scheduled in the future.

credit risk risk of default.

crowding-out effect effect of government borrowing on market interest rates.

debt instrument legal statement of debtor's obligation which may be issued and sold like a commodity to provide a vehicle of credit.

debt management decisions by the Treasury and the Federal Reserve relating to the maturity of the Treasury debt held by the public; may influence the term structure of interest rates.

debt monetization modern process by which governments garner spendable funds without legislating new taxes or borrowing from the public; government debt is purchased by the central bank with issues of new currency or reserve balances.

debt money a medium of exchange which is a debt instrument or deposit balance redeemable on demand in another asset of value (usually issued by commercial banks as checkable deposits) and backed less than 100 percent by reserves of the other asset.

deficit entities entities which are net absorbers of external funds.

deflation a fall in the general price level of the economy.

demand curve ceteris-paribus relationship between quantity demanded and an influencing variable, usually the price variable.

demand function one of the fundamental components of the supply and demand model; states all important variables which influence quantity of a good or service desired.

dependent variable influenced variable.

depression severe and widespread decline in economic output; no precise degree of severity distinguishes a depression from a recession.

discount credit a credit arrangement where the interest charge is effected by discounting the face amount of the obligation when advancing funds to the borrower.

discount rate interest rate Federal Reserve charges on loans to depository institutions.

discount yield rate of discount applied to face value of a discount credit.

disintermediation withdrawals of funds from financial intermediaries for direct investment in the obligations of deficit entities.

elastic elasticity more than 1 in absolute value.

electronic funds transfer (EFT) transfer of funds among individual accounts by remote electronic signal, directly from the location of a transaction in some applications.

endogenous variable variable determined within the model.

equation of exchange equation linking the money supply, velocity, prices, and transactions; $M^SV^T = P^TT$.

equilibrium condition condition where the central variables of a model are at a state of rest.

equilibrium for money model quantity of money demanded equals quantity supplied.

equity finance involves financing through issuance (sale) of new shares of ownership in a corporate enterprise, either common or preferred stock.

Eurodollar deposits dollar-denominated time deposits available at foreign branches of U.S. banks and at some foreign banks abroad.

exogenous variable variable determined outside the model.

external finance the drawing by one entity on the current resources of another to meet current expenses.

Fannie Mae market jargon for Federal National Mortgage Association.

Federal Deposit Insurance Corporation (FDIC) agency created by Congress during the Great Depression to provide deposit insurance for banks.

federal funds rate rate of interest charged on unsecured, short-term loans of immediately available funds, principally among banks.

Federal Home Loan Board and Bank System regulatory and reserve bank system for savings and loans and mutual savings banks.

Federal Home Loan Mortgage Corporation government agency which buys residential mortgages, funded with debt issues in the credit markets; administratively under the Federal Home Loan Bank Board.

Federal National Mortgage Association once a semigovernment agency, now a private institution which buys residential mortgages with funds raised in the national credit mar-

kets.

Federal Open Market Committee (FOMC) principal policymaking unit of the Federal Reserve; meets monthly to provide guidance to the manager of the System Open Market Account for open market operations.

Federal Reserve Bank one of 12 banks chartered by Congress to perform central banking functions; provides credit to U.S. government and depository institutions, issues currency and reserve balances and performs clearing and other services for U.S. government, foreign central banks, and U.S. banks.

Federal Reserve float source of interest-free credit to the banking system from the Federal Reserve, which arises as a result of the Federal Reserve's check-clearing operations.

Federal Reserve system system of 12 Federal Reserve Banks, one in each of 12 Federal Reserve districts, and the Board of Governors of the Federal Reserve.

Federal Savings and Loan Insurance Corporation (FSLIC) government agency which provides deposit insurance for savings and loan associations; administratively under the Federal Home Loan Bank Board.

fiat money money made legal tender by government fiat; has significantly less intrinsic value than its face value but is accepted in transactions at face value because it has legal-tender status.

financial intermediaries entities which engage in intermediation in the flow of funds between surplus and deficit entities.

financial sector financial markets such as stock and bond markets and institutions such as banks, savings and loan institutions, credit unions, brokerage firms, and investment banks.

financial stabilization refers to actions by the central bank to prevent extreme fluctuations in credit and equity markets.

fiscal policy discretionary posture of federal government spending and taxes, intended to influence aggregate demand.

Fisher effect phenomenon which occurs when prices continue to rise over time and cause interest rates to rise to compensate lenders for the expected loss in the purchasing power of money; more generally, the effect of expected inflation on interest rates.

510

fixed-weight price indexes index numbers which express weighted prices in the current period as a percentage of prices with the *same* weights in a base period.

flow-of-funds data data measuring financial flows among surplus and deficit entities and financial intermediaries, reported in Federal Reserve's Flow-of-Funds Accounts.

Freddie Mac Federal Home Loan Mortgage Association.

free reserves excess reserves less borrowed reserves.

Free Silver movement political movement in the 1880s and early 1890s to restore the monetization of silver.

Ginnie Mae market jargon for the Government National Mortgage Association.

Ginnie Mae pass-throughs certificates representing shares in pools of government guaranteed (FHA and VA) mortgages; certificates are guaranteed by the Government National Mortgage Association.

GNP gross national product, the market value at current prices of all final goods and services produced in the economy over a specific period; current-dollar GNP is the broadest measure of the economy's output at current prices; real GNP measures final output at constant, base-period prices.

GNP deflator price index for all goods and services which comprise gross national product; derived indirectly from nominal GNP series.

gold standard a monetary system in which the unit of account is established in terms of gold of certain weight and fineness and in which the supply of money is effectively linked to gold in circulation or held in the form of reserves.

Government National Mortgage Association government-owned agency which buys mortgages and guarantees and arranges pass-through of payments to investors in mortgage pools.

Gresham's Law usually stated as "bad money drives out good money" meaning that less intrinsically valuable money tends to replace more valuable money in circulation; occurs when the money which is more intrinsically valuable is also more valuable in other uses than it is as money and when

the two monies are fixed in parity.

hyperinflation name of condition which occurs when the price level in an economy rises at a rate 50 percent per month or more.

identity of exchange version of the equation of exchange which uses actual values and, hence, which is true by definition.

induced consumption that part of consumption demand which is influenced by disposable income.

indicators variables which provide information to policymakers about the state of the economy and/or the thrust of policy.

inflation a rise in the general price level of the economy.

income velocity of money the ratio of current-dollar GNP to the money supply.

independent variable influencing variable.

inelastic elasticity less than 1 in absolute value.

inside lag the lag between the need for a specific policy action and the adoption of the policy action.

interest rate the cost to a borrower for the use of funds, expressed in terms of percent per period; also, the return to a lender of funds.

interest to follow (ITF) credit conveys specified interest payments at the end and, in most cases, periodically over the life of the credit.

interest-to-follow yield yield on an ITF credit; for assets of greater than one year maturity and which vary in offered or market price, it is the annual rate of interest which when applied directly to the original investment and compounded annually would produce the terminal value of the instrument, assuming all interim income is reinvested at that same rate of interest.

international gold standard system where two or more countries have a gold standard and permit relatively free flows of trade, including gold, across their borders.

International Monetary Fund (IMF) organization created by 44 western countries following World War II to facilitate the operation of a fixed-exchange rate system; serves as valuable source of information on world economies and on monetary issues.

IS curve curve which traces the combinations of income and the interest rate which are equilibrium combinations for the goods market.

Keynesian   economist who subscribes to the views of John Maynard Keynes (author of *The General Theory of Employment, Interest, and Money*), as generally expressed in Keynesian literature; stresses the power of fiscal policy (government spending and taxes), rather than the importance of the supply of money and credit, in managing aggregate demand.

L   broad monetary aggregate equal to M–3 plus certain Eurodollars of U.S. residents, bankers acceptances, commercial paper, savings bonds, and liquid Treasury obligations.

lagged-reserve accounting   the Federal Reserve's accounting practice, adopted in 1968, which allows depository institutions to meet reserve requirements each week based upon their reservable liability levels two weeks prior to the current week.

law of demand   usual inverse relationship between price and quantity demanded.

law of diminishing returns   over the relevant range of the production function, further additions to employed resources will yield smaller additions to output than was obtained from prior additions to employed resources.

legal tender   money designated by government as lawful money for settling specific or general transactions.

Libor   London interbank offered rate, offering interest rate on interbank loans of Eurodollar deposits.

liquidity   an asset quality reflecting the perceived speed, ease, closeness, and certainty with which an asset can be exchanged for other assets, goods, or services at a price such that the asset earns as high a return as that expected for it over a short-term holding period.

liquidity effect   effect of the Federal Reserve's actions on interest rates, via changes in the supply of money and credit.

liquidity-premium hypothesis   hypothesis that a positive spread between short- and long-term interest rates may be accounted for by a risk (liquidity) premium or by a combination

of: (1) a liquidity premium and expectations of a rise in the long-term interest rate, or (2) a liquidity premium and expectations of a fall in the interest rate where the liquidity premium effect is stronger; a negative spread between long-and short-term assets is accounted for by expectations of a fall in the interest rate sufficient to outweigh the liquidity premium.

liquidity trap   segment of the Keynesian demand-for-money curve where the curve is perfectly horizontal (infinite interest-rate elasticity); implies a trap where an increase in the money supply cannot bring about lower interest rates and stimulate the economy.

liquid-store-of-value function   function of money as a store of value which can be drawn upon on short notice to finance spending.

LM curve   curve which traces the combinations of income and the interest rate which are equilibrium combinations for the money market.

M–1   medium-of-exchange measure, defined prior to 1980 as currency plus commerical bank demand deposits owned by the "nonbank public," where the nonbank public refers to anyone except domestic commercial banks, the Federal Reserve, and the U.S. Treasury; in early 1980, this measure was replaced by M–1A, a very similar measure, and M–1B, a more accurate measure of the entire stock of medium-of-exchange assets; M–1B adds other checkable deposits, such as NOW and ATS accounts, and travelers checks to M–1A.

M–1A   new medium-of-exchange measure introduced by the Federal Reserve in February, 1980; same as old M–1 measure except that it excludes deposit holdings of foreign commercial banks and foreign official (government) institutions.

M–1B   M–1A plus other checkable deposits (that is, NOW, ATS, and credit union share draft balances and demand deposits at thrift institutions) and travelers checks.

M–2   M–1B plus overnight RPs issued by commercial banks, overnight Eurodollar deposits held by U.S. nonbank residents at Caribbean branches of U.S. banks, money-market mutual fund shares, savings deposits at all depository institutions, and small time deposits at all depository institutions.

M–3 M–2 plus large time deposits at all depository institutions, term RPs issued by commercial banks, and term RPs issued by savings and loan associations.

marginal efficiency of investment business expectations regarding the likely rate of return at the margin on capital expenditures.

marginal propensity to consume the incremental change in desired consumption induced by an incremental change in disposable income.

marginal propensity to save the incremental change in personal savings induced by an incremental change in disposable income.

marketability speed, ease, and closeness with which an asset can be exchanged for other assets, goods, or services at the best obtainable price.

market-clearing equilibrium condition where quantity supplied equals quantity demanded, which occurs when the market is free of legal restrictions on the price that can be charged or the quantity that can be sold.

maturity of an asset length of time before an asset is redeemable at a specified price for more liquid or intrinsically valuable assets, goods, or services.

medium-of-exchange function also called means-of-payment function and transactions function; function of money as a means of payment in transactions.

mint ratio ratio of gold to silver implicit in the metal values specified for the monetary unit in a bimetallic system.

modern quantity theory of money theory that the demand for money is stable in the sense that it is stably related to a limited number of standard macro variables, that specific motives for holding money are not important, that the influence of money on real income is temporary, and that the influence of money on prices, therefore, is paramount.

monetarist economist who subscribes to the view that changes in the economy have powerful effects on interest rates, real income, and, particularly, prices; also stresses view that the Federal Reserve can effectively control the money supply.

monetary base aggregate quantity of money which is used or can be used as reserves for debt money; also known as "high-powered money."

monetary standard standard that is chosen by a society for its unit of account and serves as the asset of value which backs debt money.

money whatever is used in making payments in transactions in the economy; other, broader definitions incorporate various liquid assets.

money commodity commodity which serves both monetary and other uses.

money-market mutual funds short-term liquid funds managed mainly by brokerage firms; funds are placed in commercial paper, CDs, and other "money market" instruments; interest earnings, less a small management fee, are passed on to the investor; investors can withdraw funds on short notice, in some cases by a check of $500 or more.

money-stock multiplier the ratio of the money stock to the monetary base.

money supply outstanding stock of money in the economy.

multiple-commodity standard specification of the monetary unit in terms of more than one commodity.

municipal bonds long-term ITF obligations issued by state and local governments, nontaxable (federally).

National Credit Union Administration Federal agency which charters and regulates federal credit unions, extends funds to members, and administers the National Credit Union Share Insurance Fund.

National Income Accounts (NIA) data produced by the Department of Commerce which provide estimates of GNP, national income, and their components.

negotiable instrument debt instrument which must be signed by the creditor to transfer payment rights to another party.

net-borrowed reserves borrowed reserves less excess reserves.

nonborrowed reserves total reserves less borrowings of depository institutions from the Federal Reserve.

nonnegotiable instrument by prior agreement or law, instrument cannot be transferred to third party.

NOW accounts negotiable-order-of-withdrawal accounts; checkable deposit accounts authorized nationwide by the Federal Reserve in January, 1981; essentially demand deposits which bear interest and carry a different label to get around federal regulations which have prohibited interest payments on demand deposits.

OPEC Organization of Petroleum Exporting Countries, a cartel of oil-producing countries located mainly, but not exclusively, in the Middle East.

open-market operations purchases and sales of debt instruments (mostly U.S. government securities) in the open market by the Federal Reserve; purchases add to reserves in the system; sales absorb reserves from the system.

outside lag lag between the time policy action is taken and the timing of its effects.

Phillips curve curve tracing the relationship between inflation and unemployment.

PPI producer price index for finished goods, a monthly price index constructed by the Bureau of Labor Statistics; designed to measure changes in prices of finished goods prior to distribution.

precautionary motive one of three motives for holding money identified by Keynes; demand for money as a liquid store of value to be drawn upon when unexpected needs or opportunities arise and to avoid risk.

preferred-habitat hypothesis hypothesis that the spread between short- and long-term interest rates reflects both expectations of interest rate changes and the maturity preferences of borrowers and lenders, which cannot be generalized.

price ceiling maximum legal price for goods or services; when effective, it creates a state of excess demand or, in other words, a shortage.

price elasticity of demand percentage change in quantity demanded divided by the percentage change in price.

price floor minimum price for goods or services; when effective, it creates a state of excess supply or, in other words, a glut.

price level average of prices in one period, usually weighted by quantities; used to make comparisons of prices and the general purchasing power of money between periods.

primary commodity-money system one of four basic monetary systems which consists of one or more commodity monies.

primary fiat-money system one of four basic monetary systems which consists solely of fiat money.

prime bank rate rate normally used by banks as their base rate for loans to commercial and industrial customers; it is adjusted from time to time to reflect the cost of funds to banks.

production function defines the physical relationship between real output and employed resources.

pure-expectations hypothesis hypothesis that a positive spread between long- and short-term yields on otherwise equivalent assets is entirely accounted for by an expected rise in the long-term interest rate; a negative spread (the short rate above the long) is fully accounted for by an expected fall in the long-term interest rate.

purchasing power parity relationship where exchange rate between two countries' currencies is such that each currency has equal purchasing power in either of the two countries

rational expectations expectations which are based on a rational assessment of the economic and other factors affecting the expected variable.

real-bills doctrine theory that central-bank loans linked to rediscounting real bills will ensure an adequate supply of money and credit without encouraging inflation.

real disposable personal income household real income after taxes.

real GNP broadest indicator of real economic activity; measures gross national product at constant, base-period prices.

real income money income deflated by price changes; in other words, income in terms of command over real resources; roughly equivalent to real output for the U.S. economy.

real return return after allowing for changes in the purchasing power of money; roughly the money rate of return less inflation.

realized yield actual yield on an investment for the actual holding period.

recession a fall in economic output of sufficient magnitude and duration to qualify as a recession as determined by the National Bureau of Economic Research, a private nonprofit organization.

Regulation Q Federal Reserve regulation which sets ceilings on interest rates member banks can offer on savings and time deposits.

repurchase agreement (RP) short-term (often overnight), secured loans effected through simultaneous purchase and later-dated sale arrangements for debt instruments.

reserve adjustment magnitude (ram) the magnitude added to or subtracted from the monetary base to arrive at the adjusted monetary base (St. Louis Federal Reserve version).

reserve ratio ratio of reserves to debt money.

reverse causation condition where the variable specified as the dependent variable in a relationship happens instead or also to be an important influencing variable for one or more of the designated independent variables.

reverse repurchase agreement also called a matched sale-purchase agreement; short-term borrowing effected through simultaneous sale and later-dated purchase arrangement for debt instruments.

Sallie Mae market jargon for Student Assistance Loan Association.

scrip emergency money not legal tender.

seasoned debt instruments previously issued debt instruments which trade regularly in the secondary markets.

secondary commodity-money system one of four basic monetary systems which consists of a combination of commodity and debt monies.

secondary fiat-money system one of four basic monetary systems which combines fiat and debt money.

seigniorage net revenue obtained from minting coins; originally a designation for the rights of the king or feudal lord; sometimes applied generally to all government revenue from fiat money creation.

special drawing rights (SDRs) created by IMF to augment international liquidity; unit of account and medium for reserve loans; value is tied to a basket of currencies.

speculative motive one of three motives for holding money identified by Keynes; the demand for money to avoid expected losses on risky assets such as long-term bonds.

St. Louis equation econometric equation formulated and estimated at the Federal Reserve Bank of St. Louis; relates changes in GNP to current and lagged changes in monetary and fiscal variables.

sterilization operations by a central bank or government treasury which offset the effects of autonomous changes in the public's holdings of high-powered money so as to leave the monetary base unchanged.

Student Assistance Loan Association government-owned agency which buys college student loan paper from commercial banks.

supply curve ceteris-paribus relationship between quantity supplied and an influencing variable, usually the price variable.

supply function one of the fundamental components of the supply and demand model; states all relevant variables which seem likely to affect quantity producers desire to sell.

surplus entities entities which are net suppliers of external funds.

targets parameters which define the objectives of policymakers for variables over which they exercise some measure of control.

tax and loan accounts government demand deposits in accounts with commercial banks.

thrift institutions financial institutions originally chartered to encourage thrift, namely savings and loans, mutual savings banks, and credit unions.

total reservable liabilities all deposits and other liabilities subject to reserve requirements.

total reserves reserve deposits with the Federal Reserve plus currency held by depository institutions to meet Federal Reserve reserve requirements.

transactions motive one of three motives for holding money identified by Keynes; demand based upon the medium-of-exchange function of money.

transactions velocity average number of times per period that a dollar of the money supply turns over or changes hands.

unemployment rate percent of the labor force which is unemployed based on a monthly household survey by the Bureau of Labor Statistics.

unitary elastic elasticity equal to +1 or −1; proportional (+1) or inversely proportional (−1) relationship.

unit-of-account function also called standard-of-value function; function of money as the unit in which prices are conventionally stated.

U.S. Treasurer's general account government deposits with Federal Reserve Banks from which most government expenditures are made.

U.S. Treasury bonds long-term ITF obligations issued by the U.S. Government in denominations of $5,000 and higher.

U.S. Treasury bills government obligations, payable at dates ranging from 90 days to 1 year of issue, in minimum denominations or par value of $10,000, and sold at discount from $10,000.

wild-cat banks banks in the frontier areas of the U.S. prior to the Civil War which issued notes with little or no reserves to back them.

yield curves curves tracing interest rates or yields according to maturity for assets which are otherwise the same.

yield to maturity yield earned if financial instrument is held to maturity.

Index

524

This book has been set VIP, in 10 and 9 point Caledonia, leaded 2 points. Part numbers are 20 and 30 point Optima bold; part titles are 20 point Optima bold. Chapter names are 44 point Optima bold and chapter titles are 18 point Optima bold. The size of the type area is 31 by 48 picas.